# THE
# COURT ROLLS
## OF
# WALSHAM LE WILLOWS

## 1303–1350

# THE
# COURT ROLLS
## OF
# WALSHAM LE WILLOWS
## 1303–1350

Edited by

# RAY LOCK

General Editor

MARK BAILEY

The Boydell Press
_____

Suffolk Records Society
VOLUME XLI
1998

A Suffolk Records Society publication
First published 1998
Reprinted 2002
The Boydell Press, Woodbridge


ISBN 0 85115 616 9


Issued to subscribing members for the year 1997–8


The Boydell Press is an imprint of Boydell & Brewer Ltd
PO Box 9, Woodbridge, Suffolk IP12 3DF, UK
and of Boydell & Brewer Inc.
PO Box 41026, Rochester, NY 14604–4126, USA
Website: www.boydell.co.uk


A catalogue record for this book is available
from the British Library


This publication is printed on acid-free paper


Printed in Great Britain by
Antony Rowe Ltd, Chippenham, Wiltshire

# CONTENTS

# LIST OF ILLUSTRATIONS

# ACKNOWLEDGMENTS

First I have to acknowledge the debt I owe to two very inspirational teachers, who taught Latin and History respectively at Eastbourne Grammar School, which I attended from 1930 to 1937. They were Patrick Kingham BA (London), who was then in the last decade of his career, and John Harrison BA (Durham), who began his first teaching appointment there on the day I arrived as a pupil. Particularly in my last two years, when I was alone in studying Arts subjects for the Higher Schools Certificate Examination, they passed on to me a great deal of their love for, and knowledge of, their subjects, without which I could not have embarked on the translation of the Walsham court rolls almost fifty years later.

I am very much indebted also to David Dymond, who in 1979–80, through the medium of his course of lectures entitled 'An Introduction to Local History', re-kindled my interest in English history, and later helped me to resurrect my knowledge of Latin. He showed me the way when I was first confronted by medieval Latin and the court hand, and as work on this book has progressed, his help in translating passages which were obscure or difficult to read has been most valuable. His suggestions for the maps, so elegantly interpreted by Philip Judge, and for the illustration on the front of the dust-cover, have greatly enhanced the book's appearance.

Another Durham graduate I have to thank is Mark Bailey, who from our first meeting in the Bury Record Office, when he was working on his doctorial thesis, showed great enthusiasm for the work I was doing. Not only did Mark encourage me to prepare this work for publication, but, in a very busy life, he has made time to make valuable contributions to the Introduction and the Glossary. I also wish to mention Audrey McLaughlin, who, when secretary of the Walsham Local History Society, first raised with David her hope that the rolls would be translated, and then involved me in making a start on the realisation of that hope. My thanks go also to Peter Northeast for his help on many occasions in deciphering 'illegible' words, and for his contribution to the Glossary. In this latter connection, I also thank Dr Sandra Raban, whose help on one of the more arcane subjects was enlisted by Mark Bailey. While recording these acknowledgments of help, I unreservedly accept that the responsibility for any inaccuracy in this book is my own.

I wish to thank Amanda Arrowsmith, Director of Libraries and Heritage in Suffolk, for granting permission for the publication of the Walsham Court Rolls, and to record my appreciation of the friendly helpfulness at all times of Gwyn Thomas and all his staff in the Bury Record Office. It has been a congenial place in which to spend so much of my retirement. Finally, my thanks to my wife Jean for all the writing in the Record Office of every item as it was translated, for the typing and re-typing of two editions of the original transcripts, for her help in reading proofs and compiling indexes, and above all, for her constant support and encouragement.

Ray Lock

# INTRODUCTION

Walsham le Willows, hereafter referred to as Walsham, lies about ten miles north-east of Bury St Edmunds and a similar distance north-east of Stowmarket and south-west of Diss. It is fortunate in not being on, or near, any major road, and apart from a malting, converted to flats in the 1980s, and a large builders merchant's offices and stores, it has never attracted industrial development. The village centre, which is a Conservation Area, is at the west end of the parish, with the church dominating a cross roads. The main street, running eastward from the church has a number of medieval and 16th century timber-framed houses interspersed with a smaller number of brick-built houses of the 19th century. There are a few larger modern houses to the west and north of the church, and some modern housing on the outskirts to the east and south, but the shape of the village remains substantially as it has for centuries.

The Lay Subsidy Return of 1283 for Blackbourne Hundred shows Walsham with 90 tax-payers, and the neighbouring vills of Bardwell and Stanton, with 128 and 99 respectively.[1] These figures, compared with an average of 36 for the other 30 vills in the Hundred, indicate an area of dense and wealthy population. In 1349, immediately before the Black Death, the population of Walsham is estimated to have been between 1250 and 1500, with mortality in that year between 45 and 55 per cent.[2] Population at this level was not approached again until the mid-19th century, the highest recorded figure being 1294 in the Census of 1851. Thereafter the population declined, and today it stands at about 900.

Apart from its above-average population, Walsham in the 14th century was unremarkable. It had no great house, and no noble family resident in the vill to dominate the lives of its inhabitants. Except during the period 1361–82, when the manor of Walsham was held by Robert de Ufford, Earl of Suffolk, and later by William, his son, the lords of the manors were comparatively minor gentry, and only the de Walsham family, successively lords of High Hall from before 1300 to 1351, lived in the vill. We are fortunate, therefore, that there survives, among fifty-six bundles of court rolls dated from 1303 to 1710, an almost complete series from 1316 to the end of the 14th century, throwing light on the lives, and deaths, of members of a Suffolk rural community.

## THE MANORS OF WALSHAM

The manorial structure of medieval East Anglia was highly complex, and many vills contained a number of small and fragmented manorial holdings. Similarly, lands pertaining to one manor were often dispersed among the fields of other vills.

1  E. Powell, *A Suffolk Hundred in the Year 1283* (Cambridge, 1910).
2  R. Lock, 'The Black Death in Walsham le Willows', *Proc. Suffolk Inst. Archaeol.* (PSIA) vol.XXXVII (1992), pp.316–336.

1

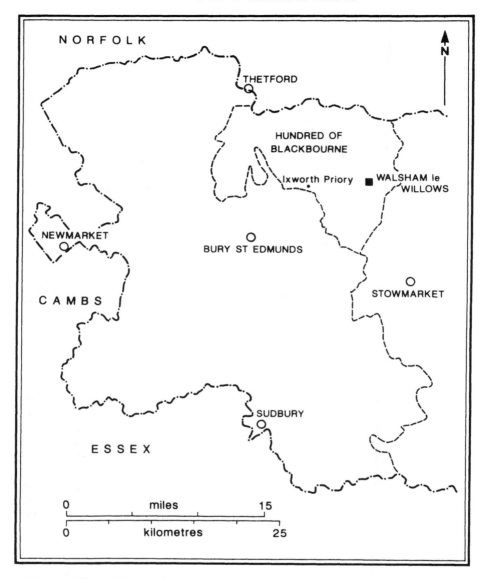

Map 1. THE LIBERTY OF ST EDMUND IN WESTERN SUFFOLK, showing the position of Walsham le Willows within the hundred of Blackbourne

K.M. Dodd argued that Walsham conformed to this pattern and claimed to have identified seven manorial units: Walsham manor, Walsham Churchhouse, High Hall (*alias* Wildecattes or Overhall), Walsham Hall, the manor of Alexander de Walsham and Easthouse ('Esthous'), as well as the holding of the Prior of Ixworth.[3] This conclusion was based on records of the descent of these 'manors', which are not continuous. However, it is clear from the continuity of business in the court rolls that Walsham Hall was, in fact, a rarely used alternative name for Walsham manor, and only one other manor existed, namely, that referred to in this volume as High Hall. All the other names quoted by Dodd were alternative names for this manor, which was at the eastern end of the vill, bordering on Westhorpe and Finningham. The exception to this is Walsham Churchhouse, which is the name given to the holding of the Prior of Ixworth, which first appears in a court roll dated 1409.[4] On this, and the succeeding rolls until the dissolution of the priory in 1537, the lord is shown as the Prior of Ixworth: thereafter it continued to exist as a lay manor.

Dodd abandoned an attempt to identify the manors of Walsham and Churchhouse with the respective holdings in Domesday Book of Robert Blunt and the Abbot of St Edmunds. However, it is probable that the one carucate of land and eight acres of meadow in the abbot's hands in 1086 was later held by the Prior of Ixworth, and became the manor of Walsham Churchhouse; and that Blunt's holding in Domesday, combined with the two carucates which he held from the abbot, equated with Walsham manor as it was in the 14th century; and that the much smaller holding of Roger Malet, who was lord of Westhorpe and Finningham, equated with the manor of High Hall.

## THE ROLLS

For the two manors 255 rolls from the 14th century survive, 176 for Walsham Manor and 79 for High Hall. They are written on 196 membranes, of which 48 are for High Hall, where much less business was conducted than at Walsham, and a single membrane often sufficed for more than one court. The earliest roll is that for the High Hall court of 16 October 1303, the survival of which may be due to its being sewn together with rolls of 1327, because the year of its dating was misinterpreted as 1 Edw.III instead of 31 Edw.I. From 1316 to 1352, a series of 68 rolls survives for High Hall, but from 1354 to 1379 there are only ten. For this later period, during which the lordship changed many times, and some lords were not resident, the contents of the rolls indicate that the court sat much less frequently, rather than that a large number of rolls have not survived. For Walsham manor, 13 rolls exist for the period from 1316 to 1319, a series of 78 from 1327 to 1351, single rolls for 1353 and 1354, and a series of 83 from 1359 to 1399.

With the exception of a few rolls for High Hall, which are smaller, the membranes used are of a roughly uniform width between 9 and 9½ inches, but vary greatly in length, most being between 18 and 30 inches long. That used for the court of 15 June 1349, when the deaths of 103 victims of the Black Death were recorded, is 4 feet long, and is made of two skins.

3   K.M. Dodd, *The Field Book of Walsham le Willows, 1577*, SRS vol.XVII (1974), p.13.
4   Suffolk Record Office, Bury St Edmunds (SRO(B)): HA504/1/21.A.

Hector, describing the format of English parchment rolls associated with the Exchequer and courts of common law, says 'the Roll was made up by piling the component sheets of parchment (here themselves described individually as rolls or *rotuli*), and securing them by cords passing through the heads, the lower ends being left free, so that quick reference is comparatively easy'.[5] This is the method used for assembling up to 50 manor court rolls (meaning the records of individual courts) into Rolls, each of which, broadly speaking, covers a decade of the king's reign. Thus, Roll 3 (HA504/1/3) contains 34 membranes, on which are inscribed the rolls of 43 courts, dating from 1 Edw.III to 9 Edw.III; Roll 4 (HA504/1/4) consists of 50 rolls on 38 membranes, dating from 10 Edw.III to 19 Edw.III. Throughout this volume, the distinction between a court roll and a Roll of court rolls, will be marked by this use of the lower case *r* and the upper case *R*.

The rolls calendared in this volume are contained in five Rolls (HA504/1/1 to HA504/1/4 and part of HA504/1/5). They are not segregated between the two manors, and with a few exceptions, including all eight courts in Roll 2 (HA504/1/2), they are in chronological order following the date of the first court of each membrane. The dates of the five Walsham and three High Hall courts in Roll 2 range from October 1317 (no.9) to May 1349 (no.146). There is no apparent reason for their separation from other rolls of similar dates, or for the random order in which they were bound together.

In addition to roll no.1, referred to above, one other was misplaced because its date was misinterpreted [HA504/1/4.13 (no.17)], and one where the date was incorrectly expressed by the clerk of the court [HA504/1/1.19 (no.37)]. The latter is referred to again later in this Introduction, under the heading 'Walsham and the World Outside'. A footnote, explaining the misinterpretation, appears against each of them in the edited text. The interchange of HA504/1/5.13 (no.149) and HA504/1/5.14 (no.147) was probably the result of a mistake in the sorting. The chronological order of the rolls is further distorted in most cases where a single membrane was used for more than one court.

The condition of the rolls is, generally, very good. Fading or damage has occasionally made a word or short passage illegible, but, for documents now more than 650 years old, which until their arrival in the Suffolk Record Office were unlikely to have been stored in ideal conditions, they are remarkably well-preserved. The text is written in Latin in cursive court hand, with no great variation between the hands of individual scribes, except in two High Hall courts in 1330/31 (nos.54 and 56) where the quality of calligraphy and accuracy are well below standard. The style of the writing remained very consistent throughout the century. The rolls are, for the most part, of very pleasing appearance, and, despite their heavy abbreviation, reasonably easy to decipher.

As with other manors, the court rolls were designed as working documents. In the left hand margin (always about 1½ inches wide) are recorded the amounts of amercements and fines; and later insertions, frequently indecipherable, indicate the regular use to which the record was put in collecting and accounting for the sums due. Marginal notes also draw the attention of court officials to orders, and to unfinished business: many rolls end with a memorandum 'to execute the orders of the preceding court, marked with a cross, and not acted upon'.

---

5    L.C. Hector, *The Handwriting of English Documents* (London 1958), p.18.

The rolls were not solely for the benefit of the lord and his officials. Tenants of, or claimants to, villein or customary land could request that earlier rolls be scrutinised for evidence to support a claim, and such applications were not uncommon. The evidence of court rolls was also of great value when a man's status, free or unfree, was in dispute, but no such cases occur in this volume. An example of a dispute in which the defendant asked for scrutiny of earlier rolls appears in the Walsham manor rolls of 17 January 1318 and 28 March 1318 [nos.11 and 13], where the entries read:

> Robert Godefrey pays 12d. fine for the rolls of the 26th, 27th and 28th years of King Edward [Nov. 1297 – Nov. 1300] to be scrutinised concerning a messuage, 1 acre of land which Alice le Fener acquired by the surrender in court of Simon le Fener, and the suit between Walter le Fener and Robert is adjourned until the next court; ordered to summon [them] before the enquiry etc.

and

> Robert Godefrey is amerced 6d. for unlawful deforcement of a messuage, 1 acre of land from Walter le Faber, as was found by the enquiry, before which Robert and Walter placed themselves; therefore ordered to take the said tenement [into the lord's hands] etc., Robert's pledges are Walter the reeve and John le Man. Thereupon Walter comes and pays 5s. fine for having entry, rendering due and accustomed services, and he swore customary fealty.

Although the name of the plaintiff appears in the second entry as 'le Faber' (the smith), there is little doubt that this was either an error on the part of the clerk, or is an example of the confusion between family names and occupational names, referred to later under Editorial Methods.

The use of earlier rolls by the lord is illustrated in the roll of 24 January 1329 (no.46):

> Ordered [the enquiry] to scrutinise the rolls [to ascertain] whether William Kebbil, John Wyswyf and Peter Sawyer disposed of land before their deaths, and therefore do not owe heriots.

Evidence of much later use of the rolls appears occasionally on rectangular pieces of parchment measuring roughly 3½ by 1 inch, which have been stitched to the left hand margin of individual rolls against particular entries. All but three of the entries marked by these tabs record a transfer of land, and on each is written, in a hand no earlier than 16th-century, the name of the grantor recorded on the roll. On three occasions a second name appears, and on two of these the words 'et alii' (and others) are added: none of the additional names is that of the other party to the land transaction recorded. The inference is that these rolls were being used as evidence in disputes some 200 years after the relevant transfers of land took place. Marginal annotations, in even later hands, such as 'gavelkind', 'warren', 'dower' and 'escheat by bastardy', also appear occasionally, but they appear to have been added to note a point of interest to a historian rather than for the work of the court.

## THE COURTS

### Jurisdiction

The right of manorial lords to hold courts was not established by statute; nor were the powers exercised by these courts, which initially were limited to matters affecting the tenants' holdings, the services due from them and the settling of disputes between them. It was considered to be the natural right of any lord to hold a court with these limited powers for his tenants, but in the course of time many lords were granted other local powers by the king, for example, the oversight of the assizes of ale and bread and the liberty of warren, so giving the manor court jurisdiction in cases of brewing and baking offences and the poaching of small game.

More significantly, many lords assumed powers proper to the hundred courts, in which the sheriff held the view of frankpledge and the jury took presentments of offences against the king's peace made by the capital pledges of each vill. In some cases the assumption was legalised retrospectively by the lord claiming that the powers had been vested in his predecessors from pre-conquest times by right of 'sake and soke, toll and team and infangthef'. The full meaning of this phrase is obscure, except the final word which means the right to have a private gallows, and entitlement to the chattels of a hanged thief. In short, a lord who legitimately held a view of frankpledge had jurisdiction not only over matters affecting the relationship between the lord and his tenants and between the tenants themselves, but also some criminal offences within his manor. The latter, together with brewing and baking and poaching offences, were dealt with either in a separate court, called a Court Leet, or at a sitting of the Court Baron, with a separate roll being kept.

Within the Liberty of St Edmunds the abbot ensured that manorial lords did not assume additional powers, except when they were granted by the king. The lord of Walsham manor was granted jurisdiction over brewing, baking and poaching offences, and instances of them are common in the rolls of Walsham manor; they are not recorded separately. Neither of the Walsham lords was authorised to hold a Court Leet.

### Frequency

An ancient formula required manorial courts to be held 'from three weeks to three weeks' (de tribus septimanis in tribus septimanas), and over the centuries this degree of frequency was found necessary in the larger manors. For example, in the manor of Wakefield, which included twelve surrounding vills, and where in the mid-14th century the lordship was divided between two royal ladies, the Court Baron of each lord sat regularly at three-weekly intervals. For smaller manors the amount of business may not have justified more than, say, three courts per year. Excluding the period 1319–1326, for which no rolls survive, the average frequency of courts in Walsham manor was between two and three per year, and in High Hall from 1316 to 1350 two per year.

### Court Officials

The presiding official was normally the lord's steward (senescallus), the most important administrator in the lord's household and estates. The headings of certain rolls, however, suggest that in Walsham manor, whose lords were non-resident, it was the custom for the lord to preside over the first court during his lordship, but very rarely thereafter. In comparison with Walsham, High Hall was a small manor, where the lords were both resident and held no other manors. Almost all of its rolls are headed with the lord's name, either for every court individually, or, where more than one court appears on a single roll, on the first court thereon. It may be inferred from this that the lord of High Hall presided over his own courts.

The steward was assisted by his clerk, and, since the proceedings of the court were formal and in conformity with those of higher courts, they both needed to have knowledge of the law and of local custom. The clerk recorded the proceedings of the court on the roll, but not always, it would seem, as the business progressed. It is clear from instances where an item was dealt with in two stages in the same court, and the entries appear in the roll separately but in the wrong order, that the clerk made notes on separate scraps of parchment, as the court proceeded, and compiled the roll from them after the sitting had ended.

The steward also had the assistance of the principal manorial officials, the reeve (*prepositus*) and the hayward (*messor*), who were elected annually by, and from among, the villein tenants. In some rolls for High Hall, the latter office appears as *collector*. Their duties were concerned mainly with husbandry, but included special functions in the court – ensuring the attendance of all who owed suit of court, and of those summoned, or attached, to answer an offence against the lord or a complaint by another tenant, and, after the court, executing its orders. The hayward was also responsible for ensuring the payment of fines and amercements: this may account for the alternative title for his office in High Hall. Two other officials, called 'affeerers', were appointed by the tenants to advise the steward on the scale of amercements. Their duties, and those of the jury, are described more fully below.

*The Conduct of Business*

The court opened with applications from suitors to be excused attendance. All tenants were required to be present at the court, villein tenants at every court, and free and customary tenants at the courts specified in the rental of the manor, usually once per year. A tenant unable to attend a court could apply to be essoined, the application being made on his behalf by another tenant, referred to as an essoiner, who could not act in a similar capacity for any other applicant in the same court. In Wakefield a suitor could be essoined for a maximum of three courts in succession, but in Walsham he was allowed only one, because his reason for not attending could not have remained valid for the long interval between courts. The applications for essoin were always the first items on the roll, and frequent spaces on the parchment after these items indicate that the clerk had expected more applications than were made. Remarkably, the space is greatest in the roll of 15 June 1349 (no.147), in which the deaths of most of the victims of the Black Death are recorded; the clerk left a space of 3½ inches for essoins, but there were no applicants. That nobody was too ill to seek to be excused suggests that the severity of the plague was subsiding in Walsham by that date.

After the essoins, business appears to have been despatched in no set order; cases of damage to the lord's crops, absence from court, or from the manor, land transactions etc., followed one after another at random. However if the business of a typical Walsham court, such as that of 12 October 1316 (no.2), is analysed, a discernible, though by no means rigid, pattern does emerge. The business conducted, extensive in both volume and breadth, especially in Walsham manor, falls into four categories

7

which were probably segregated in the court, but only erratically, if at all, in the rolls. The method of compiling the roll, referred to above, made it almost inevitable that the record would not follow the order in which the business was conducted.

The four categories of business were:

(a) the punishment of offenders against the court, the lord, and other members of the community, and the collection of fines due to the lord,
(b) the settling of disputes between tenants,
(c) the approval, and recording, of land transactions, including the succession of heirs, and
(d) administrative matters, for example, the election of manorial officials, and supervising the performance of their duties.

As noted above, the Walsham manor court also dealt with breaches of the assizes of ale and bread.

The first of these categories occupies all the first three pages of the transcript of roll no.2, except the last line on p.35. The matters dealt with include absence from court, and from the manor, damage to the lord's crops and woods and to his warren, stealing the lord's crops, tenants owing fealty to the lord, an application from a female villein for leave to marry, and the attachment of another who married without leave, repeated orders to retain in the lord's hands land seized at earlier courts and the progressing of disputes between tenants. Most of these were matters which would be known to the reeve and the hayward, and it is probable that the presentments were made in court by one, or both, of them.

The remainder of the roll deals mainly with land transactions, six of which followed the death of tenants, and offences against the assizes of ale and bread, but interspersed with these items are many which fall into category (a). The only five items from category (d) are to be found on page 43: they concern a dispute about services owed to the lord by a tenant, an instruction to the jurors to enquire and report about pannage in the lord's woods, two fines paid to be excused from the offices of woodward and reeve, and an amercement of the woodward for not performing his duties.

## Procedures

Every offence, dispute, and land transaction was brought to the notice of the court by presentment, but the roll frequently does not show who made the presentment. Sometimes the phrase 'it was presented that' is used, but frequently no introductory words appear. The procedure of presentment follows that used in Hundred courts, where offences notified by tithingmen to the capital pledges of each vill were presented to the court by a jury. In Hundred courts this procedure had long been obligatory, but in manorial courts it was adopted gradually and by the 14th century had become common practice. As with all procedures which evolve, that of presentment became ill-defined, and subject to local variation.

It has already been said that a jury assisted the steward, but it is important to note that this was not a jury in the modern sense of the word. Many Walsham rolls include the words 'General Enquiry made by' (*Generalis Inquisitio facta per*) followed by a list of names, varying between ten and eighteen, then followed by 'jurors, who say on their oath that' (*juratores qui dicunt super sacramentum suum quod*), and finally followed by the first of a number of presentments. *Inquisitio* has been translated in this volume as 'enquiry', to reflect its function as a jury of enquiry and presentment, rather than one of hearing evidence presented by lawyers, and giving a verdict. The list of jurors does not appear on every roll, and it seems that, once appointed, they conducted their enquiries both inside and outside succeeding courts, until a new general enquiry was set up. This is confirmed in the roll of a court where no enquiry was empanelled (no.52). The entry immediately preceding the presentments by the enquiry reads:

> The enquiry, sworn at the last court, as shown there by their names, had a day to report on several defaults pertaining to the manor.

There are no instances in the High Hall rolls of a general enquiry being named, but the settlement of disputes over land tenure there makes it clear that an enquiry was held when necessary, probably with all the villein tenants, of whom there were less than twenty, acting as the jury.

The list of jurors' names usually appears after the presentment of offences against the court and the lord, and after disputes between tenants settled out of court, or not pursued by the plaintiff. This is the point where a clear division can be seen in roll no.2, after which nearly all the business is appropriate for the enquiry to present. The division is rarely as clear-cut as on this roll.

Whether the presentments were made by an official or by the jury, villeins were presumed to be guilty and were amerced. They were said to be in the mercy of the court, and required to pay a penalty, called an 'amercement', agreed between the steward and the affeerers. In recommending to the steward the amount due from each offender, the affeerers took into account his circumstances and ability to pay. Offenders other than villeins may have had the opportunity to dispute the facts as presented, but only one instance of dispute has been found, and the accused appears to have been a free man, not resident in Walsham. In the court of 22 March 1328 (no.41), it was presented that 'Henry of Saxlingham took a hare in the lord's warren, inside the messuage and close of Sir Alexander de Walsham.' This was an offence against the lord of Walsham, who had the liberty of free warren, the right to hunt small game. The order was given to distrain Henry to satisfy the lord for the trespass, and at the court of 30 May (no.43) he denied taking the hare, and asked for an enquiry. The enquiry was held: the jurors said that he was not guilty, and he was discharged. No fine was levied for holding the enquiry, as it would have been had he been found guilty, in addition to any penalty for the offence.

The presumption that most offenders presented by the enquiry were guilty contradicts, to some extent, the statement above that the jury was one of enquiry and presentment, rather than one of hearing evidence and giving a verdict. In most cases falling under category (a) they acted more as a jury of enquiry and judgment, with the steward having no function other than setting the penalty. The scales of justice seem to have been heavily weighted against the accused, even though he may have had some opportunity to defend himself to the jury, or the officials, before the court sat. The not uncommon use, after the description of the offence, of the phrase 'which he cannot deny' implies that he did. The accused also had some protection in that all of those making presentments were themselves villeins, and victimisation of an individual could rebound on the perpetrator, when it was the victim's turn to hold office.

The procedures of the court were at their most formal when they applied to disputes between individuals, but many such actions were concluded informally at an

9

early stage. Nevertheless, each step in the proceedings followed a pattern. The plaintiff's first step was to enter a plea, specifying his complaint. As in the king's courts, where pleas had to conform with the prescribed forms of action, those in the manorial court were limited to pleas of debt, detention of chattels, land, covenant and trespass. The first three of these are self-explanatory; covenant would today be termed 'breach of contract'; trespass is defined by Pollock and Maitland as 'a wrong done to the plaintiff in his body, his goods or his land', a definition so broad as to encompass almost any other complaint.[6] John Fraunceys complained in a plea of trespass against Avice Deneys that she had damaged his status by saying that his wife wore her short jacket (*curtepia*) before Easter (no.45), and several other complaints of defamation appear under similar pleas. Contempt of the lord by insulting his bailiff, refusing to make a linen cloth for the lady, and even fornicating within his manor were also interpreted as trespass.

If the defendant did not deny the accusation, he was amerced and required to pay damages, if any. If he entered a defence with the enquiry, and they decided that the complaint was false, or if the plaintiff, not having been essoined, did not attend the court to pursue his case, he was amerced, and the defendant was quit. If both parties agreed to settle, they asked the court for leave to agree, and this was granted, on payment of an amercement. If they failed to agree, they could be granted a limited period of time to reach agreement: the roll would say 'At the request of the parties, a day [or sometimes, 'a love-day'] was given to A and B, in a plea of . . . until the next court, to come without essoin.'

If the parties failed to agree, the defendant could ask for a special enquiry, or offer to wage law. Both these procedures were comparatively uncommon, probably because the expertise of an attorney might be necessary. The stilted language in the following entry, in the roll of 2 December 1332 (no.62), matches in its precision, and in its form of words, the examples of pleading in the king's courts, quoted by Pollock and Maitland.[7]

Robert the cooper and Robert Man were summoned to reply to Richard of Belhawe in a plea of land, in various complaints; on which he says that Robert the cooper forcibly deprived him of ¼r. of land, and Robert Man forcibly deprived him of 1r. by estimation of uncultivated land. And he says that Cristina Grous, his grandmother, was seised of the said land, as of right and her inheritance; that she demised the land to Richard Reve and Cristina, his wife, for a term of years, and within that term, Richard Reve sold it to Robert the cooper and Robert Man, who now hold it unlawfully, and thereupon he produces suit. Robert and Robert come and say that Cristina Grous sold the land to Richard and Cristina Reve, and they held the land by that sale, and not by demise; that Richard Reve afterwards sold it to Robert and Robert, and that they hold it by that right, and not otherwise. On this, they ask that an enquiry be held, and the other party agrees; a day is given to them until the next court, in the status in which they now are. Afterwards, because the complaint is not sound, Richard has leave to withdraw it.

[6]   F. Pollock and F.W. Maitland, *The History of English Law*, 2nd edition (Cambridge 1968), vol.2, p.526.
[7]   *Ibid.*, p.605 *et seq.*

The phrase 'he produces suit' means that he, the plaintiff, has character witnesses, who would be subject to examination by the special enquiry if, as in the case above, the defendant asked for it. If the defendant offered to wage law, he would do so with the support of five or eleven compurgators, by his swearing on oath that his denial of the charge was truthful, and by their swearing that they believed him.[8] The formula sometimes used in the rolls, but never in those in this volume, is 'he offered to wage law six-handed, or twelve-handed', the sixth or twelfth hand being the defendant's own.

These long and complicated processes were only used as a final resort, and many of the cases ended in the same way as the one quoted above. It is clear that all concerned did their best to get the parties to settle their differences amicably, and without recourse to the complications of the law.

Formality, accuracy and certainty were of great importance in the recording of land transactions, both to the lord and to the tenants. If villein A wished to part with his tenement to villein B, both wanted to be certain that the transfer was properly recorded; the lord wanted it understood that the land was his to transfer, and not the tenant's, and that the terms of villein B's tenure were fully understood and recorded. Villein A came into the court and formally surrendered the tenement into the lord's hands, stating that he wished it to be granted to the use (i.e. benefit) of villein B. Transfers were often made by a tenant nearing the end of his life to another member of his family; he could then make the surrender outside the court, through the hands of a manorial official, in the presence of other tenants. If villein A held his tenement jointly with his wife, she was questioned privately by the steward, to ensure that she was a willing party to the transfer, and not acting under coercion. Seisin of the tenement was then granted to villein B, to hold to him and his heirs in villenage, by services and works, at the lord's will, saving the right of whomsoever etc., and he paid a fine for having entry to the tenement. As the new tenant, he had to swear fealty to the lord, or, in the lord's absence, through his steward.

This was the commonest and simplest form of land transfer, and others were slightly different: for example, if the land was customary, and not of villenage, seisin was then said to be 'by the rod', and the services would be specified, and the words 'at the lord's will' omitted. The system was very effective, and served both landlord and tenant very well over many centuries, finally emerging as the progenitor of copyhold tenure.


## THE LORDS

### Walsham Manor

At the beginning of the 14th century, the lordship of Walsham manor was in the hands of Lady Rose (*Roesia*) de Valognes (*alias* Valence), one of two granddaughters of Sir Robert de Valognes and Rose le Blund (*alias* Blunt). The latter was daughter of William le Blund, who was the fifth successor in direct line from Robert Blunt, holder of the manor in 1086. At William's death, the manor had passed to his sister Rose, the wife of Sir Robert; and from them to their son Robert.

---

8 Pollock and Maitland give 'oath-helpers' as a synonym for 'compurgator', *History of English Law*, p.634.

Rose and Cecily, her sister, were infants when their father died in 1282, and their mother, Eve de Valognes (*née* Criketot), had custody of the children, and of the manor, until they came of age. The rolls calendared in this volume contain several references to earlier events as having been 'in the time of Lady Eve de Valence'. The date of her death is unknown, but it is certain that Rose had succeeded to the lordship by the year 1307,[9] and probable that, at that time, she was the wife of Sir Edmund de Pakenham, an ancestor of the present Earl of Longford.[10]

Lady Rose held the manor, jointly with Sir Edmund, until his death at the end of 1331. The last court in his name was held on 24 September, and the first, in Lady Rose's name, on 11 December of that year. She then married Sir Hugh de Saxham, and early in 1332, they enfeoffed the manor to Thomas de Saxham and Robert de Rickinghall, in whose names a court was held on 11 June. The manor was subsequently regranted to Sir Hugh and Lady Rose, and her heirs; and they held it jointly until Sir Hugh's death in 1349. Lady Rose then held it alone until her death in 1353, when she would have been over 70 years old.

Her heir was her son Thomas de Pakenham; her other sons, Edmund, Robert and Harvey, had pre-deceased her. In 1355, after only two courts under his lordship, Thomas enfeoffed Sir John de Ufford, William de Wichingham, John de Cavendish and John de Gonville clerk with the manor,[11] and in 1358, following Thomas' death, they granted it to Mary, the widow of Edmund, his brother. The first court in her name was held on 4 July 1359, and four more courts followed, in all of which the holder of the lordship was named as 'the lady'. Lady Mary is remembered as a benefactor of the Cambridge college named after Edmund de Gonville, a kinsman of one of the feoffees named above: she bequeathed a moiety of her estate to the maintenance of the Hall of the Annunciation of Our Lady, part of the college.

The last of Lady Mary's courts was dated 24 September 1360, the year of her death, when the manor reverted to Robert de Ufford, Earl of Suffolk, the son of Cecily, sister of Lady Rose.[12] On the earl's death in 1369, he was succeeded by his son William, who held the manor until 1375 when it was acquired by Robert de Swillington ('Swelyngton'), Sir Roger Boys (*alias* Bois) and two associates, their first court being noted in the roll of 12 September of that year. No mention of the earl, as lord of Walsham, appears in the rolls after that date, and the descent of the lordship is unclear.

Dodd says that it was held by Sir William de Elmham and his wife from 1393 to at least 1415, but quotes no sources. There is evidence of Sir William's earlier tenure in his letter (in Norman French), attached to the roll of 19 January 1389, and dated four days before, with the salutation 'William Elmham, knight and Lord of Walsham, to his very dear and well beloved Steward of his lands, Edmond Lakynghith, greetings'. Sir William died in 1403 and his wife in 1419, but there is no evidence in Inquisitions Post Mortem that either of them then held the manor. The roll of 30 March 1391 is headed as 'The first court of Henry Grene, [*illeg.*] de Wingfield, Edmund de Lakenheath, Robert Hotet, Richard dil Church, and Alexander

---

9  Edmund de Pakenham and Rose his wife *v* Richard son of Robert Hawys of the freedom of Richard – 20m. of silver. Feet of Fines, 35 Edw.I 29.
10  An illuminated pedigree of the Pakenham family, approved by the College of Heralds, is to be seen in St Mary's Church, Pakenham. The date of Sir Edmund's marriage is given there as 'before 1306'.
11  SRO(B): HA504/8.2.
12  SRO(B): HA504/8.3.

Broun, lords of the manors of Walshamhall and Wyldecattes'. After 300 years in the hands of the descendants of Robert Blunt, it appears that Walsham manor was held by feoffees in the final quarter of the century, apart from the few years of the lordship of Sir William de Elmham.

## High Hall Manor

Confusion over the local manors is worse confounded by Copinger, who assumed that there were two manors, identified as 'Walsham' and 'Churchhouse or Easthouse'. He gives evidence of fines to show that a manor was vested in John de Walsham and Alice his wife in 1293 and 1307, and says that, after their deaths, it passed 'to their son and heir, Nicholas, and Margaret his wife'.[13] An order of the court in the Walsham manor roll of 12 October 1316 'to retain a bullock, taken upon the heirs of John de Walsham, and to take more for fealty demanded of them', indicates that John had recently died. His death coincides with the first of many rolls between 1316 and 1324, headed 'The court of Alexander de Walsham'. One of them, dated 11 May 1321, bears the additional comment, 'held at East Hall ['le Esthal']'.

Copinger's evidence for Nicholas de Walsham succeeding John is a fine of the manor of 'Walsham *juxta* Westhorpe', between Nicholas de Walsham and Margaret his wife, and Ralph de Rydlingfeld and John son of Peter de Welle, dated 1325/26.[14] The description 'next to Westhorpe' is unusual among references to the Walsham manors in the Feet of Fines, and it confirms that this is the manor of High Hall. An earlier fine, of Alexander son of Ralph de Walsham *versus* William Sparsho and Agnes his wife, in Walsham *juxta* Ixworth, clearly relates to Walsham manor, in which Alexander de Walsham, lord of High Hall from 1316 to 1324, had substantial holdings.[15]

Copinger gives no evidence that Nicholas de Walsham was the son and heir of John, nor that he succeeded him when he died. His first court was held on 18 April 1325, immediately after Alexander's death; and the continuity of business from Alexander's to Nicholas' courts make untenable any case for Alexander's manor being a separate entity.

Nicholas held the manor until 1347, and was then succeeded by Edmund de Welles and Margery, Edmund's sister, whose tenure lasted until September 1352. During this time, which spanned the Black Death, they held only five courts, but single courts were held in May 1349 by John Talbot, parson of Rickinghall, and in July 1351, by Robert Spenser, parson of the church of Ellough, Ralph Fatoun, Bartholomew Fraunceys and William of Shelton, chaplain. It is possible that Margery, sister of Edmund de Welles, was the widow of Nicholas de Walsham, her Christian name having been misread in the Feet of Fines quoted above, and that Edmund also had a claim to the manor, as a relative of John, son of Peter de Welle; but this is conjecture, of which the example of Copinger should make us wary.

Only eight rolls survive for the period between 1352 and 1379, two in 1354–5 in the names of Lord Emeritus de Wellington and Hawisia, his wife, one in 1356 in that of Andrew Baylock, two in 1365–6 in that of John Brinkley ('Brinkelee'),[16] and

---

13  W.A. Copinger, *The Manors of Suffolk* (London 1905), vol.I, p.388.
14  W. Rye, ed., *Calendar of Feet of Fines for Suffolk* (Ipswich 1900), ref. 19 Edw.II, 24.
15  *Ibid.*, ref. 30 Edw.I, 17.
16  Abbot of St Edmunds 1362–78.

three between 1371 and 1374, in which no lord was named. The final roll for High Hall as a separate manor was that of 27 April 1379, which is headed 'Walsham Overall, the first court of Sir William de Ufford, Earl of Suffolk, Sir Roger Boys knight, Sir John de Peasenhall ('Pyshale') clerk, Robert Ashfield, Thomas de Wroxham and Roger de Woolverstone'.

## The Tenants

Dodd wrote that 'there was an absence or virtual absence of servile tenures, for Walsham was without bondage or villenage', and he referred to an unknown number of large freehold tenements, in addition to the manors and the holdings of the Prior of Ixworth.[17] It is difficult to reconcile this view with the evidence in the rolls, where land is frequently said to be 'of bondage' or 'of villenage' and the unfree tenants heavily outnumber the free. Furthermore, almost all the surnames of tax-payers in the Lay Subsidy of 1283 can be identified with those of unfree tenants in the rolls.

The demographic data derived from the rolls show that immediately before the Black Death, out of a male population of about 650 to 750, 153 were in possession of land.[18] In this estimated population, the assumed ratio of those aged under 16 years, the minimum age at which heirs were admitted to their inherited land, to those 16 years old and over was 40:60. Thus the adult male population was between, say, 360 and 450, of whom between 42 and 34 per cent were tenants.

Among those tenants who died before 1349 holding a messuage and land, the average holding was 9½ acres; the average for those whose holding did not include a dwelling was 3½ acres. The pressures on local officials, immediately before the court of 15 June 1349, prevented the recording of many details of individual holdings; the figures for that year were therefore excluded from the above calculations. The holding of three messuages, two half-messuages, 64 acres of land in Walsham manor, by Alexander de Walsham, lord of High Hall, was also excluded, to avoid distortion of the average figure. Included in the calculation were only three holdings well above the average (of 20, 30 and 40 acres respectively), the last of which belonged to William Lene, who is discussed later. Among the holdings of victims of the Black Death was one of 40 acres, held by William Hawys. Comparing the foregoing figures with those in the Survey of 1577,[19] which listed 86 individual tenants holding in total much more land, the earlier average is very much lower. The holdings of Lene and Hawys would have put them twenty-first equal in the table of 1577.

In the decade before the Black Death, the average number of land transactions was 20 per year. This indication of a healthy market in land tends to conceal the pressures brought about by high population and the fragmentation of peasant holdings caused by the local custom of partible inheritance. Only a reduction of population such as that experienced in Walsham in 1349, followed by two centuries with no great increase, could have changed the pattern of land tenure where the average holding of about 170 tenants was well below 10 acres (and the great majority held much less than the average), to one where 86 tenants each held, on average, 30 acres.

[17] Dodd, *Field Book of Walsham le Willows*, p.12.
[18] Lock, 'Black Death in Walsham le Willows', p.318.
[19] Dodd, *Field Book of Walsham le Willows*, pp.40–41.

## The Relationship Between Lords and Tenants

All tenants, free and unfree, had certain obligations to the lord, depending upon their status and their tenure. Free tenants owed fealty to the lord, and suit of court at specified sittings; that is to say they had to be present at the manor court at times stated in the rental, usually once per year at Michaelmas. They also had to swear fealty at the first court of a new lord, and at the court at which they were granted possession of a tenement. They were also liable for annual rent, and for 'relief', usually equal to one year's rent, when the tenement descended to an heir. Their liability for labour services was limited to a few days labour at harvest and, possibly, at ploughtime.

Villein tenants owed fealty and suit at all courts; their tenure was always at the lord's will and carried the burden of labour services at the lord's summons. In Walsham there is no evidence that the call to work was anything other than when needed, but in some manors the arrangements for labour services were highly regimented.[20]

Labour services were unavoidable and deeply unpopular, because work on the lord's demesne was inevitably demanded at times when tenants most wanted to tend their own land. On the other hand, the lord's intervention in the villein land market appears to have been minimal, and his influence there to have been benevolent; granted that the lord benefited financially by entry fines paid into the court on completion of land transfers, and by the permanence of the record of landholding. There is no evidence in the rolls of permission to transfer a tenancy ever being refused; the interests of a wife who held land jointly with her husband, and of the widow of a tenant, or his under-age heirs were all protected. The wife was examined in private to ensure that she willingly agreed to the transfer of land in which she had an interest; in Walsham the widow was entitled to hold in dower a half-share of her late husband's tenement for life; and the land inherited by minors was taken into the lord's hands until the court approved custody of them and their inheritance during their minority.

If a villein left the manor he was declared to be a fugitive, and the court ordered him to be 'attached by the body wherever he might be found', but he could be granted permission to remain outside the manor on payment of *chevage*, or *head-pence*, usually 1d. per year. The fact of living outside the manor was not treated later as a bar to his entry as heir to his father's land. If a villein's daughter wished to marry, a fine had to be paid, which elsewhere is usually called *merchet* but never so in the Walsham rolls. The amount of the fine varied widely, probably based on ability to pay. The lowest was 6d. and the highest £1, but between 1335 and 1349 6s.8d. was the usual figure. The highest fines were demanded when the bridegroom lived outside Walsham, and the lord was losing the benefit of the bride's labour, and that of her children in the future. The fine was also high when the bride was a landed widow, who was a villein by blood (*nativa de sanguine*), that is to say the daughter of a villein. If the lord's leave to marry had not been sought a fine was levied by the court, usually similar in amount to those mentioned above. Examples occur in the rolls of the jury being amerced for failing to present cases of marrying without leave.

20  See R.H. Hilton, *A Medieval Society* (Past and Present Publications 1983), pp.131–135, for details of an example in Buckland near Evesham, a manor of Gloucester Abbey.

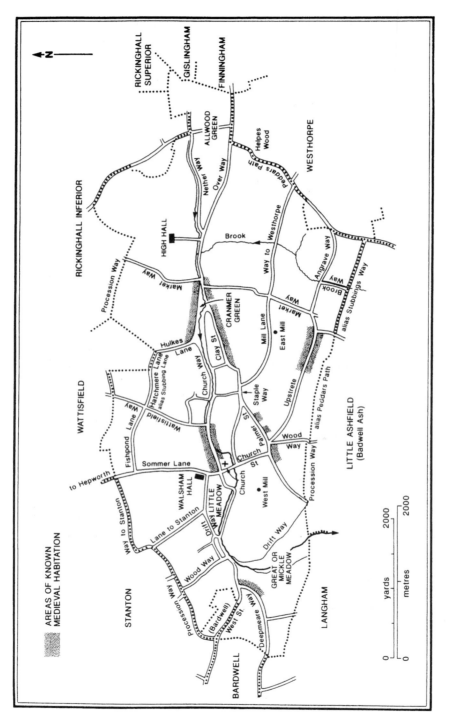

Map 2. THE PARISH OF WALSHAM LE WILLOWS, showing the halls of its two manors, roads and other identifiable topographical features mentioned in the court rolls of 1303–50. Also shown are areas of known medieval settlement revealed by archaeological fieldwork in the 1980s

The lord also collected a fine from a villein whose daughter had a bastard child; in the rolls it is called *childwite* and usually fixed at 2s.8d. In Wakefield a similar fine called *lecherwite* was imposed, but there the offence was related to the loss of the girl's chastity, and both parties were punished, financially and corporally. To this editor the former punishment seems fair, but the latter might more justly have been applied only to the man.

When a villein tenant died the lord was entitled to a *heriot*, the surrender of the dead man's best beast as a sort of death duty; if he had no beast a fine was paid. The payment of the heriot, or the fine in lieu, relieved the heirs from paying an entry fine, when they succeeded to their inheritance. As will be seen in the inventory of William Lene in roll no.52, the church also took a beast after the death of a villein; this was called a *mortuary*. No heriot was payable on customary land, but the heirs paid a *relief*, usually equal to one year's rent.

Tenants were required to take their corn to the lord's mill to be ground, the miller taking a proportion of it as payment; the payment was called *multure*. In Wakefield the proportion taken was one measure in sixteen from 1 August until Christmas and one in twenty thereafter. With all these obligations in terms of labour and cash, the living which the average villein made from his small tenement must have been very meagre, but some families flourished, and all who survived the Black Death showed remarkable resilience in its aftermath.

*Non-tenants*

Since the origin of manor courts lay in the need for a seat of jurisdiction over all matters affecting tenants' holdings, and the most important local activity was agriculture, most of the court's time was devoted to matters connected with land; it follows that non-tenants feature in the rolls much less than tenants. It may seem therefore to someone reading this volume that most adult males held land, but in fact the number of non-tenants at any one time far exceeded that of tenants. Immediately before the outbreak of the Black Death in Walsham there were 176 tenants (153 male and 23 female); using the mean of the population figures already referred to (c.1400), the non-tenants numbered 1224 (547 male and 677 female).

However this 'snapshot' statistic, from which one might deduce that seven out of eight of the population were landless throughout their lives, does not present the true picture, which is more complex. Some of those without land in Walsham may have been tenants in neighbouring manors. The custom of partible inheritance ensured that all surviving sons of tenants, or daughters where there were no sons, could expect to become tenants; and in many cases they did not remain landless until they inherited. It was not unusual for a tenant to transfer part of his tenement to a son, or to a daughter at the time of her marriage.

The population estimate above was based on the assumption (the validity of which was acknowledged to be in some doubt) that those under 16 years of age amounted to 40 per cent of the whole. A more realistic picture of the ratio of tenants to non-tenants emerges if this percentage, numbering c.560 is excluded. This leaves an adult population of 940, of whom 176 were tenants and 764 were non-tenants (317 male and 447 female). Notwithstanding this adjustment, it remains true that among adults tenants were greatly outnumbered by non-tenants, particularly among women: two out of every three men, and 19 out of every 20 women, were landless.

Inevitably, the rolls tell us very little about the non-tenants. Many of them, of course, were members of a tenant's family and worked on the family tenement;

some worked for other tenants, and some for the lord. The rolls contain many instances of a trespass against the lord by an individual who is referred to as the servant of a named tenant, and of the amercement of a female who was pledged by her employer, 'because in [his] house'. There is more evidence of the employment of non-tenants by the lord in many examples of his crops being damaged by them when working on his land, and in references to his shepherds, cowherd, swineherd and goatherd. In manors with a resident lord, particularly if he was a nobleman, there was employment for many in the castle, or the manor house, but the lords of Walsham manor did not live there, and those of High Hall were no more than gentry.

Some tenants can be seen to have employed shepherds, as well as house-servants, and labourers to work on their tenements and to perform customary services for them. Women appear frequently among those amerced for breaking the assize in the brewing or selling of ale, and on one occasion, for trespass in refusing to make cloth for the lady of the manor. Most of the tradesmen who are named were tenants; they too would have provided some work for non-tenants, but preference was probably given to their own families.

Most of the landless must have been heavily dependent on the farming activities of the lord, or of their family, or of other tenants, most of whom held relatively small tenements. With Walsham's high level of population, life was hard for the majority, but it was particularly so for the non-tenant and his family, especially in the second decade of the century when there were several years of famine. After the Black Death the opportunities for the landless must have improved dramatically.


WALSHAM AND THE WORLD OUTSIDE

Although the courts' business was wide-ranging, it has to be admitted that the rolls tend to be repetitive and extremely parochial (in a non-ecclesiastical sense). Of 155 rolls calendared, only two are markedly different from the rest; one (no.52), because it contains a very informative inventory of the goods of William Lene, and the other (no.147), because it contains a wealth of information about 103 victims of the Black Death.

William Lene was a villein; both the inventory and the accompanying list of funeral expenses indicate that he may have been a butcher, as was at least one of his descendants.

The roll, dated 11 December 1329, states

They say that William Lene, villein, who recently died, held from the lord a messuage \and a cottage/, 37a. of arable land, 1a.2r. of meadow and 1a.2r. of wood, as is shown in the particulars of the rental. His sons, William, aged 10, and Robert, aged 6, are his nearest heirs, and he gives an ox, worth 13s.4d. as a heriot. They say that Hilary, William's wife, should have in dower half of the messuage, cottage, land, meadow and wood; and she comes to ask for custody of the heirs, their lands and chattels, until their full age, she being answerable to them, and to the lord, when they come of age, for the income from the land and chattels, over and above the maintenance and repair of the buildings and land; and she pays 40s. fine for entry and custody,[21] pledges for

---

[21] Shown in the margin of the roll as 30s.

the fine and custody, as above, Nicholas Goche, John Syre and Matthew Hereward.

There is nothing unusual here, but the inventory of his goods and the list of his funeral expenses which appear at the end of the roll give William's death great interest. The gap in Walsham rolls between 1319 and 1327 has probably deprived us of a great deal of information about him. In seven rolls between 1316 and 1319 his name appeared 33 times, many of them in connection with land acquisitions; afterwards we have only the notice of his death. The existence of the inventory prompts the questions 'Why was it taken?' and 'For whose use?' It would have been of use to the lord only if William's land and goods were to be escheat to him, and this could only have been so if William had been a felon. The description and value of his goods, and of his funeral expenses, exclude any such possibility; and one must assume that William's death was not from natural causes, and the coroner had to decide whether it was suicide, the legal Latin for which is *felo de se*, a felony. However, the inventory contains a clue to the cause of his death, *una vacca in arsura deprehensa*, 'one cow caught in the blaze'. William, most probably, suffered the same fate as the cow, and the coroner's verdict was 'accidental death'.

Having concentrated, for a long time, on these Walsham rolls, one tended to feel that, because all the contents are concerned with local affairs, the people were isolated from, and unaware of, national events, whether of greater or lesser importance. Nowhere is the deposition of Edward II mentioned; even the recording of 119 deaths in the Black Death is limited to a few details of the land and heirs of each victim. But the list of expenses following William Lene's death gives clear evidence that he had been aware of, and took sides in, the civil war between Edward II and Queen Isabella. The last item of expenditure reads *pro expensis unius euntis Sancto Thoma Lancastris – ignoratur quantum*, 'for the expenses of one going to [the shrine of] St Thomas of Lancaster – the amount unknown'. This journey would not have been undertaken, except on the instructions of William himself on his death-bed, or of his widow.

Thomas, Earl of Lancaster and Hereditary Steward of England, led the rebel army which was defeated at the battle of Boroughbridge in March 1322; he was taken prisoner, and beheaded at Pontefract Castle. With the king's leave, the monks of the priory there removed his body and buried it before the high altar of their church. Before long, the earl was accounted a saint by supporters of the queen, who had fled to France, and pilgrims began to visit the tomb in sufficient numbers for the king to order an armed guard to be placed on it. In the following year, two of the guard were killed by a mob of pilgrims from Kent, and the relics of Lancaster were reported as being venerated in St Paul's in London. A substantial cult was established, and after Edward's deposition, the Commons pressed for the earl to be canonised. Nothing came of this because the Vatican did not even bother to respond. Nevertheless, the cult continued until the Reformation, and it was thought that his hat and belt, preserved at Pontefract, had curative properties.

Four years after Lancaster's death, the queen and Mortimer landed with an army at Walton near Felixtowe, and marched through Suffolk, staying a night in Bury St Edmunds, before moving on to Cambridge and into the West Country. The king was formally deposed on 20 January 1327, and murdered in September of that year. As the queen's army, consisting mainly of Hainaulters, came so close to Walsham, it would be surprising if none of the local people had taken sides, and while William

19

Lene favoured Queen Isabella, there is some ground for believing that Nicholas de Walsham, or his clerk, favoured the king.

The heading of roll no.37 gives the date as 'Wednesday after the feast of the Finding of the Holy Cross 20 Edw.II' [6 May 1327], but Edward's reign had ended on 27 January. Comparison of the business of courts immediately before and after this court, confirm that the calendar date was correct, and, since errors in dating in this form are so rare, it is likely that the mode of dating was deliberate. The king was deposed, but still lived, and those loyal to Edward II did not recognize the new Edward III. In the light of what was said earlier about the lord of High Hall presiding over his own courts, this apparent display of adherence to a lost cause could only have been made with Nicholas' approval. Is it possible that Walsham gave either side material support, in the way that their descendants, in the troop of Ironsides raised by Captain Ralph Margery, did for the Parlamentarian cause three centuries later?

# EDITORIAL METHODS

The following editorial conventions are used throughout this volume:

| | |
|---|---|
| Insertions in the original rolls are shown between oblique lines, thus | \ . . . / |
| Deletions are shown in angled brackets, thus | < . . . > |
| Editorial insertions in English are shown in square brackets, thus | [. . .] |
| Illegible words, or passages, are shown thus | [*illeg.*] |
| Words, or passages, made illegible by damage are shown thus | [*damaged*] |

Where uncertainty exists about a word or phrase, the Latin is shown in round brackets, preceded by a question mark, thus  (*?capit'*)

All Latin words used are shown in italics, letters inserted to interpret contractions are underlined.

The rolls are presented in five Sections, as shown in the Table of Contents, and numbered in chronological order, unsegregated between the two manors. Each roll is given in English translation. However, the first two rolls, fortuitously one for each manor, are transcribed in the original Latin, and, except in the marginal notes, with all abbreviations extended. Opposite, on the facing page, each entry is translated into English *verbatim*. The dates are in the standard format for the period, namely, by reference to the nearest saint's day or festival, and to the regnal year of the king; and they illustrate the convention for distinguishing kings of the same Christian name from one another. The king known to later generations as Edward I, was known to his own as 'King Edward'. His son was known as 'King Edward, the son of King Edward'; and the use of the ordinal numeral in the title did not occur until the third king of the same name. The confusion over the date of the first roll would have been avoided if the abbreviated word *tricesimo* (30th) had not been read as *tertio* (3rd) and taken to refer to the king's title, and *uno* (1), to his regnal year.

In succeeding rolls, the date, in its original format, has been omitted from the heading, and appears only in its modern form, with the year beginning on 1 January. In the text, dates are given as in the original, followed by the modern form; where a date is repeated for an identical entry in a subsequent roll, only the modern form is given.

The wide margin has been dispensed with, and the details of amercements, fines, etc. are embodied in the text. Where a marginal note provides additional information, for example 'and no more because poor' after the amount of an amercement, it is given in a footnote.

In the interest of economy some changes have been made to the layout of the rolls, but, except in the case of land transactions, the content has been altered only by reducing excess verbiage, and condensing into a single paragraph consecutive entries, where the business, or the person or persons involved, are identical. Where an offence, for example, is the subject of consecutive entries, and only the names of offenders are different, the word 'likewise' is inserted. Elsewhere, 'likewise' is used only where *similiter* appears in the original. No entry has been omitted, and the order of entries within the rolls has not been disturbed. Changes to the order of wording have only been made where necessary in the interest of clarity. Punctuation, which is rarely used in the original, has been inserted sparingly with the same objective.

Reference has already been made, under Procedures, to the complexity of entries dealing with land transactions, and as they occur so frequently, and individually occupy so much space, they have been reduced to a simple formula, as in the following example:

> Surrender: John Kebbil, to John Terwald and his heirs, a cottage, with a garden 8p. long and 5ft. wide, at Hatchmere, granted to him to hold in villenage at the lord's will, fine 2s., pledge the hayward.

Appropriate changes are made in the formula to cater for the circumstances of each transfer. A similar approach is taken in condensing entries following the death of tenants. Special care has been taken to ensure that no detail, especially of the terms of tenure, has been omitted from all changes of land holding.

Inconsistency is frequently to be found in the recording of transactions involving a messuage, land on which a dwelling is built. For example, the tenement may be described as 'a messuage and 3 acres of land' or as 'a messuage 3 acres of land', but whether the variation is merely one of practice between individual clerks, or is of greater significance is not clear. It is possible that the convention for all clerks was to include the conjunction 'and' only when the land being transferred was additional to the messuage, and that where 'and' was not used, the measured land was that in the messuage. Evidence elsewhere of failure by clerks to conform with other conventions suggests that this is unlikely, and in view of the uncertainty, the description used for each transaction in the original is reproduced in the edited text.

*Etc.* is used extensively in the original, but is generally omitted from the transcript. Square brackets are used to enclose appropriate substitutions for *etc.*, where clarity demands it, and on the rare occasions when it has been introduced by the editor. Three formulae are used to indicate that an order from a preceding court is repeated: *adhuc* is translated 'again', *sicut alias* 'as elsewhere' and *sicut pluries* 'as many times'.

The titles of two manorial officials with no responsibilities in the courts, occur infrequently in the rolls: the bailiff (*ballivus*) in Walsham manor, and the serjeant (*serviens*) in High Hall. Manorial lords, and especially those holding more than one manor, usually employed a bailiff to supervise the activities of the reeve and other local officials, and it is to be expected that one would be employed by Sir Edmund de Pakenham, and his successors. However, the title is more frequently used in the plural as a generic term for 'officials', as in the phrase *in contemptu domini et suorum ballivorum*, in contempt of the lord and his officials, namely, the reeve and the hayward. It is sometimes used together with the name of an official who is known to be the reeve. *Ballivus* has been translated as 'bailiff', only when it is clear that no other official was intended. A similar rule is applied in the translation of the word *serviens* as 'serjeant' in High Hall.

The spelling of identifiable place-names is shown in their modern form, followed, in brackets, by the original, for example Bardwell ['Berdewelle'], when it occurs for the first time: thereafter, only the modern form is used. Where a doubt exists, the original appears between single quotation marks, preceded by a question mark. Place-names which cannot be equated to a modern form appear as in the original. This formula is also used where a place-name forms part of a surname, with *de*, *del* and *atte* being translated as 'of', 'of the', and 'at the'. Thus *Wilelmus de Cranemere* becomes 'William of Cranmer', and *Rogerus del Brok*, 'Roger of the Brook', the styles by which they were probably known to their peers.

This, however, does not apply to those of higher social status, but one cannot be sure at what point in the social scale a family would use the French *de* as part of their surname. The letter from Sir William Elmham [*sic*] to Edmund Lakenheath, referred to above, indicates that French was the common usage of the sender, who had held high military rank in the disastrous Norwich Crusade of 1383, and of the recipient, his steward. Lady Rose de Pakenham would surely have been known as 'de Valognes', before she married Sir Edmund, and probably they too would have been French-speaking. To translate *de* as 'of' in their surnames, and those of similar status, is thought inappropriate, and all such names are as in the original. This formula is applied to all those who held the lordship of either manor.

Many surnames in the text are preceded by the word *le* meaning 'the', followed in most cases by an indication of a physical characteristic, or of an occupation, for example 'le Longe' or 'le Smith', descriptive of either the holder of the name or, more probably, of one of his or her forebears. The exceptions to this rule present an editor with a problem, in that the word *le* appears in names which, in translation, would result in such absurdities as Agnes the Man, John the King and William the Typtot. There are also many instances of a person being referred to in different styles in the same roll, for example John Wodebite and John le Wodebite.

The occupational names too can be very misleading, as in the case of Robert le cooper, who appears in the rolls under that name ten times. At his death in January 1339, his daughter Alice had entry to his tenement, the reversion of which she had, by purchase, before he died. No surname was given for Alice in the roll. In July 1339, six months later, the roll records the transaction by which Robert surrendered his tenement to the lord, who then granted seisin of it to Robert for life, and the reversion to Alice, on payment of a fine of 20s. In 1346, Alice, still described as the daughter of Robert the cooper, was given leave to marry Matthew Gilbert. When she died in the Black Death, her heir was found to be Robert Hereward, the son of her father's brother. Although, before her marriage, she was never described in a roll as anything but the daughter of Robert the cooper, her surname was Hereward, or Terewald, the two being interchangeable.

It becomes apparent, as one works through the rolls, that the word *le* is, more often than not, superfluous; and that the only reliable indication of a man's occupation is when his surname is expressed in Latin, and usually without a capital letter, e.g. *faber* for 'the smith', *bercarius* for 'the shepherd'. The word *le* does not appear in these forms, because the direct article did not exist in Latin.

When the word *le* appears in the rolls as part of a descriptive surname or an occupation, it has been translated on the first occasion it is used for an individual, and thereafter omitted; thus *Johannis le Longe* when he first appears, is given as 'John Long [le Longe]', afterwards as 'John Long'. When a name indicating an occupation appears in its Latin form, it has been translated and, on the first occasion, the original follows, in brackets. Thus, *Robertus cissor* appears first as 'Robert the tailor (*cissor*)', and subsequently as 'Robert the tailor'.

In the original, sums of money are expressed in pounds (*libri*), shillings (*solidi*), pence (*denarii*), half-pence (*oboli*) and farthings (*quadrantes*), and occasionally in marks (*marce*). The following table shows the relationship between them, with to-day's decimal currency:

| | | | |
|---|---|---|---|
| 1 pound (£) | = 20 shillings (s.) | = 240 pence (d.) | = 100 new pence (p.) |
| 1 shilling | = 12 pence | = 5 new pence | |
| 1 penny | = 2 half-pence (½d.) | = 4 farthings (¼d.) | |
| 1 mark (m.) | = 13s.4d. | | |

In the text amounts are shown in lower case Roman numerals. The figure *i* (1), when it appears alone, or as the last digit, is shown as *j*; 4 appears as *iiij*, and not as *iv*. For example, 1 mark is sometimes shown as *xiijs iiiijd*, and is then transcribed as 13s.4d.

Land areas are measured in acres, roods and perches; 1 acre (1a.) being equal to 4 roods (4r.) and 1 rood to 40 perches (40p.). The only unfamiliar unit of linear measurement is the perch (p.), which was equivalent to 5½ yards. Despite the use of the same abbreviation for both usages of the word 'perch', they are easily distinguished when read in context. Corn is measured in quarters, bushels and pecks; 1 quarter being equal to 8 bushels and 1 bushel to 4 pecks.

# THE
# COURT ROLLS
## OF
# WALSHAM LE WILLOWS

## 1303–1350

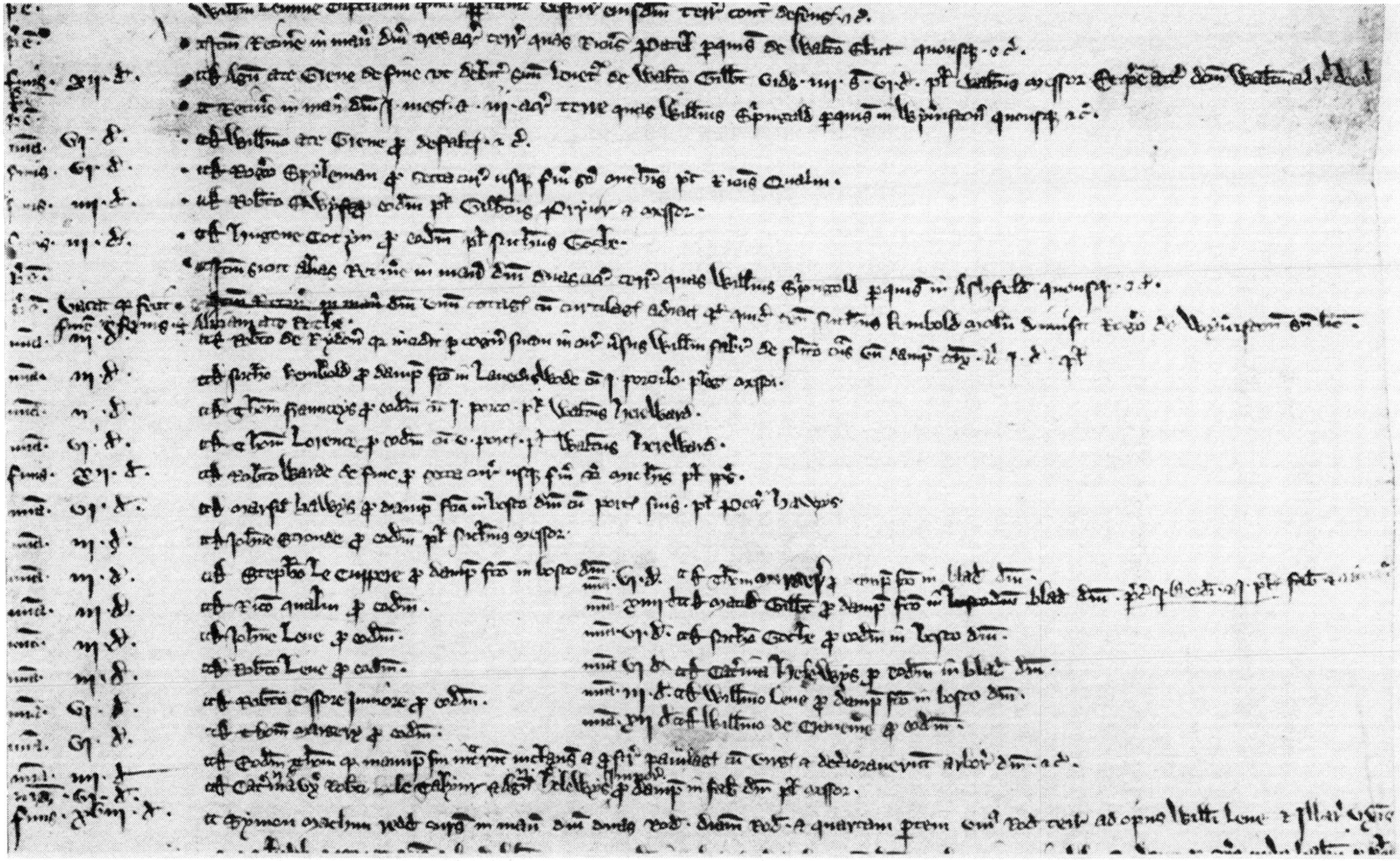

Plate 1. Extract from the court roll of Walsham manor dated 12 October 1316 [SRO(B) HA504/1/1.1].
See Latin transcription and full translation of this extract on pp. 28–43

# Section 1

## 16 October 1303 and 12 October 1316

### 1. HIGH HALL Court, 16 October 1303 [HA504/1/3.4]

Curia apud Walsham die mercurii proximo ante festum Sancte[*sic*] Luce Evangelisti anno regni regis Eadwardi tricesimo uno

Essonia    Henricus de Mers essoniat se de secta curie per Robertum Trusse.

   Johannes Stronde essoniat se de commune [secta] per Walterum Hosbern.

mia[1] *iiijd*    Willelmus Goche conquiritur se super Rogerum April de placito debiti, et dictus Rogerus invenit plegium ad respondendum, videlicet Gilbertus Helpe, et quittur per Walterum Wodebite et alios juratos quia Willelmus non verum dicit, et ideo in misericordia, plegius Gilbertus Helpe.

mia *vjd*    Willelmus Brodeie manucepit Galfridum le Doo, et non venit ad proximam curiam ad faciendum quod fecisse debet domino, et ideo Willelmus in misericordia, et precipitur ponere Galfridum ad meliores plegios, et dictus Willelmus invenit plegios Gilbertum Helpe et Reginaldum mercatorem.

mia *iiijd*    Petrus de Angeral et Willelmus Goche fecerunt pactum inter se de quadam pecia terre [h]abendam ad usum dicti Petri, prout fuerunt in unum, et dictus Willelmus fregit pactum inter se factum, et curia dixit quod dictus Petrus recuperabit pecuniam captam et [dampna sua] ad valorem *vjd*, et dictus Willelmus in misericordia, plegii Walterus le Wodebite et Gilbertus Helpe.

mia *iiijd*    Willelmus Goche et Simo Dolale fecerunt pactum inter se de quadam pecia terre [h]abendam ad usum Simonis ad seminendam per spatiam trium annorum, et dictus Willelmus fregit dictum pactum ad dampnum *x* denarios, et dicitur per curiam quod Simo recuperabit, et ideo Willelmus in misericordia, plegii Walterus Wodebite et Gilbertus Helpe.

mia *vjd*    Robertus Kempe invenit plegium ad respondendum Simoni Kembald *xxxvjd* de debito, et Simo recuperabit dampna sua ad valorem predictum, et ideo [Robertus] in misericordia, et invenit plegios Walterum Wodebite, Walterum Payn, Wilelmum de Angerale et Gilbertum Helpe ad solvendum dictos tres solidos dicto Simoni ad certos terminos, videlicet *xijd* ad natalem domini, et ad pascham *xijd* et ad purificationem *xijd*, sub pena *xijd* ad solvendum domino.

mia *iiijd*    Walterus le Wodebite fecit dampnum in blado domini, plegius Walterus Payn.

pre est[2]    Vicini de Opstrete fecerunt dampnum in blado domini et preceptum est athachare eos.

mia *ijd*    Willelmus Marlere fecit dampnum in blado domini.

mia *xijd*    Willelmus Burchard fecit dampnum in blado domini per viam quam vocatur Longe Weie.

---

1   misericordia.
2   preceptum est.

## 1. HIGH HALL Court, 16 October 1303 [HA504/1/3.4]

Court at Walsham, Wednesday next before the feast of St Luke the Evangelist, the
  31st year of the reign of King Edward [I][3]

Essoins   Henry of [the] Marsh essoins himself of suit of court by Robert Trusse.
  John Stronde essoins himself of common [suit] by Walter Osbern.

mercy 4d.   William Goche complains against Roger April concerning a plea of
  debt, and the said Roger finds a pledge to reply, namely Gilbert Helpe. And he
  [Roger] is acquitted by Walter Wodebite and the other jurors, because William
  does not speak the truth, and therefore in mercy, pledge Gilbert Helpe.

mercy 6d.   William Brodeie mainperned for Geoffrey le Doo, and he [Geoffrey]
  did not come to the following court to do that which he should have done to the
  lord,[4] and therefore William in mercy. And it is ordered to appoint better pledges
  for Geoffrey, and William finds as pledges Gilbert Helpe and Reginald the
  chapman.

mercy 4d.   Peter of Angerhale and William Goche made an agreement between
  themselves, concerning a piece of land, to have to the use of the said Peter as they
  had agreed, and the said William broke the agreement made between them. The
  court said that Peter shall recover the money taken, and [his losses] to the value
  of 6d., and the said William in mercy, pledge Walter Wodebite and Gilbert
  Helpe.

mercy 4d.   William Goche and Simon Dolale made an agreement between themselves, concerning a piece of land, to have to the use of Simon for sowing, for the
  span of three years. And the said William broke the said agreement to the loss of
  10d, and it is said by the court that Simon shall recover, and therefore William in
  mercy, pledges Walter Wodebite and Gilbert Helpe.

mercy 6d.   Robert Kempe finds a pledge to reply to Simon Kembald concerning a
  debt of 36d., and Simon shall recover his losses to the aforesaid value, and therefore [Robert] in mercy, and he finds as pledges Walter Wodebite, Walter Payn,
  William of Angerhale and Gilbert Helpe, to pay the said 3s. to the said Simon at
  fixed terms, namely 12d. at Christmas, and at Easter 12d., and at the [feast of the]
  Purification [2 February] 12d., under penalty of 12d. to be paid to the lord.

mercy 4d.   Walter Wodebite did damage in the lord's corn, pledge Walter Payn.

ordered   The inhabitants of Upstreet did damage in the lord's corn, and it was
  ordered to attach them.

mercy 2d.   William Marler did damage in the lord's corn.

mercy 12d.   William Burchard did damage in the lord's corn by the way which is
  called Long Way.

---

3   Before accession to SRO, interpreted as the first year of the reign of Edward III.
4   *viz.* to swear fealty.

mia *jd*  Thomas Suter fecit dampnum in blado domini.

mia *iijd*  Hugo Harre fecit dampnum in blado domini.

pre est  Alicia de Fornham fecit dampnum in bosco domini cum vacca, \preceptum est atachare eam/.

def.[5] mia *vjd*  Johannes Helpe non venit ad curiam ad sectandum ut debet et ideo in misericordia.

mia *iijd*  [De] Galfrido Payn pro eodem.

Summa Curie iiij solidi, vij denarii

## 2.  WALSHAM Court, 12 October 1316 [HA504/1/1]

Curia Generalis de Walsham die Martis proximo ante festum Sancti Luce Evangelisti anno regni regis Edwardi filii regis Edwardi decimo

[Essonia]  Gilbertus Sare de commune per Robertum Sare. Affidat super summonitionem.

| | |
|---|---|
| Thomas le Kyng versus Johannem de Hunterstone | |
| de placito debiti per Henricum Grym.[6] | habent |
| Johannes Margery de commune per Thomam Margery. | diem super |
| Johannes Stronde de commune per Adam Margery. | summonitionem. |

mia *vjd*  De Martino Bakun quia non warrantat suum essonium etc.

mia *vjd*  De Johanne Lene et messore secundis plegiis Thome le Kyng de Wattisfeud quia non habuerunt ipsum ad respondendum Johanni Maheu de Sancto Edmundi de placito debiti prout manuceperunt. Et preceptum est ponere ipsum per meliores plegios ad respondendum eidem de eodem, et Johannes Maheu ponit loco suo Walterum Osebern.

finis di marc[7]  De Agnete filia Roberti Hawys pro licentia se maritandi Radulpho Sesare \si dominus consensiat/, plegii Walterus Osebern et Nicholaus Goche. Et postea Willelmus Hawys et Marsilia Hawys manucapiunt quod querantur de domino.

mia *vjd*  De Gilberto Sare et suis plegiis de prosecutione versus Simonem fabrum de placito transgressionis \quia non est prosecutus/. Et dictus Simon inde quittur versus eum et suos plegios Johannem Lene et messorem.

finis[8]  Roberto Lene pro ingressu habendo in dimidiam rodam et quartam partem unius rode terre quam perquisivit de Radulpho le Ryche tenendum sibi et heredibus suis in vilnagio ad voluntatem domini, et dat per plegia Walteri prepositi et Nicholai messoris.

mia *vjd*  De Thoma le Suter et Simone Kembald primis plegiis Galfredi Kembold ad respondendum Olyvero Bercario de placito plegii. Et preceptum est ponere ipsum per meliores plegios.

pre est  Adhuc sicut pluries attachare Willelmum Wyswyf, Johannem Robetel et Johannem Goche nativos domini quia subtrahunt se de domino, et pro chevagio etc.

mia *iijd*  De Ada Warde pro transgressione facta Anne que fuit uxor Petri Warde prout cognovit in curia, dampnum taxatur ad *iijd*, plegius de dampno et misericordia Nicholaus Goche.

---

5  'defectus'.
6  Margin: 'non jacet quia per (?magn' ?distr')'.
7  'finis dimidia marca'.
8  Margin: 'vacat quia mortus'.

mercy 1d.   Thomas Suter did damage in the lord's corn.

mercy 3d.   Hugh Harre did damage in the lord's corn.

ordered   Alice of Fornham did damage in the lord's wood, with a cow, \it was ordered to attach her/.

default, mercy 6d.   John Helpe does not come to court to make suit as he ought, therefore in mercy.

mercy 6d.   Geoffrey Payn [in mercy] for the same.

Sum of the court 4s. 7d.

## 2.   WALSHAM Court, 12 October 1316 HA504/1/1]

Court General of Walsham Tuesday next before the feast of St Luke the Evangelist the 10th year of the reign of King Edward son of King Edward [10 Edw.II]

[Essoins] Gilbert Sare of common [suit] by Robert Sare. He pledges faith on summons.

| Thomas King versus John of Hunston concerning a plea of debt, [essoins] by Henry Grym.[9] | They have |
| John Margery of common [suit] by Thomas Margery. | a day on |
| John Stronde of common [suit] by Adam Margery | summons. |

mercy 6d.   From Martin Bakun because he did not warrant his essoin etc.

mercy 6d.   From John Lene and the hayward, the second pledges of Thomas King of Wattisfield, because they did not have him reply to John Mayheu of Bury St Edmunds concerning a plea of debt, as they undertook. And it was ordered that he appoint for himself better pledges to reply to him concerning the same. And John Mayheu appoints in his place Walter Osbern.

fine ½ mark From Agnes, the daughter of Robert Hawys, for leave to marry Ralph Sesare, \if the lord gives consent/, pledges Walter Osbern and Nicholas Goche. And afterwards William Hawys and Marsilia Hawys undertook that they would enquire of the lord.

mercy 6d.   From Gilbert Sare and his pledges concerning a prosecution against Simon the smith in a plea of trespass,\because he did not proceed/. And the said Simon is cleared of this [complaint] against him and his pledges, [viz.] John Lene and the hayward.

fine[10]   <Robert Lene> for having entry into three quarters of a rood of land which he purchased from Ralph le Ryche, to hold to him and his heirs in villenage, at the lord's will etc, and he gives by the pledges of Walter the reeve and Nicholas the hayward.

mercy 6d.   From Thomas the Suter and Simon Kembald, the first pledges of Geoffrey Kembald, to reply to Oliver the Shepherd concerning a plea of pledge. And it was ordered that he appoint for himself better pledges.

ordered   Again as many times, to attach William Wyswyf, John Robetel and John Goche, villeins, because they absent themselves from the lord, and for chevage.

mercy 3d.   From Adam Warde for trespass done to Anne, who was the wife of Peter Warde, as he acknowledges in court, the damage is assessed at 3d. Pledge for the damage and the amercement Nicholas Goche.

---

9   Margin: 'it does not lie because by (?great ?distraint)'.

10   Margin: 'void because dead'.

pre est   Item sicut pluries attachare Walterum parsonam inferioris ecclesie Stantune pro dampno facto in warenna domini etc.

pre est   Item sicut pluries retinere in manibus domini *xxiiij* acras terre apud Gyselyngham quas Templarii tenuerunt et respondere de exitibus quousque etc.

pre est   Item sicut pluries retinere stramen et pannos arestatos in custodia Johannis Lene, et capere plura quousque Robertus Jagge attachetur ad respondendum Marsilie Hawys de placito debiti.

pre est   Item sicut pluries attachare Ricardum Patel per corpus suum quod sit ad proximam curiam ad facere domino quod facere debet etc.

pre est   Item sicut pluries retinere in manibus domini dimidiam acram terre quam Johannes de Culyngge perquisivit de Petro Springald, et respondere de exitibus.

pre est   Item sicut pluries attachare Willelmum Kembold capellanum ad respondendum Petro Clyvehog de placito debiti etc.

pre est   Retinere unum bovettum captum super heredes Johannis de Walisham, et capere plura pro fidelitate ab eis exacta etc.

pre est   Sicut pluries retinere in manibus domini dimidiam acram terre quam Walterus Pye clamat versus Gilbertum Sare, et respondere de exitibus quousque etc.

respectum   Omnia tangentia Priorem de Bresete et Priorem de Ixwrthe ponuntur in respectum usque ad proximam curiam etc

pre est   Adhuc sicut pluries attachare Ceciliam Machun quia maritavit se sine licentia domini etc.

pre est   Item retinere in manibus domini proportionem Willelmi de Cranemere junioris de duabus acris quas perquisivit cum Willelmo Lemme capellano, et attachare dictum Willelmum Lemme capellanum quia asportavit vesturam ejusdem terre contra defensionem etc.

pre est   Item retinere in manibus domini tres acras terre quas Ricardus Patel perquisivit de Waltero Skut quousque etc.

fin *xijd*   De Agnete ate Grene de fine ut debitum suum levetur de Waltero Gilbert, videlicet *iiijs vjd*, plegius Walterus messor. Et preceptum est attachare dictum Walterum ad respondendum de eodem.

pre est   Retinere in manibus domini unum messuagium et *iij* acras terre quas Willelmus Springald perquisivit in Wyverstone quousque etc.

mia *vjd*   De Willelmo ate Grene pro defalto etc.

fin *vjd*   De Rogero Spileman pro secta curie usque festum Sancti Michaelis plegius Ricardus Qualm.

fin *iiijd*   De Roberto Swyft pro eodem, plegii Gilbertus Pryur et messor.

fin *iijd*   De Hugone Cotyn pro eodem, plegius Nicholaus Goche.

pre est   Item retinere in manibus domini duas acras terre quas Willelmus Springald perquisivit in Ashfeld quousque etc.

pre est   <Item retinere in manibus domini> unum cotagium cum curtilagio adjacente quod quidem tenementum Nicholaus Kembald molendarius dimisit Rogero de Wyverstone sine licentia.[11]

---

[11]  Margin: 'vacat quia fecit finem in forinse per Aliciam ate Roche'.

ordered    Also as many times, to attach Walter, the parson of the lower church of Stanton,[12] for damage done in the lord's warren etc.

ordered    Also as many times, to retain in the lord's hands 24 acres of land at Gislingham, which the Templars held, and to report the profits until etc.

ordered    Also as many times, to retain straw and cloths taken into the custody of John Lene, and to take more, until Robert Jagge is attached to reply to Marsilia Hawys concerning a plea of debt.

ordered    Also as many times, to attach Richard Patel by his body, that he be at the next court to do to the lord that which he should do.

ordered    Also as many times, to retain in the lord's hands ½ acre of land, which John of Cowlinge purchased from Peter Springald, and to report the profits.

ordered    Also as many times, to attach William Kembold chaplain to reply to Peter Clyvehog concerning a plea of debt.

ordered    To retain a bullock taken upon the heirs of John de Walsham, and to take more, for fealty demanded of them etc.

ordered    As many times, to retain in the lord's hands ½ acre of land, which Walter Pye claims against Gilbert Sare, and to report the profits, until etc.

respite    All matters touching the Prior of Bricett and the Prior of Ixworth [are] in respite until the next court etc.

ordered    Again as many times, to attach Cecilia Machun because she married without the lord's leave etc.

ordered    Also to retain in the lord's hands the share of William of Cranmer the younger of two acres of land, which he purchased with William Lemme chaplain, and to attach the said William Lemme chaplain, because he took away the crop from the same land, contrary to the prohibition etc.

ordered    Also to retain in the lord's hands three acres of land, which Richard Patel purchased from Walter Skut until etc.

fine 12d.    From Agnes ate Grene as a fine that her debt be raised from Walter Gilbert, namely 4s.6d., pledge Walter the hayward, and it was ordered to attach the said Walter [Gilbert] to reply concerning the same.

ordered    To retain in the lord's hands a messuage and 3 acres of land, which William Springald purchased in Wyverstone, until etc.

mercy 6d.    From William ate Grene for default etc.

fine 6d.    From Roger Spileman for [respite of] suit of court until the feast of St Michael, pledge Richard Qualm.

fine 4d.    From Robert Swyft for the same, pledges Gilbert Pryur and the hayward.

fine 3d.    From Hugh Cotyn for the same, pledge Nicholas Goche.

ordered    Also to retain in the lord's hands two acres of land, which William Springald purchased in Ashfield[13] until etc.

ordered    <Also to retain in the lord's hands> a cottage with a curtilage adjoining, which same tenement Nicholas Kembold the miller demised to Roger of Wyverstone without leave.[14]

---

12  All Saints church.

13  Probably Little Ashfield, now Badwell Ash.

14  Margin: 'void because he paid a fine in an outside court by Alice atte Roche'.

mia *iijd*   De Roberto de Rydon quia incidit per cognitionem suam in curia versus Willelmum fabrum de placito transgressionis unde dampnum taxatur ad *jd*, plegius [blank].

mia *iijd*   De Nicholao Kembald pro dampno facto in Lanediswode cum uno porculo, plegius messor.

mia *iijd*   De Thoma Fraunceys pro eodem cum uno porco, plegius Walterus Hereward.

mia *vjd*   De Thoma Lorence pro eodem cum v porcis, plegius Walterus Hereward.

fin *xijd*   De Roberto Warde de fine pro secta curie usque festum Sancti Michaelis, plegius prepositus.

mia *vjd*   De Marsilia Hawys pro dampno facto in bosco domini cum porcis suis, plegius Petrus Hawys.

mia *iiijd*   De Johanne Stronde pro eodem, plegius Nicholaus messor.

mia *iijd*   De Stephano le Cuppere pro dampno facto in bosco domini.

mia *iijd*   De Ricardo Qwalm pro eodem.

mia *iijd*   De Johanne Lene pro eodem.

mia *iijd*   De Roberto Lene pro eodem.

mia *vjd*   De Roberto Cissore juniore pro eodem.

mia *vjd*   De Thoma Margery pro eodem.

mia *iiijd*   De eodem Thoma quia manupasti sui intraverunt in clausum et prostraverunt pannagium cum virgis et deterioraverunt arbores domini etc.

mia *vjd*   De Thoma Margery pro dampno facto in blado domini.

mia *xiiijd*   De Matilda Gilbert pro dampno facto in blado domini pretito uno buscello ordei et una pecca fabarum asportatis.

mia *vjd*   De Nicholao Goche pro eodem in bosco domini.

mia *vjd*   De Caterina Helewys pro eodem in blado domini.

mia *iijd*   De Willelmo Lene pro dampno facto in bosco domini.

mia *xijd*   De Willelmo de Cranemere pro eodem.

mia *vjd*[*sic*]   De Caterina uxore Roberti le Talyour \\*ijd*/ et Agneta Helewys juniore \\*ijd*/ pro dampno facto in fabis domini, plegius messor.

fin *xviijd*   Symon Machun reddidit sursum in manus domini duas rodas, dimidiam rodam et quartam partem unius rode terre ad opus Willelmi Lene et Illarie uxoris sue et heredum eorum, et seisina sibi deliberatur tenendum in vilnagio ad voluntatem domini, salvo jure cujuslibet, et dant pro seisina inde habenda per plegia Walteri prepositi et Nicholai Goche.

mia *iijd*   De Radulpho Crane pro dampno facto in ordeo domini ad valorem unius garbi ordei, plegius Willelmus de Cranemere.

Compertum est per inquisitionem quod Willelmus Springald nativus domini trahit bona crescentia in bondagio de Walsham usque ad Wyverstone super feodem domini Hugonis Hovel. Ideo preceptum est capere in manus domini totum bondagium quod dictus Wilelmus tenet de domino quousque etc.

mia *vjd*   Item quod Symon Kembold trahit bona et catalla de bondagio domini in liberum tenementum ubi manet. Ideo ipse in misericordia.

mia *iijd*   De Robert Godefrey pro assisa panis fracta.

mercy 3d.   From Robert of Rydon because by his own admission he intervened in the court against William the smith concerning a plea of trespass, for which the damage is assessed at 1d, pledge [blank].

mercy 3d.   From Nicholas Kembald for damage done in Lanediswode with a piglet, pledge the hayward.

mercy 3d.   From Thomas Fraunceys for the same with a pig, pledge Walter Hereward.

mercy 6d.   From Thomas Lorence for the same with five pigs, pledge Walter Hereward

fine 12d.   From Robert Warde as a fine for [respite of] suit of court until the feast of St Michael, pledge the reeve.

mercy 6d.   From Marsilia Hawys for damage done in the lord's wood with her pigs, pledge Peter Hawys.

mercy 3d.   From John Stronde for the same, pledge Nicholas the hayward.

mercy 3d.   From Stephen the Cooper for damage done in the lord's wood.

mercy 3d.   From Richard Qualm for the same.

mercy 3d.   From John Lene for the same.

mercy 3d.   From Robert Lene for the same.

mercy 6d.   From Robert the Tailor the younger for the same.

mercy 6d.   From Thomas Margery for the same.

mercy 4d.   From the same Thomas [Margery] because his servants entered the close, and knocked down the pannage with rods, and damaged the lord's trees etc.

mercy 6d.   From Thomas Margery for damage done in the lord's corn.

mercy 14d.   From Matilda Gilbert for damage done in the lord's corn, assessed at 1 bushel of barley and 1 peck of beans taken away.

mercy 6d.   From Nicholas Goche for the same in the lord's wood.

mercy 6d.   From Catherine Helewys for the same in the lord's corn.

mercy 3d.   From William Lene for the same in the lord's wood.

mercy 12d.   From William of Cranmer for the same.

mercy 6d.[15]   From Catherine, the wife of Robert Tailor, \2d./ and Agnes Helewys the younger \2d./ for damage done in the lord's beans, pledge the hayward.

fine 18d.   Simon Machun surrendered into the lord's hands 2¾ roods of land to the use of William Lene and Hilary his wife and their heirs, and seisin is delivered to them to hold in villeinage at the lord's will, saving the right of whomsoever, and they give for having seisin thereof, by the pledges of Walter the reeve and Nicholas Goche.

mercy 3d.   From Ralph Crane for damage done in the lord's barley, to the value of 1 sheaf of barley, pledge William of Cranmer.

It was found by the enquiry that William Springald, villein of the lord, took crops growing in the bondage of Walsham as far as Wyverstone, on the fee of lord Hugh Hovel. Therefore ordered to take into the lord's hands all of the bondage which the said William holds of the lord until etc.

mercy 6d.   Also that Simon Kembold took goods and chattels from the lord's bondage into the free tenement where he lives, therefore he [is] in mercy.

mercy 3d.   From Robert Godefrey for breach of the assize of bread.

---

[15] [sic.]

mia *iijd*   De Ada Noble pro eodem.

mia *iijd*   De Petro Pynful pro eodem.

mia *iijd*   De Roberto Kembold pro eodem.

mia *iijd*   De Gilberto Pryur pro eodem.

mia *iijd*   De Simone fabro pro eodem, plegius Petrus Robbys.

mia *vjd*   De Willelmo Lene pro assisa cervisie fracta.

mia *vjd*   De Matilda Kembold pro regrateria cervisie.

mia *iijd*   De Matilda uxore Galfridi Kembold pro eodem.

mia pauper   De Johanne Albry pro eodem.

mia *iijd*   De Agneta Fuller pro eodem, plegius Wilelmus Marlere.

mia *iijd*   De Alicia Warde pro eodem, plegius Adam Warde.

herieta jumentum *ijs vjd*   Walterus Puddyng tenuit de domino die quo obiit unum messuagium quinque acras terre custumarie per servicium in redditale contentum. Et quod Matilda et Cecilia filie ejusdem Walteri Puddyng sunt heredes ejusdem Walteri, que veniunt in curiam et petunt dictum tenementum ut hereditarium suum. Per cujus mortem dominus habuit unum jumentum pretitum *ijs vjd*, et preceptum est retinere dictum tenementum in manibus domini quousque etc. et preceptum est preposito quod respondeat de exitibus.

herieta jumentum *vs*   Item Petrus Warde tenuit de domino die quo obiit mediatem unius messuagii et *xij* acrarum terre cum bosco et pastura, per servicium etc, per cujus mortem dominus habuit unum jumentum post fetum, pretitum *vs*. Et dicunt quod Robertus et Willelmus filii ejusdem Petri sunt heredes ejus propinquos etc. Et preceptum est retinere dictum tenementum in manibus domini quousque etc. et respondere de exitibus.

fin *xijd*   Item dicunt quod Alicia le Doo obiit seisita de uno cotagio quod perquisivit de Radulpho le Doo et aliis. Et dicunt quod Walterus le Doo est heres ejusdem Alicie, qui venit in curiam et fecit finem pro dicto tenemento habendo sibi et heredibus suis, per plegium Nicholai Goche.

fin dim marca   Radulphus le Ryche obiit seisitus in uno cotagio et *iij* acras terre custumarie, per cujus mortem dominus nichil habuit quia nichil habuit in bonis. Quod quidem tenementum preceptum est retinere in manibus domini quousque veniet etc. Et dicunt quod Basilia ate Broke est propinquior heres ejusdem tenementi, habet diem usque ad proximam curiam etc. \Et postea fecit finem pro dicto tenemento habendo, plegius Wilelmus Lene./

fin *xijd*   Alicia le Longe obiit seisita in quarta parte unius curie unius acre et dimidie terre custumarie. Matilda, Agatha et Alicia sorores ejusdem Alicie sunt heredes ejusdem Alicie, que fecerunt finem pro dicto tenemento habendo, per plegios Willelmi de Cranemere et Walteri filii Simonis.

pre est   Seisire in manus domini unum cotagium continens unam rodam et dimidiam, quod quidem tenementum Radulphus Heryrof vendidit Alicie Spilman, quousque veniet et reddet sursum dictum tenementum.

fin *xijd*   Willelmus Payn junior reddidit sursum in manus domini unam rodam et dimidiam terre ad opus Wilelmi filii Galfridi Payn et heredum ejus, et seisina sibi deliberatur tenendum in vilnagio ad voluntatem domini, salvo jure cujuslibet etc. et dat pro ingressu habendo per plegium Nicholai Goche.

mercy 3d.    From Adam Noble for the same.

mercy 3d.    From Peter Pynful for the same.

mercy 3d.    From Robert Kembold for the same.

mercy 3d.    From Gilbert Pryur for the same.

mercy 3d.    From Simon the smith for the same, pledge Peter Robbys.

mercy 12d.   From William Lene for breach of the assize of ale.

mercy 6d.    From Matilda Kembold for the regrating of ale.

mercy 3d.    From Matilda, the wife of Geoffrey Kembold, for the same.

mercy[16]   From John Albry for the same.

mercy 3d.    From Agnes Fuller for the same, pledge William Marler.

mercy 3d.    From Alice Warde for the same, pledge Adam Warde.

heriot a mare 2s.6d.   Walter Pudding held from the lord on the day on which he died a messuage, five acres of customary land by the service contained in the rental, and Matilda and Cecilia, the daughters of the same Walter, are the heirs of the same Walter, and they come into court and seek the said tenement, as their inheritance. By whose death the lord had a mare priced 2s.6d., and it is ordered to retain the said tenement in the lord's hands until etc. and the reeve is ordered to report the profits.

heriot a mare 5s.   Also Peter Warde held from the lord, on the day on which he died, half of a messuage and 12 acres of land with wood and pasture, by the service etc., by whose death the lord had a mare after foaling, priced 5s. And they say that Robert and William, the sons of the same Peter, are his nearest heirs etc., and it is ordered to retain the said tenement in the lord's hands, until etc. and to report the profits.

fine 12d.   Also they say that Alice le Doo died, seised of a cottage, which she purchased from Ralph le Doo and others, and they say that Walter le Doo is the heir of the same Alice, and he comes into court and pays a fine for having the said tenement to himself and his heirs, by the pledge of Nicholas Goche.

fine ½ mark   Ralph le Ryche died seised in a cottage and 3 acres of customary land, and by his death the lord had nothing because he [Ralph] had nothing in goods. And it is ordered that this same tenement be retained in the lord's hands until [the heir] comes etc. And they say that Basilia at Broke is the nearest heir to the same tenement, and she has a day until the next court etc. \And afterwards she pays a fine for having the same tenement, pledge William Lene/

fine 12d.   Alice Long died seised in a quarter part of a courtyard, 1½ acres of customary land; Matilda, Agatha and Alice, sisters of the same Alice, are heirs of the same Alice, and they pay a fine for having the said tenement, by the pledges of William of Cranmer and Walter, the son of Simon.

ordered   To seize into the lord's hands a cotland containing 1½ roods of land, which same tenement Ralph Heryrof sold to Alice Spilman, until he shall comes and surrender the said tenement.

fine 12d.   William Payn the younger surrendered into the lord's hands 1½ roods of land to the use of William, the son of Geoffrey Payn, and his heirs, and seisin is delivered to him to hold in villeinage, at the lord's will, saving the right of whomsoever, and he gives for having entry, pledge Nicholas Goche.

---

[16]  Margin: 'poor'; the amercement was waived.

fin *xijd*  Thomas Echeman reddidit sursum in manus domini unam rodam et dimidiam terre ad opus Radulphi Echeman et heredum suorum et seisina sibi deliberatur tenendum in vilnagio ad voluntatem domini, salvo jure cujuslibet, et dat etc. plegius messor.

fin *xviijd*  Rogerus of Wode[*sic*] et Alicia uxor sua reddiderunt sursum in manus domini dimidiam acram terre jacentem in le Syke, sicut jacet inter terram le Peyntour et terram Hugonis Clyvehog, ad opus Johannis Patyl et heredum ejus, et seisina sibi deliberatur tenendum in vilnagio ad voluntatem domini, salvo jure cujuslibet etc. et dat pro seisina inde habenda per plegium Nicholai Goche.

fin *ijs*  Walterus le Machun reddidit sursum in manus domini unum messuagium cum duobus domis et omnibus pertinentibus ad opus Roberti de Rydon et Matilde uxoris ejus et heredum eorum, et seisina sibi deliberatur tenendum in vilnagio ad voluntatem domini, salvo jure cujuslibet etc. et dant de fine pro ingressu habendo, plegius messor.

fin *xijd*  Petrus Qualm reddidit sursum in manus domini unam rodam terre jacentem in Wellefeld ad opus Symonis Peyntour et heredum ejus, et seisina sibi deliberatur tenendum in vilnagio ad voluntatem domini, salvo jure cujuslibet etc. et dat de fine, plegius Nicholaus Goche.

fin *xviijd*  Alicia le Longe et Agatha le Longe reddiderunt sursum in manus domini dimidiam acram terre jacentem apud Estmelne ad opus Ade le Noble et heredum suorum, et seisina sibi deliberatur tenendum in vilnagio ad voluntatem domini, salvo jure cujuslibet etc. et dat etc. plegius messor.

mia *iijd*  De Nicholao Kembold quia incidit per inquisitionem versus Petrum Springald de placito transgressionis unde dampnum taxatur ad *iijd*, plegium pro dampno et misericordia [blank].

mia *xijd*  De Ade Warde quia incidit per inquisitionem versus Edmundum Patel de placito transgressionis unde dampnum taxatur ad *jd*, plegius pro dampnum et misericordia [blank].

fin *ijs*  De Basilia Pays de fine pro seisina habenda in tenementa que fuerunt Radulphi Hulke, que capta fuerunt in manus domini in curia precedente, plegius Willelmus de Cranemere.

pre est  Summonere Radulphum Heryrof quod sit ad proximam curiam ad respondendum [de] cotagio quod vendidit Alicie Spilman etc.

pre est  Adhuc retinere in manibus domini unam rodam prati quam Willelmus Lene perquisivit de Radulpho de Walsingham quousque etc.

fin *xijd*  Beatrix ate Broke reddidit sursum in manus domini unam rodam terre jacentem juxta terram Willelmi de Cranemere et Willelmi Hawys ad opus Wilelmi de Cranemere junioris et heredum ejus, et seisina sibi deliberatur tenendum in vilnagio ad voluntatem domini, salvo jure cujuslibet, et dat etc. plegius Willelmus de Cranemere.

fin *vjd*  De Petro le Peyntour de fine pro secta curie usque festum Sancti Michaelis, plegius Simon Peyntour.

fin *vjd*  De Johanne Lene pro eodem, plegius Robertus Lene.

fin *iijd*  De Willelmo Rampolye pro licentia concordandi cum Waltero fabro in placito transgressionis, plegius Walterus Rampolye.

mia *iijd*  De Simone Roty pro vasto facto, plegius messor.

fine 12d.   Thomas Echeman surrendered into the lord's hands 1½ roods of land to the use of Ralph Echeman and his heirs, and seisin is delivered to him to hold in villeinage, at the lord's will, saving the right of whomsoever etc. and he gives for having entry, pledge the hayward.

fine 18d.   Roger of Wood and Alice, his wife, surrendered into the lord's hands ½ acre of land, lying in the Syke between the land [of] le Peyntour and the land of Hugh Clyvehog, to the use of John Patyl and his heirs, and seisin is delivered to him to hold in villeinage, at the lord's will, saving the right of whomsoever etc. and he gives for having seisin thereof, pledge Nicholas Goche.

fine 2s.   Walter le Machunn surrendered into the lord's hands a messuage with two buildings and all appurtenances, to the use of Robert of Rydon and Matilda, his wife, and their heirs, and seisin is delivered to them to hold in villeinage, at the lord's will, saving the right of whomsoever etc. and they give as a fine for having entry, pledge the hayward.

fine 12d.   Peter Qualm surrenders into the lord's hands 1 rood of land, lying in Wellfield, to the use of Simon Peyntour and his heirs, and seisin is delivered to him to hold in villeinage, at the lord's will, saving the right of whomsoever etc. and he gives as a fine, pledge Nicholas Goche.

fine 18d.   Alice Long and Agatha Long surrendered into the lord's hands ½ acre of land, lying at Eastmill, to the use of Adam Noble and his heirs, and seisin is delivered to him to hold in villeinage, at the lord's will, saving the right of whomsoever etc. and he gives etc. pledge the hayward.

mercy 3d.   From Nicholas Kembold because he intervened through the enquiry against Peter Springald concerning a plea of trespass, the loss from which is assessed at 3d., pledge for the loss and the amercement [blank].

mercy 3d.   From Adam Warde because he intervened through the enquiry against Edmund Patel concerning a plea of trespass, the loss from which is assessed at 1d., pledge for the loss and the amercement [blank].

fine 2s.   From Basilia Pays as a fine for having seisin in the tenements which were of Ralph Hulke, which were taken into the lord's hands in the preceding court, pledge William of Cranmer.

ordered   To summon Ralph Heryrof that he be at the next court to reply [concerning] a cottage which he sold to Alice Spilman etc.

ordered   Again to retain in the lord's hands 1 rood of meadow which William Lene purchased from Ralph of Walsingham until etc.

fine 12d.   Beatrice ate Broke surrendered into the lord's hands 1 rood of land, lying next to the land of William of Cranmer and William Hawys, to the use of William of Cranmer the younger and his heirs, and seisin is delivered to him to hold in villeinage, at the lord's will, saving the right of whomsoever, and he gives etc. pledge William of Cranmer.

fine 6d.   From Peter le Peyntour as a fine for [respite of] suit of court until the feast of St Michael, pledge Simon Peyntour.

fine 6d.   From John Lene for the same, pledge Robert Lene.

fine 3d.   From William Rampolye for leave to agree with Walter the smith in a plea of trespass, pledge Walter Rampolye.

mercy 3d.   From Simon Roty for waste made, pledge the hayward.

fin *vjd*   Agatha le Longe reddidit sursum in manus domini unam rodam terre ad opus Alicie le Longe et heredum ejus, et seisina sibi deliberatur tenendum in vilnagio ad voluntatem domini, salvo jure cujuslibet etc. et dat de fine per plegium [blank].

fin *vjd*   Simon faber reddidit sursum in manus domini dimidiam rodam terre jacentem Aboventhebroke[*sic*] inter terram Johannis Lene ex parte una et terram Roberti Spilman, ad usum Stephani Godefrey et heredum ejus, et seisina sibi deliberatur tenendum in vilnagio ad voluntatem domini, salvo jure cujuslibet etc. et dat de fine per plegium Nicholai messoris.

fin *vjd*   De Alicie ate Roche pro termino habendo de uno cotagio, quod conducit de Nicholao Kembald ad terminum vj annorum, plegius Olyverus Bercarius.

fin *vjd*   De Nicholao molendario pro secta curie usque festum Sancti Michaelis, plegius messor.

fin dim. marca   Basilia ate Broke reddidit sursum in manus domini unum messuagium et totam terram unde Radulphus le Ryche obiit seisitus, quod quidem tenementum jure hereditarie contigit ad opus Wilelmi Lene et Illarii uxoris sue et heredum suorum, et seisina sibi deliberatur tenendum in vilnagio ad voluntatem domini, salvo jure cujuslibet etc. et dant de fine pro seisina inde habenda, plegii Walterus prepositus et Nicholaus Goche.

mia *vjd*   De Willelmo ate Grene pro secta curie usque festum Sancti Michaelis.

mia *iijd*   De tenentibus tenementi Jacobi Bercarii pro defalto.

mia *iijd*   De Johanne Fraunceys pro eodem.

fin una marca   De Willelmo Osebern pro ingressu habendo in tenementa que fuerunt Mathei ate Broke, tenendum sibi et heredibus suis in vilnagio ad voluntatem domini, per plegia Walteri prepositi et Willelmi de Cranemere.

R.[17]   Jurati habent diem usque ad proximam curiam ad respondendum de *vjd* annuale redditu et iiij diebus metendis in autumpno.

fin *iijs*   Rogerus of Wode[*sic*] et Alicia uxor sua reddiderunt sursum in manus domini unam acram et dimidiam acram terre jacentes in *xj* peciis, quarum *iiij* pecie jacent in Hordeshage, et *v* pecia jacent circa Hordeshage, et in Coppeloweslond aboven[*sic*] Sudbroke jacet una pecia, et super Wellefeld jacet una pecia, ad opus Petri Clyvehog et heredum suum, et seisina sibi deliberatur tenendum in vilnagio ad voluntatem domini, salvo jure cujuslibet etc. et dat etc. plegius Walterus prepositus.

Electio   Nicholaus Kembold electus est in officio custodis bosci et warenne, et recepit dictum officium et juravit.

fin *ijs*   De Willelmo filio Galfridi Payn de fine ne sit in officio messoris.

fin *ijs*   De Ricardo Kebbel pro eodem.

fin *xijd*   De Roberto Rampolye ne sit in officio custodis bosci.

fin *ijs*   Walterus Goselyng reddidit sursum in manus domini unam peciam pasture que continet ad unum caput *iiij* perticas et ad aliud caput *iij* perticas, et pratum jacentem in prato vocato Miclemedwe, ad opus Willelmi Lene et Illarii uxoris sue et heredum eorum, et seisina sibi deliberatur tenendum in vilnagio ad voluntatem domini, salvo jure cujuslibet etc., et dant per plegium Walteri Osebern.

---

17 'Respondere'

fine 6d. Agatha Long surrendered into the lord's hands 1 rood of land, to the use of Alice Long and her heirs, and seisin is delivered to her to hold in villeinage, at the lord's will, saving the right of whomsoever etc. and she gives as a fine, pledge [blank].

fine 6d. Simon the smith surrendered into the lord's hands ½ rood of land, lying above the brook between the land of John Lene on one side and the land of Robert Spilman, to the use of Stephen Godefrey and his heirs, and seisin is delivered to him to hold in villeinage, at the lord's will, saving the right of whomsoever etc. and he gives as a fine by the pledge of Nicholas the hayward.

fine 6d. From Alice ate Roche for having her term of a cottage, which she leases from Nicholas Kembald, to a term of six years, pledge Oliver the Shepherd.

fine 6d. From Nicholas the miller for [respite of] suit of court until the feast of St Michael, pledge the hayward.

fine ½ mark Basilia ate Broke surrendered into the lord's hands a messuage and all the land of which Ralph le Ryche died seised, which same tenement belonged by hereditary right to the use of William Lene and Hilary, his wife, and their heirs, and seisin is delivered to them to hold in villeinage, at the lord's will, saving the right of whomsoever etc. and they give as a fine for having seisin thereof, pledges Walter the reeve and Nicholas Goche.

mercy 6d. From William ate Green for [respite of] suit of court until the feast of St Michael.

mercy 3d. From the tenants of the tenement of James the Shepherd for default.

mercy 3d. From John Fraunceys for the same.

fine 1 mark From William Osbern as a fine for having entry into the tenements which were of Matthew ate Broke, to hold to him and his heirs in villeinage, at the lord's will, by the pledges of Walter the reeve and William of Cranmer.

Reply The jurors have a day until the next court to reply concerning 6d. annual rent and four days reaping in autumn.

fine 3s. Roger of Wood and Alice, his wife, surrendered into the lord's hands 1½ acres of land, lying in 11 pieces, of which 4 pieces lie in Hordeshage, and 5 pieces lie around Hordeshage, and in Coppelowesland above Southbrook lies 1 piece, and above Wellfield lies one piece, to the use of Peter Clyvehog and his heirs, and seisin is delivered to him to hold in villeinage, at the lord's will, saving the right of whomsoever etc. and he gives etc. pledge Walter the reeve.

Election Nicholas Kembold was elected to the office of keeper of the wood and warren, and he accepted the said office and was sworn.

fine 2s. From William, the son of Geoffrey Payn, as a fine that he shall not be in the office of hayward.

fine 2s. From Richard Kebbel for the same.

fine 12d. From Robert Rampolye that he shall not be in the office of keeper of the wood.

fine 2s. Walter Goseling surrendered into the lord's hands a piece of pasture, which contains at one head 4 perches and at the other head 3 perches, and meadow lying in the meadow called Micklemeadow, to the use of William Lene and Hilary, his wife, and their heirs, and seisin is delivered to them to hold in villeinage, at the lord's will, saving the right of whomsoever etc. and they give by the pledge of Walter Osbern.

fin *vjd*   De Waltero Osebern et Willelmo Hawys de fine pro termino habendo de uno messuagio et vj acras terre, quod quidem tenementum habuerunt ex dimissione Willelmi Osebern, a festo Sancti Michaelis ultimo preterito usque ad dictum festum pro vij annis proximis sequentibus et completis. Et facere omnia opera et consuetudines de dicto tenemento debita infra dictum terminum, et dant de fine, plegius alter alterius.

R.      Willelmus ate Grene per uxorem suam invenit plegios ad satisfaciendum dominum ad proximam curiam de messionibus, aruris et aliis serviciis ab eo exactis, vel ad ostendum quare facere non debet, videlicet Willelmus de Cranemere et Willelmus Cocus.

R.      Datus est dies juratis ad inquirendum et certificandum ad proximam curiam de valore pannagii in omnibus boscis domini hoc anno.

mia *iijd*   De Roberto Spilman pro dampno facto in bosco domini, plegius prepositus.

fin *iijs iiijd*   De Roberto capellano de fine ne sit in officio prepositi, per plegium Walteri Osebern.

mia *xijd*   De Petro Springald quia non fecit officium custodis bosci nec fecit attachamenta prout facere debuit etc.

mia *vjd*   De Ade Coppelowe pro dampno facto in blado domini cum porcis etc.

pre. est   Attachare Robertum Warde respondendum Waltero Pye de placito detentionis bidentium.

Summa iiij libri vij solidi vj denarii, preter herietas

*From this point the court rolls are only translated into English.*

fine 6d.   From Walter Osbern and William Hawys as a fine for having a term in a messuage and 6 acres of land, which same tenement they had by the demise of William Osbern from the feast of St Michael last past to the said feast of St Michael after the next seven years following and completed. And to perform all works and customs due from the said tenement within the said term, and they give as a fine, pledge each of the other.

Reply   William ate Green by his wife finds pledges to satisfy the lord at the next court concerning reapings, ploughings and other services demanded of him, or to show on what grounds he should not do so, namely William of Cranmer and William Cook.

Reply   A day is given to the jurors to enquire and to certify, at the next court, concerning the pannage in all the lord's woods this year.

mercy 3d.   From Robert Spilman for damage done in the lord's wood, pledge the reeve.

fine 3s.4d.   From Robert [Shepherd] the chaplain as a fine that he shall not be in the office of reeve by the pledge of Walter Osbern.

fine 12d.   From Peter Springald because he did not perform the duty of keeper of the wood, nor make attachments as he ought etc.

mercy 6d.   From Adam Coppelowe for damage done in the lord's corn with pigs etc.

ordered   To attach Robert Warde to reply to Walter Pye concerning a plea of detention of sheep.

Sum £4 7s. 6d., except the heriots

43

# Section 2

## December 1316 – November 1326

**3. HIGH HALL Court of Sir Alexander de Walsham, 16 December 1316 [HA504/1/1.2.i]**

The whole homage pays ½ mark to the lord for recognition, pledges each for another.

William Hawys amerced 12d. for trespass with his pigs in the lord's wood, pledge William of Cranmer.

Ordered to retain in the lord's hands a messuage 5r. of land of villeinage, [taken] after the death of Peter the son of Richard of Angerhale villein, who died one year ago, and 2a. of the fee of Sir Hugh Hovel, which Richard held free, and 2a. of the lord of Westhorpe, which he also held free. Margery Peter's sister is his nearest heir, and she pays 3s. for entry, pledges Gilbert Helpe and John Wodebite.

Simon Kembald and Thomas Suter each amerced 3d. for trespass in the tenement, formerly of William Kembald, by Catherine Simon's daughter for whom they were guarantors, pledges each for the other.

William the son of Geoffrey Payn amerced 6d. for trespass with cows in the orchard formerly of Geoffrey Kembald, now in the lord's hands; Thomas Suter 3d. and Simon Kembald 3d. for the same, pledge for all William of Cranmer.

Gilbert Helpe is elected to the office of reeve, and John Wodebite to that of collector; John will receive nothing for his office and no remission of services and customs, and he will collect rents and the fines and amercements of the court.

Ordered to take into, and retain in, the lord's hands a messuage 8½a. of land which Geoffrey Kembald held in villeinage, and a messuage 8a. which Ralph Issabel held likewise, for services and customs withheld, and for many defaults.

Ordered to distrain John Stronde, Geoffrey Doo, Robert of House, Robert Carpenter, William, the son of Reginald Chapman, William Thurbern, Richard Herbert, William Noreys, Andrew Colt, Richard the shepherd [of Westhorpe] \he swore fealty/, Roger Martin and Henry Puppin to swear fealty.

SUM 12s. 5d.

**4. WALSHAM Court, 18 January 1317 [HA504/1/1.3]**

William [Goche] of Westhorpe, plaintiff v Simon Roty in a plea of debt, essoins by Gilbert Sare.[1]

Ordered as many times to attach William Wyswyf, John Robetel and John Goche, villeins and fugitives, because they remain absent, and for chevage; also to attach Walter the parson of the lower church of Stanton for damage in the lord's warren.

Ordered as many times to retain 24a. of land at Gislingham which the Templars held, and to report the profits.

---

[1] Margin: 'They agree as shown below'.

44

Simon Kembald and the hayward, the first pledges of the Prior of Bricett, amerced 2s. because they did not have him do homage and fealty to the lord. Ordered to appoint better pledges.

John Ketel and the hayward amerced 12d. because they did not have the Prior of Ixworth satisfy the lord concerning many summonses as they undertook; ordered to appoint better pledges.

Ordered to adjourn until the next court a complaint against William of Cranmer the younger, concerning land which he and William Lemme chaplain purchased jointly; the bailiff to report the profits.

William Springold amerced 6d. because he took away growing crops from the lord's villeinage to Wyverstone, in the domain of Sir Hugh Hovel, pledge Nicholas Goche.

Ralph Heryrof amerced 3d. because he sold a cottage to Alice Spileman without leave of the court, pledge Walter Pye.

Ordered as many times to retain in the lord's hands straw and cloths taken into the custody of John Lene, and to take more until Robert Jagge is attached to reply to Marsilia Hawys in a plea of debt.

Ordered to retain in the lord's hands 1r. of meadow, which William Lene purchased from Ralph of Walsingham, and that William is to show his charter at the next court, pledges Nicholas Goche and the reeve.

Ralph Heryrof amerced 3d. for withholding 1 bushel of beans, worth 6d., from Robert Spileman, pledge Walter Pye.

Walter Pye, plaintiff, amerced 6d. for leave to agree with Gilbert Sare in a plea of land, pledges William Lene and Nicholas Goche.

The summons against William at the Green and Agnes his wife is adjourned until the next court, pledges William of Cranmer and William Lene.

Adam Warde amerced 3d. for detention from Walter Typetot of 1 bushel of barley, as he admitted in court; Walter to recover for the corn and the loss, pledges Peter Jay and John Warde.

Robert Deneys amerced 3d. for leave to agree with Gilbert Prior in a plea of debt, loss 1d., pledge for the loss and the amercement the hayward.

Ida Pays amerced 3d. for damage in the lord's corn in autumn, pledge the hayward.

Nicholas Kembald pays 6d. fine to be released from the office of woodward, and because he did not perform his duties, pledge William Hawys.

Simon Roty amerced 3d. for leave to agree with William Goche of Westhorpe, pledge Peter Pynfoul.

As many times, ordered Thomas King to appoint for himself better pledges to reply to John Mayheu of Bury St Edmunds in a plea of debt; John appoints as his pledge Walter Osbern.

Ordered to take into the lord's hands chattels taken upon Geoffrey Kembald, and to take more until he is attached to reply to Oliver the shepherd in a plea of pledge.

Ordered as many times to attach Richard Patel ['Patil'] by the body, to be at the next court to swear fealty to the lord.

Ordered as before to retain in the lord's hands ½a. of land which John Cowlinge purchased from Peter Springold, and to report the profits.

Surrenders: Ralph Heryrof to Walter Pye and Alice Spileman and their heirs, a messuage 1½r. of land, seisin is delivered to them to hold in villeinage at the lord's will, fine 18d., pledges Nicholas Goche and William Lene; and to William Lene and Hilary his wife, and their heirs, 1½r. of land abutting on the Waterway next

45

to the croft [*illeg.*], seisin is delivered to them in the same form, fine 12d., pledges the reeve and the hayward.[2]

John Rede the elder to John Syre and his heirs, 3a. of land in the field called Newhawe, abutting on the Hundredsmere at one head, and at the other on Willowmere ['Wilwemere'], next to the land formerly of John de Walsham to the south, seisin is delivered to him in the same form, fine 7s., pledge Nicholas Goche.

Robert Kembald to William and Hilary Lene and their heirs, 1a. of land in Machonscroft next to Lytleemme, and abutting on the Kingsway ['Kyngesweye'], and 1r. at the head of the same land, and 1a. at Eastmill ['Estmelne'] next to the land of Sir Alexander de Walsham, seisin is delivered to them in the same form, rendering the services due to the lord and ¼d. increased rent, fine 5s., pledge the reeve.

Agatha Long to Nicholas Goche and his heirs, 1r. of land in Eastfield ['Estfeld'], abutting at one head on the Mill way, seisin is delivered to him in the same form, fine 6d., pledges William Lene and the reeve.

The jurors have a day until the next court to enquire into the felling and removal of trees from the common, and to report on such trespasses, and on the trespassers etc.

Surrenders: Walter Goselyng to William and Hilary Lene and their heirs, 2a. of land lying opposite the gate of Thomas at the Gore next to the land of William the miller, seisin is delivered to them in the same form as above, fine 4s., pledges the reeve and the hayward.

Cristina Machon (Machun) to Robert Lene and his heirs, 1½r. of land, seisin is delivered to him in the same form, fine 12d., pledge the hayward.

Robert Godefrey amerced 3d. for detention from Alice Hereward of 3 sheaves of wheat, worth 6d., as he admitted etc, pledge for the loss and the amercement the hayward.

Ordered as many times to attach William Kembald chaplain to reply to Peter Clevehog in a plea of debt.

Surrenders: Emma Peyntour to Simon Peyntour and his heirs, 1½r. of land lying below the yard of Hugh Clevehog, and next to the land of Robert Pudding on the other side, seisin is delivered to him in the same form as above, fine 12d., pledge Walter Rampolye.

Peter Pynfoul to Walter Rampolye and his heirs, 1½r. of land in Millfield ['Melnefeld'], seisin is delivered to him in the same form, fine 12d., pledge the hayward.

John Man amerced 3d. for his false complaint against Walter Peyntour in a plea of trespass.

Ordered as many times to retain a bullock taken upon the heirs of John de Walsham, and to take more for fealty etc. demanded of them.

<Walter Pye pays for leave to marry Alice Spileman, pledge Nicholas Goche>.\void/.

Alice Spileman pays 2s. fine for leave to marry Walter Pye, pledge the reeve.

Ordered as many times to attach Cecilia Machon because she married without leave etc.

---

2 Tab between this item and the next: 'Rafe Heryrof, John le Rede'.

Ordered to retain in the lord's hands 10a. of land which Richard Patel purchased from Walter Skut etc.

Surrenders: John Fraunceys to William Payn the younger and his heirs, ½r. of land, seisin is delivered to him in the same form as above, fine 3d., pledge Nicholas Goche.

Henry Crane to Hugh Crane and his heirs, ½a. of land with a cottage, seisin is delivered to him in the same form, fine 18d., pledge the hayward;

Walter Clevehog to Hugh Clevehog and his heirs, ½a. of land, seisin is delivered to him in the same form, fine 18d., pledge the hayward.

It was found that William at the Green withheld two autumn works every year of the 16 years of this lord's lordship, each work worth 1d., therefore etc. William finds pledges to show at the next court on what grounds he owes nothing etc., *viz.* William of Cranmer and William Lene.

John Stronde amerced 6d. for default at this court.

John Fraunceys amerced 3d. because he did not perform the works for which he was summoned, pledges William Payn and the hayward.

John Dun the servant of the Prior of Ixworth amerced 2s. for damage in the lord's wood cutting down branches.

Walter Heryrof, when he died, held from the lord a messuage 3a. of land by the services specified in the rental. William and Robert his sons are his nearest heirs; and, because Walter had no beast, they are to satisfy the lord for the heriot by the next court.

Peter Qualm, when he died, held from the lord a messuage 1½a. of land by services etc.; Walter his son, aged 3 years, is his nearest heir; therefore ordered to retain in the lord's hands until etc.

Ordered to attach John Margery for damage in the lord's warren with his dog, as witnessed by John Child and (*?Inginar'*).

Surrenders: Basilia Pays to William of Cranmer the younger and his heirs, 1a.½r. of land lying in three pieces, of which 2r. lie between the land of Peter Jay and that of William of Cranmer [the elder], 1½r. lie between Basilia's land and that of William [the elder], and 1r. lies in the Bottom ['Botme'] between land of William Hawys and that of John Hulke, seisin delivered to William [the younger] in the same form as above, fine 2s., pledge William of Cranmer [the elder].

Alice the widow of Stephen Spileman surrendered to the lord, 2a.1r. of land lying in two pieces, one at the Regway ['Regweye'] and one at the Stubbing; the lord granted the tenement to Walter Pye and Alice, and the heirs born to them, in the same form, fine 4s.; if they die without such heirs, the land shall revert to the lawful heirs of Alice.

William of Cranmer the elder to Walter Osbern the younger and his heirs, a messuage with a yard adjoining formerly of William Bullock, seisin is delivered to him to hold in villeinage at the lord's will, fine 6d., pledge William Lene.

Simon Roty and Joan his wife to Matthew Hereward and Emma his wife and their heirs, 1r. of land in the Bottom, seisin is delivered to them in the same form, fine 2d, pledges Nicholas Goche and William Lene.

Walter Gilberd amerced 3d. because he sold 1r. of land to Matthew Hereward without leave, ordered to take into the lord's hands until etc.

William Machon, when he died, held from the lord ½r. of land by services etc.; Richard his brother and nearest heir is a beggar, and his whereabouts unknown. Ordered to take into the lord's hands until etc.

47

Walter the son of James the shepherd, when he died, held a cottage from the lord; Alice his sister, aged 14, is his nearest heir. Ordered etc.

Ordered to attach Peter Pynfoul to reply to Agatha Pynfoul in a plea of detention of chattels.

Robert Godefrey and Richard of Wortham each amerced 3d. because they ground their corn away from the lord's mill, pledges the hayward and William Hawys respectively.

Simon Stritt amerced 3d. because he intervened with the jury against Geoffrey Lenne, the loss assessed at 6d., pledges for the loss and the amercement Richard Kembald and the reeve.

Ordered to attach Gilbert the miller to reply to Robert Godefrey in a plea of trespass, to the value of 3 pecks of corn, and to Robert of Reydon and his wife in a similar plea, value ½ bushel of corn.

Surrender: Robert Kembald to Walter the smith and his heirs, 3½r. of land, seisin is delivered to him in the same form as above, fine 2s., pledge Robert Godefrey.

Agnes Machon pays 12d. fine for entry to a third part of a messuage and 2a. of land, which were of Agnes Machon, the wife of Simon Stritt, of whom she is the heir.

Surrenders: Roger of the Wood ['Wode'] and Alice his wife to Peter Clyvehog and his heirs, 11a. of land with a messuage, seisin is delivered to him in the same form as above, fine 20s.; and they made it known that they granted to Peter all their tenements in Walsham, with none retained.

Basilia Pays to William Hawys and his heirs, ½r. of land, seisin is delivered to him in the same form, fine 3d., pledge the reeve.

Roger of the Wood and Alice his wife to William Typetot and Philippa his wife, ¼r. of land, seisin is delivered to them in the same form, fine 3d.

William Robhod to Robert Hereward and his heirs, half a messuage with appurtenances, seisin is delivered to him in the same form, fine 12d., pledge Nicholas the hayward.

Simon Roty and Joan his wife to Thomas Fuller and his heirs, 1r. of land, seisin is delivered to them in the same form, fine 9d., pledges etc.[sic].

Walter Pye amerced 3d. for his false claim against Robert Warde in a plea of detention of sheep as attested by the jurors, and Robert [is quit] indefinitely.

John Warde amerced 3d. because he sold wood to free men, when the lord's men wished to buy it etc.

Surrender: Isabella Reve to Thomas Fuller, ½r. of land, seisin is delivered to him in the same form as above, fine 3d., pledges Nicholas Goche and the reeve.

Ordered to attach Richard Warde to reply to Agnes Hulke in a plea of land.

Richard Qualm is elected woodward and he takes the oath.

Surrender: Agnes Machon to Thomas Suter and his wife, and their heirs, 1r. of land lying in the Blackacre ['Blakaker'], seisin is delivered to them in the same form as above, fine 9d.

[Ordered] to take into the lord's hands all the lands and tenements which the lord's customary tenants acquired of [illeg.] tenement.

Surrender: John Lene and Robert Lene to John Margery and Mabel his wife and the heirs born of their bodies, 2a. of land in the field called Culynges, fine 2s., seisin is delivered to them in the same form as above, pledges the reeve and the hayward, and they will pay ¼d. increased rent at Michaelmas.

Ordered to attach Nicholas Kembald the miller and Matilda his wife to reply to Thomas Harre in a plea of [detention of] a cow, pledge for Thomas the reeve.

It was found that Sir Robert de Morle formerly held 24a. of land from the lord for services 2s. per year, and that the Templars afterwards rendered the services formerly rendered by Sir Robert.

Amice[3] the widow of Peter Warde pays 2s. fine for leave to marry Peter Jay, pledges Robert Warde and Peter Jay.

Ordered to retain in the lord's hands a messuage in Wyverstone and 2a. of land in Ashfield, which William Springold purchased, until etc.

SUM 76s. 6d.

Affeerers: Walter Osbern, Nicholas Goche and William Lene

### 5. HIGH HALL Court, 1 March 1317 [HA504/1/1.2.ii]

Robert Kembald essoins of common suit by William of Cranmer, likewise Walter Osbern, by Gilbert the Miller, and Walter of the Marsh ['del Merch'], by Richard Shepherd; they pledge faith.

Surrender: Margery, the daughter of Richard of Angerhale and sister and heir of Peter, Richard's son, to William Wodebite and his heirs, a messuage 5r. of villein land, 2a. of free land of the fee of Sir Hugh Hovel and 2a. of land of the fee and villeinage of the lord of Westhorpe, granted to William and his heirs to hold in villeinage by services and customs, fine 5s., pledges John Wodebite and Gilbert Helpe; and William will house Margery for her lifetime.

Geoffrey Kembald pays 3d. fine to repossess from the lord a messuage 8½a. of villein land, pledges Simon Kembald, William Goche and John Wodebite.

Robert House amerced 3d. for default, ordered to distrain him for fealty.

William Wodebite amerced 6d. for unlawful detention of the dower of Alice, the widow of Roger April, pledge John Wodebite.

William Wodebite pays 20d. fine for entry to half a messuage and 5a. of villein land which he leased from Richard Gothelard, of the tenement formerly of Walter Payn of Angerhale, to hold to William for Richard's lifetime, and for the reversion of the other half of the said messuage and 5a., after the death of Mabel Walter's widow, who holds the tenement in dower. If Mabel dies within the said term, William is to hold the tenement for Richard's lifetime, rendering for Richard the due and accustomed services, and 6d. annually at Michaelmas, pledges John Wodebite and Hugh Angerhale.

Ordered as elsewhere to retain in the lord's hands a messuage 8a. of land with appurtenances, which Ralph Issabel held in villeinage, for services and customs withheld.

Ordered as elsewhere to distrain John Stronde, Geoffrey Doo, Robert House \he swore fealty/, Robert Carpenter, William, the son of Reginald Chapman, William Thurbern, Richard Herbert, William Noreys, Andrew Colt, Roger Martin and Henry Puppin for fealty withheld.

SUM 7s. 8d.

### 6. WALSHAM Court General there, 21 April 1317 [HA504/1/1.4]

Martin Bakonn essoins of common suit by Peter Margery; he pledges faith.

Surrenders: Robert Herirof and William Herirof to William of Cranmer and his heirs, 2½r. of land, seisin is delivered etc., fine 18d., pledge William Hawys; and

---

3 In court no.2 she was named 'Anne'.

to William Hawys and his heirs, a messuage 3a., seisin is delivered etc., fine ½ mark.

Again as many times ordered to attach William Wyswyf, John Robetel and John Goche, fugitive villeins, who remain absent from the lord, and Walter, the parson of the lower church of Stanton, for damage in the lord's warren; and to retain in the lord's hands 24a. of land in Gislingham which the Templars held, and to report the profits.

All matters touching the Prior of Ixworth are adjourned until the lord is present, as ordered by the lord's letter.

Again ordered to summon the Prior of Bricett to do homage and fealty.

Again as many times ordered to retain straw and cloths taken into the custody of John Lene, and to take more until Robert Jagge is attached to reply to Marsilia Hawys in a plea of debt.

William of Cranmer and William Lene did not have William at the Green and Agnes his wife to satisfy the lord concerning pleas of (?*mand'*) as they undertook; ordered to summon them by better pledges.

Thomas King pays 3d. for leave to agree with John Mayheu of Bury St Edmunds, pledges the reeve and the hayward; and he complains against the said John in a plea of trespass, pledges William of Cranmer and the hayward.

Thomas Suter and the hayward, the pledges of Geoffrey Kembald, amerced because they did not have him reply to Oliver the shepherd (*bercarius*) in a plea of pledge; ordered etc.

Ordered as many times to attach Richard Patel by the body, to be at the next court to swear fealty.

Again as many times ordered to retain in the lord's hands ½a. of land which John Cowlinge purchased from Peter Springold, and to report the profits.

Again as many times ordered to attach William Kembald to reply to Peter Clevehog in a plea of debt; and to attach Cecilia Machon because she married without leave.

Again as many times ordered to retain in the lord's hands 10a. of land, which Richard Patel purchased from Walter Skut.

Surrender: Walter Suter to John Patel and his heirs, 1a. of land at Sweynsacre, seisin delivered to him to hold in villeinage at the lord's will, fine 3s., pledge the hayward.[4]

Peter Pynfoul amerced 3d. for leave to agree with Agatha Pynfoul in a plea of detention of chattels, pledges Walter Osbern and John Man.

Surrenders: John Rede to John Syre and his heirs, 1r. of land in three pieces in the field of Runimere, seisin delivered to him to hold in bondage at the lord's will, fine 3s., pledges Walter Osbern and the hayward.

Emma Pye to John Patel, ½r. of land next to John's croft, seisin delivered in the same form, fine 6d., pledge the hayward.

Peter Clevehog to John Patel and his heirs, 3r. of land in the field of Ashfield, next to the land of Emma Pye and abutting on John's land, seisin delivered in the same form, fine 2s., pledge the hayward.

John Fraunceys to Peter the son of Robert[5] and Matilda his wife and the heirs of

---

4   Tab: 'Walter Sewter, John le Rede (?*et. alii*)'.
5   Probably Robert of Reydon; Peter later known as Peter Robbes.

Matilda, a cotland, 2½p.8ft. in length and 1½p. and ¹/₃p. in width, seisin delivered in the same form, fine 6d., pledge the hayward.

Cristina Machon to William Lene and his heirs, ½a. of land in the Millfield, between William's lands on both sides, seisin delivered in the same form, fine 12d., pledge the hayward.

Agnes Machon to Robert of Reydon and his heirs, 1r. of land at the Regweye, next to that of John Lene, seisin delivered in the same form, fine 6d., pledge Nicholas Kembald.

Agnes Machon to William of Cranmer the younger and his heirs, 2½r. of land and ½r. of wood in the field of Walsham, seisin delivered in the same form, fine 2s., pledges William of Cranmer and the reeve.

Cristina Machon to William of Cranmer the younger and his heirs, 1a. of land in two pieces in the Northfield, seisin delivered in the same form, fine 3s., pledges as above.

Peter Hulke and John his brother to William of Cranmer the younger, ½r. of meadow in the Great Meadow, seisin delivered in the same form, fine 6d., pledges as above.

Simon Machon to William Lene and his heirs, ¾r. of land, seisin delivered in the same form, fine 6d., pledge the reeve.

Thomas Echeman to William Lene, ½a. of land at Glonwismere abutting on the lord's wood, seisin delivered in the same form, fine 18d., pledge the reeve.

Agnes Machon to Robert Godefrey and his heirs, 1½r. of land, seisin delivered in the same form, fine 12d., pledge the reeve.

John Fraunceys to Thomas Suter and his heirs, 3½r. of land at the Eastfield; fine 2s., seisin delivered in the same form, pledge the hayward.

Agnes Machon to Cristina Machon, a messuage ½a. of land, seisin delivered, fine 18d., and for this sale Cristina granted the tenement to Agnes to hold in bondage, at the lord's will, for her lifetime, pledge Walter Osbern.

Emma Peyntour to Simon Peyntour and his heirs, 1r. of land at Knosyl, fine 9d., pledge Walter Patel; and to Walter Patel, 1a. of land, fine 3s., pledge Simon Peyntour; and to Peter Peyntour and his heirs, ½a. of land, fine 18d., pledge Simon Peyntour; seisin delivered to all to hold in bondage at the lord's will.

Agatha Long to Alice Long and her heirs, a quarter of a messuage, seisin delivered in the same form, fine 3d., pledge Peter Pynfoul.

Walter Clevehog to William of Cranmer the elder and his heirs, 1r. of land, as aid to the light of the Blessed Mary, seisin delivered in the same form, fine 3d., pledge the hayward.

Basilia Pays to William of Cranmer the younger, a cottage 3a. of land and ¼r. of meadow, seisin delivered in the same form, fine 6s., pledges the reeve and William of Cranmer; Ida Pays surrenders to William all her right in the tenement in name of dower.

Adam Goche customary tenant, when he died, held from the lord a messuage 8a. of land and ½r. of meadow; Agnes, his daughter and nearest heir, is aged 3 years; ordered to retain in the lord's hands until etc., the bailiff to report the profits; the lord had as a heriot a cow, worth 13s.4d.

William Typetot, when he died, held from the lord half a messuage 6a. of land and ½r. of meadow; the lord had as a heriot a mare, worth 3s.4d.; Peter, his son and nearest heir, is aged six years, and Philippa, his mother, seeks custody of Peter until his full age. The jurors say that she should have custody by right and by the

51

custom of the manor, and it is granted to her on condition that she swears fealty to the lord, pledges Peter Clevehog and Peter Peyntour, and meanwhile she seeks the grace of the lord (?*querit gratiam domini*).

Surrender: John Fraunceys to Walter Osbern and his heirs, 1a. of land, fine 3s.; and 1a. to William Hawys and his heirs, seisin delivered in the same form as above, fine 3s.

Peter le Neve complains against William Wauncy in a plea of detention of 1 bushel of barley, pledge for the plaintiff Thomas Fuller.

William Lene amerced 3d. for trespass, digging on the common, pledge the hayward.

John Wyndilgard [Wyndirgard], when he died, held from the lord a quarter of a messuage 3r. of land; Richard his brother and nearest heir is aged five years, and Cecilia his mother seeks and is granted custody until his full age, fine 6d., because John had no beast for a heriot, pledges John Man and William of Cranmer.

Robert Spileman amerced 3d. for trespass digging on the common, pledge William of Cranmer.

The Prior of Ixworth amerced 12d. for trespass digging clay on the common, to the nuisance of the lord and the townspeople, ordered to distrain him to make good the pit.

Robert Champeys and Cristina Clevehog each amerced 3d. for trespass, pledge William Marler; Alice Hyte 3d. for the same, pledge Robert Tailor ['le Taylour'] for the same; Cecilia Hardevid 12d. for trespass to the value of 6d., pledge Richard Qualm.

Robert Godefrey amerced 6d., William Priour and Robert of Reydon 3d. each and Simon Kembald 6d. for breaking the assize of bread.

Robert the tailor (*cissor*)[6] amerced 6d., and Robert Godefrey and Robert Kembald 3d. each for breaking the assize of ale.

Thomas Echeman amerced 3d. because he sold 1r. of land without leave; ordered to take into the lord's hands, pledge Ralph Echeman.

Peter Peyntour amerced 6d. because he sold a messuage in Ashfield to Ralph Crane without leave; ordered to take into the lord's hands; Ralph finds surety to be at the next court to swear fealty and to reply concerning that which is claimed [from him] as a customary tenant, pledges Hugh Crane and Willliam of Cranmer.

Surrenders: William Marler and Mabel his wife, to Emma the daughter of William the shepherd, a messuage, seisin delivered in the same form as above, fine 12d., pledge Stephen Godefrey.

John Hulke and Peter Hulke to the same Emma, ¼r. of meadow in the Great Meadow, seisin delivered in the same form, fine 6d., pledge as above.

Ordered to take into the lord's hands 5a. of land which Richard Patel purchased in Finningham, and to report the profits; and to attach Richard by the body to swear fealty.

Ordered to take into the lord's hands 3a. of land which Walter Osbern purchased from Simon Kembald etc., and ½a., which Walter Payn purchased from Stephen of Allwood ['Aldewode'] and Agatha his wife until etc.

---

6    It is assumed that Robert le Taylour and Robert *cissor* are not the same person.

Ordered as many times to retain in the lord's hands the tenement which William of Cranmer [the younger] and William Lemme chaplain jointly purchased etc.

William and Robert the sons and heirs of Walter Herirof pay 2s. fine for entry to a messuage 3½a. of land, and they swear fealty, pledge William of Cranmer.

Matthew Hereward and Emma his wife pay 6d. fine for entry to ½r. of villein land purchased from Walter Gilberd, pledge the reeve.

William Lene pays 12d. fine for entry to ½a. of villein land lying in four pieces, which was of Walter and William Machon, pledge the hayward.

Surrenders: Richard Reve to Thomas Fuller and Cristina his wife and their heirs, ½r. of land, seisin delivered in the same form as above, fine 6d., pledge the hayward.

Isabella Reve to the same Thomas and Cristina and their heirs, ½r. of land abutting on Isabella's messuage, seisin delivered in the same form, fine 6d., pledge the hayward.

Robert of Fornham to Walter Payn and his heirs, 1½r. of land in the Southfield ['Soutfeld'], seisin delivered in the same form, fine 12d., pledge the hayward.

Agnes Machon to Robert Kembald and his heirs, ½r. of land, seisin delivered in the same form, fine 6d., pledge Robert Spileman.

Alice Lyf to Robert Lene and his heirs, a cottage 1r. of land, seisin delivered in the same form, fine 12d., pledge the hayward.

Gilbert the miller (*molendarius*) amerced 3d. for trespass against Robert Godefrey, damage 1 bushel of corn, worth 12d.; and 3d. for trespass against Robert of Reydon, 1 peck of corn, worth 3d., pledges Peter Clevehog and the reeve.

Agnes Hulke amerced 3d. for her false claim against Robert Warde, pledge the hayward.

William Springold pays 6d. fine for entry to a messuage 2½a. of land in Wyverstone which he purchased from Robert Carpenter and Agnes his wife, to hold from the lord by the rod, paying ¼d. at the feast of St Michael, and rendering to the capital lords of that fee the due and accustomed services, pledge the hayward; and the charter is delivered to William to hold at the lord's will.

Thomas Harre and his pledge Thomas Suter amerced 3d., because he did not proceed against Nicholas the miller in a plea of detention of a cow.

Walter Payn pays 3d. fine for entry to ½a. of land which he purchased from Stephen and Agatha of Allwood, to hold by the rod from the lord, paying ¼d. rent at Michaelmas, and rendering to the capital lords of that fee the due and accustomed services, and the charter is delivered to Walter to keep at the lord's will, pledge Walter Osbern.

Walter Typetot and his pledges amerced 3d. because he did not proceed against John Fraunceys in a plea of debt; Nicholas Coniers and his pledges [*sic*], namely Simon Kembald, amerced 3d., because he did not proceed in a plea of detention of a charter.

Elias Typetot pays 3d. for leave to agree with John Man in a plea of trespass, pledge Robert Godefrey.

Ordered to retain in the lord's hands 1r. of meadow which William Lene purchased from Ralph of Walsingham until etc, and to show [his charter].

Walter Hereward, Richard Priour, Richard Gothelard and Agatha the daughter of William Marler each amerced 12d. for trespass, to the value of 8s.; Walter's pledges are Simon the smith and Robert Spileman.

William Wilde and Richard Wynter each amerced 12d. for trespass against the lord to the value of 6d., pledge Robert Lene; and Geoffrey of Lenne amerced 2s. for harbouring the said trespassers, pledge William Hawys.

Thomas Colpon amerced 3d. for trespass, pledge the hayward; likewise Clara the wife of Richard Qualm 3d., pledge Richard; Walter Osbern 3d., pledge the reeve; Robert Broune 3d., pledge Simon the smith; and Alice Man 3d., pledge Robert Lene.

Peter Clevehog pays 3d. for leave to agree with Walter Suter in a plea of trespass, pledges the hayward and Walter Osbern.

Robert the cooper ['le couper'] complains against William Wauncy concerning the detention of 2 bushels of barley, ordered etc.

Surrender: John Fraunceys to Walter Osbern the younger and his heirs, ½a. of land, seisin delivered to him to hold in the same form as above, fine 12d.

William Payn amerced 3d for unlawful detention of 10d. from Nicholas Kembald at Southbrook ['Soutbrok'], loss assessed at 1d., ordered etc.; and amerced 3d. for unlawful detention of 3d. from William Rampolye, the loss remitted, pledge William Hawys.

Thomas Suter and Oliver the shepherd each amerced 3d. for unlawful detention from Robert Kembald of 1 bushel 1 peck of barley, worth 15d., loss 3d., pledge the hayward.

Alice Whiteman pays 3d. for leave to agree with John Lene in a plea of trespass, pledge John Springold.

SUM 69s., except the heriots

## 7. HIGH HALL Court of Sir Alexander de Walsham, 2 May 1317 [HA504/1/1.5.i]

Henry Trusse essoins of suit of court by William Dolhale, and William of Cranmer of the same by Walter Osbern.

William Wodebite amerced 12d. because he did not come at the bailiff's summons, to thresh his cut straw etc., pledges John Wodebite and Gilbert Helpe.

Geoffrey Kembald and John Chapman amerced for default [amount unstated].

Ordered as many times to retain a messuage 8a. of villein land which Ralph Issabel held.

Ordered as many times to distrain <John Stronde> \Emma, wife of the same John now hereditary tenant, because John is dead, swore fealty/, Geoffrey Doo, Robert Carpenter, William, the son of Reginald Chapman, William Thurbern, Richard Herbert, William Noreys, Andrew Colt, Roger Martin and Henry Puppin for withholding fealty.

Robert House pays 4d. fine for respite of suit of court until Michaelmas.

Cristina the widow of Walter Kembald complained against Simon Kembald in a plea of dower, pledge for Cristina the hayward; Simon came and jointly they seek leave to agree, Simon amerced 6d., pledges Robert Kembald and the hayward. Cristina granted and released to Simon all her right in dower in ½a. of villein land.

It was found by the jury that Simon Kembald villein sold 3a. of land to Walter Osbern by charter without leave; ordered to take into the lord's hands.

[SUM 1s. 10d., not stated]

## 8.  WALSHAM Court, 9 August 1317 [HA504/1/1.6]

Peter Margery essoins of common suit, by Martin Bakun; he pledges faith.

Surrender: William Marler to Walter Osbern the younger and his heirs, ½a. of land at Burfield, seisin delivered to him to hold in bondage at the lord's will, by customs etc., fine 12d., pledge the hayward.

The hayward, first pledge of Ida Pays, amerced 3d. because he did not have her reply to Robert of Reydon in a plea of trespass; ordered etc.; the first pledges of John Fraunceys amerced 3d. because they did not have him reply to Nicholas Goche in a plea of debt.

Simon Roty amerced 3d. for unlawful detention of 4½d. from Robert Rampolye, as he admitted, ordered to raise, pledges Peter Pynfoul and William Hawys.

Stephen Godefrey complained against Simon the smith concerning a plea of debt, ordered to attach Simon to reply etc.

Ordered to attach Cecilia Miller of Ashfield to satisfy the lord for trespass in Ladyswood, and Margaret Cat for the same.

Catherine Goche amerced 3d. for damage in the lord's corn, pledge Nicholas Goche; Catherine Helewys 3d. for the same, pledge William Hawys.

Alice Lefe amerced 3d. for damage in the lord's beans by her servant, pledge William Hawys.

Cristina Gilbert and William her son each amerced 3d. for damage in the lord's wood, pledge Richard Qualm.

William Wauncy pays 3d. for leave to agree with Geoffrey of Lenne in a plea of debt, pledge Robert Lene; and 3d. to agree with Peter Neve in a plea of detention of 1 bushel of barley, pledge as above.

Surrender: William Wauncy to Robert Lene and his heirs, 1a.1r. of customary land in the Cockscroft ['Cokiscroft'], granted to him to hold in bondage etc., fine 3s., pledge the hayward.

William Wauncy amerced 3d. for leave to agree with Robert the cooper in a plea of detention of 2 bushels of barley, pledge Robert Lene.

+[7]Surrender: Robert of Reydon to William of Cranmer and his heirs, 1r. of land in the Brookfield, seisin delivered in the same form as above, fine 12d., pledge the hayward.

Walter Osbern pays 6d. for entry to 3a. of land, which he purchased from Simon Kembald, to hold in bondage etc., rendering due services to the capital lords of the fee, and ½d. increased rent to the lord annually at Michaelmas, pledge William Hawys; and his charter was returned to him to be held at the lord's will.

+William the son of Richard of Cranmer pays for entry to 2a. of land which he purchased jointly with William of Elmswell.[8]

Rose [*Roysia*] Typetot amerced 3d. for damage in the lord's corn, pledge William Hawys.

Peter Tailor the (?*receptator*) of John the son of Cristina amerced 3d. for the same.[9]

+William of Cranmer brought to the court the charter by which he, with William of

---

7   The significance of the cross (+), inserted at a later date, against this and other subsequent entries, is shown in the final entry of roll no.11, and referred to in the Introduction under The Rolls.

8   Margin: 'elsewhere': further details follow after the next two entries.

9   The meaning of *receptator* is not clear; it can mean a harbourer, e.g. of criminals, or a receiver, or a lessee.

Elmswell chaplain, purchased 2a. of land from William the rector of Downham, and it was returned to him to be held at the lord's will etc.

Surrender: Peter Hulke to Peter Hawys and his heirs, ½a. of land lying below Hulkeswood, granted to him to hold in bondage, fine 12d., pledge the hayward.

William Lene pays 2d. for entry to 1r. of meadow which he purchased with Walter Osbern from Ralph of Walsingham, granted to him to hold by the rod, paying to the lord ¼d. annually at Michaelmas, and rendering to the capital lords of the fee due services etc.. Walter released and quitclaimed to William all his right and claim in the said meadow, pledge William of Cranmer the younger.

Surrenders: William Marler and Mabel his wife to Stephen Couper and his heirs, a messuage with a croft adjoining, containing in all 5r. of land, granted to him to hold in bondage, fine 4s., pledge William Hawys.

Peter Hulke to Agnes Hulke and her heirs, ½a. of land in Hulkescroft, granted to her to hold in bondage, fine 2s., pledge William Hawys.

William Hereward, who lately died, held from the lord a freehold messuage 3a. of customary land; and the lord had as a heriot a cow, worth 13s.4d.; ordered to retain in the lord's hands until Matthew and Robert Hereward [Terward], his brothers and his nearest heirs, satisfy the lord for entry etc.

Alice the widow of William Fenner [le fenere][10] complains against Matthew Hereward [Therward] and Robert his brother, in a plea of dower, and they have a day until the next court etc., pledges for Alice William Hawys and Walter Rampolye.

Walter the reeve and William Lene each amerced 3d. because they dug on the common making a dungheap, to the nuisance of the lord and the townspeople.

Surrender: Peter Hulke to Stephen Cooper and his heirs, ½r. of land at Hulkesbridge ['Hulkesbrigge']; granted to him to hold in bondage, fine 6d., pledge William Hawys.

Walter Hawys granted to Peter his brother, 6a. of land, 1r. of meadow and a quarter of a messuage, which Marsilia Hawys holds for her lifetime of Walter's inheritance, and which, after her death, shall revert to Walter, with remainder to Peter and his heirs, fine ½ mark, pledge the hayward.

Walter Hawys pays 1d. chevage, and he will come to the next court after Michaelmas every year to pay the same, pledges William Hawys and Peter Hawys.

Surrenders: John Lene the younger to John Lene the elder and his heirs, 1a.1r. of land lying in various places, fine 2s., pledge Robert Lene; and to Robert Lene and his heirs, 1a.1r. of land in various places, fine 2s., pledge John Lene the elder; granted to both to hold in bondage.

Agnes Machon to William Lene and his heirs, ½a. of land in two pieces abutting on the Regway, granted to him to hold in bondage, fine 3d., pledge William of Cranmer the younger.

+Peter Hulke to William the son of William of Cranmer, and his heirs, 1¼r. of land in two pieces in the Northfield, granted to him to hold in bondage, fine 3d., pledge the hayward.

+Simon and Joan Roty to William the son of William of Cranmer and his heirs, ¼r. of wood in Northmanswood, granted to him to hold in bondage, fine 3d., pledge the hayward.

---

[10] References to this complaint in succeeding courts indicate that William's surname was Robhood; P.H. Reaney gives Venner and Fenner to mean 'Huntsman' or 'Fen-dweller'. *Dictionary of British Surnames* (London 1961), p.363.

Ralph Crane pays 2s. for having entry to a messuage which he purchased from Peter Peyntour, granted to him to hold by the rod, paying 1d. increased rent annually at Michaelmas, and rendering, for the lord, to the capital lords of the fee the services due therefrom; Ralph swore customary fealty, and his charter was returned to him to be held at the lord's will, pledges Hugh Crane and William of Cranmer the younger.

John Stronde, who lately died, held jointly with his wife Emma, for the term of their lives, a messuage 16a. of land, by the lord's demise, and they held 3a. of customary land purchased in court by the rod, etc., the lord had a stot, worth 13s.4d., as heriot, ordered to retain in the lord's hands etc.

Millicent Qualm amerced 3d. for waste made in the lord's bondage, and because she harboured unknown wrongdoers, ordered to take her tenement into the lord's hands until etc., and to report the profits.

Robert Broune [Broune Robyn] amerced 6d. for damage in the lord's rye and beans and [in] his orchard, harboured by Simon the smith, his brother.

Cristina Clevehog amerced 3d. for damage in the lord's corn, pledges William Marler and Stephen Godefrey.

Simon Fenner in mercy for default \afterwards he came/; and amerced 6d. for services and customs withheld, ordered to distrain him to do what he should do etc.

Ordered to take into the lord's hands 1r. of land, which John Fraunceys sold to Peter the son of Robert; also 1a. sold to John Syre; also ½r. sold to Thomas Suter, until etc.

Ordered to take into the lord's hands 1r. of land, which William of Fornham sold to Walter Payn, also ½a. which Walter Goselyng sold to William Terwald, and 3r. sold to Walter Typetot, until etc, and to report the profits.

The jurors have a day until the next court to certify as to the condition of Walter Goselyng, and whether the said land is free, or customary.

Surrender: Adam Warde to Robert Warde and his heirs, ½a. of land lying at the head of Walter's wood, granted to him to hold in bondage, fine 12d., pledge William Hawys.

Alice the daughter of James the shepherd pays 6d. for having entry to a cottage formerly her father's, pledges William Hawys and Peter the son of Robert.

Surrenders: Simon Roty and Joan his wife to Adam Noble and his heirs, 1r. of villein land lying next to the pightle ['pikild'] called the Stonylond, granted to him to hold in bondage, fine 9d., pledge William Hawys.

Isabella Reve to Thomas Fuller and his heirs, 1¼r. of land in several pieces in the field etc., granted to him to hold in bondage, fine 9d., pledge the hayward.

Thomas Echeman to Ralph Echeman and his heirs, 1r. of land lying in a croft, granted to him to hold in bondage, fine 9d., pledge William Hawys.

Richard Payn to William Payn and Amice his wife and their heirs, 1¼r. of land in several places, granted to him to hold in bondage, fine 9d., pledge William Hawys.

William Payn to Richard Payn, ½a. of land in the Shortcroft, in exchange for ½a. within William Payn's croft, granted to them to hold in bondage, fines 6d. each, pledges each for the other.

Adam Warde to John Goche and his heirs, 1a. of land at Cocksdrit, granted to him to hold in bondage, fine 2s., pledge William Hawys.

Agnes Hulke pays 3s. fine for leave to marry Adam Noble, pledge William Hawys.

Surrender: Walter Qualm to Walter Osbern and his heirs, ½r. of meadow in the

Great Meadow of Walsham, granted to him to hold in bondage, fine 6d., pledge William Hawys.

The action between William Hawys plaintiff and William Lene defendant is in respite until the next court.

The Prior of Ixworth amerced 12d. because he depastured the lord's herbage with his cows.

Cristina Gilbert amerced 3d. because she grazed three cows from outside the manor without leave.

Ordered to take 3s.2d. from the goods and chattels of Robert Jagge [Jade] to the lord's use, about which the reeve will reply.

As before, ordered to attach William Wyswyf, John Robetel and John Goche villeins, who are fugitives, to be at the next court to satisfy the lord for chevage.

Again ordered to attach Walter the parson of All Saints, Stanton, to satisfy the lord for trespass in the lord's warren.

Again ordered to retain 24a. of land at Gislingham which the Templars held, and to report the profits.

All matters touching the Prior of Ixworth are in respite until the lord is present, by the lord's letter.

As before ordered to summon the Prior of Bricett to make to the lord that which he should make.

Ordered to summon William and Agnes at the Green to satisfy the lord for many summonses; in respite until the next court.

Thomas King complains against John Mayheu of Bury St Edmunds in a plea of trespass, pledges for Thomas William of Cranmer and the hayward, ordered etc.

Again ordered to summon Geoffrey Kembald to reply to Oliver the shepherd in a plea of pledge.

Ordered to attach Richard Patel by the body to be at the next court to do that which he should do.

Again ordered to retain ½a. of land, which John Cowlinge purchased from Peter Springold, and to report the profits.

Again ordered to attach William Kembald chaplain to reply to Peter Clevehog in a plea of debt.

Again ordered to attach Cecilia Machon to satisfy the lord because she married without leave.

Again ordered to retain 10a. of land which Richard Patel purchased from Walter Skut until etc.; also a messuage 1a., and 8a. of land which were of Adam Goche; and the tenement which William Typetot held at his death; and 5a. which Richard Patel purchased in Finningham; and to report the profits.[11]

Ordered to take into the lord's hands ½a. of land which Walter Payn purchased from Stephen of Allwood and Agnes his wife until etc.

Surrender: Walter Goselyng to Matthew Therewald and Robert his brother and their heirs, ½a. in the meadow of Upstreet, granted to them to hold in bondage, fine 18d., pledge William Cook (*Cocus*).

Walter Goselyng finds pledges, *viz.* Walter the reeve and William Cook, [for him] to come to the next court to swear fealty to the lord, because he is accused of being a villein.

---

[11] The earlier item ordering the attachment of Richard is repeated here.

Matthew and Robert Therewald pay 2s. for having entry to a free messuage and 3a. of customary land, of which William Hereward their brother died seised, paying to the lord 1d. increased rent annually at Michaelmas, and rendering, for the lord, to the capital lords of the fee, the due and accustomed services therefrom; they swore customary fealty, pledge the hayward.

Ordered to attach Andrew Patel to be at the next court to answer why he refused to receive the lord's beasts from the delivery of the bailiff etc., the lord not knowing where they were taken.

SUM 51s. 1d., except the heriots and increased rents

## 9. WALSHAM Court General, 11 October 1317 [HA504/1/2.4]

Sarah Margery essoins of common suit by Berard Margery.

Cecilia Miller ['la Melnere'] amerced 6d., and Margery Cat ['le Kat'] 12d., for damage in the lord's wood, pledge Richard Qualm.

Simon the smith places himself in mercy against Stephen Godefrey in a plea of debt and is amerced 3d., pledge William Hawys.

+Robert Hereward amerced 6d. because he unlawfully deprived Alice the widow of William Robhood[12] of her rightful dower of the tenement, formerly held by William in bondage, viz. half a messuage 1½a. of land; ordered the reeve and hayward to have her rightful dower delivered to Alice, following the verdict of the homage and the custom of the manor.[13] Alice pays 6d. fine for entry, pledge Walter Rampolye.

Matthew Hereward amerced 6d. because he did not attend when he was summoned, and ordered to take into the lord's hands half of 1½a., which Alice claims in dower; ordered to summon Matthew to be at the next court to reply etc., and the same day given to Alice.[14]

Ordered to retain in the lord's hands a messuage 3a. of land which Millicent Qualm holds, for waste made and for several defaults until etc., and the reeve to report the profits.

Simon the smith pays 3d. to repossess from the lord 1a. land and a quarter of a messuage which were seized for customs and services withheld, pledge William Hawys.

Robert Spileman and Walter Gilberd each pay 6d. fine for the exchange of 2r. of land and meadow: Robert exchanged with Walter a piece of meadow 6ft. wide in Badwell meadow and ½r. of land next to Walter's croft, for a piece of meadow 6ft. wide in Walsham meadow and ½r. of land in the field called Outgongishende next to the land of Ralph Neve, pledges each for the other.

The second pledges of Ida Pays amerced 3d. because they did not have her reply to Robert Reydon in a plea of trespass, ordered that she appoint better pledges; the hayward to reply concerning the pledges.

The second pledges of John Fraunceys amerced 3d. because they did not have him reply to Nicholas Goche in a plea of debt, ordered John to appoint better pledges.

Surrender: William of Fornham to Walter Payn and his heirs, 1r. of land lying in

---

12 Referred to in the preceding court as William le Fenere.
13 It was the custom in both manors in Walsham for a widow to hold half her late husband's tenement for her lifetime.
14 Tab between last two items: 'Alice Robwood' [sic].

Fornhamscroft, granted to him to hold in bondage at the lord's will, by services and customs, fine 9d., pledge William Hawys; John swore fealty.

William Wyswyf, John Robetel and John Goche each amerced 3d. for default, ordered to distrain them to satisfy the lord for their absence.

William at the Green pays 12d. for [respite of] suit of court for this year, pledge the hayward; and with Agnes his wife is amerced 2s. for withholding autumn works for 12 years, pledges Robert Swift and the hayward.

Thomas King and his pledges, William of Cranmer and the hayward, amerced 3d., because he did not proceed against John Mayheu ('Machon') in a plea of trespass, and John is quit indefinitely.

Oliver the shepherd and his pledges amerced 3d., because he did not proceed against Geoffrey Kembald in a plea of debt.

Robert of Reydon amerced 3d. for withholding a day ploughing service, worth 8d., from Hugh Rouse ['le Rous'], loss assessed at 2d., ordered to raise, pledges the hayward and William Hawys.

Surrenders: John Hulke to William of Cranmer and his heirs, 1r. of land called the Longrode, granted to him to hold in bondage in the same form as above, fine 6d., pledge the hayward.

Peter the son of Robert to William the son of William of Cranmer and his heirs, ½r. of meadow in the Micklemeadow, granted to him to hold in the same form, fine 6d., pledge the hayward.

Cristina Machon to William the son of William of Cranmer and his heirs, ½r. of wood in Northmanswood ['Northmanyswode'], granted to him to hold in the same form, fine 6d., pledge the hayward.

Walter Osbern the younger pays 6d. for having entry to 1a. of land, which he purchased from Cristina the widow of Walter Kembald, and he surrendered to the lord the charter therefor; seisin delivered to him to hold in bondage at the lord's will, rendering for the lord, to the capital lords of that fee, the due and accustomed services therefrom, and to the lord ½d. increased rent annually at Easter, pledge the hayward; and the charter was returned to Walter to be held at the lord's will.

Walter and Cristina Gilberd amerced 3d. for 2½ autumn works withheld this year, pledge the hayward; ordered to raise the value of the works.

The first pledges of Robert Suter ['le Suter'] amerced 3d., because they did not have him reply to Geoffrey of Lenne in a plea of debt, ordered to appoint better pledges.

John at the Wood, who recently died, held from the lord by the rod 4½a. of land in Ashfield ['Aysthefeld'], for services ½d. per year, and suit of court from 3 weeks to 3 weeks, William and Henry, his sons, are his nearest heirs because the tenements are partible, following the custom of the manor.[15] They are of full age and they pay 5s. for having entry, to hold in bondage at the lord's will, rendering services and customs, and they swear customary fealty, pledges Richard Qualm and Walter Patel.

William Cook ['le Ku'] pays 7d. for having entry to ½a. of land in the field called

---

[15] Inheritance was partible in both Walsham manors. Margin: in a later hand (?17th century), 'Gavelkynde'.

Brightwaldishal, which he purchased from Ralph Herirof, pledge the reeve, and seisin is delivered to him to hold in bondage etc.

William Joste amerced 3d. for damage in the lord's wood, pledge Richard Qualm.

Simon Roty amerced 6d. for waste made in the lord's bondage, and continuing to make waste, pledges William of Cranmer and the hayward; he has a day to make good the waste before the feast of the Purification [2 February] next coming.

William Robhood amerced 6d. for waste made in the lord's bondage; ordered to seize and retain all his tenement in the lord's hands until etc.

Richard of Wortham amerced 6d., Simon Kembald 6d. and Thomas the Suter 3d., because they stored on a free tenement corn grown in the lord's bondage, pledge the hayward.

Oliver the shepherd amerced 3d. for the same; ordered to take his customary tenement into the lord's hands for autumn services withheld etc.

Robert Kembald amerced 3d. for the same, pledge Robert Spileman.

Basilia of Downham amerced 3d. for trespass, because she digs on the common without leave, pledge the hayward.

Robert Lene amerced 3d. for damage in the lord's barley to the value of ½ bushel of barley with his geese, pledge [illeg.]; and the reeve 3d. for the same with the lord's colt, to the value of 1d.

Roger Spileman pays 6d. fine for [respite of] suit of court for this year, pledge the hayward.

\General Enquiry by William of Cranmer, Nicholas Goche, Peter Robhood, Peter Jay, Walter Patel, Robert Rampolye, Richard Qualm, William Fraunceys, Peter Springold, Peter Clevehog, Peter Pynfoul ['Pinfowel'] and Walter the son of Simon; they take the oath./

Robert Spileman, who purchased from Thomas at the Gore a messuage 3½a. of land, parcel of the tenement which William Cook formerly held in bondage, has a day to surrender his charter to the lord and do to the lord that which he ought, pledges the reeve and the hayward.

Ordered to distrain William at the Green in 3½a. of land, parcel of the said tenement, for services and customs withheld, and also in 1a. of land, formerly of William Springold, and in 3a., formerly Kebbil's, all of which are of the lord's bondage.

All the tenants of the tenement of Ralph Herirof amerced 12d. for 3 autumn works withheld; ordered to distrain; Walter Qualm amerced 3d. for the same.

Robert Godefrey amerced 6d. for breaking the assize of bread, pledge the hayward; Gilbert Priour 3d. for the same, pledges the hayward and Peter Robbes. Robert Godefrey and Robert the tailor each amerced 6d. for breaking the assize of ale, pledge the hayward.

John Fraunceys amerced 3d. for default; ordered to take into the lord's hands all the tenement he holds in bondage, until etc.

Ordered to retain a messuage 8a. of land, [taken] after the death of Adam Goche because his heir is under age, until etc., and the reeve to report the profits. Upon this comes Catherine Adam's widow, and finds pledges to satisfy the lord for having custody at the next court, viz. the reeve and the hayward.

Philippa the widow of William Typetot also has a day until the next court to satisfy the lord for custody of William's land and heir, pledges William Hawys and the hayward.

Surrender: William Payn and Amice his wife to William Hawys and his heirs, 3r. of land in Northfield, granted to him to hold in bondage at the lord's will, fine 18d., pledge the reeve.

Nicholas Kembald pays 6d. as a fine for [respite of] suit of court until Michaelmas, pledge William Hawys.

Alice and Matilda Longe and Henry Crane each amerced 3d. for default; Simon Stritt amerced 3d. for the same, ordered to take his tenement into the lord's hands until etc.; and Walter Machon amerced 3d. for the same, all his tenement to be seized for services and customs withheld.

Hugh Rous amerced 3d. for unlawful detention of 6d. from Robert of Reydon, the loss assessed at 2d, ordered to raise, pledge the same Robert.

Walter Doo, Robert the tailor, Walter Hereward, William Robhood and Ralph Echeman each amerced 3d. for default.

Ordered to seize all the tenement which Peter Warde held on the day he died, until Robert Warde and his brother satisfy for entry etc. following Peter's death.

William Patel pays 6d. for [respite of] suit of court until Michaelmas, pledge Walter Typetot.

Robert Warde amerced 12d. for default, and for [respite of] suit of court until Michaelmas.

Richard Patel, Thomas Patel and Robert Osbern each amerced 3d. for default. Walter Gilberd pays 6d. for [respite of] suit of court, pledge the hayward.

The tenants of the tenement Bryd amerced 6d. for withholding 1 bushel of oats as foddercorn.

Surrender: William Clevehog to Richard Qualm and his heirs, ¼r. of land at the Wellfield ['Wellefeld'], granted to him to hold in bondage, at the lord's will, fine 3d., pledge the hayward.

Ordered to retain in the lord's hands 1r. of land which Thomas Echeman sold to Richard Crane, until Richard's heirs satisfy for entry etc.

William Lene and William Hawys each amerced 3d. for trespass against the other, pledge the reeve.

Bartholomew Patel pays 3s. fine that he shall not be in the office of reeve, pledge the hayward, and Peter Hawys 2s. for the same, pledge William Hawys.

John Syre pays 2s. fine because he was elected hayward, in token of his gratitude (?*pro in gratitudine sua*),[16] pledge the hayward.

Walter Rampolye pays 2s. fine, that he shall not be in the office of hayward, and William Coppelowe and William the miller 4d. not to be keepers of the wood for this year, pledge the hayward.

Walter Osbern remains as before in the offfice of reeve; John Man is elected to be hayward; and Richard Qualm remains keeper of the wood; and they all take the oath.

Surrenders: John Fraunceys to Walter Osbern and his heirs 1a. of land in the Eastfield ['Estfeld'], granted to him to hold in bondage at the lord's will, fine 2s.6d., pledge the reeve; and to William Hawys and his heirs 1a. in Eastfield, fine 2s.6d.; and to John le Syre and his heirs 1a., lying in separate pieces, fine 3s., pledge Walter Osbern; and to Thomas Suter and his heirs 1r., granted to them in the same form, fine 6d., pledge the hayward.

---

16 Coming between instances of fine for leave to be excused taking office, this appears to be a clerical error, or a misreading of the abbreviated words *pro* and *in*.

John Lene pays 6d. fine for having entry to a plot of waste land lying opposite his messuage, which is granted to him to hold by the rod, rendering due and accustomed services, pledges the reeve and the hayward.

SUM 54s. 6d., except the increased rent

## 10. HIGH HALL Court General of Sir Alexander de Walsham, 4 January 1318 [HA504/1/1.5.ii]

William Brodheigh essoins of suit of court by John Brodheygh, he pledges faith; Walter Osbern of the same by Walter Typetot, \afterwards he came/. Thomas Suter, defendant v William Wodebite in a plea of trespass, essoins by William Suter, he pledges faith on summons, William Wodebite is present.

John Wodebite and William Totay, the first pledges of Geoffrey Doo, amerced 6d. because they did not have him swear fealty to the lord; ordered to summon him by better pledges.

Stephen Suter and John Wodebite, the first pledges of Walter the son of Eve, amerced 3d. because they did not have him reply to William Wodebite in a plea of debt; ordered to summon him by better pledges.

It was found by the enquiry, before which Simon Kembald placed himself, that William Hardonn, Simon's servant, broke into the lord's pound and abducted two cows, against the will of the bailiffs, amerced 6d., pledges John and William Wodebite.

Alice the widow and executrix of Peter of Angerhale amerced 3d. for unlawful detention of 5s. from Gilbert Helpe; and Gilbert conceded to Alice that she should pay him 2s.6d. at Michaelmas next following, and 2s.6d. at Michaelmas a year later, pledge William Wodebite.

William Hawys amerced 3d. for trespass in the lord's pasture with his pigs, pledge William of Cranmer.

Ordered as before to attach Robert Carpenter, William the son of Reginald Chapman, William Thurbern, Richard Herbert, William Noreys, Andrew Colt, Roger Martin and Henry Puppin for fealty withheld.

The profits from a messuage 8a. of land, [taken] into the lord's hands for default by Ralph Issabel villein, and for services and customs withheld, are 3s.5d., ordered to retain the said tenement.

Geoffrey Kembald amerced 3d. for default. Ordered to attach him to reply to Oliver the shepherd in a plea of debt, pledge for Oliver John Wodebite.

Hugh of Angerhale villein, when he died, held from the lord a messuage 10½a. of villein land, also 3r. of free land of the fee of Bartholomew de Elmham and of Sir Hugh Hovel, of which 1r. is of the fee of Sir Hugh, paying for service 1½d. rent per year, to Bartholomew and Sir Hugh. The heriot is a mare, worth 3s. or more; and John and Adam, Hugh's sons and heirs, who swore fealty, give nothing for entry, as is customary.

William Goche villein, when he died, held in villeinage from the lord a messuage 10a. of land by services and customs, also he held 1a.3r. of free land of the fee of Sir Hugh Hovel, paying him 3d. per year. William had no beast, therefore he gives no heriot; John and Peter his sons and nearest heirs are under age; therefore ordered to take the tenement into the lord's hands. Upon which Alice William's widow came and paid 40d. for John and Peter to have entry, pledges Gilbert Helpe and John Wodebite.

Ordered to distrain William and Nicholas Deneys because, in the autumn, they withheld a reaping service with one man for one day.

Ordered to attach William Hawys to make amends for trespass with his cows in the lord's wheat and herbage at Allwood, and Peter Robbes for trespass in the lord's oats at the Hamstale ['Hamstachel'], and in the lord's wood at Lenerithsdel ['Leneresdel'] with his cows.

John Wodebite pays 10s. for leave to marry, pledges Gilbert Helpe and William Wodebite.

It was found that the capons and hens of the Prior of Ixworth trespassed in the lord's barley, damage 1 bushel of barley, and that [those of] William Hawys did likewise, damage 1 bushel.

SUM 18s. 9d., 1 mare and 2 bushels of barley

### 11. WALSHAM Court held there, 17 January 1318 [HA504/1/1.7]

Martin Bakun essoins of common suit by Berard the son of William, he pledges faith; Gilbert the miller [defendant] v Robert of the Peartree ['del Pertre'] in a plea of debt, essoins by Richard of Wortham; Robert is present and appoints William Hawys as his pledge.

Surrender: William Payn the younger to Walter Osbern and his heirs, 3r. of customary land with a toft, lying at the east end of the vill, granted to him to hold in bondage by services and customs etc., fine 2s., pledge John Man; Walter swore customary fealty.

John Fraunceys amerced 3d. for unlawful detention of 10d. from Nicholas Goche, which he could not deny, the loss is remitted; ordered to raise, pledges William Fraunceys and John Man.

Again as many times ordered to summon Ida Pays to reply to Robert of Reydon in a plea of trespass.

Simon Fenner in mercy for default. Afterwards he came.

Ordered to retain in the lord's hands the tenement which Millicent Qualm held from the lord, for waste in a messuage 3a. of land.

Matthew Hereward amerced 6d. for leave to agree with Alice the widow of William Robhood in a plea of detention, pledge the hayward.

William Chapman pays 18d. for entry into ½a. of customary land in Meadowfield ['Medwefeld'], which was purchased from William and Agnes at the Green etc., pledge John Man; William swore customary fealty.

Robert Suter amerced 3d. for leave to agree with Geoffrey of Lenne in a plea of debt, pledges John Man and Walter Osbern.

Simon Roty amerced 3d. for default. Ordered to take all his tenements into the lord's hands until etc., for waste made etc.

Ordered as elsewhere to distrain William at the Green in 3½a. of land, parcel of the tenement of William Cook, for services and customs withheld, and also in 1a. formerly of William Springold and Robhood [sic], and also in 3r. formerly Kebbel's, all tenements of the lord's bondage; and also in ½a. of land, formerly of William Echeman.

Simon Peyntour amerced 3d. for unlawful detention of ½d. rent from Walter Patel, which he could not deny; ordered to raise, pledge the hayward.

Robert Godefrey pays 12d. for the rolls of the 26th, 27th and 28th years of [the reign of] King Edward [Nov.1297–Nov.1300] to be scrutinised, concerning a messuage which Alice Fenner acquired by the surrender in court of Simon Fenner, and the plea between Walter Fenner and Robert is adjourned until the next court; ordered to summon before the enquiry etc.

John Rede amerced 3d. for leave to agree with John Hulke in a plea of trespass, pledge William Hawys; likewise Robert Godefrey 3d. to agree with William Rampolye in a plea of debt; and William Rampolye 3d. to agree with Robert Godefrey in a plea of trespass; pledge for both Robert Rampolye.

Surrenders: Adam Noble to Walter Osbern the younger and his heirs, 1r. of wood lying at Agneshedge ['Agneysheg'], fine 12d., granted to him to hold in the same form as above; he swore customary fealty.

Matilda, Agatha and Alice Long to the same Walter and his heirs, a cottage with 1½a. of customary land abutting on Clay street ['Cleystrete'], granted in the same form, fine 4s.; he swore customary fealty, pledge for both fines John Man.

Hugh Clevehog, who recently died, held from the lord 4a. of land and half a customary messuage; his brother Peter is his heir, and he pays ½ mark fine for entry, pledge Walter Osbern; granted to him to hold in bondage by customs and services; and Peter swore customary fealty.

Ordered to take into the lord's hands a messuage in Ashfield which Ralph Crane customary tenant sold to William Broun without leave etc., the bailiff to report the profits; also 3r. of land which Basilia Coppelowe held, because it is attested that she is dead and it is not known who is her nearest heir. The jurors have a day to certify etc.

Matilda Long amerced 3d. for unlawful detention of ½ bushel of barley from Robert Kembald, which she could not deny, pledges Peter Pynfoul, Hugh Crane and Walter Rampolye, ordered to raise.

Surrender: Matilda Long to Peter Pynfoul and his heirs, 1r. of customary land at the Millmere ['Melnemere'], granted to him to hold in bondage by services and customs, fine 2d., pledge William of Cranmer; Peter swore customary fealty.

Ordered to take into the lord's hands ½r. of customary land which Walter Gilbert demised to William and Agnes at the Green; afterwards they sold the land to William Chapman, as part of the ½a. shown above.

Surrenders: Robert of the Brook to John Patel and his heirs, ½a. of meadow in Hordeshawe ['Hordishawe'], granted to him to hold in the same form as above, fine 2s., pledge John Man; John Patel swore customary fealty.

+Cristina and Agnes Machon ['Masonn'] to William of Cranmer the younger and his heirs, ½r. of meadow in two pieces in the Great Meadow, granted to him to hold in the same form, fine 6d., pledge John Man; William swore customary fealty.

+Peter Hulke to William of Cranmer the younger and his heirs, 1r. of land in Northfield, granted to him to hold in the same form, fine 6d., pledge John Man; William swore customary fealty.

Robert the cooper to Matthew Hereward and Emma his wife and their heirs, a plot of land in his customary messuage, 4p. long and 2p. wide, granted to them to hold in the same form, fine 6d., pledge John Man; they swore customary fealty.

Peter Pynfoul to Matthew Hereward and his heirs, ½r. and ¼r. of land in the Bottom, granted to him to hold in bondage, fine 6d., pledge John Man; Matthew swore customary fealty.

Robert Godefrey amerced 3d. for leave to agree with Peter Jay in a plea of trespass, pledge John Man.

Robert the chaplain amerced 3d. for damage with his cows in the lord's wheat, pledge Walter Osbern; also Cristina Clevehog 3d. for damage in the lord's willows taking away etc. pledge Peter Clevehog.

Ralph Echeman amerced 3d. for leave to agree with Alice Whiteman ['Quyteman'] in a plea of trespass, pledge Matthew Hereward.

Surrender: Cristina Machon to William Lene and his heirs, 1r. of land in the Syke, granted to him to hold in the same form as above, fine 6d., pledge John Man; William swore customary fealty.

Robert Godefrey amerced 6d. because he deprived Alice the widow of Hereward Gunter[17] of her rightful dower, as he acknowledged in court, pledge John Man; the bailiff was ordered that she should have that which was hers by right.

Surrenders: Robert of Reydon to William Cook and his heirs, half a customary messuage in Clay street formerly of Walter Machon, granted to him to hold in the same form as above, fine 6d., pledge John Man; William swore customary fealty.

Alice Long to Nicholas Goche and his heirs, 1a.½r. of customary land lying in the Millfield at Tofts, granted to him to hold in the same form, fine 3s., pledge John Man; Nicholas swore customary fealty.

Matilda and Alice Long to Hugh Crane and Cecilia his wife and their heirs, 1a. of customary land, lying in pieces [sic] in the Millfield, granted to them to hold in the same form, fine 2s.6d., pledge John Man; they swore customary fealty.

Peter Pynfoul and Matilda and Alice Long to Walter Rampolye and his heirs, 1a. of customary land at the Millmere, granted to him to hold in the same form, fine 3s., pledge Walter Osbern; Walter [Rampolye] swore customary fealty.

William at the Wood and Henry his brother to John Patel and his heirs, ½a. of land near Mabelotiscroft, granted to him to hold in the same form, fine 2s., pledge John Man; John swore customary fealty.

Robert of Reydon amerced 6d. for unlawful detention of 16d. from Walter Machon, for which the loss is assessed at 2d., ordered to raise, pledge John Man.

Surrender: Emma Pye to Richard Qualm and his heirs, a piece of customary meadow, 40p. long and 2ft. wide, granted to him to hold in the same form as above, fine 6d., pledges John Man and Walter Osbern; Richard swore customary fealty.

Walter Machon amerced 3d. for a false claim against Robert of Reydon concerning the detention of chattels, pledges Robert of Reydon and Robert Spileman.

Surrender: Richard Qualm to Walter Osbern the younger and his heirs, a piece of customary meadow next to the Jaysacre ['le Jayisaker'], 40p. long and 10ft. wide, fine 6d., in exchange for ½r. of meadow in Bradmeadow ['Brademedwe'], lying in separate pieces, surrendered to Richard and his heirs, granted to each of them to hold in the same form as above, fine 6d., pledges each for the other; they swore customary fealty.

Peter Tailor in mercy[18] for trespass against Robert of Reydon, of which he was convicted by the enquiry, pledge Walter Osbern.

John Suter amerced 3d. for a false claim against William Frаunceys in a plea of debt, pledge William Payn.

Surrenders: Richard Payn to Robert Lene and his heirs, ½a. of customary land in the

---

17 MS: 'Buntir', but later references are clearly 'Gunter'.
18 Amount not stated.

Netherfield, granted to him to hold in the same form as above, fine 18d., pledge John Man; Robert Lene swore customary fealty.

John Fraunceys to Peter the son of Robert and his heirs, ½a. of land called the Shorthalfacre ['le Schortehalfaker'] lying at the Brook ['le Broke'], granted to him to hold in the same form, fine 20d., pledge John Man; Peter swore customary fealty.

Simon Fenner to Peter Hawys and his heirs, 1a. of land in Thediscroft, granted to him to hold in the same form, fine 2s., pledge John Man; Peter swore customary fealty.

Peter Clevehog to Peter Springold and his heirs, ½r. of customary meadow in the Great Meadow, granted to him to hold in the same form, fine 6d., pledge Robert Spileman; Peter Springold swore customary fealty.

Peter Clevehog, Rose Typetot, Simon Peyntour, Walter Qualm, Elias Typetot, Robert of the Brook, John Wysdom, Walter Lete and Robert Rampolye amerced 18d. for damage in the herbage of William Fenner with their beasts, for which they were convicted by the enquiry, the loss assessed at 18d., ordered to raise, pledge each for another; William to pay the lord 6d. from the 18d. for the raising thereof.

Surrender: John Patel to William the son of William of Cranmer, ½r. of customary meadow in the Great Meadow, granted to him to hold in the same form as above, fine 6d., pledge John Man; William swore customary fealty.

Robert Tailor and William Robhood each paid 3d. fine for [respite of] suit of court until Michaelmas, pledge for Robert John Man, for William Nicholas Kembald.

Surrender: William Payn to Walter Payn and his heirs, 1a. of customary land at Burnscroft, granted to him to hold in the same form as above, fine 12d., pledge Walter Osbern, Walter Payn swore customary fealty.

Ordered to execute all the orders of the court not yet acted upon, marked with a cross in the roll of the preceding court.

SUM 48s. 1d.

## 12.   HIGH HALL Court of Sir Alexander de Walsham, 28 February 1318 [HA504/1/1.8.i]

As elsewhere ordered to summon Geoffrey Doo by a better pledge to swear fealty; and Walter the son of Eve to reply to William Wodebite in a plea of debt.

As elsewhere ordered to attach Robert Carpenter, William the son of Reginald Chapman, William Thurbern, Richard Herbert, Walter Noreys \he swore fealty/, Andrew Colt \he swore fealty/, Roger Martin and Henry Puppin for fealty withheld.

As elsewhere ordered to retain a messuage 8a. of land taken into the lord's hands for defaults by Ralph Issabel, villlein, [and] for services and customs withheld.

As elsewhere ordered to attach Geoffrey Kembald \dead/ to reply to Oliver the shepherd concerning a plea of debt, \therefore indefinitely/.

As elsewhere ordered to attach William and John Deneys to make amends to the lord, because in the autumn they withheld one reaping service with one man.

Ordered to attach Peter Robbes to make amends for trespass in the lord's oats at the Hamstal, and in his wood at Lenerithsdel with cows.

William Wodebite amerced 4d. for a false claim against Thomas Suter in a plea of trespass, pledge Gilbert Helpe.

It was found by the enquiry that Andrew Warin with 2 cows, John Scot with a cow and a calf, Helena Aylmer with 2 cows, Katherine Warin with 2 cows, and all the

67

aforesaid with 5 bullocks, caused damage in the lord's wheat at Borefeld; and that the beasts were impounded in a certain building of the lord, and had escaped by night. Therefore ordered to attach Andrew and the others to make amends.[19]

Ordered to distrain Cristina Gilbert because she withheld one hen [rent] for two years; also John, the son of Hugh of Angerhale and Agnes, his mother, tenant in dower, amerced 3d. for the same for this year, pledge John Wodebite.

Ordered to attach John Syre for trespass in the lord's corn and herbage; and as elsewhere to attach William Hawys to make amends for trespass with his cows in the lord's wheat and herbage at Allwood.

SUM 7d.

### 13.   WALSHAM Court, 28 March 1318 [HA504/1/2.3]

Peter Margery essoins of common suit by John Hernyng; likewise John Margery by William at the Wood, and Sarah Brian ['Brionn'] by Berard Margery; they pledge faith.

William at the Wood amerced 6d. for leave to agree with John Hernyng in a plea of covenant, pledge Peter Jay.

Surrender: Nicholas Goche to William Chapman and his heirs, 1r. of land at the Maypole ['le Mapol'], granted to him to hold in bondage by customs and services, fine 9d., pledge John the hayward; William swore customary fealty.

Again ordered to attach Ida Pays to reply to Robert of Reydon in a plea of trespass.

+Gilbert the miller amerced 3d. for unlawful detention of 2 bushels of corn, worth 2s., from Robert of the Peartree, which he could not deny, the loss is remitted; ordered to raise.

Simon Roty pays 3d. fine to repossess his tenement from the lord's seisin, taken for waste made in the said tenement, pledges Peter Pynfoul and Hugh Crane; Simon has a day until Michaelmas to make good the waste and to perform services and customs etc., pledges as above.

Ordered to retain a horse taken upon Robert of Reydon and to take [more] etc. so that he shall reply to Adam Warde in a plea of detention of chattels.

Ordered to retain in the lord's hands 2a. of land of his demesne formerly demised to Robert Arnald, of which Martin Bakun holds 1a., and Peter Margery and his brothers hold the other 1a., until etc., and to distrain Martin and Peter and the others to be at the next court to show by what right they entered into the said tenement.

Surrender: Thomas Fuller, Cristina his wife and Isabella [Reve] her sister, to William Coppelowe and his heirs, 3r. of land in the meadow called the Stubbyng, granted to him to hold in the same form as above, fine 2s., pledge Walter Osbern; William swore customary fealty.

Millicent Qualm pays 3d. fine to repossess her tenement from the lord, taken because she sheltered wrongdoers in the vill by night, and for waste made etc., pledges Richard Qualm and Simon Peyntour; she has a day to make good the waste by Michaelmas, pledges as above.

Again ordered to retain in the lord's hands a messuage in Ashfield which Ralph Crane, customary tenant, sold to William Broun without leave, the bailiff to report the profits.

---

[19] Margin: 'void because the lord intervened by royal writ'.

Robert Warde and Richard and William his brothers pay 5s. fine for having entry into a messuage 5a. of land which Peter Warde held on the day he died; they are Peter's heirs, and the tenement is granted to them to hold in the same form as above; and Richard and William swore customary fealty; the fealty of Robert is postponed until etc., pledge John the hayward.

Walter Machon pays 3d. fine to repossess his tenement from the lord, taken for customs withheld etc., and he finds surety to do henceforth that which he should do, pledge John Man.

Surrender: John and Robert Lene to John Herning and his heirs, 2a. of land in one piece at Brunnthweyt, granted to him to hold in bondage etc. rendering to the lord 1d. increased rent annually at Michaelmas, and one appearance annually at the Court General at Walsham after Michaelmas, and, for the lord, to the capital lord of the fee the due and accustomed services. John pays 2s. entry fine, pledge John the hayward, and he swore customary fealty.

+John Man the hayward amerced 6d. because he did not present the trespass by Thomas Margery removing a certain tree, pledge the reeve. Thomas now amerced 12d. because he cut down a tree, worth 2s., in the lord's bondage, and sold it to William Chapman, without leave; ordered to raise the [value of the] tree to the use of the lord. And William Chapman amerced 7d. because he bought the tree without leave.[20]

Again ordered to retain in the lord's hands 1r. of land which Thomas Echeman sold to Richard Crane, until the heirs of Richard satisfy the lord for entry etc.

Agatha Robhod pays 6d. to have entry into 1r. of land, which Robert Robhod, her [late] husband, held from the lord etc.

Surrender: William Payn to Walter Payn and his heirs, a plot of land from a curtilage, 8p. long and 4½p. wide, granted to him to hold in the same form as above, fine 12d., pledge Walter Osbern; Walter Payn swore customary fealty.

The summonses against Catherine the widow of Adam Goche concerning a messuage 8a. of land, to do that which she should do, because Adam's heir is under age, and against Philippa, the widow of William Typetot, to satisfy the lord for custody of William's land and heir, are adjourned until the next court, pledges for Catherine the reeve and the hayward, for Philippa William Hawys and the hayward.

Nicholas Kembald and William Marler each amerced 3d. for default.

Robert Godefrey amerced 6d. for unlawful deforcement of a messuage 1a. of land from Walter the smith,[21] as was found by the enquiry before which Robert and Walter placed themselves; therefore ordered to take the said tenement etc., pledges of Walter the reeve and John Man; and thereupon Walter pays 5s. for having entry, rendering the due and accustomed services, and he swore customary fealty.

Elias Typetot and Matilda his wife and Emma Matilda's sister pay 2s. fine for having entry into 3r. of land after the death of Basilia Coppelowe kinswoman of Matilda and Emma, who are her heirs, granted to them to hold in bondage by

---

[20] Tab: 'Thomas Margerie' (?17th century).

[21] MS: 'Faber', probably in error. This appears to be the follow-up to the entry in the roll of 17 January 1318 (no.11) concerning a dispute over a messuage 1a. of land, where the defendant's name was Robert Godefrey, and the surname of the plaintiff and earlier tenants of the land was 'le Fenere'.

customs and services; and they swore customary fealty, pledges the reeve and the hayward.

Cecilia the daughter of Gilbert Reve pays 32d. for childwyte, pledge John Hewe.

William Coppelowe amerced 3d. for digging on the common, pledge the hayward, and 3d. for ploughing on the common way, pledge the reeve.

Walter Machon surrendered to William of Cranmer the younger all the right and claim he has by inheritance in 1½a. of land in the Millfield, which Cristina his mother holds in dower for her lifetime, and he granted that this 1½a., which should revert to him after Cristina's death, shall revert to William and his heirs. Granted to William to hold in bondage by customs and services, after the death [of Cristina] etc., fine 40d., pledge the reeve and the hayward. And the same William of Cranmer surrendered to William Cook 1r. of land to hold in the same form, after Cristina's death, and seisin is granted to him, fine 6d., pledge the reeve; and he swore customary fealty.

Walter[22] Machon, villein of the lord, finds pledges for 1d. per year chevage and for making one suit at the Court General after Michaelmas, *viz.* William of Cranmer and William Cook. Walter swore customary fealty.

Richard Patel and William Clevehog each amerced 3d. for default.

Thomas Fuller amerced 3d. because he tilled within customary land without leave, pledge William of Cranmer.

Robert of Reydon amerced 6d. because he ploughed on the common at Therwalds, and also appropriated to make an enclosure from the common there; Nicholas Kembald, Peter Springold, Ralph Echeman, Walter Goselyng, William at the Green, Gilbert Sare and Robert Lene each amerced 3d. for the same.

Agatha Robhood amerced 3d. for withholding one hen [rent] for two years, ordered to raise, pledge Robert Spilman.

The jurors have a day until the next court to certify concerning all the customary men who took wives at any time past, without the lord's leave etc., and moreover to certify concerning trespassers ploughing upon the common, or cutting down trees there.

SUM 33s., except increased rent and chevage

\As elsewhere ordered to distrain William and Agnes at the Green in 3½a. of land, parcel of the tenement of William Cook, and in 1a. formerly of William Springold and Robhood, and in 3r. formerly Kebbil's, and in ½a. formerly of William Echeman, for customs and services withheld, all of which tenements are of the lord's bondage./

## 14. WALSHAM Court, 15 June 1318 [HA504/1/1.9]

Martin Bakonn essoins of suit of court by Berard Margery.

Again ordered to retain in the lord's hands 2a. of his demesne formerly demised to Robert Arnald, of which Martin Bakonn holds 1a., and Peter Margery and his brothers hold the other 1a., and to distrain Martin and Peter and the others to be at the next court to show by what right they entered the lord's fee etc.

Again ordered to distrain William and Agnes at the Green in 3½a., parcel of the tenement of William Cook, also in 1a. formerly of William Springold and

---

22 MS: 'William', but this is certainly an error. The only other mention of William Machon in the rolls records his death in 1317; Walter Machon appears many times as a fugitive.

Robhood [*sic*], also in 3r. which were Kebbil's, and ½a. formerly of William Echeman, all tenements of the lord's bondage, for services and customs withheld.

Again ordered to retain in the lord's hands a messuage in Ashfield which Ralph Crane sold to William Broun without leave, the reeve to report the profits.

Again ordered to retain 1r. of land which Thomas Echeman sold to Richard Crane, until Richard's heir satisfies the lord for entry.

Robert of Reydon and Matilda his wife amerced 6d., for leave to agree with Adam Warde in a plea of detention of chattels; and Robert and his pledges amerced 4d. because he did not proceed against Ida Pays in a plea of trespass.

The summonses against Catherine the widow of Adam Goche to do that which she should do concerning custody of Adam's heir and his land, and against Philippa the widow of William Typetot for the same, concerning custody of his land and heir, are in respite until the next court, pledges the reeve and the hayward.

Thomas King complains against Walter Gilberd in a plea of debt; his pledges are John Margery and the bailiff. Ordered to attach him [Walter].

Catherine Helewys amerced 3d. because she entered the lord's wood without leave to take away spoil (?*spol*') etc., pledge the hayward.

Ordered to attach the Prior of Ixworth to satisfy the lord for damage with his beasts in the lord's corn and pasture.

The jurors say that a certain William Barel of Walsham, 40 years before, in the time of Sir William de Blund, lord of Walsham, gave by charter to Ralph Patel villein, with Alice his daughter, in marriage, 7a. of land, [Ralph] rendering annually to William Barel and his heirs 13d. of silver, and to scutage when it was due etc., and Ralph held this land for the rest of his life, and died seised thereof. After his death Henry his son and heir received the 7a. by the rod in court, with other tenements of the lord's bondage, to hold in villeinage at the lord's will etc. Afterwards Henry, brought into the court, surrendered half of the 7a. to Agnes his daughter, who married a certain Roger of St Edmunds; and Roger and Agnes surrendered that land to John Patel, Agnes' brother.

Surrender: Agnes Machon to Thomas Fuller and his heirs, 1½r. of land in one piece in the Millfield, next to the land of William Hawys, granted to him to hold in bondage by customs and services etc., fine 12d., pledge John Man; Thomas swore customary fealty.[23]

William Rampolye amerced 3d. for leave to agree with Simon Kembald in a plea of trespass, pledge Robert Rampolye.

Nicholas Kembald amerced 6d. for damage in the lord's meadows, pledge the reeve; and Elena Aylmer 12d. for damage in the lord's herbage, pledge Walter Osbern the elder.

Surrender: Gilbert Priour to Richard his brother and his heirs, a piece of land in Priorscroft, containing ¾r., granted to him to hold in the same form as above, fine 12d., pledge Gilbert Priour; Richard swore customary fealty.

Thomas Echeman, who recently died, held from the lord by the rod half a cotland ½a. of land; because Thomas had no beast, Ralph his son and heir, who is of full age, pays 2s. fine for having entry to the tenement, which is granted to him to hold in the same form as above, pledges John Man and Nicholas Kembald; Ralph swore customary fealty.

---

23 Tab: 'Agnes le Machon, William Prior *et alii*'.

Emma Shepherd amerced 3d. for damage done in trampling the lord's corn while hoeing and treading etc., pledges John Man and Stephen Cooper; likewise Catherine Coppelowe 12d., and Nicholas Goche 3d.; likewise Thomas Margery 12d. for the same with his beasts; and Peter Tailor by his servants trampling, pledge for all John Man.

The jurors say that the Abbot of St Edmunds and his community made an unlawful way outside the land of the lord, going towards Redgrave and Rickinghall.

Walter Typetot says in court that he holds nothing from the lord in bondage etc., and the jurors have a day until the next court to certify thereon; and ordered to attach Walter to reply to Robert Warde in a plea of detention of cattle, *viz.* 6 sheep.

Ordered to attach Simon Cooper ['le Cupper'] to reply to Bartholomew Patel in a plea of trespass, pledge for Simon the reeve, and for Bartholomew Walter Osbern.

A day is given to Nicholas But, plaintiff, and Simon Fenner in a plea of land until the next court, to come without essoin. The jurors have the same day to enquire etc.

Adam Noble, Peter Pynfoul, Hugh Crane and Robert Kembald each amerced 3d. for unlawful detention of 1 bushel of barley, 1 bushel of peas and 1 bushel of oats from Emma Straunge,[24] which they cannot deny, and the loss is remitted, ordered to raise, pledges each for another.

Surrenders: Simon Fenner to Thomas Fuller and his heirs, 1½r. of land in Rafelescroft, granted to him to hold in the same form as above, fine 18d., pledge John Man; Thomas swore customary fealty.

Richard Reve to Thomas Fuller and his heirs, a piece of land in Scherewyndescote, 20p. long and 7½ft. wide, granted to him to hold in the same form, fine 3d., pledge John Man; Thomas swore customary fealty.

Alice Whiteman to Matthew Hereward and his heirs, a cottage and ½a. of land in the adjoining croft, and a piece of land at the Leyton, 30p. long and 7ft. wide, granted to him to hold in the same form, fine 20d., pledge Robert Spileman; Matthew swore customary fealty; and upon this Matthew, by the lord's leave, granted the said cottage and land to Alice to hold for life, and the lord granted [seisin] to her; after her death the cottage and ½a. of land shall revert to Matthew and his heirs.

Adam Warde to Nicholas Goche and his heirs, ½a. of land at Cocksdrit, granted to him to hold in the same form, fine 18d., pledge John Man; Nicholas swore customary fealty.

Thomas Clevehog surrendered, granted and released to his brother Peter, in perpetuity, all the claim which he had, or in any way could have had, in half a messuage and 4a. of land after the death of their brother Hugh; with the condition that neither Thomas, nor his heirs, nor anyone in his name shall henceforth be able to demand or justify anything of right or claim in the said tenement; granted to Peter to hold in the same form as above, fine 40d., pledge John Man; Peter swore customary fealty.

---

[24] Probably Emma Stronde.

Again the jurors have a day until the next court to certify concerning all the customary men who have taken wives at any time in the past without the lord's leave; also to certify in future concerning trespass, ploughing and felling trees on the common etc.

SUM 18s. 10d.

### 15. HIGH HALL Court, 13 July 1318 [HA504/1/1.8.ii]

Walter of the Marsh essoins of suit of court by Henry Trusse, likewise Robert of House by William Brodheigh, and Walter Osbern by William of Cranmer; they pledge faith and have a day on summons.

As elsewhere ordered to summon by better pledges Geoffrey Doo for fealty withheld, and Walter the son of Eve to reply to William Wodebite in a plea of debt.

As elsewhere ordered to distrain Robert Carpenter, William, the son of Reginald Chapman, William Thurbern, Richard Herbert, Roger Martin and Henry Puppin for fealty withheld.

As elsewhere ordered to retain in the lord's hands a messuage 8a. of land which Ralph Issabel held, for many defaults and services and customs withheld.

William Deneys and John, his brother, amerced 4d. because they withheld one reaping service in the previous autumn, pledges William of Cranmer and William Hawys.

Peter Robbes amerced 3d. for trespass with his cows in the Lord's oats at Hamstal, and 3d. for the same in his wood at Lenerithsdel, pledge William of Cranmer.

As elsewhere ordered to distrain Cristina Gilbert because she withheld 1 hen annual rent for two years.

John Syre amerced 3d. for trespass in the lord's corn and herbage, pledges John Wodebite and the hayward; and William Hawys 3d. for the same in the lord's wheat and herbage at Allwood with cows, pledge William of Cranmer.

It was found by the enquiry that Geoffrey Kembald villein, when he died, held in villeinage a messuage 8a. of land by the services and customs contained in the terrier etc., and that he had no beast by which a heriot could be paid. Matilda his sister, who married Nicholas the miller freeman, Alice the daughter of Oliver the shepherd free woman, and his wife Agatha, Geoffrey's sister, are Geoffrey's nearest heirs; therefore ordered [to retain] the tenement in the lord's hands.

Also that William Makenoyse freeman held from the lord at his death ½a. of free land lying in the furlong called Kerfeld by services, ¼d. to ward service, homage and fealty; ordered to take etc.

SUM 16d.

### 16. HIGH HALL Court, 5 August 1318 [HA504/1/1.8.iii]

William of Cranmer essoins of common suit by Oliver the shepherd, he pledges faith on summons.

As elsewhere ordered to summon Geoffrey Doo for fealty still withheld, and to attach Walter the son of Eve to reply to William Wodebite in a plea of debt.

John Wodebite amerced 3d. because he did not attach Richard Herbert for fealty as ordered, and he admits that he could have attached him. Ordered to attach Richard.

As elsewhere ordered to distrain Cristina Gilbert for one hen annual rent withheld for two years; and to retain in the lord's hands ½a. of land in the furlong called

Kerfeld which William Makenoyse, who recently died, held free from the lord by services, ¼d. to ward service, and homage and fealty.

Walter Osbern amerced 3d. because he did not warrant his essoin from the last court.

John Wodebite was elected by the whole homage to the office of reeve.

Henry Puppin was attached to swear fealty to the lord and did not come, his pledges amerced 3d.; ordered to summon Henry, and afterwards he came and swore fealty.

As elsewhere ordered to attach Robert Carpenter, William Chapman, William Thurbern and Roger Martin for fealty withheld.

Matilda the sister of Geoffrey Kembald and Alice the daughter of Oliver the shepherd, Geoffrey's heirs, pay 3s. fine for entry to a messuage 8a. of land, following Geoffrey's death, pledges Gilbert Helpe and Simon Kembald; because Alice is under age Oliver pays 6d. for having custody etc., pledges as above.

Matilda the widow of Geoffrey Kembald to pay 6d., so that her dower be granted to her, \waived by the lord/.

Robert Spileman, the keeper of the cows, amerced 3d. because they did damage in the lord's wheat above the wood.

The Prior of Ixworth did damage in the lord's oats with sheep, likewise Sir Edmund de Pakenham and Agatha of Allwood with heifers[25], and likewise Thomas Suter with cows at Allwoodgreen, ordered to attach them to satisfy for the damage.

Eda Rede did damage in the lord's oats on the Fourteenacres with cows and pigs, likewise Thomas Suter on the Fifteenacres, ordered to attach them to satisfy the lord for the trespasses.

Gilbert [Helpe] the reeve amerced[26] because he accepted 3 pecks of oats from certain villeins who trespassed in the lord's corn.

William Wodebite amerced 6d. because he did not come to [perform] boonworks when summoned, pledge John Wodebite; likewise John Wodebite 3d. and Simon Kembald 3d.

Ralph Issabel pays 2s. fine for entry to a messuage 8a. of land of villeinage, pledges Gilbert Helpe, William and John Wodebite.

SUM  7s. 3d. and 3 pecks of oats

## 17.  WALSHAM Court, 6 September 1318 [HA504/1/4.13]

Walter Typetot, defendant v Robert Warde in a plea of debt, essoins by Berard Margery; he pledges faith, and Robert is present by attachment.

+Again ordered to retain in the lord's hands 2a. of land of the lord's demesne formerly demised to Robert Arnald to hold at the lord's will, of which Martin Bakonn holds 1a., and Peter Margery and his brothers hold the other 1a.; the bailiff reports the profits, viz. 1a. sown with rye in April at 6 bushels of rye, and 1a. sown with barley in April at 5 bushels, and flax to the value of 3d.

+William of Cranmer and Robert Spileman, the first pledges of Martin Bakonn, amerced 6d. because they did not have him show by what right he entered the lord's fee, and to do that which he ought; ordered to distrain him as before concerning 1a. of land formerly of Robert Arnald. +Likewise, as pledges of Peter

---

25  MS: *boviculis* = either heifers or bullocks.
26  Amount illegible.

Margery and his brothers, William and Robert, amerced 6d. for the same; ordered etc. concerning the other 1a.

+Again ordered to distrain William and Agnes at the Green in 3½a. of land, parcel of the tenement formerly of William Cook, and in 1a. formerly of William Springold and Robhood, and in 3r. which were Kebbil's, and in 1a. formerly of William Echeman, for customs and services withheld; all the land is of the lord's bondage.

+Walter Gilberd amerced 3d. for leave to agree with Thomas King in a plea of debt, pledge Robert Spileman.

Again ordered to retain in the lord's hands a messuage in Ashfield, which Ralph Crane customary tenant sold to William Broun without leave, the reeve to report the profits.

Sarah Margery amerced 9d. for leave to agree with Nicholas Goche in a plea of trespass, in 3 complaints, pledges the reeve and the hayward.

Ordered to attach the Prior of Ixworth to satisfy the lord for damage in the lord's corn and pasture with his beasts.

Again ordered to retain 1r. of land which Thomas Echeman sold to Richard Crane until Richard's heir satisfies the lord for entry.

Simon Cooper amerced 6d. for leave to agree with Bartholomew Patel in a plea of trespass, pledge John Man; and Thomas Salvetayl 6d. to agree with John Boniard in a plea of debt, pledge Thomas King.

+Concerning the summonses against Catherine the widow of Adam Goche to do to the lord that which she ought for the custody of Adam's heir and land, and against Philippa the widow of William Typetot for the same for his land and heir, they have a day until the next court etc., pledges the reeve and the hayward.

+Catherine Goche pays ½ mark for leave to marry Simon Peyntour villein, pledges Robert Spileman and Walter Osbern.

+The Abbot of St Edmunds and his servants made an unlawful way outside the lord's land, going towards Redgrave and Rickinghall, in respite etc.

Simon Fenner amerced 3d. for leave to agree with Nicholas But in a plea of land, pledge Thomas Fuller; and Catherine Goche 4d. for the same with Stephen Broun in a plea of trespass, pledge John Man.

Robert the chaplain amerced 3d. for damage in the lord's peas with his pigs; likewise Stephen Cooper 3d. for the same in the lord's oats with his cows, pledge for both John Man; and Basilia of Downham 6d. for the same in the fold with her pigs; Walter Qualm 3d. for the same in the lord's rye with a stot in his keeping; Robert Lene 3d. for the same with geese; William Shepherd 4d. for the same in the corn with sheep, pledge for Walter, Robert and William, the reeve; Peter Tailor 3d. for the same with a pig, and Thomas Margery 3d. for the same with pigs, pledge for both John Man.

Ordered to distrain the Prior of Ixworth to satisfy the lord for damage done, laying flat the lord's oats with his carts, the loss assessed at ½ bushel of oats.

+Galiena Houthon amerced 3d. because outside the court she demised to William and Agnes at the Green ½a. of customary land without leave, ordered to seize.

The tenants of the tenement of Ralph Herirof amerced 3d. for the withholding of service, [viz.] 1 bushel of oats for one year; ordered to distrain them to satisfy etc.

Surrenders: William the son of Emma at the Brook to William Hawys and his heirs, half a messuage 3a. of customary land formerly his mother's, granted to him to hold in bondage by customs and services, fine 8s.; he swore customary fealty;

likewise, to Walter Osbern and his heirs, the other half of the messuage and 3a., granted to him to hold in the same form, fine 6s.; he swore customary fealty, pledge each for the other.

The tenants of the tenement of Roger Suter amerced 3d. for withholding one autumn work for one day, ordered to distrain them for the work.

+The jurors say that Walter Typetot holds from the lord 3r. of land of the lord's bondage, lying within Walter's croft and close, rendering for services 1¼d. and half of one autumn work per year priced at 3d., and that Hugh Typetot, Walter's father, purchased these 3r. from Estrilda Pye and Basilia, her sister; Walter refuses in court to hold any land from the lord by the rod; ordered to seize etc.

Surrender: Avice Deneys to Gilbert Helpe and his heirs, 1r. of customary land, granted to him to hold in bondage, fine 12d., pledge Walter Osbern; Gilbert swore customary fealty.

The jurors have a day until the next court to certify concerning all customary men who have taken wives at any time in the past without leave, and to certify henceforth concerning offences of ploughing on the common, and cutting wood on common land.

SUM 28s. 4d.

## 18. WALSHAM Court General there, 18 October 1318 [HA504/1/1.10]

Robert Warde, plaintiff v Walter Typetot in a plea of debt, essoins by John Tothman, he pledges faith on summons; Martin Bakon essoins of common suit by Thomas Margery; likewise Sarah Brian by Berard Margery and John Herning by John Margery.

Roger Spileman pays 3d. fine for leave of suit of court until Michaelmas, pledges Robert Spileman and others, likewise Walter Gilbert 6d., pledge Robert Spileman, Nicholas the miller 4d., pledge the hayward, William Patel 6d., pledge John Man, and William at the Green 6d., pledge the hayward, for the same at the same time.

The Prior of Ixworth amerced 12d. for damage in the lord's corn and pasture, and ½ bushel of oats for damage in the lord's oats.

The summonses against Catherine the widow of Adam Goche to make to the lord that which she ought for the custody of Adam's heir and his land, and against Philippa widow of William Typetot for the same of his land and heir, are in respite until the next court etc., pledges the reeve and the hayward.

Matthew Hereward pays 3s. for having leave from the office of reeve, pledge Walter Osbern; likewise Peter Jay 3s., pledge John Margery.

Simon Peyntour and Walter Payn each pay 2s. for having leave from the office of hayward, pledge the hayward.

At the request of the parties, a love day is given until the next court concerning a plea of trespass between Marsilia Hawys and Peter Neve and Alice his wife.

Thomas Fuller pays 12d. for having leave from the office of keeper of the wood, pledge the hayward.

Ordered to distrain Martin Bakonn to show by what right he entered the lord's tenement, and to do etc.

Again ordered to distrain William and Agnes at the Green in 3½a. of land, parcel of the tenement formerly of William Cook, and in 1a. formerly of William Springold and Robhood, and in 3r. which were Kebbil's, and in 1a. formerly of

William Echeman, for customs and services withheld, all the land is of the lord's bondage.

Surrender: Peter Pynfoul to Robert Godefrey and his heirs, 6r. of land in the field called Southfield ['Suthfeld'] between Adam Noble's land on each side, granted to him to hold in bondage at the lord's will, by services and customs, fine 9d.; Robert swore fealty.

Again ordered to retain in the lord's hands a messuage in Ashfield, which Ralph Crane customary tenant sold to William Broun without leave, the reeve to report the profits.

Again ordered to retain 1r. of land which Thomas Echeman sold to Richard Crane, until Richard's heir satisfies the lord for entry etc.

The Abbot of St Edmunds and his servants made an unlawful way outside the lord's land, going towards Redgrave and Rickinghall, in respite etc.

Again ordered to seize ½a. of land of villeinage which Galiena Houthon demised to Wiliam and Agnes at the Green, and to report the profits.

Ordered to seize 3r. of land of villeinage which Walter Typetot holds, and to report the profits, as shown in the preceding court at the end of the roll.

William Hawys complains against Adam Noble in a plea of trespass, that Adam unlawfully appropriated from his land [a piece] 5ft. wide and 30p. long to his loss of 2s.; Adam denies that he appropriated the land, and says that Walter Hulke had died seised of it, and that Walter's heirs were under age and in custody etc.; therefore in respite until the next court, meanwhile the heirs to be warned to be at the next court.

Robert the miller pays 3d. fine for leave of suit of court until Michaelmas, pledge John Syre.

The jurors say that Walter of the Marsh of Westhorpe unlawfully took ten partridges in the lord's warren, and five partridges next to the wood of John de Walsham.

Also that, concerning the 2a. of land which Robert Arnald and his brother held, a former lord of the manor before the time of Sir William de Blund gave the land by charter to hold free by due services, of which nothing is in arrears; adjourned indefinitely.

Simon Roty amerced 6d. for default of suit of court; and it is ordered to seize a quarter part of a messuage 3a. of land for waste made and customs still withheld, and Simon warned to be at the next court to satisfy [the lord] if he wishes.

Simon Kembald amerced 6d., Robert Godefrey 6d., Robert Kembald 3d., William Cook 6d., Alice Warde 3d., pledge John Warde, and Nicholas [Kembald] the miller 3d. because they brewed in breach of the assize.

The jurors have a day to certify concerning the tenement Herirof, and 1 bushel of oats and other services owed therefrom.

William Clevehog and Hugh Cotyn each pay 3d. for leave of suit of court until Michaelmas, pledge the hayward.

Gilbert Prior surrendered to the lord a messuage ½a. of land of villeinage, and the lord grants it to him and his wife Alice to have and to hold at the lord's will, for the term of the life of each of them; and after their decease [damaged] the tenement to the heirs issuing from the bodies of the said Gilbert and Alice.

Robert Warde pays 12d. fine for leave of suit of court until Michaelmas.

Surrender: William Syre to Walter Syre and his heirs, 1 [damaged] in the field called Newhawe within Walter's land at one side, granted to him to hold in bondage at the lord's will by customs and services, fine 6d.; he swore fealty.

Ralph Hawys amerced 3d. for trespass in the lord's wood, burning sticks (?*cinendis virgis*),[27] pledge William Hawys.

Surrender: Emma Peyntour to Robert Godefrey and his heirs, 1r. of land lying next to Walsham mill, granted to him to hold in bondage at the lord's will, fine 9d.; he swore fealty.

SUM 21s. 2d., and ½ bushel of oats

Affeerers: Walter Osbern, William Cook

## 19. WALSHAM Court General of Sir Edmund de Pakenham, 16 January 1319 [HA504/1/1.11]

[The manuscript is torn on one side, affecting the left margin *recto* and some text *verso*.]

Eda the widow of Robert Rede, pays 2s. for leave to marry John of Stonham, pledges William of Cranmer and the hayward.

The summonses against Catherine the widow of Adam Goche to do to the lord that which she ought for the custody of Adam's heir and land, and against Philippa the widow of William Typetot for the same of his land and heir, are in respite until the next court etc.

Robert Warde and his pledges, concerning whom the hayward presents, amerced 6d. because he did not proceed against Walter Typetot in a plea of debt.

The summons against William and Agnes at the Green concerning various articles, as shown in the preceding court, is in respite until the next.

John Hernyng amerced 6d. for default.

Again ordered to retain in the lord's hands a messuage in Ashfield, which Ralph Crane customary tenant sold to William Broun without leave, the reeve to report the profits.

John Man and Robert Rampolye each amerced 3d. for default.

Thomas Suter amerced 3d. for leave to agree with Walter Osbern in a plea of debt, pledge the hayward; likewise Peter Neve and his wife Alice 3d. to agree with William Hawys in a plea of trespass, pledge the same William.

Galiena Houthon pays 3d. for repossessing ½a. of land out of the lord's hands, which she demised to Agnes at the Green without leave.

Agatha Pynfoul amerced 3d. for waste in the lord's bondage, ordered to take into the lord's hands until etc.

Ordered to retain in the lord's hands all the tenement which Simon and Joan Roty hold from the lord in bondage, for waste made and for customs and services withheld, and that the reeve report the profits. \Upon this he came./[28]

Oliver the shepherd and Alice his wife surrender into the lord's hands to the use of Juliana Deneys and her heirs, 2a.1r. of land and a sixth part of a messuage in Paynistreet, and it is granted to her to hold in bondage at the lord's will, fine [*damaged*]; and she swore fealty; and for this surrender Juliana granted the said land and sixth part of a messuage to Oliver and Alice to hold for their lifetime etc.

Basilia of Downham amerced 3d. for damage with her cows in the lord's meadow, pledge Thomas Fuller; likewise Thomas Fuller 3d. and Nicholas Goche 3d.,

---

27 Possibly, 'making charcoal'.

28 See court of 7 August 1319 (no.22).

pledges each for the other; Richard Reve 3d., pledge Nicholas Goche; and Geoffrey the swineherd 3d., pledge the hayward.

The summons against Martin Bakonn to show by what right he entered the fee of the lord, and to do etc. is in respite until the next court.

Robert Spileman and Walter Pye pay [*damaged*] fine that they be apportioned in the tenement formerly of Ralph Spileman, that they are not [*damaged*][29] for services and customs in any other way than as joint partners in the same tenure, and that they shall render no service or custom for other land which they do not hold.

John Man pays [*damaged*] fine for having entry to ½r. of land taken into the lord's hands because Thomas Echeman sold it to Richard Crane without leave, and it is granted to him to hold in villeinage by services and customs, pledge the hayward.

Ordered to distrain Walter at the Marsh because he took 15 partridges in the lord's warren.

John Fraunceys in mercy for default \afterwards he came/, Walter Deneys amerced 2d., John Reve 3d. and John Hulke 2d. for the same.

Robert Tailor the younger pays 6d. for [respite of] suit [of court].

Robert Hereward amerced 6d., William the son of Alice Robhood 3d., William the smith \afterwards he came/, Richard Patel 6d. and Bartholomew Patel 3d. for default.

Gilbert Prior amerced 3d. because he brewed and sold ale in breach of the assize, pledge the reeve; likewise, Simon Kembald, Robert Godefrey and Robert Kembald, pledge for all the reeve; Alice Warde, pledge John Warde, and Nicholas the miller, pledge the hayward.[30]

William Hawys amerced 6d. for a false claim against Adam Noble in a plea of trespass; Adam amerced 6d. for damage done to William, as was found by the enquiry, the damage assessed at 6d., which is ordered to be raised to the use of William etc.; likewise Wiliam amerced 3d. for damage done to Adam, assessed at 3d.; ordered etc.

It was found by the enquiry, to which John and Thomas Margery submitted, that Thomas trespassed against John, the damage assessed at 3d., Thomas amerced 6d., ordered etc., pledge the hayward.

William Fraunceys, who recently died, held from the lord a messuage 5a. of customary land, and his heir is his son Nicholas, aged 18 years, who gives as a heriot a cow, worth 10s. Seisin is delivered to him to hold in bondage at the lord's will, by customs and services; and he swore fealty. And upon this claim (?*calumpnio*) for entry fine, the jurors say that he will give nothing for entry if the lord had a heriot, in accordance with the custom of the manor.

The whole homage amerced 6s.8d. because they did not present concerning waste and strip in the tenement formerly of William Payn, and other tenements which are wasted and stripped.

William of Cranmer amerced 6d. for waste in the tenement formerly of Basilia Payn, damage 2s., ordered [to raise] 2s., pledge William Hawys; likewise William Hawys 6d. in the tenement formerly of Walter Herirof, damage 3s., ordered 3s.; and 6d. in that of John Wyswyf, damage 12d., ordered 12d., pledge William of Cranmer; likewise Agnes Hulke 6d. in the tenement of William Wyswyf,

---

[29] MS: ?*arcantur*; the tear appears to have removed only the first letter of this word.
[30] Details of amercements removed by the tear.

damage 12d., ordered 12d., pledges Adam Noble and William of Cranmer; likewise William Cook 6d. in the tenement formerly of Peter Machon, damage 2s., ordered 2s.; and 12d. in that formerly of Richard Machon, damage 18d., ordered 18d., pledge the hayward; likewise Robert the cooper 6d. and Agatha Robhood 6d. in the tenement formerly of Robert Robhod, damage 2s., ordered 2s..

Peter Springold amerced 6d. because he did not make good waste in the tenement formerly of Hugh Marewe, and he has a day until Michaelmas to repair the waste, pledges Robert Spileman and William Hawys.

William Hawys pays 2s. for scrutinising the court rolls for the 2nd, 3rd, 4th and 5th years of the reign of King Edward [Nov.1273–Nov.1277], for a certain enrolment concerning the exchange of lands between Ralph Herirof and Marsilia [Hawys] the daughter of Richard Terewald, pledge the bailiff.

Surrender: Elias Typetot and Matilda his wife and Emma Matilda's sister to Robert of Reydon and his heirs, [damaged]r. of land in the field called the Bottom, within the land of John Terwald, granted to him to hold in bondage as above, fine 6d., pledge Walter Osbern and the hayward; Robert swore customary fealty.

Walter Pye pays 2s. fine for having entry to 3r. of land taken into the lord's hands from those of Walter Typetot, for services and customs withheld, seisin delivered to Walter Pye to hold in bondage, fine 2s., pledge Walter Osbern.

Walter [Osbern] the reeve amerced 6s.8d. because he did not repair buildings in the courtyard and other (?n'ccia) of the manor etc., and for other offences etc.

The jurors have a day until the next court to certify concerning the tenants of the tenement Herirof [damaged] and concerning others, for which services and customs are withheld, together with carting service etc.

John Goche amerced 6d. because, by his defective custody, he allowed a stot in his keeping, worth 40d., to escape, ordered to raise, pledge the reeve.

Walter Qualm amerced 6d. because a stot, worth 5s., died as a result of his defective custody; ordered to raise 5s. to the lord's use.

> SUM  51s. 1d., except 2 stots, worth 8s. 4d., which died,
> and a cow, worth 10s., as a heriot

## 20.  HIGH HALL Court of Sir Alexander de Walsham, 7 March 1319 [HA504/1/1.12.i]

Henry Trusse essoins of common suit by Walter of the Marsh, and Robert of House of the same by Adam Dolhale; they pledge faith on summons.

Eda Rede amerced 3d. because her servant took away the lord's straw without leave, pledge William of Cranmer.

Thomas Suter amerced 3d. for damage in the lord's corn with oxen; John Syre 3d. for damage in the lord's corn and pasture with oxen; and Thomas Suter 3d. for damage by his servants taking away the lord's straw, pledge for both William of Cranmer.

Ordered as elsewhere to attach Geoffrey Doo for fealty still withheld; and Walter the son of Eve to reply to William Wodebite in a plea of debt.

Cristina Gilbert in mercy for services and customs withheld, pledge the reeve. \Condoned by the lord/.

Richard of Wortham amerced 4d. for damage in the lord's corn and herbage, pledge William of Cranmer; also Thomas, the shepherd of the lord Prior [of Ixworth], 3d. for damage in the lord's oats with sheep in his custody, pledge Oliver the shepherd; also Thomas Suter 3d. for damage with cows in the lord's oats, pledge

William of Cranmer; also Robert Spileman 6d. for damage in the lord's wheat above the wood with cows in his custody, pledge Gilbert Helpe; also Eda Rede 3d. for damage in the lord's oats at Fourteenacres, and Thomas Suter 3d. for the same with cows and pigs at Fifteenacres, pledge for both William of Cranmer.

Richard Gothelard amerced 3d. for trespass against Gilbert Helpe, the damage assessed at ½d., pledge John Wodebite.

Adam Noble amerced 3d. for trespass in the lord's pasture within the close, pledge Robert Kembald.

+Ordered to attach Walter Osbern the elder to reply to the lord because his servants took away the lord's straw.

Ordered to retain in the lord's hands ½a. of land lying in the furlong called Kerfeld which William Makenoyse, who recently died, held free from the lord by service, ¼d. to ward service, homage and fealty.

Ordered to distrain John Fraunceys the keeper of the beasts of Sir Edmund de Pakenham and Agatha of Allwood for damage in the lord's corn.

The jurors present that the lord's pigs, as a result of not being tended, damaged the lord's wheat stooked in the field, estimated at 1 bushel. The reeve had custody and therefore he was responsible; the reeve was Gilbert Helpe, and he is amerced 9d.

Also that Robert Spileman in summer and autumn had six pigs in the lord's peas, without a keeper, the damage assessed at 3 bushels; Gilbert Helpe, the reeve, was responsible because he should have prevented the offence, Robert being the keeper of the cows under Gilbert, who is amerced 3s.4d.

Gilbert Helpe the reeve amerced 6s.8d. because he allowed Robert Spileman to have six pigs in his custody cause damage to the lord, pledge William Wodebite.

Presented that the lord's pigs caused damage in his peas estimated at ½ bushel, Gilbert Helpe, then reeve, was responsible and is amerced 6d.

Also that the servant of Walter Osbern the younger took away the lord's straw, ordered to attach him.

Gilbert Helpe amerced 6d. because he intervened against John Wodebite in various complaints.

SUM 15s. 4d.

## 21.   WALSHAM Court General, 20 April 1319 [HA504/1/1.13]

Martin Bakonn essoins of common suit by Berard Margery, he pledges faith; and William Reve, defendant v Robert Spileman, by Walter Typetot in a plea of trespass, he pledges faith, and Robert is present.

William Springold amerced 3d. for trespass in the Ladyswood ['Lanedyswode'], pledges the hayward and the reeve, and Emma Whiteman 3d. for the same in the lord's corn, pledges Simon the smith and the reeve.

John Margery amerced 6d. for leave to agree with Thomas Margery in a plea of covenant, pledge Walter Osbern.

Robert Godefrey amerced 3d. for a false claim against Alice Gunter in a plea of covenant, pledge William Hawys.

The [tenants of the] tenement formerly of Hereward Gunter amerced 3d. for withholding one hen at Christmas, ordered to raise, pledge the hayward. Robert Godefrey amerced 3d. for waste made in the same tenement, pledge William Hawys; he has a day to make good the waste until the next court, pledge as above.

The summonses against Catherine the widow of Adam Goche and Philippa the widow of William Typetot, concerning the custody of the land and heirs of Adam and William, are in respite until the next court, pledge William Hawys.

John Hernyng amerced 3d. for default.

The summonses against William and Agnes at the Green concerning various articles are in respite until the next court.

Ordered to retain in the lord's hands a messuage in Ashfield, which Ralph Crane customary tenant sold to William Broun without leave, and to report the profits; also the tenement which Simon and Joan Roty hold in bondage, for waste made and services and customs withheld, and to report the profits.

Surrenders: Robert Spileman to William Springold and Isabella his wife, and William's heirs, 1a. of land at Staple way ['Stapilweye'], granted to them to hold in bondage at the lord's will, fine 3s., pledge William of Cranmer; they swore servile fealty; and to +William the son of William of Cranmer and his heirs, ½a. of land, granted to him by the lord to hold by services and customs etc., fine 18d., pledge the hayward; William swore servile fealty.

Isabella Reve to Agnes her daughter and her heirs, a cotland containing ½r. of land, granted to her to hold in bondage at the lord's will, by services and customs, fine 12d., Agnes swore fealty, and she willed and granted that Isabella should hold the cotland for her whole life, pledges William of Cranmer and the hayward.

John Reve to Thomas and Cristina Fuller and Thomas' heirs, 1r. of land and ¼r. of meadow lying at Longelond, granted to them to hold by customs and services etc., fine 15d., pledge the hayward; they swore customary fealty.

Agnes Wither amerced 6d. for waste made in the lord's bondage, and she has a day to repair the waste, pledge Adam Noble.

Surrenders: Robert Neve to Ralph Neve and his heirs, a piece of a toft in the messuage formerly of Robert Neve, 1½p. long and 1p. wide, granted to him to hold in bondage at the lord's will, fine 6d., pledge the hayward; Ralph swore servile fealty.

Geoffrey of Lenne to Robert Lene and his heirs, 1r. of land, granted to him in the same form, fine 12d., pledges William Springold and the hayward; Robert swore servile fealty.

Robert Godefrey amerced 3d. for unlawful detention of ½ bushel of corn from Alice Gunter, pledge the hayward.

Simon Kembald amerced 3d. because he brewed ale in breach of the assize, likewise Robert Kembald 6d., pledge the hayward, Robert Godefrey 6d., pledge the reeve, William Cook 3d., pledge the hayward, Gilbert Priour 6d., pledge Walter Osbern, and Robert the tailor[31] for the same. Matilda Kembald amerced 3d. for gannocking ale.

Simon the dairyman ['le deye'] amerced 6d. for damage in the lord's wood with the lord's beasts, to the value of 3d.

Agnes at the Green amerced 12d. for digging on the common.

William Payn amerced 12d. for waste in the tenememt formerly of Walter Payn, to the value of 2s.6d., and [because] he sold [the tenement] to Walter Osbern; ordered [to raise] 2s.6d.; also William amerced 3d. for default.

---

[31] No amount stated.

Avice Deneys amerced 6d. for waste in the tenement formerly of Hugh Deneys, and she has a day until Michaelmas to make it good, pledge William Hawys.

Walter Osbern in mercy[32] for waste in the tenement formerly of Peter Sawyer, and he has a day until Michaelmas, pledge William of Cranmer, also amerced 6d. for the same in the tenement formerly of Matthew at the Brook, to the value of 12d., ordered etc.

William Robhood amerced 6d. for waste in the lord's bondage, and he has a day to make it good until Michaelmas, pledges Nicholas Kembald and William Cook.

Ordered to attach the Prior of Ixworth for damage in the lord's meadow with his cart.

Robert of Fornham amerced 3d. for default.

Robert Spileman amerced 40d. because he bought land and sold it to William Hawys without leave of the court etc.; and 3d. for trespass ploughing the common, pledge William of Cranmer.

Surrenders: Nicholas Kembald and Alice his wife to Nicholas Fuller and his heirs, 1r. of land at the Toft, granted to him to hold in bondage at the lord's will by services and customs, fine 8d., pledge the hayward; Nicholas [Fuller] swore servile fealty; and to Nicholas Goche and his heirs, ½a. of land at Northrow ['Northwro'], granted to him to hold in bondage, fine 18d., pledge the hayward; Nicholas [Goche] swore servile fealty.

William Rampolye amerced 6d. because two years ago he sold 1a. of land to his brother Walter without leave; ordered to take the land into the lord's hands. And upon this Walter pays 3s.6d. fine for having the land, and it is granted to him to hold in the same form, pledges Walter Rampolye the elder and the hayward; Walter swore servile fealty.

The whole homage amerced 6s.8d. for concealment of the same, and of the sale of the land of Robert Spileman as appears above.

SUM 36s. 11d.

## 22. WALSHAM Court of Sir Edmund de Pakenham, 7 August 1319 [HA504/1/2.5]

Sarah Brian essoins of common suit by Berard Margery; she pledges faith and they [*sic*] have a day on summons.

The summons against William and Agnes at the Green is adjourned until the next court.

Ordered to retain in the lord's hands a messuage in Ashfield, which Ralph Crane customary tenant sold to William Broun without leave, and to report the profits.

Agnes Wither has a day to make good waste in the lord's bondage until Michaelmas, pledge Adam Noble, likewise Walter Osbern in the tenement formerly of Peter Sawyer, and that of Matthew at the Brook, pledges William of Cranmer and William Hawys.

William Robhood amerced 3d. for default, and he has a day to make good waste in the lord's bondage until Michaelmas, pledges Nicholas Kembald and William Cook.

The first pledge of the Prior of Ixworth in mercy because he did not have him satisfy the lord for damage in the lord's meadow with his cart; ordered to make him

---

[32] Margin: 'nothing because permitted by the bailiff'.

come. He came and is amerced 18d. [for this offence], and for damage in the lord's pasture with beasts, pledge the bailiff.

William Reve amerced 3d. for leave to agree with Robert Spileman in a plea of trespass, pledge William of Cranmer.

Simon Peyntour pays 6s.8d. fine for having custody of the land and heir of Adam Goche until his full age; he will render services and customs etc., and will keep the house and land in as good condition as he received it, without waste or destruction.

Nicholas Goche amerced 6d. for damage in the lord's meadow with his horse, pledge William of Cranmer.

Philippa the widow of William Typetot pays 12d. fine for having custody of the land and heir of William until his full age; she will render services and customs, and will keep the house and land without waste or damage and in as good condition as when she received it, pledge Robert of the Brook.

Simon and Joan Roty pay 12d. for repossessing their land out of the lord's hands, taken for waste in the lord's bondage and for withholding services and customs; they have a day to make good the waste until the feast of All Saints [1 November], and henceforth they will render services and customs etc., pledge Robert Godefrey.

Surrenders: John Neve to Robert of Reydon and his heirs, 1½r. of land lying in the Bottom, Robert was admitted, to hold by customs and services etc., fine 12d., pledge the hayward; Robert swore servile fealty. Also John gives to the lord 1d. for chevage, and 1r. of land which he holds by charter, pledges Robert of Reydon and Nicholas Kembald.[33]

Cristina Machon to Catherine her daughter and her heirs, a messuage 2a. of land in two pieces, granted to her to hold in bondage by services and customs, fine 2s., pledges Nicholas Goche and Nicholas Kembald; fealty postponed.

Robert Lene to Peter Springold and his heirs, 1a.1r. of land, granted to him in the same form, fine 4s., pledge the hayward; Peter swore servile fealty.

Agnes Machon amerced 3d. for default. Ordered to take into the lord's hands 1½a. of land which Agnes sold to Cristina Machon without leave, and to report the profits.

Thomas Fuller amerced 9d. for leave to agree with Peter Jay in a plea of trespass, in three complaints, pledge the hayward; likewise Alice Warde 3d. to agree with Peter in a plea of trespass, pledge John Warde.

Peter Tailor and his wife amerced 6d. for damage in the lord's corn and pasture, pledge the hayward.

Catherine Helewys amerced 3d., Nicholas Kembald 3d., William the shepherd 3d., Emma Shepherd 3d., Stephen Cooper 3d., Adam Noble 6d., Peter Springold 3d., Robert Spileman 3d., William Coppelowe 3d., Peter Neve 3d., Basilia of Downham 3d. and Walter Man 3d., for damage in the lord's corn, pledge the hayward.

Peter Robbes, Walter Deneys, Walter Osbern the elder, Richard Kebbil, Walter Man, John Hewe, William Rampolye, Robert Kembald, Marsilia Hawys and Geoffrey of Lenne, each amerced 3d., because they did not perform their works in the lord's meadow, as they had been summoned to do, pledges each for another and the hayward.

---

[33] Tab: 'John le Neve, Robert Levy(?t)'.

Henry the son of John at the Wood amerced 3d. for default; ordered to attach him to reply to Walter Patel in a plea of trespass.

Peter Peyntour amerced 3d. for leave to agree with Walter Pye in a plea of trespass.

Surrender: Robert Lene to William Lene and his heirs, 3r. of land lying at Calfthweyt, seisin granted to him to hold by services and customs etc., fine 2s.; he swore fealty.

Walter Doo amerced 6d. for trespass against Peter Hulke, the loss assessed at 12d., ordered to raise, pledge William of Cranmer.

The Prior of Ixworth amerced 6d., William Coppelowe, William Cook, Nicholas Kembald, Matthew Hereward, Robert Spileman, Walter Pye, Richard Qualm, Alice Warde and Peter Springold, 3d. each for damage in the meadows of William Hawys and Robert of Reydon.

The lord's swineherd, William Cook, Robert Spileman, Alice Warde, Richard Qualm, Walter Pye and Robert Tailor each amerced 3d. for damage in the lord's meadows and in his customary land with their pigs etc., pledges each for another.

Stephen Bronn ['Baronn'], Peter Jay, William Shipman of Wicken ['Wykys'], Thomas Margery and Marsilia Hawys each amerced 3d. for damage in the lord's corn with their beasts, pledges each for another.

Ordered to take into the lord's hands all the tenement which Isabella Reve held from the lord on the day she died, until the heir does to the lord that which he ought etc.

<John Fraunceys complains against Thomas Suter and John Syre in various pleas, ordered that they be summoned etc.>[34]

The jurors say that the servant of William Cook borrowed from the lord's swineherd a boar, valued at 3s.4d., for William's use, and he undertook to keep the boar safe and unharmed, and that a boar of Sir Alexander de Walsham attacked the lord's boar, and as a result it died; adjudged that William should compensate the lord for the value of his boar.

Also that the dog of Robert Ketil, the servant of the Prior of Ixworth, did damage in the lord's warren, [to the value of] 7d., and the same dog and that of Robert of Reydon killed four lambs, worth 5s., in the lord's fold, pledges of Robert of Reydon Peter Clevehog and William Cook, pledge of Robert Ketil the Prior of Ixworth.[35]

Robert the chaplain amerced 6d. for damage in the lord's corn with his pigs; likewise Stephen Couper 3d. for damage at Aylenestoftrowe, and the wife of Nicholas Goche 3d. for the same, pledge for all the hayward; also Simon Deneys, Basilia of Downham, Geoffrey Carter, Richard Reve, Emma Stronde and Simon the dairyman 3d. each, for the same, pledge for all the reeve.

William and Agnes at the Green amerced 3d. because they sold 1a. of customary land to William Springold without leave; ordered to take into the lord's hands etc.

Cecilia Wyndilgard pays 12d. for leave to marry Manser of Shucford, pledge William of Cranmer.

Walter Hereward amerced 3d. for damage in the lord's meadows, pledge the reeve.

---

[34] Margin: 'see below'.

[35] There is no reference to an amercement in any of these three offences involving animals; only the value of the damage caused is recorded in the margin for each case.

William of Cranmer amerced 3d. for waste in the tenement formerly Hunns, ordered to make good the waste.

Thomas Suter amerced 6d. because he occupied, outside the 1r. of land, which he bought from John Fraunceys, ¼r. more than he bought; ordered to take into the lord's hands etc., pledge the reeve. And upon this John comes and gives 3d. fine for having the said land out of the lord's hands, granted to him to hold in bondage, pledge the hayward. Likewise John Syre amerced 12d. because he occupied ½a. of land more than he bought from John Fraunceys, and John gives 3d. for having this land out of the lord's seisin, granted to him to hold by services and customs, pledge for both the hayward.

Thomas Patel amerced 6d. because he worked in 5a. of land of villeinage from the surrender of Richard Patel without the lord's leave, ordered to take into the lord's hands, and to report the profits.

Walter Osbern pays 6d. for having entry to 1a. of land, which he purchased from Almary Grym, rendering to the lord ¼d. at Michaelmas, and, for the lord, to the capital lords of the fee the services and customs etc., Walter has a day to show his charter at the next court.

Walter and Richard, the sons of Geoffrey Payn, in mercy for default, condoned because they are poor.

William Hawys amerced 6d. for withholding services and customs, *viz.* 1 bushel of oats, from the tenements formerly Herirof's and Spileman's, as was found by the enquiry, pledge the hayward; and William will henceforth pay the said bushel of oats.

Walter Pye, Cristina Gilbert, Robert Spileman, William of Cranmer, Robert of Reydon, John Fraunceys, John Rede, Walter Payn the elder and Robert Lene each amerced 3d. for services and customs withheld, and now they are to be apportioned by the enquiry.

Ordered to take into the lord's hands the tenement which Eda Rede holds from the lord, to show by what right she entered into the lord's fee.

Walter Osbern has a day to make good waste in the tenement formerly of Peter Sawyer, until the next Michaelmas after the completion of these presents, pledge William Hawys; and Walter gives to the lord 12d., for leave to build the tenement formerly of Matthew at the Bridge ['Brig'], two buildings and no more, pledge as before.

SUM 54s. 9d., except 1d. chevage and ¼d. new rent

### 23. HIGH HALL Court of Sir Alexander de Walsham, 9 October 1319 [HA504/1/1.12.ii]

The first pledges of John Fraunceys, concerning whom Gilbert Helpe reports that they did not have him reply for trespass in the lord's corn, amerced 3d.; ordered him to appoint better pledges. \Afterwards he appointed William of Cranmer/.

Ordered to attach Agatha of Allwood for damage in the lord's corn.

Thomas the shepherd of the Prior of Ixworth amerced 3d. for trespass in the lord's herbage with sheep; and Peter Robbes 6d. for the same in the lord's pasture, pledge for both Gilbert Helpe; and William Payn 3d. for the same in the lord's corn, pledge John Wodebite.

Thomas the shepherd complains against Simon Cooper in a plea of debt, his pledges are Oliver the shepherd and the reeve; ordered to attach Simon to reply to Thomas.

Ordered to attach John Syre for trespass in the lord's corn by his servant.

John Wodebite, the first pledge of the Prior of Ixworth, amerced 12d. because he did not have him satisfy the lord for trespass adjusting a boundary, and for trespass with his cows in the lord's corn; ordered to appoint better pledges.

Robert Godefrey amerced 3d. for damage with horses, pledge Simon Rampolye; and Walter Osbern the younger 3d. for damage in the lord's corn.

Ordered as elsewhere to attach Geoffrey Doo for fealty still withheld; and Walter the son of Eve to reply to William Wodebite in a plea of debt; and Walter Osbern the elder to reply to the lord because his servant took away the lord's straw.

Ordered as elsewhere to retain in the lord's hands ½a. of land in the furlong called Kerfeld, which William Makenoyse, who lately died, held free from the lord by services, ¼d. to ward service, and for homage and fealty.

Alice Goche pays 3s. for leave to marry, pledge Gilbert Helpe.

Presented that the lord's cows, in the keeping of Robert Lene, caused damage in the lord's wheat, estimated at ½ bushel, worth 3d., Robert amerced 3d., pledge the reeve; and that the lord's geese caused damage in his oats, estimated at ½ bushel, worth 1½d., Robert Lene amerced 3d. because they were in his keeping, pledge the reeve; and that the lord's stots, in the keeping of Stephen Bronn, caused damage in the lord's oats, estimated at 4 bushels, worth 12d., Stephen amerced 15d., pledge the reeve.

Also that Matilda Kembald took away the lord's corn, amerced 2s., pledge Simon Kembald, and took away the crops from villein land into a free tenement, amerced 3d., pledge Gilbert Helpe.

Also that the lord's pigs, in the keeping of Geoffrey the carter, caused damage in the lord's peas, estimated at 4 bushels, worth 14d., amerced 18d., pledge the reeve.

Walter Osbern the younger amerced 3d. for trespass taking away the lord's straw, pledge William Hawys.

Margery of Angerhale surrendered into the lord's hands, and released and quit-claimed to William Wodebite all the right and claim which she had in all the lands and tenements which were of Richard of Angerhale her father. The lord granted the said tenements to William and his heirs, to hold in villeinage, by services and works etc., fine 12d., pledge John Wodebite.

Presented by the bailiff that the lord's ploughs were dismantled (?*disjunct'*) for two days to the lord's loss, by the default of John Wodebite, amerced 12d.

Margery of Angerhale pays 12d. for leave to marry, pledge William Wodebite.

It was found by the enquiry that William Wodebite was summoned to perform works but did not come, and as a result Gilbert Helpe lost 8d.;[36] adjudged that Gilbert shall recover his loss, and ordered to raise, William amerced 3d., pledge Gilbert Helpe.

Also that Alice the widow of Peter of Angerhale and executrix of his testament, unlawfully withheld from Agnes Helpe 2s., which Peter had received as a loan from Agnes; adjudged that Agnes shall recoup the said 2s. and 3d. damages, Alice amerced 3d.; ordered to raise, and afterwards Agnes remitted the debt to 6d.

---

[36] Gilbert Helpe was reeve in 1318–19, and was liable to the lord for the value of services withheld; hence his loss of 8d.

William Wodebite is elected by the whole homage to the office of reeve, and Gilbert Helpe to the office of hayward.

Alice of Angerhale the widow of Peter pays 2s. for leave to marry, pledges Gilbert Helpe and William Wodebite. Agnes the widow of Hugh of Angerhale pays 40d. for the same, pledges Gilbert Helpe and John Wodebite

Emma Stronde amerced 6d. for default.

SUM 20s. 11d.

Affeerers: Walter Typetot and Gilbert Helpe

### 24. HIGH HALL Court of Sir Alexander de Walsham, 20 January 1320 [HA504/1/1.12.iii]

Robert of House essoins of common suit by John Brodheigh, he pledges faith; likewise Walter of the Marsh by John Wood \Afterwards he came/, and Robert Kembald by Geoffrey the carter, he pledges faith, and William of Cranmer by Walter Osbern \Afterwards he came/.

Ordered as elsewhere to attach Agatha of Allwood for damage in the lord's corn.

John Syre amerced 3d. for trespass in the lord's corn by his servant, pledges Gilbert Helpe and William Wodebite.

Ordered as elsewhere to attach the Prior of Ixworth for damage in the lord's corn, and to reply to the lord why he moved a certain boundary between himself and the lord.

Simon Cooper amerced 6d. for leave to agree with Thomas the shepherd in a plea of debt, pledge Gilbert Helpe.

Ordered as elsewhere to attach Geoffrey Doo for services and customs and fealty [withheld], also Walter the son of Eve to reply to William Wodebite in a plea of debt, and Walter Osbern the elder for damage by his servant taking away the lord's straw.

Ordered as elsewhere to retain in the lord's hands ½a. of land in the furlong called Kerfeld, which William Makenoyse held free from the lord by services, ¼d. to ward service, and for homage and fealty.

It was found by the enquiry that Gilbert Helpe unlawfully withheld 7d. from Geoffrey the carter from his pay; adjudged that Geoffrey shall recover the debt and damages of 1d., Gilbert amerced 3d., pledges William and John Wodebite; ordered to raise the damages.

Richard Gothelard pays 6d. for leave to marry, pledge Gilbert Helpe.

Ordered to attach the Prior of Ixworth for damage at Allwood with sheep.

The jurors have a day until the next court to enquire who caused [damage] in the lord's wood at Lenerithesdel.

They say that Catherine and Alice the daughters of Simon Kembald gave birth outside wedlock, and that Simon is free, and his daughters are not with him, and were not with him for five years before the time of the births; therefore advice to be taken etc. by the next court.

SUM 18d.

Affeerers: John Wodebite and Richard Gothelard

## 25. HIGH HALL Court of Sir Alexander de Walsham, 10 July 1320 [HA504/1/1.14.i]

William of Cranmer essoins of common suit by Ralph of Hinderclay ['Hildercle']; likewise Henry Trusse by Walter of the Marsh, and Walter Osbern the younger by John Margery; they pledge faith.

Agatha of Allwood amerced 3d. for trespass in the lord's corn, pledge Walter of the Marsh; and Geoffrey, the shepherd of the Prior of Ixworth, 3d. for the same with sheep, pledge Oliver the shepherd, and the cowherd of the Prior 6d. for the same with cows, pledge John Wodebite.

The distraint upon the Prior of Ixworth for moving a boundary between the lord and himself next to the Thirtyacres, is in respite until the next court; meanwhile [the jurors] will petition the lord to set the boundary; [the Prior is] to satisfy for the trespass.

Ordered to distrain Geoffrey Doo for services and customs withheld and for fealty; and to attach Walter the son of Eve to reply to William Wodebite in a plea of debt; and to attach Walter Osbern the elder for trespass by his servant taking away the lord's straw; and to retain in the lord's hands ½a. of land in the furlong called Kerfeld, which William Makenoyse held free from the lord by services, ¼d. to ward service, and for homage and fealty.

It was presented elsewhere that Catherine and Alice the daughters of Simon Kembald gave birth outside wedlock etc., and that Simon is free etc., and his daughters did not live with him for five years before etc., the lord to be consulted.

The enquiry present that William Thurbern freeman held from the lord 1a. of freehold land for fealty and service 1d. per year, that his son Thomas aged two years is his nearest heir, and the lord will have relief of 1d.

Robert of House and Robert Kembald each amerced 3d. because they were essoined [at the last court], and did not come [to this].

The keeper of the cows amerced 9d. for damage in the lord's wheat, estimated at 1 bushel, and 5d. for damage by the lord's beasts in the lord's oats, estimated at 1 bushel, pledge the reeve.

William Deneys amerced 3d. for default, likewise John Packard, who married Alice the widow of Peter of Angerhale, 3d., and Henry Broun, who married Alice Goche, 3d.

SUM 3s. 5d.<br>Affeerers: John Wodebite and Oliver the shepherd

## 26. HIGH HALL Court, 5 October 1320 [HA504/1/1.14.ii]

Robert of House essoins of common suit by John Brodheigh.

Again the summons against the Prior of Ixworth, concerning the moving of a boundary between himself and the lord, is respited until the next court; meanwhile the lord to be asked to set the boundary, and the Prior to satisfy the lord for trespass. \Afterwards the Prior came and replaced the boundary, as is attested by the court; therefore the summons dismissed./

Again ordered as before to distrain Geoffrey Doo for services and customs withheld and for fealty; and to attach Walter the son of Eve to reply to William Wodebite in a plea of debt; and Walter Osbern the elder for trespass by his servant taking away the lord's straw; and to retain in the lord's hands ½a. of land in the furlong called Kerfeld, which William Makenoyse held free from the lord by services, ¼d. to ward service, and for homage and fealty.

Presented that John Syre caused damage in the lord's peas with his pigs, to the value of 2 bushels; ordered to distrain him to satisfy the lord.

Peter Clevehog amerced 4d. because he caused damage in the lord's oats at Anger-hale, pledge Oliver the shepherd; Elias Typetot did likewise, ordered to distrain him to satisfy the lord; William Wodebite did likewise, amerced 4d., pledge Gilbert Helpe; John Wodebite did likewise, amerced 4d.

William of Cranmer and Walter Osbern each amerced 6d. because they did not perform the works to which they had been summoned.

Again the summons against Catherine and Alice, the daughters of Simon Kembald because they gave birth outside wedlock, is in respite until the next court, the lord to be consulted, as before.

The whole homage elected Gilbert Helpe to the office of reeve, and John Wodebite to the office of hayward.

Ordered to distrain Roger Martin for homage and fealty and for services withheld.

SUM 2s.

Affeerers: William Wodebite and Gilbert Helpe

### 27. HIGH HALL Court of Sir Alexander de Walsham, held at East Hall ['Esthal'], 11 May 1321 [HA504/1/1.15.i]

Peter Pynfoul essoins of common suit by Robert Kembald.

Robert of House amerced 3d. because he was essoined at the last court, and does not come.

Again ordered as many times to distrain Geoffrey Doo for services and customs withheld and for fealty; and to attach Walter the son of Eve to reply to William Wodebite in a plea of debt; and Walter Osbern the elder for trespass by his servant taking away the lord's straw; and to retain in the lord's hands ½a. of land in the furlong called Kerfeld, which William Makenoyse held free from the lord by services, ¼d. to ward service, and for homage and fealty.

John Syre finds a pledge, viz. John Wodebite, to satisfy the lord for damage in the lord's peas with his pigs at Burchardscroft, and is amerced 6d.

Elias Typetot amerced 3d. for damage in the lord's oats at Angerhale with his oxen, pledge the hayward.

Again, the summons against Catherine and Alice the daughters of Simon Kembald because they gave birth outside wedlock, is adjourned until the next court.

Gilbert Helpe and William Broun amerced 3d. because they did not have Roger Martyn do to the lord that which he ought, as they undertook; ordered him to appoint better pledges for homage and fealty to the lord.

William Fisser of Rickinghall ['Rekinghal'], pledge of a certain [blank] of Ricking-hall, amerced 6d. for damage in the lord's pasture with a foal.

John Syre amerced 3d. for damage in the lord's wood with sheep, and 3d. for the same with heifers, pledge the hayward.

Gilbert Sare pays 3d. for leave to sow part of 5a. of land at Bodishawe to the third sheaf \of Richard Gothelard/,[37] until the end of three years complete and full, pledge the hayward.

William Wodebite amerced 3d. because he intervened through the enquiry against Gilbert Helpe in a plea of trespass, ordered to raise 2s. from William to the use of

---

[37] MS: *pro licentia seminenda ad partem ad tertiam garbam \de Ricardo Gothelard/ quinque acrarum in campo'*. This has been translated literally, the meaning is unclear.

Gilbert as damages, as assessed by the enquiry. William also amerced 3d. because he proceeded against Oliver the shepherd in a plea of debt,[38] pledge the hayward.

SUM 3s.

Affeerers: Gilbert Helpe and John Wodebite

## 28.   HIGH HALL Court, 25 September 1321 [HA504/1/1.15.ii]

[This membrane is damaged; small but material sections affecting this and the next court are missing.]

Henry Trusse essoins of common suit by Bartholomew Dolhale; he pledges faith.

Again as many times ordered to distrain Geoffrey Doo for services and customs withheld and for fealty; and to attach Walter the son of Eve to reply to William Wodebite in a plea of debt; and Walter Osbern the elder for trespass by his servant taking away the lord's straw; and to retain in the lord's hands ½a. of land in the furlong called Kerfeld, which William Makenoyse held free from the lord by services, ¼d. to ward service, and for homage and fealty.

Again the summons against Catherine and Alice Kembald because they gave birth outside wedlock, is in respite until the next court.

Again as before ordered to distrain Roger Martyn for homage and fealty.

Presented by the enquiry that John Syre caused damage in the lord's barley in Catherinescroft ['Katerinescroft'] with his pigs and other beasts, to the value of 1 bushel, amerced 9d., also 2d. for damage in the lord's oats at Doucedeux, to the value of 1 sheaf, pledge for both John Wodebite; also 2d. for damage in the oats with pigs, to the value of 2 sheaves, pledge Gilbert Helpe.

[damaged] caused damage with cows and geese in the lord's barley to the value of 2 sheaves, in Gilbert Helpe's time as reeve, therefore Gilbert [is responsible] and is amerced 4d.; likewise [damaged] of the lord to the value of 1 sheaf of wheat, Gilbert responsible and amerced 1d.

The [damaged] of the Prior of Ixworth at Easthall amerced 2d. for the same with cows in the lord's wheat and peas, to the value of 1 sheaf.

Robert of [damaged] and Emma Stronde each amerced 3d. for default.

William Wodebite and Peter Clevehog have reached an agreement, Peter amerced 4d.

Catherine the daughter of Simon Kembald and Hilary Kembald took away handfuls of the lord's oats, ordered to attach them.

The whole homage elected John Wodebite to the office of reeve, and William Wodebite to the office of collector, and he shall collect services, customs, rents and fines of the court, and shall have nothing from the lord for the said office.

SUM 2s. 10d.

## 29.   HIGH HALL Court, 26 December 1321 HA504/1/1.15.iii]

Robert of House essoins of common suit by Gilbert Reve, and Robert Kembald of the same, by John Reve; they pledge faith.

Henry Trusse amerced 3d. for default.

+Again as many times ordered to distrain Geoffrey Doo for services and customs

---

[38] It is likely that the word *non* was omitted by the clerk, and this should read 'did not proceed'.

91

withheld and for fealty; +and to attach Walter the son of Eve to reply to William Wodebite in a plea of debt.

Roger Martyn swore fealty to the lord for ½a. of land of the lord's fee, which he has by inheritance after the death of his father, and he gives 1d. relief, pledge William of Cranmer.

+Again as many times ordered to attach Walter Osbern the elder for trespass by his servant taking away the lord's straw; and to <retain in the lord's hands> \distrain in/ ½a. of land in the furlong called Kerfeld, which William Makenoyse held free from the lord by services, ¼d. to ward service, and for homage and fealty.

+Again the summons against Catherine and Alice Kembald, because they gave birth outside wedlock, is in respite until the next court.

Nicholas Fraunceys amerced 6d. for damage in the lord's wood, pledge John Syre; also Peter the son of Robert 3d., Walter Payn 3d. and Richard of Wortham 6d. for the same, pledge for all the bailiff; Walter Rampolye to be attached, and Simon Kembald amerced 2d. for the same, pledge the bailiff.

+Again as before ordered to attach Catherine the daughter of Simon Kembald and Hilary Kembald for taking away handfuls of the lord's straw.

Henry Goche amerced 2d. because he intervened through the enquiry against Robert Suter in a plea of debt; adjudged that Robert shall recover from Henry 4d. for the debt and ½d. damages, as assessed, ordered etc.

William Wodebite was attached to reply to John Bande of Ipswich ['Gippeswic'] concerning a plea of debt, and the jurors say that on Monday before the feast of St Barnabas, 12 Edw.II [4 June 1319], in Ipswich, John delivered to William 12 marks [£8] of silver to trade and profit for John's benefit, and William was required to render faithfully a true account thereof quarterly, in accordance with the Law Merchant \and by a certain written agreement/. William was requested many times to render his account for the 12 marks together with the profits from the same, but he refused to render his account, and he withheld, and still withholds, the debt and the profits therefrom, to the loss of 100s. to John, who brings suit. William came and acknowledged himself indebted to John [damaged] marks of silver. Adjudged that John shall recover from William [damaged] assessed at [blank]. And that he be etc. and ordered the reeve [damaged].

SUM 2s. 5d.

### 30.  HIGH HALL Court, 26 January 1324 [HA504/1/1.16.i]

Walter of the Marsh essoins of common suit by William Deneys, he pledges faith; likewise Walter Osbern by William Kembald \void, afterwards he came/.

William Hawys amerced 3d. for damage in the Brook pasture with his sheep, pledge the bailiff.

John and William Wodebite, the pledges of Peter Robbes, amerced 3d. because they did not have him reply to the lord for damage in his corn at Hamstale, and in the herbage at Brook pasture with his foals; ordered to produce Peter [in court] by four mainpernors. Afterwards Peter came and satisfied the lord by his pledge, Walter Osbern the younger, at the instance of the lady.

Again ordered, as elsewhere, to attach John Man for damage in the lord's corn at Hamstale, to the value of 1 sheaf.

Oliver the shepherd and John Wodebite, the pledges of John Syre, amerced 12d. because they did not have him reply to the lord for damage in his pasture at the Brook, grazing and driving cows; ordered to produce John Syre [in court] by four mainpernors. He comes and pays the amercement, by the said pledge, at the instance of the lady.

John Syre and William Wodebite, the pledges of Robert Deneys, amerced 3d. because they did not have him reply to the lord for damage in the Brook pasture with cows; ordered as above, and Robert pays the amercement, pledge John Syre, at the instance of the lady.

Again ordered, as many times, to attach Alice the daughter of Simon Kembald because she gave birth outside wedlock etc.; and to distrain Geoffrey Doo for services and customs withheld and for fealty; and to attach Walter the son of Eve to reply to William Wodebite in a plea of debt.

Gilbert Helpe and Anne Typetot came to an agreement in a plea of debt, Anne amerced 3d., pledges William of Cranmer and the bailiff.

Again as many times ordered to distrain in ½a. of land in the furlong called Kerfeld, which William Makenoyse held free from the lord by services, ¼d. to ward service at the castle, still in arrears, and for homage and fealty.

Henry Goche and his pledges amerced 3d. because he did not proceed against Anne Typetot in a plea of debt.

At the request of the parties, a love day is given between sir[39] William Kembald chaplain, plaintiff, and Matilda Kembald, defendant in a plea of trespass, to come to the next court, without essoin.

William Kembald and Robert of House each amerced 3d. for default.

Presented that John Chapman the lord's granger delivered oats to John Wodebite the reeve, 2 bushels over the tally, John amerced 18d., pledges Gilbert Helpe and William Wodebite.

Also that John Wodebite has grazed his bullocks in the lord's pasture at Angerhale for two years past, amerced 18d., pledges William Wodebite and the hayward.

William of Cranmer amerced 3d. for damage in the lord's wheat with sheep, pledge the hayward.

Matilda Kembald amerced 6d. because she took away straw and firewood from the lord's yard, pledge William Wodebite.

John Chapman and the reeve each amerced 2s.3d. because they had and took away 3 bushels of oats over the tally, for which they are to answer, pledges Gilbert Helpe and William Wodebite. Also John amerced 9d. because he took away 1 bushel of oats, with which he sowed his land, and 18d. because he delivered oats to the gooseherd, 2 bushels over the tally, pledges as above.

The bailiff amerced 10d. because he sold ½ bushel of corn to Peter Cook over the tally of the outgoings.

Henry Trusse amerced 3d. for default.

Alice Kembald acknowledged herself in debt to Walter Osbern for 6s.8d.; half of the debt was conceded by Walter to the lord, and the other half is to be raised to the use of Walter; ordered the debt to be raised to the use of the lord and Walter, pledge William Kembald chaplain.

SUM 18s. 2d.

Affeerers: Walter of Trowse and John Packard

---

[39] The courtesy title given to non-graduate clergy in the Middle Ages.

## 31. HIGH HALL Court, 2 August 1324 [HA504/1/1.16.ii]

Walter Osbern essoins of common suit by William Kembald; likewise Walter of the Marsh by Bartholomew Dolhale.[40]

Again as many times ordered to attach Alice the daughter of Simon Kembald, to distrain Geoffrey Doo, to attach Walter the son of Eve and to distrain in ½a. of land in the furlong called Kerfeld, as appears in preceding courts.

Matilda Kembald amerced 3d. for leave to agree with William Kembald chaplain in a plea of trespass, pledge the bailiff.

Robert Rampolye amerced 3d. for trespass in the lord's pasture.

John Man amerced 3d. for damage in the lord's wheat at Hamstale, pledge William Kembald chaplain.

William Clevehog, Rose Typetot, Elias Tiptot, Crispiana Qualm and John of Cowlinge each amerced 3d. for damage in the lord's meadow with cows; William Marler amerced 6d. for the same in the same place, and Nicholas Fraunceys, Simon Peyntour, Anne Typetot and Robert of the Brook all amerced for the same.[41]

Walter of the Marsh in mercy for default \afterwards he came/; Robert Kembald amerced 2d. for the same.

William Wodebite amerced 6d. for trespass grazing the lord's herbage in Smallbrook ['Smalbroke']; also John Wodebite 3d. for the same; and John Man 4d. for damage in the lord's oats, to the value of 8d.; the gooseherd and swineherd of the manor 8d. for the same in the lord's peas, to the value of 2 bushels; the driver of the plough 2d. for the same, ½ bushel of beans and peas; the gooseherd 3d. for the same with geese in the wheat, 3 sheaves, and 1d. for the same with cows, 1 sheaf; the gooseherd of Westhorpe 2d. for the same with cows, 2 sheaves of wheat; the gooseherd of the Prior of Ixworth 3d. for the same in the lord's barley, 3 sheaves; the keeper of the cows 1d. for the same in the barley at the Hulver, 1 sheaf; the gooseherd 1½d. for the same in the oats at Ulviswell, 3 sheaves; the servants and shepherd of Sir Edmund de Pakenham 3d. for the same in the same place with a plough and sheep, 3 sheaves; and Bartholomew Patel 8d. for the same with heifers, 2 bushels of oats.

Ordered to attach Walter Osbern because he made an encroachment, ploughing on the demesne at Allwood, 1p. wide and 6p. long; upon this Walter comes and pays 3d. for setting the bounds between the lord and himself by the custom of the manor, and is quit; the bailiff ordered to set the bounds of the said land.

Isabella, who lives in the house of Walter Payn, amerced 3d. for damage in the lord's beans, and for trespass taking away the straw of the lord's shepherd, pledge the bailiff.

William of Cranmer in mercy for default \afterwards he came/.

Alice the widow of John Suter pays 3d. fine for having her dower of half of 2a. of land with a customary messuage, in the hands of John Wodebite until the crop has been taken; ordered the bailiff to have Alice's rightful dower given to her, when the crop has been taken.

Gilbert Helpe the younger pays 12d. for leave to marry Agnes Whiet [sic], pledge William Wodebite.

---

40 Margin: 'It does not lie because essoined at the last court'.
41 The amounts of these amercements are obliterated by the torn margin.

Alice the widow of John Suter in open court granted, released and surrendered and quitclaimed to John Wodebite all the right and claim which she had, or could have had, by right and in name of dower, in 2a. of land with a messuage, which John recently purchased from John Suter, to have and to hold to John Wodebite and his heirs by services and customs etc.; and he pays 3d. entry fine; and John acknowledges himself bound to Alice for the whole of her life, for 1 bushel of barley annually at Michaelmas, the term beginning at that feast next year.

Matilda Kembald pays 3d. fine for having an enquiry between herself and William Kembald chaplain, concerning an agreement made between them for the sowing of their land; William amerced 3d. because he intervened against Matilda in a plea of covenant; and Matilda amerced 3d. for a false claim against William in a plea of debt.

SUM 10s. 8½d.

### 32.  HIGH HALL Court, 18 December 1324 [HA504/1/1.16.iii]

John Packard, the hayward, amerced 3d. because he did not come to perform his office as he ought.

Again ordered as many times to attach Alice the daughter of Simon Kembald, and to distrain Geoffrey Doo, and to attach Walter the son of Eve, as appears in preceding courts.

Richard the shepherd [of Westhorpe] amerced 3d. for leave to agree with Gilbert Helpe in a plea of trespass.

William Wodebite amerced 3d for default; Agnes and John of Angerhale and Ralph Isabel in mercy for the same, \afterwards they came/; William Kembald, Robert of House and Henry Trusse, each amerced 3d. for the same.

Surrender: John of Angerhale to John Packard and his heirs, a messuage containing ½r. of land, half a wood containing ½r., half of 2a. of customary land and 1a. of land of mollond,[42] and of this, ½a. of land [is] of the fee of the Abbot of St Edmunds; granted to John to hold in villeinage by services and customs, fine 6s.8d., pledges John and William Wodebite.

William of Ipswich, when he died, held from the lord 4a. of free land for services 12d. per year; Edmund, his son and nearest heir, is 13 years old; ordered to take and retain the land in the lord's hands, because the heir is under age, and to report the profits.

The gooseherd amerced 3d. for damage in the lord's peas, to the value of 1 bushel; also Walter Osbern 3d. for damage with stots in the lord's oats at Ulviswell, 1 bushel; and the gooseherd 1d. for the same with cows in the same place, 2 sheaves.

Walter Kembald, when he died eight years ago, held from the lord a messuage 3a. of customary land by services etc.; Alice and Agatha Kembald were his nearest heirs, and because at that time Alice was under age, the tenement was taken into the lord's hands, and granted out of his seisin to Oliver the shepherd until her full age. Alice is now of full age, and she comes and seeks to be admitted to the said tenement; seisin is granted to her, fine 10d.,[43] pledge Oliver the shepherd.

---

[42] *OED* gives 'molland – land on which rent is paid in commutation of servile customs'.

[43] Margin: 'and no more because [the land] is poor, and because she should have entry following the custom of the manor [*illeg.*]'.

John Wodebite amerced 3d. because he did not proceed against William Wodebite in a plea of [*illeg.*], and William gives to the lord 3d. freely for having [*illeg.*].

SUM 10s.

### 33.  HIGH HALL Court of Nicholas de Walsham, 18 March 1325 [HA504/1/1.17]

Free tenants: Walter of the Marsh holds a messuage and 2½a. of land by services, suit [of court] and 4s. per year; he swore fealty.

Henry Trusse holds a part of a messuage and 1r. of land by suit of two courts, *viz.* at Easter and Michaelmas, and he pays ½d. per year on the feast of St Edmund [20 November].

William Deneys holds a certain close and a certain piece of land, containing 1a., by services, suit [of court], and 4d. at the feast of St Catherine [25 November]; he also gives a hen at Christmas and 20 eggs at Easter.

Ordered to distrain William of Cranmer, Walter Osbern \1 messuage 5r. of land, paying 2d. at the Purification of Mary, rendering suit, 1 hen and 20 eggs the day before/,[44] Robert Kembald, Cristina Gilbert, Agnes Pinfoul, Emma Stronde, Robert of House, Robert Benett, Geoffrey Doo, Thomas Thurbern, the widow of William of Ipswich, William Chapman, Richard the shepherd of Westhorpe, William Noreys, Andrew Colt, Adam Dolhale, Bartholomew Dolhale and Henry Puppin to be [at the next court] etc.

Villein tenants: William Wodebite, John Wodebite, Gilbert Helpe, Gilbert Helpe [the younger], John Packard, Richard Gothelard, John of Angerhale, John Chapman, Ralph Isabel, Oliver the shepherd, Matilda Kembald, Alice Kembald, William Kembald, Agnes of Angerhale, Alice Goche, Matilda Fraunceys and William Kembald chaplain.

John Wodebite was elected to the office of reeve and took the oath; Gilbert Helpe was elected collector and took the oath.

William of Cranmer holds [*sic*].

### 34.  HIGH HALL Court of Nicholas de Walsham, 22 May 1325 [HA504/1/2.6]

William of Cranmer essoins of common suit by William Kembald, likewise Walter of the Marsh by William the son of Hugh.

Robert of House pays 3d. for respite of his suit of court until Michaelmas.

The whole homage offers to pay 1 mark to the lord for recognition.

The jurors present that Walter Osbern occupied and appropriated from the lord's land at Netherway, 14ft. wide and 10p. long; ordered to distrain him to make good the said trespass.

<Walter Osbern amerced 3d. for default.> [see below.]

Cristina Gilbert amerced 3d. for default; Emma Stronde in mercy for the same, afterwards she came.

John of Angerhale sold ½a.½r. of land of villeinage with a messuage to John Packard freeman, after the death of John de Walsham, and John now comes and pays 6d. entry fine, to hold to himself and his heirs, at the lord's will by services and customs etc.

William Wodebite pays 2s. fine for leave to hold in peace a messuage 9a. of villein

---

44  The insert is almost illegible and heavily contracted, for example *p.m.* for the feast day.

land, which he purchased in the time of Alice de Walsham, to hold to himself and his heirs in the same form.

John Wodebite pays 18d. for leave to hold in peace a messuage and 2a. of land, which he purchased in the time of Alice de Walsham, to hold to himself and his heirs, in the same form.

William Wodebite pays 3d. for leave to hold in peace a messuage 5a. of land, which he leased from Richard Gothelard, to hold to himself and his heirs for the whole lifetime of the same Richard.

William Kembald amerced 6d. because he took away underwood from the lord's wood after the death of Alice de Walsham.

The jurors present that John the dairyman,[45] of Halesworth, and Gilbert Reve of Westhorpe cut down a maple tree in the lord's wood, after the death of Alice de Walsham; and that Walter of Trowse cut down a tree and a willow, and that he also cut down, and caused to be cut down, four elm trees, after the death of Alice.[46]

Gilbert Helpe villein purchased 4a. of land of the fee of Sir Hugh Hovel, from William Dun and Thomas Patel, and 1a. of free land of the fee of Sir Edmund de Pakenham, from Robert Broun, and 2a. of land of the fee of Bartholomew de Elmham, from John Chapman; ordered to take all the tenements into the lord's hands.

William Wodebite villein purchased 2a. of land of the fee of lord Hugh Hovel from Margery of Angerhale; ordered to take into the lord's hands etc.

Walter Osbern amerced 6d. for default of [suit of] court, ordered to distrain him to swear fealty to the lord.

The jurors present that Roger de Walsham, formerly lord of this manor, enfeoffed John de Walsham and Joyce ('Joysia'), his wife, of all this manor, with all its appurtenances, to hold to the same John and Joyce his wife, and the heirs issuing from their bodies etc., and afterwards John released a certain William Brodheigh of Cotton, his villein, and 10a. of land of his villeinage, with all its appurtenances, to a certain Laurence Compeygne by his charter; therefore a remedy to be sought by writ, if the lord sees fit.

Agnes Pynfoul [is granted] leave to have in peace the custody of two parts of 3a. of land, and of John, the son and heir of Peter Pynfoul, who was aged five years last Easter, to hold to Agnes until the lawful coming of age of John, following the custom of England, and she will pay nothing for rent, or service owed to the lord therefrom for the whole time. She gives 40d., paying half at the Gules [1st] of August next, and the other half at Michaelmas.

Ordered to distrain William of Cranmer, Cristina Gilbert, Robert Deneys, Geoffrey Doo, Thomas Thurbern, Albreda the widow of William of Ipswich, William Chapman, Richard the shepherd of Westhorpe, William Noreys, Andrew Colt, Adam Dolale, Bartholomew Dolale and Henry Pupping to be at the next court to do homage and swear fealty to the lord.

[SUM 14s. 6d., not stated]

---

45 'le Deye'; 'Goldere' inserted above.
46 Note against these three presentments: 'Therefore a remedy to be sought by writ'.

### 35. HIGH HALL Court of Nicholas de Walsham, 17 November 1326 [HA504/1/1.18]

Robert Kembald essoins of common suit, by Oliver the shepherd, and Walter Osbern of the same by Robert Sare.

Gilbert Helpe the hayward amerced 3d. because he did not raise the damages caused in the lord's corn, as was ordered.

The jurors say that the tenement formerly of William Payn is wasted and damaged by William Wodebite, to the value of 5s., William amerced 3d., and ordered 5s. [to be raised].

Robert Deneys amerced 3d. for damage in the lord's corn, 1 peck of wheat, worth 1½d., ordered to raise; likewise William Kembald 3d. for damage in the lord's corn.

They say that the tenement Kembald is wasted and damaged by William Kembald chaplain and Nicholas and William Kembald, amerced 12d.; ordered to warn them to rebuild by the next court, under penalty etc. Also that Matilda Kembald has made waste in her tenement, amerced 6d.; ordered that she repairs it by the next court.

John Wodebite amerced 3s.4d. because for five days he ploughed lands other than those of the lord.

It was found that William Wodebite withheld 1½d. per year of his services and customs for 14 years, and for the said time Agnes Fytte performed the services for him, William amerced 3d. Adjudged that Agnes shall recover from William the value of the services, which amounts to 21d.; ordered the hayward to raise to Agnes' use 17d., and no more, because William paid the residue. Agnes pays 5d. fine for raising the said money.

The whole homage elected William Kembald the younger to the office of reeve for the whole tenement Kembald, which contains 12a. of land; and Gilbert Helpe the younger to the office of hayward for the tenement Helpe, which contains 9a. Because William declined to hold office as elected, ordered that his tenement be taken into the lord's hands \order cancelled as below/.

The same Gilbert Helpe pays 12d. fine for relief from the office of hayward, and no more because he is poor.

William Kembald chaplain amerced 3d. for default; ordered to distrain him to reply to the lord concerning apple and other wood, taken away by him from the manor house.

William Kembald the younger pays 5s. fine to be relieved of the office of reeve.

SUM 16s. 9d.

# Section 3

## April 1327 – January 1336

**36.   HIGH HALL Court, 22 April 1327 [HA504/1/3.1]**

William of Cranmer essoins of common suit by Robert Kembald, and Walter
Osbern of the same by William Deneys; afterwards he came.

Gilbert Helpe amerced 3d. because he did not present the book[1] for the account of
his office.

William Kembald chaplain, Nicholas Kembald and William Kembald have a day,
*viz.* the Gules [1st] of August,[2] to repair and make good the aforesaid [*sic*] tenement, under penalty of forfeiting all the crops of their tenements; Matilda Kembald also has a day until Michaelmas to rebuild, repair and make good her
tenement.

Bartholomew Patel amerced 3d. for damage in the lord's wheat, pledge Gilbert
Helpe.

From Robert Kembald for damage in the lord's wheat, to the value of 8 sheaves;
likewise Walter Osbern 2 sheaves, Walter Payn 2 sheaves and Walter Deneys
1 sheaf.

Simon Cooper amerced 6d. for damage in the lord's barley, to the value of 6d., and
for damage in his oats, 2 sheaves.

The shepherd of Bartholomew de Elmham amerced 6d. for damage in the lord's
wheat with sheep, valued at 6d., pledge John Wodebite.

Ordered the whole homage that none of them shall store any corn in any tenement
not in the lord's villeinage, under penalty of forfeiting all the crops growing on
the villeinage.

Matilda the wife of Oliver [the shepherd] amerced 6d. for a false claim against
Nicholas and William Kembald, in two complaints.

Ordered to take into the lord's hands 1a.3r. of land which John and Alice Goche, villeins, demised to Bartholomew Dolhale to a term of five years, without leave,
and to report the profits etc., and custody by the whole homage.

Ordered to take into the lord's hands 1a. of land of villeinage which William Kembald demised to Robert Kembald without leave, and to report the profits; and
upon this he finds pledges to surrender[3] his charter to the lord, *viz.* Gilbert Helpe
and Nicholas Kembald. \Afterwards William comes and pays a fine for holding
this land, as appears below./

Henry Goche amerced 12d. for taking away a gate worth [*blank*], and 3d. for damage taking away the boards of a bench from the manor house; ordered to distrain
him to repair the bench.

---

1   *librum* translated as 'book', but 'parchment' would appear more appropriate; the roll of 17 November
1343 (no.118) recording a similar offence gives *percamentum*.
2   This date substituted for 'Michaelmas', which was deleted.
3   Substituted for 'show' which was deleted.

John Wodebite amerced 3d. for taking away a mortar from the manor house, ordered that another mortar be purchased by John.

Ordered to take into the lord's hands 2½a. of land of villeinage which Richard Gothelard demised to William Kembald without leave, and to report the profits; and [the land] is sown with peas. Afterwards he pays 6d. fine [to repossess] and is amerced 3d. for demising the land without leave.

A day is given to the whole homage to measure all the lands of the manor, and also to certify by the next court which [tenements] each holds, how much [land], and by which services and customs, and concerning the terms etc., and how much they should, as of right, take back (?*resumere*) from the lord for customs and services performed, under penalty of 40s. payable to the lord; and also concerning a swan, taken from the manor house.

Bartholomew Brunn amerced 3d. for trespass taking away a swan from the manor house.

The reeve amerced 12d. because he did not plough for a third time (*non rebinavit*) 3a. of the lord's land.

Ralph Isabel amerced 2s. because he did not perform ploughing work in the demesne, and did not lie in the manor.[4]

Henry Goche and his wife amerced 12d. because they remained in the court, in breach of the lord's prohibition.

John Wodebite amerced 12d. because he carted his corn in the carts of the manor for 2 days, without leave.

Ordered to distrain the wife of William of Ipswich to reply to the lord for rent and services in arrears etc.

Surrender: William the son of Walter Kembald to Robert Kembald and his heirs, 1a. of land lying next to Hingelondiscroft, granted to Robert to hold in villeinage by services and customs, at the lord's will, fine 2s., pledges Nicholas and William Kembald.

Alice Kembald pays 3d. fine for raising her debt to the lord, concerning a plough of the manor.

SUM 11s. 9d.

## 37. HIGH HALL Court of Nicholas de Walsham, 6 May 1327 [HA504/1/1.19][5]

The jurors say that Geoffrey Doo of Cotton, when he died, held from the lord a messuage in Cotton with a croft adjoining, containing 1a., for homage and services 12d. and scutage when demanded; John his son, aged 20 years, is his nearest heir; ordered to take the tenement into the lord's hands. John pays 2s. fine for leave to marry.

It was ordered to take into the lord's hands 1a. of land which Walter Kembald [deceased] purchased from the lord without charter, to hold at the lord's will, for services 2d. at Michaelmas, and at Christmas one hen, and one boonwork in

---

4 The word *curia* occurs twice here, and is translated as 'demesne' and 'manor', 'court' or 'courtyard' seeming inappropriate. In the next entry it appears again, and is translated as 'court', though the reason for the prohibition is not clear.
5 The date given is 'Wednesday after the feast of the Finding of the Holy Cross, 20 Edw.II'. As Edward II's reign ended on 20 January 1327, this appears to be an error; see Introduction, under The Rolls.

autumn with food provided by the lord; William, his [Walter's] son, pays 2s. fine for entry.

Matilda the widow of Simon Kembald holds in dower 6a. of land of villeinage, and she pays 12d. fine for leave to marry.

Oliver the shepherd pays 12d. fine for the same.

The damage in the lord's corn in the autumn by divers men, is assessed at 17 sheaves of wheat, ½ bushel of barley and 4 sheaves of peas.

Matilda Kembald in mercy for damage in the lord's corn, condoned.

William Wodebite amerced 3d. for default; <William Kembald in mercy for the same>, \condoned at the instance of William [Kembald] chaplain./

John Wodebite and William Wodebite each amerced 3d. for damage in the lord's herbage.

A day is given to the jurors to reply concerning the articles above.

<Ordered to take into the lord's hands 3a. of land with a messuage, which Eve Payn held.> \void/.

Ordered to distrain William Wodebite for waste in the tenement formerly of Walter Payn, and that the homage inspect the waste.

SUM 6s. 9d.

## 38.   HIGH HALL Court, 29 August 1327 [HA504/1/3.2.i]

The enquiry present that William Kembald chaplain, Nicholas Kembald and William Kembald did not fully repair their tenement held in villeinage, and they stored corn grown in the villeinage in another tenement, in breach of the lord's prohibition; therefore they are amerced the whole crop for trespass, which was valued by the homage at 6s. They have a day to repair the tenement in full by Michaelmas under penalty of ½ mark; likewise Matilda Kembald, under penalty of ½ mark.

Walter Deneys gives 2 sheaves of wheat for damage next to Allwood Green; Walter Osbern gives 5 sheaves for the same there with sheep and cows; William Payn, the Prior of Ixworth, William Kembald, Matilda Kembald, Simon Cooper and William Kembald caused damage there, to the value of 7 sheaves; and Agatha of Allwood and John Syre caused the said damage, together with the others. William of Cranmer, William Hawys, Walter Osbern, William Payn, Simon Cooper and Walter Deneys caused damage in the wheat in the same place, to the value of 2 bushels.

John the dairyman gives ½ bushel of barley for damage in the lord's barley at St Catherine's croft;[6] and Nicholas Fraunceys and his mother, 3 sheaves of oats for the same at Hordeshagh, \condoned by the lord/.

Ordered the reeve to have the bench repaired, which Henry Goche took away from the manor house and broke, and to buy a mortar [to replace that] which the reeve took away, by the next court, under penalty of 40d.

William Wodebite amerced 6d. because he did not come to work in the autumn as summoned; Ralph Isabel 3d. and Gilbert Helpe 6d. for the same.

Ordered to seize 1a. of land, which Robert Kembald held in villeinage, because he claims to hold it free, and he says that he does not owe servile fealty.

The whole homage amerced 40d. because they did not certify which tenements each

---

6   MS: '1½ bushels' deleted, '½ bushel' substituted above.

villein holds, how much [land], and by which services and customs, and concerning terms etc., and how much they should take back from the lord for services and customs etc.; and they have a day until the next court to certify concerning the aforesaid, under penalty of 40s.; and to enquire, and certify, which lands of the manor are sown, and ploughed for the third time, and cultivated in other ploughings; memorandum that they shall certify, by schedule, the measurements of the lands of the manor.

Ordered to attach Albreda the wife of William of Ipswich for rent and services in arrears.

Ordered to retain 1a. of land of villeinage which John Goche and Alice Goche villein[?s] by blood demised to Bartholomew Dolhale without leave; and the profits are remitted for this year.

Ordered to seize all the tenements which John of Angerhale, villein, held from the lord, with all the chattels found in them, because in contempt of the lord, he refused service (?renunciavit servicium). Afterwards he came and paid 40d. fine for the trespass.

Richard Gothelard in contempt of the lord, declining (nolend') to serve him but [serving] others. Afterwards he came and paid 12d. fine.

SUM 13s. 11d.

### 39. WALSHAM Court General, 10 October 1327 [HA504/1/3.3]

Walter Trowys amerced 6d. for leave to agree with Alice Kembold in a plea of debt, pledge Robert Spileman.

Again ordered to attach Richard Horn to reply to John Aubry in a plea of debt; afterwards agreement is reached and John puts himself in mercy; condoned because poor.

Again ordered to attach Gilbert the miller and Cristina his wife to reply to Peter the son of Robert in a plea of debt. \Attached by a horse./

Denis Aleyn amerced 6d. for damage in the lord's wood, pledges the hayward and the woodward.

Robert of Fornham and his pledges amerced 3d. because he did not proceed against Geoffrey Brantham in a plea of debt; Manser of Shucford and Cecilia his wife and their pledges amerced 6d. for the same in a plea of trespass.

Walter Gilbert pays 6d. fine for respite of suit of court until Michaelmas, pledge the hayward.

Simon Peyntour amerced 12d. because he sold 1a. of land to Walter de Wells ['Welles'] without leave; ordered to take the land into the lord's hands.

Walter Deneys amerced 4s. because he took away two horses from the pound without leave, pledge the hayward and the reeve.

Surrenders: Emma Stronde to Stephen Cooper and his heirs, 1a.¼r. of land, next to the Churchway, granted to Stephen to hold by services and customs, fine 4s.; he swore servile fealty.

Robert Godefrey to William Rampolye and his heirs, 1a. of land in the Millfield, granted to him to hold in the same form, fine 3s.; he swore fealty.

Simon Rampolye to Walter the Smith and his heirs, three parts of 1a. of land, granted to him to hold in the same form, fine 18d.; he swore servile fealty.

Robert Godefrey to Richard Suter and Alice his wife and their heirs, 1½r. of land in the Millfield, granted to them to hold in the same form, fine 18d.; they swore servile fealty.

Walter Pye, Peter Tailor and Stephen Cooper each amerced 3d., Emma Shepherd 2d, and Gilbert Priour and John Lene 3d. each, for damage in the meadows with cows.

William Gobold amerced 6s.8d. because he took the crop from 3r. of land of the lord's bondage in Finningham, out of the lord's possession, in breach of the orders of the lord's bailiffs. This land was formerly of John Patel, villein of the lord; and the crop is valued at 6s.8d., ordered to raise.

Robert Warde pays 18d. fine for respite of suit of court until Michaelmas, pledge William of Cranmer; Robert Robetel pays 4d. fine for the same.

Surrenders: Walter Osbern to William Hawys and his heirs, 1r. of land at Wylegmere, granted to William to hold by services etc., fine 9d.; he swore servile fealty;

William Hawys to Walter Osbern and his heirs, 1½r. of land at Langethweyt, granted to Walter to hold in the same form as above, fine 12d.; he swore servile fealty.

Ordered to summon Walter Osbern to reply to William Gilbert in a plea of land.

Richard Patel, the pledge of Geoffrey of Burgate, amerced 6d. because he did not have him to swear to the lord that which he ought, as he undertook; and ordered to distrain Geoffrey for homage and other service, *viz.* 8½d. rent for Scuttisfee in arrears; and to appoint a better pledge.

The jurors say that Olivia of Cranmer, when she died, held from the lord a quarter of a messuage 3a. of land by services, as by others of the same tenure; Eleanor, the wife of William Wither, is her nearest heir, and the heriot is a cow, worth 4s.; therefore nothing for entry as is customary.

Ordered as elsewhere to attach Walter of the Marsh because he took partridges without leave; and the hayward amerced 6d. because he did not attach Walter [for the same].

Adam Trounce amerced 6d. for damage in Ladyswood cutting branches, pledge Richard Warde.

Ordered to attach John Trempe for damage in the same place with cows.

Ordered to attach William Garlek and William the warrener because they grazed on the common where they had no right of common, and also overstocked the common with sheep, as shown in the roll of the court of Tuesday before the feast of St Nicholas, 8 Edw.II [5 December 1313].[7]

Robert of Reydon amerced 6d. for trespass, digging on the common.

Peter, the son of Robert, amerced 3d. because he had sheep outside the lord's fold.

Ordered to distrain William Kembald the younger for unlawfully withholding one reapale in the autumn, and one hen at Christmas.

Oliver the servant of Marsilia Hawys amerced ½ mark because, in the autumn, he unlawfully took corn from the lord, assessed at 1 peck.

Thomas Fuller amerced 3d. for damage in the lord's meadows.

The son[8] of Robert Lene amerced 6d. for the same in the courtyard,[9] taking away pears; and William Goseling 3d. for the same, pledge Walter Goselyng.

William Hawys pays 2s. fine for having entry into 1a.1¼r. of land lying at Clayhill ['Cleyhel'] and Stonyland ['Stonylond'], which Robert, William and Simon

---

[7] The year given is 8 Edw.II, but in subsequent references it is 7 Edw.II; the latter is taken to be correct.
[8] Possibly 'sons'; Robert had two sons – John and William.
[9] *curia.*

[Kembald] surrendered into the lord's hands, to the use of William Hawys; granted to him to hold by services and customs etc.; he swore servile fealty.

William Clevehog amerced 6d. because he had 30 sheep outside the lord's fold.

William Cook and Walter Pye each amerced 9d. because they brewed and sold ale in breach of the assize; Walter Rampolye 6d. and Robert Spileman 3d. for the same.

Alice Warde and Matilda Kembald each amerced 2d. for gannocking ale.

Robert Spileman amerced 3d. because he baked bread in breach of the assize.

Ralph Echeman aletaster amerced 3d. because he did not perform his duties; and upon this Nicholas Fraunceys was elected as aletaster.

Surrender: Richard Reve to Robert Man and his heirs, 1r.4p. of land in Sywardiscroft, granted to him to hold in the same form as above, fine 12d.

Robert the cooper pays 6d. fine for respite of suit of court until Michaelmas.

Surrenders: Peter Jay to Robert of Reydon and his heirs, 1½ r. of land next to the land of Robert at the Brook, granted to him to hold in the same form as above, fine 12d.

John Terwald to Peter Jay and his heirs, ½a. of land in the Meadowfield, granted to him to hold in the same form, fine 15d.

Richard Kebbil to Nicholas Goche and his heirs, 3r. of land in Overstubbing, granted to him to hold in the same form, fine 6d.

Nicholas Goche to Richard Kebbil and his heirs, 1½r. of land, granted to him to hold in the same form, fine 6d., and he swore servile fealty.

SUM 46s. 8d.

## 40.  HIGH HALL Court, 21 October 1327 [HA504/1/3.2.ii]

William Kembald chaplain, [plaintiff] v Matilda Kembald in a plea of trespass essoins by Robert Kembald.

Robert Kembald amerced 3d. because he refused to perform the services and customs due from the land which he holds from the lord in villeinage, pledge [*blank*]; he swore fealty.

Matilda Kembald has a day until the next court to make good the tenement in S[*sic*] under penalty of ½ mark.

Nicholas and William Kembald <amerced 6d.[10]> because they did not fully repair their villein tenement, as they undertook in the preceding court; and ordered William and others to repair before the next court, under penalty of ½ mark, in S[*sic*].

John Wodebite amerced 3d. because he did not raise 2 bushels of wheat from William of Cranmer and his associates.

William of Cranmer, Walter Osbern, Emma Stronde and William Kembald in mercy for default because they did not come when summoned \condoned/, Nicholas Kembald amerced 3d., and Alice and William Kembald each amerced for the same.[11]

Ordered to attach Albreda the widow of William of Ipswich for rent and services in arrears.

Ordered to retain in the lord's hands 1a. of land, which John and Alice Goche, villeins of the lord, demised to Bartholomew Dolhale freeman, without leave, for a

---

10  Margin: *alibi*, meaning '[dealt with] elsewhere'.
11  Amounts illegible.

term of 5 years, of which 3 years are past; John and Alice are in mercy, so long as they conceal this demise.

The whole homage elect William Wodebite to the office of reeve for the tenement Aprilles, and John of Angerhale to the office of collector.

All the lord's villeins, being sworn, say upon their oath that Henry Goche beat an ox of the lord and as a result it lost an eye, to the lord's loss of 12d., for which the reeve is liable; also Henry was ordered by John Wodebite, the reeve, to keep the lord's plough horses, and by his negligent custody, the lord lost a horse, valued by the homage at 16s.; the reeve is liable for this, and for the loss of 4s. from defective ploughing.

Gilbert Helpe pays 2s.6d. fine for leave to marry.

The abovesaid jurors say that damage was done in the lord's oats in the Thirtyacres to the value of 3 bushels, for which John Wodebite must answer.

William Kembald chaplain and his co-tenants pay 40d. fine, for not repairing their houses, and they have a day to repair until the feast of St Peter's Chains [1 August], and to replace (*reponend*) the corn grown in the lord's villeinage.

SUM 31s. 7d.

### 41. WALSHAM Court of Sir Edmund de Pakenham, 22 March 1328 [HA504/1/2.1]

Bartholomew Patel, plaintiff v Geoffrey of Burgate in a plea of debt, essoins by Richard Patel, he pledges faith. Ordered to attach Geoffrey to reply to Bartholomew concerning this plea.

William Kembald chaplain, defendant v Walter Petipas \he is present/ in a plea of debt, essoins by Walter the clerk, he pledges faith.

Again ordered to attach Gilbert the miller and Cristina his wife to reply to Peter the son of Robert in a plea of debt; and also to retain a horse, worth ½ mark, taken upon Gilbert and Cristina until etc., and to take more etc.

Ordered to retain 1a. of land, which Simon Peyntour villein sold to Walter de Wells, by charter, without the lord's leave, and to report the profits, until etc.

William Gilbert and his pledges amerced 6d. because he did not proceed against Walter Osbern in a plea of land; Walter is quit indefinitely.

Walter Osbern and John Syre, the first pledges of Geoffrey of Burgate, amerced 12d. because they did not have him do homage to the lord, and satisfy him concerning the annual rent of 8½d. for his tenement in Finningham, called Scuttisfee, in arrears for one year; ordered to distrain Geoffrey to appoint four pledges for himself.

+Ordered as elsewhere to distrain Walter of the Marsh because he took partridges in the lord's warren without leave.[12]

Ordered as elsewhere to distrain John Trempe for damage done with his cows in Ladyswood; and William Garlek[13] because he grazed beasts on the common where he had no right of common, and also overstocked the lord's common with sheep. The summons for the same against William the warrener is in respite until the next court, the roll for the court of 5 December 1313 to be scrutinised,

---

12 Margin: 'warren' (?17th century).
13 The Prior of Ixworth, see no.44.

pledges William of Cranmer and Simon Cooper; and to find in that court how many sheep the Prior of Ixworth had grazing in Wathesham.[14]

Nicholas Kembald, the pledge of William Kembald the younger, amerced 3d. because he did not have him satisfy the lord regarding the withholding of one hen and one reapale, as is the custom for the common[15] etc.; ordered William to appoint four pledges.

Nicholas Kembald, William Springold and Peter Springold amerced 6d. for unlawful detention of 10 bushels of wheat, which Walter Gilbert was ordered to give to Thomas of the Beck on Tuesday before the feast of the Purification, 1 Edw.III [29 January 1327], which they cannot deny; granted to Thomas that he shall recover the 10 bushels and damages of 12d.; ordered to raise.

William Cook and Peter Springold each amerced 3d. for trespass in Ladyswood with their pigs, pledge the hayward.

William Coppelowe amerced 12d. for trespass in the same wood, cutting down and taking away the lord's young ash-trees and underwood, as found by the enquiry before which he put himself, pledge the hayward.

Walter Pye pays 3d. fine to have the jurors enquire which malefactors did damage in his barley near Ladyswood; and the jurors say that William Cook, Matthew Hereward, Robert Spileman and William the miller did the damage.

An enquiry was held by William Hawys, William of Cranmer the younger, Walter Osbern, John Man, Richard Kebbil, William Springold, Peter Springold, Simon Peyntour, Walter Payn, Simon Rampolye, Elias Typetot and Robert of Reydon, and they say that Richard Reve villein, when he died, held in villeinage by services and customs a cottage and 3r. of land adjoining, and that there is no heriot because he had no beast. Upon this Walter and Robert his sons claim that they are his heirs, which the jurors confirm, and being of full age they seek possession. Seisin is granted to them and their heirs, to hold at the lord's will etc.; and they swore servile fealty; and because there was no heriot, they pay 3s. fine for having the enquiry as well as for entry, pledge Thomas Fuller.

Robert Osbern the tanner purchased a cottage and 1r. of land of the lord's fee; ordered to take it into the lord's hands until he satisfies the lord for entry, and shows his charter for the purchase, and for fealty and homage.

Ordered to distrain Alice the daughter of Robert Rede villein because she married, without leave.

Robert Champneys amerced 3d. because he took away fodder and straw, worth ½d., from the lord's courtyard, pledge the hayward.

Henry of Saxlingham took a hare in the lord's warren, inside the messuage and close of Sir Alexander de Walsham, ordered to distrain him to satisfy etc.[16]

William of Cranmer the elder, John Man, William Springold, Walter Springold, Walter Payn and Elias Typetot, jurors, to certify whether John Spileman holds ½r. of land of the tenement Robetels, and Simon Peyntour holds 3r. of the tenement Swiftes, and Thomas Fuller holds ½r. of the tenement Gores, and whether Stephen Cooper owes 4d. annual rent for the tenement Robhood, which the tenants of these tenements say they do not hold, and seek an enquiry. They say, under oath, that John Spileman does not hold ½r. of land, and is therefore quit,

---

14 Probably a copying error by the clerk; 'Walsham' is frequently spelt 'Walesham' in the rolls.
15 MS: *pro ut mos est pro communa*; in this context, the meaning is obscure.
16 Margin: 'warren' (same hand as in footnote 12).

but William the miller holds that land; and that Simon Peyntour holds 3r. of the tenement Swiftes; he is therefore amerced 3d., pledge the hayward; and they say that Thomas Fuller holds ½r. in the tenement Gores, which he had denied, and is amerced 3d., pledge the hayward; that Stephen Cooper owes part of the 4d. rent for ½a. and he has a co-tenant; he pays 3d. fine for the rent to be apportioned; ordered Walter Osbern and his associates that it be done under penalty of 2s.

Ordered the bailiff to distrain Peter Springold to reply to Walter Gilbert in a plea of trespass, and for damage done in distraining in Walter's house, taking his horse away from the house, against Walter's will, without complaint.

Ordered to take into the lord's hands 3a. of land now in the possession of Walter Osbern the younger, which the predecessors of Nicholas Goche, villein, demised at farm, without enrolment in the court; therefore ordered to show his charter for the purchase etc., <and to take into the lord's hands 1a. of land, of which Eda Rede villein was enfeoffed by charter in frank-marriage> \void because pleaded before William de la Chambre/; and to distrain Geoffrey of Burgate for contempt of the lord, and his bailiffs, in pleading and [*illeg.*] in courts outside that of the lord, and in the Hundred.

Robert Warde pays 3d. fine for scrutiny of the court rolls concerning the tenement Wyswyf.

Surrenders: +Beatrice of the Brook to Ralph Echeman and his heirs, a messuage 2½a. of land, granted to him to hold by services and customs at the lord's will, fine 5s., pledge the hayward, under this form, *viz.* that Ralph shall provide for Beatrice a room suitable to her status, and 1 quarter of barley annually, measured in the market at Bury St Edmunds, for her lifetime.

Walter Rampolye to Walter the smith and his heirs, 1a. of land, granted to Walter to hold at the lord's will, fine 40d., pledge the reeve; Walter swore servile fealty.[17]

Walter Osbern the elder to Walter Osbern the younger and his heirs, ¾r. of land, granted to him to hold at the lord's will etc., fine for entry 9d., and for having his term in 1a. of land for six years, from the surrender of Beatrice of the Brook, the term having begun at Michaelmas last past.

Cecilia Pudding to Robert of Reydon and his heirs, ½r. of land 4p. long in Upstreet, granted to him and his heirs to hold at the lord's will, fine 4s., pledge the hayward.

Robert Warde to William of Cranmer the younger, 10p. of meadow in the Micklemeadow; likewise Simon Rampolye to William, [a piece of] land 18p. long and 1p. wide; and Robert, William, Simon and Walter Rampolye to William, 5p. of meadow in the Micklemeadow; granted to him to hold to him and his heirs, at the lord's will, fine 2s.[18]

William of Cranmer the younger to Thomas Fuller, 1r. of land next to the Regway, likewise Stephen Cooper to Thomas, 1¼r. of land at the same place, granted to Thomas to hold to him and his heirs at the lord's will etc., fine 20d.

Robert Godefrey to William Wither and his heirs, 3r. of land, granted to him to hold at the lord's will, fine 2s., pledge the hayward; William swore servile fealty.

17 Tab: 'Walter Rampolye'.
18 Margin: 'fealty'.

Richard Warde the parker pays 3d. fine to be relieved of his office, and not to be the parker this year, pledge the reeve, and because he is poor.[19]

Surrender: Walter Gilbert to William Springold and Isabella his wife and their heirs, 3r. of land in two pieces, one lying near Ladyswood, and the other in the Stubbing; granted to them to hold at the lord's will, fine 2s.; they swore servile fealty.

William Coppelowe who, at the Court General held this year, was elected to be the parker after Michaelmas, is amerced 12d. because he did not perform his duties, and concealed wrongdoers in the said wood, and trespasses there with beasts. Nevertheless, he took the oath to uphold the office, under penalty of 20d., pledge the whole homage.

+Memorandum to enquire regarding messuages, cottages and lands demised, or sold in exchange, or demised at farm, without leave of the court; and regarding tenements formerly built, and the names of the buyers and sellers, and what rents are to be paid to the lord, hens, boonworks etc.

Surrenders: William the miller to Matthew Hereward and his heirs, ½r. of land, granted to him to hold at the lord's will, fine 3d., he swore servile fealty;

Walter Gilbert to William Cook and his heirs, 1r. of land abutting on the Oldtoft, granted to him to hold at the lord's will by services and customs, fine 12d.

Matthew Hereward to Robert Hereward and his heirs, 3r. of land lying in the furlong between William Coppelowe and Walter Goselyng, in exchange for 1½a. lying in the furlong called Leyton ['Leyhtone'], which Robert surrendered to Matthew and his heirs; granted to them in the same form as above, fine 20d., pledge the hayward.

The whole homage in mercy for concealment, because they failed to present that for a long time Sir Alexander de Walsham withheld rents and services for various tenements held from the lord, condoned.

The reeve and the hayward in mercy because they did not dismantle a fold, unlawfully raised by Sir Alexander de Walsham on the free land of Master John de Walsham, where he had no liberty of fold, nor right to common his sheep; condoned by order of a letter from the lord. The whole homage in mercy for concealment of the same, because they did not present the unlawful raising of the fold, nor the fact that it was not dismantled, as ordered; condoned.

SUM 29s. 9d.

Affeerers: Nicholas Goche, Robert of Reydon, John Syre, William Cook

## 42. WALSHAM Court there, 11 May 1328 [HA504/1/3.5.i]

Geoffrey of Burgate, defendant v Bartholomew Patel in a plea of debt, essoins by John of Stonham; it does not lie, because following default, it cannot lie until he has appeared in court; therefore Geoffrey's second pledges amerced 8d., because they did not have him reply to Bartholomew, ordered to make him do so by eight pledges. Also, William Hawys and Nicholas Kembald, Geoffrey's first pledges, amerced 8d. because they did not have him reply to Bartholomew Patel in a plea of trespass; ordered to make him do so by four pledges.

Surrender: Emma Stronde to Letitia her daughter and her heirs, 1a. of land lying in Northcroft on the north side of Emma's messuage, and abutting at one head on the way leading towards Strondislane and Hawyslane, granted to her to hold in

---

[19] It is not clear whether Richard's poverty is the reason for his wish not to be parker, or for the level of the fine.

villeinage at the lord's will, fine 12d., pledges Stephen Cooper and the hayward; she swore servile fealty.

Simon and Robert Rampolye were summoned to reply to Bartholomew Patel in a plea of debt, concerning which Bartholomew says that on Saturday after Epiphany 1 Edw.III [8 January 1328], in Westhorpe, the aforesaid Simon and Robert bought from Bartholomew a wood for 5s., to be paid on the feast of the Purification [2 February]; on which day they paid, except 13d., which they withheld, and still withhold, to his loss of 10d.; and he produces suit. Simon and Robert say that Bartholomew can have no right of action, because he prevented them from having the wood, and they seek an enquiry, and Bartholomew likewise; ordered the bailiff to summon the enquiry.

William Rampolye was summoned in the aforesaid form to reply to Bartholomew Patel for 14d., and he conceded for Bartholomew to wage law that he [Bartholomew] did not prevent him [William] from having the wood which he had bought etc., to the loss of 6d.

William Hawys and Nicholas Kembald, the pledges of Geoffrey of Burgate, amerced 2s. because they did not have him do homage to the lord and pay rent of 8½d. for his tenement called Scuttisfee; ordered to appoint four pledges; also William and Nicholas, Geoffrey's pledges, to pay 40d. to the lord as aid for his first-born son to be knighted, and for the relief of William the son and heir of Thomas Auncel following Thomas' death, for the tenement, of which he died seised, and of which Geoffrey is the tenant, and for contempt of the lord and his bailiffs in pleading against them outside the lord's court, and in the Hundred; ordered to summon him by better pledges.

Ordered to distrain Robert of Reydon to reply to Thomas of the Beck in a plea of debt, pledges for Thomas John Noreys and the hayward.

William Coppelowe, when he died, held from the lord a messuage 7a. of land of the lord's bondage by services etc.; the lord had a cow, worth 8s., as a heriot; William his son, aged two years, is his nearest heir, and the jurors have a day to certify whether his mother will have custody until he comes of age, without fine.

Walter Osbern the elder, when he died, held from the lord 4a. of land and half of a messuage of the lord's bondage by services etc.; the lord had a calf, worth 12d., as a heriot; John his son aged 12 years, is his nearest heir, and the jurors have a day to certify whether his mother will have custody until etc., without fine.

George of Brockley ['Brokkeley'] and Alice his wife complain of Gilbert Priour in a plea of land, pledges the reeve and the hayward; ordered to distrain Gilbert to reply.

Ordered to execute the old orders of the preceding court as marked by a cross.

Surrender: William Robhood to Matthew Hereward and his heirs, [a piece of] land, 7ft. wide and 30p.2ft. long, lying between Matthew's land on both sides, granted to him to hold in villeinage at the lord's will, fine 2d.; he swore servile fealty.

Peter Jay villein was attached because he demolished an old barn in the lord's bondage, and he asks for a day until next Easter to rebuild it, pledges Nicholas Goche and Robert Spileman, granted under penalty of ½ mark.

SUM 7s. 10d.
Affeerers: the reeve and the hayward.

## 43. WALSHAM Court, 30 May 1328 [HA504/1/3.5.ii]

Again as before ordered to attach Geoffrey of Burgate to reply to Bartholomew Patel in a plea of debt, and to appoint for himself eight pledges; and to summon him by four pledges to reply to Bartholomew in a plea of trespass; and to retain in the lord's hands 1a. of land, which Simon Peyntour sold to Walter de Wells without leave, and to report the profits.

The summons against William Kembald the younger, because he withheld one hen and one autumn reapale, as is the custom for the common, is in respite until the next court, pledges Walter Osbern and Nicholas Kembald.

Ordered to attach John Trempe for damage with his cows in Ladyswood.

The summonses against William Garlek and William the Warrener, because they grazed on the lord's common with their sheep where they had no right of common, and because they overstocked the lord's common with their sheep, as is found in the roll of the court of 5 December 1313, are in respite until the next court, pledges William of Cranmer and Simon Cooper.

Ordered to distrain Alice the daughter of Robert Rede villein because she married without the lord's leave.

Henry of Saxlingham was accused of taking a hare within the messuage of Sir Alexander de Walsham, and he said that he was not guilty, and asked for an enquiry, which was held, and the jurors say that he is not guilty, and he is acquitted.

[The enquiry ordered] to enquire concerning messuages, cottages and land, sold, or exchanged, or demised at farm without the court's leave, or in exchange etc., an enquiry was held before the steward, William de la Chambre, as shown in the roll of the court held on Wednesday before the feast of St Matthew, 19 Edw.II [18 September 1325], and also, in the same court, regarding tenements formerly built, and the names of the buyers and sellers, and for which they are accustomed to render hens and boonworks to the lord.[20]

Simon, Robert and William Rampolye each amerced 6d. for leave to agree with Bartholomew Patel in pleas of debt, pledge Bartholomew Patel.

Robert of Reydon fined 1d. for the same, to agree with Thomas of the Beck, pledge the hayward.

Ordered to attach Richard Horn, and to appoint better pledges for him to reply to John Aubry in a plea of debt.

Ordered to distrain in the tenements, of which Ralph Broun of Westhorpe died seised, for homage, fealty and relief; Idonia of Holkham is now the tenant and she comes and swears fealty, and pays 12d. fine as aid for the lord's first-born son to be knighted, pledges the reeve and the hayward.

Ordered to distrain Geoffrey of Burgate to do homage to the lord, and to pay 8½d. rent for his tenement called Scuttisfee; and to pay a fine as aid for the lord's first-born son to be knighted, and for the relief of William, the son and heir of Thomas Auncel, following Thomas' death, for the tenement of which he died seised, of which Geoffrey is now the tenant; and to attach Geoffrey, villein of the lord, to reply to the lord for contempt of the lord and his bailiffs and men in pleading outside [his] lord's court, and in the Hundred etc.

Ordered to attach Walter Machon villein because he has withheld 1d. chevage for four years, and to enquire regarding his first pledge.

---

[20] Margin: 'concluded'.

Cristina the daughter of Simon the Smith pays 32d. childwite, because she is a villein.

Alice Schetenhait,[21] when she died, held from the lord a cottage of the lord's bondage by services and customs; and there was no heriot, because she had nothing in goods. Agnes her daughter, aged four years, is her nearest heir; and it was ordered to enquire whether Robert Salvetail Alice's husband should hold the tenement for his lifetime, because he was never seised thereof, he is not the heir, nor has he paid a fine for entry. They say that he can claim nothing in the cottage, as of right. Upon this Robert comes, and pays 3d. fine to hold the cottage from the lord for his lifetime, pledge the hayward; he swore servile fealty.

Robert Osbern [the tanner] pays 3d. fine for having [the court's] aid in raising from Juliana the widow of Adam Suter 4s.6d., which she owes him, as appears in a plea [of debt] between them, in the [roll of the] last court but one, ordered to raise.

Surrender: John Fraunceys to William Payn and his heirs, ¾r. of land abutting on Lenerethsdel, granted to him to hold at the lord's will, fine 9d., he swore servile fealty.

William Cook pays 3d. fine to be relieved of the office of woodward from now until Michaelmas. William Springold was elected by the whole homage to be woodward in his place, and he swore fealty.

William of Cranmer pays 3d. fine for having his term, \for him and his heirs,/ for the lifetime of Eleanor, the wife of John Man, in half a messuage with gardens and a pightle, by the demise of John and Eleanor; granted to William to hold in that form, to him and his heirs, for Eleanor's lifetime, on condition that he or they manage and maintain the half-messuage during the said term, in as good a condition as they received it.

John at the Green pays 3d. fine for having an enquiry concerning damage in his corn. The jurors have a day until the next court to certify, and they say that the lord and Sir Alexander de Walsham caused the damage.

Ordered to distrain Walter Osbern the younger to reply to the lord, because he maliciously accused William Hawys, defendant v Sir Alexander de Walsham, for which William was amerced ½ mark, to the use of Sir Alexander, as [illeg.] by the inquiry, for destruction by William in Sir Alexander's wood.

Richard the son of Stephen the reeve of Gislingham pays 2s. fine for having entry to 3r. of land of bondage, with Emma the daughter of William the shepherd; Richard has a day to come to the next court to swear fealty, pledges the reeve and the hayward. Richard swore servile fealty.

Ordered to retain in the lord's hands a messuage 7a. of land of villeinage, of which William Coppelowe died seised, and half a messuage and 4a. of which Walter Osbern the elder died seised, until etc.

George of Brockley and Alice his wife claim a cottage against Gilbert Priour; in respite until the next court.

SUM 9s. 3d.

Affeerers: Nicholas the reeve and John Syre

---

21 Surname substituted for 'Salvetail', which is deleted.

## 44.  WALSHAM Court, 27 July 1328 [HA504/1/3.6]

Ordered as many times to distrain Geoffrey of Burgate to reply to Bartholomew
Patel in a plea of debt, and to appoint eight pledges, and to make him come to the
next court by four pledges to reply to Bartholomew in a plea of trespass.

Simon Peyntour who sold 1a. of free land to Walter de Wells without leave, is
allowed to sell to him, by the lady's letter.

Ordered as elsewhere to distrain John Trempe of Ashfield for trespass in the lord's
wood with his cows.

The summonses against William Garlek \Prior of Ixworth/[22] and William the warrener concerning the fact that they grazed on the lord's common with their sheep
where they had no right of common, and also that they overstocked the lord's
common with their sheep, as was found at the court of 5 December 1313, are in
respite until the next court, pledges William of Cranmer and Simon Cooper.

Ordered to distrain Alice the daughter of Robert Rede villein because she married
without leave; and to attach Richard Horn to reply to John Aubry in a plea of debt
by better pledges; and to distrain in the tenements which were of Ralph Broun of
Westhorpe and of which Idonia of Holkham is now the tenant, for homage to the
lord and relief. \Afterwards Robert Spileman came and confirmed that she had
received [the tenements] by extract of the court [roll], in the time when he was
hayward, and therefore she is quit./

Ordered to distrain Geoffrey of Burgate to do homage to the lord, and to pay 8½d.
rent for his tenement called Scuttisfee; and to pay a fine as aid for the lord's
first-born son to be knighted, and for the relief of William the son and heir of
Thomas Auncel following Thomas' death, for the tenement of which he died
seised, of which Geoffrey is now the tenant; and to attach Geoffrey villein to
reply to the lord for contempt of the lord and his bailiffs, in pleading outside the
lord's court, and in the Hundred etc.

Ordered to distrain Walter Machon, villein, because he absents himself, and for 1d.
chevage for [each of] the past four years.

Ordered to raise 4s.6d. from Juliana the widow of Adam Suter to the use of Robert
Osbern, under penalty of 40d.

Walter Osbern and Nicholas Kembald, the first pledges of William Kembald the
younger, each amerced 3d. because they did not have him reply to the lord,
because he withheld one hen and one autumn reapale, as is the custom for the
common; ordered to appoint better pledges to reply at the next court.

Nicholas Goche complained against Geoffrey of Burgate in a plea of discharge of a
debt, pledges for Nicholas the hayward and Walter Osbern, and Geoffrey was not
attached, therefore ordered to distrain him to reply to Nicholas.

Robert Man amerced 3d. for damage in the lord's corn by his wife gathering herbage, pledges the reeve and the hayward.

<Ordered to execute the orders of the last court marked with a cross and not acted
upon.>

Richard Qualm and Robert of the Brook ask for leave to agree in a plea of trespass;
Robert is amerced 6d., pledge Simon Peyntour.

Stephen Cooper amerced 2d. for trespass in the lord's corn by his daughter gathering
herbage, pledges the reeve and the hayward.

---

22  Insert over the first name.

Matilda the widow of William Coppelowe received from the lord a messuage 7a. of land, of which her husband died seised, and half of which she has in dower following the custom of the manor; Matilda now seeks to have custody until his full age of William, her late husband's son and heir, who is aged two years; granted to her to hold in that form by services and customs, on condition that she maintains the house and messuage in as good a state as she received it, pledges Walter Osbern, William Cook and Ralph Echeman, fine for custody 40d., pledge the reeve; she swore servile fealty.

Isabella the widow of Walter Osbern received from the lord 4a. of land and half of a messuage, of which her husband died seised, and half of which she has in dower following the custom of the manor; Isabella now seeks to have custody until his full age of John, her husband's son and heir, who is aged 12 years; granted to her to hold in the same form, and on the same condition, pledges Walter Osbern, William Hawys, fine 2s., pledge the hayward; she swore servile fealty.[23]

John Lene amerced 2d. for trespass in the lord's corn by his maidservant, pledge the hayward.

Gilbert Priour amerced 6d. for damage in the lord's pasture below a certain spinney, pledge the reeve; Nicholas Goche in mercy for the same, condoned.

The jurors present that Gilbert Helpe withheld suit and services, therefore ordered etc.

Surrender: Peter Springold to Elias Typetot and his heirs, ½a. of land in the field called Schetebusk, granted to him by the rod, to hold at the lord's will by services and customs, fine 20d., pledge the hayward; he swore servile fealty.

The aletasters present that all the brewers refuse to send for them when they brew etc., therefore ordered etc.

Thomas of the Beck complains against John at the Green in a plea of debt and a plea of trespass, pledges for Thomas, Walter Osbern and the hayward; ordered to distrain John to reply to Thomas in the two complaints.

George of Brockley and Alice his wife, in open court, claim against Gilbert Priour a cottage in Walsham, as of Alice's right and purchase, because, they say, a certain Richard Priour, a former tenant thereof, outside the court surrendered it into the hands of William Hawys and Walter Osbern, to the use of Alice and her heirs in fee, and Gilbert has no entry to the cottage except by trespass. Gilbert says that George and Alice should not be given judgment in their claim, because the surrender of the cottage should not prejudice him unless it was made in the lord's court; and he asks that an enquiry be made, and likewise George and Alice. And the enquiry says that in the time of John of Scardelowe, formerly steward of this court, a similar case was heard before him between William Cook, claimant, and Ralph Rich, the tenant of a tenement in Walsham, concerning the surrender of it into the hands of William of Chevington ['Cheventone'], clerk of the lord of this court. And that Ralph Rich died before the next court held here after that surrender, and Basilia at the Brook, Ralph's niece and heir, claimed the tenement by her right and inheritance from the death of her uncle. And that, because Ralph died before the said court was held, the surrender was wholly annulled, and the tenement was delivered to Basilia, as Ralph's niece and heir, to hold in bondage at the lord's will etc. In the case of George and his wife Alice, claimants, and

---

[23]  Margin: 'dower' (?17th century).

113

Gilbert, tenant, [they say] that Richard Priour, brother and heir of Gilbert, came to the court, held in the said form, and claimed as his right and inheritance from the death of the above-named Richard Priour, as his brother and heir.[24] Adjudged that George and Alice shall recover nothing, but are amerced 6d. for a false claim, pledge the reeve; and Gilbert is to be quit indefinitely.

Surrender: Richard Suter and Alice his wife to William Springold and Isabella his wife and their heirs, 1½a. of land in the field of Walsham, granted to them to hold at the lord's will by the rod, by services and customs, fine 4s., pledge the reeve and the hayward; they swore servile fealty.

SUM 13s. 7d.

Affeerers: Walter Osbern, Nicholas Goche and John Syre

Memorandum to enquire concerning messuages, cottages and lands sold, exchanged or demised at farm without leave of the court; and as in the court of 18 September 1325 tenements formerly built, the names of buyers and sellers of them, and for which they were accustomed to render to the lord hens, boonworks, autumn works etc.

### 45. WALSHAM Court of Sir Edmund de Pakenham, 8 October 1328 [HA504/1/3.7]

Ordered as elsewhere to distrain Geoffrey of Burgate to reply to Bartholomew Patel in pleas of debt and trespass, and to summon him by better pledges; and to attach John Tremp to reply to the lord concerning trespass in his wood with cows.

Again as elsewhere ordered to attach Alice the daughter of Robert Rede villein because she married without leave.

John Aubry and his pledges amerced 2d. for leave to withdraw his complaint against Richard Horn, pledge the hayward.

Ordered to distrain in the tenements which Geoffrey of Burgate holds, for homage to the lord and for 8½d. rent withheld for his tenement called Scuttisfee; and for aid for the lord's first-born son to be knighted, and for the relief of William the son and heir of Thomas Auncel, following Thomas' death, for the tenement of which he died seised, and of which Geoffrey is now the tenant; and to reply to the lord concerning trespass against the lord and his bailiffs.

Again as elsewhere ordered to attach Walter Machon the chapman villein, because he absents himself from the lord's fee, and has withheld 1d. chevage per year for the past four years.

The hayward amerced 3d. because he did not execute the court's order to attach William Kembald the younger etc.; ordered William to appoint better [pledges] to reply to the lord for the withholding of a hen and an autumn reapale, as is the custom for the common.

Ordered as elsewhere to distrain Geoffrey of Burgate to reply to Nicholas Goche in a plea of discharge of a debt.

Ordered as elsewhere to take into the lord's hands \1¼r./ of land, which Gilbert Helpe holds, for services and customs withheld, until etc., and to distrain him in the free tenement \1½r./ which he holds from the lord.

The distraint taken on the Prior of Ixworth for overstocking the lord's common with

---

24 The judgment is confused because the clerk has written 'Richard', at least once, instead of 'Gilbert'. Gilbert was correctly named as the tenant before and after the judgment, and he and Richard his brother were probably the heirs of the Richard cited by the claimants, as having surrendered the tenement.

114

his sheep and because he grazed his sheep where he had no right of common is in respite to the next court, pledges William of Cranmer the elder and Simon Cooper. And be it known that it is shown in the court of 5 December 1313 where his sheep may graze, and how many.

Peter Jay, the first pledge of John at the Green, is amerced 3d. because he did not have him reply to Thomas of the Beck in a plea of trespass and another of debt; ordered John to appoint better pledges.

Robert the chaplain amerced 3d. for trespass in the lord's several meadow with his cows, pledge the reeve, likewise Walter Pye 3d., Peter Tailor 3d., Robert Lene 2d. and John Lene 3d. for the same at the same place, pledge for all the hayward.

John Lene amerced 2d. for contempt of the steward of the lord's court, pledge the hayward.

Gilbert Prior amerced 3d., Nicholas Goche 2d. and the Prior of Ixworth 6d. for trespass in the lord's several meadow, pledge the hayward.

William of Cranmer and William Hawys each amerced 6d. for trespass with their pigs rooting in Micklemeadow, pledge the hayward.

Ordered to attach John at the Green to reply to the lord for damage with his pigs rooting and turning up the lord's meadow in Micklemeadow; Robert Spileman, William Cook and Nicholas Kembald each amerced 3d., William Springold 1d. and Peter Springold 2d. for the same, pledge for all the hayward.

Peter Springold in mercy for contempt of the steward in bearing false witness (*afferend' fals'*) contrary to his oath, condoned because poor.

Robert of Reydon amerced 3d. for trespass in Micklemeadow with his pigs rooting and turning up as above, pledge the hayward.

Peter Neve, Stephen Cooper, Richard the son of Stephen Reve and Thomas Fuller each amerced 3d. for trespass in the severalty of the lady, pledge the hayward.

William Payn amerced 4d. for trespass in the lord's oats with his beasts; Robert Lene 6d. for the same in the lord's barley, assessed at 1 bushel; Peter Tailor 3d. for the same, 1 peck of barley, pledge for all the hayward.

Robert of Reydon amerced 12d. for trespass in Ladyswood with his cows, pledge the hayward; the swineherd of the lord and the swineherd of Sir Alexander de Walsham in mercy for trespass in the lord's meadow with pigs, condoned.

Walter Goseling amerced 3d. because he harboured William Goseling with a sheaf of wheat from the lord's corn, pledge the hayward.

The enquiry *viz.* Robert Warde, \Walter Osbern,/ Matthew Hereward, Walter Hereward, Robert Tailour, Elias Typetot, Simon Peyntour, Walter Payn, William Payn, Simon Rampolye, Ralph Echeman, Walter Pye, \William Springold/, jurors, with other jurors associated with them, *viz.* Peter the son of Robert, William Springold [*sic*], William Hawys, Robert Deneys, John Patel, Peter Jay, William Pach, Walter Osbern [*sic*] and Robert Spileman, say on oath that Hugh Rouse of Ashfield trespassed in Ladyswood with his cows, amerced 3d., pledge William Springold.

The Prior of Ixworth trespassed with his sheep on fallow (*frisca*) land at Allwood, ordered to attach him.[25]

Robert the shepherd of Sir Alexander de Walsham amerced 6d.[26] for damage with sheep in the lord's severalty at Allwood, and Matilda Kembald amerced 3d. for

---

[25] Margin: 'ordered' deleted, 'afterwards' inserted.
[26] Amount deleted.

the same at Currescroft with cows, pledge the hayward. Ordered to attach the Prior of Ixworth for damage in the same place with his plough oxen. William of Cranmer and John Syre amerced 3d. for damage in the same place, pledge each for the other.

The swineherds of the lord and of Sir Alexander de Walsham did damage with pigs in the lord's wheat at Nineacres next to the Micklemeadow, condoned; Peter Jay and Peter Springold each amerced 3d. for the same, pledge the hayward.

Robert the chaplain withheld eight autumn works, worth 8d., in mercy;[27] Emma Stronde withheld nine autumn works, worth 9d., in mercy.[28]

Ordered to attach the Prior of Ixworth because he overstocked the lord's common with sheep, and grazed where he had no right of common, in the field called Scuttbrook.

Robert of Reydon, villein, amerced ½ mark because he prejudiced villeins of the lord, telling the bailiffs of Sir William Criketot that they caused damage in Sir William's meadow, pledges William Hawys and John Syre.

Avice Deneys amerced 3d. because it was found that she damaged the reputation of John Frounceys, damage assessed at 3d., which John is to recover; ordered to raise.[29]

William Hawys amerced 12d. for demolishing and taking away a house on the lord's bondage, pledge the hayward, and ordered concerning a plea to rebuild, pledge as before.

Agnes Helewys amerced 2d. because she took away coppice wood out of the lord's demesne (*curia*), pledge the hayward.

Sir Alexander de Walsham withheld the service of one man being over the lord's great boonwork in autumn, and he withheld one suit for a tenement called Master Johns, which he holds by [suit of] two Courts General per year, and one other suit for another tenement, and that he withholds the rent for a tenement which he holds, of unknown name \called Crutlanes/. Ordered to attach [him].

Walter Gilbert pays 3d. fine for respite of suit of court until Michaelmas, pledge Nicholas Kembald; likewise Robert Robetel, Robert Salvetail, Geoffrey of Lenne, and William Deneys 3d. each, and Robert Warde 12d. for the same, pledge for all the hayward.

Walter Man amerced 1d. because he exchanged 1½r. of land with Walter Hereward without the court's leave; afterwards they come and pay 3d. fine for the exchange, to hold at the lord's will.

William Cook and his wife amerced 12d. because they brewed and sold ale in breach of the assize, and because they did not send for the ale-tasters; Walter Rampolye amerced 12d., Walter Pye 2d. for the same; Emma Kembald 6d. for the same, pledge John Robhood because in [his] house; Joan the brewster 12d. for the same, pledge Walter Osbern because in [his] house; and Gilbert Priour 3d. for the same, pledge the hayward. Ralph Echeman and Nicholas Frounceys the ale-tasters each amerced 3d. because they did not perform their duties in the due manner. William Kembald amerced 12d. because his wife brewed and sold ale in breach of the assize. Matilda Kembald, gannocker, and seller of ale in breach of the assize, amerced 3d., pledge Peter Robbes because in [his] house.

---

[27] Margin: no amount shown; note: 'because sold by the hayward'.
[28] As above; note: 'because the hayward [?records] in the account'.
[29] See below.

John Terwald has a day until the next court to come to receive his inheritance, and to do to the lord that which he should do for entry into the lord's bondage.

Robert of Reydon finds pledges for custody of the goods and chattels in the messuage and land which he holds from the lord in villeinage, without removing or disposing of them, until the next court, to which the heir should come and receive his inheritance, with the profits from it. The pledges are William Hawys and John Syre.

William the son of Walter Patel and Walter Qualm have the same day, \pledge for not removing goods, William of Cranmer/; William Deneys and Nicholas Deneys have the same day, \pledge as above William Helpe/;[30] Agnes and Alice Typetot have the same day, \pledge as above John Syre/; John Robhood, \pledge William Hawys/, Agnes Goche, \pledge Walter Osbern/; John and Robert Crane and Robert, the son of Peter Warde, \pledge for all the hayward/; have the same day.

The enquiry has a day to certify concerning a water course obstructed and blocked, because they did not clean part of it, and concerning wasted tenements, which were accustomed to render to the lord reaping service, hens and many other necessaries (?*necc'a*), and which now pay nothing, whether any services are withheld; and whether any customary tenants withhold customs in autumn, summer or winter, and do not come to work when forewarned; and concerning land sold or disposed of, free or villein.

Surrender: Cecilia Pudding to Robert of Reydon and his heirs, ½r. and ¼r. of villein arable land lying in the field called Broomfield ['Bromefeld'], at the head of [the land of] John Terwald, granted to Robert to hold by the rod at the lord's will, fine 9d, pledge the hayward; he swore servile fealty.

The enquiry has a day to enquire concerning the [lord's] fold, and to certify by what right it is entered. They say that (?*non grav' n de Priore*).

Richard of the Wood pays 3d. fine for respite of his suit of court until Michaelmas, pledge the hayward.

Hugh Crane in mercy for default, condoned because infirm; John Lene the younger amerced 3d. for the same; John Wisdom condoned because infirm; John at the Green 6d.; Millicent Qualm condoned because infirm; Gilbert Helpe condoned; and Thomas Patel amerced 12d.; all for the same.

John Frlaunceys complains of Avice Deneys that she accused his wife of wearing her short jacket (*curtepia*) for a long time before (?*citra*) Easter this year, and that the damage to his reputation is assessed at 2s., and on this he produces suit. Avice defends and says that she is guilty of nothing, and asks for an enquiry to be held; and John asks likewise. The enquiry has a day until the next court.[31]

Walter the smith pays 5s. fine not to be in the office of reeve, pledge the hayward.

Nicholas Goche and John Noreys come into court and by mutual consent pay 3d. to the lord for leave to exchange 3p. of land, and it is granted to them, one and the other, to hold at the lord's will by services and customs etc.

SUM 34s. 11d.

---

[30] These two entries are bracketed together, and, against them, the word *quientur* – 'they are quit' – inserted. The name 'Helpe' has been illegibly overwritten.

[31] The earlier entry in this roll appears to have disposed of this matter.

117

## 46. WALSHAM Court held there, 24 January 1329 [HA504/1/3.8]

Peter Margery essoins of common suit, by John Noreys; he pledges faith.

Bartholomew Patel, [plaintiff] v Geoffrey of Burgate[32] in a plea of debt, essoins by Richard of Langham, and likewise, in a plea of trespass, by Walter of Higham ['Heigham']; they pledge faith \order below/.

Again as elsewhere ordered to attach John Tremp to reply to the lord concerning damage in the lord's wood with cows; and to attach Alice daughter of Robert Rede villein because she married without leave; and to attach Walter Machon the chapman, villein, because he absents himself, and for withholding 4d. in chevage, 1d. per year, for the past four years.[33]

Again as elsewhere ordered to retain in the lord's hands ¼r. of villein land and 1½r. of land which Gilbert Helpe held, for services and customs withheld and in arrears, and to report the profits.

The distraint taken on the Prior of Ixworth for overstocking the common with his sheep, and because he grazed them where he had no right, is in respite, pledges William of Cranmer and Stephen Cooper.[34]

Again as elsewhere ordered to attach John at the Green to reply to Thomas of the Beck in a plea of debt.

The summons on the Prior of Ixworth for overstocking the common, and grazing his sheep in the meadow called Southbrook, where he had no right, is in respite until the next court.

The summons touching Emma Stronde for nine autumn works and for 1 quarter of oats, to come to show why she claims to be quit of the tenement formerly of John Brytwyne, for the lifetime of John and Emma [was] in respite until the next court. Upon this, Emma comes and places herself before the enquiry, who say that the present lord released her and her husband, from all customs from the tenement of John Brytwyne, in return for 6s. which was allocated to the same in the account, but that they hold other tenements not covered by the relief, on which they owe 17d., and five autumn works and seven winter works.

Again as elsewhere ordered to attach Alice the daughter of Robert Rede to reply to the lord because she married without leave.

Ordered to retain in the lord's hands a messuage 4a. of free land, and 3r. of villeinage which Walter Typetot held from the lord, when he died, because John, the son and heir of the said Walter,[35] was under age, until he <marries at the lord's direction and> pays relief to the lord, and does as he ought etc. Afterwards, seisin of the land [is granted] to the heir, and the lord's leave to marry where he wishes, saving the relief on the free land.[36]

Ordered as elsewhere to distrain Geoffrey of Burgate to reply to Bartholomew Patel in pleas of debt and trespass; and to attach in the tenements which Geoffrey of Burgate holds, for homage to the lord; and for 8½d. rent withheld for his tenement called Scuttisfee; and for aid for the lord's first-born son to be knighted, and for the relief of William the son and heir of Thomas Auncel, following Thomas' death, for the tenement of which he died seised, of which Geoffrey is now the

---

32  MS: 'ordered below' inserted above 'Geoffrey'.
33  Margin: 'To enquire'.
34  Margin: 'To enquire'.
35  MS: 'Thomas' in error.
36  Margin: 'To enquire concerning heriot'.

tenant; and to reply to the lord concerning trespass against the lord and his bailiffs; and to reply to Nicholas Goche in a plea of discharge of a debt.

Again as elsewhere ordered to attach John at the Green for damage in Micklemeadow with his pigs.

Surrender: Emma Stronde to Ralph Echeman and his heirs, ½r.5p. of land, granted to him to hold at the lord's will by services and customs, fine 6d., pledge the hayward; he swore servile fealty.

Again as elsewhere ordered to attach Walter of the Marsh and Stephen of Allwood for two autumn reapales, carrying rods over the reapers,[37] on the day of the boonwork, and to raise from them 6d., for two reapings for the past year.[38]

Robert the cooper pays 3d. fine for respite of suit of court until Michaelmas, pledge the hayward.

The lord's swineherd in mercy for damage in the lord's rye with pigs \condoned/, and the lord's shepherd amerced 6d. for the same in the Meadow with sheep, on several occasions.

+An enquiry held by William Hawys, William of Cranmer the younger, Robert Spileman, William Springold, Robert Tailor, Simon Peyntour, Richard Kebbil, Walter Payn, Peter Springold, Peter the son of Robert, Walter Osbern and Robert of Reydon, jurors, who say that Peter Hulke, who recently died, held from the lord a messuage 10a. of land, wood, meadow and pasture of villeinage by services and customs, and he gives a heriot. At his death he held, in goods, a pig, worth 3s. and 2 calves, worth 4s.; and during his lifetime he sold his messuage 10a. of land etc. to William of Cranmer the elder, to hold to William and his heirs after Peter's death.

Cristina Patel gave birth outside wedlock, childwyte 32d., pledges John and Edmund Patel.

Walter Rampolye amerced 3d. because he sold 1½r. of land to Walter the smith without leave; ordered to take the land into the lord's hands until he shall receive it by fine etc.; afterwards he comes and pays 3d. fine for having the land out of the lord's possession.

Again as elsewhere ordered to attach John Herning for works withheld, for 2a. of land of the lord's fee, purchased from John and Robert Lene.

Surrender: Emma Stronde to Letitia her daughter and her heirs, 1a. of land lying and abutting on the wood of Sir Alexander de Walsham, and at the other head on the lord's land; granted to her to hold at the lord's will by services and customs, fine 2s.6d., pledge Stephen Cooper; she swore servile fealty.[39]

John Man was elected by the whole homage to the office of reeve, and he takes the oath.

Simon Rampolye pays 3d. fine for respite of suit of court until Michaelmas.

Surrender: Simon Deneys to Thomas Fuller and his heirs, ½r. of land in six pieces, granted to him to hold at the lord's will by services and customs, fine 8d.; he swore servile fealty.

Ordered to attach Simon Glisse of Ashfield for taking coppice wood away by night

---

[37] Mention of this service owed by these two tenants occurs before and again hereafter. See Glossary under 'rod'.

[38] Margin: 'To enquire'.

[39] Tab: 'Emma Stronde'.

from the lord's wood called Ladyswood, by the daughter of Walter Alleyn and Simon's son [John]; and to attach the wife of Peter Dilke for the same.

Surrenders: Beatrice of the Brook to Walter Osbern and his heirs, 1a. of land called Woodmansacre ['Wodemannysakir'] at the Brook, granted to him to hold at the lord's will by services and customs, fine 3s.; he swore servile fealty.

Avice the widow of Hugh Deneys to William Hawys and his heirs, ½r.7p. of land, of which 12p. lie in the garden called Terwald's yard, and 15p. lie in the field called Musewell, granted to him to hold in the same form, fine 6d., pledge the hayward; he swore servile fealty.

SUM 11s. 4d.

Memorandum:[40] [The enquiry] to scrutinise the rolls [to ascertain] whether William Kebbil, John Wyswyf and Peter Sawyer disposed of land before their deaths, and therefore do not owe heriots.

### 47. WALSHAM Court of Sir Edmund de Pakenham, 17 March 1329 [HA504/1/2.2]

John Margery essoins of common suit by Peter Margery, he pledges faith.

Again as elsewhere ordered to attach John Tremp to reply to the lord concerning damage in the lord's wood with cows \fine in the next court/, and +to attach Alice the daughter of Robert Rede villein because she married without leave; and to attach Walter Machon the chapman, villein, because he absents himself, and for withholding 4d. in chevage, 1d. per year for the past four years.

It was ordered at the last court to take into the lord's hands ¼r. of land of villeinage, which Gilbert Helpe held, for suit of court withheld; later he came into court and sought to recover the land; he was admitted at the instance of Nicholas de Walsham, and he pays 2d. for [respite of] suit of court from this day for one year, pledge the hayward.

+Again as elsewhere to attach John at the Green to reply to Thomas of the Beck in a plea of debt.

John the son of Walter Typetot, being of full age, and, by the lord's leave, marrying at will, came and swore fealty for a messuage 4a. of free land and 3r. of villeinage; he gives 5¾d. relief \for the free tenement/, pledges the hayward and John Man. Afterwards John Typetot, one of the heirs of the same Walter, pays 18d. fine, for himself and his brothers [Robert and Richard] to have entry [to the 3r. of villeinage], in the name of heriot, pledges Warren Brether, the hayward and Richard Qualm.[41]

John Herning amerced 3d. for services and customs withheld from 2a. of land which he holds, pledges the hayward and Walter Pye.

The shepherd of the manor amerced 2s. for damage in the lord's meadow with his sheep for six consecutive weeks after the [feast of] the Purification [2 February], and also 3s. for the same at the same time, entering the Newhawe and breaking the latch, pledges the reeve and the hayward.

---

[40] Inserted later, in margin.

[41] Again, the name of John's father is given as Thomas. Although John was mentioned as Walter's sole heir in the last court, he appears to have been sole heir to the free land, and co-heir with Robert and Richard to the villein land, which, in 1339, when the lord claims that no heriot was paid, was described as customary (no.102).

Peter Digge amerced 3d. for damage in the lord's wood cutting and taking away coppice wood, and William Fleg 3d. for the same, pledge for both William Springold.

Amice Hawys gives 13s.4d. to the lord for leave to marry John Terwald, pledge William Hawys.

Surrender: Robert Spileman to Peter Neve and his heirs, 1a.1r. of land, granted to him to hold at the lord's will by services and customs, fine 4s., pledges the hayward and Stephen Cooper; Peter swore servile fealty.

+Again as elsewhere ordered to distrain Geoffrey of Burgate to reply to Bartholomew Patel in pleas of debt and trespass; and to attach in the tenements which Geoffrey of Burgate holds, for homage to the lord; and for 8½d. rent withheld for his tenement called Scuttisfee; and for a share of the aid for the lord's first-born son to be knighted, and for the relief of William the son and heir of Thomas Auncel, following Thomas' death, for the tenement of which he died seised, of which Geoffrey is now the tenant; and to reply to the lord concerning trespass against the lord and his bailiffs; and to reply to Nicholas Goche in a plea of discharge of a debt.

+Again as elsewhere ordered to attach John at the Green to reply to the lord for damage in Micklemeadow with his pigs.

Again as elsewhere ordered to attach Walter of the Marsh and Stephen of Allwood for one autumn reapale, bearing rods in charge of the boonworkers reaping and binding the lord's corn, and to raise from them 3d. for the autumn reaping for the past year.

Ordered to attach John Glisse of Ashfield for taking away coppice wood from the lord's wood called Ladyswood, pledge William Springold.

Amice the daughter of Walter Hulke came into court and received her inheritance, and swore servile fealty.

Surrenders: Walter Goselyng to Peter Hawys and his heirs, 2r.32p. of arable land, granted to him to hold at the lord's will by services and customs, fine 18d., pledge the hayward; he swore servile fealty; also to Robert Hereward and his heirs, ½a. of arable land, granted to him in the same form, fine 20d., pledge Peter Hawys; he swore servile fealty.

An enquiry having been held, the jurors say that the Prior of Ixworth purchased from Alan of Gislingham the liberty of a fold containing 40 sheep and a ram, which feed as far as Southbrook towards Angerhale; also he purchased from Adam the shepherd, with 1a. of land, another liberty of fold containing 30 sheep and a ram, which feed in the fields towards Rickinghall; also he purchased from Hugh the clerk, with 2r. of land, another liberty of fold containing 40 sheep and a ram, which feed in the fields called Ashfield as far as Staple way,[42] and the Prior also had, from time out of mind, the hay every year from 1 measured rood, 3p. wide, of meadow in the Littlemeadow.

They present that a cottage, formerly of Hilary Cook, fell down on account of old age, and there is no loss to the lord from vacating it, therefore granted, without fine.

Hilary the widow of William Cook pays 12d. for leave for 60 sheep to lie in the fold on her own land, pledge the hayward.

---

[42] These details of the prior's grazing rights are those being sought by reference to the court of roll of 5 Dec. 1313; see roll no.39 and several subsequent courts.

The shepherd of the manor amerced 12d. for damage with his sheep, in the wood at Northawe, and diverting the ditches there.

Cecilia Herning amerced 6d. for damage, removing parts of the lord's hedge at Damyerd, pledge William of Cranmer.

+The present reeve, hayward and woodward amerced 2d. because they cut down two poplars and a willow, and sold them secretly (?*sine visum*).

Alice Hereward gave birth outside wedlock, childwyte 32d., pledge Robert of Reydon; Cecilia Puddyng 32d. for the same, pledge the hayward.

Margaret Spileman in mercy because she married without leave, condoned by the lady.

The jurors say that the tenement Margery withheld two ploughing services for six years, valued at 15d., because [the tenants] had only three horses for that time, which comprised half a ploughteam; the tenants are amerced 3d., and 15d. is to be raised for the six ploughing works withheld.

+The jurors have a day until the next court to certify concerning a heriot following the death of Peter Hulke, who sold all his tenements and lands to William of Cranmer before his death.

William Robhood pays 12d. fine for leave to sell by charter 1a. of free land in Ashfield, pledges the hayward and Hilary, the widow of William Cook.

William, Peter, Ralph, Nicholas and John Hawys chaplain, sons and heirs of William Hawys, were summoned to this court to receive their inheritance, because they are of full age. Nicholas and John say in open court that they claim nothing from the lord of the inheritance; William, Peter and Ralph seek to be admitted, and seisin is delivered to them. A division is made \between them/, and William says that he will take as his share a toft called the Eastyard ['Estyerd'] 10a.3r. of arable land, of which 3a. lie at the Eastyard, 4a. at Thediscroft, 1½a. at Middlewent, 1a.1r. at Musewell, ½a. at Marledhalfacre, and ½a. at Bluntishawe, and ½a. of meadow in the Micklemeadow. He concedes the remainder to Peter and Ralph. Upon this Ralph grants all his right and claim in the inheritance to Peter, who will pay to him annually therefor, for his lifetime, 1 quarter of wheat, 1 quarter of barley and 1 quarter of beans and peas at Michaelmas and Easter, in equal parts. If Peter shall default in this payment for a month or more after one of these feasts in any future year, then it shall be allowed to Ralph to repossess his portion of the inheritance; if Peter pays the rent at the said terms, Ralph grants to him and his heirs that his portion shall remain to them. The lord granted that Peter should hold the said tenement in the above form by services and customs, fine 6s.8d., pledge the hayward; they [Peter and William] swore servile fealty.

Surrenders: John and Walter, the sons of William Clevehog, to John Man and his heirs, 1a. of land, granted to him to hold at the lord's will by services and customs, fine 18d., pledge the hayward; John swore servile fealty.

Matilda and Cecilia Puddyng, 1a. of land, and Cecilia, ½r., to Robert of Reydon and his heirs, granted to him in the same form, fine 40d., pledge the hayward; Robert swore servile fealty.

Nicholas Kembald and Alice his wife to Walter Reve and his heirs, ½r. of land, granted to them in the same form, fine 6d., pledge the hayward; Walter swore servile fealty.

Memorandum concerning nine mares and foals grazing in the wood at Northawe, from the feast of the Purification until this day, at 3d. per head, \not included in the sum of this court/.

Nicholas Goche, Adam Margery and Peter Margery each amerced 6d. for damage breaching the lord's ditches at Littlemeadow and in the common way there, by them and their servants; John Noreys to be attached for the same, \acquitted by the jury/, pledges Nicholas Goche and the hayward; the servant of Simon Peyntour amerced 6d. for the same, and the jurors have a day to enquire about other wrongdoers there by the next court.

Nicholas Fraunceys pays 3d. fine for respite of suit of court until Michaelmas.

SUM 53s. ¾d., except the grazing of the foals and mares

## 48. WALSHAM Court General, 8 June 1329 [HA504/1/3.9.i]

Robert Tailor amerced 3d. for damage in the lord's corn by his wife gathering herbage, pledge Nicholas Kembald; William the Miller 2d. for the same, pledge Peter Springold, and Ralph Neve, John Lene, Stephen Cooper and Robert Man each amerced 3d. for the same, pledge for all the hayward.

Peter Neve amerced 6d. for trespass in the lord's garden, pledge Nicholas Kembald.

John Glisse of Ashfield amerced 3d. for damage in the lord's wood called Ladyswood, taking away coppice wood, pledge William Springold.

Henry Draper and his first pledges amerced 3d. because they did not have him reply to William Hawys in a plea of debt, ordered to appoint better pledges.

William Godyene[43] amerced 3d. for trespass in the lord's herbage, pledges Adam Fraunceys and William Springold.

Surrenders: Robert of Fornham to William Payn and his heirs, 3r. of land, granted to him to hold in villeinage by services and customs, fine 2s.3d., pledges William Hawys and the hayward; William swore servile fealty; and to Walter Payn and his heirs ½a. of land, granted to him in the same form, fine 18d., pledge William Payn; Walter swore fealty.

Robert Swift and Agatha his wife to Thomas Dormour and his heirs, 1a.1r. of land and 20p. of meadow, granted to him to hold in bondage by services and customs, fine 40d., pledge William of Cranmer; he swore servile fealty.

John Lene amerced 3d. for damage in the Syke next to the Littlemeadow with his sheep, pledge Walter Pye, and Robert Lene amerced 3d. for the same, pledge William of Cranmer.

On or about the feast of St John before the Latin Gate, 2 Edw.III [6 May 1328], at Walsham church John Reve surrendered into the lord's hands, through the hands of the hayward, ½r. of land, to the use of Thomas Fuller and his heirs, who now seeks to be admitted; granted to him to hold in bondage by services and customs, fine 5d., pledge the hayward; Thomas swore servile fealty.[44]

Surrenders: Robert of Fornham to William Hawys and his heirs, 1r. of land, granted to him to hold in villeinage at the lord's will by services and customs, fine 6d., pledge the hayward.

Walter Goselyng to Peter Hawys and Agnes his wife and Peter's heirs, ½a. of land, granted to them in the same form, fine 18d.; William Miller to Peter and Agnes and Peter's heirs, 1r.12p. of land, granted to them to hold in the same form, fine 12d., pledge for both fines William Hawys, they swore servile fealty.

---

43 The 'y' is not clear, and may be a 'z' or a *yogh*.
44 Tab: 'John le Reve'.

General enquiry by William Hawys, William of Cranmer the younger, Robert Spileman, William Springold, Robert Tailor, Simon Peyntour, Richard Kebbil, Walter Payn, Peter Springold, Peter the son of Robert, Walter Osbern and Robert of Reydon, jurors, who say that Walter the son of Letitia, when he died, held from the lord a messuage 7a. of land, meadow and pasture by services and customs; there is no heriot because Walter had no beast. Richard his son and nearest heir is of full age, and he pays 6s.[45] fine for entry, pledges Simon Peyntour and Richard of Wortham.

John Tremp was attached by 2 cows brought into the lord's pound by William Springold, and for this attachment the reeve and the hayward are answerable; John is amerced 3d. for damage in the lord's wood with his cows, pledge the reeve and the hayward.

Robert Man amerced 6d. for damage in the Micklemeadow with his sheep, and Robert Shepherd 3d. for the same in Northrow, pledge for both the hayward; Geoffrey de Lenne 3d. for damage in the lord's herbage by his servant, pledge William Hawys.

Eleanor Osbern amerced 6d. \because poor/ because she gave birth out of wedlock, pledge Walter Osbern because in [his] house.

Geoffrey of Lenne amerced 3d. for damage in the lord's herbage by his servant, pledge William Hawys.

They present that Bartholomew de Elmham took a hare within the lord's warren; therefore ordered to attach him to reply; afterwards he came, and demanded a second enquiry; the jurors [now] say that the hare was taken in Ashfield, and he is acquitted.

The wife of Walter Pye amerced 6d. because she brewed and sold ale in breach of the assize; the wife of Walter Man 12d. for the same, pledge William of Cranmer; the wife of Walter Osbern \condoned/; Walter Rampolye 6d.; Hilary, the widow of William Lene \condoned/; and Gilbert Priour 6d. for the same; Gilbert Priour amerced 6d. because he baked and sold bread in breach of the assize.

Ralph Echeman ale-taster amerced 3d. because he did not perform his duties, and Nicholas Fraunceys, the other ale-taster, in mercy for the same, condoned.

John Margery in mercy for default, condoned because infirm.

The jurors have a day until the next court to certify concerning a heriot following the death of Peter Hulke, who, before his death, sold all his tenements and lands to William of Cranmer; and concerning the tenement of John Noreys which he holds of the lord's fee, how big it is, and the services and customs by which it is held.

Ordered to raise 4s. from Juliana the widow of Adam Suter, to the use of Robert Osbern, which he was to recover in the preceding court, as the debt of Adam her husband, and to attach in Juliana's tenement for the debt.

William Springold complains against Robert Lene, John Lene and Walter Hereward in three separate pleas of trespass, ordered to attach Robert, John and Walter to reply.

Surrender: Alice Warde to Nicholas Goche and his heirs, 1¼r. of wood, granted to him to hold in bondage by services and customs, fine 10d., Nicholas swore servile fealty, pledge [*blank*].

---

[45] The fine was recorded as '6s.8d.', amended by deletion of '8d.'.

The jurors have a day to certify concerning 1¼d. arrears of annual rent, withheld from the tenement of John Terwald, to the use of John Man, for a certain tenement etc.; and to attach Robert Lene because he impounded (?*imparcavit*) pigs outside the lord's pound, in prejudice to the lord.

Surrender: Alice Warde to John Warde and his heirs, 1r. of land, granted to him to hold in bondage by services and customs, fine 10d.; he swore servile fealty.

William Clevehog pays 12d. fine to have 60 sheep lying in a fold on his land until Michaelmas, pledge William of Cranmer.

Surrender: William Warde to William Springold and Isabella and their heirs, ½ old acre[46] of land, granted to them to hold in bondage by services and customs, fine 12d.; they swore servile fealty.

A day was given, at the request of the parties, to Warren Bret, plaintiff, and William Clevehog, defendant, in a plea of trespass, to come to the next court without essoin.

Robert Spileman amerced 3d. for unlawful detention from Emma Stronde of services and customs from a certain tenement.

Ordered to attach Matilda the widow of William Coppelowe, to satisfy Hilary William's daughter [concerning] goods and chattels bequeathed to Hilary by William, which are in Matilda's keeping.

John Albry, Geoffrey of Lenne and John Warde in mercy because they regrated bread, selling it in breach of the assize, condoned.

The wives of Walter Pye and Walter Man each amerced 3d., because they did not send for the ale-tasters, and sold [ale] in measures not marked by seal, the wife of Walter Osbern in mercy for the same, condoned, Walter Rampolye amerced 3d., Hilary Cook condoned and Gilbert Priour amerced 3d. for the same.

Ordered to execute all the old orders marked by a cross in [the roll of] the last court.

Exchange: Stephen Cooper and Alice his wife surrendered to Gilbert Priour and his heirs, a messuage containing 21p., which they held at the lord's will by services and customs and rent of ¾d.; in exchange for 5r.3p. of land, which Gilbert held at the lord's will by services and customs; granted to them to hold to them and their heirs in bondage in the same form, fine 3s.4d.; they swore servile fealty.

John Typetot and Cecilia, his wife, in open court surrendered all their right and claim in a messuage containing 15p. to the use of Elias Typetot. And Matilda Puddyng surrendered all her right in the same messuage to Elias and his heirs to hold at the lord's will by the rod, by services and customs; seisin is delivered to him, fine 12d.; Elias swore servile fealty.[47]

SUM 32s. 11d.

Affeerers: William Springold and John Man

## 49. HIGH HALL Court of Nicholas de Walsham, 14 June 1329 [HA504/1/3.10]

Walter Osbern essoins of common suit by William Deneys, he pledges faith.

William the smith amerced six fowls for trespass in the lord's corn, pledge John Syre.

---

46 See Glossary, under 'Old acre'.

47 The first of these two transactions appears to be a quitclaim, and the second a land transfer. Normally, the former would precede the latter. Matilda and Cecilia were sisters.

Ordered to distrain Robert of the Peartree for 16 years of arrears of 2d. annual rent from 2a. of land of his tenement.

Bartholomew Dolhale amerced 12d. because he intervened through the jury against Agnes Fitte in a plea of trespass, the loss assessed at ½d., ordered to raise, pledges Gilbert Helpe and Walter of the Marsh.

The whole homage amerced 12d. because they did not distrain Robert of the Peartree, and allowed him to plough and sow the said tenement.

Nicholas Kembald came and took from the lord all the land which his brother William held in villeinage, to hold by the rod at the lord's will by services etc., fine six fowls, pledge Gilbert Helpe.

William Kembald chaplain pays 12d. fine to have entry to 1a. of land, taken from John Wodebite, paying ½d. increased rent at Easter.

William of Cranmer, Robert Kembald and Robert Sare amerced 6s.8d. because they did not return \at this court/ the distraint taken on Walter Osbern, viz. 36 sheep, as they undertook.

Olivia Isabel gives six fowls as fine for leave to scrutinise [the rolls for] the demise of ½a. of customary land to Walter of the Marsh, pledge Gilbert Helpe.

John Wodebite villein, when he died, held from the lord, 2½ messuages and 23a. of land by services etc., John, his son and nearest heir, is aged 8 years; afterwards [Matilda] John's widow came and paid 6s.8d. fine for custody of the land until the legal age of the heir, rendering services and customs etc., pledge [blank].

William Wodebite amerced 6d. for trespass in the lord's meadows, Matilda Wodebite 3d. for the same.

The whole homage have a duty to distrain in the lord's meadow and in the field at Hordeshawe for the unlawful sowing there by various people of the neighbourhood, and to reply concerning the damage.

Ordered to attach Walter Osbern to reply to and satisfy the lord for damage in the lord's herbage at Hordeshawe and for trespass in the lord's wood at Lenerethsdel with his sheep, and for damage in the lord's herbage in 3a. at Boteshagh with beasts.

Cecilia Kembald amerced 3d. for default.

Ordered to take into the lord's hands all the land which William Kembald chaplain holds from the lord in villeinage, because he absents himself from the lord, and to report the profits.

Gilbert Helpe amerced 4d. because he intervened through the jury against William Hawys in a plea of detention of 1½ bushels of barley, the loss assessed at 1d., and 4d. for the same in a plea of trespass, loss 1½d., and 4d. for the same in a plea of trespass, loss 6d.; ordered to raise.

SUM 18s. 4d., except 18 fowls and ½d. increased rent

### 50. WALSHAM Court, 28 July 1329 [HA504/1/3.9.ii]

Walter the cooper, plaintiff v Robert Martin in a plea of trespass, essoins by John Typetot, he pledges faith; Robert is present.

Walter Rampolye and William Wither, the second pledges of Henry Draper, amerced 6d. because they did not have him reply to William Hawys in a plea of debt; ordered to appoint better pledges.

Warren Brether amerced 2d. for leave to agree with William Clevehog in a plea of trespass, pledge the hayward.

Ordered to take into the lord's hands all the tenement \in Pakenham/ which John Marsil enfeoffed to Alice the wife of Walter the smith villein, and to report the profits.

Roger the baker (*pistor*) of St Edmunds, and his pledges, amerced 12d. because he did not proceed against Roger the carter in a plea of debt; Walter Little (*parvus*) of St Edmunds, and his pledges amerced 12d. for the same in a like plea; the defendant [is quit] indefinitely.

Robert Osbern the tanner amerced 2d. for default.

Robert Lee amerced 3d. for leave to agree with William Springold in a plea of trespass, and for contempt of the lord, pledges the reeve and the hayward.

Edmund Lene amerced 3d. for trespass against William Springold, the loss assessed at 6d.; ordered to raise, pledges the hayward and John Lene.

Surrender: Robert Godefrey to William Rampolye and his heirs, 3r. of land, granted to him to hold in villeinage at the lord's will by services and customs, fine 2s.6d., pledge the hayward; William swore servile fealty.

William Springold amerced 3d. for a false claim against Walter Hereward in a plea of trespass, and 3d. for the same against John Lene in a similar plea.

Agnes at the Green pays 3d. fine for having an enquiry concerning damage in her pasture, pledge William Springold.

Surrenders: Walter Peyntour to Alice Typetot and her heirs, 1r. of land lying below the Brook, granted to her to hold in the same form as above, fine 10d., pledge the reeve; she swore servile fealty.

Walter Rampolye to William Rampolye and his heirs, a piece of land containing ¾r., granted to William to him in the same form, fine 6d., pledge the hayward; he swore servile fealty.

Robert Godefrey to Walter the smith and Alice his wife and Walter's heirs, a portion of two messuages which contain in all 1½r., with houses built on them, and also 2a. of land lying separately in divers places; granted to them to hold in villeinage by services and customs, fine 6s., pledge the reeve; they swore servile fealty.

Robert Godefrey in court appoints Walter the smith and William Rampolye as his pledges to come to court annually at Michaelmas to pay 1d. per year chevage, for his whole lifetime.

Peter Neve amerced 4d. for damage in the Churchcroft and in the lord's wheat, assessed at 1 bushel of wheat and ½ bushel of rye, pledge the reeve.

Surrender: Robert of Fornham to Walter Payn and his heirs, 1r. of land lying in the croft, granted to him to hold in villeinage at the lord's will by services and customs, fine 10d., pledge the reeve; he swore servile fealty.

The lord's cowherd amerced 3d., Peter Tailor 2d. and the lord's shepherd 2d. for damage in the lord's corn in Churchcroft and below the Hall, pledges the the hayward and the reeve.

Peter Tailor, Peter Neve and Robert Man each amerced 6d., and the keeper of the lord's calves 3d., for damage in the lord's peas, loss 1 quarter of peas. Nicholas Goche amerced 2d. for damage in the oats at the Stubbing, pledge the hayward; Matthew Terewald 2d. for the same in the barley below the manor, Robert Man 2d. for the same below Northawe, the dairymaid 9d. for the same, below the manor with geese; and the keeper of the plough beasts in mercy for the same opposite the Church gate, condoned.

Ordered to attach Alexander de Walsham for damage by his servants, John Pach and Adam Trounce, in the barley opposite the Church gate.

The lord's cowherd amerced 2d. and Massilia Hawys 3d. for damage in the barley next to the Meadow, and Robert Lene 1d. and John Lene 1d. for the same at Ayleldestoft.

Ordered to attach the Prior of Ixworth for damage in the wood at Oldtoft ['Oldetuft'] and in the cow-pasture with cows; Robert Spileman amerced 2d. for the same, at Oldtoft, pledge the hayward; likewise Matthew Terewald 1d. at Ayleldestoft, Robert Lene 1d. and John Lene 1d., at Millmount ['Mellemunt'], and Nicholas Goche 3d. at Howistuft.

Matilda Coppelowe amerced 3d. for unlawful detention of a cow, worth 5s., 2 piglets, worth 8d., 4 bushels of wheat, worth 5s., 4 bushels of oats, worth 2s., 1 tub, worth 3d., 1 brass bowl containing 1½ gallons, worth 7d., and 2 hens from Hilary, the daughter of William Coppelowe, who bequeathed the goods to her, the loss assessed at 2d.; ordered to raise. Memorandum that the goods together with Hilary were delivered to Walter Osbern for custody, because he is her blood relation; he is to answer to her [for the goods] when she comes to full age.

Ordered to execute all the old orders marked with a cross in the [roll of the] court of 17 March 1329 [no.47].

Surrender: Nicholas Kembald and Alice his wife, in full agreement, to Thomas Fuller and his heirs, 1r. of land in several pieces, granted to him in the same form as above, fine 10d.; he swore servile fealty.

William Robhood pays 6d. fine [*sic*].

Surrender: Walter Payn \the younger/ to William Hawys and his heirs, ½a. of land at Butteshawe, granted to him in the same form as above, fine 18d.; he swore servile fealty.

John Lene amerced 1d. for damage in the cow-pasture with his cows, pledge the reeve; Robert Lene 1d. and Robert Man 1d., for the same.

The keeper of the oxen amerced 3d. for damage in the lord's wheat with the oxen, and Richard Reve 3d. for the same opposite the Church gate, pledge William of Cranmer the younger.

The jurors say that Robert Spileman \villein/, when he died, held from the lord 9a. of land, 3r. of meadow and 1r. of wood; and that, of this, the heir to 2a.1½r. of land and 1½r. of meadow is not known to anyone (?*de caus'*). They have a day to enquire by the next court. They say that the heir to [the remaining] 1½r. of meadow, 1r. of wood and 6a. 2½r. of land is John the son of Stephen Man aged 14½ years; and that the heriot after Robert's death was a mare, worth 8s.6d.

William Springold amerced 6d. for damage to the lord deceiving him in choosing the said heriot.

+Again, the lord to be consulted whether villeins, who have beasts and other animals in the lord's demesne and hold no land, owe relief or not, because Peter Hulke and others were in this situation.

The jurors have a day until the next court to certify concerning 1¼d. arrears of annual rent, withheld from the tenement Terewald, to the use of John Man, for certain tenements, and to certify which tenements they are.

Walter the smith received from the lord a smithy and a cottage situated next to it in front of the gate, formerly of Robert Tailor, to hold for his lifetime without waste, on condition that he keeps the house roofed, ridged, plastered, carpentered and timbered as shall be necessary, for 2s. annual rent, to be paid at the usual terms;

and next Michaelmas, the lord will give to Walter timber, worth 12d., and a cart-load of straw, worth 6d., fine 6d., pledge the hayward.

Manser of Shucford amerced 3d. for leave to agree with Robert Godefrey in a plea of debt, pledge William Hawys.

William Robhood amerced 2d. because he sold 1a. of land to William Springold without leave; ordered to take into the lord's hands, and to report the profits.

Surrenders: John Terwald and Amice his wife to William Hawys and his heirs, ½r. of meadow, and to Peter Hawys and Agnes his wife and their heirs, another ½r. of meadow, granted to them in the same form as above, fine 6d. each; they swore servile fealty.

Matilda Puddyng to Matthew Hereward and his heirs, ¾r. of meadow lying in Risbymeadow ['Rysebymedwe'], granted to him in the same form, pledge the hayward; Matthew swore servile fealty.

SUM 26s. 6d.

### 51. HIGH HALL Court of Nicholas de Walsham, 4 December 1329 [HA504/1/3.11]

Walter Osbern amerced 3d. because he was essoined at the last court, and he does not come to warrant his essoin

Ordered to distrain Robert of the Peartree for arrears of 2d. annual rent from 2a. of land of the lord's fee for the past 16 years.

The whole homage amerced 6d. because they did not <enquire> distrain nor present concerning trespass in the meadows and fields at Hordeshawe, and unlawful sowing there by various local inhabitants (*patriensibus*).

William Wodebite in mercy for trespass in the Lord's meadows with his cart, condoned.

Ordered to take into the lord's hands all the land which William Kembald holds in villeinage, because he absents himself from the lord, and to report the profits.

Hilary Kembald in mercy for default, condoned; Alice Kembald and John of Anger-hale each amerced 3d. and Catherine Gothelard 2d. for the same.

Oliver the shepherd amerced 3d. for unlawful detention from Walter Petipas of 2 bushels of wheat and 2 bushels of barley, worth 12d.; ordered to raise to [Walter's] use etc., payment to be made at Michaelmas without delay, pledges William and Nicholas Kembald.

John Goche and Matilda Wodebite ordered to repair a ditch at Angerhale next to Highwood ['Heywod'], by the next court, under penalty of 12d.

Ordered to be raised from Gilbert Helpe 48s.9¼d. arrears from the last account, at the time when he stood as hayward, to the use of John Wodebite, so that he can discharge his account for the time when he stood as reeve.

+William Wodebite amerced 1d. for damage in the lord's wheat at Hordeshawe, to the value of 1 sheaf; Walter Osbern, John Packard, Matilda Wodebite, John Albry, John Goche and Gilbert Helpe each amerced 1d. for the same.

Ordered to attach Simon Rampolye to reply to the lord for damage with beasts in the lord's wheat at Hamstale; and John Syre and Simon Cooper for damage in the lord's dredge at Doucedeux.

John Goche amerced 3d. for damage in the lord's wheat, with the lord's oxen.

Ordered to attach the servant of Alexander de Walsham for damage in the lord's wheat below the wood with oxen and stots; and William Hawys to reply for

129

damage with beasts in the Lord's oats, to the value of 1 bushel; and the servant of the Prior of Ixworth for damage in the lord's wheat, to the value of 2 sheaves, at the shepherd's house, and for a further 2 sheaves there.

William Wodebite amerced 3d. for trespass against Matilda Wodebite; and 1d. for waste in the messuage called Grennard, ordered to make good; and 1d. for unlawful detention of 7d. from Peter Priour, ordered to raise to Peter's use.

John and Alice Goche amerced 2d. for waste in the lord's bondage, ordered to make good the said messuage [sic].

Surrender: William Wodebite to John Packard and his heirs, all the tenement formerly of Richard Blobbe, granted to him to hold by services and customs, fine 2s.

Matilda Wodebite has a day until the next court to repay without delay 5s.7½d. for 4½ bushels of wheat borrowed from William Hawys.

William Wodebite was elected by the whole homage to the office of reeve.

Oliver the shepherd has a day until the next court to pay without delay for 4 bushels of barley, worth 3s., and 4 bushels of oats, worth [blank], borrowed from William Hawys; and he is to be attached for damage in the lord's wheat in the street.

Memorandum that because the steward travelled 3 times to take the account, and the reeve had been summoned to have the clerk render it, it was ordered to have the clerk at the next court, under penalty of 20s.

SUM 5s. 1d.

Richard Banlone complains against Adam Dolhale in a plea of debt, his pledges are Richard the shepherd and the bailiff; ordered that Adam be attached by William Wodebite and the bailiff.

Matilda Wodebite complains against Ralph Wybert in a plea of detention of goods, her pledge is the bailiff.

The pledges of John Cayly and Alice his wife, plaintiffs v Matilda Kembald in a plea of detention of chattels, [are] William Wodebite and the bailiff.

The pledges of Walter Petipas, plaintiff, concerning whom the lord (?*respondebit*) v Ralph Wybert in a plea of debt.[48]


## 52.   WALSHAM Court, 11 December 1329 [HA504/1/3.12]

Again as elsewhere ordered to distrain Geoffrey of Burgate to reply to Bartholomew Patel in pleas of debt and trespass; and to distrain John Tremp to reply to the lord, concerning trespass in the lord's wood with his cows; and to attach Alice the daughter of Robert Rede villein, because she married without the lord's leave; and to distrain in the tenements, which Geoffrey of Burgate holds, for homage and fealty to the lord, and for 8½d. rent withheld for the lord's tenement of Scuttisfee, and for aid for the lord's first-born son to be knighted, and for the relief of William the son and heir of Thomas Auncel, following Thomas' death, for the tenement of which Thomas died seised, and of which Geoffrey is now the tenant; and concerning trespass against the lord and his bailiffs etc.; and to attach Walter Machon the chapman, because he absents himself from the lord's fee, and for 1d. per year chevage for the past four years; and to attach Geoffrey of Burgate to reply to Nicholas Goche in a plea of discharge of a debt.

Again as elsewhere ordered to retain in the lord's hands ¼r. of land of villeinage and

---

48 This order of words is that of the original.

a ditch, and to attach in 1½r. of free land which Gilbert Helpe held, for customs and services withheld [and] in arrears, and to report the profits.

The distraint taken on the Prior of Ixworth for overstocking the lord's common with his sheep, and because he grazed them where he had no right of common, [is] in respite until the next court, pledges William of Cranmer and Stephen Cooper.

Again, as elsewhere, ordered to attach John at the Green to reply to Thomas of the Beck in a plea of debt.

The Prior of Ixworth amerced 3d. for damage with his beasts at Currescroft, and 3d. for the same with sheep at Allwood, pledges the hayward.

Robert the chaplain amerced 3d. for withholding four autumn works, worth 8d., remitted by the lady; ordered to raise the said four works.

The summons on Emma Stronde for nine autumn works and for 1 quarter of oats, to come to show the charter by which she claims to be quit, is in respite until the next court, pledges Nicholas Goche and Peter Hawys.[49]

The summons on the Prior of Ixworth to come to the next court for overstocking the lord's common, in that he grazed his sheep in Southbrook field where he had no right,[50] is in respite, pledge the hayward.

Richard the son of Stephen Reve and Walter Reve each amerced 3d. for damage in the lord's corn with a cow; Stephen Cooper, Walter Pye and Peter Tailor each amerced 3d. for the same at Northawe in the Launde, pledge for all the hayward.

Robert the farmer (*le fermer*) amerced 6d. for damage in the lord's wood with his cows, pledge Nicholas Kembald; Robert of Reydon 3d. for the same in Launde, William Springold 3d., Peter Springold 3d., Robert Spileman 4d., William Cook 6d. and Nicholas Kembald 3d., for the same in the same place with pigs, pledge for all the hayward.

+William Kembald was summoned to reply to Robert Spileman and Alice his wife in a plea of debt, and they say that on Saturday after the feast of the Nativity of St John the Baptist, 1 Edw.III [27 June 1327], William and Alice, while she was single, made a reckoning of various debts and contracts between them, and on this reckoning William remained in debt to Alice for 1 bushel of wheat, worth 10d., and 14d. for ale bought from Alice, 3s. for 1 iron chain and a bowl, 3s. for 2 casks and a vat, and 6d. for a sieve, to be paid on the coming Saturday, or within 8 days. On this day, Alice sought payment in full, which William withheld, and still withholds, to her loss of ½ mark, and upon this she produces suit. William could not deny the said debt; and it is adjudged that Robert and Alice shall recover the debt and the damages, William amerced 6d. for unlawful detention, pledge Nicholas Kembald.

Surrenders: Walter Goselyng to Robert Tailor and his heirs, 2a. of land in the field called Calfthweyt, granted to him to hold at the lord's will by services and customs, fine ½ mark, pledge the hayward; he swore servile fealty.

Robert Kembald to Hilary his daughter and her heirs, 1r. of land, granted to her to hold in the same form, fine 12d., pledge John Man; she swore servile fealty.

Robert of Fornham to William Payn and his heirs, 26p. of land, granted to William to hold in the same form, fine 9d., pledge the hayward; he swore servile fealty.

Richard Warde to William Springold and Isabella his wife, ½a. of land, granted to

---

[49] The order of wording has been amended to achieve clarity. Margin: '<Reply>, condoned'.
[50] Margin: '<Reply>, condoned'.

them to hold in the same form, fine 18d., pledge the hayward; they swore servile fealty.

Nicholas Goche to Robert the chaplain, ½a. of land, granted to him to hold in the same form, fine 12d., pledge the reeve; he swore servile fealty.

Robert Shepherd chaplain to Nicholas Goche, 3r. of land lying at the Longlonde, granted to him to hold in the same form, fine 12d., pledge the hayward; he swore servile fealty.

Robert the chaplain to Richard the son of Stephen Reve, ½a. of land which he lately purchased from Nicholas Goche, granted to him to hold in the same form, fine 12d., pledge the hayward; Richard swore servile fealty.

The enquiry sworn at the last court, as shown there by their names, had a day to present several defaults pertaining to the manor.

+They say that William Lene villein, who recently died, held from the lord a messuage, \and a cottage/ and 37a. of arable land, 1a.2r. of meadow, and 1a.2r. of wood, as is shown in the particulars of the rental. His sons, William, aged 10, and Robert, aged 6, are his nearest heirs; and he gives an ox, worth 13s.4d., as a heriot. They say that Hilary William's wife should have in dower half the messuage, cottage, land, meadow and wood; and she comes and asks for custody of the heirs and their lands and chattels until their full age, she being answerable to the lord and to them, when they come of age, for the income from the land and chattels over and above the maintenance and repair of the buildings and land; and she pays 40s.[51] fine for entry and custody, pledges for the fine and custody Nicholas Goche, John Syre and Matthew Hereward.

Peter Neve amerced 3d. for damage in the lord's severalty with his beasts, pledge the hayward.

Matilda Coppelowe, Richard Qualm and Nicholas Kembald each amerced 4d., because they did not clean out the ditch where the water course turns above the demesne, pledge the hayward.

Again as elsewhere ordered to attach Alice the daughter of Robert Rede, because she married without leave.

A day is given to the enquiry until the next court to certify concerning a ditch next to the Great Meadow, which has not been cleaned out, and the meadow is so wet that the tenants cannot measure the tenements around the meadow there.

William Kembald the younger amerced 12d. for withholding a hen for the past two years, as found by the enquiry before which he put himself, pledges for the amercement as well as the hens, priced at 4d., Nicholas Kembald and the hayward. Ordered to raise the said hens or [their] value.

Again as elsewhere ordered to attach John at the Green to reply to the lord for damage in Micklemeadow with his pigs.

They say that William Hawys demolished without leave a house on the lord's bondage, worth 18d., and he comes and by paying a fine of the said 18d., asks that he should not rebuild on the site, pledge the reeve and the hayward; granted because nobody dares to live there because of thieves.

And that Simon Rampolye demolished without leave a house on the tenement Whitemans, worth 18d.; ordered to raise; he is amerced 12d. and no more, because he rebuilt the house elsewhere on the lord's villeinage.

---

[51] Shown in the margin as 30s.

+Walter of the Marsh and Stephen of Allwood withheld two autumn reapales, bearing rods over the reapers on the day of the boonwork; ordered to attach them to reply to the lord, and to raise from them the two reapings, priced at 6d..

John Fraunceys amerced 32d. for a false claim against Alice Deneys, as found by the enquiry, pledge Peter the son of Robert.

They say that Robert of Reydon and his wife are in debt to John Terwald ['Therewald'] for 20s., the profits on his land for the past 15 years, over and above his maintenance, and that they are now bound to satisfy him for a 16th year, and they find as pledge William Springold; John Terwald received his inheritance without a fine, as is the custom of the manor; and he swore servile fealty.

William the son of Walter Patel, in the custody of Walter the cooper and his wife for the past six years, is entitled to recover 2s. from the profits on his land from them. He received his inheritance without fine, as is the custom of the manor, because the lord had a heriot following the death of his father; he swore servile fealty. Likewise William and Nicholas Deneys, Walter Qualm, Agnes and Alice Typetot, and Agnes Goche received their inheritances without fine, following the custom of the manor, and swore servile fealty. It was adjudged that Agnes Goche should recover \from Simon Peyntour/ and her mother half of all the land sown at 1 August.

Ordered to attach John Robhood villein to receive his land, and to do to the lord that which he should. Afterwards he came and swore servile fealty.

John and Robert Crane swore servile fealty for their inheritance, received without fine as above.

Ordered to raise 2s. from Peter Jay to the use of Robert Warde, for the profits on his land while it was in Peter's custody; and upon this Peter shall surrender his lands well-sown in the autumn; Robert received his inheritance, and swore servile fealty.

+The jurors have a day until the next court to certify to the lord concerning various trespasses or damages, if there were any such.

The swineherd of the manor in mercy because the pigs rooted in the lord's orchard, condoned.

Surrenders: William the miller to Matthew Hereward ['Therewald'] and his heirs, 2r. of land, granted to him to hold in the same form as above, fine 18d., pledge the reeve; William swore servile fealty.

Juliana Deneys to William Hawys and his heirs, 3½r. of land in two pieces, one piece lying at Butteshawefield ['Buddishawefeld'], and the other in the headland called Bornscroft, granted to him to hold in the same form, fine 2s.9d., pledge the reeve; William swore servile fealty.

Ordered to attach John Herning for services and customs withheld for a certain tenement which he holds etc.; and John, the son of Walter Typetot, to swear fealty to the lord, to pay relief for a free tenement, and to show by what right he entered the lord's tenement without paying a fine.

+Memorandum: The Inventory of the goods of William Lene, on the day on which he died, *viz.* Saturday before the feast of All Saints [28 October 1329].

In his principal house: 3 brass pots containing 7½ gallons, price 11s.10½d.; 2 brass pans containing 10 gallons, pr. 6s.8d.; 1 posnet containing ½ gallon, pr. 12d.; 1 basin and ewer, pr. 21d.; 1 board with trestles and 3 forms and 1 chair, pr. 12d.

Item 2 oxen, pr. 30s.; 8 cows, pr. 53s.4d.; 1 bullock, pr. 6s.8d., 3 calves, pr. 4s.

Item 2 stots, pr. 16s.; 1 mare, pr. 5s.; 1 filly, pr. 20d.

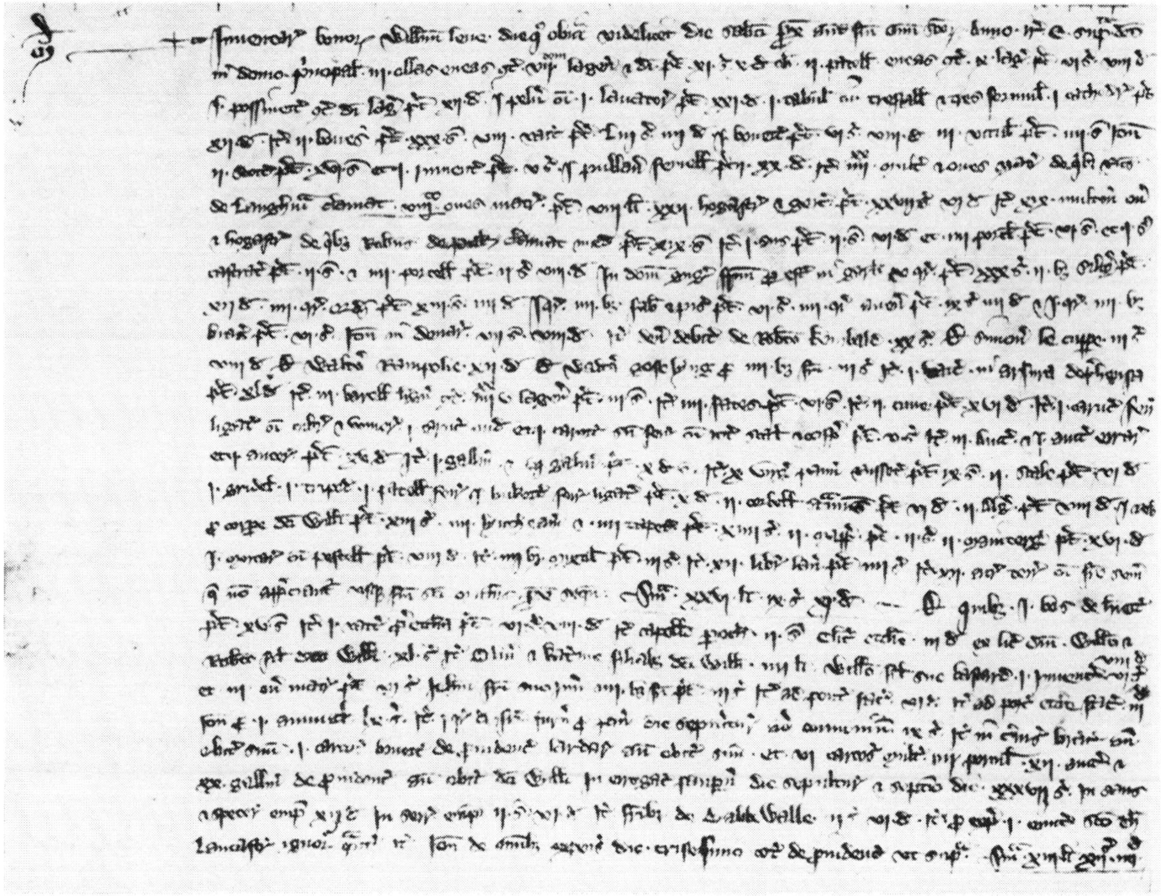

Plate 2. Inventory of the goods of William Lene, villein of Walsham manor, who died in 1329, and account of expenditure on his funeral etc. [Ref. SRO(b) HA504/1/3.12]. See pp. 133–135

Item 4 score wethers and ewes, of which Richard of Langham claims 8 ewes, pr. £8; 22 hoggets and gimmers, pr. 27s.6d.; 19 wethers and hoggets, of which Robert of Pakenham claims half, pr. 19s.

Item 1 sow, pr. 2s.6d.; 4 piglets, pr. 6s. and 1 castrated swine pr. 2s., 4 piglets, pr. 2s.8d.

In the granary house: Wheat in sheaves, by estimation 5 quarters, pr. 30s.; 2 bushels of rye, pr. 12d.; 4 quarters of barley, pr. 13s.4d.; 1 quarter 4 bushels of beans and peas, pr. 6s.; 4 quarters of oats, pr. 9s.4d.; and 1 quarter 4 bushels of malt, pr. 6s.

Item in money 7s.8d.; money owed from Robert Kembald 20s.; from Simon Cooper 3s.8d.; from Walter Rampolye 12d.; from Walter Goseling for 4 bushels of wheat, 3s.

Item 1 cow, trapped in the blaze, pr. 40d.[52]

Item 3 wooden barrels containing 85 gallons, pr. 3s.; 4 vats, pr. 6s.; 2 tubs, pr. 16d.

Item 1 plough bound with iron, with the coulter and the ploughshare, 1 unshod plough, 1 cart with unshod wheels,[53] ladder and cosp, pr. 5s.

Item 3 geese, 1 nesting goose and 2 ganders, pr. 15d.; 1 cockerel and 6 hens, pr. 10½d.

Item 10 yards of russet cloth, pr. 9s., 2 ladders, pr. 6d., 1 griddle, 1 tripod, 1 iron pan, 1 iron-bound bucket, pr. 10d.; 2 straw baskets, pr. 6d.; 2 troughs, pr. 8d.; 1 robe[54] for William's body, pr. 13s.; 4 linen sheets and 4 coverlets (*tapete*), pr. 14s.; 2 table-cloths (*mappe*), pr. 2s.; 2 towels, pr. 16d.; 1 mortar with pestle, pr. 8d.

Item 4 bushels of maslin, pr. 3s.

Item 12 lbs. of wool, pr. 4s.

Item 12a. of land sown with wheat, which will not be appraised until Michaelmas.

SUM £26 9s. 11d.

From which - 1 ox for a heriot, pr. 15s.; 1 cow for the church, pr. 6s.8d.; to the parish chaplain 2s.; to the clerk of the church 3d.; by the lord's leave, to William and Robert, William's sons, 40s.; to Olivia and Catherine, his daughters, £4.; to William, his bastard son, 1 mare, pr. 6s.8d. and 3 ewes, pr. 6s.; to John, his younger brother, 4 bushels of wheat, pr. 3s. To repairing the bridge 6d.; to repairing the church door 3d. For one annual[55] 60s. Item 1½ quarters of wheat for baking bread for the common feast on the day of burial, pr. 9s. Item in ale brewed before his obit,[56] 1 bullock carcase, to be provided from the meat-stock (*de providente lardare*) before his obit, and 6 carcases of wethers, 4 of piglets, 12 geese and 20 cockerels, to be provided [from the same] before his obit. In alms given to the poor on the day of his burial, and the 7th day 37s., in salt and spices bought 12d., in wax bought 2s.6d. Item to the Friars of Babwell 2s.6d. Item for the expenses of one going to [the shrine of] St Thomas of Lancaster, an unknown amount. Item for all the foreseeable expenses at the 30th day, as above. SUM £13 12s. 4d.

SUM [excluding the inventory and expenses] 57s. 7d.

---

[52] See Introduction under Walsham and the World Outside.

[53] Literally, 'without iron'.

[54] MS: *roba*, possibly 'shroud', but 13s. seems too high a value for a shroud.

[55] A mass said daily for one year after a person's death, or yearly on the anniversary thereof.

[56] A service in commemoration of, or on behalf of the soul of, a deceased person on the anniversary of his death.

**53.  HIGH HALL Court of Nicholas de Walsham, 7 May 1330 [HA504/1/3.13]**
Henry Trusse essoins of common suit by Walter of the Marsh; he pledges faith.

Thomas the shepherd, defendant v Walter of the Marsh plaintiff, in a plea of trespass, essoins by Robert Pynchon; he pledges faith; Walter is present, and has William Wodebite and the bailiff as pledges; pledges for Thomas John Goche and William Wodebite.

William Wodebite [in mercy] because he did not distrain Robert of the Peartree for the arrears of rent at 2d. per year for 16 years, from 2a. of land of the lord's fee. <Ordered as elsewhere to distrain in the said tenement for the said services>. Afterwards the said William is made liable for the said rent, as shown in the margin.[57]

<Ordered>[58] to retain in the lord's hands all the tenement which William Kembald held in bondage until etc.; the tenement contains 1½a., excluding the 1½a. which Matilda the wife of Oliver the shepherd holds in dower; and to report the profits, from which ½a. sown with small oats is excluded. Afterwards Nicholas Kembald received the 1½a., to hold at the lord's will, fine 2s., pledge William Wodebite.

John Goche amerced 2d. for default.

John Goche and Matilda Wodebite are ordered to complete digging and repairs at Angerhale next to Highwood, under penalty of 12d., if it is not fully completed on the 30th day from this court,.

Ordered to attach John Goche by his body, wherever he may be found in the lord's domain, because he refused to serve the lord, absenting himself from the lord and his service in contempt of the lord.

Oliver the shepherd has a day until Michaelmas to pay to Walter Petipas 2 bushels of wheat and 2 bushels of barley.

Memorandum - John Syre and Simon Cooper, John Goche, and William Hawys to satisfy the lord for damage in his dredge at Doucedeux.

Ordered to distrain Simon Rampolye to reply for damage in the lord's wheat with his beasts, afterwards he made satisfaction.

Ordered to take and retain in the lord's hands all the tenement which John Goche held in villeinage, which contains 2½a., and to report the profits.

Ordered to attach the servant of Sir Alexander de Walsham for damage in the lord's wheat below the wood.

The shepherd of the Prior of Ixworth pays 4d. fine to satisfy William Wodebite for damage, estimated at 4d.

<Ordered> to retain in the lord's hands all the tenement which William Wodebite holds in villeinage of the tenement Grennard, for waste made there, <and to report the profits>. +Afterwards William pays 40d. fine so that he should not be required to rebuild for his lifetime, and he has a day to pay until Michaelmas.

+Ordered to retain in the lord's hands all the tenement which Henry Goche and Alice his wife hold in dower, for waste made in it, and to report the profits. Henry amerced 2d. for several defaults.

Matilda Wodebite has a day until Michaelmas to pay 5s.7½d. to William Hawys for 4½ bushels of wheat, under penalty of 12d., to the use of the lord, pledge William Wodebite.

---

57  Margin: 'Arrears of rent 2s.8d.'.
58  Margin: '<Order>'.

Oliver the shepherd amerced 3d. for trespass in the lord's wheat in the street, pledge William Wodebite.

Ordered to take into the lord's hands 5a. of land which Alice the daughter of Oliver the shepherd held in villeinage, because she married John Caley freeman, without leave, and to report the profits.

Oliver the shepherd and Matilda his wife amerced 3d. for a false claim against Walter Osbern in a plea of dower.

Richard Banlone places himself in mercy in a plea of debt against Adam Dolhale, amerced 3d., pledges Adam Dolhale and William Wodebite.

Ordered to raise from Oliver the shepherd 4 bushels of barley, worth 3s., and 4 bushels of oats to the use of William Hawys, to which William has proved his claim, as shown in the preceding court.

Matilda Wodebite places herself in mercy in a plea of debt against Ralph Wybert, amerced 2d., pledge William Wodebite.

Ralph Wybert amerced 3d. for leave to agree with Walter Petipas in a plea of debt, pledge Walter of the Marsh.

Matilda Kembald amerced 3d. for unlawful detention from John Caley and Alice his wife of ½ bushel of wheat, 2 bushels of barley and 1 bushel of peas; adjudged that they shall recover, and the loss assessed at 2d., ordered to raise, pledges Gilbert Helpe and Nicholas Kembald.

Matilda Wodebite amerced 6d. because she caused damage to her house with pigs.

Ordered to take and retain in the lord's hands 1½a. of land which Nicholas Kembald the elder appropriated to himself, from the land of Nicholas Kembald the younger, without leave, and to report the profits for the past three years.[59]

Surrender: Oliver the shepherd and Matilda his wife to Matilda Kembald, a plot of land for rebuilding, 44ft. long and 32 ft. wide, granted to her to hold in villeinage at the lord's will, paying annually to the lord a new increased rent of 1d. at Michaelmas, and a hen at Christmas, fine 6d..

<Gilbert Helpe villein in mercy> because he sold to John of Banham 1½a. of land from the free tenement of his wife, without leave; <ordered to take into the lord's hands> all the said land, and for contempt, and to report the profits. Afterwards Gilbert is given leave to sell the land by charter, because in the lifetime of his father, the said Gilbert, [who was] his heir, made a charter for the purchase thereof, fine 2s.

The lord's shepherd amerced 6d. for damage in the lord's wheat next to his wood, by the escape of his sheep from the fold at night.

Gilbert Helpe villein amerced 12d. because he built outside the manor a house, worth 12d., of timber from the tenement which he holds of the lord's bondage.

Adam of Angerhale villein in open court swore servile fealty to the lord.

Ordered to take into the lord's hands all the tenement of Robert of Angerhale villein because he does not come to swear fealty to the lord now that he is of full age; and to report the profits; ordered to warn Robert as above. The tenement contains 2½r. and the area of the sown part is 1r.; to report the profits on the buildings and the herbage.

SUM 13s. 6d.

---

[59] Margin: 'Void as above. Profits 6d.'.

## 54. HIGH HALL Court, 30 July 1330 [HA504/1/3.14.i]

Walter Osbern essoins of common suit by William of Cranmer. Ralph Wyberd, defendant, v William Wodebite in a plea of debt, essoins by Henry Trusse; and against Gilbert Helpe in a plea of debt, by Robert of the Peartree.

Thomas the shepherd amerced 3d. for leave to agree with Walter of the Marsh in a plea of trespass; and Matilda Wodebite 3d. for the same, with William Rampolye in a plea of debt; pledge for both William Wodebite.

John Goche villein came and made an end to his contempt of the lord; condoned.

Oliver the shepherd has a day to pay to Walter Petipas 2 bushels of wheat and 2 bushels of barley by Michaelmas, under penalty of 2s.

William Wodebite amerced 3d. because, as he could not deny, he could have distrained the servant of Sir Alexander de Walsham for damage done to the lord; again ordered to distrain him for the damage.

A day is given to Matilda Wodebite to pay to William Hawys 5s.7½d. for 4½ bushels of wheat by Michaelmas, under penalty of 2s. payable to the lord.

All the tenement Goche, viz. \a cottage with/ 10a. of land, of which 1½a. is sown with peas, is delivered to the homage, on condition that they make good the waste in the tenement, and they render[60] services and customs, until the lawful heirs come to receive etc.

Matilda Kembald pays 2s.6d. fine to receive from the lord 5a. of land, which had been taken from Alice the daughter of Oliver the shepherd, because she married a freeman without leave, pledge the hayward.

Ordered to distrain Robert of the Peartree in a piece of land which he holds of the lord's fee at Banbrigg, for homage and fealty, and arrears of 1½d. annual rent. Afterwards, he did homage and fealty, and paid 7½d. rent. Likewise to distrain Catherine Machon for the same in a piece of land at Tunbrigg.

Ordered to take and retain in the lord's hands ½a. of land, sown with barley, which William Noreys held in villeinage, until the lawful heirs come to swear fealty.

John Packard comes and receives from the lord all the tenement of Robert of Angerhale, to hold by the rod until Robert comes to render to the lord the services and customs owed [from him] as a villein.

John of Angerhale and Peter Goche each amerced 3d. for default.

John the dairyman amerced for damage in the lord's wheat with the beasts of Sir Alexander de Walsham, 2 sheaves; John Goche for the same, 1 sheaf; Roger the dairyman for the same with the beasts of the Lord Prior, 2 sheaves; Thomas the shepherd for damage at Allwood, 1 sheaf of wheat and 1 of oats; Walter Osbern and William of Cranmer, 2 sheaves of oats; the shepherd of the Prior for damage at Doucedeux, 2 sheaves of peas; Walter Payn at Angerhale, 1 sheaf of oats; William Wodebite, 1 sheaf of peas; the inhabitants of Upstreet at Angerhale, 3 sheaves of peas; John Goche at Hordeshawe, 2 sheaves of oats.

Ordered to distrain the heirs of William Thurbern for homage and fealty withheld; and Simon White for the same, and for ½d. arrears of rent.

Robert Sare amerced 6d. for damage in the lord's meadow at the Micklemeadow.

Ordered to distrain Oliver the shepherd because Alice his daughter married without leave.

SUM 6s. 10½d.

---

60 The word used for both 'make good' and 'render' is *perficiant*: the second usage is taken to be a clerical error.

**55. HIGH HALL Court, 15 November 1330 [HA504/1/3.14.ii]**

William of Cranmer essoins of common suit by William Deneys; William Elys of the same, by Robert Kembald.

Richard the shepherd and Gilbert Helpe, the first pledges of Ralph Wybert, amerced 6d. [because he did not] reply to William Wodebite in a plea of debt; ordered to appoint better pledges. The first pledges of Ralph Wybert amerced 6d., because he did not reply to Gilbert Helpe in a plea of debt; ordered etc.

Robert Sare and John of Angerhale each amerced 3d. for default, pledge Robert Kembald; Olivia Isabel amerced 3 fowls for the same, pledge as above; <Nicholas Kembald and Peter Goche for the same> condoned.

Matilda Wodebite did not satisfy William Hawys concerning 5s.7½d. for 4 bushels of wheat; ordered to raise the debt.

A day is given to John Goche to repair a house and building which are wasted, by 1 August.

Ordered as elsewhere to distrain William Thurbern for homage and fealty withheld, and Simon White for the same.

William Wodebite in mercy because he cannot deny 2 bushels of wheat [*sic*], by the pledge of William Wodebite; ordered to raise to the use of William Rampolye;[61] condoned.

Matilda Kembald amerced 3d. because she did not proceed against Matilda Wodebite in a plea of debt.

Ordered to attach Henry of Littlehaugh to reply to John Roty in a plea of debt; and to distrain Oliver the shepherd because Alice his daughter married without leave.

Nicholas Kembald amerced 3d. because he did not rebuild on the tenement Kembald; ordered to rebuild by [*blank*].

Gilbert Helpe amerced 6d. because he stored his corn away from the lord's fee.

William Wodebite amerced 3d. for damage in the lord's corn. Ordered to distrain William Hawys for the same.

Catherine Payn and William Wodebite each amerced 3d. because they did not perform autumn works; John Packard, Matilda Wodebite and Mabel Payn each amerced 6d. for the same, Gilbert Helpe the younger in mercy for the same; condoned.

The whole homage elected John of Angerhale \and all his tenement[62]/ to the office of collector, fine 12d.

Alice of Heythe amerced 3d. for default.

SUM 6s. 6d.

**56. WALSHAM Court of Sir Edmund de Pakenham, 24 September 1331 [HA504/1/3.15.i]**

[This membrane is damaged in the right margin *verso*, and the left margin *dorse*, and small sections of this roll, and the next, are illegible.]

William Rampolye, defendant v Nicholas de Walsham in a plea of covenant, essoins by John Noreys; he pledges faith; Nicholas is present.

---

61 This entry is one of several in the roll where apparent errors and omissions make them difficult to comprehend. The person in mercy was probably Matilda Wodebite, and the dispute with William Rampolye was that on which Matilda paid 3d. for leave to agree in the last court.

62 Presumably this should read 'for all his tenement'.

Manser of Shucford, defendant, v John Pynchon and Olivia Kembald, plaintiffs, in a plea of trespass, essoins by Thomas Hereward; he pledges faith.

Robert of Reydon amerced 3d. for leave to agree with John Terwald in a plea of trespass, pledge William Hawys.

John at the Green of St Edmunds amerced 6d. because he did not proceed against Walter Goselyng and Alice his wife in a plea of trespass.

John Noreys amerced 6d. because he withheld four ploughing services for two years, pledge William Hawys.

Gilbert Priour amerced 3d. for leave to agree with William Shepherd in a plea of debt, pledge the hayward.

Simon Peyntour amerced 6d. for leave to agree with Sir William Gyfford in pleas of agreement and trespass, pledge the hayward.

Mabel Bonde pays 6d. fine for scrutinising the rolls to enquire whether she purchased with John Margery her [late] husband 2½a. of land, [and] whether she is a co-tenant or not, as appears in the last court, pledge John Noreys.

Surrenders: Matilda Coppelowe to John Typetot and his heirs, ½r. of customary land lying in Brookfield, with one head abutting on Otoftwell,[63] granted to John to hold in villeinage by customs and services etc., fine 6d., pledge Richard Kebbil.

Robert at the Wood to Alice at the Wood and her heirs, ½a. of land with a cottage, granted to her in the same form, fine 18d., pledge Richard Kebbil.

Simon Rampolye amerced 3d. for damage in the Littlemeadow with three pigs, and 6d. for damage in the lord's rye with his geese, pledge Richard Kebbil. Massilia Hawys amerced 3d. for damage in the Littlemeadow with her pigs; Richard of Langham in mercy for the same, condoned. Mabel Bonde and Peter Jay each amerced 4d., William Elys 2d., Robert the shepherd 3d. for the same, each with one pig, pledge for all the hayward.

Nicholas Kembald amerced 4d. for leave to agree with Matilda Coppelowe in two pleas of trespass; likewise Ralph Echeman 3d., with William Springold in a plea of trespass, and William 3d., with Ralph in a plea of debt, pledge for all the hayward.

Surrenders: Matilda Coppelowe to William Deneys, half a messuage 5a. of customary land, granted to him to hold to himself and his assigns by services and customs. Afterwards William surrenders the said half a messuage 5a. to the use of Geoffrey Rath and Matilda Coppelowe, to hold to them and their heirs and assigns by services etc., and entry was granted to them, fine 10s., pledges William Hawys and John Typetot.

+Again a day is given to William the servant of the parson of Langham to come to the next court to make amends for trespass in Ladyswood taking away trees etc., pledge Richard of Langham.

+A day is given to Nicholas de Walsham to come to the next court to make amends for trespass in the lord's wheat in the autumn with his pigs and geese, and also because he took a hare in the lord's warren.

+A day is given to Catherine Mayheu to come to the next court to show by what

---

63 Possibly 'Oldtoftwell', but the original is clearly as transcribed.

right she entered into 4a. of land, which she purchased from Agnes of Angerhale by charter, pledge Nicholas de Walsham.

William Wither amerced 2d. because he defamed Alice Ape, damaging her to the value of 1d., ordered to raise the damages, pledge the hayward.

Matilda Coppelowe pays 12d fine for leave to marry Geoffrey Rath, pledges William Hawys and the hayward.

It was found that Robert at the Brook villein, when he died, held from the lord a messuage 12a. of land by services and customs etc., and the lord had a mare as a heriot, and that Roger and Robert his sons are his nearest heirs, and are of full age. They seek admittance and are admitted without fine, because Robert gave the heriot, according to custom; they swore servile fealty.

Walter Gilbert, when he died, held from the lord a messuage 4a. of land by services and customs etc., and the lord has a calf, worth 18d., as a heriot. Peter and Matthew his sons are his nearest heirs; and Peter, of full age, seeks admittance, and is granted entry by the heriot; Matthew is 11 years of age, and accordingly a quarter part of the tenement will remain in the lord's hands until etc.

Richard Kebbil, the hayward, amerced 3d. because he did not attach Walter Osbern to reply to Aubrey of Wyken in a plea of debt; ordered to attach Walter to reply.

+Alice Schetenheyt, when she died, held from the lord a cottage by services etc.; the lord had no heriot, because she had no beast. She has no heirs, therefore ordered to take the cottage into the lord's hands, and to report the profits.[64]

Peter Gilbert amerced 3d. for damage harvesting wheat in the autumn, pledge Peter Springold; Richard Winter amerced 3d. for the same, pledge Robert Lene because [Richard is his] servant.

Catherine the wife of Robert Tailor amerced 3d. for damage in the lord's barley gathering herbage, pledge the hayward.

William Tailor the ploughman of the manor amerced 6d. for damage in the lord's wheat at Ayleldestoft taking away 2 sheaves; John Lene amerced 3d. because he sheltered William with the sheaves.

Catherine the wife of Robert the tailor[65] amerced 3d. for damage in the lord's meadow gathering herbage, and 3d. because she took away the lord's corn, pledge the hayward.

Robert the chaplain amerced 3d. for damage in the lord's peas with a cow, pledge Nicholas Goche; Thomas Fuller 3d. for damage in the lord's rye with his pigs; Richard Reve 4d. for damage in the lord's peas with his cows and pigs, pledge William of Cranmer.

Ordered to attach Gilbert Sare for damage with his cows in the lord's corn at Boynhawe.

Adam Noble amerced 3d. for damage in the lord's meadow with his pigs, pledge Thomas Fuller; Henry of Saxmundham 6d. for the same in the lord's meadow with four pigs, pledge the hayward; Robert the tailor 3d. for the same with two pigs, pledge as above; Nicholas Kembald 3d. for the same with pigs, pledge as above; Robert Wauncy the servant of Warren Bret for damage in the meadows

---

[64] Margin: 'heriot' (?16th century).
[65] It is uncertain whether this is the Catherine Tailor referred to above; in this and the next entry, the surname is given as *Cissor*; in the earlier entry, as 'Taylour'.

with cows, and Warren himself 1d. for damage in the lord's barley at Millwong ['Mellewong'] with geese, pledge for both, the reeve.

The Prior of Ixworth amerced 18d. because he overstocked the common, and because he grazed his sheep where he had no right of common.

William Clevehog amerced 2s. because he had 7 score sheep in his fold over the fixed number, pledge William of Cranmer.

<Ordered> to attach Adam Sket because he overstocked the lord's common with his sheep.[66]

Henry of Saxmundham amerced 12d. because he had 50 sheep in his fold over the fixed number.

The lord's swineherd amerced 1d. for damage in the lord's meadow, pledge the reeve.

Henry the servant of Ralph Echeman amerced 3d. because he took away apples from the lord's courtyard; Ralph Echeman and Robert Wauncy each amerced 3d. because they sheltered him, pledge the reeve.

Henry of Saxmundham amerced 6d. because he took away timber out of the lord's bondage.

+<William Goselyng> John and Peter the sons of Robert Tailor amerced 6s.8d. because they took and carried away out of the lord's granary 2 bushels of wheat and 4 bushels of barley, pledge Robert Tailor; and ordered to raise the said corn to the lord's use. Robert amerced 3s.4d. because he sheltered them with the same.

William the miller, by the lord's leave, sold to William Springold 1½a. of customary land to hold to himself and Isabella his wife and the heirs issuing from their bodies, by services and customs; in exchange for 1a. of land [damaged ?which William] Springold sold to William the miller, to hold to himself and his heirs in the same form. Entry was granted to them, fine for the exchange 18d., pledge [damaged].

Ordered to execute the orders of the preceding court marked with a cross, and not yet acted upon.

SUM 41s. 1d., except the heriots: a mare and a calf


## 57. WALSHAM Court of Lady Rose de Pakenham, 11 December 1331 [HA504/1/3.15.ii]

[See the note, preceding no.56, re. damage to the membrane, to which 7 inches were added to make space for the last four items in this court. This area is badly faded and stained.]

Robert of Reydon, plaintiff v Edmund Patel in a plea of trespass, essoins by Nicholas Goche; and as defendant v Geoffrey Rath in a plea of covenant, essoins by John Bret; he pledges faith.

John Pynchon[67] and Olivia Kembald, plaintiffs v Manser of Shucford in a plea of trespass, essoin by Robert Kembald; they pledge faith.

---

66 Only the words *pre. est* in the margin are deleted; it is assumed that the order was cancelled.

67 MS: John is named in this court, and the next, as John the Shearman ('Sherman'), but in the last court and subsequently he appears as John Pynchon. In 1334 (no.73) Olivia is referred to as John Pynchon's wife.

William Rampolye amerced 3d. for leave to agree with Nicholas de Walsham in a plea of covenant, pledge the hayward.

Robert Sare amerced 2d. for trespass in the lord's corn at Boynhawe with his cows, pledge the hayward.

Oliver the shepherd amerced 3d. because he did not proceed against Willliam Payn in a plea of trespass, and the said William [is quit] indefinitely.

Walter Deneys amerced 3d. for leave to agree with John Man in a plea of trespass, pledge John Man.

John Syre amerced 2d. for unlawful detention of 18d. [from] \Thomas of the Beck/, for the mainprise of Agnes Wodebite, which he cannot deny, the loss assessed at 2d., ordered to raise.

Peter Tailor, Stephen Cooper, Richard Reve, Nicholas Kembald and Margaret Margery each amerced 2d. for damage in the lord's wheat with their cows; the Prior of Ixworth amerced 3d. for damage in the Litttlemeadow with his geese, and 3d. for the same with his cows; Stephen Cooper and Peter Tailor 2d. each for the same with pigs, pledge for all the hayward.

Agnes Helewys amerced 3d. for taking away the lord's straw, pledge as above.

Ralph Echeman amerced 2d. for leave to agree with Henry of Saxmundham in a plea of debt, pledge Thomas Fuller; Matthew Hereward, Nicholas Kembald and John Man each amerced 2d. for the same, pledge for all the hayward.

Robert Warde, Roger of Southwold and John Wymond pay 6d. each as fines for respite of suit of court until Michaelmas, pledge the hayward; likewise Simon Deneys pays 3d., pledge John Syre, William Patel 3d., pledge Richard Patel, Robert the chaplain 4d., pledge the hayward, Bartholomew Patel 6d., pledge Richard Patel, Henry of Saxmundham 4d., William of the Wood and Richard Patel 3d. each, pledge the hayward, for the same.

Walter Osbern amerced 3d. for leave to agree with William Wither in a plea of trespass, pledge the hayward.

+It was found that John Man withheld from Robert Crane 1 quarter 2 bushels of wheat, worth 10s., 3 pairs of linen sheets, worth 12d., and a tester, worth 18d., the damages assessed at 6d.; and that he took away a quern, worth 1d., a Lanksetel, worth 1d., a building, worth 18d. and a pair of doors, worth 2d.; adjudged that Robert shall recover the debt and the damages from John, who is amerced 12d. +John also amerced 2d. because he cut down an ash tree and a pear tree, worth 10d., in Robert's tenement, ordered to raise.

Robert Crane amerced 3d. for his false claim against John Man.

Adam Sket amerced 2d. because he overstocked the lord's common.

William the miller held from the lord, when he died, a messuage 2a. of customary land by services etc.; the lord has no heriot because William had no beast; Isabella William's daughter, aged two years, is his nearest heir; ordered that the tenement remain in the lord's hands because she is under age.

Robert Lene amerced 2d. for damage in the lord's herbage with his pigs, pledge the hayward; William Springold, Peter Springold, Walter Hereward, Henry of Saxmundham, Robert Tailor and Nicholas Kembald each amerced 3d. for damage in the Great Meadow with their pigs.

Robert the cooper amerced 6d. because he stored corn grown on the lord's bondage, in a free tenement; Peter Neve amerced 3d. for the same, and 3d. for overstocking the lord's common with his sheep, pledge the hayward.

Ordered to distrain the Prior of Ixworth because he overstocked the lord's common, and grazed his sheep where he had no right of common.

Henry the chaplain amerced 2d. for damage in Ladyswood with his pigs, pledge the hayward; Henry of Saxmundham in mercy for the same with a cow, condoned; Robert Tailor amerced 2d. for the same.

Walter Pye and Henry of Saxmundham each amerced 12d. because they brewed and sold ale in breach of the assize; Edmund Lene amerced 6d. because he baked and sold bread in breach of the assize; Joan Brewster, gannocker, Gilbert Salvetail and Alice Warde each amerced 2d. because they sold ale in breach of the assize.

John Lene and Robert Lene amerced 6d. because they withheld works and services to the value of 3d..

+Ordered to distrain William Kembald because he diverted a path within his land, to the detriment of the lord and his neighbours.

+William Kembald chaplain complains against William Hawys and William of Cranmer the elder, in a plea of debt, pledge for the plaintiff Nicholas Kembald; ordered to attach them.

Surrenders: Ralph Echeman to Thomas Fuller and his heirs, 4a.1r. of customary land, granted to him to hold in villeinage by services and customs, fine 12s., pledge the hayward.

Richard of Wortham to Walter the smith and his heirs, 1r. of customary land, granted to him in the same form, fine 9d.

Geoffrey Rath and Matilda Coppelowe to John Typetot and his heirs, 1a. of customary land, granted to him in the same form, fine 3s..

Henry of Saxmundham pays 12d. for having 4 score sheep in his fold until next Michaelmas, pledge the hayward.

Richard the son of Letitia, Robert Crane, Richard Spileman and William Deneys each pay [damaged] fine for respite of suit of court until next Michaelmas.

Surrender: Robert Swift and Agatha his wife to Thomas Dormour and his heirs, ½r. of pasture at Hordeshawe, granted to him in the same form as above, fine 6d..

The whole homage gives 100s. grace payment (in gratia) as recognition of the lady, [see below].

Thomas Dormour pays [damaged] fine for respite of suit of court until next Michaelmas, pledge the hayward.

Surrenders: Emma Pye to John Patel and Beatrice his daughter and their heirs, the reversion of ½a. of land with a cottage in Walsham, granted to them in the same form as above, fine 18d., pledge the hayward.

John Patel to Richard the son of Thomas of the Beck and his heirs, 1½r. of land in the field of Ashfield, in the furlong called the Dales, granted to him in the same form, fine 12d., pledge the hayward.

Stephen Cooper and Alice his wife to Amice their daughter and her heirs, [illeg.] 1r. of customary land in the Tailorscroft, granted to her in the same form, fine 10d., pledge the hayward.

John Wymond and Agnes his wife, by leave of the court, demised to William of Cranmer the younger 20a. of land, 2r. of meadow and 1a. of pasture to hold at farm, from last Michaelmas for four years full and complete; William gives 12d. fine for having his term, pledge the hayward.

Surrender: John Wymond to William of Cranmer the younger and his heirs, 1½a. of land in Edwardstoft, granted to him to hold in villeinage by services and customs, fine 3s.6d., pledge the hayward.

SUM 42s. 10d., except 100s. customary fine, waived by the lady.

## 58. WALSHAM Court, 20 February 1332 [HA504/1/3.16]

William of Cranmer essoins of common suit by Henry of Saxmundham, and, as defendant v William Kembald chaplain, in a plea of debt, by Richard Kebbil; he pledges faith; William Kembald is present.

The first pledges of Edmund Patel amerced 3d. because they did not have him reply to Robert of Reydon in a plea of trespass, ordered to summon him by better pledges.

Geoffrey Rath amerced 3d. because he did not proceed against Robert of Reydon in a plea of covenant; and Robert [is quit] indefinitely.

Alice Miller pays 12d. fine for having custody of Isabella the daughter of William miller until her full age, pledges Matthew Hereward and William Springold.

Robert Ryvel amerced 6d. for damage in the lord's rye with his sheep, pledge the hayward; Robert the shepherd of Wattisfield amerced 3d. for the same in the lord's common. pledge the bailiff.

John Man amerced 3d. for chattering in court.

+Richard of Langham amerced 2s. because he did not have Robert the parson of Langham make amends for trespass in Ladyswood, [by his servant] cutting and taking away trees etc.; ordered to attach him by better pledges.

Manser of Shucford amerced 3d. for unlawful detention of 8s. from Alice Long, as he admitted in open court; ordered to raise, and the loss assessed at 12d..

Nicholas Fraunceys pays 3d. fine for respite of suit of court until Michaelmas, pledge the hayward.

+A day was given to the Prior of Ixworth to come to the next court to satisfy the lord for overstocking the common with his sheep, and because he grazed them where he has no right of common, pledge the hayward.

John Man amerced 3d. for leave to agree with Robert Kembald in a plea of trespass, pledge the hayward.

Manser of Shucford amerced 3d. for unlawful detention of wool, worth 22d., from John Pynchon[68] and Olivia Kembald; ordered to raise 3d. loss, pledge the hayward.

Walter Osbern was attached to reply to William Wither in a plea of covenant, and thereupon he [William] complains that on Monday before Michaelmas 12 Edw.II [25 September 1318], it was agreed between them that Walter was in debt to him for 1 quarter 1 bushel of barley, worth 10s., 3 cloths, worth 6s., and 1 quarter of barley and oats, worth 8s., to be paid to him on the feast of All Saints next following [1 November]. On this day he did not pay but withheld and still withholds, to William's loss of 10s.; and he produces suit. Walter comes and defends (*defendit vim*), and says that he owes William nothing, and thereupon he offers [to wage] law, pledges of the law Nicholas Goche and the hayward.

John Man was attached to reply to Walter Noreys in a plea of debt, and thereupon he

---

68 See footnote 67.

[Walter] complains that on Monday before the feast of the Assumption 4 Edw.III [13 August 1330], John acknowledged himself in debt to Walter for 2½ bushels of wheat, worth 2s., 2 bushels of peas, worth 18d., 1½ bushels of barley, worth 18d., a cap,[69] worth 4d., a hen, worth 2d., and 15d. rent, to be paid to Walter at the following Michaelmas. On this day he did not pay but withheld and still withholds, to Walter's loss of 40d., and he produces suit. John comes and says that he owes him nothing, as he is accused, and thereupon he offers to wage law, pledge for the law the hayward.

Surrenders: Roger of the Brook and Alice his wife [and] William of the Wood to William and Robert the sons of William Cook and their heirs, a messuage with 1a. of customary land, granted to them to hold in villeinage by services and customs, fine 3s., pledge the hayward.

Robert Swift to Robert Man and his heirs, 3r. of customary land lying at Strondeslane, granted to him in the same form, fine 2s., pledge the hayward. Afterwards, Robert Man granted the said land to Robert Swift, to hold for his lifetime, and after his death the land to revert to Robert Man to hold in the aforesaid form.

John Patel to Richard the son of Thomas of the Beck and his heirs, ½a. of customary land in Ashfield, in the field called the Stubbing, granted to him in the same form as above, fine 8d., pledge the hayward.

William Wither to William Rampolye and his heirs, ½r. of customary land at Clay street, within the land of William Rampolye, granted to him in the same form, fine 6d., pledge the hayward.[70]

John Lene amerced 2d. for damage done to Alexander de Walsham cutting down a hedge, to the value of ½d., ordered to raise, pledge the hayward.

Again a day is given to William Kembald chaplain, plaintiff, and William Hawys and William of Cranmer the elder, defendants, to come to the next court without essoin.

Peter the son of Robert villein, when he died, held from the lord, with Matilda his wife, a cottage and 2r. of customary land by services; the heriot is a cow, worth 10s.; Matilda shall hold the tenement for her lifetime.

Agnes the widow of William the miller, when she died, held from the lord a third part of a messuage 5a. of land, 1r. of wood and 1r. of customary meadow by services and customs; the lord had a cow as a heriot. John her son was her nearest heir, but he died on the same day as his mother, and he gave no heriot because he had no beast. John Spileman is his nearest heir, and is of full age. He seeks admittance to the tenement, and it is granted to him to hold by services and customs, fine 10s., pledge William Hawys.

Presented that the tenement of Peter Pynfoul is wasted, to the lord's loss of 16s.; ordered to raise from Henry the chaplain and Walter Osbern, the executors of Agnes Pynfoul, because the tenement was wasted in her time, and to take it into the lord's hands.

Matilda Coppelowe amerced 3d. because she did likewise [sic], ordered to take the tenement into the lord's hands.

William Kembald amerced 6d. for damage done to the lord diverting a boundary, pledge the hayward.

---

[69] MS: *capit'*; in this context, this may be a clerical error for *capo*, a capon.
[70] Tab between last two items: 'John Patell, William Wither'.

Surrender: Simon Rampolye to John Noble and his heirs, 1½r. of customary land in the Millfield, granted to him in the same form as above, fine 15d., pledge Adam Noble.

Ordered to execute the orders of the court of 13 February 1331, [not yet acted upon].

+Again a day is given to Nicholas de Walsham until the next court to satisfy the lord for damage in his wheat in autumn with pigs and geese; and to Catherine Mayheu to show by what right she entered into the lord's fee.

Ordered to retain in the lord's hands a cottage which Alice Shetenheyt held from the lord on the day she died.

SUM 39s. 10d., except a cow, worth 10s., as heriot

From this in the expenses of Peter the clerk for holding the court, together with those of Edmund de Pakenham and William of Langham, 3s.4d.; in fodder 3 pecks of oats

## 59.  WALSHAM Court, 28 April 1332 [HA504/1/3.17]

Edmund Patel amerced 3d. for leave to agree with Robert of Reydon in a plea of trespass, pledge the hayward.

William of Cranmer and William Hawys were attached to reply to William Kembald chaplain, [plaintiff], in a plea of debt; and on this he complains that on Sunday before the feast of the Assumption 4 Edw.III [12 August 1330], in the vill of Walsham, William and William became mainpernors and principal debtors of himself for 27s. for his service, to be paid at Michaelmas next following. On this day they did not pay but withheld and still withhold, to his loss of ½ mark; and thereupon he produces suit. William of Cranmer and William Hawys come and say that they owe no money to him, nor did they stand as mainpernors, as he imputes; and on this they ask that an enquiry be held, and the other party likewise. The enquiry say on their oath that William and William did not become mainpernors nor debtors to the said William as he imputes; and he is in mercy for his false claim, condoned; William and William [are quit] indefinitely.

Robert Tailor and Henry of Saxmundham, the first pledges of John, the son of Agnes at the Green, amerced 6d. because they did not have him do homage and fealty to the lord. Ordered to summon him by better pledges.

Again ordered to retain in the lord's hands a messuage built which John Clevehog villein sold without the lord's leave, and to report the profits.

Ordered to distrain Robert Hovell in the tenements which were formerly of Henry the son of Bartholomew de Elmham, to do homage and fealty.

Matthew Hereward amerced 6d. because he did not rebuild his wasted tenement, as he undertook; ordered to take the tenement into the lord's hands.

Again a day is given to the Prior of Ixworth to come to the next court, and satisfy the lord for overstocking the common with his sheep, and because he grazed them where he had no right of common, pledge the hayward.

Ralph Echeman amerced 3d. because he did not rebuild the tenement Spileman as he undertook; ordered to take the whole tenement into the lord's hands, and to report the profits.

A day is given to Robert the parson of Langham to make amends for trespass in Ladyswood cutting and taking away trees etc., or to pay compensation of a horse, worth 6s.8d., on the Friday of Whitsun week [12 June], pledge William of Cranmer the younger.

Walter Osbern amerced 3d. for leave to agree with William Wither in a plea of covenant, pledge the hayward.

Geoffrey Rath complains of Robert of Reydon in a plea of covenant, pledge for the plaintiff the hayward, ordered to attach [Robert].

Stephen Cooper amerced 3d. for damage in the lord's corn collecting herbage, pledge the hayward.

Walter Noreys amerced 6d. for leave to agree with John Man in a plea of debt, pledge John Man and the hayward.

Peter Tailor, Joan the servant of Robert Shepherd chaplain, and Emma Shepherd each amerced 3d. for damage in the lord's corn collecting herbage, pledge for all the hayward.

Again a day is given to Nicholas de Walsham until the next court to satisfy the lord for damage in his wheat in the autumn with his pigs and geese.

Again ordered to retain in the lord's hands a cottage which Alice Shetenheyt held when she died, and to report the profits.

+Again as elsewhere ordered to attach Geoffrey of Burgate to do homage and fealty to the lord, and for 8d. annual rent for the tenement Scuttisfee, and for other summonses as shown in the [roll of the] court of 13 February 1331.

Again as elsewhere ordered to attach Alice the widow of Walter Goselyng, and Thomas and William his sons, to reply to John at the Green of St Edmunds in a plea of trespass.

+Mabel Bonde, Robert Osbern, Robert Suter, William Suter and Simon Suter each amerced 3d. for default; ordered to distrain them to swear fealty to the lord.

+Geoffrey Rath amerced 2d. for waste in the lord's tenement; a day is given to him to make good the waste by 1 November next following, pledges Nicholas Kembald and the hayward.

Peter Neve amerced 12d. because he overstocked the lord's common with his beasts.

Ordered to distrain Henry of Saxmundham because he grazed his sheep where he had no right of common.

Edmund Lene amerced 12d. because he baked and sold bread in breach of the assize, and Simon Rampolye 6d. for the same, pledge for both the hayward.

Great Joan ['Gretejone'] amerced 6d. because she brewed and sold ale in breach of the assize, pledge Walter Rampolye because in [his] house; likewise Henry of Saxmundham 6d., and Alice Pye 12d., pledge for both the hayward.

Agnes Ryvel amerced 3d. because she sold ale in breach of the assize, pledge Robert Robetel because in [his] house; Alice Warde 2d. for the same, pledge the hayward.

Geoffrey of Lenne and John Warde each amerced 6d. because they sold bread in breach of the assize, and Henry Smith 3d. for the same, pledge for all the hayward.

Stephen Cooper and William Payn the ale tasters amerced 6d. because they did not perform their duties, pledge each for the other.

William Robhood amerced 2d. because he withheld 1d. annual rent.

Adam Noble amerced 3d. because he removed his sheep from the lord's fold.

All the tenants of the tenement formerly of Master John de Walsham amerced 6d. for default; and all the tenants of the tenement formerly Outlawe, 6d. for the same.

Agnes the widow of Peter Hawys pays 13s 4d. fine for leave to marry Thomas William.

John Robhood amerced 3d. for default; William Robhood and William Warde 2d. each for the same.

Surrender: William Patel to Richard the son of Thomas of the Beck and his heirs, ½a. of land lying in Ashfield next to the land of Roger Clerke, and one head abutting on the garden of John of Micklewood, granted to him to hold in villeinage by services and customs, fine 8d., pledge the reeve.

Alice Warde demised to Thomas of the Beck a messuage 3r. of customary land, to hold from that day until she clears herself [of a debt] to Thomas of geese and hens, in the manor of Alexander de Walsham, fine for that demise 3d., pledge the reeve.

William Hawys received from the lord a cottage, which was of Alice Shetenheyt and was escheat to the lord after her death, to hold to William and his heirs and assigns at the lord's will, by services and customs, fine 2s., pledge the hayward.

Surrender: John Wymond and Agnes Stronde[71] to William of Cranmer and his heirs, 1r. of meadow lying in Ashfield meadow, granted to him to hold in villeinage by services and customs, fine 12d., pledge the hayward.[72]

Walter Osbern received from the lord a messuage with all the land and tenements which were of Peter Pynfoul, to keep John, Peter's son, in all his needs until his full age, in this form, *viz.* that Walter shall maintain the tenements in as good condition as he received them, and in the last year of the said term, Walter shall pay to John 4 bushels of wheat, 4 bushels of peas and 1 quarter of large oats, good corn and clean, a cow, worth 9s., a gelded calf, worth 2s., 2 ewes, worth 4s., 2 linen sheets, and 1 of hemp, worth 6d., and other small necessities as shown by an indenture made between them.

SUM 31s. 1d., less the expenses of the clerk for holding the court, and for overseeing the account: 2s. 11½d.

### 60. WALSHAM Court of Thomas de Saxham and Ralph de Rickinghall, 11 June 1332 [HA504/1/3.18.i]

William Kembald, defendant v Nicholas de Walsham in a plea of trespass, essoins by John Note; he pledges faith; Nicholas is present.

The first pledges of Robert of Reydon amerced 3d. because they did not have him reply to Geoffrey Rath in a plea of covenant; ordered to summon him by better pledges.

Nicholas de Walsham in mercy for damage in the lord's wheat, assessed at 2d.; condoned by the lord.

The first pledges of Robert of Reydon amerced 3d. because they did not have him reply to John Typetot and Geoffrey Rath in a plea of trespass; ordered to summon him by better pledges.

The first pledges of Robert Warde amerced 3d. because they did not have him reply to Henry of Saxmundham in a plea of debt; ordered to summon him by better pledges.

---

71 John's wife.
72 Tab: 'John Wymonde'.

Ordered to attach John Noreys to reply to Henry of Saxmundham in a plea of debt.

Manser of Shucford amerced 3d. for leave to agree with John Underwood in a plea of debt; and Simon Peyntour 3d. for the same with Thomas of the Beck in a plea of trespass, pledge for both the hayward.

Henry the chaplain in mercy for damage on the lord's common where he had no right of common.[73]

William Kembald freeman withheld one hen rent and one reapale for two years; ordered to distrain him to make amends.

+Robert of Fornham villein withheld various services for two years, ordered to take his tenement into the lord's hands.

Matilda the wife of Peter Robbes amerced 6d. because she withheld one hen in rent.

Simon Peyntour amerced 2d. for his false claim against William Clevehog in a plea of detention of a lamb; William [is quit] indefinitely.

+Again ordered to attach John the son of Agnes at the Green to do homage and fealty to the lord.

+Again as elsewhere ordered to retain in the lord's hands a messuage built which John Clevehog villein sold without leave, and to report the profits.

+Again as elsewhere ordered to distrain Robert Hovell in the tenements which were of Henry the son of Bartholomew de Elmham, to do homage and fealty to the lord.

+Ordered to retain in the lord's hands the tenement of Matthew Hereward, because he did not rebuild it as he undertook, and to report the profits.

+Again a day is given to the Prior of Ixworth until the next court to come and satisfy the lord for overstocking the common with his sheep, and because he grazed them where he had no right of common.

+Ordered to retain in the lord's hands the tenement Spileman \in the hands of Ralph Echeman/, because he did not rebuild it as he undertook, and to report the profits.

Again a day is given to Robert the parson of Langham until the next court, to make amends for trespass in Ladyswood cutting down and taking away trees valued at 40d., or to make recompense of a horse, worth 6s.8d. for the same, pledges Henry of Langham and William of Cranmer the younger.

Ordered to execute all the orders of the preceding court, marked with a cross and not acted upon.

SUM 23d.;

from this, in the expenses of Thomas de Saxham, Philip de Gelham
and Peter the clerk and others for holding one court, and taking
seisin of the manor: 4s. 2¾d., and one capon from stock.

### 61. WALSHAM Court of Sir Hugh de Saxham and Lady Rose de Pakenham, 15 September 1332 [HA504/1/3.18.ii]

Adam Noble, defendant v William Hawys in a plea of trespass, essoins by Thomas Fuller; he pledges faith, and William is present.

The first pledges of William Kembald amerced 6d. because they did not have him reply to Nicholas de Walsham in a plea of trespass; ordered etc.

---

[73] Margin: 'condoned because [*illeg.*] cause'.

The first pledges of Robert Warde amerced 6d. because they did not have him reply to Henry of Saxmundham in a plea of debt; ordered etc.

The first pledges of John Noreys amerced 6d. because they did not have him reply to Henry of Saxmundham in a plea of debt; ordered etc.

+The first pledges of William Kembald amerced 12d. because they did not have him satisfy the lord for withholding one hen in rent and one reapale in arrears for two years; ordered to summon him by better pledges.

+Henry of Langham and William of Cranmer the younger, the first pledges of Robert \the parson/ of Langham, amerced 12d. because they did not have him reply for damage in Ladyswood, cutting and taking away trees, valued at 40d., and because they did not make recompense of a horse, worth 6s.8d., for the trespass, as they undertook; ordered to summon him by better pledges.

Edmund Patel amerced 3d. for leave to agree with Nicholas de Walsham in a plea of trespass, pledge the hayward.

Peter Jay amerced 3d. for unlawful detention of 12d. from John Herning, which he cannot deny, to the loss of 6d.; ordered to raise, pledge the hayward.

Geoffrey Rath amerced 3d. for leave to agree with Robert of Reydon in a plea of covenant; Robert of the Brook 3d. for the same with Alice Draweswerd in a plea of debt; Avice Hulke 3d. for the same with William Hawys in a plea of trespass, and Agnes, the daughter of Thomas Suter, 3d. for the same with Walter Payn the younger in a plea of trespass, pledge for all the hayward.

Walter Osbern and Robert the chaplain each amerced 6d. because they did not mill [their corn] at the lord's mill; Peter Jay 3d., Amice Echeman 3d., Simon Peyntour 6d., Nicholas Fraunceys 3d., John Terwald 6d. and Stephen Cooper 3d. for the same, pledge for all the hayward.

Robert Ryvel the shepherd of the manor amerced 6d. for damage in the lord's wheat at Summerway ['Somerweye'] and in the lord's barley at the Cross.

The farmer of the cows amerced 6d. for the same in the lord's wheat at Oldtoft and in the lord's barley at Prioursgate; the keeper of the cows of the Prior 6d. for the same, and in the lord's barley at Oldtoft ['Aldistoft']; Alexander de Walsham 3d. for damage in the lord's barley at the Cross; Robert Man the keeper of the beasts of Alexander de Walsham, Massilia Hawys, Adam Noble, Walter Osbern, William Payn, William Deneys and John Syre each amerced 3d. for the same, pledge for all the hayward.

Adam Margery amerced 3d. for damage in the Littlemeadow with a mare, pledge the hayward.

Robert Ryvel the shepherd of the manor amerced 3d. because he put the lord's sheep in the fold of Robert Sare, pledge the hayward.

Ordered to distrain the Prior of Ixworth because he overstocked the lord's common with 100 sheep.

Alice Warde amerced 3d. because she sold to John Warde a plot of land, 8ft. wide; ordered to seize.

Surrender: Matilda the widow of Peter Robbes to Adam Hardonn and Alice his wife, and their heirs, a cottage next to the tenement of Nicholas Fraunceys, granted to them to hold in villeinage by services and customs etc., fine 12d., pledges Walter Payn and the hayward.

Presented that Peter Warde [dec'd.] sold to Robert Warde 1¼r. of pasture and 1r. of meadow without leave; ordered to take into the lord's hands.

Surrender: Ralph Neve to William Springold and his heirs, 1r. and ½r. of land, lying separately and abutting on Ladyswood, granted to him in the same form as above, fine 12d., pledge the hayward.

Richard Wyndilgard sold to William Payn 1r. of customary land without leave; ordered to take into the lord's hands.

Robert Salvetayl comes into court and seeks admittance to a cottage, which Alice Shetenheyt his wife held when she died; adjudged that he should hold the cottage for his lifetime, and after his death it shall revert to the lord as the nearest heir; entry granted, fine 2s., pledges Nicholas Kembald and the hayward.

Adam Margery and Peter Margery pay 18d. fine for the apportioning of their tenements, pledge the hayward; ordered to attach all the tenants.

Richard of Wortham amerced 6d. because he stored corn grown on the bondage, in a free tenement, pledge the hayward; Robert Kembald 2d., John Typetot 3d., Peter Neve 3d. and Henry of Saxmundham 6d. for the same.

Henry of Saxmundham amerced 3d. for damage in the lord's oats with a cow, pledge the hayward. Adam Sket did likewise at the Micklemeadow with a foal, ordered to distrain him; John Hernyng amerced 3d. for the same with a mare, pledge the hayward.

Richard Qualm and William of Cranmer the younger were elected to the office of reeve, and Richard gives ½ mark as fine to withdraw from the said office. Richard Kebbil and William Wither were elected to the office of hayward, and William pledges (?assurat) 2s. as fine to withdraw. William Springold and Peter Springold were elected to the office of woodward, and William gives 12d. as fine to withdraw.

Richard of Belhagh complains of Robert the cooper and Robert Man in a plea of land, ordered to summon them etc., pledge for the plaintiff [illeg.].

Henry the chaplain amerced 3d. because he dug a pit on the common, causing nuisance to the lord and the townspeople.

The whole homage in mercy for various concealments.[74]

The jurors have a day until the next court to enquire concerning 2a. of land formerly Clevehogs, whether it should be customary or not, and concerning alienation [of it]; also concerning trespass against John Typetot and Geoffrey Rath by Robert of Reydon, viz. the appropriation from their messuage of land, 3ft. wide and 4p. long.

Ordered to execute all the orders of the preceding court, marked with a cross, and not acted upon.

Ordered to attach Walter Craske to reply to Nicholas de Walsham in a plea of trespass, and Robert Salvetayl to reply to William Hawys in a like plea.

Geoffrey Rath and Matilda Coppelowe his wife come into open court and surrender into the lord's hands the custody and care (?nutr') of William Matilda's son, aged five years, together with all her dower, until his full age; and entry was granted to John of Stonham in the aforesaid form, rendering the annual services due therefrom, fine 2s.6d., pledge the hayward.

SUM 32s. 4d.

---

74 No amount shown.

## 62. WALSHAM Court, 2 December 1332 [HA504/1/3.19]

<William Hawys plaintiff v Robert Salvetayl> in a plea of trespass, essoins by Walter Payn, he pledges faith; Robert did not come. \as appears below/ Roger Hauker, defendant v John Hernyng in a plea of debt, essoins by John Frere, he pledges faith; John is present. Robert Kembald essoins of common suit by Manser of Shucford, he pledges faith.

Adam Noble amerced 3d. for leave to agree with William Hawys in a plea of trespass, pledge the hayward.

Robert Warde amerced 3d. for unlawful detention of 2s.6d. from Henry of Saxmundham for John Noreys; ordered to raise, pledge the hayward.

William Kembald amerced 3d. for leave to agree with Nicholas de Walsham in a plea of trespass, pledge Nicholas Kembald.

The second pledges of William Kembald amerced 6d., because they did not have him satisfy the lord concerning the withholding of one hen in rent for two years; ordered to summon him by better pledges.

Walter Craske amerced 3d. for leave to agree with Nicholas de Walsham, pledge the hayward.

Robert the cooper <and Robert Man[75]> was summoned to reply to Richard of Belhawe in a plea of land, in various complaints; on which he says that Robert the cooper forcibly deprived him of ¼r. of land, and Robert Man forcibly deprived him of 1r. by estimation of uncultivated (?fera) land. And he says that Cristina Grous his grandmother was seised of the said land as of right and inheritance; that she demised the land to Richard Reve and Cristina his wife for a term of years, and within that term Richard Reve sold it to Robert the cooper and Robert Man, who now hold it unlawfully, and thereupon he produces suit. Robert and Robert come and say that Cristina Grous sold the land to Richard and Cristina Reve, and they held the land by that sale, and not by demise; that Richard Reve afterwards sold it to Robert and Robert, and that they hold it by that right, and not otherwise. On this they ask that an enquiry be held, and the other party agrees; a day is given to them until the next court, in the status in which they now are. Afterwards, because the complaint is not sound, Richard has leave to withdraw it.

Robert Lene amerced 20s. for trespass against the lord, beating Euphemia the daughter of Robert Ryvel villein, pledges Richard Kebbil and John Lene.

John Man was attached to reply to Robert Crane in a plea of debt, and thereupon Robert complained that John unlawfully withheld from him 5s., which he ought to have paid him, and on this he brought suit. John said that he owed Robert nothing, as he was accused, and on this he offered to wage law. He waged law [successfully] that he owed nothing; therefore it was adjudged that Robert Crane be amerced 6d. for his false claim; John is quit indefinitely, pledge Manser of Shucford.

Robert the chaplain amerced 6d. for damage in the lord's wheat with three cows; Henry of Saxmundham 3d. for damage in the lord's wood with a cow; William of Cranmer the elder and Robert Sare 3d. each for damage in the lord's wheat with their sheep; Adam Noble 3d. for the same with two horses; Richard Lorence, William Godyene and Nicholas Goche 3d. each for damage in the lord's pasture

---

[75] This deletion of 'Robert Man' must be intended to apply to all the later references to him in this entry.

with their horses; and Henry the chaplain 6d. for damage in the lord's corn and pasture with his beasts; pledge for all the hayward.

Robert Warde pays 6d. fine for respite of suit of court until Michaelmas; William Noreys and Mabel Bonde pay 3d. each, John of Cowlinge and John Crane pay 4d. each, Bartholomew Patel pays 6d., Richard Patel, Richard of Cranmer and William Patel pay 3d. each for the same, pledge for all the hayward.

It was found that <Henry of Saxmundham trespassed in the lord's wood with his dog and> that Henry the chaplain caused damage on the common, with his sheep grazing where he had no right of pasture; ordered to attach him etc.

Henry of Saxmundham amerced 3d. because he raised a fold and kept it beyond the fixed day granted to him by the lord, pledge the hayward.

Walter Osbern amerced 12d. because he had a fold to the number of 6 score sheep from Michaelmas until this day.

Nicholas Goche purchased from John Noreys 3r. of land by charter; a day is given to him until the next court to surrender the said charter.

William Clevehog amerced 3d. because he overstocked the common with sheep of the cullet, pledge the hayward.

<Presented that the Prior of Ixworth has the liberty of a fold formerly of Adam Syre to the number of 30 sheep and 1 ram, the jurors to enquire>. [see below]

The first pledges of Robert Salvetayl amerced 3d. because they did not have him reply to William Hawys in a plea of trespass; ordered etc.

Surrender: Alice Warde to Robert Warde and his heirs, 12p. of land abutting on the tenement of William Chapman, granted to him to hold in villeinage by services and customs, fine 3d., pledge the hayward, fealty.

Walter Pye amerced 12d. because he brewed and sold ale in breach of the assize; Walter Rampolye 6d. for the same; Geoffrey of Lenne and John Warde each amerced 3d. because they baked and sold bread in breach of the assize, pledge for all the hayward.

John Typetot and Geoffrey Rath amerced 4d. for their false claim against Robert of Reydon, pledge each for the other.

William Payn and Stephen Cooper the ale-tasters in mercy because they did not perform their duties, condoned by the lord.

Simon Deneys pays 3d. fine for respite of suit of court until Michaelmas, pledge John Syre; Roger Southwold and John Wymond each pay 6d. for the same, pledge for both William of Cranmer.

Again ordered to retain 1¼r. of meadow which Peter Warde sold to Robert Warde, without leave; and to seize 1r. of land which Richard Wyndilgard sold to William Payn, without leave.

A day is given to the whole homage to enquire concerning the tenement Skut, who holds and how much each one holds separately, and to apportion the said tenement; and to enquire concerning a fold, which was formerly of Adam Syre, and is now in the hands of the Prior of Ixworth, how many sheep belong to this fold, and where should they graze; and also concerning two folds, formerly of William the shepherd and Hugh the clerk, now in the hands of the Prior, how many sheep belong to these folds, and where they should graze; <and to enquire whether Henry of Saxmundham disposed of (*alienavit*) his goods outside the lord's bondage into a free tenement, under penalty of 20s.>. And to enquire concerning the tenants of <the tenement of Robert of Fornham and> the tenement formerly Margery's tenement, who holds it, and to apportion it; and also concerning all the tenants who should be apportioned to 3s.8d. of Sheriff's aid, which pertains to the Abbot of St Edmunds, with the condition that they are apportioned by Sunday before the feast of St Thomas the Apostle [20 December], under penalty of 20s.

Surrender: John Typetot and Cecilia his wife to John Bolle and his heirs, half a messuage 2a.1r. of land, of which 1a.7r. lie in Puddyngscroft and ½a.13p. lie in the croft of Elias Typetot, granted to him to hold in villeinage, by services and customs, fine 7s., pledge William of Cranmer.

Ordered to attach Walter Pye and Walter Rampolye brewers because they did not send for the ale-tasters as they ought.

Robert Noreys, Robert Osbern, <Robert Sutor and John Sutor>, John Green, Richard Spileman, William Warde and Robert the chaplain of Walsham each amerced 3d. for default.

A day is given to the whole homage until Sunday before the feast of St Thomas the Apostle [20 December], to apportion the tenement formerly of Robert of Fornham, according to the value of each acre separately, under penalty of 20s.

Surrender: John Lene and Edmund his son to Thomas Fuller and his heirs, ½r.3p. of land lying in the Brookfield, abutting on Kebbelsbrook, granted to him to hold in the same form as above, fine 3d., pledge the hayward.

William Clevehog pays 3s. fine for having a fold to the number of 8 score sheep until next Michaelmas, pledge William of Cranmer.

Matilda Robbes pays 3s. fine for leave to marry William Deneys, pledge the hayward.

Robert and William Sutor pay 6d. fine for respite of suit of court until Michaelmas, pledge the hayward.

[SUM 48s. 6d., not stated]

### 63. WALSHAM Court, 3 February 1333 [HA504/1/3.20]

Robert Kembald essoins of common suit by John Typetot, and Manser of Shucford of the same by Richard Gileman. Ralph Echeman, defendant v Thomas King in a plea of debt, essoins by Richard of Langham, he pledges faith; Ralph is represented by his attorney.

The first pledges of Roger Hauker amerced 3d. because they did not have him reply to John Hernyng in a plea of debt; ordered to summon him by better pledges.

Walter Pye and Walter Rampolye brewers each amerced 3d. because they did not send for the ale-tasters, pledge for both the hayward.

Robert Kembald amerced 3d. because he did not warrant his essoin.

Surrenders: William Warde to Richard Warde and his heirs, 3⅓r. land, granted to him to hold in villeinage by services and customs etc., fine 2s., pledge the hayward.

Walter Rampolye to William Rampolye and his heirs, ½r. of land next to Goselyngesyerd, with one head abutting on the Bury way, granted to him to hold in the same form, fine 6d., pledge the hayward.

Again as elsewhere ordered to attach Robert Salvetayl to reply to William Hawys in a plea of trespass.

Simon Cooper in mercy for unlawful detention of 20s. from Henry de Elmham, from the time when he was Henry's dairyman, which he could not deny in open court, condoned, and ordered etc.

Surrender: William Warde to William Springold and his heirs, 25p. of land abutting on Ladyswood, granted to him in the same form as above, fine 6d., pledge the hayward.

The jurors say that the servants of Henry the chaplain and John Underwood took the lord's rabbits; ordered to distrain Henry and John; and that Robert the farmer of Ashfield gathered and took away withies (?*virgas*) out of Ladyswood; ordered to distrain him.

The servants of John Lene amerced 3d. because they broke and took away the lord's hedges, pledge the hayward; Alice Whyteman 3d. for the same, pledge Robert Lene.

The gooseherd \of the farmer/ of the Prior of Ixworth amerced 3d. for damage in the lord's rye, pledge the hayward.

The servant of Robert Shepherd chaplain amerced 6d. because he blocked the stream at the Hedge ['Heg'], causing a nuisance to the lord etc., pledge the hayward.

The servant of Nicholas Kembald amerced 3d. because he broke into the lord's pound, pledge the hayward.

Clarice the wife of Andrew Patel held from the lord, when she died, 6½a. of land which she and Andrew purchased jointly, to hold to them and the heirs issuing from their bodies. The jurors say that Richard Patel is her nearest heir, and he is of full age; and that the land is held from the lord by the rod, because at some time it was taken into the lord's hands, and returned to them to hold at the lord's will. After Clarice's death the lord had a bullock, worth 5s., as a heriot, by which Richard claims entry without fine, following the custom of the manor. Entry is granted and he swore servile fealty.

Alexander the son of Sir Alexander de Walsham purchased from John Noreys 4½a. of land and ½r. of pasture; ordered to distrain him to swear fealty.

Ordered to distrain Sir Edmund de Pakenham[76] and Sir Alexander de Walsham to swear fealty.

William Elys purchased from Peter Margery 2a.1r. of land of the lord's fee; a day is given to him to come to the next court to show his charter, and to do that which he should do, pledge the hayward. Afterwards he comes and shows his charter in due form, and swears fealty.

Robert Shepherd chaplain pays 6d. fine for respite of suit of court until Michaelmas, pledge the hayward.

Surrender: Roger of the Brook to John Man and his heirs, 21p.4ft. of land, abutting on the Southway, granted to him in the same form as above, fine 6d., pledge the hayward.

William Hawys amerced 40d. because this year he had a fold of 200 sheep, without the lord's leave. Walter Osbern amerced 2s. because this year he had 100 sheep lying outside the lord's fold, without leave.

Thomas Patel of Finningham chaplain complains of William Clevehog the son of Stephen Reve the elder of Walsham, in a plea of debt in two complaints, pledges for Thomas, Richard and Bartholomew Patel; ordered to attach William to reply.[77]

---

76 Son of the late Sir Edmund and Lady Rose.
77 Margin: 'ordered' is deleted.

Robert of the Brook, by leave of the court, demised to Walter Osbern ½a. of meadow at Southbrook, to hold from last Michaelmas to a term of three years, fine 2d.; and Roger of the Brook, by leave of the court, demised to Walter Osbern ½a. of meadow at Southbrook to a term of five years, fine 2d., pledge for both fines the hayward.

Surrender: Robert Sare and Idonia his wife to Letitia Stronde and her heirs, a quarter of a messuage formerly of John Stronde, granted to her in the same form as above, fine 6d., pledge the hayward.

Ordered to attach Sir Hugh Hovel to swear fealty to the lord, for half a quarter of a knight's fee, which he holds of the lord in Wyverstone.

Ordered to take into the lord's hands ½a. of customary land which Richard de Walsham purchased by charter from [blank], with another free tenement.

Ordered to attach Thomas Patel chaplain for services and customs withheld, to the value of 46s.

Henry de Wells ['Welles'] chaplain pays 12d. fine so that he can graze his sheep on the common of Walsham, in the fold of Thomas of Badwell, until next Michaelmas, pledge the hayward.

Again ordered to take into the lord's hands 1r. of land, which Richard Wyndilgard sold to William Payn, without leave, and to report the profits.

A day is given to Walter Osbern and his fellow-jurors until the next court to enquire concerning the tenement Skut, who holds, and how much each one holds separately, and to apportion the tenement; and to enquire concerning the fold formerly of Adam Syre, and now in the hands of the Prior of Ixworth, how many sheep belong to the fold, and where ought they to graze; also concerning the two folds formerly of William the shepherd and Hugh the clerk, now in the Prior's hands, how many sheep belong and where they should graze; and to enquire concerning the tenants of Margery's tenement, who holds, and to apportion; also concerning the tenants who should be apportioned to 3s.8d. of Sheriff's aid which pertains to the Abbot of St Edmunds, with the condition that they are apportioned by Sunday next before the feast of Thomas the Apostle [21 December],[78] under penalty of 20s.

A day is given to the parson of Langham until the next court to satisfy the lord for trespass, taking away wood out of Ladyswood, pledges Richard of Langham and William of Cranmer.

SUM 13s. 8d., except a bullock, worth 5s., as a heriot
From this, in the expenses of Thomas de Saxham and the clerk, 22d.

## 64.   HIGH HALL Court of Nicholas de Walsham, 5 May 1333 [HA504/1/3.21.i]

Catherine Mayheu, defendant v Roger Brush in a plea of debt, essoins by Walter of the Marsh, he pledges faith; Roger is present, and afterwards he appoints in his place William Wodebite.

+Gilbert Helpe amerced 3d. because he did not distrain Simon Wright in a certain pightle in Cotton with a piece of pasture adjoining, opposite Simon's wood, and

---

[78] This date appears to have been copied from the entry in the last court, and is probably an error; it is unlikely that the time allowed would be 3 weeks on the first occasion, and 10 months on the second.

in a certain piece of land in the same vill, abutting on the said pightle to the east, for homage, fealty, \and ½d. rent/ and suit of court. Again ordered to distrain.

Nicholas Kembald pays 3d. fine for postponement of the rebuilding of a certain house in the lord's bondage until Michaelmas, pledges Gilbert Helpe and the hayward.

Ordered to distrain Richard Banlone because he appropriated to himself from the land of the lord's bondage at Angerhaleway, 3p. in length and 10ft. in width, digging and making ditches, as shown in the last court.

Adam Crane amerced 3d. for default of suit of court.

John of Foxley amerced 2s. for leave to agree with William Wodebite in a plea of debt, pledge William Wodebite.

Gilbert Helpe and John Packard each amerced 3d. because they did not allocate enough drivers to drive the lord's plough, as they had been ordered, on the contrary (?immo) they took John Goche, less than enough, to the lord's great loss.

Nicholas Kembald amerced 6d. because he demised to William Hawys 3r. of land of bondage without leave; ordered to seize the said land for contempt etc. and to report the profits to satisfy the lord.

Ordered to raise from the hayward 3d. [and] three hens, the arrears of rent of 1d. and 1 hen outstanding for three years, from a plot of land, 43ft. long and 32ft. wide, of the tenure of Matilda Wodebite; Nicholas Kembald is now the tenant of it, and the arrears to be raised from him, as shown in the court of 7 May 1330 [no.53].

Ordered to distrain in a messuage 3r. of land in Westhorpe at the Marsh, which Simon Erl purchased from William Wodebite villein of this manor, in the time of Alice de Walsham, formerly tenant of this manor, [to hold] for his lifetime by services and ½d. increased rent, and to satisfy for entry, and to show by what right he entered into the said messuage 3r. of land.

The jurors present that William Hawys caused damage with his sheep at the Thirty-acres, and in the lord's headlands and the thorn hedges (*dumetis*) growing there, to the loss of 1d.

Walter Payn, Nicholas Kembald and Nicholas Fraunceys in mercy because they entered the lord's wood at Lenerethsdel and \trampled down and/ broke the banks, and caused damage. Also they took a hare against the lord's will etc.; remitted by the lady at the instance of Sir Hugh de Saxham.[79]

Adam Crane amerced 3d. because he demised to William Kembald ½a. of pasture of the lord's bondage without leave; ordered to seize until etc.

Ordered \to distrain John of Foxley/ and to take into the lord's hands 1a. of land in a certain pightle, which his fold manures, until he shows by what right he claims to hold and have the said 1a.

William Wodebite \and his fellow jurors/ amerced 8d. because they failed[80] to present the damage done by William Hawys \with his sheep/, in the wood and pasture, and for several concealments.

[SUM 2s. 10d. not stated]

---

[79] Margin: 'Ordered'.
[80] MS: *nolitterunt*, presumably in error for '*noluerunt*'.

## 65. WALSHAM Court, 17 May 1333 [HA504/1/3.22]

Nicholas Kembald, defendant v Geoffrey Rath in a plea of debt, essoins by John Typetot, he pledges faith; Geoffrey is present. William Clevehog <the elder of Walsham> \the son of Stephen Reve the elder of Walsham/, defendant v Thomas Patyl of Finningham, chaplain, in a plea of debt, essoins by Peter Neve, he pledges faith. Willliam Clevehog of Walsham, the son of Stephen Reve the elder of Gislingham,[81] essoins by Peter Tailor, he pledges faith; Thomas is represented by J. Bret, his attorney. Nicholas Kembald, plaintiff v William Rampolye in a plea of covenant, essoins by William Kembald, he pledges faith.

Walter the smith and the hayward, the first pledges of Robert the parson of Langham, amerced 12d. because they did not have him satisfy the lord for damage in Ladyswood; ordered to summon him by better pledges.

Robert the farmer amerced 12d. for damage in Ladyswood taking away withies, pledges William Hawys and Robert of Reydon.

Surrender: Robert Crane to Manser of Shucford and his heirs, ½a.22p. of land in one piece in Cranescroft, abutting on Clay street, granted to him to hold in villeinage by services and customs, fine 18d., pledge the hayward.

Ralph Echeman amerced 3d. for leave to agree with Thomas King in a plea of debt, pledge the hayward.

The second pledges of Roger Hauker amerced 6d. because they did not have him reply to John Hernyng in a plea of debt, ordered to summon him by better pledges.

Again as elsewhere ordered to attach Robert Salvetayl to reply to William Hawys in a plea of trespass.

Ordered to raise from Simon Cooper 20s. to the use of Henry de Elmham.

Again ordered to distrain Sir Hugh Hovel \to distrain by 1 horse/, to swear fealty to the lord for half a quarter of a knight's fee, which he holds from the lord in Wyverstone.

Gilbert Helpe amerced 20s. for various trespasses and contempt to the lord, pledges Walter Pye and Bartholomew Patel.

<Ordered to raise> from Gilbert Helpe 6s.8d. in respect of various amercements for trespass against the lord.

Ordered to attach Nicholas de Walsham to reply to William Rampolye in a plea of covenant.

Walter the miller amerced 3d. for leave to agree with Nicholas de Walsham in a plea of trespass. Walter Man amerced 3d. for the same with William Hawys in a plea of debt, pledge for both the hayward.

William Hawys amerced 3d. for unlawful detention of 1 quarter of malt, worth 9s., from Adam Syre chaplain, which he could not deny in open court, pledge the hayward, with the loss, which is assessed at 3d.; ordered to raise.

Eleanor Windilgard pays 6d. fine to repossess 1r. of land out of the lord's seisin, which was taken because Richard Windilgard sold it without leave, pledge Manser of Shucford.

William Wither amerced 3d. for his false claim against Manser of Shucford in a plea of trespass, pledge the hayward.

---

[81] There is some confusion here; it is clarified in roll no.69, in which the first William is referred to as the elder, and the second as his brother, and Stephen Reve only as 'of Gislingham'.

Robert Ryvel amerced 4d., Robert Lene, Peter Jay and John Herning 3d. each for damage in the Great Meadow, pledge the reeve.

John King amerced 3d. for damage in the lord's herbage with his sheep at Strondesway, pledge William Hawys.

Edmund Lene amerced 6d. because he baked and sold bread, and 6d. because he brewed and sold ale, in breach of the assizes; Walter Pye 12d. and Walter Rampolye 6d. for the latter, and Geoffrey of Lenne 3d., Henry Smith 3d. and George Swan 2d. for the former, pledge for all the hayward.

<The jurors say that Gilbert Helpe trespassed in the lord's warren, and is in mercy, pledges Walter Pye and Bartholomew Patel>, see above.

William Hawys amerced 12d. because he sold 1a. of customary land to Alan Stritt without leave, ordered to take the land into the lord's hands.

Mabel Bonde, when she died, held from the lord 2½a. of land by the rod; Agnes the wife of Adam Sket is her nearest heir and is of full age; ordered to take the land into the lord's hands.

William Payn and Stephen Cooper the ale-tasters amerced 6d. because they did not perform their duties.

Surrenders: +John Wymond and Agnes Stronde [his wife] to William of Cranmer the younger and his heirs, 3r. of pasture and 1r. of land, granted to him to hold in villeinage by services and customs, fine 3s., pledge the hayward.

+Letitia Stronde to William of Cranmer the younger and his heirs, 3r. of pasture and 1r. of land, granted to him in the same form, fine 3s., pledge the hayward.

John Wymond and Agnes his wife to Letitia Stronde and her heirs, 3r.30p. of land, lying in a croft in two pieces, granted to her in the same form, fine 3s.4d., pledge the hayward.

Robert Sare and Idonia his wife to William of Cranmer the younger and his heirs, 1r. of meadow lying in Ashfield meadow, granted to him in the same form, fine 12d., pledge the hayward.

Henry de Wells chaplain and John Underwood amerced 6s.8d. for trespass in the lord's rabbit warren by their servants, pledges William of Cranmer and the hayward.

Surrender: William Robhood to Thomas of the Beck and his heirs, 1a. of land in Stowemerefield, granted to him in the same form as above, fine 12d., pledge the hayward.

The Prior of Ixworth amerced 3d. for damage with his sheep in the lord's corn and pasture at Allwood; William Hawys, William Payn and William Kembald 2d. each, Walter Osbern 3d., Walter Deneys 2d. and John Syre 3d. for the same with their beasts, pledge for all the hayward. Robert Ryvel amerced 2d. for damage with his sheep on the bank at the gate of the manor, pledge the hayward. Adam Noble and Robert Man each amerced 3d., Peter Tailor 2d., and Nicholas Goche 3d. for damage in the lord's corn by their servants collecting herbage, pledge the hayward.

William Hawys pays 12d. fine for having a fold of 6 score sheep from the feast of the Finding of the Holy Cross [3 May] until Michaelmas, pledge the hayward.

Again ordered to distrain Sir Edmund of Pakenham, Sir Alexander de Walsham and Alexander his son to swear fealty to the lord.

William Hawys pays 12d. fine for entry into ½a. of land after the death of Peter Hawys, which Richard, his brother, appropriated to himself with a free tenement, pledge the reeve.

160

The first pledges of Thomas Patel chaplain amerced 6s.8d. because they did not make compensation for a distraint taken on Thomas, for 46s. for services and customs withheld, which is again ordered to be raised \6s.8d./.

Again a day is given to Walter Osbern, William Hawys, William of Cranmer and their fellow jurors until the next court, to enquire concerning 3 folds, which were formerly of Adam Syre, William the shepherd and Hugh the clerk, now in the hands of the Prior of Ixworth, how many sheep belong to the folds and where they should graze; and to enquire concerning all the tenants of Margery's tenement, who holds, and to apportion that tenement; and to enquire concerning 4a. of land, 1a. of meadow and 3r. of wood which Andrew Patel held, on the day he died, whether it should be shared among Andrew's four sons, or not, \Afterwards the jurors say that it should not be shared/, under penalty of 20s. And to apportion the tenement Skut.

> SUM 60s. 6d., except 6s.8d., for which Gilbert Helpe is liable for
> various fines. From the sum – 2s.6½d., the expenses of holding
> the court, and ½ bushel of oats

## 66.  WALSHAM Court, 18 October 1333 [HA504/1/3.23]

<William Rampolye> \a day on request, as below/, defendant v Nicholas de Walsham in a plea of covenant, essoins by John Hayloke; likewise in a plea of covenant, by Gilbert Sare.

Thomas William, defendant v William Hawys in a plea of trespass, essoins by Geoffrey the bailiff, he pledges faith; William is present.

Roger Hauker, defendant v John Herning in a plea of debt, essoins by Henry Whitemor;[82] John Man, defendant v Alan, the bailiff of Sir William Gyfford, in a plea of debt, essoins by Richard Patel; and Walter the smith, by Thomas Patel; and Thomas Fuller, by Walter Osbern; and Richard Kebbel, by John Syre; and John Typetot, by William Springold, all defendants v the same Alan in like pleas. \Afterwards all came/.

Nicholas Kembald amerced 3d. for leave to agree with Geoffrey Rath in a plea of debt, pledge the hayward.

A day is given, at the request of the parties, to Nicholas de Walsham, plaintiff, and William Rampolye in a plea of covenant, and to William, plaintiff, and Nicholas, defendant, in a like plea, to come to the next court without essoin.

Ordered to raise from Simon Cooper 20s. to the use of Henry de Elmham, to be recovered from Simon.

A day is given, at the request of the parties, to Thomas Patel chaplain, plaintiff, and William Clevehog, defendant, in a plea of debt, to come to the next court without essoin.

John Man amerced 3d. for leave to agree with Walter the smith in a plea of debt, pledge the hayward.

John Typetot, Thomas Fuller, Stephen Cooper, Richard Kebbil and Walter the smith each amerced 2d., for unlawful detention of 3s. from Alan Stritt, for Roger Hauker; ordered to raise, pledges each for another. Afterwards they paid in court.

---

82  Margin: 'It does not lie because *?ad magn' distr'*: this may refer to the unspecified order later in this court, in which Roger's pledges are amerced.

Ordered to raise from William Hawys 1 quarter of malt, worth 9s., and 3d. for damages, to the use of Adam Syre, chaplain, as awarded in the last court.

The third pledges of Roger Hauker amerced 6d. because they did not have him reply to John Hernyng in a plea of debt; ordered etc. and the hayward to reply concerning the pledges.

Simon Peyntour amerced 3d. for leave to agree with William Clevehog in a plea of trespass, pledge the hayward. <John Man in mercy for the same, with Walter the smith in a plea of debt> \because recorded above/.

John Lester ['Lyster'] amerced 6d. for unlawful detention of 21s.8d. from Richard of Layham ['Leyham'], which he could not deny in open court; ordered to be raised, and he finds a mainpernor to pay the money at the next court, *viz.* Robert of Reydon.

John Syre amerced 3d. for leave to agree with Robert Lene in a plea of debt, and 3d. for the same with William Goselyng; Simon Peyntour 3d. for the same with John Man, and 3d. for the same with Elias Typetot in a plea of trespass, pledge for both the hayward.

John Robhood pays 3d. fine for respite of suit of court until Michaelmas, pledge Robert Tailor.

Simon Peyntour amerced 3d. for leave to agree with Robert Rampolye in a plea of trespass, and 3d. for the same with John Typetot, pledge the hayward.

Amice the servant of the Prior of Ixworth amerced 9d. for damage in the lord's corn with her geese; Robert Ryvel 6d. for the same, with his wethers, pledge for both the hayward.

Robert the son of Peter Warde pays 4d. fine for respite of suit of court until Michaelmas, pledge Robert Warde; Robert Warde pays 6d. fine for the same, pledge the hayward.

Surrender: William of Cranmer the elder and William of Cranmer the younger to Walter the smith and his heirs, 2a. of land in the Millfield, abutting on the Bury way, granted to him to hold in villeinage by services and customs, fine 8d., pledge the hayward.

John Crane pays 3d. fine for respite of suit of court until Michaelmas, pledge the reeve; likewise Roger of Southwold 6d., John Wymond 6d., Simon Deneys 3d., William Noreys 3d., pledge for all William of Cranmer; Richard the son of Letitia 3d., pledge Richard of Wortham; Robert of the Brook 3d., pledge the hayward; Robert Shepherd chaplain 6d., and William Chapman 3d., pledge the reeve.

John Syre, Walter Payn, William Hawys, Walter Osbern, Stephen Cooper, Nicholas Goche, Matthew Hereward, William Springold, Peter Springold, Simon Peyntour, John Man, Elias Typetot, Robert Tailor and John Terwald, jurors on the Enquiry, say on oath that Richard the shepherd of Westhorpe, \on the day he died/, held a pightle from the lord by charter, for services 3½d. per year, and that his heir is unknown; ordered to take into the lord's hands until etc.

Robert the son of Richard Reve villein, when he died, held by the rod 1a.½r. of land and half a cotland. After his death the lord had <an ewe as heriot> no heriot, and they say that Walter Robert's brother is his nearest heir and of full age; and he comes and seeks admittance. Granted to him to hold by the rod by services and customs; <but they say that he should not pay a fine for entry because the lord had a heriot> and he pays 2s. fine, pledge the hayward.

Henry of Saxmundham amerced 6d., and Walter Hereward, Robert Tailor, Matthew

Hereward, William Springold and Peter Springold 3d. each, for damage in the lord's meadows with their pigs; John of Banham did likewise with his pigs in the same place, and in Ladyswood with his sheep, ordered etc.; Simon Cooper amerced 6d., and Nicholas Kembald 3d. for damage in Ladyswood with their cows, and John Typetot 3d., for damage cutting and taking away withies; John Warde 3d., for damage in the Little Meadow with his sheep, pledge for all the hayward.

<Ralph Echeman was summoned to perform works and did not come, and is in mercy.>

Robert of Reydon holds 2r. of land of the tenement of William of the Wood, which renders 1d. per year and half an autumn work, which have been withheld, therefore he is in mercy, condoned by the steward; ordered to raise. Robert purchased the land from Ralph Echeman.

Agnes Sutor the widow of Thomas Sutor stored corn grown on the bondage, in a free tenement; Richard of Wortham did the same, both in mercy, condoned. Robert Kembald and Peter Neve amerced 3d., Robert Sare 2d. and John Typetot 3d. for the same, pledge the hayward.

Henry de Wells chaplain and John Underwood overstocked the lord's common with their sheep, ordered etc.; and they grazed with the Prior's fold where they had no right of common. Henry also, under the (?*colar'*) of farm, which he has from Thomas of Badwell, grazed where he had no right of common; afterwards, he came and paid 5s. fine to have a fold of 6 score sheep there until next Michaelmas, pledge the hayward.

Henry of Saxmundham amerced 12d. because he took his sheep out of the lord's fold, pledge the hayward; ordered to return them to the lord's fold.

The jurors present that Adam Sket can and should graze in the open season with the fold which he has, which was formerly of Robert Bonde, as far as Rahawe, Kolnhawe and Waryneshawe, and not beyond; amerced 3s.4d. because he grazed beyond, pledges Nicholas Goche and the hayward.

Walter Osbern amerced 6s.8d. because he had 5 score sheep outside the lord's fold, and William Hawys 6s.8d. because he had 60 sheep outside.

Robert Ryvel amerced ½ mark because he unlawfully grazed on the common of Walsham, with the fold which he holds in Langham, pledge the hayward.

Edmund Lene amerced 6d. because he baked and sold bread in breach of the assize; Alice Pye amerced 12d. because she brewed and sold ale in breach of the assize; Isabella Lene and Walter Rampolye 6d. each, and Alice Warde 3d. for the same; Geoffrey of Lenne amerced 2d. because he sold bread in breach of the assize; pledge for all the hayward.

Stephen Cooper and William Payn the ale-tasters amerced 6d. because they did not perform their duties.

Adam Hardonn pays 2d. fine for respite of suit of court until Michaelmas, pledge Walter Osbern.

Catherine Machon gave birth outside wedlock; therefore the fixed [fine] 2s.8d.[83]

Robert of Reydon amerced 3s.4d. because he gave his daughter in marriage without leave.

---

[83] Margin: '2s.8d.' deleted, and 'amerced 12d.' substituted.

William Hawys pays 10s. fine to have leave to alienate in fee 1½a. [of land] in the field of Wattisfield to a certain Alan Stritt and his heirs, to hold as it was held for all time before the land came into William's hands, pledge the hayward. And it was granted by the lord etc.

It was ordered to take into the lord's hands 2a. of land which was held, on the day she died, by Mabel Bonde, whose nearest heir is Agnes the wife of Adam Sket until Adam and Agnes came to receive it by the rod, because, at some time, it was in the hands of John Lene villein, who held it by the rod, although before that time the land was free from all time. Adam and Agnes [now] come into court and ask that they be admitted to hold that land free, as of old it was accustomed to be, and notwithstanding that it was at some time in the seisin of the said villein, and that this should not in any way count against them. And it was granted to them [to hold] by the due and accustomed services therefrom, fine 20s.; Adam swore fealty. And, because it was found by process and the record of the roll of the preceding court, that he has in the same place ½a. more than the said 2a., ordered to take the ½a. into the lord's hands etc. Afterwards because the land was measured by Nicholas Goche and others of the lord's men, and it was found by the testimony of Nicholas, at his peril, that he has no more than 2a. and possibly less, the above order is void, and it is adjudged that Adam be quit of this charge.

Ordered to attach Richard Patel to satisfy the lord because he occupied the tenement of his father Andrew Patel, after his death, without the lord's leave, and because he did not swear fealty nor receive the tenement by the rod.

Robert of Reydon surrendered into the lord's hands a messuage 3a. of land to the use of John the Dyester[84] and Rose his wife and their heirs, who do not pursue the matter; ordered to retain in the lord's hands until etc. and to report the profits.

William Hawys amerced 6d., and John Man 3d., because they did not come to plough, as customary, when summoned, pledge for both the hayward.

Ordered to execute the orders of the last court marked with a cross and not acted upon.

Robert Sare pays 2s.6d. fine for having a fold of 5 score sheep until Michaelmas, viz. 6d. per score, pledge the reeve.

Robert Warde and John Warde pay 2s.4d. fine for a fold of 6 score sheep until Michaelmas, and no more because 8d. is allowed to them, on condition that they go on behalf of the reeve of the manor to the old Tower[85] and the king's Court of Justice, for the delivery of prisoners and the discharge of others.

Nicholas Goche pays 2s. fine for a fold of 4 score sheep until Michaelmas, pledge the reeve.

Peter Neve customary tenant amerced 3d. because he had 40 sheep outside the lord's fold for a whole year; ordered to make him return his sheep to the lord's fold. Memorandum that he is not now amerced because he is resident on a free tenement; the order could not be executed at the present time, because they will not be moved until the summer.

William of Cranmer pays 3s. fine for a fold of 8 score sheep until Michaelmas, and no more because he has 20a. of land to which one fold belongs, for which it was granted to him to hold 40 sheep free and to be quit of 6d. per score, 12d. in total, pledge the reeve.

---

84 Earlier named as 'Lyster' and later as 'Lester'.
85 Probably the Norman Tower of the Abbey of Bury St Edmunds.

Peter Jay pays 2s. fine for a fold of 4 score sheep until Michaelmas, pledge the reeve.

William of Cranmer and John Terwald were elected to the office of reeve, Richard Kebbil and Robert Rampolye to the office of hayward, and Peter Springold and Ralph Neve to the office of woodward.

SUM 103s. 5d.

## 67.   HIGH HALL Court, 24 November 1333 [HA504/1/3.21.ii]

<Robert Sare [and] William of Cranmer essoin of common suit by Walter Osbern, and William Ellis by Robert Kembald>; afterwards they came. William Deneys essoins of the same by Peter Priour, he pledges faith. Ralph Wybert v Thomas Shepherd in a plea of debt, essoins by Henry Trusse; and in another plea of debt, by Richard Patel, he pledges faith; Thomas is present.

Catherine Mayheu amerced 3d. for leave to agree with Roger Brush in a plea of debt; likewise 3d. to agree with John Man in a like plea, pledges Gilbert Helpe and the bailiff.

Robert Sare amerced 3d. for default.

Gilbert Helpe, John Packard \and William Wodebite/ were summoned to reply to Adam Syre in a plea of detention of 3 quarters of barley, worth 8s., concerning which Adam says that on Thursday after the feast of Epiphany in the 4th year of the reign of the present king [10 January 1331], he and William agreed a price of 10s., for a cow delivered to William, and for other debts owed by him to the same William; and on this agreed price, William remained indebted to Adam for the 3 quarters of barley, to be paid at the following Michaelmas; at this date they did not pay, but unlawfully withhold until now, to the loss etc.. Gilbert, John and William came into open court, and could not deny \that they owe the said 3 quarters of barley, as they are accused/. Adjudged that Adam shall recover the said corn, with the condition that it be paid at the feast of the Purification and at Easter next in equal portions, and that Gilbert, John and William be amerced 9d. If they default in the payment of the debt on the said days they shall pay to the lord 40d. as a penalty.

Matilda Wodebite, John Packard and William Wodebite amerced 3d. for unlawful detention of 40d. from John Chapman, by the hands of the said Matilda, adjudged that John shall recover the 40d., the loss is remitted.

Matilda Wodebite amerced 3d. for unlawful detention of 4s.6d. from Adam Syre; ordered to raise; the loss is remitted.

+Gilbert Helpe amerced 3d. because he did not distrain in a messuage 3r. of land for ½d. increased rent from the time when William Wodebite received the tenement from the lord, as shown in the last court; ordered to retain.

The profit from ½a. of pasture of the lord's bondage, lately taken into the lord's hands because Adam Crane sold it to William Kembald without leave, is 1d.; ordered to retain.

Adam Crane and Henry Goche each amerced 6d. for many defaults.

William Isabel is admitted to his inheritance without fine after the death of his father Robert, by the relief paid, following the custom of the manor.

John of Foxley amerced 2s. because he depastured the lord's herbage.

John the son and heir of John Wodebite, of full age, is admitted to his inheritance after his father's death, by a heriot, therefore nothing for entry. Likewise

165

Nicholas Kembald the son and one heir of Simon Kembald to his portion of the inheritance. <Mabel, the daughter and heir of Richard Gothelard, pays 6d. for having her inheritance at Michaelmas>, \void/.

Nicholas Kembald has a day until the next court to repair a certain house in the lord's bondage, pledges Gilbert Helpe and the hayward.

Ordered to distrain Richard Banlone to reply to the lord [to explain] why he appropriated to himself from the lord's land at Angerhaleway, 3p. long and ½[p.] wide, digging and causing damage, making a ditch.

William Revel amerced 12d. for damage in the lord's oats at Allwoodgreen with sheep, to the value of 3 sheaves, ordered to raise, and because he depastured the corn and herbage of the lord by night and day. Richard Winter did damage with sheep in the oats at Allwoodgreen, to the value of 1 sheaf, and William Payn the same with cows and geese, ordered to raise. +Avice Horn did damage in the lord's peas at Netherhawe with seven cows, to the value of 2 sheaves; ordered to distrain. Agnes the house servant of the lord amerced 6d. for damage in the lord's oats at Netherhawe with cows, 2 sheaves, and with a beast in the wheat, 1 sheaf. Nicholas Kembald the elder did the same in the lord's barley 3 sheaves, order waived by the lord. Richard Winter and William Isabel amerced 6d. for damage in the lord's wheat at Hordeshawe with pigs and sheep and other animals, to the value of 3d. William Wodebite amerced 6d. for damage in the lord's meadow at Smallbrook with beasts, to the value of 2d.; and John Man 6d. for the same, to the value of 3d. <William Hawys and William of Cranmer did damage at Lenerethsdel with their pigs rooting in the woods>.

Adam Crane amerced 12d. because he did not perform works for which he had been forewarned; John Chapman 6d. because he did not perform reaping works.

Peter Goche villein is a fugitive and withholds 1d. for chevage, ordered to distrain him by the body, wherever he may be found in the lord's domain.

Richard of Garboldisham broke the lord's ricks in the field, and took away sheaves to the mansion of the Lord Prior at the Easthouse; and Henry the chaplain and John Underwood are the receivers; ordered.

Matilda Wodebite and John Packard each amerced 6d. because they did not perform works which etc.; and all the villeins are amerced 6d. for concealing the said works.

Olivia Isabel in mercy for unlawful detention from the Prior of Ixworth, to the use of the sacrist, of 10s. of her rent; adjudged that the Prior shall recover the 10s., the loss is remitted; condoned.

All the customary tenants elect Adam Crane to the office of hayward[86] for the tenement Kembald; and the tenant of the tenement formerly of John Wodebite, to the office of hayward; ordered to distrain them to take the oath and assume their office.

[SUM 9s. 4d., not stated]

---

[86] In error for 'reeve'.

## 68. WALSHAM Court General, 13 January 1334 [HA504/1/3.24]

William Hawys, plaintiff v Thomas William <of Stanton> in a plea of trespass, essoins by Nicholas Fraunceys, he pledges faith; Thomas is present. William Hawys, tenant v Thomas William of Stanton[87] in a plea of dower, by Robert Kembald. Afterwards, Thomas did not proceed and he and his pledges are amerced 3d., William [is quit] indefinitely.

William Rampolye in mercy for leave to agree with Nicholas de Walsham in a plea of covenant in two complaints, condoned by the lord.

Richard Kebbil the hayward amerced 2s. because he did not raise from William Hawys 1 quarter of malt, worth 9s., and 3d. loss, to the use of Adam Syre as he was ordered; again ordered to raise; Adam established his claim to this malt against Richard in this court last year.

+Thomas William of Stanton and Agnes his wife complain of Wiliam Hawys in a plea of dower, pledges for the plaintiffs, Richard Kebbil and Geoffrey Stephen; ordered to summon William to reply, Agnes appoints Thomas in her place.

+Ordered as elsewhere to raise from John Lester 21s.8d., to the use of Richard of Layham, to which Richard established his claim in the preceding court, pledges Robert of Reydon and Richard Kebbil.

Again a day is given, at the request of the parties, to Thomas Patel, plaintiff, and William Clevehog, defendant, in a plea of debt, to come to the next court without essoin.

The fourth pledges of Roger Hauker amerced 4d. because they did not have him reply to John Hernyng in a plea of debt; ordered etc.

John of Banham amerced 6d. for damage with pigs in the lord's meadows, and 3d. for damage in the lord's wood with sheep, pledge Henry de Wells, chaplain.

+The summons on Henry de Wells and John Underwood concerning trespass in the lord's pasture by overstocking with sheep from the fold, which he had at farm from the Prior, is in respite until etc., pledge the hayward.

+Ordered that William of Cranmer the elder, William Hawys, Walter Osbern and Nicholas Goche, having co-opted as many others of the homage as are necessary, apportion the tenement Margery before the feast of the Purification [2 February], under penalty of 2s. from each of them.

William Hawys pays 3s.6d. fine to have this year a fold of 8 score sheep, *viz.* at 6d. per score, save 1 score which he has free; Walter Osbern pays 2s. for a fold of 6 score sheep, 6d. per score, save 40 free; Elias Typetot and Richard Qualm pay 2s. for a fold of 4 score sheep, pledge for all the hayward.

Thomas Mittewynd complains against Margaret Hawys in a plea of debt, pledge for the plaintiff the hayward; ordered to retain one woollen cloth, worth 3s.6d., taken upon Margaret and to take [more] etc. to reply etc.

Robert Kembald and his pledges amerced 3d. because he did not proceed against John Man in a plea of trespass.

Walter Noreys complains against John Man in a plea of debt, pledge for the plaintiff the hayward; ordered etc.

General Enquiry by William of Cranmer, Walter Osbern, Matthew Hereward, Nicholas Goche, William Springold, Peter Springold, Simon Peyntour, Walter Payn, John Syre, Elias Typetot, Simon Rampolye and John Terwald, sworn etc.

---

[87] 'of Stanton' not deleted.

Ordered as many times to attach Robert Salvetayl to reply to William Hawys in a plea of trespass.

Ordered as many times to distrain Sir Hugh Hovel to swear fealty for half a quarter of a knight's fee, which he holds from the lord in Wyverstone; and Sir Edmund de Pakenham and Sir Alexander de Walsham <and Alexander his son> to swear fealty to the lord.

Ordered as many times to distrain Robert the parson of Langham church for damage in Ladyswood with his sheep.

Ordered as many times to attach Thomas Patel, or Richard Patel and Bartholomew Patel, his mainpernors, if he himself is not subject to jurisdiction, to return three horses with a cart, worth 30s., taken on Thomas for 46s. owed for services and customs withheld from the lord, for which Richard and Bartholomew are mainpernors, and notwithstanding, to take more distraints on Thomas to satisfy for the same.

Surrender: William Hawys to Thomas Hereward and his heirs, 1a. of customary land at the Goresgate, granted to him to hold by the rod in bondage, by services and customs, fine 3s., pledge Walter Hereward; Thomas swore customary fealty.[88]

Robert Robetel, when he died, held from the lord a customary cottage by services and customs; the lord had no heriot because he had no beast. John, his son, is his nearest heir, and is of full age; he comes into court and pays 12d. fine for entry, to hold in bondage at the lord's will, by services and customs. Seisin is delivered to him by the rod, and he swore customary fealty, pledge for the fine William Hawys. And John pays 2d. fine for respite of suit of court this year, pledge as above.

Memorandum that John Hernyng holds 2a. of land at Brounthweyt which he purchased from Robert Lene and John Lene villeins, and although this land was formerly free, Robert and John held it by the rod. Because the lord was given to understand that John Hernyng claims free status in the said land, and does not make suit of court, or anything else which should pertain to customary tenure, it was ordered to seize the land into the lord's hands until etc. Afterwards, at the next court, John says that he received the land by the rod, by leave of the court, for increased rent of 1d., and on this he submits to the record of the roll, and pays a fine for the roll to be scrutinised. \The fine appears in the next court./

John Hernyng amerced 12d. for many defaults.

Robert Osbern villein sold to John at the Church of Rickinghall a messuage in Rickinghall, which he held by the rod; ordered to take into the lord's hands until etc.

Ordered to attach Nicholas Fraunceys to reply to Gilbert Salvetayl in a plea of debt, pledge for Gilbert William Kembald.[89]

<Robert [Osbern] amerced 20s. because he sold the aforesaid messuage without leave of the court.>[90]

John at the Green amerced 6d. for default.

William the shepherd and Thomas of the Beck amerced 6d. for damage with sheep in the Launde at Ladyswood, pledge Peter Springold.

---

88  Tab: 'William Hawys'.
89  This entry is in a different hand, that of the scribe of the next roll, and is followed by a space of about 2in. before the next entry. The remainder continues in the original hand.
90  Margin: 'because elsewhere in subsequent roll'.

Walter [Craske] the miller in mercy[91] for damage in the lord's wood cutting down an ash tree.

Robert Rampolye exchanged ½a. of customary land with William Wodebite, villein of Nicholas de Walsham, without leave; ordered to take into the lord's hands until etc.

William Patel the younger in mercy for false testimony, condoned.

Walter the cooper amerced 3d. because he demised to John Underwood 1½r. of customary land in Dalefield, for a term of four years, without leave. Ordered to take into the lord's hands until etc.

Henry de Wells and John Underwood grazed their sheep where they had no right of common; ordered to attach them for the same.

Peter Neve amerced 6d. because he overstocked the common with his sheep, pledge the hayward.

Surrenders: Robert Crane to John Crane and his heirs, 1¼r. of customary land lying in two pieces in Brookfield, granted to him to hold in bondage at the lord's will by services and customs, fine 12d., pledge Manser of Shucford, John swore customary fealty.

William Hawys and Massilia his wife to Thomas Fuller and his heirs, ½r. of meadow at the Turfpits ['Turfpettis'], granted to him in the same form, fine 9d., pledge the hayward, Thomas swore customary fealty.

<Adam Syre chaplain amerced 12d. for many defaults.> Deleted because in subsequent court.

Adam Syre chaplain holds ½a. of customary land in the Syrescroft, formerly of Norman of Cranmer, and 1r. in the Southfield, and 1r. of customary land at Agneshedge ['Anneyshedge'], and he claims free status in the said land, and makes no suit of court or anything else which should pertain to customary land. Ordered to take into the lord's hands until etc. Afterwards at the next court, *viz.* Thursday after the feast of the Purification [3 February, no.69], Adam came into open court and declined (?*renuit*) absolutely to hold the land in future, but refused to keep that in mind (*illud recusat ?animo tenere*). Therefore ordered to take into the lord's hands, and to report the profits. Adam in mercy for trespass, because he cultivated the land for 10 years without leave, pledge John Fraunceys. The amercement is shown in the next court.

Agatha the daughter of William Marler amerced 6d. because she married Robert Swift without the lord's leave, and she holds customary land; Edith Agatha's sister 12d. because she married Thomas Dormour; Alice the daughter of John Stronde 40d. because she married Roger of Southwold; and Agnes the daughter of John Stronde 12d. because she married John Wymond, all without the lord's leave and holding customary land. And the same Agnes to reply for childwite, on two occasions.

Idonea the daughter of John Stronde amerced 18d. because she married Robert Sare without the lord's leave, and holds customary land; Rose the daughter of John Stronde in mercy for childwite, she holds customary land, condoned, and Letitia daughter of John Stronde amerced 2s. for the same on two occasions; Letitia and Alice the daughters of William the shepherd each amerced 2s. because they married Nicholas Goche and Stephen Cooper respectively, without leave; Emma the

---

[91] Margin torn, amount illegible.

daughter of William the shepherd 12d. because she married Richard Reve without leave, and she then held customary land; Walter Osbern amerced 20s. because Alice his daughter married Bartholomew Jerico freeman, pledge the hayward.

Ordered to execute all the orders of the preceding court not yet acted upon, marked by a cross.

SUM 54s. 4d.

### 69.  WALSHAM Court, 3 February 1334 [HA504/1/3.25]

Nicholas Fraunceys, defendant v Gilbert Salvetayl in a plea of debt, essoins by Stephen Cooper; he pledges faith; Gilbert is present. Robert Kembald essoins of common suit by William Elys; he pledges faith.

The first pledges of Margaret Hawys, about whom the hayward will report, amerced 6d. because they did not have her reply to Thomas Mittewynd in a plea of debt; ordered to appoint better pledges.

John at the Green amerced 6d. for default; ordered to take into the lord's hands all the tenement which John holds \from the lord/ in villeinage, *viz.* 3a. by estimation, for services and customs in arrears.

Walter Osbern comes into court and surrenders to the lord a capital messuage situated in Walsham, with a croft adjoining, together containing 2½a. by estimation. The lord granted all the tenement to Walter, to hold for the whole of his lifetime by services and customs etc., and that after Walter's death, all the tenement will revert to Bartholomew Jerico and Alice his wife and their heirs, to hold from the lord by the rod, by services and customs etc., and they pay 20s. fine for entry and reversion in the said form, pledges Walter Osbern and the hayward.

William Hawys amerced 6d. for leave to agree with Thomas William in a plea of trespass, pledge the hayward.

Thomas William and Agnes his wife amerced 6d. for leave to agree with William Hawys in a plea of dower, pledge the hayward. And the agreement is such that William granted and surrendered to them the dower of Agnes in all his lands and tenements, with which Peter Hawys, former husband of Agnes, was able to endow her; and each of the parties remits to the other all other actions, complaints and summonses whatsoever, from the beginning of this world to this day.

Thomas of the Beck purchased from Alexander the son of Sir Alexander de Walsham all the tenement which he had bought from John Noreys; he showed his charter and swore fealty to the lord.

William Clevehog the elder and William his brother amerced 6d. for leave to agree with Thomas Patel chaplain in a plea of debt, and the agreement is such that William and William acknowledged themselves to be in debt of 10s. to Thomas, on behalf of Stephen Reve of Gislingham, to be paid at Michaelmas, pledges William of Cranmer the elder and Richard Kebbil the hayward. And they will and grant that if they do not pay on the day etc., the lord's bailiff shall cause the debt to be paid out of the land and goods of William and William.

John Man amerced 4d. for leave to agree with Walter Noreys in a plea of debt, pledge the hayward.

Bartholomew Patel pays 6d. fine for respite of suit of court until Michaelmas.

John Typetot and Geoffrey Rath pay 4d. fine for the tenement Puddyngs, of which they each hold a part, to be apportioned; ordered the homage to apportion, pledge the hayward.

Peter Springold amerced 3d. for damage in Ladyswood by his sons cutting down an ash tree, worth 2d..

William Kembald amerced 3d. for digging a pit on the common at Cranmer, pledge the hayward.

+John Spileman amerced 3d. for making waste in the lord's bondage by allowing the decay of buildings, pledge the hayward.

William Revel amerced 6d. for trespass depasturing the herbage of Walsham with 'foreign' sheep from the vill of Westhorpe;[92] and 2s. because he overstocked the common of Walsham with his sheep, pledge the hayward.

Gilbert Salvetayl holds ½a. of land by the right of Alice his wife, and it is not known whether the land is customary or not, and they have a day etc. \The jurors say on oath that the land is customary; therefore ordered to seize./

William the son and one of the heirs of William Cook comes into open court, and since he is of full age he is admitted to his inheritance without fine, by the heriot given after his father's death, following the custom of the manor; he swore customary fealty.

Adam Syre amerced 3s.4d. for many defaults, and because he cultivated 1a. of customary land for 10 years, or more, without leave, as shown in the last court, pledge the hayward. Ordered to retain in the lord's hands, and to report the profits.

John Hernyng pays 6d. fine for the rolls to be scrutinised, concerning 2a. of land at Brounthweyt, which he bought from John Lene and Robert Lene, pledge the hayward. The process of the claim to this land and the cause are shown in the last court. Memorandum: that the rolls to be examined are those of the 11th and 12th years of the father of the present king [Jan.1337–Jan.1339], or about that time.

Ordered to retain in the lord's hands a pightle which Richard the shepherd of Westhorpe, when he died, held from the lord by charter, and for services 3½d. per year, until it is known who is the nearest heir, and his age.

Ordered to retain a messuage 3a. of land which Robert of Reydon gave to John Lester and Rose his wife and surrendered into the lord's hands to their use, until they come and receive it from the lord.

Ordered to execute the orders of the preceding court, marked with a cross, and not acted upon.

[SUM 37s. 9d., not stated]

## 70.   HIGH HALL Court of Nicholas de Walsham, 22 February 1334 [HA504/1/3.26.i]

Ralph Wybert gives two capons as a fine that he shall not dispute (*calumpnietur*) concerning his amercement in a plea of debt against him by Thomas the shepherd.

William Wodebite amerced 3d. for leave to agree with Adam Syre, chaplain, in a plea of debt, pledge Ralph Wybert; Ralph Wybert 12d. for the same with Thomas the shepherd, pledge [*blank*].

---

92 The remainder of this entry, and of the next, after 'a day etc.', and of the roll, after 'William Cook', are in a different hand.

Ralph Wybert in mercy for leave to agree with Thomas the shepherd in a plea of debt, pledge William Wodebite, condoned by the lord. Ralph acknowledges that he owes Thomas 8s. to be paid at Michaelmas, under penalty of 40d., paying the said 8s. and 40d., at the same term after the date of this court.[93]

Ordered to seize into the lord's hands all the tenement which Adam Crane holds from the lord in villeinage, for many defaults and services withheld.

Nicholas Kembald had a day until Michaelmas to rebuild a building wasted and taken outside the lord's bondage; he has a day until Christmas, pledges Gilbert Helpe and Robert Kembald.

+Again ordered to distrain in a messuage 3r. of customary land in Westhorpe, at the Marsh, which Simon Erl recently acquired from William Wodebite, villein of this manor, for the whole of his lifetime by services and ½d. increased rent, to satisfy for entry, and to show by what right Simon entered the fee of the lord.

Avice Horn amerced 3d. for damage in the lord's peas at Netherhawe, [and] in the lord's oats, to the value of 2 sheaves, with seven cows.

Ordered to attach by the body Peter Goche villein, a fugitive, wherever he may be found in the lord's domain, because he withholds from the lord 1d. for chevage.

John of Angerhale villein amerced 6d. for default.

Matilda Wodebite made waste in the lord's bondage which she holds by reason of wardship from the lord's demise, until the lawful age of her son John, and is amerced 12d. because she allowed the house to decay; she has a day to rebuild before next Michaelmas, pledge Gilbert Helpe.

John Goche villein amerced 3d. for waste in the lord's bondage, allowing a house to decay; he has a day until Michaelmas etc.

William Revel amerced 12d. for damage with his sheep at Angerhalefield, estimated at 1 sheaf; John Man amerced 6d. for the same. William Gostelen amerced 9d. for damage with his sheep in the lord's wheat at the Hulver ['Holver']; Robert Lene did the same there, ordered to distrain him to reply.

John Packard amerced 3d. for waste in the lord's bondage allowing a house to decay; ordered to repair, and he has a day until next Christmas.

William Revel overstocked the lord's commons and pastures with sheep from outside the manor, ordered to distrain him.

John Man pays ½ mark fine for entry to the tenement of Matilda his wife which she holds from the lord in villeinage, pledge Walter Osbern.

Robert the son of Gilbert Helpe villein amerced 6d. because, against the lord's orders, he sold fowls when the lord wished to keep them, pledge Gilbert Helpe.

The servant of John Man, with the consent of John and Matilda his wife, cut down and took away two ash trees from the lord's bondage, John and Matilda amerced 6d., pledge Gilbert Helpe.

All the customary tenants elect John Goche to the office of collector, and he gives two capons as fine not to be in that office this year, pledge Gilbert Helpe.

SUM 13s. 5d. and four capons

## 71. WALSHAM Court General, 29 April 1334 [HA504/1/3.27.i]

Elias Typetot, defendant v William Wodebite in a plea of trespass, essoins by John Typetot, he pledges faith; William is present. Robert Shepherd, chaplain, tenant v

93 The wording of this entry, and of that concerning the fine of 2 capons, is difficult to comprehend.

Stephen Cooper and Alice his wife, claimants, in a plea of land, essoins by Robert Kembald, he pledges faith. John the son of Adam Margery essoins of common suit by Peter Margery, likewise Robert Crane by Manser of Shucford, they pledge faith. Robert Shepherd chaplain, tenant v Richard Reve and Emma his wife, claimants, in a plea of land, essoins by Robert Sare, he pledges faith. Gilbert Salvetayl, plaintiff v Nicholas Fraunceys in a plea of debt, essoins by Walter the cooper, he pledges faith.

The first pledges of Henry de Wells chaplain <and John Underwood>\dead/ amerced 12d. because they did not have them satisfy the lord for grazing where they had no right of common. Ordered etc.

Surrender: Walter Osbern to William Ramploye and Agnes his wife and their heirs, 1a. of land with a pightle adjoining, granted to them to hold in villeinage by services and customs, fine 3s., pledge the hayward.

Again ordered to raise from John Lester 21s.8d., to the use of Richard of Layham, to which Richard established his claim against John in the court here, pledges Robert of Reydon and Richard Kebbil.

+Again as elsewhere ordered to attach Roger Hauker to reply to John Hernyng in a plea of debt.

+The summons against Henry de Wells chaplain and John Underwood concerning trespass in the lord's pastures, overstocking with sheep of the fold which they have at farm from the Prior, is in respite until etc.

<Again, as many times, ordered to attach Robert Salvetayl to reply to William Hawys in a plea of trespass.>

Ordered as many times to attach Sir Hugh Hovel to swear fealty for half a quarter of a knight's fee, which he holds from the lord in Wyverstone. +Also to attach Sir Edmund de Pakenham and Sir Alexander de Walsham to swear fealty to the lord, and Nicholas de Walsham for the same.

+[94]<Ordered as many times to distrain Robert the parson of Langham church for damage in Ladyswood with his sheep.>

Ordered to retain in the lord's hands ½a. of customary land which Robert Rampolye transferred to William Wodebite, villein of Nicholas de Walsham, without leave, in exchange etc.[95]

Again ordered to retain in the lord's hands ½a. of customary land in Dalesfield which Walter the cooper demised to John Underwood for a term of four years, without leave; and upon this John comes and pays 4d. entry fine, pledge the hayward.

<Again, as many times, ordered to attach Margaret Hawys to reply to Thomas Mittewynd in a plea of debt.>

+Again as elsewhere ordered to retain in the lord's hands all the tenement which John at the Green holds, for services and customs withheld.

Again ordered the whole homage to apportion the tenement Puddyngs.

William the son of William Cook complains of William Springold in a plea of land, pledges for the plaintiff Henry of Saxmundham and the hayward; ordered to summon William. \Void because [the plaintiff is] under age/.

---

[94] It is odd that this deleted entry was marked as an order not executed, but see footnote 95.

[95] Margin: 'Ordered \because [the transfer] was not approved, each of them is to keep his own [land]/'. It seems that this entry should have been deleted, and not that preceding.

Henry de Wells chaplain amerced 9d. for damage in the lord's rye at Dovehouse-wong ['Dufhouswong'] and in the lord's pasture at Allwood with his beasts; Amice Horn 3d. for the same; Robert Lene 6d. for damage in the lord's wheat at Brouneswong with his sheep; Peter Neve 12d. for damage in the lord's pasture with his beasts, on many occasions; Edmund Lene 3d. for damage in the lord's wheat at Ayleldestoft; Nicholas Goche 6d. for damage in the lord's pasture next to the Littlemeadow, with his beasts; pledge for all the hayward.

Simon Peyntour amerced 3d. for trespass against William Wodebite, assessed at 3½ farthings, ordered to raise, pledge the hayward.

Robert of Reydon, when he died, held from the lord by the rod 3a. of land, by services and customs; Rose his daughter is his nearest heir and of full age, and she is married to John Lester. They do not come; therefore ordered to take into the lord's hands until etc.

Matilda the wife of Elias Typetot, when she died, held from the lord by the rod 4a. of land and half a messuage, by services and customs; the lord had a cow as a heriot; Elias will hold the tenement for his lifetime.

Henry de Wells amerced 3d. for damage in the lord's herbage at the Oldtoft, pledge the hayward.

The whole homage amerced 10s. because they concealed 2a.3r. of land of the tenement Goselyngs, excluded from the rental.

+Mabel Springold amerced 6d. because she sold the reversion of 3r. of land to Agnes her sister without leave, ordered etc.

Robert Salvetayl sold a cottage to William Hawys without leave, ordered etc.

Peter Margery amerced 9d. because he withheld 2 ploughing services.

Walter Pye amerced 12d. because he brewed and sold ale in breach of the assize; Isabella the daughter of John Lene 6d., Walter Rampolye 6d. and Alice Warde 3d. for the same; Geoffrey of Lenne amerced 3d. because he sold bread in breach of the assize, pledge for all the hayward.

Stephen Cooper and William Payn the ale-tasters amerced 6d. because they did not perform [their duties], pledge the hayward.

Surrender: Robert Kembald to William Elys and Hilary his wife and their heirs, 1a. of land in Clay street between Robert's land and that of Catherine Machon, granted to them to hold in villeinage by services and customs, fine 3s., pledge the hayward.

John Man amerced [*damaged*] for unlawful detention from Walter Noreys of 1 bushel of peas, worth 8d.; ordered to raise, pledge the hayward.

Walter Noreys amerced [*damaged*] for his false complaint, pledge the hayward.

Agnes Springold pays [*damaged*]<sup>96</sup> fine for leave to marry John of Stonham, pledges the reeve and the hayward

<Ordered to retain in the lord's hands 1a. of customary land, which Adam Syre chaplain held for 10 years or more, without leave.> \because afterwards/.

+Ordered to retain in the lord's hands a pightle which Richard the shepherd of Westhorpe, when he died, held from the lord by charter and for services 3½d. per year, until it is known who is his nearest heir, and his age.

---

96 Damage to the margin has obscured two amercements and one fine, totalling 6s.3d.: the amercement of Walter Noreys suggests that John Man's was waived. An amercement of 3d. would be typical for Walter's offence, and 6s. for Agnes' leave to marry would not be unusual.

<Ordered to retain in the lord's hands a messuage 3a. of land, which Robert of Rey-
don gave to John Lester and Rose his wife, and surrendered into the lord's hands
to their use, until they come and receive it from the lord.>

Ordered to retain in the lord's hands 1a. of customary land which Adam Syre chaplain held for a long time without leave. Adam remitted all his right to the said
land, and upon this John Syre came and received it from the lord, to hold to him
and his heirs in villeinage by services and customs, fine 5s., pledges the reeve
and the hayward.

SUM 33s. 10d., except a cow as a heriot

### 72.   WALSHAM Court, 19 July 1334 [HA504/1/3.27.ii]

Peter Sparrow ['Sparwe'], defendant v William the son of Robert Ryvel, in a plea of
trespass, essoins by Peter Margery, he pledges faith. <John the son of Adam
Margery essoins of common suit, by Robert Sare.> \It does not lie because
essoined elsewhere[97]/. William the son of Robert Ryvel, plaintiff v Peter Sparrow
in a plea of trespass, essoins by Nicholas Kembald, he pledges faith. Manser of
Shucford essoins of common suit by Robert Kembald, he pledges faith.

John the son of Adam Margery amerced 3d. for default pledge the hayward.

Elias Typetot amerced 3d. for leave to agree with William Wodebite in a plea of
trespass, pledge the hayward.

<A day is given, at the request of the parties, *viz.* Richard Reve and Emma his wife,
and Stephen Cooper and Alice his wife, claimants, and Robert the shepherd,
defendant, in a plea of land in various complaints, until the next court, to come
without essoin>.

Sir Alexander de Walsham <to pay 12d. fine> for having easement with his carts for
carting dung in the Stubway, which is in the lord's severalty, as far as Sir Alexander's land in Wattisfield called Pinchonneslond. \waived by the lord./

Robert Kembald amerced 4d. for unlawful detention of 1 bushel of wheat from
Alice of Angerhale, pledge Walter the smith.

After the death of Robert of Reydon, a messuage 6a. of land, which he held in bondage by services and customs, was retained in the lord's hands; Robert's nearest
heir is Rose his daughter, who is of full age, and married to John Lester. They
come into court and pay 20s. fine for having entry, rendering services and customs. Seisin is delivered to them by the rod, and John swore customary fealty,
pledges the hayward and John Terwald. Memorandum that the lord had no heriot
because Robert had no beast.

Gilbert Salvetayl in mercy for a false claim against Nicholas Fraunceys in a plea of
debt. \condoned/.

Henry de Wells fined 12d. for trespass grazing the lord's common where he had no
right of common, pledge the hayward.

Robert Salvetayl, who holds from the lord, by the law of England, a cottage the
reversion of which belongs to the lord, comes into court and surrenders all the
title he has in the cottage to the use of William Hawys and his heirs; and because
the reversion belongs to the lord, he must be consulted. Afterwards the cottage

---

[97] In the last court.

175

was granted to William and his heirs to hold in perpetuity by services and customs, *viz.* 5d., for rent one hen, and a boon reapday ['bedrepeday'] in autumn with one man, entry fine 3s., pledge the hayward.

+Ordered to attach the holder of the manor of Wyverstone for relief and fealty, following the death of Sir Hugh Hovel, lately the lord [there]; likewise for half a quarter of a knight's fee.

Presented by the General Enquiry that Amice Horn caused damage with the Prior's geese in the lord's wheat at Ayleldestoft, amerced 6d, pledge Henry the chaplain. The same Henry amerced 9d. for damage with sheep in the lord's pasture at Boliskote; Nicholas Goche 9d. and John Warde 6d. for the same; Robert Sare 9d. for the same in the Stubway with sheep, cattle and oxen; Walter Syre 6d. for the same with a cow grazing there; William of Cranmer 9d. for the same with sheep, pledge for all the hayward.

Hilary the daughter of Anne Typetot, the servant of Henry of Saxmundham, amerced 3d. because she burned the lord's herbage in the meadows of the vill, and gathered the hay of the men of the town, and took it away against their will, pledge Henry; John the son of Peter Neve amerced 3d. for the same, pledge the hayward, also John Noble 3d., pledge William Wither.

Surrenders: Peter Springold and Mabel his wife to John of Stonham and Agnes Peter's daughter and their heirs, 3r. of land lying at Calfthweyt, granted to them to hold in bondage at the lord's will by services and customs, fine 2s.; and 1½a. of land lying in three places at Upstreet, and a third part of a messuage at Upstreet next to the messuage of Elias Typetot, granted to them in the same form, fine 4s., pledge the hayward.[98]

William Wither to William Rampolye and Agnes his wife and their heirs, 1½r. of land lying next to Bury way, granted to them in the same form, fine 12d., pledge the hayward.

William Springold pays 12d. fine for having a fold of 40 sheep until next Michaelmas, pledge the hayward.

Peter Tailor amerced 12d. for damage with his beasts around the manor, pledge the hayward; Simon Deye 6d. for damage in the lord's rye with cows, pledge the reeve; the servant of William Pach and Margaret Margery 3d. each for damage in Micklemeadow burning the herbage, pledge for both the hayward; Alice Whiteman 3d. for breaking the lord's hedges, pledge Robert Lene.

Eleanor Wyndilgard pays 3s.4d. fine for leave to marry, pledge Manser of Shucford.

Nicholas de Walsham complains against Nicholas Fraunceys in a plea of trespass, ordered to attach Nicholas [Fraunceys], pledge for the plaintiff, Richard Kebbil.

Mabel the daughter of Peter Springold pays 3s. fine for leave to marry, pledges Peter Springold and the hayward.

SUM 46s. 7d.

### 73. WALSHAM Court General of Sir Hugh de Saxham, 25 October 1334 [HA504/1/3.28]

Ralph of Rudham chaplain, defendant v Bartholomew Jerico in a plea of trespass, essoins by Nicholas Fraunceys, he pledges faith; Bartholomew is present.

---

98 Margin: 'customary fealty'.

Nicholas de Walsham, plaintiff v Nicholas Fraunceys in a plea of trespass, essoins by William Kembald, he pledges faith; Nicholas [Fraunceys] is present. John Hernyng essoins of common suit by Peter Margery. John Rath, defendant v John Warde in a plea of debt, essoins by John Typetot, he pledges faith; John Warde is present. William Hawys, plaintiff, v Ralph of Rudham chaplain, in a plea of trespass, essoins by Richard Patel; Ralph of Rudham, defendant in the same plea, essoins by Robert Sare, they pledge faith.

Bartholomew Patel pays 6d. fine for having respite of suit of court until Michaelmas, pledge Richard Patel.

William the son of Robert Ryvel and his pledges amerced 6d. because he did not proceed against Peter Sparrow in a plea of trespass, Peter is quit indefinitely. Afterwards they came, and Peter presented himself for leave to agree with William, pledge the hayward.

Manser of Shucford amerced 3d. because he did not warrant his essoin.

Adam Hardonn pays 3d. fine for respite of suit of court until Michaelmas; John Robetel 2d. for the same, pledge for both the hayward.

John Terwald amerced 3d. for leave to agree with Thomas of the Beck in a plea of trespass, pledge the hayward.

John Typetot in mercy for his false claim against Olivia Kembald in a plea of trespass; waived because he renews his complaint.

Walter Syre amerced 6d. for trespass in the lord's oats, pledge the hayward.

Walter Noreys amerced 6d. for his false claim against John Man in a plea of trespass, pledge the hayward.

Ordered to attach all the tenants of the tenement Allwood for one autumn boonwork withheld.

John Robhood \and Thomas Fuller/ amerced 3d. because they did not come to work when summoned in the autumn; Simon Peyntour 3d. because he did not come to gather the lord's hay.

A day is given, at the request of the parties, to Walter the smith, plaintiff, and Adam Noble, defendant, in a plea of trespass, until the next court to come without essoin.

Richard Cranmer amerced 3d. because he did not come to work when summoned. Robert Rampolye, William Patel the younger, John Terwald, John Robhod, <Henry of Saxmundham,> William Springold, Richard and William Warde, and John Man each amerced 3d. for the same.

Henry de Wells chaplain and Thomas Fuller each amerced 3d. for trespass in the lord's herbage at Littlemeadow, pledge the hayward; Richard Lorence 3d. for damage in Northawe with his cows, pledge the reeve; Nicholas Harnays 3d. for damage in Ladyswood, pledge Thomas of the Beck; John Digge 3d., Henry de Wells 6d., Matthew Hereward 3d., Robert Tailor 3d., William Springold 12d., Walter Hereward 3d. and Peter Springold 3d. for damage in Ladyswood with their pigs, pledge for all the hayward; William Godyene 3d. for damage in Northawe with his cows, pledge Thomas William.

Ordered to raise from William Clevehog the elder and William his brother 10s. to the use of Thomas Patel, chaplain.

Surrenders: William Chapman to Robert the son of Peter Warde and his family (*sequela*), a messuage 2½a. of land \and 1r. of meadow/, granted to him to hold by services and customs etc., fine 23s.4d., pledge Robert Warde the elder. And

177

for this surrender, fine and concord, Robert the son of Peter granted to William all the said tenement to hold for his lifetime.[99]

Walter Osbern to Thomas Fuller and his heirs, 1a.½r.6p. of land, granted to him to hold in villeinage by services and customs etc., fine 4s., pledge the hayward.

Robert the son of Peter Warde to William his brother, and his heirs, ½r. of land and a quarter of a messuage, granted to him in the same form, fine 12d., pledge Robert Warde the elder.

Walter Osbern to Walter Rampolye and his heirs, 1r. of land, granted to him in the same form, fine 10d., pledge the hayward.

Simon Rampolye to William Rampolye and his heirs, 3½r. of land, granted to him in the same form, fine 3s., pledge the hayward.

Peter Jay to Alice, Agnes and Catherine his daughters and their heirs, 1a. of land, granted to them in the same form, fine 3s., pledge the hayward.

Richard Patel pays 3d. fine for respite of suit of court until Michaelmas, pledge the hayward.

Simon Deneys, when he died, held from the lord a messuage 10a. of land by services and works, and the lord had nothing because he had no beast; Catherine and Alice his sisters are his nearest heirs, and they do not come; ordered to take into the lord's hands. Afterwards they come and pay 10s. fine for entry, pledge the hayward.

Mabel Springold pays 2s.8d. childwite, because she gave birth out of wedlock, pledge Peter Springold because in [his] house.

Henry of Saxmundham amerced 4d. for damage in Ladyswood with his pigs.

The jurors say that Sir Alexander de Walsham holds two folds in the west end ['westinde'] of the vill of Walsham, which is too many, and to the detriment of the lord and his customary tenants, and also of the whole neighbourhood on that side. And [they say] that he can have there, together with his co-tenants in the tenement Margery, no more than the single fold which was formerly of Warin Outlawe. Ordered etc.

William Cook the shepherd and John Wauncy caused damage in the lord's pasture with sheep, [*damaged*] they illegally recovered from Robert Lene, the lord's shepherd of the said sheep. Ordered.

Elias Typetot and Richard Qualm amerced 6d. because they had in their fold 20 sheep over the fixed number, pledge the hayward.

Richard Typetot amerced 12d. for damage in the lord's wheat with the pigs of Henry the chaplain, Robert Tailor, Walter Hereward and Henry of Saxmundham, to the value of 6d.. Henry the chaplain amerced 6d. for damage in the lord's peas at the Oldtoft with pigs and sheep, to the value of 3d..

John Typetot amerced 3d. and Robert Kembald, Richard of Wortham, William Elys \and Robert Sare/, 2d. each because they took their cattle out of the lord's bondage.

Robert Warde amerced 6d. for damage in the lord's hay with his beasts; Peter Margery 3d., Henry the chaplain 6d. and William Pach 3d. for the same.

Walter Hawys amerced 12d., and William Wyswyf, Henry Crane, John Rede and

---

99 Margin: 'Therefore a term, because [the tenement] should be escheat to the lord after William's death, for lack of an heir'. This insertion is very faded.

Walter Doe, all villeins, 3d. each because they absent themselves from the lord; ordered to attach them by the body if they are found in the lord's domain.

Marsilia Hawys <amerced 9d.> because she had 30 sheep outside the lord's fold, \condoned because they are in the fold of William Hawys/. Robert Tailor amerced 3d. for 5 sheep, William Pach 2d. for 2 sheep, and Peter Neve 9d. for 30 sheep outside the lord's fold.

Walter Pye amerced 12d., Walter Rampolye 6d., Walter Man 3d., Isabel Lene 6d. and Henry of Saxmundham 6d. for breach of the assize of ale. Alice Warde amerced 3d. because she sold ale in breach of the assize. Geoffrey of Lenne amerced 2d. because he sold bread in breach of the assize. William Payn and Stephen Cooper the ale-tasters amerced 3d. because they did not perform their duties, waived.

John Typetot complains of John Pynchon and Olivia his wife, in pleas of debt and trespass, pledges for the plaintiff, Richard Kebbil and the hayward.

Richard the son of Letitia pays 4d. fine for respite of suit of court until Michaelmas, pledge Richard Qualm.

William of Cranmer and John Terwald were elected to the office of reeve; and Richard Kebbil and Robert Warde to the office of hayward.

John Crane pays 4d. fine for respite of suit of court until Michaelmas, pledge Manser of Shucford.

Peter Springold was elected to the office of woodward.

<The jurors present that Catherine Mayheu free woman, held from the lord 4a. of free land by fealty, and services 18d. per year; and that, during her lifetime, she gave this land to Henry of Meryshalle, chaplain, \who did not present himself to the lord/. Therefore ordered to distrain him for fealty, and because he did not offer services, while his feoffor was alive.>[100]

Robert Crane pays 4d. fine for respite of suit of court until Michaelmas, pledge the hayward.

Walter Osbern pays 18d. fine for having a fold of 4 score sheep until Michaelmas, and no more, because he has allowance of 6d. for half a fold, for which he pays 6d. William Springold pays 2s.6d. fine for a fold of 5 score until Michaelmas, 6d. per score; Peter Jay pays 18d. for 60 sheep; Richard Qualm and Elias Typetot pays 2s.6d. for 5 score sheep; Robert Sare and Robert Warde each pay 2s.6d. for 5 score, pledge the hayward; Nicholas Goche pays 2s. for 4 score, pledge the reeve, William Hawys pays 3s.6d. for 8 score sheep, and no more because he has an allowance of 6d. for half a fold, for which he pays 6d.; William of Cranmer pays 3s. for 8 score sheep, and no more because he has an allowance of 12d. for a fold, to which belong 40 sheep; all until Michaelmas.

Marsilia Hawys, Richard Warde, William Springold and Ralph Echeman each amerced 3d. because they did not come to perform labour services when summoned.

Again as elsewhere ordered to attach Roger Hauker to reply to John Hernyng in a plea of debt.

Again the summons against Henry de Wells chaplain <and John Underwood> for overstocking the lord's common is adjourned until the next court.

---

[100] Margin: 'because he died'.

As elsewhere ordered to attach Sir Edmund de Pakenham and Sir Alexander de Walsham to swear fealty to the lord.

Ordered to retain in the lord's hands all the tenement of John at the Green for services and customs withheld; and to retain a pightle which Richard the shepherd of Westhorpe held from the lord when he died, by services 3½d. per year, until his heir satisfies for relief.

Ordered to raise from William Hawys 3s.4d. for the crop from 1a. of land of the tenement Goselyngs, which he took away unlawfully (?*minus juste*).

SUM £4 15s. 8d.

Affeerers: William of Cranmer the younger, Richard Kebbil

The jurors present that Catherine Machon, when she died, held from the lord 4a. of free land, for fealty and services 18d. per year, and that she held that [land] by the rod, and that it is not known who is her nearest heir. Ordered to seize into the lord's hands, and to report the profits.

### 74.  HIGH HALL Court, 16 November 1334 [HA504/1/3.26.ii]

William of Cranmer essoins of common suit by Walter Osbern; Walter of the Marsh of the same by Henry Trusse, and William Lene of the same by Robert Sare; they all pledge faith.

The profits in money for various crops from the land and tenements of Adam Crane, taken into the lord's hands for many defaults, [amount to] 4s.4d.. Ordered again to retain all the tenements of which 1r. is sown with oats, and to exploit them.[101]

Gilbert Helpe and Robert Kembald, the pledges of Nicholas Kembald, amerced 6d. because he did not rebuild a certain wasted house before Michaelmas; ordered etc..

1½ bushels of wheat from William Gostelen and Robert Lene, for damage in the lord's wheat at the Hulver, as shown in the last court.[102]

John Man amerced 1d. for damage in the oats of William Wodebite, to the loss of 2 bushels, which he admits; adjudged that William shall recover the 2 bushels. John also amerced 1d. because he stored wheat in the bondage of Westhorpe, to the detriment of the lord's villeinage.

John Man pays 12d. fine for having his term in all the lands and tenements of John Wodebite, following his death, from last Michaelmas to the same feast three years immediately following, pledge Gilbert Helpe.

John of Angerhale amerced 6d. for many defaults.

John Pynfoul amerced 3d. for default. Ordered to distrain him for homage and fealty, and for relief, *viz*. ½lb. of pepper.

John Man amerced 1d. for damage in his[103] wheat to the value of 2 bushels, and 1d. for damage in the garden, in the corn and elsewhere to the value of 3d.. William Wodebite amerced 1d. for damage with pigs in the courtyard, to the value of 1d., and 1d. for damage in John Man's barley at Nottynggiscroft, 2 sheaves, and in the oats at Stonylond, 1 sheaf, and 1d. because his horse bit John Man's horse, to

---

[101] This entry is garbled: after 'oats' it reads 'and estimated in the lord's granary, viz. the aforesaid tenements containing 6 acragges [*sic*]', and the order to retain is repeated.

[102] William was amerced 9d. and Robert ordered to be distrained.

[103] i.e. William Wodebite's; this entry is a continuation of that three entries above.

the loss of 1d.. John Man amerced 1d. for damage in William Wodebite's wheat at Packardswood, 2 sheaves, and 1d. because he gathered William's straw at Allwood field to the value of ¼d, and 1d. for the same at the Reddinge.

Ordered to execute the old [orders] of the last court, as shown by a cross.

Mabel Gothelard pays 40d. fine to be admitted to the tenement which Richard Gothelard, her father, held in villeinage by services etc. <Catherine her sister refuses to apportion with Mabel.> Ordered to warn Catherine to come to apportion as she ought.

Oliver Shepherd the younger, when he died, held a cottage from the lord in villeinage by services etc., ordered etc.

William Wodebite pays 3d. fine for leave to receive from John Wodebite a garden 6p. long and 6p. wide, and for having entry for himself and his heirs, rendering services etc., John Wodebite pays 3d. fine for leave to receive from William a plot [illeg.] in exchange, and for entry in the same form; seisin is delivered by the rod.

John Man and John Goche amerced 2d. because they did not repair a bank at Stonylond, as they were ordered, to the lord's loss of one sheep.

Margery of Angerhale villein pays 2s.8d. childwite, because she gave birth outside wedlock.

Ordered to distrain Richard of Depham to do homage for a tenement which he purchased from Edmund of Ipswich.

Walter Sylvester ['Selestire'] caused damage in the lord's wheat at Angerhalefield, and in the oats there, damage 1 sheaf of each.[104]

[SUM 9s. 11d, except 4s. 4d. profits; not stated]

## 75. WALSHAM Court, 3 February 1335 [HA504/1/3.29]

John Pynchonn, defendant v John Typetot in a plea of debt, essoins by Robert Kembald, John is present; and Olivia his wife, defendant in the same plea, essoins by William Hernyng; they both pledge faith.

Roger Hauker amerced 3d. for leave to agree with John Hernyng in a plea of debt, pledge the hayward.

The first pledges of Ralph of Rudham chaplain amerced 3s.4d. because they did not have him reply to Bartholomew Jerico in a plea of trespass; and 2s. for the same to William Hawys in a similar plea; ordered to summon him by better pledges.

Adam Noble amerced 3d. for trespass against Walter the smith in a plea of trespass [sic], pledge the hayward.

Nicholas Fraunceys amerced 2d. for trespass against Nicholas de Walsham, valued at 3d.; ordered to raise, pledge the hayward.

Ordered to seize into the lord's hands all the tenement which Robert the shepherd demised to Peter Neve without leave. Robert amerced 2s. for [making] the demise without leave, and Peter 12d. because he worked the land without leave.

The first pledges of John Pynchon and Olivia his wife amerced 6d. because they did not have them reply to John Typetot in a plea of trespass; ordered etc.

<Roger Brook in mercy because he sold ½r. of land to Robert his brother without leave, and Robert in mercy because he demised ½a. of pasture to Walter Osbern without leave>; both condoned because afterwards they came and paid fines.

104 The last five entries are badly faded.

Walter Osbern surrenders into the lord's hands 1a. of land, to the use of Bartholomew Jerico and Alice his wife and the heirs begotten of their bodies. And if it
happens that they die without such heirs, this land shall remain to the rightful
heirs of Alice, to hold by services and works etc., fine 3s.4d., pledge Walter
Osbern.

Walter Osbern, who has a term of the next three years in ½a. of pasture at Southbrook, by the demise of Roger Brook, the term beginning at Michaelmas last
past, gives 3d. fine for having a term of [a further] two years in the said land,
pledge the hayward.

John Pynfoul, who is of full age, seeks admittance to a messuage 20a. of land, which
were of Peter Pynfoul his father; he was admitted, and has entry by the heriot
after Peter's death.

The General Enquiry presents that William Chapman held from the lord on the day
he died[105]

They say that Eleanor the daughter of Walter Osbern the younger, and Olivia the
daughter of Walter Osbern the elder, gave birth out of wedlock. \Because they
have nothing, ordered to attach them by the body to satisfy for childwite./

Walter Petipas holds 1a. of land by the demise of Robert Deneys and Simon Deneys
without leave; ordered to seize into the lord's hands.

Henry de Wells chaplain unlawfully overstocked the common of Walsham by the
right of fold of Thomas of Badwell; ordered etc.

William Hawys and his co-tenants amerced 3d., for half of one autumn work
withheld.

Robert the hayward <amerced 6d.> \condoned/, because he did not raise 10s. from
William Clevehog the elder and William his brother, to the use of Thomas Patel
chaplain; ordered to raise.

Isabella the daughter of John Lene pays 3s.4d. fine for leave to marry William
Underwood, pledge the hayward.

Surrenders: Peter Jay to Agnes Typetot and her heirs, ½a. of land, granted to her to
hold in villeinage by services and works etc., fine 18d., pledge the hayward.

William Hawys to John Pynfoul and his heirs, 1r. of land, granted to him in the
same form, fine 12d, pledge the hayward.

John Lester and Rose his wife to Robert Hereward and his heirs, 1a.½r. of land,
granted to him in the same form, fine 3s.4d.; also to John Terwald and Amice his
wife, a cottage and 4a.3½r. of land, granted to them and the heirs of John, in the
same form, fine 13s.4d., pledge for both fines the hayward.

John Terwald to Robert Hereward and his heirs, 1a. of land, granted to him in the
same form, fine 3s.4d., pledge the hayward.

Roger Brook to Robert Brook and his heirs, ½r. of land in the Syke, granted to
him in the same form, fine 6d., pledge the hayward.

Walter Osbern to William Rampolye and Agnes his wife and their heirs, 2a. of
land with a cottage, granted to them in the same form, fine 8s., pledge the hayward.[106]

+William of Cranmer the younger to Walter the smith and his heirs, 3r. of land
and half a toft, granted to him in the same form, fine 3s.4d., pledge the hayward.

---

[105] A space of 2in. was left after this entry for its completion; margin: 'Nothing here because in a preceding court'.
[106] Margin: 'Memo. that in future that tenement owes 1 hen and 1 reaping per year'.

+William of Cranmer the elder to Thomas Fuller and his heirs, 3r. of land, granted to him in the same form, fine 3s., pledge the hayward.

John Syre amerced 3d. because he did not properly repair a watercourse, pledge the hayward.

Peter Neve amerced 6d. for damage in the lord's corn with his cows; Thomas Fuller 6d. for the same with his pigs; Richard Kebbil 2d. for damage in the lord's pasture with a colt; Nicholas Goche in mercy for the same \condoned by the lord/; Stephen Cooper 3d. for the same with a cow; Robert Ryvel 3d. for the same with a cow; Basilia of Langham 3d. for damage in Ladyswood with pigs, pledge for all the hayward.

[The lord had] a cow as a heriot after the death of Alice the wife of Walter the smith, because she held, jointly with her husband, 1r. of land;[107] and a cow, worth 10s., after the death of William Chapman; and let it be known that they held nothing other than for their lifetime.

[The lord had] a cow, worth 6s., after the death of Walter Man.

Ordered to execute the orders of the preceding court marked with a cross, and not yet acted upon.

Ordered to raise from Walter Osbern 3s.9d. for one hen and one reapale for the tenement Longes, withheld for 15 years.

Memorandum concerning land exchanged with Robert the shepherd to the lord's loss, the rebuilding of two buildings of John Spileman on the lord's bondage, valued at 5s., and one hen and one autumn boonwork from the tenement Longes, to be charged in the account.

SUM 59s. 11d., except 3 cows as heriots, value 22s.
Affeerers: Robert Warde and John Terwald

## 76. HIGH HALL Court of Nicholas de Walsham, 9 June 1335 [HA504/1/3.30]

Gilbert Helpe the hayward reports that the tenements of Adam Crane, taken into the lord's hands at the last court for many defaults, are sown by the lord; ordered to exploit them, and to report the profits.

<William of Cranmer in mercy because he did not warrant his essoin from the last court by Walter Osbern>; condoned by the steward.

Gilbert Helpe the bailiff [sic] amerced 1d. because he falsely testified that he had sight of William of Cranmer being present etc.

It was ordered to seize into the lord's hands all the tenement which Nicholas Kembald, when he died, held in bondage, for the heriot. The jurors [now] say that he had an ox, worth 10s., and they report on this and, concerning the profits, that 3a. of the tenement are sown with wheat, and 1½a. with oats and peas; and that William and Robert and 2 other sons of Nicholas are co-heirs and entitled to share (*participes*), and they are all under age.

Gilbert Helpe amerced 3d. because he did not distrain William Revel, who overstocked the lord's several pastures with sheep from outside the manor; ordered as elsewhere to distrain William for the same.

Memorandum that Mabel Gothelard was admitted, after the death of Richard Gothelard, to all her share of the inheritance, *viz.* 6a. of land of bondage. Catherine the

---

[107] No value is given for this cow, but the note at the end of the roll refers to 3 cows as heriots valued at 22s.; Alice's cow must have been worth 6s.

183

daughter of Richard and co-heir to the inheritance, was given notice to receive her share, but she does not come, and is therefore precluded from having seisin. The lord therefore took possession of the 3a. of land which was her share. Ordered to report the profits.

Ordered to retain in the lord's hands a cottage which Oliver the shepherd, when he died, held from the lord in bondage, and to report the profits.

John Packard is ordered to repair and rebuild a certain ruined house in the lord's bondage before Michaelmas one year hence.

+John Man amerced 3d. because he did not repair a certain house in the lord's bondage, wasted in the time of his wife; again ordered to rebuild and sufficently repair as new.

<Ordered to seize> into the lord's hands a third part of 3a. of land which Agnes the widow of Peter Pynfoul, \when she died/, held in dower, of the inheritance of John, Peter's son and heir, because he was under age; John is now 15. Afterwards Henry de Wells comes and gives 3d. fine to hold all the said 3a. of land, rendering services and customs therefrom.

Ordered to distrain Walter Osbern, who took the profit from 1a., of the said 3a. for three years after Agnes' death.

Peter Goche villein, fugitive from the lord, pays 4d. chevage for the past four years, pledge John Goche.

Ordered to distrain the tenant of the tenement of Andrew Veyse to show his charter, and for homage and fealty and services withheld.

Ordered to seize into the lord's hands ½a. of land, sown with oats after the death of the aforesaid [sic] Sarah, who held it in bondage, until etc. and for a heriot.

John Man defendant amerced 3d. for leave to agree with John Wodebite in a plea of trespass in two complaints, pledge the hayward; and 3d. because he did not repair a bank at Stonylond as ordered, to the lord's loss; and 1d. because he made an unlawful road on the lord's land at Angerhalefield.

Ordered to distrain all those crossing by the way called Angerhalefield, on the lord's severalty there.

The jurors present that by the defective custody of Peter Goche two piglets, worth 2s., died, and were buried; ordered to raise 2s. to the lord's use, pledge John Goche.

John Man amerced 3d. because his servant John Wodebite cut down hazel boughs in the woods of John Packard, John of Angerhale and Adam of Angerhale.

A certain outsider amerced 3d. for crossing on Angerhalefield, pledge John Man.

[SUM 14s. 3d., not stated]

## 77.  WALSHAM Court, 13 June 1335 [HA504/1/3.31]

Thomas of the Beck essoins of common suit by Robert Sare. \Afterwards he came./

The second pledges of Ralph of Rudham chaplain amerced 4s., because they did not have him reply to Bartholomew Jerico in a plea of trespass. Ordered to summon him by better pledges.

John Pynchon and Olivia his wife amerced 6d. for leave to agree with John Typetot in pleas of debt and trespass, pledge Robert Kembald.

The second pledges of Ralph of Rudham chaplain amerced 4s. because they did not have him reply to William Hawys in a plea of trespass. Ordered to appoint better pledges.

Henry de Wells chaplain amerced 12d. because he depastured the lord's common with sheep, where he had no right of common, \viz. in Clay street, Palmer street and Upstreet, pledge the hayward/.

Thomas Lorence amerced 12d. for illegal recovery from the lord's bailiff, taking a stray ewe outside the lord's domain, pledges Thomas William and the hayward, who guaranteed to return the ewe to the lord.

Henry de Wells chaplain amerced 12d. for damage in the lord's rye at Churchgate with his sheep, pigs and geese; Alice Kembald 6d. for trespass in the lord's corn at Nineacres with her beasts; Walter Pye 3d. for trespass in the lord's severalty; Peter Tailor 3d. for trespass in the lord's rye with his beasts; Peter Jay 6d. for trespass in the Micklemeadow with his sheep; Thomas Fuller 6d. for trespass in the lord's warren with his dogs; Robert Tailor 3d. for damage in the Micklemeadow with his sheep, pledge for all the hayward.

Ordered to attach Alexander de Walsham for damage in the Micklemeadow with his sheep.

Henry the chaplain amerced 3d. for trespass in the lord's herbage at the Eastend with his sheep, pledge the hayward.

John Hawys chaplain came into open court and granted that 5a. of land and ½r. of pasture and a sixth part of a messuage, which descended to him after the death of Robert his father, and which Marsilia Hawys holds for her lifetime, and after her death should revert to John, shall remain to William Hawys and his heirs. Furthermore John granted that 4a.1r. of land, ½r. of pasture and a quarter of a messuage, which descended to him after the death of Peter his brother, and which Marsilia Hawys holds for her lifetime, and after her death should revert to John, shall remain to William Hawys and his heirs. Furthermore, John granted that 1a.1½r. of land, ½r. of pasture and a 12th part of a messuage, which Agnes the wife of Thomas William holds in dower for her lifetime, and after her death should revert to John, shall remain to William Hawys and his heirs. The lord granted that William shall have the reversion of the said tenements after the deaths of Marsilia and Agnes, to hold to him and his successors at the lord's will, by services and works etc., fine waived by the lord.

William Payn amerced 3d. for damage in the lord's herbage at the Eastend with his sheep; Nicholas Goche 3d. for damage in the Littlemeadow with his sheep, pledge for both the hayward.

William Clevehog amerced 3d. because he did not come to perform labour service when summoned, pledge the hayward.

General Enquiry by John Syre, Walter Payn, William Hawys, William of Cranmer, Walter the smith, Simon Rampolye, John Man, Simon Peyntour, Robert Tailor, Matthew Hereward, William Springold and Nicholas Goche, who say upon their oath that Richard of Wortham surrendered into the lord's hands 1r. of land in the Millfield, to the use of John Noble and his heirs, to hold in villeinage by services and works etc., fine 9d., pledge the hayward.

Surrenders: Robert Crane to Manser of Shucford and his successors, 2a. of land and half a messuage, granted to him to hold by services and works etc., fine 10s., pledge the hayward.

William Hawys to Emma Fraunceys and Matilda her daughter and their heirs, a cottage formerly of Robert Salvetayl, granted to them to hold in villeinage by services and works etc., fine 12d., pledge the hayward; and 1½r. of land at Stonylond, granted to them in the same form, fine 12d., pledge William Hawys.

John Syre to William Syre and his heirs, ½a. of land, granted to him in the same form, fine 2s., pledge the hayward.

William Hawys to Walter Noreys and William Noreys and their heirs, 8p. of land at the Hewen, in exchange for 8p. of land at Paynesoutgond, granted to them in the same form, fine 3d. [for each transaction], pledge the hayward.

William Wither to Walter the smith and his heirs, ½a. of land in the Eastmillfield, abutting on Hevedacre, granted to him in the same form, fine 18d., pledge the hayward.

Walter Osbern surrendered into the lord's hands a cottage called Bullocks, and ½a. of land adjoining, and the lord granted the tenement to Walter to hold for his lifetime, and that after his decease, it shall revert to Isabella his daughter, to hold to her and the heirs begotten of her by services and works etc.; and if she shall die without such an heir, that the tenement shall revert to the rightful heirs of Walter, to hold in villeinage by services and works etc., fine 4s., pledge the hayward.

Agnes Machon to Catherine Machon and her heirs, 1r. of land lying in the Millfield in two pieces, of which one abuts on the king's highway, and the other piece at Windellond ['Whynnylond'], granted to her to hold in villeinage by services and works, fine 9d, pledge the hayward.

John Pynfoul, by leave of the court, demised to Henry de Wells chaplain a messuage 20a. of land for a term of three years, the term beginning at Michaelmas last past, rendering services and customs for the said term; and Henry shall find for John during that term all necessities in food and clothing, and he shall maintain the houses and buildings in the tenement in as good conditon as, or better than, he received them; fine for having his term 5s., pledge the hayward.

Surrender: Walter Hereward to Robert Hereward and his heirs, a toft 9p. long and 2p. wide, granted to him to hold in villeinage by services and works, fine 9d., pledge the hayward.

Nicholas de Walsham and his pledges amerced 6d. because he did not proceed against Edmund Patel in a plea of covenant.

Thomas Lorence amerced 3d. for damage in the lord's herbage on the land of John at the Green and Richard the shepherd, now in the hands of the lord, pledges William Hawys and the hayward.

Nicholas Kembald, when he died, held from the lord 3r. of customary land, and the lord had as a heriot an ox, worth 12s.; William, Thomas and Robert [his sons] are his nearest heirs, and are under the age of 12 years, and they do not come. The jurors say that following the custom of the manor the lord shall have custody until their full age; ordered to take the land into the lord's hands, and to report the profits.

Sir Alexander de Walsham, when he died, held from the lord a messuage 20a. of land which was formerly his father's, by fealty and services of one second ploughing, for which he ploughed at the Ploughale at the time of sowing wheat, and provided a man to carry a rod over the reapers for a day, called Reapale, etc.

Also he held a messuage 22½a. of land, 1a. of meadow and 1a. of pasture of the tenement formerly of Warin Outlawe by homage and fealty and suit of court, rendering for services 2s.5d. per year, two autumn ploughings and one autumn boonwork, two ploughings and one second ploughing at the time of sowing wheat, 3 bushels of oats at each tallage, if the lord wished, 3d. to each mark.

Also he held 1r. of meadow of the tenement of Adam Shepherd ['Berchard'] rendering for services 1d. per year.

Also he held a messuage 22a. of land \and pasture/ and 2a.1r. of meadow of the tenement, formerly of Master John, by homage, fealty and suit of court, paying for services 4s.10½d. per year, and scutage to the king, amounting to 40s.6d., or as demanded.[108]

Also he held a messuage 1½a. of land, which was formerly of Adam Pinchonn, by fealty and services, one ploughing at Ploughale, one autumn boonwork at Reapale, and one hen at Christmas and eggs at Easter.

Also he held ½r. of customary land of the tenement Kebbel's, which he purchased from John Stronde, by services and works as for others held in the same tenure. Alexander his son is his nearest heir, and he does not come; ordered to distrain him for relief, homage and fealty.

Ordered to attach Denis the son of Michael Nichole for damage in the lord's meadow, taking away herbage.

Ralph Echeman amerced 3d. because he demised, \and mortgaged for 9s./, to John the chaplain of Newmarket 3r. of land, without leave; John Robhood amerced 3d. because he demised, \and mortgaged for 12s./, to the same John, 1a. of land, without leave; ordered to take into the lord's hands etc. Memorandum that the land is sown with wheat.

John Robhood amerced 3d. for default.

Catherine and Alice Deneys amerced 4d. because they demised to Alexander the bailiff \freeman/ a garden, until 1 August, without leave; ordered etc.

Ordered to distrain Nicholas de Walsham for damage in the lord's pasture at Currescroft, with his pigs.

Presented that a house in the tenement of William and Robert Cook is laid waste by a tempest of wind; ordered to distrain them to repair it.

Walter Pye amerced 12d., Isabella Lene 6d., Walter Rampolye 9d., Olivia Kembald, in the house of Walter Osbern, 3d., because they brewed and sold ale in breach of the assize. Alice Warde gannocker amerced 1d. because she sold ale in breach of the assize. Geoffrey of Lenne amerced 3d. because he sold bread in breach of the assize. William Payn and Richard Kebbil the ale-tasters amerced 6d. because they did not perform their duties.

Ordered to distrain the Prior of Ixworth to make good a watercourse which he diverted, to the detriment of a free tenement of the lord, where the sheepcourse lies, and the tenement of John Syre.

Ordered to seize and retain 1r. of land which Nicholas Goche purchased from Thomas of the Beck without leave. Nicholas comes and surrenders his charter for this land, and it is returned to him to keep etc.

Isabella Lene amerced 2d. because she did not send for the ale-tasters, \John Man and Robert Tailor/.

Robert Warde and Simon Peyntour were elected to the office of reeve; Robert took the oath.

Ordered to retain in the lord's hands ½a. of land which Alice, the wife of Gilbert Salvetayl, held for her lifetime. Afterwards, Nicholas Fraunceys Alice's brother and heir comes and is admitted to the land to hold by customs and services etc., fine 3s., pledge the hayward.

Surrenders: Stephen Cooper to Edmund Lene and Amice, Stephen's daughter, and

---

[108] *ad plus plus et ad minus minus*, literally, 'at a higher rate more, at a lower rate less'.

their heirs, ½a. of land in Marlerescroft, granted to them to hold by customs and works etc.; and if it happens that Edmund and Amice shall die without such heirs the land shall revert to the rightful heirs of Stephen, fine 2s., pledge Stephen Cooper.

Stephen Cooper surrenders into the lord's hands 1a.1r. of land with a cottage, of which 3r. with the cottage lie in Marlerescroft and 2r. lie in Stephen's croft abutting on Churchstreet; the lord granted the land with the cottage to Stephen to hold for his lifetime by services and works etc. And after Stephen's decease, the tenement shall revert to Edmund Lene and Amice Stephen's daughter, to hold to them and the heirs born of them; and if they die without such heirs, the tenement shall revert to the rightful heirs of Stephen, to hold by services and works etc., fine 5s., pledge Stephen Cooper.

Amice the daughter of Stephen Cooper pays 6s.8d. fine for leave to marry Edmund Lene, pledge the hayward.

Surrenders: +John Wymond and Agnes his wife, she being examined in court, to William of Cranmer the elder and his heirs, 3a. of land, granted to him to hold in villeinage by services and works etc., fine 9s., pledge the hayward.

+William Hawys to William of Cranmer the elder and his heirs, 3r. of land, granted to him in the same form, fine 2s.6d., pledge the hayward.

Margaret the daughter of Robert Warde pays 6s.8d. fine for leave to marry John Nowel of Harling ['Herelynge'], pledge the hayward.

Ordered to execute the orders of the last court marked with a cross and not acted upon.

SUM £4 2s. 2d., except a heriot worth 12s.<br>Affeerers: Robert Tailor and Robert Warde

## 78.  WALSHAM Court, 27 September 1335 [HA504/1/3.32]

John Pynchon, defendant v Manser of Shucford in a plea of trespass, essoins by Robert Sare; Olivia Kembald, defendant v Manser in a similar plea, essoins by Robert Kembald; they pledge faith, Manser is present.

Warin Cokeman[109] the hayward amerced 3d. because he did not attach Ralph of Rudham chaplain, as ordered; again ordered to attach Ralph to reply to William Hawys and Bartholomew Jerico in a plea of trespass.

+A day is given to the Prior of Ixworth until the next court to make amends to the lord because he diverted a watercourse at Trendelwood to the lord's detriment etc., pledge Henry the chaplain.

Basilia Pays and her pledges amerced 4d. because she did not proceed v John Smith in a plea of trespass.

Robert the son of Elias [Typetot] amerced 6d. for leave to agree with John Man in a plea of trespass, pledge Elias Typetot.

John Noble amerced 3d. for damage in the lord's peas with his pigs, pledge Richard Kebbil; Simon Cooper 6d. for damage in the lord's wheat with his beasts, pledge the reeve; Robert Lene 3d. for damage in the lord's oats with sheep, pledge Richard Kebbil; Nicholas Goche 2d. for damage in the lord's peas with pigs, pledge the hayward.

---

[109] In the court of 27 September 1334 (no.73), Richard Kebbil and Robert Warde were elected hayward; in those of 7 February and 13 June (nos.75 and 77), there is no mention of a change; and in this court, Richard Kebbel and Robert Warde are elected again. Warin Cokeman does not appear in any other court.

John the son of Adam Margery pays 4d. fine for respite of suit of court until Mich-aelmas one year hence, pledge Peter Margery.

John Man amerced 3d. for leave to agree with William Rampolye in a plea of debt, pledge Richard Kebbyl.

Thomas of the Beck amerced 3d. because he did not come to perform labour service when summoned, pledge the hayward.

Mabel Ape amerced 4d. for leave to agree with Robert Sare in a plea of trespass in two complaints. William Elys amerced 3d. for the same with William Wither in a similar plea, pledge for both Richard Kebbil.

William Warde amerced 4d. because he was summoned for labour service and did not come, pledges the hayward and William Cook. Simon Peyntour and Alice the widow of Peter Peyntour 4d. for the same, pledge Richard Kebbil.

Surrender: William Hawys to Walter Deneys and his heirs, 1p. of land at Culpon-nescroft, granted to him to hold in villeinage by services and works etc., fine 3d., pledge Richard Kebbil.

John Terwald amerced 3d. because he was summoned for labour service and did not come, pledge the hayward.

Surrenders: John Robetel to Walter Deneys and his heirs, a cotland containing ½r. of land, granted to him to hold in villeinage by services and works etc., fine 12d., pledge the hayward. Walter acknowledges on behalf of himself and his heirs to be bound to pay William Hawys 12d. per year for the cotland. John, having demised all his tenement to Walter Deneys, finds pledges [for him] to come to the lord's Court General every year, and to pay 1d. as chevage, *viz.* Walter Deneys and Nicholas Fraunceys.

Nicholas Fraunceys to Emma Fraunceys and her heirs, a piece of land at Stony-lond, 6ft. wide and 25p. long, granted to her to hold in villeinage by services and works etc., fine 6d., pledge the hayward.

+William of Cranmer the younger to Walter Rampolye and his heirs, 1a.1½r. of land in the Millfield, granted to him in the same form, fine 4s., pledge the hayward.

Walter Osbern to William Wither and his heirs, 1r. of wood, granted to him in the same form, fine 12d., pledge the hayward.

Joan the daughter of William Hawys pays 20s. fine for leave to marry John of Fox-ley, pledge her father. Isabella the daughter of Walter Osbern pays 20s. fine for leave to marry William the son of Thomas of Mileham ['Mylham'], pledge her father. Alice the daughter of Robert Deneys pays 6s.8d. for leave to marry Robert Hereward, pledge the hayward.

Robert Rampolye and Richard Qualm pay 2s. fine for having a fold of 4 score sheep, at 6d. per score, until Michaelmas one year hence; William Clevehog 6d. for a fold of 20 sheep, pledge for all the hayward.

Surrender: John Terwald to Manser of Shucford and his heirs, 3r. of land in two pieces, of which 1r. lies at the head of Kembald's croft and 2r. lie at the head of Furnenescroft, granted to him to hold in the same form as above, fine 3s., pledge the hayward.

William of Cranmer pays 2s. fine for having a fold of 6 score sheep until Michael-mas one year hence, and no more because he is allowed 12d. for a fold of 40 sheep.

Surrenders: John Man to John Terwald and his heirs, 7½p. of meadow, granted to him in the same form as above, fine 3d., pledge the hayward.

John Terwald to William Springold and his heirs, 1a.1½r. of land lying in two places, granted to him in the same form, fine 5s., pledge the hayward.

Robert Kembald surrenders into the lord's hands 1a.2r. of land, and the lord granted the land to him to hold for his lifetime; and after Robert's decease it shall revert to Olivia Robert's daughter, to hold to her and her heirs in the same form as above, fine 5s., pledge Robert Warde.

Robert Kembald surrenders into the lord's hands 1a.2r. of land, and the lord granted the land to him to hold for his lifetime; and after Robert's decease it shall revert to William Elys and Hilary his wife, to hold to them and the heirs of Hilary in the same form as above, fine 5s., pledge the hayward.

General Enquiry by John Syre, Walter Payn, Walter Osbern, William Hawys, Wiliam Wyther, Nicholas Goche, Robert Tailor, William Springold, Matthew Hereward, Stephen Cooper, Simon Peyntour, Peter Springold, jurors.

Henry of Saxmundham and Henry de Wells chaplain each amerced 3d. for damage in the lord's peas at Howestoft, pledge the hayward.

Alice the servant of Henry of Saxmundham amerced 4d. for taking away 1 sheaf of the lord's oats; Alice the wife of Ralph Echeman 4d. for taking away 1 sheaf of wheat at the Oldtoft, pledge for both the hayward.

William Godyene ('Gudgeon') and Henry of Saxmundham each amerced 4d. for damage in the lord's meadow with their pigs, pledge the hayward; Henry de Wells chaplain 3d. for the same, pledge the hayward; and John Noble the swineherd of the manor 3d. for the same, pledge the reeve. Walter Osbern amerced 3d. for damage in the lord's oats at Micklemeadow, pledge the hayward.

+Robert the chaplain demised, without leave, to Alexander the bailiff a messuage 20a. of customary land; ordered to take into the lord's hands, and to report the profits.

+Ordered to take into the lord's hands the tenement Pynfoul because it is wasted, the house being in ruins.

Henry the chaplain who holds the tenement amerced 6d. because he took corn to a free tenement outside the bondage; likewise Peter Neve 6d., William Elys 3d., Robert Kembald 3d., Richard of Wortham 2d., Robert Sare 2d., pledge for all Richard Kebbil; likewise Thomas William 12d. and Agnes Suter 2d., pledge the hayward; likewise John Typetot 3d., pledge Henry the chaplain, and Bartholomew Jerico 8d., pledge Walter Osbern .

The servant of Henry the chaplain amerced 2d. for damage in the lord's rye at Churchgate with geese, pledge Henry; Henry de Wells chaplain 2d. for the same with his pigs, pledge the hayward.

Alice the daughter of Geoffrey of Lenne freewoman, who lives on the lord's bondage by consent, gave birth out of wedlock, therefore she pays the fixed fine 2s.8d..

Walter Pye amerced 12d., Walter Rampolye 6d. and William Underwood 6d., because they brewed and sold ale in breach of the assize, pledge the hayward. Alice Ward in mercy because she sold ale in breach of the assize, condoned because poor. Geoffrey of Lenne 3d. because he sold bread in breach of the assize. Richard Kebbil and William Payn the ale-tasters amerced 3d. each, because they did not perform their duties.

Peter Neve amerced 12d. because he had 26 sheep lying outside the lord's fold.

+Alexander de Walsham dug on the common land, and made a pit there to the detriment of the lord and the townspeople; ordered etc.

Walter Osbern amerced 6d. because he made an encroachment at Godefreysyerd, appropriating to himself from the common land 7p. long and 2ft. wide; also 6d. for the same at Sawyersyerd, 11p. long and 2ft. wide; ordered to make amends, pledge Richard Kebbil.

Sir Alexander de Walsham, in his lifetime, made a pit on the common at Stubway, and it remains unfilled; ordered etc.

A day is given to the enquiry until the next court to enquire and present concerning various encroachments on the lord's common.

Robert Warde and Walter Payn were elected to the office of reeve, Walter took the oath; Richard Kebbil and William Wither are elected to the office of hayward, William took the oath; Peter Springold and Ralph Echeman are elected to the office of woodward, Ralph took the oath.

Peter Jay pays 18d. fine for having a fold of 60 sheep until Michaelmas one year hence, pledge the hayward.

Matthew the son of Walter Gilbert, who is now of full age, comes and seeks admittance to his father's tenement. He is granted admittance by the heriot after his father's death following the custom of the manor, he swore fealty.

William Springold and Nicholas Goche each pay 2s. fine, for each having a fold of 4 score sheep until Michaelmas one year hence, pledge the hayward.

Surrenders: William Hawys and Massilia his wife, she being examined in court, to John Terwald and his heirs, 1½r. of meadow, granted to him in the same form as above, fine 12d., pledge the hayward. John Terwald to William and Massilia Hawys and their heirs, 1½r. of meadow, granted to them in the same form, fine 12d. William Hawys to John Terwald and his heirs, ½r. of meadow, granted to him in the same form, fine 6d., pledge the hayward.

Ordered to execute all the orders from the preceding court not yet acted upon.

SUM 103s. 3d.

Affeerers: Nicholas Goche and John Terwald

## 79. HIGH HALL Court General of Nicholas de Walsham, 23 November 1335 [HA504/1/3.33]

Walter Osbern essoins of common suit, by William Osbern; void because the essoiner did not expect a day at the last court,[110] and nevertheless defaulted there; amerced 3d.

William of Cranmer essoins of common suit, by Robert Sare.

Ordered to retain in the lord's hands and to exploit all the tenement of Adam Crane until etc., and to report the profits.

+Again as elsewhere ordered to retain in the lord's hands and to exploit all the tenement which Nicholas Kembald held from the lord, for a heriot, viz. a bullock, worth 10s., and for arrears of rent, until the heirs come and pay to the lord that which they owe; and to report the profits.[111]

William Ryvel was distrained for overstocking the pasture, and he satisfied the lord.

+Ordered as elsewhere to retain in the lord's hands and to exploit the land, which Matilda Gothelard held from the lord, as her share of an inheritance, viz. 3a., and all the tenement which Catherine her sister held in villeinage, as her share of the

---

[110] MS: *diem*, probably a clerical error.
[111] Margin: 'heriot' (?17th century) against this item and the next but one.

inheritance, \viz. the other 3a./, because they do not come, and demand nothing of the inheritance for the heriot; and for many defaults; and [ordered] to report the profits.

Again as elsewhere ordered to retain in the lord's hands and to exploit the cotland which Oliver the shepherd held when he died, and to report the profits.

John Packard amerced 3d. because he did not rebuild a ruined house in the lord's bondage, as ordered at the last court, pledge Gilbert Helpe. John Man amerced 6d. because he did not repair a house in the lord's villeinage, as ordered at the last court, pledge Gilbert Helpe.

Gilbert Helpe amerced 14d. because he did not distrain Walter Osbern, who took the crops from 3a. of land for three years from the time of the death of Agnes the widow of Peter Pynfoul; ordered to distrain Walter. The crops were valued by the court at 14d.

Ordered as elsewhere to distrain in the tenements, which were of Andrew Veyse and are now held by Agnes Veyse; Robert Veyse the son of Agnes finds pledges to show his charter for the tenement, under penalty of 6s.8d., viz. Gilbert Helpe and William Wodebite.

Agnes the daughter of William Noreys, now of full age, comes into open court, and receives from the lord ½a. of land as her inheritance from her father, seisin is delivered to her to hold by the rod, rendering services and one hen annual rent.

All the tenants of Angerhale amerced 3d. because they did not distrain men crossing by the road of Angerhale, as they were ordered.

It was found by the enquiry that John Man and Matilda his wife were guilty of damage against John Packard, as he alleged in three complaints against them, to his loss of 25d.; adjudged that John shall recover the loss from John and Matilda, and ordered to raise; John and Matilda amerced 6d. Also that John Packard was guilty of damage against John and Matilda Man, as they had alleged against him in seven complaints, to the loss of 10d.; adjudged that they shall recover the loss, and ordered to raise; John amerced 7d.

Henry de Wells chaplain amerced 6d. for default.

It was found by the enquiry that John and Matilda Man were guilty of damage against John Packard, as he alleged against them in two complaints, to the loss of 2½d.; adjudged that John shall recover, and John and Matilda amerced 3d. Also that John Packard was guilty of damage against John and Matilda, taking away three cheeses, to the loss of 3d.; John Packard amerced 1d.; also that he was guilty of damage against them as alleged in five complaints, to the loss of 2½d.; amerced 1d.; ordered to raise the losses.

John Man amerced 3d. for his false claim against John Packard, pledge the bailiff.

John Packard was elected to the office of reeve for this year, and pays 12d. fine for the office. Gilbert Helpe was elected to the office of collector for this year.

Gilbert Helpe the younger amerced 1d. because he absented himself from labour service in autumn.

John Wodebite amerced 6d. for default.

Ordered to distrain William Deneys, Simon Petyt, Thomas Frere, Robert Deneys and the shepherd of Walter Osbern for damage to the lord in Sheepcotecroft; and Simon Petyt for damage at Gothelardslond; <and Henry de Wells chaplain at the Hulver at Netherhawe.>

Agnes Wodebite in mercy for damage to the lord in three pieces [of land], condoned by the lord. John Syre amerced 4d. for damage in the croft with his chickens;

John Syre and William Kembald 1d. for damage in the lord's corn, and on a certain boundary; William Deneys 1d. for damage in the lord's corn at Hamstale; Simon Petyt 1d. for damage in the lord's meadow; Simon Peyntour, William Smith, William Clevehog, Richard Qualm, Millicent Qualm, Cristina Qualm, Elias Typetot, John Cowlinge, John Bolle, Robert Rampolye and John Patil each amerced 1d. for damage in the lord's meadows at Hordeshawe; John Syre amerced 6d. for damage with his pigs in Gothelardsyerd.

The whole homage at Angerhale amerced 12d. because they did not perform their labour service, in gathering straw badly.

William of Cranmer and Robert Kembald each amerced 3d., because they did not perform their boonworks in autumn when summoned.

Robert Kembald was elected by the whole homage to collect and pay the Castle ward.

Peter Goche the son and one of the heirs of William Goche pays 6d. fine for entry to half a messuage 9a. of land after Willliam's death, pledge John Goche; seisin delivered to him to hold in villeinage by services and works etc., he swore fealty.

The whole homage amerced 12d. for various concealments.

SUM 11s. 4d.

## 80.   WALSHAM Court, 17 January 1336 [HA504/1/3.34]

<Ralph of Rudham chaplain, defendant v Bartholomew Jerico in a plea of trespass, essoins by Richard Banlone.> \Deleted because in error/.

Bartholomew Jerico, plaintiff v Ralph of Rudham in a plea of trespass, essoins by Wiliam the son of John; he pledges faith.

<John Man, defendant v Robert Kembald in a plea of debt, essoins by Thomas of the Beck.> \It does not lie because he holds customary land./

John Pynchon and Olivia his wife amerced 6d. for leave to agree with Manser of Shucford in a plea of trespass, pledge Robert Kembald.

Simon Cooper amerced 1d. for leave to agree with William Warner of Botesdale ['Botelisdale'] in a plea of debt, pledge the hayward.

Manser of Shucford amerced 3d. for unlawful detention of 4s. from William Hawys, which he acknowledged in open court; ordered to raise, the loss is remitted, pledge the hayward.

Peter Tailor, Richard of Cranmer and Stephen Cooper each amerced 2d. for damage in the herbage around the manor with their beasts, pledges for Peter and Stephen the hayward, for Richard, William of Cranmer.

John of Westley ['Westle'] was attached to swear fealty and he has a day until the next court, pledges William Wither and Peter Reve.

Massilia Hawys and Alexander Geldenefot each amerced 3d., and Robert Man 2d. for damage in the herbage around the manor with their beasts.

Surrender: Walter Osbern to Walter Reve and his heirs, 1r. of meadow and pasture, granted to him to hold in villeinage by services and works etc., fine 12d., pledge the hayward.

John Man amerced 3d. for leave to agree with Robert Kembald in a plea of debt, pledge the hayward.

Bartholomew Patel pays 6d. fine for having respite of suit of court until Michaelmas; Richard Patel pays 3d. for the same, pledge for both the hayward.

John Terwald amerced 3d. for his false claim against Richard Kebbil in a plea of trespass, pledge the hayward.

Henry Barker ['le Barker'] of Langham amerced 3d. for damage in the lord's rye at the Conynger,[112] pledge Thomas Fuller.

Robert the servant of Henry of Saxmundham amerced 3s.4d. because he unlawfully drove the lord's sheep, pledge Robert Warde.

Thomas William amerced 9d for unlawfully withholding a ploughing service at the Ploughale, pledge John Hernyng.

Ordered to attach Agnes Grym for damage in the lord's wheat at Boynhawe with sheep.

John Crane pays 4d. fine for respite of suit of court until Michaelmas, pledge Manser of Shucford.

John Tailor amerced 3d. for damage in the corn of William Elys, as found by the enquiry, to the loss of 6d.; ordered to raise.

Surrender: John Cowlinge and Alice his wife, she being examined in court, to John Stonham and his heirs, a cotland containing ¼r., and 2a.1r. of land, granted to him to hold in villeinage by services and works, etc.; and John wills and grants that John and Alice shall hold all the tenement for the term of their lives, fine 6s., pledge the hayward.

John Tailor amerced 1d. for unlawful detention of 1 peck of barley from William Elys for damage done to him, pledge the hayward; ordered to raise.

Henry de Wells amerced 3d. for damage in the lord's herbage with his beasts at Oldtoftrow, pledge the hayward.

Catherine Machon pays 6s.8d. fine for leave to marry John Tailor, pledge the hayward.

Ordered to attach Ralph of Rudham chaplain to reply to William Hawys in a plea of trespass.

General Enquiry by John Syre, William Hawys, Nicholas Goche, Robert Tailor, William Springold, Matthew Hereward, Simon Peyntour, Peter Springold, John Terwald, Walter the smith and Richard Kebbil.

Richard the son of Letitia pays 4d. fine for respite of suit of court until Michaelmas, pledge Richard Qualm.

Surrender: Peter Neve to Peter Tailor and his heirs, 2a.1½r. of land, granted to him to hold in the same form as above, fine 8s., pledge the hayward.

The jurors say that Roger Brook held from the lord, when he died, 6a. of land, 2r. of meadow and half a messuage by services and works etc., and that the lord had no heriot because Roger had no beast. Roger's son John aged three is his nearest heir, and he pays no entry fine. Ordered to take the tenements into the lord's hands, and to report the profits. Upon this came Alice Roger's widow and paid a fine for holding the tenements until John's full age. The fine is entered in the next court.

++They say that the cottage of Hereward Gunter is wasted; therefore ordered to take it into the lord's hands. \Profits 12d./ +Likewise the tenement Pynfoul is wasted; ordered to seize etc.

Ralph Echeman in mercy for having 2 sheep outside the lord's fold, condoned because poor; Henry of Saxmundham amerced 3d. for 7 sheep for 5 weeks. William Springold in mercy for having 10 sheep in his fold over the fixed number,

---

112 i.e. the rabbit warren.

\waived because satisfied in preceding court/. Isabella Osbern amerced 1d. for 2 sheep outside the lord's fold; likewise Avice Deneys 1d. for 3 sheep.

Henry de Wells chaplain amerced 12d. because he withheld one ploughing service and one ploughale for the tenement Pynfoul.

Surrender: John Terwald and Amice his wife, she being examined in court, to Thomas Hereward and Alice the daughter of Thomas Fuller and their heirs, 3r.35p. of land \at Longelond/, granted to them to hold in the same form as above, fine 3s., pledge the hayward.

Roger of Southwold pays 6d. fine for having respite of suit of court until Michaelmas, pledge William of Cranmer.

+The jurors present that Robert Shepherd chaplain purchased a messuage in Debenham; therefore the lord to be consulted.

Surrenders: Robert Hereward to Thomas Hereward and his heirs, 1r.24p. of land at Broadland ['Brodelond'], abutting on the Stubbing, granted to him to hold in the same form as above, fine 12d., pledge the hayward.

Walter Hereward to Thomas Hereward and his heirs, a plot of land of his messuage on the east side, containing 20p., granted to him to hold in the same form, fine 6d., pledge the hayward.

Alice the daughter of Thomas Fuller pays 6s.8d. fine for leave to marry Thomas Hereward, pledge the hayward.

William Hawys and Marsilia Hawys pay 2s.6d. fine for having a fold of 6 score sheep until Michaelmas, and no more because they are allowed 20 sheep, pledge the hayward.

SUM 46s. 1d., except 12d. for profits;
from this in expenses, 2s. and 2 pecks of oats
Affeerers: Walter Payn and William Wither

# SECTION 4

## May 1336 – November 1345

### 81. WALSHAM Court General, 17 May 1336 [HA504/1/4.1]

<John Man, defendant v Alexander Geldenfot in a plea of debt, essoins by Thomas of the Beck>, \void because he holds customary land/. John Manning, defendant v Henry the chaplain in a plea of debt, essoins by Thomas de Walsham; he pledges faith; Henry is present. <Ralph Wybert, defendant v John Man in a plea of debt, essoins by Robert Sare>, \void because the plaintiff did not proceed/. Walter Osbern, defendant v Simon Cooper in a plea of trespass, essoins by Robert Kembald; he pledges faith; Robert is present. Michael Nichole, plaintiff v Matilda of Reydon in a plea of debt, essoins by Walter de Wells; he pledges faith; Matilda is present.

Again ordered to attach Ralph of Rudham chaplain to reply to Bartholomew Jerico in a plea of trespass, and to William Hawys in a like plea.

Agnes Grym amerced 3d. for damage in the lord's wheat at Boynhawe, pledge William of Cranmer.

General Enquiry by John Syre, William Payn, William of Cranmer, Nicholas Goche, Matthew Hereward, John Terwald, Richard Kebbil, Peter Springold, Robert Tailor, Walter the smith, Simon Rampolye and Robert Warde; they took the oath.

John Man and his pledges amerced 3d. because he did not proceed v Ralph Wybert in a plea of debt.

Peter Jay amerced 3d. for leave to agree with Henry Whitemor in a plea of debt, and 3d. to agree with Nicholas Goche in a like plea, pledge the hayward.

Agnes Goche amerced 3d. for unlawful detention of 16d. from Henry Albry, which she admitted in open court, to the loss of 3d.; ordered to raise, pledge Simon Peyntour.

The first pledges of John Man amerced 6d. because they did not have him reply to Alexander Geldenfot in a plea of debt; ordered to appoint better pledges.

William Hawys complains against Matilda of Reydon, executrix of Robert of Reydon, in a plea of debt; ordered etc.; pledge for William the hayward.

Agnes the daughter of Simon Stritt claims ½a. of land from John Tailor and Catherine his wife, and she says that Alice Machon her aunt was seised of the land, as of fee and of right, following the custom of the manor, and that she died seised of it; that right descended from Alice to Agnes, who now claims etc., and she produces suit. John and Catherine come and say that Catherine, while single, purchased the land from Agnes, and now has entry by that purchase; and on this they ask that an enquiry be made by means of the court rolls, and the other party likewise. Ordered that the rolls of the 9th, 10th and 11th years of the reign of Edward II [July 1315–July 1318] be scrutinised; and they have a day until the next court.

Surrender: John Syre to Robert Warde and his heirs, 10p. of meadow in the

Micklemeadow, next to the meadow of William of Cranmer, granted to him to hold in villeinage, by services and works, fine 6d., pledge the hayward.

William Payn amerced 3d. for leave to agree with Simon Cooper in a plea of trespass; John Syre 3d. for the same, with Simon Cooper in a like plea, pledge for both the hayward. Agnes Goche 3d. for the same, with Henry Albry in a plea of debt, pledge Simon Peyntour; Bartholomew Jerico 3d. for the same, with Richard the Shepherd in a plea of debt, pledge the hayward.

Surrender: William Hawys to Thomas Fuller and his heirs, 1r. of meadow in the Micklemeadow, abutting on the Hevedacre, granted to him in the same form as above, fine 12d., pledge the hayward.

Ordered to attach William Cook the shepherd and John Wauncey for damage in the lord's pasture with sheep, and because they illegally recovered the sheep from Robert Lene the shepherd of the said sheep.

Ordered to attach Sir Edmund de Pakenham and Alexander de Walsham for fealty to the lord.

Ordered to retain in the lord's hands all the tenement of John at the Green, for services and customs withheld.

Ordered to retain in the lord's hands a pightle, which Richard Shepherd of Westhorpe, when he died, held from the lord, for services 3½d. per year, until the heir satisfies for relief etc. Afterwards came Alice, Richard's widow, and showed that she has title in the pightle for her lifetime; she swore fealty.

Ordered to retain in the lord's hands 4a. of land which Catherine Mayheu, when she died, held for services 18d. per year; but they say that she held the land by the rod, and that her nearest heir is not known.

Ordered to attach by the body Eleanor and Olivia the daughters of Walter Osbern[1] because they gave birth outside wedlock.

Ordered to retain in the lord's hands all the tenement which Robert the shepherd demised to Peter Neve without leave; and to retain 1a. of land which Walter Petipas holds by the demise of Robert Deneys and Simon Deneys, without leave.

The lord is to be consulted about land exchanged with Robert the shepherd to the lord's loss; and about the rebuilding of two houses on the lord's bondage, valued at 5s.

Ordered to retain in the lord's hands 3r. of customary land, after the death of Nicholas Kembald, because the heirs do not come; afterwards came Alice, Nicholas' widow, and custody is granted to her until the full age of the heirs.

Ordered to distrain Alexander de Walsham for relief, homage and fealty, and for other demands, as shown in the court of 13 June 1335 [no.77].

Ordered to attach Denis the son of Michael Nichole for damage in the lord's meadow.

Ordered to retain in the lord's hands a garden which Catherine and Alice Deneys demised to Alexander the serjeant freeman, without leave.

Ordered to distrain William and Robert Cook to make good waste in the lord's bondage.

William Springold villein, when he died, held from the lord a messuage, 30a. of land and ½a. of meadow; the lord had an ox, worth 13s.4d., as a heriot. Isabella William's wife will hold, for her lifetime, 5a. of land, ½a. of meadow and half of the

---

[1]  In roll no.75 they were named as the daughters of Walter sen. and of Walter jun. respectively.

messuage, which she and William purchased jointly. Walter, Walter and Robert William's sons are his nearest heirs, and they have entry by the heriot.[2]

Amice Echeman, when she died, held from the lord ½a. of land by services and works, Ralph Echeman her son is her nearest heir and is of full age; he pays 6d. entry fine, pledge Peter Springold.

Matthew Hereward amerced 2d. and Ralph Echeman 1d. for damage in the lord's wood with their beasts, pledge the hayward. Ordered to attach Robert the farmer for damage in Ladyswood, with his pigs, and John of Banham for the same with his beasts and pigs. William Springold amerced 2d. for the same with his pigs, pledge the hayward.

Massilia Hawys amerced 12d. for making an encroachment on the lord's pasture at Hatchmere ['Hachemere'], ploughing an area, 12p. long and 3ft. wide, pledge William Hawys; Robert Sare 3d. for the same at the Broadway ['Brodeweye'], 4p. long and 1½ft. wide, pledge the hayward; Massilia Hawys 3d. for the same there, 12ft. long and 2ft. wide, pledge William Hawys; Peter Tailor 2d. for the same there, 4p. long and 2ft. wide; Richard Kebbil 2d. for the same there, 3p. long and 2ft. wide; the ploughmen of Alexander de Walsham 6d. for the same at Stubway, 12p. long and 2ft. wide; John Spileman 3d. for the same at the Oldtoft, 4p. long and 12ft. wide; Robert and William Cook 3d. for the same there, 2p. long and 12ft. wide; Robert Tailor 3d. for the same there; Alice Helewys 3d. for the same there, 2p. long and 2ft. wide, Ralph Neve 3d. for the same there, 1p. long and 3ft. wide; Ralph Echeman 1d. for the same there; pledge for all the hayward; [all the foregoing were] ordered to make good.

Massilia Hawys amerced 2d. for damage in Boynhawe way with her sheep, pledge William Hawys; Peter Neve 2d. for the same, pledge the hayward.

Peter Neve in mercy for overstocking the lord's common with 26 sheep; waived because he had the lord's leave.

Ordered to attach Robert the shepherd because he cut timber, worth 5s., [in land] in the lord's possession, and sold it outside the lord's bondage.

Walter Pye amerced 6d., Walter Rampolye 6d., Alice Kembald 3d., Walter Osbern 6d., John Tailor 3d., and William Underwood 2d. for breach of the assize of ale; Geoffrey Lenne 6d. for breach of the assize of bread; Alice Warde 1d. for gannocking ale; Richard Kebbil and William Payn the ale-tasters each amerced 3d. because they did not perform their duties.

Richard Qualm finds pledges to make good waste in the lord's bondage at Upstreet, which was of Walter Clevehog, viz. William of Cranmer and William Wither. William Hawys finds pledges to rebuild a house on the tenement Doo, before Michaelmas one year hence, viz. William of Cranmer and William Rampolye.

Thomas William amerced 12d. for waste in the lord's bondage, allowing a house on the tenement Goselyng to fall into ruin; ordered to make good, pledge William Hawys. Robert Hereward amerced 6d. for the same, demolishing a barn there, to the value of 3s.6d., pledges the hayward and Matthew Hereward; ordered to take the tenement into the lord's hands.

Robert Sare in mercy for withholding one ploughing service for the tenement Stronde, condoned.

Surrender: Peter Springold to Ralph Echeman and his heirs, a plot of pasture,

2   Margin: 'villein (*nativa*) of the lord' (later hand).

containing 7p., in Palmer street, granted to him to hold in villeinage, by services and works, fine 2d., pledge the hayward.

Alice the widow of Roger of the Brook pays 18d. fine for entry to the lands and tenements, which were Roger's, to hold until the full age of John, Roger's son and heir, rendering works and customs for the whole term, pledges John Typetot and William Wither.

Avice Hulke pays 6s.8d. fine for leave to marry John Bonde, pledges Thomas Fuller and William Wither.

Ordered to attach Walter Hawys, William Wyswyf, Henry Crane, John Rede and Walter Doo, villeins, because they absent themselves from the lord.

Ordered to execute the orders of the preceding court, marked with a cross, and not acted upon.

SUM 22s. 2d., except an ox, worth 13s.4d., as a heriot
Affeerers: Walter Payn and William Wither

## 82.   HIGH HALL Court General of Nicholas de Walsham, 11 June 1336 [HA504/1/4.2.i]

John Man, plaintiff v Ralph Wybert in a plea of trespass, essoins by Walter Osbern; he pledges faith; Ralph is present.

Ordered to retain in the lord's hands all the tenement of Adam Crane until etc.; and that which Nicholas Kembald held, for an ox, worth 10s., as the heriot, and for arrears of rent; and the 3a. of land which Mabel Gothelard held in villeinage, as her share of an inheritance, and the 3a., which her sister Catherine held in the same form, because they did not come to claim their inheritance. All the said lands and tenements are sown by the lord; therefore nothing in the account for profits.

Ordered to retain in the lord's hands a cotland held by Oliver the shepherd, when he died, and to report the profits.[3]

John Packard amerced 3d. because he did not rebuild a ruined house in the lord's bondage, as ordered at the last court; John Man 3d. for the same in the lord's villeinage, pledge for both, the reeve.

John Man amerced 3d. for default, pledge the reeve.

Ordered to distrain Walter Osbern for taking the crops from 3a. of land, for three years after the death of Agnes the widow of Peter Pynfoul, valued by the court at 14d.; ordered to raise.

Gilbert Helpe and William Wodebite in mercy because they did not have Robert Veyse chaplain to show the charter for the tenements, formerly of Andrew and Agnes Veyse, which are of the lord's bondage; ordered to seize the tenements, and to report the profits.

Ordered to distrain Simon Petyt, <Thomas Frere> \remitted by the lord/, Robert Deneys and the shepherd of Walter Osbern, for damage at Sheepcotecroft; and Simon Petyt for the same at Gothelardslond.

Thomas Kyng plaintiff v Robert Wybert in a plea of debt, says that Ralph bought from him, in Botesdale ['Botelisdale'], on Saturday after the feast of St Botolph 8 Edw.III [18 June 1334], an ox priced at 13s., to be paid at the following Michaelmas; and on that day he did not pay, and has not yet paid, to Thomas' loss of

---

3   Margin: 'Exploited by the lord'.

2s. Ralph defends and says that Thomas sold him an ox priced at 12s.. Thomas says it was priced at 13s., as he said, and asks that a verdict be given, and Ralph likewise. Adjudged that Thomas shall recover 13s. and the loss of 2s., and Ralph to be amerced 6d., pledges William Wodebite, Adam of Angerhale and the reeve.

Thomas Kyng plaintiff v Ralph Wybert in a plea of debt, says that he undertook, for Ralph, to pay John Kyng 10d, and he owes 3d. for a fish sold to him, to be paid at Michaelmas, and that he did not pay and has not yet paid. Ralph defends and says that he owes nothing, and asks for an enquiry, and Thomas likewise. The enquiry says that Ralph owes 13d. as Thomas said, and Thomas shall recover 13d. and the loss of 1d.; Ralph is amerced 3d., pledges as above.

Richard Banlone plaintiff v Ralph Wybert in a plea of covenant, says that he and Ralph agreed that they would plough their lands jointly with their oxen, on condition that Ralph had the first two days following the agreement; but for the next two days Ralph withdrew his oxen, so that Richard could not plough his land, in accordance with the agreement. He says that Ralph refused to keep the agreement, to Richard's loss of 6s., and he asks that the agreement be enforced. Ralph comes and defends, and says that he has not broken any agreement, as he is accused, and asks for an enquiry; Richard likewise. The enquiry says that Ralph broke no agreement, and Richard is in mercy for his false claim \condoned/. Ralph is quit indefinitely.

Richard Banlone received from the lord 4a. of land, which Catherine Mayheu held when she died, to hold to him and his heirs in villeinage at the lord's will, by services and works, pledge William Wodebite.

John Man amerced 6d. because he did not repair a bank as he was ordered in court; and also because a certain path was made outside the lord's land by his default; also amerced 12d. because he did not rebuild a house as ordered, and 6d. for waste in the lord's bondage.

John Goche and Peter his brother amerced 3d. because they did not repair a house as ordered.

The jurors present that John Packard holds a quarter part of a messuage and 2½r. of land, and ½a. of land, from the inheritance of Robert of Angerhale; ordered to seize until Robert comes etc., and to report the profits.

William Isabel the lord's swineherd amerced 5s. for damage to the value of 5s., caused by his defective custody of the pigs; ordered to raise, pledges the whole homage.

<Robert Kembald amerced 3d. because he left the court without leave.> \condoned/.

Ordered to attach John Man to reply to John the son of John Wodebite, in pleas of agreement, waste and detention of 1 quarter of wheat, pledge for John [in all the complaints] William Wodebite.

Ordered to execute all the orders of the preceding court marked with a cross, and not yet acted upon.

SUM 9s. 9d.

## 83.   HIGH HALL Court, 6 July 1336 [HA504/1/4.2.ii]

William Elys essoins of common suit, by William of Cranmer. Ralph Wybert, defendant v John Man in a plea of trespass, essoins by William Deneys.

Robert the son of Peter of Angerhale pays 6d. fine for entry to a quarter part of a messuage and 2½r. of land, following Peter's death, granted to him and his heirs to hold in villeinage, by services and works, pledge John Packard.

John the son of John Wodebite complains of John Man in a plea of detention of 1 quarter of wheat, worth 6s.8d., due to be paid last Michaelmas, when nothing was paid, or is yet paid, to the loss of 6d., which John Man cannot deny; adjudged that John Wodebite shall recover from John Man 1 quarter of wheat and 6d. damages; John Man amerced 3d.

John the son of John Wodebite, plaintiff v John Man in a plea of covenant, says that they agreed that John Man would find for the plaintiff's son his reasonable upkeep in food, clothing and all necessities from Michaelmas for three years to Michaelmas next coming; but John Man refused to keep the agreement and still does, to the loss of John Wodebite of 40s. John Man comes and defends, and says that he has broken no agreement as accused, and offers to wage law. He has a day until the next court to complete the [waging of] law, pledges for the law William of Cranmer and Gilbert Helpe.

A day is given, at the request of the parties, to John the son of John Wodebite and John Man in a plea of waste until the next court, to come without essoin. Afterwards, they agreed, amercement waived by the lord.

Ordered to execute the orders in the preceding court marked with a cross and not acted upon.

[SUM 9d., not stated]

### 84. HIGH HALL Court General of Nicholas de Walsham, 17 October 1336 [HA504/1/4.3]

<The first pledges of John Man amerced 4d. because he did not proceed against Ralph Wybert, in a plea of trespass; ordered to appoint better pledges, pledge the reeve.>

Ordered to retain in the lord's hands all the tenement of Adam Crane, and to report the profits.

John Packard amerced 3d. because he did not rebuild a ruined house in the lord's bondage, as ordered at the last court; again ordered to rebuild.

Ordered to retain in the lord's hands all the tenement, which Nicholas Kembald held, for the heriot, viz. an ox, worth 10s., and for arrears of rent, until the heir comes or pays a fine; and the 3a. of land, which Mabel Gothelard held in villein-age, as her share of an inheritance, and the 3a., which her sister Catherine held in the same form, because they did not come, and for a heriot and many defaults; and to retain a cotland held by Oliver the shepherd, when he died; and to report the profits in each case.

It was found by an enquiry of the whole homage that John Man and Matilda his wife made waste, valued at 12d., in the lord's bondage, in the dower which Matilda holds from the endowment of John Wodebite, her late husband; and their pledges, at the last court, for the rebuilding were the reeve and the hayward. Therefore they are in mercy; and, furthermore, they are liable for the waste three-fold,[4] and because John did not come to satisfy the lord and the parties opposing him in many matters (*et partibus de pluribus sibi obiciend'*), for which he had a day. Ordered to seize the tenement which Matilda holds in dower, and to report

---

4    Margin: 'Mercy. \condoned by the lord/.' followed by 'Waste <3s.>', 3s. being three times the assess-ment of the waste at 12d.

the profits. Afterwards, John Man paid 3s.4d. fine for the waste and for divers amercements, pledge the reeve and by the testimony of Robert de Saxham.[5]

Margery of Angerhale villein amerced 12d. for trespass and contempt to the lord, pledges Agnes and Adam of Angerhale.

Ordered to attach Simon Petyt for damage at Sheepcotecroft and Gothelardslond, and Walter Osbern for the same with his sheep, at the former.

Ordered to raise from Ralph Wybert 13s., which Thomas King was to recover from him, together with 2s. damages, in a complaint of debt, and 13d., with 1d. damages, which he was to recover in another complaint.

John Goche and Peter his brother amerced 6d. because they did not rebuild a ruined house as ordered; ordered as before.

John Man was unsuccessful in waging law against John, the son of John Wodebite, in a plea of covenant; it was adjudged that John the son of John shall recover 40s. damages as he claimed; John Man in mercy because he broke the agreement, condoned by the lord.

Margaret Sadwine, plaintiff v John Man in a plea of debt, says that he unlawfully withheld 20d., which he owes her because she stood in his service in the autumn of the 9th year of the reign of Edward III [1335], for three weeks, until she was entitled to that money. He still withholds it, to her loss of 2s.; and she produces suit. John comes and defends, saying that he witholds no money from her, and on this he asks to wage law, pledges for the law, William of Cranmer and Walter Osbern.

John Pynfoul does homage and fealty for the tenement he holds from the lord.

Ordered to retain in the lord's hands all the tenements of the lord's villeinage held by Andrew Veyse, which John Veyse purchased without leave.[6]

John Man cannot deny that he owes John the son of John Wodebite 1 quarter 4 bushels of wheat, worth 10s.; adjudged that he shall recover together with 2s. damages, and ordered to raise. John Man in mercy for unlawful detention, \condoned/.

The General Enquiry present that William Isabel the lord's swineherd caused damage in the lord's wheat at Stonylond, to the value of 1 sheaf; John Syre and William Hawys did the same, each 1 sheaf; Walter Osbern in the lord's peas at Hamstale, 1 sheaf; Walter Gyle and Henry de Wells chaplain in the lord's oats at Sheepcote, each 1 sheaf; Walter Deneys in the lord's wheat at Ulvesrowe, 2 sheaves; Bartholomew Goche in the lord's oats at Netherhawe, 1 sheaf, and in his barley there, 1 sheaf.

John of Angerhale amerced 3d. for default.

John Man in mercy because he did not perform winter works for the lord as ordered, condoned; Nicholas Kembald amerced 6d. because he did not perform autumn works as ordered.

The whole homage elect William Wodebite to the office of reeve, and Gilbert Helpe to the office of collector or hayward; he took the oath. William Wodebite pays 3s.4d. fine for not being in the office of reeve this year, pledge the hayward.[7]

SUM 9s. 2d.

---

5    Margin: 'dower' (?16th century).
6    Margin: 'Profits 2 bushels'.
7    Traces of two entries follow, which appear to have been deliberately obliterated.

## 85. WALSHAM Court General of Sir Hugh de Saxham, 5 November 1336 [HA504/1/4.4]

Robert Sare, defendant v Henry de Wells \in a plea of debt of 3s.1d. payable at Easter 1335/, essoins by John Herning; he pledges faith; Henry is present. Geoffrey Wright ['le Whrytthe'], plaintiff v Nicholas Goche, William of Cranmer and William Hawys in a plea of debt, essoins by Henry Wells; he pledges faith; the defendants are present. Robert Sare essoins of common suit by Peter Margery. Bartholomew Jerico, plaintiff v Ralph of Rudham chaplain in a plea of trespass, essoins by Hugh Rous; ordered to attach Ralph to reply to Bartholomew. <William Wodebite defendant v John Man in a plea of trespass, essoins by Walter Marsh, and v John Man in another plea, by Richard Banlone> \Afterwards he came/. John Pynchon defendant v Henry de Wells chaplain in a plea of debt, essoins by Richard Lorence, he pledges faith; and Olivia, John's wife, v Henry in the same plea, by Peter Neve; he pledges faith. \A day was given to Robert Kembald in the same plea./ <William of Cranmer, defendant v Richard the shepherd of Gislingham in a plea of debt, essoins by William Godyene.> \Afterwards he came./

Manser of Shucford, defendant v Henry de Wells chaplain in a plea of covenant, essoins by Adam Noble; William Hawys, plaintiff v William Godyene in a plea of trespass, essoins by John Typetot, and v Matilda of Reydon, executrix of Robert of Reydon, by Robert Clerk, and v Ralph of Rudham in a plea of trespass, by John of Foxley; ordered Ralph to reply to William; Alexander Geldenfot, plaintiff v John Man in a plea of debt, essoins by Richard the serjeant; Robert Rampolye, defendant v Richard Qualm in a plea of trespass, essoins by Robert Sare. All pledged faith; the respondents are present.

The first pledges of John Manning amerced 3d. because they did not have him reply to Henry the chaplain in a plea of debt; ordered to appoint better pledges[8]. Afterwards John comes and places himself in mercy for leave to agree.

Walter Osbern amerced 3d. for leave to agree with Simon Cooper in a plea of trespass, pledge the hayward.

Surrender: Roger of Southwold and Alice his wife, she being examined in court, to William of Cranmer the younger and his heirs, 5a. of land, 1r. of meadow, 1a. of pasture and a fifth part of a messuage, lying in various places, granted to him to hold in villeinage, by services and works, fine 13s.4d., pledge the hayward.

William Cook the shepherd amerced 6d. for trespass against the lord, in the illegal recovery of sheep in the lord's pasture, pledge Robert Hereward. Ordered as elsewhere to attach John Wauncy for the same.

After the death of Catherine Mayheu, [it was ordered to retain] in the lord's hands 4a. of land, which she held from the lord for services 18d. per year, at the usual terms. Nobody came to claim the tenement by inheritance, and it is wholly unknown who is the heir. Richard Banlone comes to receive the tenement, to hold at the lord's will, by services and works. Seisin is delivered to him by the rod, fine waived.

General Enquiry by John Syre, Walter Osbern, William Rampolye, William of Cranmer, Richard Kebbil, Stephen Cooper, Nicholas Goche, Matthew Hereward,

---

8  Margin: 'ordered' deleted.

Robert Tailor, Peter Springold, John Terwald, Simon Peyntour and Elias Typetot.

The first pledges of Manser of Shucford amerced 3d. because they did not have him reply to Henry de Wells chaplain, in a plea of debt; ordered to appoint better pledges.

Robert Tailor complains of Robert the parson of Langham in a plea of trespass, pledge the hayward; ordered.

Nicholas Drake amerced 3d. for leave to agree with Peter Jay in a plea of trespass, pledge Simon Peyntour.

Alice Helewys complains of Robert the parson of Langham in a plea of trespass, pledge for the plaintiff the hayward; ordered etc.

Richard the shepherd, plaintiff, amerced 3d. for leave to agree with John Man in a plea of debt, pledge the same John.

Walter de Wells and his pledges amerced 6d. because he did not proceed against John Lester in a plea of debt.

Richard the shepherd, plaintiff, and his pledges amerced 6d. because he did not proceed against Walter Osbern in a plea of debt, in two complaints, and against William of Cranmer in a plea of debt, pledge Thomas Dormour.

Robert Shepherd chaplain amerced 3d. for a false claim against William Clevehog in a plea of debt, pledges Edmund Lene and Nicholas Goche. William Clevehog amerced 1d. for damage to Robert Shepherd chaplain, assessed at 2d.; ordered to raise, pledge John Man.

Walter Payn amerced 4d. for unlawful detention of 1 bushel of peas, worth 6d., which he undertook to pay, by John Syre, for damage in the peas of Walter of the Marsh; ordered to raise.

William Clevehog amerced 1d. for damage to Thomas of the Beck, assessed at 1d.; ordered to raise, pledge Walter Cooper. Thomas of the Beck amerced 2d. for damage to William Clevehog, assessed at 2d.; ordered to raise, pledge the hayward.

The action between Agnes the daughter of Simon Stritt, claimant, and John Tailor and Catherine his wife, tenants, in a plea of land, which appeared in the last court, is again adjourned until the next court. Meanwhile the rolls are to be examined. \Catherine is dead./

Richard Warde amerced 3d. for trespass against Richard Kebbil assessed at 12d.; ordered to raise.

Henry Whitemor amerced 3d. for leave to agree with Gilbert Priour in a plea of trespass, pledge Walter the smith.

William Clevehog amerced 3d. for trespass against Thomas of the Beck, assessed at 12½d., in his withdrawal (*recess'*) from the service of the said William concerning (*de*) the sheep of the said William, freeman, pledge John Man; ordered to raise.[9]

Robert the farmer amerced 2d. for damage in Ladyswood with pigs, pledge Peter Springold.

Henry of Saxmundham amerced 6d. and John Typetot 3d. for damage to William Clevehog, because they took away hay from his meadow, valued at 2s.; ordered to raise.

---

9   This entry is recorded *verbatim*; its meaning is unclear.

Richard Qualm in mercy for a false claim against Henry of Saxmundham and John Typetot in a plea of trespass, condoned.

Ordered to retain in the hands of John Man 1 quarter 4 bushels of wheat taken on John Wodebite, and to take more, for him to reply to John Man in a plea of trespass.[10]

Olivia the daughter of Gilbert Priour amerced 3d. for damage in the lord's wheat at Fishponds, pledge Gilbert Priour.

John Wauncy, Robert Deneys and Walter Gyle the shepherd, [to satisfy] for damage in the lord's oats at Allwood, to the value of 4 bushels.

Amice Horn amerced 3d. for damage in the lord's barley with her geese, pledge Henry de Wells; John the miller ['le Meller'] 3d. for damage in the lord's pasture with his pigs, pledge Peter Margery; William Pach 1d. for damage there with a foal, and William Patel 3d. for damage there with horses.

John Robhood amerced 3d. for default.

Thomas Hereward pays 12d. fine for having, by the demise of John Robhood, a term of three years from last Michaelmas, in 3a. of land, and a term of two years, from next Michaelmas, in a messuage, pledges Robert Hereward and the hayward.

They say that John Lene, when he died, held from the lord a messuage and 3a. of customary land; and the lord had a mare, worth 6s., as a heriot. Robert and Edmund, his sons, are his heirs and they are of full age. They swear fealty, and have entry by the heriot.

Richard Reve, who died after the last court, held from the lord ½a. of land; and the lord had a cow, worth 6s., as a heriot; John and William, Richard's sons, are not of full age. Custody of the heirs is granted to their mother [Emma Reve]; they will have entry by the heriot.

Thomas of the Beck in mercy because he took away the lord's hay at Brodedole, to the value of 1d.; ordered to attach him.

William Cook amerced 3d. for damage in the lord's oats at Currescroft with his sheep, pledge the hayward; Robert Tailor 6d. for damage in the lord's wood.

Richard the son of Letitia amerced 3d. for default, and 3d. because he does not live in the lord's domain, and does not use (*expend'*) his goods in the bondage, but takes them outside.

The tenant of the tenement of William Springold amerced 3d. for default; Isabella, the widow of William Springold, amerced 3d. for having the said tenement at farm this year [without leave].

Robert the shepherd demised all his tenement to Edmund Lene, for a term of six years, without leave, and Robert concealed [this demise]; he is in mercy \for the concealment as well as the demise/. <Ordered to take into the lord's hands, and to report the profits.> Afterwards, Edmund came and paid 12d. fine for having his term, pledge Stephen Cooper. Later, Robert came and granted the tenement to Edmund to hold for his [Robert's] lifetime, as shown on the reverse of this roll.

Matilda Terwald amerced 3d. because she demised 5r. of land to John Lester freeman, without leave; <ordered to seize.> \because John paid a fine at the next court./

Thomas William and John Typetot each amerced 2d. for taking away corn from the

---

[10] A very unusual example of conflict between the two manors: in the last High Hall court (no.84), the lord sided with John Wodebite, his villein, in the dispute; here the lord of Walsham manor sides with John Man, his villein.

bondage into a free tenement; <Richard of Wortham did likewise> \condoned because poor/; Agnes Suter amerced 1d., Robert Kembald 2d., Henry de Wells chaplain 12d., and Robert Sare 3d. for the same.

Thomas Hereward amerced 6d. for digging on the common.

William Wodebite grazed in Walsham [manor] where he had no right to graze, because he should not graze beyond Angerhalebandon.

Henry of Saxmundham amerced 3d. for cutting down an ash tree on the lord's bondage, which is in the inheritance of the heir of William Cook, and 6d. for taking away new timber, worth 3s., which was felled for a house, in the lifetime of William Cook; ordered to raise.

Bartholomew Jerico amerced 6d. because he has sheep outside the lord's fold, and outside the demesne; Robert Sare 3d. for the same.

William Kembald purchased from John Foxley of Westhorpe all the tenement, which he held from the lord, [damaged]; he swore fealty.

Walter Pye amerced 6d., John Tailor 6d., Walter Osbern 12d., Walter Rampolye 6d. and William Rampolye 6d. [damaged '?for breaches of the assize of ale']. Geoffrey Lenne amerced 6d. for regrating bread. [Alice] Warde amerced [damaged] for gannocking ale, Bartholomew Jerico 6d. for breach of the assize of ale.

Walter Reve villein purchased from Robert Shepherd chaplain [damaged], and shows his charter, and surrenders it to the lord. Afterwards the lord returns it to him to keep [damaged] of Walter Payn and William Wither, and also surrenders into the lord's hands the said [damaged] by the rod, at the lord's will, fine 6d., pledge the reeve.

Walter Payn and Thomas Fuller were elected to the office of [damaged '?reeve']; William Wither and William Deneys \or Robert Tailor/ were elected [damaged '?hayward']; Ralph Echeman and William Payn [damaged '?were elected woodward'].

Richard Lorence amerced 3d. for damage in the lord's pasture with horses and pigs; William Godyene 3d. for the same with horses, pledge for both Robert Kembald; the shepherd of Geoffrey of Burgate 12d. for the same with sheep, pledge Nicholas Goche; Margery of the Wood 2d. for the same with her beasts, pledge the reeve; Peter Tailor 2d. for damage in the lord's barley with chickens, pledge the hayward.

John Tailor and Catherine his wife amerced 2d. for damage to Walter Robhood, assessed at 3d.; ordered to raise.

Richard Kebbil amerced 3d. for a false claim against Robert Warde in a plea of taking away beasts.

Catherine Lorence amerced 3d. for damage in the lord's pasture with her horses, pledge William Hawys; Thomas Whyte 1d. for the same with his beasts, pledge John Herning.

<William Patel in mercy for damage in the lord's wood with a cow, pledge the hayward.> \condoned/. Thomas Manning amerced 2d. for the same, pledge the reeve; William Wauncey 3d. for damage in the lord's corn with his pigs, and Ralph Echeman 1d. for damage in the lord's wood with his pigs, pledge for both the reeve.

John Rath amerced 6d. because he took timber outside the manor, pledge the reeve.

Geoffrey Lenne amerced 3d. because he made an unlawful road outside the lord's pasture.

John the son of Adam Margery pays 3d. fine for respite of suit of court until Michaelmas, pledge Peter Margery.

Marsilia Hawys pays 3d. fine for having an easement, pledge the reeve.

William Cook and Robert his brother find pledges for making good waste in the lord's bondage before Michaelmas, *viz.* Henry of Saxmundham and William Wither.

Walter Petipas received from the lord 1a. of land in Westhorpe, which Robert Deneys sold to him, during his lifetime, and seisin was granted to him by the rod etc., making annually, in the hall here, one suit of court at the Court General next after Michaelmas, fine 2s., pledge Thomas Patel. Walter swore customary fealty.

Matilda of Reydon was attached to reply to Michael Nichole in a plea of debt, concerning which he complains that she unlawfully withheld from him 14s.6d., and that on Wednesday in Easter week, 9 Edw.III [9 April 1335], they made an agreed calculation of a debt of Robert, Matilda's late husband, and on this calculation, Matilda remained in debt to Michael for the said 14s.6d., and agreed to pay at the feast of the Nativity of St John the Baptist last past [24 June 1336]. On this day, she did not pay, but withheld and still withholds, to Michael's loss of ½ mark, and on this he produces suit. Matilda says that she owes him no money, and offers to wage law, pledge for the law, Henry de Wells.

Surrenders: William of Cranmer the younger to Walter Syre and his heirs, ½a. of land, granted to him to hold in villeinage, by services and works, fine 18d., pledge the reeve; and to William Syre and his heirs, ½a. of land at Hulkesbridge, granted to him in the same form, fine 18d., pledge the hayward.

Robert Shepherd chaplain pays 6d. fine for respite of suit of court until Michaelmas. Ordered to raise 5s. from Robert for wood, which he cut down in the lord's bondage, while it stood in the lord's possession, and which he sold, without cause of maximum necessity, because he purchased, with that money, a free tenement in Debenham, pledges William of Cranmer the younger and Edmund Lene.

Ordered to raise 10s. from William Clevehog and his brother William, to the use of Thomas Patel, which he was to recover from them last year.

Surrenders: William Hawys and Massilia his wife, she being examined in court, to Walter the smith and his heirs, 2a.3½r. of land at the Millfield, granted to him to hold in villeinage, by services and works, fine 10s., pledge the hayward.

John Man to William and Massilia Hawys and John their son, and their heirs, ½ r. of meadow at the Hevedacre, granted to them in the same form, fine 8d., pledge as above.

Richard Spileman to Edmund Lene and his heirs, a piece of meadow 60p. long and 6ft. wide, granted to him in the same form, fine 12d., pledge as above.

Peter Jay and William Clevehog each pay 18d. for having a fold of 60 sheep, Robert Rampolye 12d. for 40 sheep, Nicholas Goche 2s. for 4 score sheep, William and Massilia Hawys 2s.6d. for 6 score sheep, and no more because 1 score is allowed to them, William of Cranmer 2s. for 60 sheep, and no more because 2 score are allowed to him.

William Rampolye pays 8s. fine for leave to marry his daughter [Alice] to John Pynfoul, pledge William Wither.

Ordered to attach Sir Edmund de Pakenham and Alexander de Walsham to swear fealty to the lord.

<Ordered to attach Eleanor and Olivia the daughters of Walter Osbern because they

gave birth outside wedlock.> \Condoned because poor, at the instance of Thomas of Bardwell./

The lord to be consulted concerning land exchanged with Robert Shepherd chaplain, to the lord's loss.

Ordered to distrain Alexander de Walsham for relief, homage and fealty, and for other summonses, as shown in the court of 13 June 1335 [no.77].

Ordered to attach Denis the son of Michael Nichole for damage in the lord's meadow.

William Hawys finds pledges to repair a house on the tenement Doo by Michaelmas one year hence, viz. William of Cranmer and William Rampolye.

Ordered to make good the waste which Thomas William made on the lord's bondage, viz. on the tenement Goselyng.

Ordered to seize into the lord's hands the tenement of Robert Hereward, which he held of the tenement Goselyng, because he demolished a barn there.

Ordered to attach Walter Hawys, William Wyswyf, Henry Crane, John Rede and Walter Doo, villeins, because they absent themselves from the lord.

A day is given to the Prior of Ixworth, until the next court, to make amends to the lord, because he diverted a watercourse at Trendelwood, to the nuisance of the lord and the townspeople, pledge Henry de Wells.

Ordered to retain in the lord's hands a messuage 20a. of customary land, which Robert the chaplain demised to Alexander the serjeant without leave, and to report the profits.

Ordered to attach Alexander de Walsham because he dug on the common, to the nuisance of the lord and the townspeople, and because he made a pit there.

Ordered to retain in the lord's hands the cottage of Hereward Gunter, for waste there, and to report the profits.

The lord to be consulted about a messuage in Debenham, which Robert Shepherd chaplain purchased.

Robert Shepherd chaplain surrendered to Edmund Lene and Amice his wife all his tenement in Walsham, to hold for Robert's lifetime, paying annually to him 12s. of silver at Michaelmas, and rendering all services and customs owed therefrom. Edmund and Amice shall maintain it and and bear all other expenses whatsoever arising, without seeking, or having, any allowance; and they shall maintain the tenement without waste or destruction. And if it happens that they, or either of them, shall fail in the said payments in any way, it shall be allowed to Robert to enter the tenement, and hold it, until he is fully satisfied for the payment. Edmund and Amice give 20s. fine for having the tenement in the said form, pledge Stephen Cooper. Moreover, they found guarantors for all these premises, and for swearing fealty, viz. Stephen Cooper and Robert Tailor.

Walter Osbern pays 3d. fine for having a term of one year in 1a. of land, by the demise of Walter the son of William Springold, pledge the hayward.

Edmund Lene pays 3d. fine for respite of suit of court until Michaelmas.

John Man in mercy for leave to agree with William Wodebite in a plea of trespass, in two complaints, and with John Wodebite in a plea of trespass \both in respite until the next court./

Catherine the daughter of Robert Deneys amerced 6s.8d. for leave to marry William Cook the shepherd, pledge William Deneys.

Ordered to attach Thomas William for waste on the lord's bondage.

SUM 107s. 10d., except a mare and a cow, each worth 6s., as heriots
Affeerers: Walter Payn and William Wither

## 86.  WALSHAM Court, 14 February 1337 [HA504/1/4.5]

Robert Ryvel, plaintiff v Agnes Helewys in a plea of debt, essoins by Peter Margery.
William the son of William Rampolye, defendant v Walter Cooper in a plea of
trespass, essoins by Robert Sare; he pledges faith; Walter is present. Gilbert
Helpe, defendant v John Man in a plea of trespass, essoins by William Wodebite;
he pledges faith; John is present. William Rampolye, defendant v Robert Swyft
in a plea of trespass, essoins by William Kembald; and William the servant of
William Rampolye, defendant in the same plea, essoins by Richard the serjeant;
they pledge faith; Robert is present. William Grym, defendant v Ralph Wright in
a plea of trespass, essoins by Bartholomew Jerico; he pledges faith; Ralph is
present.

Again as elsewhere ordered to attach Ralph of Rudham chaplain to reply to Bartholomew Jerico in a plea of trespass.

William Wodebite and his pledges in mercy because he did not proceed against John
Man in a plea of trespass, condoned.

John Pynchon and Olivia his wife amerced 6d. for leave to agree with Henry de
Wells chaplain, in a plea of debt; and Manser of Shucford 3d. for the same in a
like plea.

A day is given, at the request of the parties, to William Hawys, plaintiff, and William Godyene, defendant, until the next court, to come without essoin. A day is
given to William Hawys and Matilda of Reydon, executrix of Robert of Reydon,
in a plea of debt, in the same form.

Ordered to attach Ralph of Rudham to reply to William Hawys in a plea of trespass.

Thomas William and Agnes his wife, she being examined in court, granted to William Hawys and his heirs, all the tenement which they held in Walsham, in dower
as well as by purchase, to hold for the lifetime of Agnes, paying 8s. annually at
Pentecost and at the feast of the Assumption [15 August], in equal parts, and rendering all services and customs, save the ploughing, due from the said tenement,
fine 20s., pledge the hayward. And if it happens that William defaults in payment
of the said rent, then he wills and grants that Agnes shall enter into the tenement
and hold it until etc., fine 12d., pledge the hayward.

Robert Rampolye amerced 2d. for leave to agree with Richard Qualm in a plea of
trespass, pledge the hayward.

A day is given, at the request of the parties, to Alexander Geldenfot, plaintiff, and
John Man, defendant, in a plea of debt, until the next court, to come without
essoin.

Surrender: William Hawys to Thomas Fuller and his heirs, 6p. of meadow in the
Micklemeadow, granted to him to hold in villeinage, by services and works etc.,
fine 3d., pledge the hayward.

Manser of Shucford amerced 3d. for leave to agree with Henry de Wells chaplain in
a plea of debt, pledge the hayward.

Michael Nichole and his pledges amerced 6d. because he did not proceed against
Matilda of Reydon in a plea of debt.

Manser of Shucford amerced 3d. for leave to agree with Henry de Wells chaplain, in
a plea of taking beasts.

Alice[11] Priour amerced 3d. for leave to agree with Robert Swyft in a plea of trespass, pledge Walter the smith.

William Rampolye the elder amerced 3d. for leave to agree with Walter Cooper in a plea of trespass, pledge the hayward.

Cristina Smith amerced 3d. for leave to agree with John Pynfoul in a plea of trespass, pledge Walter the smith.

Ordered to attach Richard Jote to reply to William Clevehog in a plea of debt.

Thomas William amerced 3d. for waste in the lord's bondage, pledge the hayward.

Thomas Fuller made waste in a cottage called Brookhouse ['Brokhous']; <in mercy and ordered to make good>.[12] \He has a day to make good the waste before next Christmas./

Peter Springold, who died after the last court, held from the lord 11a. of land and 1½r. of customary meadow, and the lord had a mare, worth 5s., as a heriot. His son Robert is his nearest heir, and is of full age; he has entry by the heriot, following the custom of the manor, and swore servile fealty.

Hilary Cook, who died after the last court, held from the lord 5r. of customary land; the lord had an ox, worth 12s., as a heriot. William and Robert her sons are her nearest heirs, and are of full age; they have entry by the heriot, and swore fealty.

Surrender: Robert the son of Peter Springold to Hilary Springold and her heirs, 1a.1r. of customary land, granted to her to hold in villeinage by services and works etc., fine 4s., pledge Matthew Hereward.

Catherine Tailor held from the lord, when she died, a messuage, 3a.1½r. of land, and the lord had half a stot, worth 5s., as a heriot. John Tailor, who was married to Catherine, will hold the tenement for his lifetime, in accordance with law and custom, and John their son will have entry by the heriot, when he has come to full age.

Henry de Elmham took rabbits in the lord's warren; ordered etc.

Robert Lene amerced 12d. for damage in the lord's pasture with sheep of the cullet, pledge the hayward.

Henry de Wells chaplain did damage with his cart, flattening the lord's meadow; ordered etc.; Walter the reeve and Robert Tailor the hayward each amerced 12d., because they allowed Henry to flatten the meadow.

John the son of Walter Osbern the elder seeks to be admitted to the tenement formerly his [father's], and he is admitted without paying a fine, because a heriot was paid for Walter.[13]

Peter Margery amerced 3d. for damage in the lord's wheat, with his beasts, pledge Nicholas Goche.

Surrenders: John Man to Manser of Shucford and his heirs, ½r. of land abutting on Kembaldscroft, granted to him to hold in villeinage, by services and works, fine 10d.

John Osbern to Walter Syre and his heirs, 1r. of land at Langethweyt, granted to him in the same form, fine 10d.

William Wither to Walter Rampolye and his heirs, 2r. of customary land at the Millfield, granted to him in the same form, fine 20d., pledge for all the hayward.

---

11  MS: 'Alex', but there is no other reference to an Alexander Priour in the rolls; and this is assumed to be a clerical error.

12  Margin: 'condoned'.

13  MS: *Walter heriettebatur*, literally – Walter 'was herioted'.

Richard Qualm, John Man and William Patyl the younger mainperned for William Clevehog the elder, to pay 30s. to Richard de Walsham in the next three years, *viz.* the first term, beginning at All Saints Day [1 November], paying 10s. from year to year, on that day.

Robert Ryvel amerced 12d. because he grazed the herbage of the severalty with the sheep of the cullet. Robert Lene amerced 12d. because he allowed Robert Ryvel to do so.

Robert Sare was attached to reply to Henry de Wells chaplain in a plea of debt, and thereupon Henry complains that on Monday after the feast of St Gregory the Pope 10 Edw.III [18 March 1336], he and Robert agreed, concerning the hire of two oxen and their (?*minutar'*),[14] so that Robert was indebted to him for 3s.1d., to be paid at the following Easter day; on this day Robert withheld, and still withholds, to Henry's loss of 12d., and on this he produces suit. Robert comes and defends, saying that he owes Henry nothing, as accused; and he offers to wage law, pledges for the law, Robert Tailor and Walter Payn.

Matilda of Reydon pays 3d. fine to repossess 5r. of land out of the lord's hands, which she sold to John Lester freeman, without leave, pledge John Terwald.

Ordered to execute the orders of the last court, marked with a cross, and not acted upon.

General Enquiry by William of Cranmer, William Hawys, Nicholas Goche, John Syre, John Terwald, Stephen Cooper, Matthew Hereward, Simon Peyntour, Elias Typetot, Richard Kebbil, Walter Payn, Robert Tailor, Richard Qualm, William Wither.

Ordered that they and Robert Warde and Peter Margery apportion the tenement Outlagh, the tenement Margerys and the tenement of Master John before the feast of St Matthew the Apostle [21 September].

SUM 37s., except 1 ox, 1 mare and half a stot, worth 22s;

less the expenses of Peter of Euston for holding the court, 20¼d.

Affeerers: Walter Payn and Robert Tailor

## 87. WALSHAM Court General, 7 May 1337 [HA504/1/4.6]

Robert Sare, defendant v Henry de Wells chaplain, in a plea of debt, essoins by Simon of Weston, concerning which [he wages] law; he pledges faith; Henry is present. Henry Whitemor, defendant v Peter Neve in a plea of debt, essoins by John Typetot; he pledges faith; Peter is present. Agnes Helewys, defendant v Robert Ryvel in a plea of debt, essoins by Roger Hauker; she pledges faith; Robert is present. Richard Jote, defendant v William Clevehog the elder in a plea of debt, essoins by William Kembald; he pledges faith; Richard is present. <Manser of Shucford essoins of common suit, by Adam Noble> \It does not lie, because he holds by the rod/. Bartholomew Jerico, plaintiff v Ralph of Rudham, chaplain, in a plea of trespass, essoins by Gilbert Helpe; ordered to distrain Ralph to reply. John Man, plaintiff v Gilbert Helpe in a plea of trespass, essoins by Michael Nichole; he pledges faith; Gilbert is present.

William the son of William Rampolye amerced 3d. for leave to agree with Walter Cooper in a plea of trespass, pledge William Rampolye.

William Rampolye amerced 3d. for leave to agree with Robert Swyft in a plea of

---

14 Latham gives *minutorius* – 'blood-letter'; it is probable that the clerk intended *minatori* – drivers.

trespass, and William the servant of William Rampolye amerced 3d. for the same, pledge for both the hayward.

Ralph Wright amerced 3d. for leave to agree with William Grym in a plea of trespass, pledge William Rampolye.

The first pledges of John Man amerced 6d. because they did not have him reply to Alexander Geldenfot in a plea of debt; ordered to appoint better pledges.

The first pledges of William Godyene of Stanton amerced 6d. because they did not have him reply to William Hawys in a plea of trespass; ordered to appoint better pledges.

Matilda of Reydon \she has [since] died/ was attached to reply to William Hawys in a plea of debt, concerning which, he complained that, on Monday after Pentecost, 9 Edw.III [5 June 1335], he and Matilda together computed various debts, and as a result, [agreed] that she was indebted to him for 8s. of silver, to be paid at the following Michaelmas. On that day, she did not pay, but withheld, and still withholds, to William's loss of 40d., and on this he produces suit. Matilda came and defended, saying that she did not compute with William, and did not become indebted to him as accused; and she offered to wage law, pledge for the law John Terwald.

Ordered to retain a horse taken upon John Man, and to take more etc., for him to reply to John Clevehog in a plea of debt.

Michael Nichole amerced 6d. for damage in the lord's meadow by his servant, pledge Peter Jay.

The first pledges of Henry de Wells chaplain amerced 2s. because they did not have him make good damage to the lord's pasture, flattened by his cart; and a further 2s., because they did not have him make amends for trespass in the lord's pasture with his cart, plough, tumbril and beasts; ordered to appoint better pledges.

Manser of Shucford amerced 6d. for default.

General Enquiry by John Syre, William Payn, Walter Osbern, William Wither, John Terwald, Simon Peyntour, Elias Typetot, Nicholas Goche, Matthew Hereward, Walter Hereward, William Patel the younger, Robert Warde, William of Cranmer, William Hawys and Ralph Echeman.

John the shepherd complains of Manser of Shucford in a plea of debt, pledge for John, Robert Tailor; ordered to attach Manser.

The jurors say that[15] Thomas at the Lee caused damage in Ladyswood on several occasions, by his dog taking rabbits and hares; ordered etc.

Also that the same Thomas holds 2a.3r. of customary land, for which he should pay 7¼d. rent, and perform one winter work, one hoeing and half an autumn work, viz. 3r. of the tenement Kebbils, lying at the gate of Walter Gilbert, between the land of the Prior of Ixworth and that of Ralph Echeman, the north head abutting on Buryway, and ½a. of the tenement Springold, abutting on Ladyswood, and called the Scotheshalfacre, and ½a. of the tenement Robhood, lying on the west side of Ladyswood gate, and abutting at one head on Ladyswood, and at the other on the Grendel, and 1a. at Calvethweyt. Afterwards it was found that Robert Tailor holds this 1a. by an exchange with John at the Green, for 3r. of land, lying at the head of the same. The jurors have a day until the next court to enquire

---

15 The word 'ordered,' in the margin, and the first four words have been deleted, and endorsed 'remitted'. This refers only to the offence in Ladyswood.

concerning which tenements Thomas should hold, and his title to them. The same
Thomas holds 1r. of customary land at the Thieveshedge ['Theveshege'], of the
tenement Cook, lying between the land of Thomas Badwell and that of Alice
Hawys, and abutting on the king's highway.

The jurors say that the Prior of Ixworth holds 1a. of customary land in the Stubbing,
of which ½a. was of Robert Springold, and ½a. was of Hugh le Marwe, and that
he took the crops from this land for several years, without leave; he is amerced
6s.8d., ordered to seize etc. The Prior is amerced 3s.4d. for several defaults; and
is ordered to be attached because he grazed with his sheep the lord's pasture in
the Stubbingway in Ashfield, where he had no right of grazing.

Alexander de Walsham kept [open] (*continuit*) two pits called Marlers, dug in the
time of Sir Alexander his father, of which one is at Pynchonnes Willows ['We-
lwes'] and the other at Strondesway, ordered etc.

Henry of Saxmundham amerced 3d. because he dug in the pit at Strondesway this
year.

Robert Man amerced 6d. because he baked and sold bread in breach of the assize.
Walter Pye amerced 12d., Walter Osbern 6d., Walter Rampolye 6d., John Tailor
3d., and Robert Man 6d., because they brewed ale in breach of the assize. Geoffrey Lenne amerced 3d. for regrating bread. William Payn and Richard Kebbil
the ale-tasters each amerced 2d. because they did not perform their duties.

Ordered to attach William Wodebite because he grazed with his sheep where he had
no right of common.

The Prior of Ixworth amerced 12d. for grazing with his sheep in the lord's pasture in
the Millfield, pledge the hayward.

William Hawys pays 3d. fine to apportion the tenement Fraunceys, which was of
Peter Robbes, by the next court. A day is given to the jurors to apportion this
tenement, and the tenement Typetots.

<They present that Thomas at the Lee unlawfully drove the lord's sheep on the com-
mon to his own gates; ordered etc.> remitted.

Olivia the daughter of Walter Osbern pays 13s.4d. fine for leave to marry William
Kembald, pledge Walter Osbern.

Surrender: Walter Osbern to William Kembald and Olivia Walter's daughter and
their heirs, 4a. of land at Windellond, between Walter's land on each side,
granted to them to hold in villeinage, by services and works, fine 8s., pledges
Walter Osbern and the hayward.

Ordered to execute the orders of the last court, marked with a cross, and not acted
upon.

SUM 43s. 8d.;
less the expenses of Thomas de Saxham, 2s.2½d. and 2 pecks of oats
Affeerers: Walter Payn and Robert Tailor

**88.  HIGH HALL Court of Nicholas de Walsham, 22 May 1337 [HA504/1/4.7]**
John Man, defendant v Margery Sadwyne in a plea of debt, essoins by William
Clevehog, \concerning which [he wages] law/; he pledges faith; Margery is present. Robert Sare essoins of common suit, by John Kebbil; William Elys of the
same, by William of Cranmer; they pledge faith.

Gilbert Helpe amerced 3d. because he did not attach Walter Osbern as ordered;
again ordered to attach Walter for damage in the lord's corn at Sheepcroft, with
his sheep.

John Goche and Peter his brother pay 12d. fine for postponement of the rebuilding of a ruined house in the lord's villeinage, until Michaelmas one year hence, pledges William Wodebite and Gilbert Helpe.

William Deneys, the pledge of Nicholas Fraunceys, amerced 3d. because he did not have Nicholas satisfy the lord for damage in the herbage at the Pightle with his beasts; ordered to appoint a better pledge; pledge William of Cranmer.

John Packard pays 12d. fine for postponement of the rebuilding of a ruined house in the lord's villeinage until Michaelmas one year hence, pledge Gilbert Helpe.

Cristiana the daughter of Gilbert Helpe pays 6s.8d. fine for leave to marry Henry of Littlehawe, pledge the reeve.

Gilbert Helpe pays 2s. fine for leave to dispose of half a messuage, which was formerly of Robert Tailor, pledge the reeve.

Ordered to seize 1a. of customary land which Robert Hovel purchased without leave.

It was found that Gilbert Helpe withheld from Agnes Wodebite 1 bushel of wheat, worth 10d., to her loss of 1d.; Gilbert amerced 1d.; adjudged that she shall recover the said bushel with the loss.

Gilbert Helpe the younger has a day until All Saints day [1 November] to rebuild a certain ruined house, under penalty of ½ mark, pledges John Goche and Gilbert Helpe.

Nicholas Kembald amerced 3d. for default.

Ordered to retain a she-goat taken upon Ralph the serjeant, because he unlawfully made a path in the lord's herbage at Angerhalefield; and to take more etc.

John Pynchon and Olivia his wife purchased a messuage and 1a. of free land [without leave]; ordered to take into the lord's hands until etc.

Ordered to execute the orders of the last court, marked with a cross, and not yet acted upon.

SUM 11s. 6d.

Affeerers: William Wodebite and John Chapman

## 89.   WALSHAM Court, 24 September 1337 [HA504/1/4.8]

Thomas of the Beck, defendant v Alexander Geldenfot in a plea of debt, essoins by John the bailiff; he pledges faith; Alexander's attorney, Robert Clerk, is present.

+Manser of Shucford amerced 6d. for unlawful detention of 15s.7d. from John the shepherd, as he admitted in open court; the loss is remitted, ordered to raise.

Robert Sare amerced 3d. for leave to agree with Henry de Wells chaplain, in a plea of debt. Agnes Helewys 3d. for leave to agree with Robert Ryvel in a similar plea, pledge for both the hayward.

Henry de Wells chaplain amerced 2s. for damage in the lord's pasture with his cart, plough and tumbril, pledges Robert Sare and Robert Tailor.

William Clevehog the elder and his pledges amerced 3d. because he did not proceed against Richard Jote in a plea of debt.

The first pledges of John Man in mercy because they did not have him reply to Alexander Geldenfot in a plea of debt; ordered, as elsewhere to attach John to reply. Afterwards John comes and gives[16] to the lord for leave to agree with Alexander in the same plea, pledge the hayward. \He ackowledges himself bound

---

16  Margin: 'mercy 3d.'; this was the amercement of John for leave to agree; that on the pledges was waived.

to pay Alexander 4s.8d. on Sunday before the feast of St Luke [12 October], pledges Simon Peyntour and William Clevehog/.

+Henry Whitemor amerced 3d. for unlawful detention of 1 pound of wool, worth 4d., from Peter Neve, the loss assessed at 1d.; ordered to raise.

John Clevehog and his pledges amerced 6d. because he did not proceed against John Man in a plea of debt.

+The first pledges of William Wodebite amerced 6d. because they did not have him make amends to the lord, because he grazed his sheep where he had no right to graze; ordered to appoint better pledges.

+Ordered as elsewhere to attach Ralph of Rudham chaplain to reply to Bartholomew Jerico in a plea of trespass.

John Man amerced 3d. for unlawful detention of 6d. from Gilbert Helpe; the loss is remitted; ordered to raise.

Gilbert Helpe amerced 3d. for leave to agree with John Man in a plea of trespass, pledge the hayward.

William Wither and William Rampolye each amerced 3d. for unlawful detention of 3s.6d. from Henry de Wells chaplain, which they undertook to pay, for Manser of Shucford; the loss is remitted; ordered to raise.

Manser of Shucford amerced 3d. for unlawful detention of 2s.7d. from Henry de Wells chaplain, the loss is remitted; ordered to raise.

Henry de Wells chaplain amerced 3d. for his false claim against William Wither and William Rampolye in a plea of debt, pledge the hayward.

John Rath amerced 2d. for leave to agree with Warin Bret in a plea of trespass, pledges the reeve and hayward.

Letitia Stronde amerced 3d. for damage in the lord's oats at Boynhawe; William Hawys 2d. for the same, pledge for both, the hayward. John Golder amerced 3d. for damage by his daughter in the lord's corn in autumn, pledge the hayward. Agnes Fraunceys and Agnes Eseger of Stanton each amerced 2d. for damage in the lord's pasture, pledge the hayward. Henry de Wells chaplain amerced 3d. for damage in the lord's herbage at the Brook, pledge Peter Margery.

Robert Lene amerced 3d. for his false claim against Stephen Cooper in a plea of trespass, pledge the hayward.

Surrenders: William of Cranmer the younger to Walter Craske the miller and his heirs, 1a.3r. of land in Edwardstoft, granted to him to hold in villeinage, by services and works, fine 5s., pledge Robert Tailor, the hayward.

Walter Noreys to William Noreys his brother and his heirs, 3½r. of land at Allwoodgreen, in exchange for 2½a. of land in various places, and William's portion of a messuage, granted to them to hold in the same form, William paid 2s. fine and Walter 4s., and no more because in exchange, pledge for both the hayward.

Simon Peyntour to William Rampolye and his heirs, 3r. of land at the Regway, granted to him in the same form, fine 3s., pledge the hayward.

Peter Jay to Robert Rampolye and his heirs, 3 parts of 1r. of meadow in two places in the Micklemeadow, granted to him in the same form, fine 12d., pledge the hayward.

Ralph Hawys, when he died, held from the lord 6½a. of land, ½r. of meadow and a quarter of a messuage; the lord had no heriot because he had no beast. Ralph's nearest heirs are William and Walter his brothers, who pay 10s. entry fine, pledge the hayward.

Matilda Terwald villein, when she died, held from the lord ½a. of customary land;

the lord had a heifer, worth 3s., as a heriot, John Terwald is her nearest heir, and he has entry by the heriot.[17]

Olivia the daughter of William of Cranmer pays 2s.8d. childwyte, because she gave birth outside wedlock.

Sir William Criketot hunted in the lord's warren and took three hares; ordered etc.

Henry de Wells chaplain made waste in the lord's bondage at Pynfouls cutting down, and taking away, timber and straw to the value of 6s.8d.; ordered to attach him.

Adam Noble amerced 1d. for damage in the lord's oats with his pigs; John Tailor 3d. for allowing his pigs to graze the corn of the lord and [his] neighbours, pledge for both the hayward; Olivia Kembald 6d. for the same, pledge Robert Kembald; Henry de Wells chaplain 6d. for the same, pledge the hayward.

Henry de Wells chaplain amerced 6d. because he made an illegal road at the Regway; and 12d. because he unlawfully grazed his sheep beyond Southbrook to the west, where he had no right of common, and with more sheep than he ought to have; and 6d. because he unlawfully has his pigs rooting on the common, pledge the hayward.

John Typetot and Robert Sare each amerced 3d., and Robert Kembald 2d. because they stored their corn grown on the bondage, in free tenements, pledge for all the hayward; Olivia Kembald 2d. for the same, pledge Robert Kembald.

William Hawys was attached to reply to Henry de Wells chaplain in a plea of debt, concerning which Henry says that on Monday after the feast of the Translation of St Thomas the Martyr 9 Edw.III [10 July 1335], in Walsham, William acknowledged himself to be bound for 1 bushel of peas and ½ bushel of oats, for damage done to Henry in his corn, to be paid at the following Michaelmas, but on that day he did not pay, but withheld, and still withholds, to Henry's loss of 6d.; and on this he produces suit. William comes and defends, saying that he did not acknowledge himself bound for the said corn, nor does he owe Henry anything, as he is accused; and he offers to wage law, pledge for the law the hayward.[18]

William was also attached to reply to Henry in a plea of trespass, concerning which Henry says that on Thursday before the feast of St Peter's Chains 11 Edw.III [31 July 1337], in Walsham, William's sheep had grazed in Henry's herbage, on 3a. of land below Burchardeswood, to Henry's loss of 2s., and on this he produces suit. William comes and defends, saying that he made satisfaction to Henry for the said herbage, and that he did not graze his sheep there against Henry's will. He asks for an enquiry to be held, and the plaintiff likewise. Ordered etc.

William was also attached to reply to Henry in a plea of taking cattle, concerning which Henry says that on Thursday before the feast of St Peter's Chains Edw.III, 9 [27 July 1335] in Walsham, William took two of Henry's oxen in a common way called Burfieldway, and took them to his own house, and held them against security and pledge, to Henry's loss of 6s.8d., and on this he brings suit. William comes and says that he took the oxen in the said place, Burfieldway, in his several pasture, because he found them grazing his pasture there, and not in Henry's common, namely at such a season of the year. He asks for an enquiry, and the plaintiff likewise. Ordered etc.

---

17 Margin: 'villein of the lord' (later hand).
18 Margin: 'to enquire'.

Henry was attached to reply to William in a plea of trespass, and William says that on Monday after the feast of the Nativity of St John the Baptist 11 Edw.III [30 June 1337] in Walsham, Henry took away his [William's] hay from the Mickle-meadow, to his loss of 6s.8d., and on this he produces suit. Henry comes and defends and says that he took no hay from William, as he is accused, and he asks for an enquiry to be held, and the plaintiff likewise. Ordered etc.

Walter Payn and Nicholas Goche were elected to the office of reeve, and Nicholas took the oath. Robert Tailor and Simon Peyntour were elected to the office of hayward, and Simon took the oath.

Robert Hereward amerced 6d. for harvesting corn badly in the autumn, pledge the hayward.

Ordered to execute the orders of the last court, marked with a cross, and not yet acted upon.

The Prior of Ixworth amerced 12d. for default.

Walter Osbern pays 6d. fine for repossessing a cottage out of the lord's seisin, [taken] for waste made in the same by Alice Ape, pledge the hayward. Reversion of the cottage belongs to Walter.

William Hawys in mercy because he sold to Thomas de Saxham without leave, timber to the value of 13s.4d. and more; condoned by the lord.

Walter Osbern cut down, and caused to be cut down, timber to the value of 10s. and more, without leave; an enquiry concerning the waste to be made before the next court.

SUM 41s. 10d., except a heifer, worth 3s., as a heriot<br>
Affeerers: Walter Payn and Robert Tailor

## 90. HIGH HALL Court General of Nicholas de Walsham, 3 October 1337 [HA504/1/4.9.i]

William Deneys essoins of common suit, by William Elys.

Gilbert Helpe amerced 3d. because he did not attach Walter Osbern, as ordered.

+Ordered as elsewhere to attach Walter Osbern for damage in the lord's corn at Sheephousecroft with his sheep.

Ordered as elsewhere to attach William Wodebite to reply to the lord because he exchanged 1a. of customary land with Robert Hovel, without leave.

<John Pynchon amerced 3d. for default> \afterwards he came/.

Adjudged that Hugh de Wells should recover 20½d. from Gilbert Helpe, which Gilbert withheld from him, and damages of 2d.; ordered to raise. Gilbert amerced 3d.

Simon Peyntour and his men caused damage in the lord's oats at Angerhale, amerced 2 bushels; Walter Payn did likewise there, amerced 2 sheaves; Simon Peyntour and his men caused damage in the lord's meadow, amerced 1d.; William Payn did likewise in the lord's barley at Stonylond, amerced 1 sheaf; Walter Deneys did likewise in the lord's oats at Ulvesrowe, amerced 2 sheaves. Henry de Wells caused damage in the lord's barley at Netherhawe with his cows; ordered etc. Bartholomew Goche did damage in the lord's peas, amerced 2 sheaves; John Syre caused damage with a colt in the lord's oats, amerced 1 sheaf.

+Henry de Wells ploughed the lord's land, sown with wheat, and took away the crop from that land to the value of [blank] etc.; ordered.

John Packard amerced 3d. because he did not protect the lord's hay as ordered; and 9d. because he struck the lord's horse, and as a result it lost an eye.

William Wodebite amerced 2d. for damage in Smallbrook ['Smalbrok'] with his pigs rooting.

John and Adam the sons of Hugh and Agnes of Angerhale pay 2s. fine for repossessing 1½a. of land, which the lord exchanged with Robert Hovel, for land which he surrendered into the lord's hands, pledge the reeve.

John Goche pays 2s. for leave to marry, pledge the reeve.

William Isabel is elected reeve, and afterwards pays 12d. fine, pledge John Packard. Adam Angerhale is elected hayward, and afterwards pays 12d. fine, pledge the reeve.

Ordered to execute the orders of the last court, marked with a cross, and not yet acted upon.

Nicholas Kembald amerced 3d. for default.

SUM 8s.

## 91. WALSHAM Court General, 9 January 1338 [HA504/1/4.10]

John Terwald, defendant v Simon Cooper in a plea of debt, essoins by Robert Clerk; he pledges faith; Simon is present. <William Godyene, defendant v William Hawys in a plea of trespass, essoins by Richard Lorence> \It does not lie because after default/. Peter Cook, plaintiff v Geoffrey Whitemor in a plea of debt, essoins by Robert Sare; he pledges faith; Geoffrey is present. Bartholomew Jerico, plaintiff v Ralph of Rudham chaplain, in a plea of trespass, essoins by John Typetot; afterwards ordered to attach Ralph.

A day is given, at the request of the parties, to Alexander Geldenfot, plaintiff, and Thomas of the Beck, defendant, in a plea of debt, until the next court, to come without essoin.

Robert Tailor the hayward in mercy because he did not execute the order of the court, condoned. Ordered as elsewhere to raise from William Rampolye and William Wither 3s.6d., and from Manser of Shucford 2s.7d., to the use of Henry de Wells chaplain.

Henry de Wells chaplain amerced 6s.8d. for waste in the lord's bondage at Pynfouls, cutting down, and taking away, timber and straw, to the value of 6s.8d., pledge the hayward; and 2s. for leave to agree with William Hawys in pleas of debt and trespass, in four complaints.

Ordered to attach John Wauncy for the illegal recovery from the lord's shepherd of sheep taken in the lord's pasture.

John Margery pays 3d. fine for respite of suit of court until Michaelmas, pledge Robert Ryvel.

Robert Tailor amerced 2d. because he did not proceed against Robert the parson of the church of Langham, in a plea of trespass; and Alice Helewys 2d. because she did not proceed against Robert in the same plea, pledge for both the hayward.

William and Robert Cook amerced 6d. because they did not make good waste in the lord's bondage, as they undertook, pledge the hayward. Ordered to seize the tenement into the lord's hands, and to report the profits.

Again ordered to distrain Alexander de Walsham for homage, fealty and relief, and for many defaults.

Again a day is given to William Hawys, until next Michaelmas, to rebuild a house on the tenement Doo, pledges William of Cranmer and William Rampolye.

Ordered to attach William Wyswyf, Henry Crane, John Rede and Walter Doo, villeins, because they absent themselves from the lord.

Ordered to attach Ralph of Rudham chaplain to reply to William Hawys in a plea of trespass.

The second pledges of William Godyene of Stanton amerced 12d. because they did not have him reply to William Hawys in a plea of trespass; ordered to appoint better pledges.

Robert of Northawe amerced 18d. for leave to agree with Richard Patel in a plea of trespass, in four complaints, and 3d. for the same with Robert the son of Walter Deneys in a like plea, pledge Bartholomew Patel.

Peter Sparrow ['Sparwe'] and Robert Ryvel each amerced 3d. for leave to agree with Alexander de Walsham in pleas of trespass; Walter [Craske] the miller 6d. for the same with Ralph Echeman in a like plea, pledge for all the hayward.

Thomas Fuller, Alice Helewys and Peter Margery each amerced 3d. for damage in the lord's pasture at Northrow with horses, pledge for all the hayward.

Ralph Echeman amerced 3d. for leave to agree with Robert Springold in a plea of trespass, pledge the hayward.

William Wither amerced 3d. for damage below the warren with his horses, pledge the hayward; John the miller 3d. for damage in the lord's meadow with his pigs, pledge Peter Margery; Peter Margery 3d. for the same, pledge the hayward. Stephen Cooper amerced 3d., Peter Tailor 2d. and Edmund Lene 3d., for damage in the lord's pasture at Brouneswong with their beasts, pledge for all the hayward; Alexander Geldenfot in mercy for the same, condoned. Alexander de Walsham amerced 6d. for damage in the lord's pasture at Cowleswe with his cows, pledge the hayward. Richard Lorence and William Godyene each amerced 3d. for damage around the manor with horses, pledge John Herning, and Thomas Jote 3d. for the same, pledge William Kembald.

Adam Noble amerced 2d. for trespass against William Wither, to his loss of 2d.; ordered to raise.

Alice Helewys amerced 2d. for damage at Calfpightle with her calves; John Spileman 6d. for damage with his plough at the Oldtoft, ploughing on the lord's land; Richard Warde 2d. for damage in the lord's wheat at the Oldtoft with cows and bullocks, pledge for all the hayward.

Ralph Echeman amerced 3d. for making an unlawful way in the lord's wheat at Ayleldestoft, pledge the hayward.

General Enquiry by John Syre, Walter Payn, Walter Osbern, William Hawys, William of Cranmer, Simon Peyntour, John Terwald, Robert Tailor, Matthew Hereward, William Patel, Nicholas Goche and John Man.

Hilary Springold, who died after the last court, held from the lord 1a.1r. of customary land; the lord had no heriot because she had no beast; Robert Springold her brother is her nearest heir, and he comes and pays 3s.4d. entry fine, pledge the hayward.

Isabella Springold has a dog which took a hare in the lord's warren; amerced 3d., pledge the hayward.

Geoffrey Russel of Langham amerced 12d. for digging on the common land of Walsham at Deepmereway ['Depmerweye']; Peter Sparrow 3d., Walter Hereward 6d., and John the son of Robert Tailor 6d., for the same, pledge for all the hayward. Alexander de Walsham amerced 12d. for the same at Allwoodgreen, pledge Nicholas Goche.

Basilia Payn pays 2s.8d. childwite, because she gave birth outside wedlock.

Marsilia Hawys carted various chattels out of the lord's bondage without leave; <therefore in mercy, pledge William Hawys>;[19] ordered etc.

Gilbert Helpe[20] amerced 6d. because he uprooted and sold trees, worth 4d., out of the lord's bondage, without leave; ordered to take into the lord's hands all the tenements which he holds from the lord, and to report the profits.

Thomas of the Beck amerced 6d. for withholding from the lord one ploughing service, at the Ploughale at the time of sowing wheat.

Robert Man amerced 3d. for breach of the assize of bread, and 6d. for breach of the assize of ale. Walter Pye amerced 12d., Walter Rampolye 6d., John Tailor 3d., and John Bolle 6d. for breach of the assize of ale. Geoffrey of Lenne amerced 3d. for regrating bread. William Payn and Stephen Cooper, the ale-tasters, each amerced 3d. because they did not perform their duties.

Robert Lene and Geoffrey of Lenne amerced 12d. because they did not have Robert Loy make amends for trespass against the lord; ordered to appoint better pledges.

Richard the son of Letitia pays 6d. fine for respite of his suit of court until Michaelmas, pledge Richard Qualm.

Walter Osbern amerced 6d. for breach of the assize of ale.

Surrenders: William Hawys to Walter Reve and his heirs, 1½r. of land, granted to him to hold in villeinage, by services and customs, fine 12d., pledge the hayward. Walter Osbern to John Noble and his heirs, a plot of land 7p. long and 2p. wide, granted to him in the same form, fine 3d., pledge William Wyther.

Henry de Wells was attached to reply to William Cook in a plea of detention of chattels, concerning which William says that on Monday before Christmas Day 10 Edw.III [23 December 1336] in Walsham, he delivered to Henry a brass bowl, worth 4s., to celebrate mass for the soul of Hilary, William's mother; Henry did not celebrate the mass, and on Monday after the feast of the Nativity of the Blessed Mary [15 September 1337], he came to Henry and asked to have the bowl, but was unable to, and Henry withheld, and still withholds it, to William's loss of 40d.; and on this he produces suit. Henry comes and defends, saying that he took the bowl from William for money owed to him as computed, and he holds it for this reason and no other. He asks for an enquiry to be held, and the plaintiff likewise. Ordered etc.

John Man amerced 4d. for leave to agree with William Hawys in a plea of trespass, pledge the hayward.

Agnes Goche pays 6s.8d. fine for leave to marry Henry Albry, pledges Simon Peyntour, Nicholas Goche and the hayward.

William Noreys sold 1a.3r. of customary land by charter to John Foxley of Westhorpe, without leave; ordered to take into the lord's hands, and to report the profits.

The tenants of the tenement formerly of Master John de Walsham amerced 6d. for default; the tenants of the tenement formerly Outlagh 6d. for the same. Richard Bannelone and William Petipas in mercy for the same, condoned because poor. Thomas at the Lee amerced 6d. for the same. <Peter Gilbert in mercy for the same> \Afterwards he came/.

William of Cranmer pays 2s. fine for having a fold of 6 score sheep, and no more

---

19 Margin: 'condoned by Richard de Walsham'.
20 Insert over 'Gilbert Helpe': 'he is dead'. Tab: 'Gilbert Helpe' (?16th century).

because 40 are allowed to him; Nicholas Goche pays 2s. for a fold of 4 score sheep; Robert Rampolye 12d. for 40 sheep; William Hawys 3s. for 7 score sheep, 20 allowed; Peter Jay and William Clevehog 18d. each for 60 sheep, pledge for both the hayward.

Surrender: Nicholas Goche and Letitia his wife, she being examined in court, to Edmund Lene and Amice his wife and their heirs, a cotland 3p. long and 3p. wide, granted to them to hold in villeinage, by services and works etc., fine 12d., pledge Stephen Cooper.

Amice Reve pays 4s. fine for leave to marry John Elyot of Downham, pledges Thomas Fuller and Nicholas Goche.

SUM 60s. 1d., less the expenses of Peter of Euston, 13¾d.,

and fodder for a horse, 2 pecks of oats

Affeerers: Nicholas Goche and Richard Kebbil

## 92.   HIGH HALL Court, 15 January 1338 [HA504/1/4.9.ii]

Robert Sare essoins of common suit, by John Kebbil; William Elys of the same, by John Pynchon; they both pledge faith.

William Wodebite amerced 2s. because he exchanged 1a. of villein land with Robert Hovel, without leave, pledges Gilbert Helpe and John Packard.

+John Syre caused damage in the lord's wood at Lenerithsdel, with cows and calves; ordered etc. William Hawys caused damage in the lord's wheat at Netherhawe, estimated at 1 peck; ordered etc.

Nicholas Kembald amerced 2d. for default; Walter of the Marsh in mercy for the same, afterwards he came.

+Matthew the son of Richard Patel, the carter of Robert Hovel, drove a cart several times on the lord's land at Angerhale, which is the lord's several pasture; ordered etc.

Ordered to execute the orders of the last court, marked with a cross, and not acted upon.

SUM 2s. 2d.

## 93.   WALSHAM Court, 11 March 1338 [HA504/1/4.11]

Geoffrey Whitemor, defendant v Peter Cook in a plea of debt, essoins by William the serjeant; he pledges faith; Peter is present.

Thomas of the Beck was attached to reply to Alexander Geldenfot in a plea of debt, concerning which, Alexander says that on Monday after Michaelmas 10 Edw.III [30 September 1336], Thomas acknowledged himself indebted to him for 4s.8d., rent for a dovecote, in the manor of Alexander de Walsham, to be paid at Easter, at which date, he did not pay, but withheld and still withholds, to Alexander's loss of 2s., and he brings suit. Thomas comes and defends, saying that he owes no money as accused, and he offers to wage law, pledges for the law, Richard Kebbil and the hayward.

Again ordered to attach Ralph of Rudham chaplain to reply to Bartholomew Jerico in a plea of trespass.

John Terwald was attached to reply to Simon Cooper in a plea of debt, concerning which Simon says that on Monday after Christmas Day [30 December 1336], John acknowledged himself indebted to him for 14d. for various things, as computed between them, to be paid by the following Michaelmas, at which day he did not pay, but withheld and still withholds, to Simon's loss of 3d., and he

221

produces suit. John comes and defends, saying that he owes no money, as he is accused, and offers to wage law, pledges for the law, Richard Kebbil and the reeve.

Surrender: Agnes the daughter of Simon Stritt to William Elys and Hilary his wife and their heirs, 1a. of land in the Millfield, granted to them to hold in villeinage, by services and works, fine 3s., pledge the hayward.

Stephen Cooper amerced 2d. for his false claim against William the smith in a plea of debt, pledge the hayward.

Surrenders: William Cook to Olivia Cook his sister and her heirs, 3r. of land at Longelond, granted to her in the same form as above, fine 18d.; Olivia Cook to William her brother and his heirs, ½a. of land at Ayleldestoft, granted to him in the same form, fine 6d., pledge for both the hayward.

Henry de Wells chaplain amerced 6d. for leave to agree with William Cook in a plea of detention of chattels, pledge the hayward.

John Warde villein, when he died, held from the lord 5a. of land, 3r. of wood, ½r. of meadow and half a messuage, by services and works; the lord had no heriot because John had no beast. Alice his sister is his nearest heir, and she pays 12s. entry fine, pledges Robert Warde and the hayward.

Robert Springold sold to John of Stonham 1a.1r. of land without leave; ordered to seize etc. Afterwards he pays 12d. fine for repossessing the land, pledge the hayward.

Surrender: William Cook to Edmund Lene and his heirs, ½a. of land at Ayleldestoft, granted to him in the same form as above, fine 18d., pledge the hayward.

Walter Hawys amerced 6d. for breaking an agreement with William Hawys, as was found by the enquiry, the loss assessed at 3d.; ordered to raise.

<John Syre, Walter Payn, Walter Osbern, William Hawys, William of Cranmer the elder, Simon Peyntour, John Terwald, Robert Tailor, Matthew Hereward, William Patel, Nicholas Goche, William Wither, Thomas Fuller and John Man each amerced 6d., because they failed to present the waste in the lord's bondage at the [tenement] Doos, by Walter Hawys cutting down trees>. \Condoned by the lord/.

Ordered to raise from Richard Qualm, John Man and William Patel the younger 4s., to the use of Richard de Walsham, which they undertook to pay for William Clevehog, as shown in the court of 14 February 1337 [no. 86].

Ordered to execute the orders of the last court, marked with a cross, and not acted upon.

Alice the daughter of William of Cranmer the younger pays 6s.8d. fine, for leave to marry William Cook, pledge the hayward. Olivia the daughter of the same William [Cranmer], has leave to marry Robert the son of William Hawys, fine waived.[21]

> SUM 27s. 4d., <except 2 marriage fines above, not charged>;
> less the expenses of Peter of Euston, 15½d., and 1 peck of oats
> Affeerers: Richard Kebbil and Nicholas Goche

---

[21] Margin: Alice's fine reduced from 10s. to 6s.8d., and Olivia's from 10s. to nil.

**94. HIGH HALL Court of Nicholas de Walsham, 7 May 1338 [HA504/1/4.9.iii]**

Henry Trusse essoins of common suit, by William of Cranmer; Walter at the Marsh of the same, by William of Cranmer; John Pynchonn of the same, by William Elys; William Deneys of the same, by John Pynfoul; and Agnes Noreys of the same, by Ralph Wybert; all pledge faith.

Robert of Angerhale amerced 6d. for trespass against the lord, pledge John Packard.

John Packard amerced 2d. for leave to agree with Ralph Wybert in a plea of trespass, pledge Robert Helpe.

The jurors present that Gilbert Helpe the younger, villein of the lord, who died after the last court, held from the lord in villeinage, a messuage 9a. of land in Westhorpe, by services and works; Gilbert Helpe, his kinsman, is his nearest heir and is of full age, and should enter by fine, because the lord had no heriot. Because Gilbert died before this court, they say that Robert, John, Henry and Gilbert, his sons, are his heirs, who pay 3s.4d. entry fine, pledges William Wodebite, John Packard and John Goche.

Also that Gilbert Helpe the elder, villein of the lord, who died after the last court, held from the lord a messuage, 9a. of land \and wood/ of villeinage in Westhorpe, by services and works; that Robert, John, Henry and Gilbert are his heirs, and that the lord had, as a heriot, his better beast, a colt worth 2s.6d. They have entry by the heriot to both inheritances, and they swore fealty.

John the son of John Wodebite, who died after the last court, held from the lord, by services and works, 11a. of land, meadow and wood, with two built messuages and half a messuage; Agnes and Margery his sisters are his nearest heirs, and they seek admittance. The lord had no heriot because John had no beast, and each has entry to her share by one fine of 3s., pledge William Wodebite. <ordered to take into the lord's hands half of the said tenement etc.>. They swore fealty.

Nicholas Kembald amerced 3d. for default.

Ordered to attach Walter the parson of Gislingham for damage in the lord's meadow at Smallbrook with his cart.

Gilbert Helpe [the elder], when he died, was seised of 1½a.1r. of land, which was of Walter Enisson and Robert Broun, and held by fealty, services and 1½d. increased rent. Robert his son is his heir, and he is of full age; he has entry by relief of 1½d.

Ordered to distrain Joan the widow of Gilbert Helpe, and Cristina, Agnes and Amice, his daughters for fealty etc.

Agnes and Margery the sisters of John Wodebite came into open court, and demised all their tenement to William Wodebite, to hold from this day until next Michaelmas, and until Michaelmas in the following year.

John Chapman was elected to the office of collector.

SUM 7s. 4½d., except a colt, worth 2s.6d., as a heriot
Affeerers: John Chapman and John of Angerhale

**95. WALSHAM Court, 2 July 1338 [HA504/1/4.12]**

<Robert Hereward, defendant v Avice Deneys in a plea of debt, essoins by Thomas Hereward.> \It does not lie because he holds customary land./ Richard Patel, tenant, v Bartholomew Patel in a plea of land, essoins by Robert of Wortham; he pledges faith; Bartholomew is present. Walter Petipas essoins of common suit, by Richard Bannelone, he pledges faith.

The first pledges of Geoffrey Whitemor amerced 3d. because they did not have him reply to Peter Cook in a plea of debt; ordered to appoint better pledges.

Alexander Geldenfot amerced 3d. for his false claim against Thomas of the Beck in a plea of debt.

William Godyene amerced 3d. for leave to agree with William Hawys in a plea of trespass.

Ordered to attach Peter Neve to reply to Peter Jay in a plea of debt.

John Terwald amerced 6d. for leave to agree with Simon Cooper in a plea of debt.

John Tailor amerced 6d. for trespass in the peas of William Hawys with his pigs, to the loss of 1d.; ordered to raise.

Robert Hereward amerced 3d. for leave to agree with Avice Deneys in a plea of debt.

Surrender: Alice Warde to Robert Warde the elder and his heirs, 1½r. of land and ½r. of meadow, lying in two places, granted to him to hold in villeinage, by services and works, fine 2s., pledge the hayward.

Ordered to retain 3 horses and 14 geese taken upon Thomas at the Lee, and to take more etc., for him to reply to Thomas Hereward in a plea of trespass, to Alice Helewys in a like plea, and to John Man in a plea of covenant, and a plea of trespass in two complaints.

Surrender: Alice Warde to Nicholas Goche and his heirs, 1½a. of land at Cocksdrit, lying in three places, granted to him in the same form as above, fine 4s.6d., pledge the hayward.

+Ordered to retain a horse taken upon Nicholas de Walsham, and to take more etc., for him to reply to Walter Noreys in a plea of trespass. \Walter asks for, and has, leave to withdraw from his complaint./

William Payn amerced 6d. for damage in the lord's herbage at the ditch of Blunteslond with his beasts; Richard Spileman 2d. for damage in the lord's barley with his geese, pledge for both the hayward.

General Enquiry by John Syre, Walter Payn, Walter Osbern, William Hawys, William of Cranmer the elder, Simon Peyntour, John Terwald, Robert Tailor, Matthew Hereward, William Patyl, Nicholas Goche and John Man, who say on oath that Alice Long, who died after the last court, held from the lord by the rod, 1a. of land with a cottage, by services and works; Matilda and Agatha her sisters are her nearest heirs, and are of full age. Granted to them in the same form, fine 2s., pledges Thomas Fuller and the hayward.

+Joan the wife of Gilbert Helpe, who died after the last court, held from the lord a piece of land, 14ft. wide and 6p. long. Robert, Henry, John and Gilbert, her sons, are her nearest heirs, and they do not come; ordered to take the tenement into the lord's hands etc. The jurors say that the lord should have as heriot a mare, worth 5s. Ordered to raise.

Gilbert Helpe, who died after the last court, held from the lord 1a. of land, for fealty and services 2d. per year, but they say that he and Henry his son, who survives him, bought the land jointly from Robert Broun. Henry came and swore fealty, which he did not do before, because at the time of the purchase he was under age.

Joan the wife of Gilbert Helpe, when she died, held from the lord half a messuage, for fealty and services 1d. per year. Robert her son and nearest heir finds a pledge for 1d. relief, and swore fealty.

+Thomas at the Lee took two hares in the lord's warren since the last court, and he is in the habit of so doing (*ad hoc consuetus est*); ordered etc. Thomas did damage in the lord's herbage at the Westmill, with his horses, ordered etc.

Thomas Hereward, William Wither and Walter Goos each amerced 3d. for digging on the common to the nuisance of the lord and the townspeople, pledge for all the hayward.

Nicholas de Walsham took a hare in the lord's warren; ordered etc.

Alice Houthon married Stephen Cooper without leave, fine 5s., pledge the hayward.

+Thomas at the Lee withheld all the services and customs due for the tenements which he holds from the lord; ordered etc., and to attach him to satisfy the lord for default of suit of court.

Thomas of the Beck amerced 6d. because he withheld from the lord one ploughing service, called Ploughale, at the time of sowing wheat, pledge the hayward.

Nicholas de Walsham caused damage in the lord's herbage at Currescroft with his pigs; ordered etc.; Henry de Wells did the same there with his ewes, ordered etc.

Alice Helewys amerced 2d. because she depastured the herbage of a boundary between her land and the lord's, pledge the hayward.

Robert Man amerced 3d. for baking and selling bread in breach of the assize. The same Robert amerced 6d., Walter Pye 12d., John Tailor 6d., and Walter Rampolye 6d. for breaking the assize of ale. Alice Warde amerced 3d. for gannocking ale. Geoffrey Lenne amerced 3d. for regrating bread. William Payn and Stephen Cooper the ale-tasters each amerced 3d. because they did not perform their duties; and in their place John Typetot and Manser of Shucford were elected; they took the oath.

Robert Sare and William Kembald each amerced 2d. for unlawful destruction[22] upon William Wither, to the loss of 1d.; ordered to raise.

Agnes Robhood pays 2s. fine for leave to marry Walter Noreys, pledge Walter.

Ordered to seize into the lord's hands 1r. of customary land, which Juliana Deneys sold to John of Foxley without leave, and to report the profits. \Profits reduced to nil, because part of the field sown./

Adam Sket amerced 6d. and Robert Osbern 3d. for default.

John Man amerced 3d. for leave to agree with William Hawys in a plea of covenant, pledge the hayward.

Surrenders: John Osbern to Walter Syre and his heirs, ½a. of land at Langethweyt, granted to him to hold in villeinage, by services and works, fine 18d., pledge the hayward.

  Robert the son of Peter Springold, to Robert Lene the shepherd and his heirs, 3r. of land at the Launde ['Lound'], granted to him in the same form, fine 2s., pledge the hayward.

Ordered to execute the orders of the last court, marked with a cross, and not acted upon.

+William Hawys amerced 6d. because he sold to Thomas Fuller two cartloads of timber, without leave. Thomas Fuller amerced 12d. because he cut down the said timber, and took it out of the lord's bondage, without leave.

Alice Warde amerced 3d. because she sold timber to William Warde, without leave; and +William amerced 9d. because he took the said timber out of the lord's bondage, and disposed of it, without leave.

---

22 The literal rendering of *injusta distructio*; perhaps too strong for a loss of 1d.

+John Syre and his fellow-jurors in mercy because they concealed, and did not present, the waste from the sale of timber as above. \condoned/

SUM 30s. 9d., except a mare, worth 5s., as heriot; less the expenses of
Thomas de Saxham for holding the court, 2s.5d. and 3 pecks of oats
Affeerers: Nicholas Goche and Richard Kebbil

## 96. WALSHAM Court, 18 September 1338 [HA504/1/4.14]

John Lester, defendant v William Breton in a plea of debt, essoins by Roger Cooper; he pledges faith; William is present. John Crane essoins of common suit, by Manser of Shucford; he pledges faith.

Bartholomew Patel, petitioner, v Richard Patel in a plea of land, essoins by Richard son of Bartholomew Patel; he pledges faith. Richard Patel was essoined at the last court and does not come [to this court]; ordered to take into the lord's hands all the tenement which Bartholomew claims etc.

William the bailiff (*serviens*) of Alexander de Walsham, plaintiff v John Wauncey in a plea of debt, essoins by William Kembald; he pledges faith; John is present.

Walter Petipas amerced 3d. because he did not warrant his essoin.

Peter Jay and his pledges amerced 3d. because he did not proceed against Peter Neve in a plea of debt.

Geoffrey Whitemor amerced 3d. for unlawful detention of 3s. from Peter Cook, as he acknowledged in open court, the loss assessed at 1d.; ordered to raise.

Mabel Ape amerced 2d. for trespass in the lord's corn in autumn, taking away sheaves; Peter Margery 3d. for the same, pledge for both the hayward; Nicholas the son of William Patel 3d. for the same, pledge the same William; William the son of Peter Tailor 2d. for the same, pledge the same Peter; Walter Craske the miller 6d. for the same, by his servant, pledge the same Walter.

John the swineherd of the manor amerced 2d. for damage in the lord's wheat at the Oldtoft, pledge the bailiff. John Pykhorn ['Pykorn'] amerced 3d. for damage in the lord's oats at Allwood, pledge Robert Deneys; the same Robert 3d. for the same, pledge the hayward. William Deneys, Nicholas Fraunceys, John Syre, <Walter Payn> and William Payn each amerced 1d. for damage in the lord's herbage at Currescroft. John Man amerced 6d. for damage in the corn of the lord, and of the townspeople, at night, pledge the hayward. Stephen Cooper in mercy for damage in the lord's herbage at Calfpightle, with his beasts.\condoned/; Emma Shepherd amerced 2d. for the same, pledge for both, the hayward; Alexander Geldenfot in mercy for the same\condoned/; Edmund Lene 2d. for the same, pledge the hayward.

Thomas at the Lee amerced 2d. for damage in the wheat and barley of Thomas Hereward, to the value of 1 bushel of wheat and ½ bushel of barley; ordered to raise; the same Thomas amerced 2d. for damage in the wheat and peas of Alice Helewys, to the value of 1 bushel of wheat and ½ bushel of peas; ordered to raise.

The same Thomas amerced 3d. for damage done to John Man, beating him on two occasions, damages assessed at 3s.; ordered to raise.

Alice Helewys amerced 2d. for damage in the peas of Thomas at the Lee, to the value of 1 peck; ordered to raise.

The same Thomas amerced 1d. for breaking an agreement with John Man, [the loss] valued at 3d.; ordered to raise; and 1d. for his false claim against the same John, in a plea of covenant. John Man amerced 3d. for his false claim against Thomas in a like plea.

Peter Gudgeon in mercy for damage in Ladyswood cutting a staff.

John Wauncy amerced 3d. for damage in the lord's oats at Allwood, pledge John Syre.

Robert Lene the lord's shepherd amerced 1d. for damage in the peas of Thomas at the Lee, 1 peck; ordered to raise.

John Pynfoul amerced 3d. for damage in the lord's meadow, taking away his hay, pledge William Rampolye. Adam, the shepherd of William Hawys, Robert the swineherd of Nicholas de Walsham, John Wauncy and Robert Lene, the lord's shepherds, and Robert Hereward the cowherd each amerced 1d. for damage in the lord's herbage at Currescroft, pledge the hayward.

Walter Noreys, William Kembald, Walter Osbern, Robert Hereward, the cowherd of the rector[23] and others caused damage in the oats of the Prior [of Ixworth], at Kembaldsgate, the loss 2 bushels.

William Deneys amerced 2d. for digging on the lord's common at Allwood to the nuisance of the lord and the townspeople.

John Pynfoul amerced 3d. for persistently grazing in the corn of the lord and [his] neighbours by night, pledge William Rampolye. Simon the son of Robert Tailor amerced 2d. for taking 1 sheaf of the lord's oats; Peter Neve 3d. for the taking of 5 sheaves of the lord's barley by his wife; Robert Warde 3d. for damage in the lord's oats at Westmill with his beasts, pledge for all the hayward.

William Elys, Peter Jay and the Prior's cowherd did damage in the Prior's rye at Cocksbusk ['Cokesbusk'], with their beasts, 1½ bushels.

William Elys amerced 3d. for removing chattels from the bondage into a free tenement; Richard of Wortham 1d., John Typetot 3d., Robert Sare \condoned/, and Peter Margery 2d. for the same.

Memorandum that Alice the daughter of Geoffrey of Lenne, who is free and holds nothing from the lord, married a certain freeman; the lord to be consulted.

William Hawys, Walter Osbern, Walter Hawys, Robert Hereward and Alice Warde sold timber outside the lord's bondage, remitted.

William Hawys, by leave of the court, demised to John of Foxley 5½a. of land, to hold from last Michaelmas until next Michaelmas, fine 6d..

Matthew Hereward and William Rampolye were elected to the office of reeve; Matthew took the oath. William Warde and William Deneys were elected to the office of hayward. <John Stonham> William Cook and Ralph Echeman were elected to the office of woodward; William took the oath.

John Man amerced 2d. for damage to William the son of William Rampolye, to the value of 4d.; Simon Peyntour 2d. for the same, to the value of 2d.; ordered to raise from both.

Surrender: Robert the cooper to George of Brockley ['Brokele'] and his heirs, a cotland containing 10p. of land, granted to him to hold in villeinage, by services and works, fine 6d., pledge the hayward.

William Patel amerced 3d. for trespass against Walter Cooper to the value of 1d.; ordered to raise; and in mercy for his false claim against Walter, in a plea of trespass, condoned.

Ordered to execute the orders of the last court, marked with a cross, and not acted upon.

---

[23] Walsham had no rector; this probably refers to the rector of Westhorpe.

SUM 9s. 7d., except 1½ bushels of rye and 2 bushels of oats
Affeerers: Walter Payn and John Terwald

## 97. HIGH HALL Court of Nicholas de Walsham, 21 October 1338 [HA504/1/4.15.i]

Walter Osbern essoins of common suit, by William Deneys; and William Elys of the same, by William of Cranmer; they pledge faith.

John Pynchon amerced 6d. because he did not warrant his essoin

Ordered to seize into the lord's hands 4a. of land, called Dunneslond, which Gilbert Helpe held from the lord, when he died, until the heirs come, and to report the profits.

Ordered to attach Henry of Littlehawe the younger to reply to the lord by what right he took away, without leave, the crops from 1a.1r. and ¹/₃r. of land, which was Gilbert Helpe's, and was taken into the lord's hands.

+Ordered as elsewhere to attach Walter Osbern for damage in the lord's corn at Sheephousecroft with his sheep, and William Hawys for damage in the lord's wheat at Netherhawe with his sheep, to the value of 1 peck.

+Ordered as elsewhere to attach Matthew the son of Richard Patel, the carter of Robert Hovel, because he drove a cart outside the lord's land at Angerhale many times.

Thomas Dormour, the first pledge of Walter Osbern, amerced 3d. because he did not have him satisfy the lord for trespass in the lord's meadow and hay with a colt, at Southbrook; ordered to appoint a better pledge.

+Walter Payn did damage in the lord's wheat at Hamstale with his horses and beasts, to the value of 4 sheaves, worth 4d.; and Walter Osbern did likewise there with a colt; ordered etc. Simon Peyntour and William Clevehog did damage in the lord's wheat at Southbrook with their beasts, to the value of 1 sheaf, worth 1d.; ordered etc. William Wodebite amerced 1d. for damage in the lord's meadow with his pigs; Robert of Walpole ['Whalpol'] did likewise there, ordered etc.

William of Cranmer, William Hawys and Walter Osbern did likewise at Horde-shawe, ordered etc. Walter of the Marsh did likewise in the lord's wheat at Sheepcotecroft, to the value of 1 sheaf, worth 1d., ordered etc.

+Robert Lene, Robert Deneys, John Wauncy, Adam the shepherd, William Hawys and John Pykhorn the shepherd did damage in the lord's wheat at Allwoodgreen with their sheep, to the value of 3 sheaves, worth 3d., ordered etc. Nicholas Neve the lord's cowherd amerced 1d. for the same at Netherhawe with his beasts.

The jurors have a day to enquire concerning damage, to the value of ½ bushel, in the lord's barley at Netherhawe with beasts, and concerning damage in the manor, removing the ledges[24] from doors.

+William Cook, the cowherd and gooseherd of the manor, amerced 3d. for damage in the lord's peas with the beasts of the manor. William Kembald did damage in the lord's corn and in his wood with beasts; ordered etc.

William Wodebite amerced 2s. because he was summoned to work in the autumn

---

[24] MS: *legges*; Latham gives *lega* and *ledga* – 'ledge' or 'cross-bar of a door, door-jamb', but the clerk may have used the current spelling of the English word.

[*damaged*];[25] John Sare amerced 3d. for the same. William Wodebite amerced 6d., because he absents himself from the lord; and is in mercy for contempt [*damaged*], condoned; ordered to take into the lord's hands all the tenement which he holds until etc.

William Wodebite was elected to the offfice of reeve [*damaged*].[26] John Goche was elected to the office of hayward and took the oath.

+Ordered to retain in the lord's hands [*damaged*] he died, because the heir does not come, and to report the profits.

[SUM 10s. 7d., obliterated or not stated]

## 98. WALSHAM Court General, 2 December 1338 [HA504/1/4.16]

Bartholomew Jerico, plaintiff v Ralph of Rudham chaplain, in a plea of trespass, essoins by Peter Margery; he pledges faith. Ordered to attach Ralph to reply.

General Enquiry by John Syre, Walter Payn, William Payn, William Rampolye, Walter the smith, Simon Peyntour, William Wyther, John Man, Nicholas Goche, Robert Tailor, Robert Warde, John Terwald and Richard Kebbil.

The first pledges of John Wauncy amerced 3d. because they did not have him reply to William the serjeant of Alexander de Walsham, in a plea of debt; ordered to appoint better pledges.

John Lester amerced 3d. for leave to agree with William Breton in a plea of debt, pledge John Terwald.

William Hawys complains of Thomas at the Lee in a plea of debt, pledges for William William Deneys and the hayward. Avice Deneys complains of the same Thomas in a like plea, pledge for Avice, William Deneys.

Walter Cooper amerced 3d. for leave to agree with Alice Rous in a plea of debt, pledge the hayward.

Surrenders: William Hawys to John of Stonham and his heirs, 2a. of land in Goselingescroft, with a garden at the head of the same land, between the land of Robert Hereward and that of Thomas William, granted to him to hold in villeinage by services and works, fine 8s.; and to Robert Warde and his heirs, 1½r.5p. of pasture at Caldewellwillows, next to Robert's pasture, granted to him in the same form, fine 12d., pledge for both the hayward.

Richard the son of Letitia amerced 3d. for default.

Ordered to raise from Geoffrey Whitemor 3s. and damages of 1d., to the use of Peter Cook, as he acokwledged in the last court.

Surrenders: Walter Osbern, William of Mileham ['Mylham'] and Isabella his wife, she being examined in court, to John Barleyhand of Euston and his heirs, a messuage with a croft adjoining, called Bullockstead ['Bullokestede'], containing 1a.9p. of land, as the bounds stand, granted to him in the same form as above, fine 6s.8d., pledge Walter Rampolye.

William Hawys to Walter Hawys and his heirs, ½a.17p. of land in a messuage called the Doos, next to the messuage formerly of Emma Stronde, and the bakehouse in the messuage Hawys, with ingress and egress to and from the same, granted to him in the same form, fine 2s., pledge the hayward.

Walter Hawys to William Hawys and his heirs, all his share in the messuage of

---

[25] The right-hand side covering the last ten lines is badly stained and fragmented. Notwithstanding the excellent repair of the membrane, much is missing or indecipherable.

[26] Margin: 'fine 6s.8d.', this was probably for being excused from holding the office: William was old.

Robert Hawys his father, except the bakehouse shown above, granted to him in the same form, fine 2s., pledge the hayward. Upon this William acknowledges himself bound in 2 bushels of wheat and 2 bushels of barley to his mother, Marsilia Hawys, to be delivered to her annually at Michaelmas, for all her lifetime, for the dower which belongs to her as of right.

Geoffrey of Lenne, who died after the last court, held from the lord a cotland containing 1r.10p.; the lord had no heriot because he had no beast. Alice his daughter, wife of Robert of Thelnetham, is his nearest heir, and she pays 5s. fine for entry, and for her marriage, pledges William Wither and the hayward. Alice swore fealty.

Thomas at the Lee took a hare in the lord's warren, ordered etc.

Thomas William amerced 12d. because he withheld from the lord one hen and one autumn boonwork for the tenement Goselyngs.

Walter Pye amerced 12d. because he brewed and sold ale in breach of the assize; Walter Rampolye 6d. and Matilda Bolle 3d. for the same. Manser of Shucford and John Typetot the ale-tasters each amerced 3d. because they did not perform their duties. Alice Warde amerced 3d. for gannocking ale.

William of Cranmer pays 2s. fine for having a fold of 6 score sheep, and no more because he is allowed 40; Nicholas Goche 2s. for a fold of 4 score; Robert Rampolye 12d. for a fold of 40, William Hawys 2s.6d. for a fold of 6 score, 20 allowed; Peter Jay 9d. for a fold of 30; and William Clevehog 6d. for a fold of 20.

+Ordered as elsewhere to attach Alexander de Walsham for homage, relief and <fealty> \because he has sworn fealty/, and several defaults.

+Ordered to attach William Wyswyf, Henry Crane, John Rede and Walter Doo, villeins, because they absent themselves from the lord.

+Ordered as elsewhere to attach Ralph of Rudham chaplain, to reply to William Hawys in a plea of trespass.

+Ordered to retain in the lord's hands 1a.3r. of customary land, which William Noreys sold to John of Foxley without leave, and to report the profits.[27]

+Ordered to retain in the lord's hands a piece of land, 14ft. wide and 6p. long, which Joan the wife of Gilbert Helpe held when she died, and to report the profits. As no heriot is forthcoming, ordered to raise the mare, worth 6s, as shown in the court of 2 July 1338 [no.95].

Ordered to distrain Thomas at the Lee for trespass in the lord's warren, and for services and works withheld, and for many defaults, as shown in the aforesaid court.

Ordered to retain in the lord's hands 1r. of land, which Juliana Deneys sold to John of Foxley without leave; the profits are reduced, because part of the land is sown.

+Ordered to raise from Thomas at the Lee 1 bushel of wheat and ½ bushel of barley to the use of Thomas Hereward, 1 bushel of wheat and ½ bushel of peas to the use of Alice Helewys, and 3s.3d. to the use of John Man, which they were to have recovered from him at the last court.

+Ordered to raise from Alice Helewys 1 peck of peas, and from Robert Lene 1 peck of peas, to the use of Thomas at the Lee.

SUM 37s. 11d., less the expenses of Thomas de Saxham, 2s.6¼d.

---

[27] Margin: 'profits 10d.'.

## 99. WALSHAM Court, 27 January 1339 [HA504/1/4.17]

Robert Tailor, defendant v William the bailiff of Alexander de Walsham, in a plea of trespass, essoins by Robert of Badwell; he pledges faith; William is present. John Margery essoins of common suit, by Peter Margery; he pledges faith. Alice Helewys, defendant v William the bailiff of Alexander, in a plea of trespass, essoins by Roger of Ditton; she pledges faith; William is present. Adam of Cringleford ['Crynkilforde'], defendant v Cristiana Smith in a plea of trespass, essoins by John Hereward; he pledges faith; Cristiana is present.

The first pledges of William of Mileham amerced 6d. because they did not have him reply to John Tailor in a plea of debt; ordered to appoint better pledges.

Walter Goos ['le Gos'] amerced 3d. for leave to agree with Emma Shepherd in a plea of debt, pledges Robert Lene and Walter Payn.

A day was given, at the request of the parties, to Walter Hawys, claimant, and Walter Hereward, tenant, in a plea of land, until the next court, to come without essoin. And the agreement between the parties is that they will stand, and be bound, by the finding of 10 men of the homage, duly elected and sworn, under penalty of ½ mark, payable to the lord.

A day is given, at the request of the parties, to Walter Hawys claimant and William Hawys tenant in a plea of land, in the same form as above.

Ordered to attach Walter Goos to reply to Peter Neve in a plea of debt.

William Rampolye the younger amerced 2d. for his false claim against John Barleyhand in a plea of trespass, in two complaints, pledges Robert Rampolye and the reeve.

Elias Typetot, when he died, held from the lord a messuage and 11a. of customary land, by services and works; the lord had as a heriot a cow, worth 6s., due to calve at Christmas. Robert and William, his sons, are his nearest heirs, and of full age; they have entry by the heriot, following the custom of the manor.

Robert the cooper, when he died, held from the lord a cottage and 5a. of customary land, for his lifetime, and after his death this tenement is the right of Alice his daughter by purchase before his death, when she paid entry fine. After Robert's death the lord had as a heriot a cow, worth 5s., due to calve before the feast of the Purification [2 February].

Matilda Longe, when she died, held from the lord, by the rod, 1r. of land and half a cotland; the lord had no heriot because she had no beast. Agnes her daughter, who is married to William the smith, is her nearest heir, and she pays 9d. entry fine, pledges Nicholas Goche and Manser of Shucford.

Gilbert the smith of Badwell caused damage in Ladyswood, cutting down and taking away, etc.; ordered etc.

Richard of Wortham in mercy because he sold ½r. of customary land to Walter the smith, without leave \condoned, because poor/, ordered to seize.

Richard Kebbil amerced 2d. for unlawful detention of 9¾d. from Roger Goselyng of Ditton; ordered to raise.

The first pledges of Robert Shepherd chaplain amerced 4d. because they did not have him reply to Emma Shepherd in a plea of debt; ordered to appoint better pledges.

Ordered to execute the orders of the last court, marked with a cross, and not acted upon.

Olivia the daughter of John Man pays 10s. fine for leave to marry Thomas the son of Henry Cooper, pledges Simon Peyntour and William Clevehog.

Ordered to attach Adam Craske for trespass in the lord's oats and herbage at Currescroft, and in the lord's oats at Blunteslond, with sheep.

SUM 12s. 2d., except 2 cows, worth 11s., as heriots

Affeerers: William Rampolye and William Wither

## 100. WALSHAM Court, 12 March 1339 [HA504/1/4.18]

John Man, defendant, v Henry de Wells, chaplain, in a plea of debt, essoins by John Typetot; he pledges faith; Henry is present.

Ordered to attach Ralph of Rudham, chaplain, to reply to Bartholomew Jerico in a plea of trespass.

John Wauncy amerced 3d. for leave to agree with William the serjeant of Alexander de Walsham, in a plea of debt, pledge the hayward.

Ordered to retain three pigs taken upon Thomas at the Lee, and to take more etc., for him to reply to William Hawys and Avice Deneys in pleas of debt, and also for trespass in the lord's warren taking hares. Ordered to attach him for services and works withheld, and for many defaults.

Robert Springold amerced 6d. for leave to agree with Henry de Wells chaplain, in pleas of debt and agreement, pledge John of Stonham.

Richard Kebbil amerced 3d. for leave to agree with Walter Osbern in a plea of taking cattle, pledge the hayward.

William Payn and John Man in mercy for default; afterwards they came.

Agnes the daughter of Thomas Fuller the elder, while single, surrendered to her father all her right in a messuage with a croft adjoining, which should have been hers after the death of her mother Cristina. Granted to him and his heirs to hold in villeinage, by services and works, fine 10s. The same Agnes paid 20s. fine for leave to marry Robert Cook, pledge for both fines the hayward.

Walter [Craske] the miller amerced 3d. for leave to agree with William Hawys in a plea of trespass, pledge the hayward.

Sir William de Langham knight took a hare in the lord's warren; ordered etc.

Alice Galyon gave birth outside wedlock; she pays 2s.8d. childwyte.

Bartholomew Patel, \villein/, when he died, held from the lord 1½a. of customary land and half a messuage, by services and works etc.; the lord had a stot, worth 6s.8d., as a heriot. Richard, William and Ralph, his sons, are his nearest heirs, and they have entry by the heriot, following the custom of the manor. Bartholomew also held, from other lords, 26a. of free land, 1r. of meadow and 1r. of wood, by fealty and services etc.[28]

Alice Whiteman and Amice Terwald each amerced 3d. for breaking the lord's hedges round the Calfpightle; Hilary Typetot 2d. for the same; Agnes the daughter of John Margery, servant of John Craske, 3d. for the same, pledge John Craske.

William Hawys amerced 3d. because he had a day to repair a house on the tenement Doos before last Michaelmas, and he did not do so; ordered to attach him for the same. \He has a day until next Michaelmas to repair./ He is amerced 3d. because he withheld from the lord ½d. and half of one harvest service with one man in

---

[28] In the 1327 Subsidy Return (Suffolk Green Books no.IX, vol.II), Bartholomew is shown as paying 3s. tax, in Finningham. It is remarkable that a villein should hold so much freehold land outside the manor of his lord: the description of his status is possibly an error.

autumn, for the tenement Outlawe. He also sold to Thomas de Saxham 16 trees out of the lord's bondage, without leave; postponed until [etc.].

Robert Springold villein in mercy because he sold 1a.1r. of customary land to John of Stonham, without leave; ordered to seize, and report the profits. Memorandum that the land is sown with wheat. Afterwards Robert came and paid 6d. fine for repossessing the land, pledge John of Stonham.

Ordered to attach Thomas at the Lee for default.

Ordered to raise from Richard Kebbil 10½d. to the use of Roger Goselyng, as he acknowledged etc.

Surrenders: William the son of Peter Warde surrenders ½a. of land called Ayleldes-lond to Edmund Lene and his heirs, to hold in villeinage, by services and works, in exchange for another ½a. in the same field, which Edmund surrenders to Peter and his heirs, to hold in the same form, fine 12d., pledge Stephen Cooper.

Elias Typetot to William Typetot his son and his heirs, a piece of his garden, containing 30p., next to the garden of Walter Qualm, granted to him in the same form, fine 12d., pledge Elias Typetot.

A day is given to William Cook and Robert his brother, to repair a house in the lord's bondage called Galyones, by next Michaelmas, pledge William of Cranmer.

Surrender: Robert Springold to John of Stonham and his heirs, 1a.1r. of land at Brightwaldistoft, granted to him to hold in the same form as above, fine 4s., pledge the reeve.

Ordered to execute the orders of the last court, marked with a cross, and not acted upon.

> SUM 41s. 10d., except a heriot, a stot worth 6s.8d.; less the expenses of Peter of Euston 2s.0½d. and fodder for a horse, ½ bushel of oats

## 101.　HIGH HALL Court, 12 April 1339 [HA504/1/4.15.ii]

&lt;John Pynchon essoins of common suit, by William Elys.&gt; \It does not lie because after default./ Walter of the Marsh essoins of common suit, by Henry Trusse; he pledges faith.

John Pynchon amerced 3d. for default.

Henry of Littlehawe amerced 3d. for trespass against the lord, taking away the crops of 1a.1¹/₃r. of land, without leave, pledge John Goche, the hayward.

John Goche in mercy because he did not execute an order of the court \condoned/. Ordered as elsewhere to attach William Hawys for trespass in the lord's wheat at Netherhawe with sheep, to the value of 1 peck.

Walter Osbern amerced 1d. for damage in the lord's wheat at Hamstale with a colt, pledge the hayward.

William Isabel demised to Walter Silvester 1a. of customary land without leave; ordered to take into the lord's hands, and to report the profits.

Alice the wife of Richard the shepherd, when she died, held from the lord 1r. of free land, for services ½d. per year; Adam her son, aged 20, is her nearest heir, and he does not come. Ordered to take into the lord's hands, and to report the profits.

John Syre did damage in the gardens of Gothelards and Kembalds with his pigs and sheep; and also in the lord's wheat and peas at Doucedeux; ordered. William Cook did the same there with pigs and sheep; ordered etc.

John Pynfoul in mercy for default; afterwards he came.

Ordered to take into the lord's hands ½a. of customary land, which Agnes Noreys held before she was married to Thomas [*damaged*]. Agnes amerced 3d. because she married without leave; she swore fealty, pledge the hayward.

Ordered to distrain Thomas Thurbern of Cotton and Edmund Coppelowe for homage, relief and fealty, and several defaults.

Robert of Angerhale amerced 3d. for contempt to the lord, pledges William Wodebite and John Packard.

Walter Cristmesse and Agnes his wife came and received from the lord 1a.1¹/₃r. of land called Dunneslond, taken into the lord's hands [after the death of Gilbert Helpe], to hold to them and their heirs, for services ½d. per year, and suit of court at Michaelmas, fine 6d.. Henry of Littlehawe and Cristina his wife came and received a similar share of the tenement, to hold to them and their heirs, in the same form,29 fine 6d., pledge for both parties the hayward.

Ordered to execute the orders of the last court, marked with a cross, and not acted upon.

SUM 2s. 7d.

## 102. WALSHAM Court General, 19 July 1339 [HA504/1/4.19]

William Hawys, tenant v Walter Hawys in a plea of land, essoins by Richard Patel; he pledges faith; Walter is present. William of Mileham, defendant v John Tailor in a plea of debt, essoins by Robert Hereward; he pledges faith; John is present. William Kembald the younger, defendant v William Rampolye in a plea of trespass, essoins by John Barleyhand; he pledges faith; William is present. John Margery essoins of common suit, by Peter Margery; he pledges faith.

William [Warde] the hayward in mercy because he did not execute an order of the court \condoned/. Ordered to raise from Richard Kebbil 10½d. to the use of Roger Goselyng.

William Hawys in mercy for waste in the lord's bondage, cutting down 16 trees, and selling them to Thomas de Saxham, without leave.30

John Man amerced 3d. for leave to agree with Henry de Wells chaplain, in a plea of debt, pledge the hayward.

Henry Crane villein amerced 2s. because he absents himself from the lord, pledges William of Cranmer and Robert Kembald.

Alice at the Bridge ['atte Brigge'] amerced 3d. for leave to agree with Walter Deneys in a plea of trespass, pledge William Hawys.

Ordered to retain one woollen cloth taken upon John Tailor, and to take more etc., for him to reply to Adam of Cringleford in a plea of debt.

Thomas of the Beck in mercy for leave to agree with Nicholas Goche in a plea of trespass, condoned.

Peter Neve and his pledges amerced 6d. because he did not proceed against Thomas of the Beck in a plea of trespass, pledge the hayward.

John Noreys and his pledges amerced 12d. because he did not proceed against Nicholas Goche in a plea of trespass.

John of Stonham amerced 3d. for leave to agree with William Hawys in a plea of debt.

---

29 Amice, the third daughter of Gilbert Helpe, claims her share of the inheritance in the next High Hall court (no.103). It is strange that the daughters were heirs to this tenement, when Gilbert and his wife had male heirs, who were admitted to their other lands.

30 Tab: 'William Hawys' (?16th century).

John Pynfoul amerced 3d. for trespass against Walter the smith, the loss assessed at 6d.; ordered to raise.

John Pynfoul and his pledges amerced 3d. because he did not proceed against Walter the smith in a plea of land.

William Rampolye in mercy for chattering in court, condoned.

Robert Springold amerced 3d. for default; ordered to attach him to reply to Henry de Wells chaplain, in a plea of debt.

John Pynfoul amerced 3d. for his false claim against Walter the smith, pledge the hayward.

Catherine the daughter of William Typetot pays 6s.8d. for leave to marry Walter Qualm, pledges Richard Qualm and the hayward.

Surrenders: Walter Osbern and William of Mileham and Isabella his wife, she being examined in court, to Walter Rampolye and his heirs, 3r. of land in Sawyerscroft next to Walter Rampolye's land on the south side; granted to him to hold in villeinage, by services and works etc., fine 2s.6d., pledge the hayward. They also surrendered into the lord's hands ½a. of land in the same croft, less 5p., with half a pightle adjoining; the lord granted the tenement to Walter Osbern for his lifetime, and after Walter's death, it shall revert to Walter Rampolye to hold by services and works etc., fine 12d., pledge the hayward.

John Crane, when he died, held from the lord 3a. of customary land and half a messuage; the lord had as a heriot a cow after calving, viz. by the feast of St Mark [25 April], worth 6s.8d.. Robert Crane John's brother is his nearest heir, and he does not come; ordered to take into the lord's hands, and to report the profits.

Catherine the wife of William Cook, when she died, held from the lord 5a. of land and half a messuage; the lord had as a heriot a cow after calving, viz. by the feast of SS. Peter and Paul [29 June]. Olivia her daughter is her nearest heir, but her father will hold the land for his lifetime, following the custom of the manor etc.

Robert Hereward amerced 6d. because he dug on the common, causing nuisance to the lord and the townspeople, pledge the hayward.

Walter Typetot died 16 years ago, holding from the lord 3r. of customary land, \of which 1½r. were in a messuage/; after his death, the lord should have had a horse, worth 10s., as a heriot, but he did not. John, Robert and Richard, Walter's sons, are his nearest heirs, and John has occupied the land for all this time, and refuses to satisfy for the heriot etc. Ordered to take into the lord's hands, and to distrain John for the heriot.[31]

John Pach amerced 6d. for taking away two boards from the manor, pledge the reeve.

Hilary Typetot amerced 2d. for trespass against the lord, taking away a tripod from the mill house; she lives in the house of William Hawys, her pledge.

Peter Neve amerced 3d. for overstocking the common with his cows and sheep, pledges John Typetot and Richard Kebbil.

+William Hawys in mercy because he sold 17 trees to Thomas de Saxham without leave, condoned.[32] Walter Syre amerced 3d. for selling 16 ash trees, worth 4d., pledge the hayward; +William Syre 6d. for selling 40 ash trees, worth 8d., pledge William of Cranmer; John Pynfoul 6d. for selling one white poplar, worth 16d.

---

[31] Margin: 'heriot' (later hand).
[32] Two tabs: 'William Hawys', one torn. Margin: 'Waste in trees' (later hand).

and +William of Cranmer the elder 3d. for selling ash trees, worth 20d., all to the same Thomas, pledge for both the hayward.

Thomas Patel chaplain amerced 3s.4d. because he sold 2a. of land to John Cumpyn by charter, without leave; ordered to take into the lord's hands, and to report the profits.

Thomas Fuller amerced 12d. because he did not rebuild the tenement formerly of Beatrice at the Brook; a day is given to him to rebuild by next Easter, pledges Walter Payn and John Terwald.

+John Terwald amerced 6d. because he sold trees from his tenement, worth 2s.

Walter Pye amerced 12d., and Walter Rampolye 6d., because they brewed and sold ale in breach of the assize. Robert Lenne, regrator, amerced 3d. and Gilbert Priour 2d. for selling bread in breach of the assize. Bartholomew Jerico 6d. for brewing ale in breach of the assize; and Alice Warde 2d. for gannocking ale. Manser of Shucford and John Typetot the ale-tasters each amerced 3d. because they did not perform their duties.

The jurors say that Richard of Caldwell, bastard son of Bartholomew Patel, acquired 2½a. of customary land and half a messuage of the lord's villeinage, by the rod; because Richard is of free status, ordered to take into the lord's hands until etc.

Alice the daughter of Matthew Hereward pays 20s. fine for leave to marry Walter Fuller, pledge the reeve.

Alice Warde surrendered into the lord's hands a messuage and 4a. of land and 3r. of wood, and he granted the same to Alice and Adam Child, to hold to themselves and the heirs born of them, by services and works etc.; and if Adam and Alice die without such heirs, the tenement shall revert to Adam and his heirs, to hold in villeinage, by services and works etc., fine 10s., pledges William Warde the younger and the hayward.

Alice Warde pays 2s. fine for leave to marry Adam Child, pledge the hayward.

Surrender: John the son of Walter Osbern the elder to Bartholomew Jerico, 1a. of land at Coppedebuske, granted to him to hold in the same form as above, fine 2s.6d., pledge Walter Osbern.

William Rampolye and William Payn were elected to the office of reeve. William Warde the younger and Nicholas Fraunceys were elected to the office of hayward.

A day is given to Nicholas Goche and his fellow-jurors until the next court, to certify concerning the names of those owing Shytenesyeld.[33]

Adam Sket in mercy for default; afterwards he came.

Surrenders: Robert Hereward the cooper, into the lord's hands, a cottage and 5½a. of customary land; the lord granted the tenement to Robert to hold for his lifetime, by services and works; and after his death it shall revert to Alice his daughter, to hold in villeinage in the same form, fine 20s., pledge Matthew Hereward the reeve.

    Matthew Hereward to Thomas Hereward and his heirs, 1r. of meadow in the Micklemeadow, next to that of Thomas Fuller, granted to him in the same form, fine 18d, pledge the reeve.

    Robert Hereward the cooper to Thomas Fuller and his heirs, 1½r.14p. of land at the Berghmere, granted to him in the same form, fine 18d, pledge the reeve.

---

[33] This word has not been found in any work of reference. See Glossary.

Ordered to execute the orders of the last court, marked with a cross, and not acted upon.

SUM £4 5s. 9d.

Affeerers: Matthew Hereward and William Deneys

## 103. HIGH HALL Court General of Nicholas de Walsham, 12 December 1339 [HA504/1/4.20]

Robert Sare essoins of common suit, by William Kembald; and Henry Trusse of the same, by Walter Cristmesse; they pledge faith.

Walter of the Marsh amerced 3d. because he did not warrant his essoin.

John Goche the hayward amerced 1d. because he did not execute an order of the court. Ordered to attach William Hawys for trespass in the lord's wheat at Netherhawe with his sheep, to the value of 1 peck.

Ordered as elsewhere to seize 1a. of customary land, which William Isabel demised to Walter Silvester for a term of years, without licence, and to report the profits.[34]

Ordered to retain in the lord's hands 1r. of free land, which Richard the shepherd held from the lord, when he died, [taken] because the heir did not come to satisfy the lord for relief; and to report the profits.

Ordered as elsewhere to distrain William Cook for damage in the lord's wheat and peas at Doucedeux with his pigs and sheep, and for damage in the lord's gardens at Gothelardsyerd and Kembaldsyerd.

Ordered as elsewhere to attach Thomas Thurbern of Cotton, Richard of Depham and Edmund of Ipswich for homage, relief, fealty and several defaults.

Ordered to retain in the lord's hands ½r. of customary land, which Andrew Veyse held when he died, [taken] because the heir did not come to satisfy the lord for relief; and to report the profits.[35]

Ordered as elsewhere to attach William Kembald for damage with a sow in the lord's corn, wood and meadow.

Ordered to retain in the lord's hands 1a. 1¹/₃r. of free land of the tenement called Dunneslond, which Gilbert Helpe held, when he died, until the heir comes. And upon this came Amice, Gilbert's daughter, and took the land from the lord, to hold in villeinage, for services ½d. increased rent, fine for entry 12d., pledges Walter Cristmesse and the hayward.

Ordered as elsewhere to attach Matthew the son of Richard Patel, carter of Robert Hovel, because he drove a cart outside the lord's land at Angerhalefield several times; also to attach Walter Payn for damage in the lord's wheat at Hamstale with his horses and beasts, to the value of 4 sheaves, worth 4d.; also Robert Lene, Robert Deneys, John Wauncy, Adam Shepherd, William Hawys and John Pykhorn of Gislingham, for damage in the lord's wheat at Allwoodgreen with their sheep, to the value of 3 sheaves, worth 3d.

Ordered as elsewhere to attach John Syre for damage in the lord's gardens at Gothelards and Kembaldsyerd with his pigs and sheep, and in the lord's wheat and peas at Doucedeux with his beasts.[36]

John Packard in mercy for trespass against the lord, defaulting on one day's work with the lord's plough, condoned.

---

[34] Margin: 'Profits 12d.'.

[35] Margin: 'Profits ½d.'.

[36] Margin: 'it was attested by the lady that (?fecit grat' domino)'.

Alice Goche gave birth outside wedlock, childwite 2s.8d.

Ordered to attach John Pynfoul for damage in the lord's wood at Lenerithsdel, cutting branches, to the value of ½d.

Hubert the shepherd of the manor amerced 6d. for damage in the lord's corn at various places, and in the lord's oats at Allwoodgreen, with his sheep.

Ordered to attach William Deneys for damage in the lord's peas at Hamstale with his beasts; also Harvey Bret the keeper of the cows at Esthous.[37] Robert Hereward and Nicholas Fraunceys for damage in the lord's wheat newly sown at Gothelardslond with their beasts.

John Pynchon amerced 6d. for default; John Pynfoul, Robert of Angerhale and William Deneys 3d. each for the same.

Robert Helpe amerced 6d. because he took himself and his goods out of the lord's bondage, pledge William Wodebite.

Olivia Isabel amerced 12d. for trespass against the lord, because she did not make a linen cloth for the lady, as she was ordered; and ordered to be attached because she defamed the lady, [saying] that she did not pay for services performed [by Olivia].

William Wodebite amerced 6d. because he did not come to autumn work with five men, as he had been summoned; John Packard 2d. for the same.

A day is given to William Wodebite to rebuild a house in the tenement Aprilles until next Michaelmas.

Robert Helpe was elected to the office of reeve; afterwards he came and paid 3s.4d. fine, pledge William Wodebite. William Wodebite and John Helpe were elected to the office of hayward; John took the oath, and William paid 12d. fine, for withdrawing from the office, pledge the hayward.

A day is given to the whole homage to make a rental before the next court, under penalty of 20s.

SUM 12s. 3d., except 15½d. profits from land

## 104.  WALSHAM Court General, 12 November 1339 [HA504/1/4.21]

Walter Goos, defendant v Emma Shepherd in a plea of debt, essoins by Thomas Clerk; he pledges faith; Emma is present. Walter Hereward, tenant v Walter Hawys in a plea of land, essoins by John Hawys; he pledges faith; Walter is present. Robert Shepherd chaplain, defendant v Emma Shepherd in a plea of debt, essoins by John Typetot; he pledges faith. John Pach essoins of common suit, by Peter Neve; he pledges faith.

Walter Hawys claims against William Hawys ½a. of land, with a meadow, following the death of Agnes the daughter of Peter Hawys;[38] William asks for sight [of the rolls]; ordered etc.

A day is given, at the request of the parties, to John Tailor, plaintiff, and William of Mileham, defendant, in a plea of debt, to come to the next court without essoin.

William Rampolye and his pledges amerced 1d. because he did not proceed against William Kembald in a plea of trespass. Afterwards it was found that William Kembald committed trespass against him, to the loss of ½d.; ordered to raise.

Adam of Cringleford and his pledges amerced 3d. because he did not proceed against John Tailor in a plea of debt.

---

37  In the tenure of the Prior of Ixworth.
38  Their sister.

John Margery in mercy because he did not warrant his essoin. Afterwards he came.

Robert Springold amerced 3d. for leave to agree with Henry de Wells chaplain in a plea of debt, pledge Robert Lene.

Ordered to retain in the lord's hands 3a. of customary land and half a messuage, [taken] after the death of John Crane, because Robert Crane his brother and nearest heir did not come; and to report the profits.

+The profits from 2a. of land, remaining in the lord's hands because Thomas Patel chaplain sold them by charter to John Cumpyn without leave, are 5s., pledge Richard Patel. Ordered to retain, and to report the profits.

+A day is given to Thomas Fuller until next Easter, to rebuild a tenement formerly of Beatrice at the Brook, pledges Walter Payn and John Terwald.

[A fine of] 5s. [is paid] in lieu of a heriot from the death of Walter Typetot, pledges William Deneys and the hayward.

+The profits from 2½a. of land, remaining in the lord's hands after the death of Bartholomew Patel, because Richard Caldewell his bastard son purchased the land with Bartholomew, are waived by the lord. Ordered to retain, and report the profits.

Alexander de Walsham in mercy for default. Afterwards he came.

+Ordered as elsewhere to attach William Wyswyf, John Rede and Walter Doo, villeins, because they absent themselves from the lord.

+Ordered as elsewhere to attach Ralph of Rudham chaplain, to reply to William Hawys in a plea of trespass, and to Bartholomew Jerico in a similar plea.

+Ordered to retain in the lord's hands 1a. 3r. of customary land, which William Noreys sold to John of Foxley without leave, and to report the profits.

+There were no profits from a piece of land, 14ft. wide and 6p. long, which Joan the widow of Gilbert Helpe held, when she died, [taken] because the heir did not come. Ordered to retain, and report the profits.

+Ordered to raise from Thomas at the Lee 1 bushel of wheat and ½ bushel of barley, to the use of Thomas Hereward, 1 bushel of wheat and ½ bushel of peas, to the use of Alice Hereward, and 3s.3d. to the use of John Man. Ordered to raise from Alice Helewys and from Robert Lene 1 peck of peas each, to the use of Thomas at the Lee.

+Ordered to retain in the hands of John Typetot three pigs, taken upon Thomas at the Lee, and to take more etc., for him to reply to William Hawys and Avice Deneys in pleas of debt; and also for trespass in the lord's warren taking hares, and for services and works withheld.

General Enquiry by Nicholas Goche, Robert Tailor, Walter Osbern, Richard Kebbil, Peter Jay, Walter Hereward, Simon Peyntour, Robert Lene, Stephen Cooper, Thomas Fuller, Matthew Hereward, John Man, John Terwald, Elias Typetot and Simon Rampolye.

Richard the son of Letitia [Stronde] amerced 3d. for default.

Matthew Esiger amerced 6d. for damage in the lord's wheat at Nortonfield ['Nautonefeld'] with bullocks and cows, pledge Thomas Fuller.

The first pledges of Geoffrey of Burgate in mercy because they did not have him satisfy the lord for trespass in his wood at Northawe with his cows. Afterwards he came and was amerced 12d., pledge Thomas Fuller.

+Surrenders: Robert Springold the son of Peter Springold to Robert Lene and his heirs, 7a. of land, of which 6½a. abut on Ladyswood, and ½a. called Stonylond abuts on the Brodedole, granted to him to hold in villeinage, by services and works, fine 21s., pledges the reeve and the hayward; also, to John the son of Peter Tailor and his heirs, 1r.10p. of meadow, in the Micklemeadow, in three places, next to the Brodedole on both sides, granted to him to hold in the same form, fine 2s., pledge the hayward.

Walter Hawys amerced 3d. for his false claim against William Hawys, in a plea of trespass, pledge John Terwald. William Hawys amerced 3d. for trespass against Walter.

Surrender: Walter Rampolye to William Rampolye and his heirs, 1r. of land, granted to him in the same form as above, fine 10d., pledge the reeve.

Alice the servant of William Elys amerced 12d. for taking away the lord's straw, pledge the hayward; Robert Man 2d. for the same by Cristiana his wife.

Adam Noble amerced 3d. because he had 3 sheep lying outside the lord's fold for 6 weeks; William Pach 3d. for the same with 4 sheep; Olivia Cook and Catherine her sister 4d. for the same, pledge Robert Warde.

Peter Tailor amerced 3d. for damage in the lord's wheat in Stantonfield with his beasts, pledge the hayward; Simon Cooper 3d. for damage in the lord's oats, to the value of 1 bushel, pledge the reeve; John the servant of Walter [Craske] the miller 6d. for trespass, taking away 1 sheaf of the lord's barley, pledge the hayward.

Walter Pye amerced 12d., and Walter Rampolye 6d. for breaking the assize of ale; Robert Lenne 2d. for regrating bread; Alice Warde 2d. for gannocking ale. Manser of Shucford and John Typetot the ale-tasters each amerced 2d. because they did not perform their duties; and William the smith was elected in John's place, and he took the oath.

Robert Sare amerced 3d. because he stored corn grown in the bondage in a free tenement; William Elys 6d., and John Typetot 3d. for the same.

Richard Kebbil amerced 2d. for unlawful detention of 12d. from Simon Cooper, to the loss of 1d.; ordered to raise.

Surrender: John Terwald to Robert of Thelnetham and his heirs, 6½p. of land, granted to him in the same form as above, fine 3d., pledges the reeve and John Terwald.

Simon Cooper takes the cows of the manor at farm, paying to the lord rent as appropriate, pledges John Man, Simon Rampolye, John of Stonham, Peter Tailor, Robert Tailor, William Rampolye, Edmund Lene, Stephen Cooper and Robert Lenne.

Surrender: John Goche to Robert Lene and his heirs, ½a. of land in the Launde, granted to him to hold in the same form as above, fine 18d., pledge the reeve.

Isabella Springold pays 20s. fine for leave to marry John Tailor, pledges the reeve and the hayward.

Walter Hawys amerced 3d. for unlawful detention of 13½d. and 3½ bushels of wheat and barley from William Hawys, as he acknowledged in open court, and as was found by the enquiry, to the loss of 1d.; ordered to raise, pledge John Terwald.

It was ordered elsewhere to retain in the lord's hands 3a. of customary land and half a messuage, following the death of John Crane, because Robert his brother did not come, and it was uncertain if he was dead or not. Seisin of the tenement is now delivered to Henry Crane, John's uncle, and to Robert, the son of Peter Crane and John's nephew, to hold in villeinage, by services and works, fine 5s., pledges Robert Kembald and Manser of Shucford.

William of Cranmer pays 2s. for having a fold of 6 score sheep, and no more because he is allowed 40; Robert Rampolye and Nicholas Goche 12d. each for folds of 40 sheep.

+William Hawys in mercy because he did not rebuild a house on the tenement Doo, as he undertook, condoned; ordered to distrain him. A day is given to rebuild by next Michaelmas.

+William and Robert Cook in mercy because they did not rebuild a house on the tenement Galyones, as they undertook, condoned; ordered to distrain them. A day is given to rebuild by next Michaelmas.

Surrender: John Osbern to William Syre and his heirs, 1a. of land at Coppedebusk, granted to him to hold in the same form as above, fine 3s., pledge the hayward.

SUM 26s. 9d.

Affeerers: William Rampolye and Nicholas Fraunceys

## 105. WALSHAM Court, 19 June 1340 [HA504/1/4.22]

Adam Craske, defendant v William the serjeant of Alexander de Walsham, in a plea of trespass, essoins by Walter Craske; he pledges faith; William is present. The same Adam, defendant v William Wyther in a like plea, by John Craske; he pledges faith; William is present; and defendant v William Hawys in a like plea, by John Margery, he pledges faith; William is present.

Walter Hawys amerced 3d. for leave to agree with Walter Hereward in a plea of land, pledge the hayward.

The same Walter amerced 3d. for leave to agree with William Hawys in a like plea, pledge as above. The agreement is such that Walter says that he is content under this form: that Walter shall have as his share of all the lands, tenements, meadows, pastures and their appurtenances, following the death of Robert Hawys, their father, and the deaths of their brothers, Peter, Ralph, John and Nicholas, *viz.* 4a.2r.10p. of land, meadow and pasture, of which 3r. of land lie at the Rowesend, next to the land of Robert Sare to the east, 3½r. in Hatchmere, between the land of Peter Tailor and that of Robert Sare, 1r. of land at Saresgate and 1a.2½r. at Boynhawe, next to the land of Hugh de Saxham to the east, 3½r. at Strondeswood, between the land of William of Cranmer and that of Robert Sare, ½r. of meadow at Cocksbusk, and 10p. of meadow at the Harwe, in the Turfpits. Furthermore, William grants to Walter that he shall have, next to his house, in their late father's messuage, from the door of that house on the west side, towards the tenement formerly of Gilbert Doo, as far as the road, [a way] 7ft. wide; to hold this way for Walter's lifetime. After Walter's death the way shall revert to William and his heirs, quit of Walter and his heirs. Walter says that he is content with his portion of the said lands, and with ingress to, and egress, from the said way, for the said term, in the said form. And for this grant, he remits to William all actions, complaints and demands whatsoever, from the beginning of this world until the present day. In return William remits and quitclaims to Walter all actions etc. in the same form. They pay 3d. fine for the enrolment of this agreement, pledge the hayward.

John Man amerced 6d. for trespass against Walter Noreys, demolishing parts of a house, to his loss of 3d.; ordered to raise, pledge the hayward; and 3d. for unlawful detention from the same Walter of five lengths of linen cloth, worth 7½d., to his loss of 1d., which is ordered to be raised; and 3d. for the unlawful detention of

241

a goat, worth 3d., for which the loss is remitted, pledges William the smith and William Patel.

Adam of Cringleford amerced 3d. for leave to agree with Cristiana Smith in a plea of trespass, pledge Walter the smith; and Walter Goos 3d. for the same with Peter Neve in a plea of debt, pledge Robert Lene.

Surrender: Richard of Wortham to Walter the smith and his heirs, ½r. of land in the Millfield, granted to him to hold in villeinage, by services and works etc., fine 6d., pledge the hayward.

Robert Tailor amerced 3d. for leave to agree with William the serjeant of Alexander de Walsham in a plea of trespass, and Alice Helewys 3d. for the same in a like plea, pledge for both the hayward.

Adam Craske amerced 6d. for damage with his sheep in the lord's oats and herbage at Currescroft, and in his oats at Blunteslond, pledges William Hawys and John Terwald.

William and Robert Cook pay 8d. fine [for leave] to rebuild the tenement Galyones by next Easter, pledge the hayward; and a day is given to them until that feast, pledges William of Cranmer and Thomas Fuller.

Thomas of the Beck amerced 18d. for trespass against the lord, uprooting and taking away willows from the lord's bondage, *viz.* from the tenement formerly of Thomas at the Lee.

Robert of Walpole amerced 6d. for trespass in the lord's herbage at Allwood with his sheep and pigs, pledge John Syre.

Walter Payn the shoemaker amerced 1d. for unlawful detention of 1d. from Walter Cooper; Walter Cooper amerced 1d. for unlawful detention of 1d. from Walter Payn, as found by the enquiry, damages remitted in each instance; ordered to raise.

Surrender: William Hawys to John Noble and Alice his wife and their heirs, 1r. of land in the Millfield, granted to them to hold in villeinage, by services and works etc., fine 12d., pledge William Wither.

Manser of Shucford amerced 6d. for trespass against William Rampolye, the reeve, defaming him, the loss to William being assesssed at 6d.; ordered to raise.

Surrender: William Hawys to John Noble and Alice his wife and their heirs, a garden containing 1r.17p. of land, called Mayhewesyerd, granted to them in the same form as above, fine 4s., pledge William Wither.

Walter Noreys in mercy for his false claim against John Man in a plea of debt; condoned because poor.

General Enquiry by William of Cranmer, John Terwald, Nicholas Goche, John Syre, Matthew Hereward, William Wither, Walter the smith, Walter Payn, Simon Peyntour, Robert Tailor, Robert Lene, Nicholas Spileman, William Payn, Thomas Hereward, Robert Hereward, Richard Qualm, John of Stonham and John Tailor.

Edmund Patel, when he died, held from the lord a messuage 7½a. of customary land; the lord had as a heriot a cow after calving, *viz.* at the feast of the Finding of the Holy Cross [3 May], worth 7s.. John and Richard, Edmund's sons, are his nearest heirs, and they have entry by the heriot. They swore fealty.

Agnes the widow of Robert Godefrey, villein, who holds half of a garden and 2a. of customary land in dower, following her husband's death, amerced 6d. because, without leave, she demised this tenement to William Rampolye and Walter the smith for her lifetime; ordered to take into the lord's hands, and to report the profits.[39] The same Agnes gave birth outside wedlock, childwite 2s.8d.; pledges [for both penalties] William Rampolye and Walter the smith.

Rose Stronde amerced 12d. because she demised to Robert Sare, freeman, without leave, 5a. of customary land to a term of years; ordered to take into the lord's hands, and to report the profits.[40]

Peter Margery amerced 6d. because he ploughed over the lord's land at Cocksdrit, 4ft. wide and 4p. long, pledge the hayward; ordered to make amends.

William Wauncy in mercy for cutting and taking away dry willow wood from Ladyswood; condoned because poor.

John Man amerced 3d. because he milled his corn away from the lord's mill.

Thomas at the Lee sold by charter to Thomas of the Beck 3½a. of customary land, without leave, ordered to take into the lord's hands, and to report the profits. Thomas of the Beck purchased from Thomas at the Lee [*blank*] of the lord's fee, ordered to distrain him to show [his title to] entry, and for fealty.

William Rampolye the reeve amerced 3s.4d. because he had straw, worth 3d., carted from the lord's mill to his own house. William Wither amerced 12d. because he carted this straw to William Rampolye's house in his own cart. William Rampolye amerced 3s.4d. because he took a vat, a haircloth and a brass bowl out of the manor, and had them carried to his house for his use.

Ordered to raise from Richard Qualm, John Man and William Patel the younger 4s. to the use of Richard of Wortham, which they undertook to pay, by William Clevehog, as shown in the court of St Valentine's day, 11 Edw.III [14 February 1337].

John Tailor amerced 12d. because he occupied and cultivated a sixth part of a messuage and 3a. of customary land, of the right of Walter the son of William Springold, for four years without leave, pledge the hayward; ordered to take into the lord's hands, and to report the profits.

Walter Pye amerced 12d., and Walter Rampolye and Amice the daughter of William Patel 6d. each, because they brewed and sold ale in breach of the assize; Robert Lenne 3d. for regrating bread. Manser of Shucford and William the smith the ale-tasters each amerced 2d., because they did not perform their duties.

Walter Craske the miller amerced 3d. for trespass against John Man, assessed at 1½d., ordered to raise, pledge the hayward.

William Hawys pays 2s. for having a fold of 5 score sheep until Michaelmas, and no more, because he is allowed 20, pledge the hayward.

William Rampolye and Walter the smith were elected to the office of reeve; Nicholas Fraunceys and Walter Fuller to the office of hayward; and William Cook and Ralph Echeman to the office of woodward.

Ordered to execute the orders of the last court, marked with a cross, and not acted upon.

Agnes the widow of Robert Godefrey pays 6s.8d. fine for leave to marry William Cook, pledges William Rampolye and Walter the smith. Agnes surrendered and remitted to Walter the smith all the right she had in 1a. of land, with half a garden, held in dower after her husband's death; and in the other 1a. held in dower to

---

[39] The order is rescinded; see final entry.
[40] Margin: \'foregone (*?demiss'*) by the lady'/.

William Rampolye; granted to them to hold in villeinage, by services and works, fines 12d. and 6d. respectively, pledge for both the hayward.

SUM 31s., except a cow, worth 7s., as a heriot, and the reeve's amercements

Affeerers: Nicholas Goche and Walter Payn

### 106. HIGH HALL Court General of Nicholas de Walsham, 23 October 1340 [HA504/1/4.23]

William Elys essoins of common suit, by William Deneys; Walter Cristmesse of the same by Henry Trusse; and William of Cranmer of the same, by Robert Sare \he came/; John Wodebite, defendant v John Man in a plea of debt, essoins by Richard Patel; they pledge faith on summons.

The profits from 1r. of free land, taken into the lord's hands after the death of Richard Shepherd because the heir did not come, and for relief and fealty, and several defaults [amount to] 3d.; ordered to retain etc. And upon this Adam Shepherd comes and pays a fine for repossessing this land \condoned/; he swore fealty.

Ordered as elsewhere to attach William Kembald for trespass in the lord's wood, corn and meadow; and Matthew the son of Richard Patel, carter of Robert Hovel, because he drove a cart outside the lord's land at Angerhale several times.

John Helpe amerced 1d. because he did not execute an order of the court; and ordered as elsewhere to attach Walter Payn for damage in the lord's wheat at Hamstale, with his horses and beasts, to the value of 4 sheaves, worth 4d.

John Pynfoul amerced 1d. for damage in the lord's wood, cutting and taking away branches, pledges John Packard and the hayward.

William Deneys amerced 1d. for damage in the lord's peas at Hamstale, pledge the hayward.

Nicholas Fraunceys amerced 6d. because he did not make recompense for a cow, taken upon Robert Hereward, as he undertook for Robert, for damage with his beasts in the lord's wheat, newly sown at Gothelardsyerd. Ordered to attach Robert for the same.

Ordered as elsewhere to attach Thomas Thurbern of Cotton, Richard of Depham and Edmund of Ipswich for homage, relief and fealty.

The first pledges of Agnes Fitte amerced 3d. because they did not have her reply to John Helpe in a plea of trespass; ordered to appoint better pledges.

Olivia Isabel amerced 2s. for trespass against the lord, defaming the lady [saying] that she did not pay her for her services, pledge the hayward.

John of Angerhale amerced 3d. for his false claim against Peter Stag in a plea of trespass, pledge the hayward.

William Wodebite amerced 6d. because he did not rebuild a house in the tenement Aprilles, for which he had a day at the last court; again ordered to rebuild.

Agnes Fitte gave birth outside wedlock, childwite 2s.8d.

Robert Banlone amerced 3d. for damage in the lord's wood with the oxen of the manor, pledge John Packard; and 1d. for damage in the lord's peas, to the value of 1 sheaf.

Ordered to attach Walter the smith for damage in the lord's wood at Lenerithsdel with cows and bullocks; and Walter Payn for damage in the lord's oats at Ulversrowe with cows and calves, to the value of 1 sheaf; and William Hawys for the same with sheep, 1 sheaf; and Alice, farmer of the cows of the Easthouse, for damage in the lord's wheat at the Hulver, 1 sheaf.

John the son of John Packard amerced 1d. for damage in the lord's barley below the wood with cows and bullocks, pledge John Packard. The swineherd of the manor amerced 2d. and Robert Banlone 1d. for damage in the lord's peas at Doucedeux, pledge the hayward; ordered to attach John Syre and William Hawys for the same, 1 sheaf. Ordered to attach William of Cranmer, William Hawys, John Syre, Walter Payn, William Kembald, William Deneys, William Clevehog, Simon Peyntour and John Man for damage in the lord's peas at Hordeshawe with beasts, 4 sheaves.

Ordered to attach Robert Hereward for damage in the lord's garden, taking away the fruits of the garden [and] dung, and breaking and taking away hedges, and depasturing the herbage with his pigs; also for damage at the Newerowe with a cow; and to attach William Kembald, William of Cranmer and William Hawys for damage in the lord's wood; and William of Cranmer, William Hawys and the shepherd of the Prior for damage in the lord's peas at Dousedewes; the swineherd and shepherd of the manor each amerced 1d. for the same.

Ordered to attach Robert Typetot because he drove a stot, worth 10s., so that it died. Ordered to attach William Blunte because a stot, worth 4s., died as a result of his defective custody.

William Wodebite amerced 3d. because he did not bundle[41] enough of the lord's straw for the men, as he was ordered; and 6d. because he was summoned for autumn work and did not come; John Goche 3d. and William and Olivia Isabel 3d. for the same.

Ordered to attach Nicholas Fraunceys, Avice Deneys and Agnes Fitte for damage with their beasts in the lord's newly sown wheat at Sheephouse.

John of Angerhale demised 3a. of customary land to Henry the rector of Westhorpe without leave; ordered to take into the lord's hands, and to report the profits.

John Packard was elected to the office of reeve, and took the oath; Peter Goche was elected to the office of collector, and took the oath; he pays 2s. fine.

John Packard amerced 6s.8d. for breaking the agreement, made in the court, between Alice John's wife and Margery the wife of William Wodebite, under penalty of 13s.4d., concerning which the enquiry found that Alice struck Margery, drawing blood, pledge the hayward.

William Wodebite amerced 2s. for trespass against John Packard and Alice his wife, by Margery William's wife, as found by the enquiry, damages assessed at 6d., ordered to raise.

Ordered to attach John and Alice Packard to reply to William and Margery Wodebite in a plea of debt.

[SUM 18s. 11d., except 3d. profits; not stated]

## 107.  WALSHAM Court General, 1 December 1340 [HA504/1/4.24]

<William of Mileham, defendant v John Tailor in a plea of trespass, essoins by John of Badwell>.[42] Peter Margery, defendant v Peter Jay in a plea of trespass, by Thomas of the Beck; he pledges faith; Peter Jay is present. [A blank space 3½ inches deep follows.]

Adam Craske amerced 3d. for leave to agree with William the serjeant of Alexander de Walsham, in a plea of trespass; and 3d. for the same with Willam Wither in a

---

[41] MS: *calmare*, Latham gives 'to bundle for thatching'.
[42] Margin: 'He did not proceed, as shown below'.

like plea; and 3d. for the same with William Hawys in a like plea, pledge Walter [Craske] the miller.

John Tailor and his pledges amerced 3d. because he did not proceed against William of Mileham in a plea of trespass.

Ordered to raise from Manser of Shucford 10s.7d., of a debt of 15s.7d., to the use of Richard of Worlingworth and Joan his wife, executors of the will of John Wauncy,[43] and John the son of John Wauncy the younger, co-executor of the said will; Manser having ackowledged himself to be indebted to John in the court held on Wednesday before Michaelmas 11 Edw.III [24 September 1337], but not yet having paid. Richard comes and grants to Manser a day for payment of the said 10s.6d. [*sic*], until the 8th day after the feast of St Peter's Chains [9 August].

˙ Manser in mercy for unlawful detentiom, which is recorded in the following court.

Robert Hereward amerced 4d. for leave to agree with Nicholas de Walsham in a plea of trespass; George the skinner 2d. for the same with John Berard in a plea of debt, and Peter Neve 3d. for the same with Thomas the shepherd and Roger the servant (?*serv'*) of the rectory, in a plea of trespass, pledge for all the hayward.

William the son of William Rampolye and his pledges amerced 3d. because he did not proceed against Peter Neve in a plea of trespass.

John Stonham amerced 3d. for leave to agree with Robert Hereward in a plea of trespass, pledge the hayward.

Surrender: Robert Swyft to Robert Man and his heirs, a portion of a messuage, 6p. long and 14ft. wide, lying between their messuages, granted to him to hold in villeinage, by services and works, fine 6d., pledges the reeve and the hayward.

The lord granted to John Lester and Rose his wife a plot of land for building, 8p. wide and 10p. long, as marked by metes and bounds, lying on Tailorswong next to the land of Emma Shepherd, and abutting on the Churchway, to hold to them and their heirs, by the rod, for services 2s. per year, payable at the usual terms, fine waived.

Nicholas Fraunceys the hayward in mercy because he did not attach William of Mileham, as ordered, condoned; ordered to summon William to reply to John Taylor in a plea of debt. [A blank space 2 inches deep follows.]

John Goche held from the lord, when he died, 2a. of customary land and a third part of a messuage; the lord had no heriot because John had no beast. Nicholas his brother is his nearest heir and is of full age, he pays 6s.8d. entry fine, pledge the hayward.

+Before her death Letitia Stronde surrendered all the tenement she held in bondage, *viz.* all her share in the messuage formerly of John Stronde and 8a. of land, in the presence of Nicholas Fraunceys the hayward, William Rampolye, William of Cranmer and William his son, Stephen Cooper, Robert Lene, John Terwald and others, to the use of William Letitia's son, William the son of William of Cranmer, and the heirs of William Letitia's son. Afterwards the same William, who was a bastard, died without heirs. William the son of William of Cranmer does not pursue (*sequitur*) [?his claim] for having the tenement for his lifetime. Ordered to seize and to retain in the lord's hands, and to report the profits.[44] The

---

43  MS: Named as 'John the shepherd', but as 'John Wauncy' in roll no.89.
44  Margin: 'Profits 12d.' and in later hand 'heriot'.

lord had a mare, worth 5s., as a heriot after Letitia's death, recorded in a preceding court; but after the death of William her son, he had nothing because William had no beast.

William Rampolye and Robert of Badwell each amerced 3d. for damage in Ladyswood with their beasts; Matthew Hereward 4d., Simon Rampolye 2d., William Elys 3d., Ralph Echeman 3d., Robert Cook 3d. and Thomas Hereward 3d. for the same, pledge the hayward. Alice Helewys amerced 4d. for damage in the lord's peas at Ayleldestoft with her pigs, and for taking peas away from there in the autumn, pledge the hayward.

Robert Lenne and George the skinner each amerced 1d. for making an unlawful way at Oldtoft outside the lord's wheat, pledge the hayward; ordered to attach Simon Cokerel of Ashfield for the same.

Simon Cooper the cowherd, amerced 2d. for damage in the lord's barley with his geese, pledge William Rampolye; Walter Noreys in mercy for the same, condoned because poor. Peter Tailor amerced 3d. for damage in the lord's barley on Tailorswong, pledge the hayward.

Ordered [to attach] Robert of Walpole and Stephen of Allwood because they withheld from the lord one autumn boonwork for the tenement Allwood. Memorandum that they should go with their rods to be over the reapers, and should have their food for the whole day, as the lord's overseers.

William Syre amerced 3d. for damage in the lord's oats at Boynhawe, pledge the hayward; Robert Man 3d. for damage in the lord's peas at Ayleldestoft with beasts, pledges the hayward and the bailiff; and John the swineherd of the manor 3d. for damage in the lord's corn with pigs, pledge the bailiff.

Ordered [to attach] William the serjeant [of Alexander de Walsham], who holds the tenement of Adam Sket, because he overstocked the lord's common with his sheep, and grazed them there, where he had no right of common.

Robert Sare amerced 3d., John Typetot 2d. and William Elys 6d., because they stored corn grown in the bondage, in free tenements, pledge for all the hayward.

Ralph Echeman amerced 6d. because he baked and sold bread in breach of the assize, and 6d. for breaking the assize of ale. Walter Pye 12d., Walter Rampolye 6d. and Amice Patel 4d. for breaking the assize of ale, pledge for Amice William Patel. Robert Lenne and Gilbert Priour each amerced 2d. for regrating bread. Manser of Shucford and William the smith the ale-tasters, 2d. each, because they did not perform their duties.

William Kembald held within his messuage ½a. of customary land on which his barn was situated, which Simon Kembald William's father exchanged with William the smith for ½a. of free land, which Walter the son of William the smith now holds, this exchange being made in the time of Lady Eve de Valence; the lord to be consulted.

Thomas of the Beck purchased from Thomas at the Lee 3½a. of customary land, formerly of Thomas at the Green, and this land was taken into the lord's hands because he purchased it without leave, as well as for services and customs in arrears. And upon this Thomas of the Beck comes into open court and receives the said land from the lord, to hold by the rod in villeinage, by services and works, fine 6s.8d., pledge John Terwald, he swore servile fealty. Memorandum that the said land contains 3 acres.[45]

---

[45] MS: *rode*, but the area stated above and the amount of the fine indicate that 'roods' is an error.

William of Cranmer pays 2s. fine for having a fold of 6 score sheep, and no more because he is allowed 40; Robert Rampolye and Nicholas Goche each pay 12d. for 40 sheep; William Hawys pays 2s.6d. for 6 score, he is allowed 20.

Surrenders: William Hawys to John Noble and his heirs, 1a.1r.11p. of land in Mayhewescroft, granted to him to hold in villeinage, by services and works etc., fine 4s., pledges William Wither and Adam Noble.

Emma Shepherd to Peter Tailor and his heirs, a portion of a messuage, 3p. long and 6ft. wide, as marked by metes and bounds, lying next to Peter's messuage, granted to him to hold in the same form, fine 6d., pledge the hayward.

+Ordered as elsewhere to retain 2a. of customary land, taken because Thomas Patel sold it to John Cumpyn by charter, without leave, and to report the profits. Memorandum that the lord granted to John the crops from this land.

+Ordered as elsewhere to retain 2½a. of customary land, taken after the death of Bartholomew Patel, because Richard Caldewell, Bartholomew's bastard son, purchased this land with his father, and to report the profits. Memorandum that the lord granted the crops from this land to Richard Patel.

+Ordered as elsewhere to attach William Wyswyf, John Rede and Walter Doo, villeins, because they absent themselves from the lord; and Ralph of Rudham chaplain to reply to William Hawys and to Bartholomew Jerico, in separate pleas of trespass.

Ordered to retain 1a.3r. of customary land, which William Noreys sold to John of Foxley by charter, without leave, and to report the profits. The lord's beasts have depastured this land.

+Ordered to retain a piece of land 14ft. wide and 6p. long, which Joan the widow of Gilbert Helpe held when she died, taken because the heir did not come, and to report the profits.

+Ordered as elsewhere to raise from Thomas at the Lee 1 bushel of wheat and ½ bushel of barley, to the use of Thomas Hereward; and 1 bushel of wheat and ½ bushel of peas, to the use of Alice Helewys, and 3s.3d., to the use of John Man.

Ordered as elsewhere to retain in the hands of John Typetot three pigs, taken upon Thomas at the Lee, and to take more etc., for him to reply to William Hawys in a plea of debt, and to Avice Deneys in a like plea, and also for trespass in the lord's warren taking hares, and for services and customs in arrears.

Ordered to attach Gilbert the smith of Badwell for damage in Ladyswood, cutting and taking away [timber].

Ordered as elsewhere to attach Robert Shepherd chaplain to reply to Emma Shepherd in a plea of debt.

Thomas of the Beck purchased from Thomas at the Lee various free tenements of the lord's fee; ordered to distrain Thomas of the Beck to show [his charter for] entry into the lord's fee; and he has a day to certify how many [tenements ] there are.

+Ordered to retain 3a. of customary land and a 6th part of a messuage, of the right of Walter the son of William Springold, because John Tailor occupied and worked this land for four years without leave, and to report the profits. It was found that the profits, excluding customs and works, amounted to 6d..

+Walter the smith pays 40s. fine not to be in the office of reeve, pledge the hayward.

A day was given to William and Robert Cook to rebuild the tenement Galyones by Michaelmas.

Walter Fuller pays 26s.8d. fine for declining the office of hayward, pledge the hayward.

Memorandum that a portion of a messuage 14ft. wide and 6p. long, [remains] in the lord's hands, after the death of Joan the wife of Gilbert Helpe, who died seised of it, because her heirs did not come to claim, and did not wish to succeed. The land was held by the rod, for services 1d. per year. Also in the lord's hands, a messuage formerly of the said Joan, which Nicholas de Walsham took into his hands, and held as by his own right, because Joan's heirs are villeins of Nicholas; and the lord purchased the messuage from Nicholas by charter, and with the voluntary consent of the heirs, [to hold] to himself and his heirs for ever. Upon this the lord granted all the said tenement to Walter Pye and Alice his wife to hold for the lifetime of them both; and after their deaths, the tenement shall revert to Amice and Robert the children of Walter and Alice, and their heirs for ever, to hold by the rod, paying 2d. annually at the usual terms, *viz.* 1d. for the said portion of a messuage, as has been customary from antiquity, and for the messuage, 1d. new rent; and they give entry fine.[46]

[SUM £5 2s. 7d., not stated]

## 108.   WALSHAM Court, 6 September 1341 [HA504/1/4.25]

<William Elys, defendant v Thomas Hereward in a plea of trespass, essoins by William Kembald; and v Robert Hereward in a like plea, by Walter the miller.>[47] Robert Crane essoins of common suit, by Henry Crane; Manser of Shucford of the same, by Adam Noble; they pledge faith.

John Margery amerced 3d. because he did not warrant his essoin.

The first pledges of William Leche amerced 6d. because they did not have him reply to Bartholomew Jerico in a plea of debt; ordered to appoint better pledges.

John Spileman and his pledges amerced 3d. because he did not proceed against Robert of Thelnetham in a plea of covenant.

Ordered to retain in the lord's hands a horse taken upon William Wodebite, and to take more etc. for him to reply to the lord because he overstocked the common with 60 sheep, grazing where he had no right of common.

The first pledges of Peter Neve amerced 6d. because they did not have him reply to the lord for trespass in a stack of oats at Boynhawe, in the autumn; ordered to appoint better pledges.

Emma Shepherd and her pledges in mercy because she did not proceed against Robert Shepherd chaplain in a plea of debt, condoned because poor.

Robert Cook in mercy for default; afterwards he came.

William Rampolye amerced 3d. for leave to agree with John Sayken of Drinkstone in a plea of debt; and 3d. for the same with Nicholas Fraunceys in a plea of trespass; and 3d. for the same with William Kembald in a like plea; and 3d. for the same with Roger the servant in a like plea, pledge William Rampolye, his father.

Peter Neve amerced 3d. for leave to agree with Robert Sare in a plea of trespass, pledge the hayward.

John Man amerced 3d. for default; William Clevehog in mercy for the same; afterwards he came.

---

[46] Margin: 'fine remitted'.
[47] Margin: 'The essoins do not lie because he holds customary land'.

249

Simon Peyntour amerced 3d. for trespass against Robert at the Brook, the loss assessed at ½d.; ordered to raise.

The first pledges of William Cook the elder amerced 2d. because they did not have him reply to Robert Deneys in a plea of trespass; ordered to appoint better pledges. Afterwards, it was found by the enquiry that William Cook trespassed against Robert, to the loss of ¼d.; ordered to raise.

William of Mileham amerced 12d. for leave to agree with John Tailor in a plea of debt, pledge Walter Osbern.

Agnes the daughter of Walter Typetot pays 12d. fine for leave to marry William Patel the elder, pledge the hayward.

A day is given, at the request of the parties, to Robert the son of Elias Typetot, plaintiff, and William his brother, defendant, in pleas of trespass and agreement, until the next court, to come without essoin.

Surrenders: Edmund Lene to William of Cranmer the elder and his heirs, a piece of meadow, 6ft. wide, lying in the Micklemeadow, in the Turfpits, between the meadow of Sir William Tallemache and that of William of Cranmer; granted to him to hold in villeinage, by services and works etc., fine 6d.

Ralph Echeman to the same William and his heirs, 5p. of meadow in the Micklemeadow, lying in separate pieces, granted to him in the same form, fine 3d., pledge for both fines the hayward.

Thomas Hereward in mercy for his false claim against William Elys in a plea of trespass, condoned.

Robert Hereward and his pledges amerced 3d. because he did not proceed against William Elys in a plea of trespass.

Surrenders: Walter Osbern to Bartholomew Jerico and his heirs, half of the cotland called the Sawyers, granted to him in the same form as above, fine 12d, pledge Walter Osbern.

William of Mileham and Isabella his wife, she being examined by the lord, surrendered, through the hands of the bailiff, the reversion of 5½r. of land, and half of the cotland called the Sawyers, lying separately, to the use of the same Bartholomew; granted to him in the same form, fine 4s., pledge as above.

General Enquiry by John Syre, William Deneys, Walter Payn, Walter the smith, William Rampolye, John Terwald, Simon Peyntour, Robert Rampolye, Matthew Hereward, Ralph Echeman, Robert Tailor and Nicholas Goche.

Robert Lene the farmer of the cows of the manor amerced 6d. for damage in the lord's wheat and barley, to the value of ½ bushel of each, pledge the hayward.

Bartholomew the servant of Robert Lene in mercy because he took away a sheaf of corn at Ayleldestoft, condoned; Peter the groom of the stable and John the clerk of the chapel (*capelle*) amerced 6d. for the same, pledge Emma Shepherd, because in the house.

Peter Gudgeon amerced 3d. for damage in Ladyswood, taking away firewood, pledge Robert Springold and Walter the smith.

Ordered to distrain Robert the farmer of Ashfield and Geoffrey his servant, because Geoffrey cut ash staves and sticks, and took them away to [his] cart.[48]

Ordered to attach Richard Alot the servant of John Nugg for trespass in the lord's warren, setting snares in Ladyswood.

---

[48] MS: *ad carettam*; perhaps this means 'for a cart', that is, to make or repair it, see footnote 56.

Richard the swineherd of the manor in mercy for damage in the lord's meadow in the Micklemeadow, condoned; ordered to attach John the swineherd of Sir William Tallemache for the same; John Herning, Ralph Echeman, Alice Helewys and Robert Cook each amerced 3d. for the same, pledge for all the hayward.

Ralph Neve amerced 3d. for damage in the lord's oats at Westmill with his sheep, pledge the hayward.

John Tailor amerced 2d. for damage in the lord's meadows at Micklemeadow with his pigs, pledge the hayward; <The same John in mercy for damage in the lord's oats at Westmill with his sheep, pledge as before> \error/.

+Robert Tailor and Alice Helewys 2d. each for damage in the lord's oats at Westmill with sheep, pledge the hayward.

Cristiana the wife of Robert Man amerced 3d. because she unlawfully cut hay in the Micklemeadow and took it away, pledge the bailiff; Robert of Thelnetham 3d. for the same, pledge the hayward; Alice Whiteman 1d. for the same, pledge Robert Lene, because in [his] house.

Robert Rampolye and John Herning each amerced 3d. because each had 12 sheep in his fold over the fixed number; William Hawys and William of Cranmer 3d. each for 16 sheep over the fixed number.

Ordered to attach Thomas of Badwell for overstocking the common with his sheep, grazing where he had no right of common.

John Tailor and William Kembald were elected to the office of reeve; William Patel the younger and John Spileman to the office of hayward; and Ralph Echeman and Richard Spileman to the office of woodward.

Cristiana the widow of Edmund Patel pays 12s. fine for leave to marry William the smith, pledges Robert Rampolye and Simon Peyntour.

Surrenders: Thomas Hereward to Thomas Fuller and his heirs, 1r.10p. of meadow in the Micklemeadow, granted to him in the same form as above, fine 18d., pledge the hayward.[49]

Walter Osbern to John Noble and his heirs, ½a. of land in Mayhewescroft, granted to him in the same form, fine 2s., pledges Adam Noble and William Wyther.

John Spileman to William and Robert Cook and their heirs, 3r.18p. of land at Outhgongesende, in exchange for 3r.18p. at Galyones, abutting on Buryway, granted to them in the same form, fine 2s., pledge the hayward.

Ordered to execute the orders of the last court, marked with a cross, and not acted upon.

SUM 37s. 9d.

### 109.  HIGH HALL Court of Nicholas de Walsham, 6 October 1341 [HA504/1/4.26.i]

Robert Sare essoins of common suit by John Kebbil, and Henry Trusse of the same by Walter Cristmesse; they pledge faith, and they have a day until Monday after All Saints Day [5 November]. <William Cranmer essoins of the same, by William Kembald.>[50]

John Man and his pledges amerced 6d. because he did not proceed against John Wodebite in a plea of debt.

---

49  Tab: 'Thomas Hereward' (?16th century).
50  Margin: 'Afterwards he came'.

John Helpe the hayward amerced 1d. because he did not execute an order of the court; again ordered to attach William Kembald for trespass in the lord's wood, corn and meadows with his pigs.

Agnes Fitte amerced 3d. for default.

John Helpe and his pledges amerced 3d. because he did not proceed against Agnes Fitte in a plea of trespass.

William Wodebite amerced 12d. because he did not rebuild a house on the tenement Aprilles, for which he had a day until the next court;[51] ordered to rebuild before the next court.

Agnes Fitte amerced 1d. for damage in the lord's wheat at Sheephouse, pledge the hayward.

John Packard and Alice his wife amerced 3d. for leave to agree with William Wodebite and Margery his wife, in a plea of debt.

The profits from 3a. of customary land, demised by John of Angerhale to Henry the rector of Westhorpe, for a term of years, without leave [amount to] 5d; ordered to retain in the lord's hands.

It was presented by the whole homage that Henry of Hattele of Wyverstone and Agnes his wife purchased from Walter of the Marsh of Westhorpe all the lands in the vills of Westhorpe, Wyverstone, Finningham and Bacton, which Walter held on Wednesday after the feast of St Francis the Confessor, 15 Edw.III [30 May 1341];[52] ordered etc. Afterwards Henry and Agnes came to show their charter, and sought admittance to the lands. They swore fealty.

<William Elys purchased from John Pynchon and Olivia his wife a messuage with 5r. of land, of the lord's fee, etc. Ordered to distrain him to show [his title to] entry into the lord's fee>.[53]

John Pynchon amerced 6d. for default.

Ordered [to attach] William Lene, shepherd of the manor of Walsham, and the shepherd of this manor, and William Payn and John Syre for damage in the lord's wheat at Sheephouse; Robert of Angerhale swineherd of this manor amerced 3d. for the same there, and in the Sheepcoteyard with pigs; John White the cowherd amerced 3d. for the same at Netherhawe, and in the lord's peas below the wood. Ordered to attach John Syre, William Kembald and William Payn for the same in Stonylond, and Simon Peyntour for damage in the lord's oats at Southbrook.

Agnes Wodebite amerced 6d. for waste in the lord's bondage demolishing a certain house; ordered to rebuild.

John Helpe the hayward amerced 6d. because he did not forewarn the workers for services, as ordered.

John Packard amerced 6d. because he was summoned for work [to be done] by his daughter for money, and she did not come.

John Man complains against John Wodebite in a plea of debt; ordered.

John Chapman was elected to the office of reeve, and paid 2s. fine; William Wodebite was elected to the office of hayward, viz. for the tenement Aprilles, and paid 2s. fine, pledge for both the hayward.

The lord granted to William Wodebite half of the tenement formerly of John

---

[51] That is 'this court'.
[52] The date of Wednesday after the feast of St Francis is 8 October, two days after the date of this court; it is assumed that the clerk intended to refer to the feast of the Translation of St Francis, 25 May.
[53] Margin: 'Void because error'.

Wodebite, to hold from last Michaelmas until the end of the following nine years, paying to the lord 3s.4d. rent per year, and maintaining the house etc.. William pays for having his term.

Also to John Helpe the reeve and Gilbert his brother 3a. of land, to hold from last Michaelmas to the end of the following seven years; and they pay 12d. fine for having their term.

Agnes and Margery the daughters of John Wodebite, by leave of the court, demised to William Wodebite all the tenement, which they hold following the death of their father, to hold from last Michaelmas to the end of five years, paying to them 3s.4d. per year. William pays for having his term,[54] and he will maintain the house.

[SUM 9s. 11d., except 5d. profits, not stated]

## 110. WALSHAM Court General, 17 December 1341 [HA504/1/4.27]

Bartholomew Jerico, plaintiff v William of Mileham in a plea of trespass, essoins by Manser of Shucford; he pledges faith; ordered to attach William. The same Bartholomew, plaintiff v William Leche in a like plea, essoins by Peter Margery; he pledges faith; ordered to attach William to reply.

Robert Crane in mercy because he did not warrant his essoin.[55]

Ordered as elsewhere to retain in the lord's hands a horse taken upon William Wodebite, and to take more etc., for him to reply to the lord for overstocking the lord's common with 60 sheep, grazing where he had no right of common.

Ordered as elsewhere to attach Peter Neve for trespass with his beasts in a stack of oats at Boynhawe, in the autumn; and Robert the farmer of Ashfield for trespass in the lord's wood by Geoffrey his servant cutting down and taking away ash boughs for his cart[56] and sticks, without leave; and +John the swineherd of Sir William Tallemache for trespass in the lord's meadow in Micklemeadow with pigs; and +John Nugg for trespass in the lord's warren by Richard Alot his servant setting snares in Ladyswood; and Thomas of Badwell for overstocking the common with his sheep, grazing where he had no right of common.

Manser of Shucford amerced 6d. because he did not pay 10s.6d. to Richard of Worlingworth and Joan his wife, as he undertook; again ordered to raise.

The profits from 1a. of land, now in the lord's hands because John Robhood sold it to Thomas Hereward without leave [amount to] 12d.; ordered to retain.

Ordered as elsewhere to retain in the lord's hands part of a messuage and 8a. of customary land, which William the bastard son of Letitia Stronde purchased from his mother, with William the son of William of Cranmer, as shown in the court of the Friday after St Andrew's Day, 14 Edw.III [1 December 1340, no.107], and to report the profits. Memorandum that William of Cranmer sowed 2a. of this tenement with wheat, from which the yield is estimated at 1 quarter 4 bushels.

+The lord to be consulted concerning ½a. of land, within the messuage of William Kembald, on which his barn is sited, which Simon Kembald, William's father, exchanged with William the smith for another ½a. of free land, which Walter the

---

[54] In each of these three grants of land for a term of years, the grantee is said to have paid for having his term, but only one fine of 12d. is recorded, in the margin, between the first and second entries.

[55] Margin: 'Afterwards, he paid a fine for [respite of] suit'.

[56] MS: *pro caretta*; in an earlier reference to this offence (in roll no.108) the original was *ad carettam*, see footnote 48.

son of William the smith now holds. The exchange was made in the time of Lady Eve de Valence.

General Enquiry by William of Cranmer the elder, Walter Osbern, John Terwald, Robert Lene, Walter Payn, Nicholas Goche, Stephen Cooper, John Syre, Ralph Echeman, Matthew Hereward, Robert Tailor, William Wither, William Typetot, Walter the smith, William Rampolye, Nicholas Fraunceys, John Man and Simon Peyntour.

+Ordered as elsewhere to retain in the lord's hands 2a. of customary land, which Thomas Patel sold to John Cumpyn without leave, and to report the profits; and 2½a. taken after the death of Bartholomew Patel, because Richard Caldewell, bastard son of Bartholomew, acquired this land with his father, and to report the profits.[57]

+Ordered as elsewhere to attach William Wyswyf, John Rede and Walter Doo, villeins, because they absent themselves from the lord; and Ralph of Rudham chaplain to reply to William Hawys in a plea of trespass, and to Bartholomew Jerico in a like plea.

+Ordered as elsewhere to retain in the lord's hands 1a.3r. of customary land, which William Noreys sold to John of Foxley without leave, and to report the profits. \profits 6d./

+Ordered to retain in the hands of John Typetot three pigs taken upon Thomas at the Lee, and to take more etc., for him to reply to William Hawys in a plea of debt, and to Avice Deneys in a like plea, and also for trespass in the lord's warren etc.

+Ordered to retain 2a.3r. of customary land and a 12th part of a messuage, of the right of Walter the son of William Springold, because John Tailor occupied and worked this land for four years without leave, and to report the profits. \Profits valued at 6d., excluding 6d. for customs and works./

William the son of Elias Typetot amerced 1d. for trespass against Robert his brother, as found by the enquiry, the loss assessed at 1d.; ordered to raise; and 3d. for unlawful detention from Robert of 2s. and 6 gallons of ale, as found by the enquiry, to the loss of 2d.; ordered to raise.

Surrender: Walter Osbern to John Noble and his heirs, 15p. of land in Mayhewescroft, granted to him to hold in villeinage, by services and works etc., fine 6d., pledge the hayward.

John Herning and Robert Rampolye each pay 12d. fine for having folds of 40 sheep each, pledge the hayward; William Hawys 2s.6d. for a fold of 6 score sheep and no more because 20 allowed; William of Cranmer 2s. for 6 score, 40 allowed; Nicholas Goche 12d. for 40, pledge the hayward.

Robert Cook amerced 1d. for leave to agree with Stephen the son of Peter Tailor, in a plea of debt, pledge the hayward.

Surrender: Walter Rampolye to Walter the smith and his heirs, 1½r.8p. of land, lying next to Priestscroft, granted to him to hold in the same form as above, fine 18d, pledge the hayward.

Alice Galyon, by leave of the court, demised to Robert Hereward ½a. of pasture at Hordeshawe, to hold from last Michaelmas to the end of the following four years, full and complete, fine for the term 3d..

Surrender: Robert Sare and Idonea his wife, she being examined in court, to William

---

57  Margin: inserted in a different hand, and different ink, 'Profits 12d.': this applies to all the other insertions relating to profits, recorded in this roll and the next.

of Cranmer the younger and his heirs, 1a. of land in Strondesclose, granted to him to hold in the same form as above, fine 2s.6d., pledge the hayward.

Walter Pye, who died since the last court, held from the lord 2a.½r. of customary land, by services and works; the lord had as a heriot a cow, worth 8s., due to calve by the feast of the Conception [8 December]. William and Robert Walter's sons are his nearest heirs, and they have entry by the heriot. He also held 1a. of free land, of the fee of Robert Sare, for fealty and services 1d. per year; William and Robert [the heirs] came and paid 1d. relief, pledge the hayward; and they swore fealty.

Richard of Wortham, when he died, held from the lord 3r. of customary land with a pightle, by services and works; the lord had as a heriot an ewe, worth 16d. John, Richard's son, is his nearest heir, and he seeks to be admitted; not granted because he did not come to this court. The tenement to be retained in the lord's hands. \The entry fine is recorded at the next court./

Agnes [Noble née] Hulke, when she died, held from the lord ½a. of customary land, by services and works; the lord had as a heriot a cow, worth 5s., due to calve by All Saints Day [1 November]. It is not known who are the heirs of Agnes; therefore ordered to take the land into the lord's hands, and to report the profits. \Because no heir came, this land was granted to Adam Noble, to hold in villeinage, by services and works; the fine is recorded in the third court following in the same year./[58] \No profits this year./

Robert of Thelnetham the cowherd amerced 3d. for damage in the lord's wood with cows; Alice Helewys 3d. for the same in Ladyswood, pledge for both the bailiff; Robert Cook 2d. for the same with a colt, pledge the hayward.

William Cook the elder in mercy for having 4 sheep lying outside the lord's fold; William Cook the younger for having 3 sheep outside;[59] Nicholas Deneys amerced 1d. for having 1 sheep outside.

Ordered [to attach] Olivia Patel villein because she married Robert Page of Sapiston without leave.

Robert Sare amerced 1d., William Elys and John Typetot 2d. each, because they stored in a free tenement corn grown on the bondage.

Walter Rampolye amerced 6d., Alice Pye 9d., Rose Echeman and John Lester 6d. each, because they brewed and sold ale in breach of the assize. Robert of Thelnetham and George of Brockley each amerced 2d. for regrating bread. Manser of Shucford and William the smith the ale-tasters amerced 4d. because they did not perform their duties.

Richard the son of Walter Cranmer and John Osbern each amerced 3d. for default.

Robert the son of Elias Typetot amerced 1d. for trespass against his brother William, as found by the enquiry, to the loss of ¼d.; ordered to raise.

John Terwald[60] amerced 3d. because he consulted with men who were not sworn.

Walter Osbern surrendered into the lord's hands 1½r. of land in a garden called Mayhewesyard, between the messuage of John Barleyhand and that of John Noble; and the lord granted this tenement to Walter, to hold for his lifetime. And after Walter's death, the tenement shall revert to John Barleyhand and his heirs, to hold in villeinage by services and works etc., fine 6d., pledge the hayward.

---

58 Court of 25 September 1342, (no.114); margin: 'heriot' (later hand).

59 Margin: 'Condoned'.

60 A member of the enquiry.

William the son of Elias Typetot amerced 3d. for unlawful detention of 3s.4½d. from his brother Robert, as found by the enquiry, to the loss of 3d.; ordered to raise.

By leave of the court, Robert Crane demised to Manser of Shucford 1½a. of customary land and a quarter part of a messuage, to hold from last Michaelmas to the end of the following three years, full and complete. [Manser pays] 6d. fine for his term, pledge the hayward.

William the son of Elias Typetot amerced 3d. for his false claim against his brother Robert in a plea of covenant.

Nicholas Goche, Robert Tailor, Walter Osbern, Richard Kebbil, Peter Jay, Walter Hereward, Simon Peyntour, Robert Lene, Stephen Cooper, Thomas Fuller, Matthew Hereward, John Man, John Terwald, Simon Rampolye, John Syre, William Deneys, Walter Payn, Walter the smith, William Rampolye, Robert Rampolye, Ralph Echeman and William of Cranmer the elder, jurors on the enquiry, amerced 5s.6d.,[61] because they concealed, and did not present, that Cristiana the daughter of Walter Patel married Robert the son of Elias Typetot without leave.

Robert Typetot pays 3d. fine[62] because he married Cristiana without leave, and failed to present [the fact]; Cristiana pays 5s. fine for leave to marry Robert Typetot, pledge the same Robert.

Surrender: John Robhood to Robert Lene and his heirs, 1½r. of land at the Regway, granted to him to hold in villeinage, by services and works etc., fine 12d., pledge the hayward.

Robert Crane pays 9d. fine for respite of suit of court from last Michaelmas to the end of three years, pledge Manser of Shucford.

Ordered to attach Robert Osbern villein because he absents himself from the lord; and because he gave his daughter Margaret in marriage, without leave.

SUM 35s. 5d.,[63] with profits [included],<br>
except 2 cows, worth 13s., as heriots[64]<br>
Affeerers: Robert Tailor and Stephen Cooper

## 111.   WALSHAM Court General, 15 April 1342 [HA504/1/4.28]

[This roll is badly faded throughout, and stained in several places near the end.]

Bartholomew Jerico and his pledges amerced 3d. because he did not proceed against William of Mileham in a plea of trespass.

Ordered as elsewhere to attach William Leche to reply to Bartholomew Jerico in a plea of debt.

A day is given to William Wodebite until the next court, to make amends to the lord because he grazed the lord's common with 60 sheep, where he had no right of common, pledge Walter Osbern.

Manser of Shucford amerced 6d. for unlawful detention of 6s.6d. from Richard of Worlingworth and Joan his wife, as he admitted in open court. The loss is remitted, and Manser has a day, with Richard's consent, to pay him by next Michaelmas, pledges William of Cranmer the elder and Thomas Fuller.

---

61 Margin: 'and no more, by the lord's orders'.
62 Margin: 'and no more' as above.
63 Originally the sum shown was '33s.5d.'; the amendment is in the different hand referred to above.
64 The ewe, worth 16d., is omitted.

Peter Neve amerced 2d. for damage in a stack of oats at Boynhawe, with his beasts, pledge the hayward.

John Robhood pays 6d. fine for repossessing 1a. of land, out of the lord's hands, [taken] because he sold it to Thomas Hereward without leave, pledge the hayward.

Amice Patel and her pledges amerced 3d. because she did not proceed against Alice of the Wood, in a plea of debt.

John Terwald amerced 12d. because he allowed John Hawys chaplain to have, out of his possession, a horse which had been distrained by the lord's bailiff, [for John Hawys] to reply to Nicholas Wauncy in a plea of debt. Again ordered to attach him to reply in the same plea.[65]

Thomas Hereward amerced 3d. for unlawful detention of a gate, worth 7d., from John Robhod, the loss assessed at 8d.; ordered to raise.

Isabella Larke amerced 3d. for trespass against Walter Hawys defaming him, as found by the enquiry, pledge the hayward; the loss was assessed at 6d., ordered to raise.

Alice Fraunceys pays 2s.6d. fine for leave to marry John Deeth, pledges the hayward and Nicholas Fraunceys.

Surrenders: Nicholas Goche to Robert Lene and his heirs, 1a.1r. of land at the East-mill, granted to him to hold in villeinage, by services and works, fine 3s.4d., pledge the hayward.

Edmund Lene and Amice his wife, she being examined in court, to John Tailor and his heirs, a cotland, 3p. long and 3p. wide, granted to him in the same form, fine 6d., pledge the hayward.

The lord granted to Geoffrey Whitemor a plot of land containing 1r., in the Tailor-wong, next to the messuage of John Lester, to hold by the rod to him and his heirs, paying for services 12d. per year at the usual terms; Geoffrey swore fealty.

Hilary the daughter of William of Cranmer the younger pays 20s. for leave to marry John [the son of] William Hawys, pledge William of Cranmer the elder.

William Clevehog the elder pays 6d. fine for having a fold of 20 sheep, pledge the hayward.

Manser of Shucford amerced 6d. for unlawful detention of 7s. from Robert the son of Richard Crane, as found by the enquiry, to the loss of 3s., pledges Robert Tailor and the hayward. Ordered to raise.

Surrender: Robert and William the sons of Elias Typetot, to John Terwald and his heirs, a piece of meadow, 1½ft. wide, in the Micklemeadow, granted to him to hold in the same form as above, fine 3d., pledge the hayward.

William Clevehog the elder, by leave of the court, demised to Walter Rampolye 2a. of land, to hold from last Michaelmas to the end of six years following; Walter pays 6d. fine for having his term, pledge the hayward.

+Ordered to seize into the lord's hands 3r. of customary land with part of a messuage, following the death of John Godhouse ['Gudhouse'], because he purchased this tenement from William Patel, Robert Totay and Richard Herirof, villeins of the lord; and to report the profits. \Profits 3s./

---

[65] In the court of 19 June 1340 (no.105), an agreement between William and Walter Hawys, John's brothers, stated that John was dead, and there is no later mention of him. John Terwald's offence may have occurred in 1333–4, when he was reeve, but it is more likely that the John Hawys in question was the son of William Hawys, who is mentioned later in this roll as the husband of Hilary Cranmer.

Alice Qualm pays 2s.8d. childwite, because she gave birth out of wedlock.

+Olivia the daughter of Gilbert Peyntour, villein, married a certain [*blank*], without leave; ordered.

Thomas the son of Alice [?Agnes] Veyse freeman and Richard Patel villein purchased by charter from Robert Chapman the younger, freeman, a messuage ¼r. of land, of the fee of Robert Dormour; ordered. \Profits 3d./

+William Gobald freeman sold by charter to John Gobald his son 1a.3r. of customary land without leave; ordered to take into the lord's hands, and report the profits. \Profits 2s./.

+John Longe freeman sold by charter to Walter Pykhorn 1½a. of customary land, without leave; ordered to take into the lord's hands, and to report the profits. \Profits 12d./.

+Gundreda the widow of Bartholomew Patel amerced 6s.8d. for waste in the lord's bondage, [in the tenement] formerly Bartholomew's, cutting trees and demolishing walls, to the loss of ½ mark. Ordered to take into the lord's hands, and to report the profits.

Alice Pye amerced 9d. because she brewed and sold ale in breach of the assize, John Lester and Rose Echeman 6d. each, Walter Rampolye 3d. and John of Foxley 6d. for the same. Robert Lene amerced 2d. for regrating bread, George of Brockley in mercy for the same, condoned because poor. Manser of Shucford and William the smith the ale-tasters each amerced 2d. because they did not perform their duties.

+Walter the smith villein purchased by charter from Olivia Rampolye a piece of free land, 8p.2ft. long and 8ft. wide; ordered to seize and to report the profits. \No profits/.

John of Wortham pays 6d. fine for having entry to 3r. of land, with a pightle, following the death of Richard his father, pledge the hayward; he swore fealty. He pays the fine because he did not come on the first day.

Surrender: Richard Kebbil to Robert Lene and his heirs, ½r. of land at Staple way, granted to him in villeinage, by services and works, fine 4d., pledge the hayward.

At the court of 12 November 1339 [no.104], it was ordered to retain in the lord's hands 3a. of customary land and half a messuage, following the death of John Crane, because Robert his brother and heir did not come etc.; and because he did not come the tenement was transferred to Henry Crane, John's uncle, and Robert, the son of Peter Crane, John's nephew, to hold to them and their heirs, by the rod; and they paid 5s. entry fine. Now to this court comes Robert, John's brother, and he seeks admittance as John's heir, and the tenement is transferred to him to hold by the rod, fine 8s.,[66] pledge the hayward. Upon this, Henry Crane remitted all claim which he had in this tenement.

+Richard Patel and Joan his wife purchased from Thomas of Felsham ['Falsham'] 1a.1r. of wood in Westhorpe, called Scutteswood, of the lord's fee, *viz.* of the tenement Scuttes, to hold to them and the heirs born of Richard's body. \And if Richard dies without an heir, the tenement shall revert to Agnes the daughter of Thomas Patel chaplain; and if the said Alice [*sic*] dies without an heir the tenement shall revert to the heirs of Thomas of Felsham in perpetuity./[67]

---

[66] Margin: 'and no more because the lord had an ewe as a heriot after the death of John, his brother'.

[67] This insertion is also in the different hand, as is the amendment to the sum. It seems likely that all these insertions were the work of the clerk who audited the Account.

Richard the son of Walter Qualm comes and seeks admittance to his tenement, after the death of his father, *viz.* 3½a. of land and a third part of a messuage. He says that he should have entry without paying a fine, because entry fine was paid after his father's death. Upon this an enquiry was held by 12 [men] sworn and tried (*?triat'*), *viz.* William Rampolye, Walter the smith, John Man, Simon Rampolye, William of Cranmer the elder, John Syre, Walter Payn, Richard Kebbil, Simon Peyntour, Thomas Fuller, John Terwald and Stephen Cooper, who say that Richard, after the death of his father, paid a fine for having entry. Questioned whether they wish this to be their final verdict, under penalty as appropriate, they say that they do not. Upon this, they scrutinised the roll of the court of Wednesday the feast of St Gregory the Pope in the 18th year of King Edward, father of Edward, the present king [12 March 1325],[68] in which roll it was found that Cristiana, Richard's mother, paid 12s. fine for having custody of Richard and of the tenement until Richard's full age, and not for his entry, as heir. [*several words illeg.*] William Rampolye and his fellow-jurors for their false presentment are amerced 12s. Ordered to take the tenement into the lord's hands, and to report the profits. Afterwards, Richard comes and pays 6s.8d. fine for entry, pledges Robert Tailor and the hayward.

Surrender: William Wauncy to John his son and his heirs, a plot on the east side of William's messuage, 2½p. wide and 5p. long, granted to him to hold in villeinage, by services and works, fine 4d., pledge the hayward.

Ordered to execute the orders of the preceding court, marked with a cross, and not acted upon.

SUM 72s., except 12d. rent, as above[69]<br>Affeerers: Robert Sare and Robert Tailor

## 112.   HIGH HALL Court, 25 April 1342 [HA504/1/4.26.ii]

John Wodebite, defendant v John Man in a plea of debt, essoins by Henry Trusse. They have a day until Thursday in Whitsun week [23 May].

Ordered to attach William Kembald for trespass in the lord's wood, corn and meadow with his pigs.

William Wodebite amerced 6d. because he did not rebuild a house on the tenement Aprilles, for which he had a day etc.; ordered to rebuild before the next court.

+John Helpe the hayward amerced 12d. because he did not take into the lord's hands 3a. of land, which John of Angerhale demised to Henry the parson of Westhorpe without leave. Ordered to seize, and to report the profits.

+William Lene the shepherd of Walsham manor, and the shepherd of [this] manor caused damage in the lord's wheat at Sheephouse; William Payn and John Syre did likewise; John Syre, William Kembald and William Payn did likewise at Stonylond. Ordered.

+Agnes Wodebite in mercy for waste in the lord's bondage demolishing a house, condoned; ordered to rebuild.

Hubert the lord's shepherd places himself in mercy with Nicholas at the Hatch, in a plea of debt; amerced 3d. The same Hubert amerced 3d. for trespass in the lord's corn, with sheep in his custody, pledge the hayward.

---

[68] The year 18 Edw.II ran from 8 July 1324 to 7 July 1325; and 12 March 1325 fell on a Tuesday. There is an error in the day quoted or the year; if 'Wednesday' is correct, the year should be 1326.
[69] The sum was originally shown as '65s.3d.'; it was amended to '72s.9d.', and then '9d.' was deleted.

John Pynfoul amerced 3d. because he owes suit and does not come.

John of Angerhale villein amerced 10 sheep because he absents himself from the lord, in contempt; ordered to attach John, and to seize all the lands which he holds from the lord, and to report the profits.

Robert of Angerhale the lord's swineherd amerced 9d., because by his neglect a pig, worth 6d., died; and because his pigs caused damage in the lord's orchard, pledge the hayward.

Walter of Allwood amerced 7½d. for damage in the lord's wheat, estimated at 1 bushel.

Nicholas de Walsham complains of Nicholas at the Hatch in a plea of debt.

SUM 3s. 7½d.

### 113. WALSHAM Court, 3 July 1342 [HA504/1/4.29.i]

Robert Crane essoins of common suit, by Henry Crane; he pledges faith.

Robert the farmer amerced 6d. for damage in the lord's wood by his servant Geoffrey, cutting ash boughs and sticks, pledge Thomas of the Beck.

John Terwald and Robert Lene in mercy for default. Afterwards they came.

The jurors, whose names appear in the preceding court, say that Robert at the Brook, who died after the last court, held from the lord 7a. of land and half a messuage by the rod; the lord had no heriot, because Robert had no beast. John his son is his nearest heir, and he comes and pays 6s.8d. fine for having entry, pledges Simon Peyntour and William Typetot.

Robert Crane amerced 3d. because he sold 1½r. of customary land to Manser of Shucford, without leave; ordered to seize.

Walter Springold amerced 6d. for damage in Ladyswood, cutting down and taking away sticks, pledge John Tailor.

The servant of Robert Tailor the hayward amerced 2d. because he blocked a ditch in the lord's meadow, pledge the same Robert.

The servant of Nicholas Goche amerced 3d. for damage in the lord's corn, gathering herbage; Henry Albry 3d. for the same, pledge for both the same Nicholas. John the miller, Peter Margery and Peter Tailor each amerced 3d. for the same, pledge for all Nicholas Goche. Robert Lene amerced 3d. for the same, pledge the hayward; Robert Man amerced 3d. for the same, pledges the hayward and the bailiff.

William of Cranmer amerced 6d. because he had in his fold 20 sheep above the fixed number; William Hawys 6d. for the same with 26 sheep; Robert Rampolye 3d. for the same with 10 sheep, pledge for all the hayward.

Geoffrey Stephen ['Stevene'] of Langham dug on the common of Walsham, making a dung heap there; ordered.

Richard the son of Letitia, John of Wortham and Robert the son of Peter Springold each amerced 3d. for default.

Surrenders: William Cook and Robert his brother to John Terwald and his heirs, 1r. of land, granted to him to hold in villeinage, by services and works, fine 12d., pledge the hayward.

Walter Osbern to John Noble and his heirs, 2r. of land and 1r. of wood, called Agneshedge, granted to him in the same form, fine 4s., pledge Adam Noble.

Alice Helwys to John Terwald and his family (*sequela*) ½a. of land, granted to him to hold by services and works, fine 2s., pledge the hayward.

Ordered to execute the orders of the last court, marked with a cross, and not acted upon.

SUM 18s. 10d.

### 114.   WALSHAM Court, 25 September 1342 [HA504/1/4.29.ii]

The profits from 2a. of land, now in the lord's hands because Thomas Patel sold it by charter to John Cumpyn without leave, amount to 2d. Ordered to retain and to report the profits.

A day is given to Willliam Wodebite until the next court, to make amends to the lord, because he grazed with 60 sheep where he had no right to graze, pledge Walter Osbern.

John Tolat amerced 4d. for leave to agree with William Rampolye in a plea of debt, pledge William of Cranmer.

Surrenders: Thomas of the Beck to Matthew Gilbert and his heirs, 3r. of land below Spilemanswood, granted to him to hold in villeinage, by services and works, fine 12d., pledge the hayward; and to Walter Springold the younger and his heirs, ½a. of land, abutting on Ladyswood, granted to him in the same form, fine 2s., pledge John Tailor; and to Alice Helewys and her heirs, 1½r. of land at Thiveshedge and ½r. of meadow in the Micklemeadow, granted to her in the same form, fine 2s., pledge the hayward.

Robert Lene the farmer of the cows amerced 3d. for damage in the lord's barley, with geese; William Tailor the farmer of the Churchhouse 3d. for the same, and 1d. for the same with the Prior's pigs, pledge for both the bailiff.

Thomas Cowerde[70] amerced 3d. for trespass, taking away the lord's corn in the autumn, pledge the bailiff.

Hilary Typetot the servant of Reginald Pynfoul did damage in Ladyswood, taking away firewood; ordered; pledge the same Reginald.

Agnes Helewys amerced 3d. because she cut and took away the lord's corn, in the autumn, to the value of 1 sheaf, pledge the bailiff; John Hereward 6d. for the same, by night, pledge <the bailiff and> Roger the serjeant of the rector.

Robert Sare, William Elys, John Typetot, Agnes Suter and Thomas of the Beck each amerced 1d. because they stored corn grown on the bondage, in free tenements.

The jurors say that William Springold the elder villein, 60 years and more ago, held ½a. of land by the rod, and afterwards sold it to Bartholomew Baker, who held it for a long time, until he sold it to Ralph Sare, who held it for his lifetime, by service of one wax [candle] to the church. After Ralph's death, Gilbert Sare his son and heir entered the land, and held it by the said service to the church, until he sold it to Robert his son. Robert has now sold it to John the son of Robert Tailor, by charter. The lord to be consulted.

Robert Springold in mercy for default, afterwards he came.

William of Cranmer, William Hawys, Robert Rampolye and John Herning each amerced 2d. because they had sheep in their folds above the fixed number.

Memorandum that Peter Peyntour died 14 years ago, and after his death, the lord had no heriot, so the jurors believe; the rolls to be scrutinised.

William Kembald and John Tailor were elected to the office of reeve. \and the said William refused to perform the office; therefore ordered to take into the lord's

---

70  This may have been intended as 'the cowherd': it does not appear again as a surname.

261

hands all the tenements which he holds from the lord in villenage, and to report the profits etc./. William Warde and William Typetot were elected to the office of hayward, and William Warde took the oath. William Cook and William Warde were elected to the office of woodward, and William Cook took the oath.

Surrenders: Catherine the widow of Peter Clevehog to John Terwald and his heirs, a piece of meadow 3ft. wide, granted to him to hold in villeinage, by services and works, fine 2d.; and to John the son of Peter Tailor and his heirs, a piece of meadow containing 1r. and 8p., granted to him in the same form, fine 2d., pledge for both the hayward.

William Syre and Robert Hereward were elected to be ale-tasters.

Walter the son of William Springold pays 2s.[71] fine for entry to 2a.3r. of land and a 12th part of a messuage, following his father's death, granted to him in the same form as above, pledges John Tailor and William Springold the younger.

Adam Noble pays 3s. fine for having entry to ½a. of land, remaining in the lord's hands after the death of Agnes Hulke, because no heir came, as shown in the court held on Monday after the feast of St Lucy the Virgin in the same year;[72] granted to him to hold in villeinage, by services and works, pledge the hayward.

Ordered to execute the orders of the last court, marked with a cross, and not acted upon.

Walter the son of William Springold pays 6d. for his headpence because he has absented himself from the lord for six years, pledge the hayward, and he finds a pledge, the hayward, that he will not absent himself. He has leave of suit of court until Michaelmas one year hence.

SUM 14s. 1d.


**115. HIGH HALL Court General of Nicholas de Walsham, 22 October 1342 [HA504/1/4.26.iii]**

John Helpe the hayward amerced 1 quarter of oats because he did not take into the lord's hands 3a. of land, which John of Angerhale demised to Henry the parson of Westhorpe, without leave. Ordered to retain in the lord's hands, and to report the profits.

Ordered to attach William Lene the shepherd of Walsham manor, William Kembald and William Payn for damage in the lord's wheat at Sheephouse.

Agnes Wodebite amerced 3d. for waste in the lord's bondage demolishing a house; ordered to rebuild; and 3d. because she did not come to court.

The first pledges of John Wodebite amerced 9d. because they did not have him reply to John Man in a plea of debt; ordered to make him come by four [new pledges].

Henry of Hattele amerced 3d. because he owes suit and does not come as forewarned.

Robert the lord's swineherd amerced 9d. for damage with pigs, in the lord's wheat at Doucedeux, to the value of 1½ bushels; Bartholmew Goche 2d. for damage in the lord's peas, ½ bushel; John Packard 2d. for damage in the lord's meadow at Smallbrook, to the value of 1½d.; Hubert the shepherd 12d. for the same with sheep, to the value of 7d.

William Kembald did damage in the lord's peas at Hamstale, 2 sheaves; William

---

71 Margin: 'and no more because the lord had a heriot'.
72 This is an error; the date of the court cited (no.110) was 17 December 1341.

Cook the same in the lord's wheat at Dousedewes, 2 sheaves; William Hawys, William Payn and Nicholas Drake the same in the lord's peas at Sheepcote, 3 sheaves; John Syre, John Fraunceys and William Deneys the same with their beasts in the lord's peas at Hamstale, to the value of 3d.; Nicholas the shepherd of Robert of Walpole the same in the lord's oats, 1 sheaf; John Syre and William Payn the same with horses in the lord's oats, 3 sheaves; William Payn the same with beasts in the lord's pasture, oats and peas at Sheephouse, to the value of 1d.; William Cook the same in the lord's wheat at Ulvesrowe, 4 sheaves.[73] Bartholomew Goche amerced 2d. for damage in the lord's peas at Netherhawe, to the value of 1½d. Robert Hereward caused damage with his pigs, rooting in the lord's manor, ordered; the lord's swineherd amerced 1d. for the same.

Peter Goche villein amerced 3d. because he was warned to perform autumn works, and did not come.

Ordered to seize into the lord's hands 1r. of land, which Richard Banlone purchased from John [of] \Angerhale/,[74] and to retain; also to report the profits. The whole homage amerced 2s. because they concealed and did not present the aforesaid sale of land.

William Wodebite amerced 6d. because he did not distrain on 'outside' merchants, lying on the lord's land, making paths there, etc.

The homage have a day until the next court to certify who may raise folds, with or without leave, under penalty of ½ mark.

William Wodebite was elected to the office of reeve, and afterwards came and paid 40d. fine for the office. Robert of Angerhale was elected to the office of collector, and takes the oath. John Helpe amerced 6d. because he does not perform that office, as he is excused.

SUM 10s. 5d.

Affeerers: John Packard and Robert of Angerhale

## 116. HIGH HALL Court of Nicholas de Walsham, 26 April 1343 [HA504/1/4.30.i]

Henry Trusse essoins of common [suit], by John Man; he pledges faith.

John of Angerhale pays 2s. fine for repossessing 3a. of land from the lord's hands, taken because he demised these 3a. to Henry the parson of Westhorpe church for a term of years, without leave, and because he absented himself from the lord, and for many defaults, pledges William Wodebite and Adam of Angerhale.

Ordered as elsewhere to attach William Kembald for damage in the lord's wheat at Sheephouse with his beasts.

Agnes Wodebite amerced 6d. because she did not rebuild a house, as she was ordered, pledge William Wodebite; and ordered to rebuild the said house. \Afterwards it is rebuilt./

Ordered as elsewhere to attach William Kembald for trespass in the lord's peas at Hamstale, to the value of 2 sheaves; and Nicholas Drake for the same at Sheepcote, 3 sheaves \condoned by the lord/; and John Fraunceys for the same at Hamstale, 3 sheaves; William Deneys amerced 2d. for the same with his beasts, pledge Walter Osbern.

---

[73] Margin: against each of the last eight entries the word 'ordered' is written.

[74] MS: 'Angerhale' is inserted over 'Helpe', which was not deleted: similar entries in subsequent courts show the former to be correct.

John Man amerced 6d. for his false claim against John Wodebite in a plea of debt, pledge William Deneys.

Ordered as elsewhere to attach Nicholas the shepherd of Robert of Walpole for damage in the lord's oats, to the value of 1 sheaf.

Ordered as elsewhere to retain in the lord's hands 1r. of land, which Richard Banlone bought by charter from John of Angerhale villein, without leave, 10 years ago, and to report the profits. Memorandum that half of this 1r. is sown with barley.

Robert Sare amerced 3d. for default.

William Wodebite amerced 18d. because he raised a fold to the number of 4 score sheep, without leave, pledges John Helpe and the hayward. Robert Helpe and John Helpe each amerced 3d. for the same, for 20 sheep, pledges William Wodebite and John Goche.

Adam of Angerhale amerced 1d. because he had one ewe and one lamb lying outside the lord's fold, pledge John Packard.

John Packard amerced 2d. for having four hoggets lying outside the lord's fold, pledge William Wodebite.

Ordered [to attach] John Syre for damage by a sow, rooting in the garden of Gothelards \condoned by the lord/.

Ordered to execute the orders of the last court, marked with a cross, and not acted upon.

SUM 5s. 8d.<br>Affeerers: John Packard and Robert of Angerhale

### 117. WALSHAM Court General, 3 November 1343 [HA504/1/4.31]

Bartholomew Jerico, plaintiff v William Leche in a plea of debt, essoins by Peter Margery; and as plaintiff v Ralph of Rudham chaplain, in a plea of trespass, by Manser of Shucford; Bartholomew pledges faith; ordered, as elsewhere, to attach William and Ralph to reply.

+The first pledges of John Withon amerced 6d. because they did not have him reply to the lord concerning the illegal recovery from Richard Patel, the lord's bailiff, of 50 sheep, taken upon him [John] for services and works withheld; ordered to appoint better pledges.

+The profits from 2½a. of land, in the hands of Richard of Caldewell, a bastard,[75] after the death of Bartholomew Patel, because Richard purchased this land jointly with Bartholomew from a certain Richard Patel villein, by the rod, amount to 18d. Ordered to report the profits.

+The profits from 3r. of land, remaining in the lord's hands following the death of John Godhous, because he purchased this land from William Patel, Robert Totay and Richard Herirof, villeins, etc., [amount to] 18d.

Peter Neve amerced 3d. for grazing on the common of Walsham, where he had no right to graze, and for trespass with his sheep in the lord's pasture, pledge William Wither.

Surrenders: Robert Crane and Manser of Shucford to Walter the smith and his heirs, ½r. of land, granted to him to hold in villeinage, by services and works, fine 6d.;

---

[75] This is an error: this land was taken into the lord's hands after Bartholomew's death in 1339 (roll no.102).

Robert Crane to Manser of Shucford and his heirs, 1½r. of land lying at Chequersgate ['Chiceresgate'], at the head of the toft of Robert Kembald, granted to him in the same form, fine 18d.; Robert Hereward to Thomas Fuller and his heirs, 1½a.5p. of land, granted to him in the same form, fine 4s., pledge for all the hayward.

Walter Hawys amerced 6d. for leave to agree with John the son of William the bailiff, in a plea of debt; and Robert Cook 3d. for leave to agree with the same John in a plea of trespass; and Walter Hawys 1d. for leave to agree with Robert of Elvedon ['Helveton'[76]] in a plea of debt, pledge for both the hayward.

Alice Hore amerced 2d. for trespass in the lord's wood, and William Godyene 2d. for the same in the lord's pasture, pledge for both the bailiff.

Surrenders: Robert Rampolye and Agnes his wife, she being examined in court, to John Terwald and his heirs, a piece of meadow in the Micklemeadow, 30p. long and 8ft. wide, granted to him to hold in villeinage, by services and works, fine 6d.; Alice Typetot to John Terwald and his heirs, a piece of meadow in the Micklemeadow, 30p. long and 1½ft. wide, granted to him in the same form, fine 2d., pledge for all the hayward.

+Ralph Neve, when he died, held from the lord 4a. of land and a pightle, containing 1a. of uncultivated [land], and ½r. of meadow; the lord had as a heriot a cow after calving, worth 8s., which was charged in the last account. Robert Warde and Richard and William his brothers, kinsmen of Ralph, are his heirs, and they do not come. Ordered to take into the lord's hands. Ralph also held a messuage and ½a. of land; William the smith and Peter Neve, kinsmen, are his heirs, and they do not come. Ordered as before.

The goats of the manor did damage in Ladyswood, and the goatherd is in mercy, condoned.

John Herning amerced 3d. for having 3 sheep in his fold above the fixed number; William Hawys and William of Cranmer 3d. each, for each having 6 sheep above the fixed number.

Alice Pye amerced 6d. for brewing and selling ale in breach of the assize; Walter Rampolye 3d. and John of Foxley 12d. for the same. Robert Lenne and George of Brockley each amerced 1d. for regrating bread. William Syre and Robert Hereward, the ale-tasters, each amerced 1d., because they did not perform their duties.

John Terwald amerced 3d. for having in his fold 6 sheep above the fixed number.

Amice Hereward amerced 2d. for gleaning badly in the autumn, pledge John Hereward.

Robert Sare, William Elys, John Tipetot, Agnes Suter and Thomas of the Beck each amerced 1d. for storing corn grown on the bondage, in a free tenement.

Robert Hereward amerced 3d. for digging on the common to the common nuisance.

John Pynfoul amerced 2d. for trespass against Walter the smith, to his loss of 3d.; ordered to raise; and 1d. for leave to agree with Walter in a plea of debt, pledge the hayward.

Walter [Craske], the miller, in mercy for contempt, in that he refused to testify on oath to inform on those who milled away from the lord's mill \condoned/.

John Man amerced 2d. because he milled away from the lord's mill.

---

[76] This may be a misreading of 'Helneton', which would probably have been 'Thelnetham', sometimes written 'Thelneton'.

Robert Osbern amerced 2d. for default.

+Roger, the Prior of Ixworth, tilled 1a. of customary land of the tenement Springold, lying in the Stubbing, next to the Pedderespath, and took away the crop without leave; ordered etc.

William Typtetot complains of Robert Typetot in a plea of trespass, pledge the hayward; ordered etc.

John Terwald and Robert Rampolye pay 3s. fine for having a fold of 6 score sheep until Michaelmas; William Hawys pays 3s. fine for 7 score sheep, of which 20 are without fine; William of Cranmer 2s.6d. for 7 score sheep, 40 without fine; John Herning 18d. for 60 sheep, pledge for all the hayward.

+Ordered as elsewhere to attach John Hawys chaplain to reply to Nicholas Wauncey in a plea of debt; +and John Nug for trespass in the lord's warren by his servant, Richard Alot, setting snares in Ladyswood.

+Ordered to retain in the lord's hands part of a messuage and 8a. of land, which William the bastard son of Letitia Stronde purchased with William of Cranmer the younger from Letitia, as shown in the court of 1 December 1340 [no.107], and to report the profits.[77]

Alice Pye amerced 6d., Walter Rampolye and John of Foxley 3d. each, brewers, because they did not send for the ale-tasters.

+Ordered to attach William Wyswyf, John Rede and William Doo, villeins, because they absent themselves from the lord; and Ralph of Rudham chaplain to reply to William Hawys in a plea of trespass, and to Bartholomew Jerico in a like plea.

+Ordered to retain in the lord's hands 1a.3r. of customary land, which William Noreys sold to John of Foxley by charter, without leave.

Ordered to attach Olivia the daughter of Gilbert Priour, villein, because she married without leave.

Ordered to attach Geoffrey Stephen of Langham for making a dungheap on the common of Walsham, and for overstocking the common with his sheep.

+Ordered to retain in the lord's hands 2a. of customary land, which Thomas Patel sold to John Cumpyn by charter, without leave.

+Ordered to attach Reginald Pynfoul for damage in Ladyswood, by Hilary Typetot his servant, taking away firewood.

+Ordered to retain in the lord's hands 1a.3r. of customary land, which William Gobald freeman sold by charter to John Gobald his son without leave; also 1½ acres of customary land which John Longe freeman sold by charter to Walter Pykhorn without leave.

Ordered to attach Sir William Tallemache for four autumn works, two ploughings and suit of court [withheld] for the tenement Outlawe, and because he had 6 score sheep in the fold, formerly of Adam Richard, in which only 60 sheep are allowed.

+Ordered to retain in the lord's hands a piece of free land, 8p.2ft. long and 8ft. wide, which Walter the smith villein purchased from Olivia Rampolye by charter, without leave; +and all the tenement which William Kembald held of the lord's bondage, [taken] because he refused to perform the office of reeve, and to report the profits.[78]

Ordered to distrain John the son of Thomas of the Beck to show by what right he

---

77 Margin: 'Profits in the granary, and in the account'.
78 Margin: 'Profits in the granary'.

entered 24a. of land of the lord's fee, and for fealty etc. Afterwards he swore fealty.

Ordered to retain in the lord's hands a piece of wood, containing 3½r., which Rose Stronde sold to Edmund Lene without leave; afterwards the lord bought the said wood.

Ordered to attach Robert the farmer of Ashfield for trespass in the lord's warren by Robert and John his sons, setting nets and other traps, also with their dogs, and for trespass in the lord's wood by Robert and John, cutting down and taking away [wood]. Ordered to attach John the parson of Langham for the same, by his servants.

Ordered to attach Thomas Locksmith ['Loksmith'] for trespass by his servants, taking stakes[79] from Ladyswood, and John of Boynhawe for the same by his wife.

+Ordered to retain in the lord's hands 2a. of customary land, which Agnes the widow of Adam Sket held, [taken] because she married without leave, and to report the profits. \Profits 6s.6d./

+Ordered to distrain Geoffrey at the Lee for 1d. rent withheld, for 1½r. of meadow of the tenement Margery, and for fealty.

SUM 27s. 1d., except 1 cow, worth 8s, as a heriot,
in last year's account, also 6s.6d. profits

## 118. HIGH HALL Court of Nicholas de Walsham, 17 November 1343 [HA504/1/4.30.ii]

William Elys essoins of common suit, by Robert Kembald; Henry Littlehawe of the same, by Richard Trusse.[80] Ralph Wybert, defendant v Walter Petipas in a plea of debt, essoins by Walter Cristmesse; he pledges faith; the plaintiff is present.

The collector amerced 1d. because he did not have a parchment [for the roll].

William Isabel, Robert Helpe, John Goche, Peter Goche and John Chapman each amerced 3d. for default.

Robert [of Angerhale] the collector amerced 3d. because he did not execute the court's order to distrain William Kembald; ordered to attach William.

+Ordered to attach William Kembald for damage in the lord's peas, and Nicholas the shepherd of Robert of Walpole for the same, in the lord's oats.

Richard Banlone amerced 3d. for default. Ordered to retain in the lord's hands 1r. of land, which Richard purchased by charter from John of Angerhale villein without leave, 10 years ago, and to report the profits.[81] +Ordered to attach Richard to reply to Adam of Angerhale in a plea of trespass.

Ordered to attach <Ralph Wybert>[82] to reply to Walter Petipas in a plea of debt.

Richard Banlone pays a fine for entry to 1r. of villein land, which John of Angerhale surrendered to the use of him and his heirs, to hold at the lord's will, by services and works; \fine waived by the lord/. The lord granted to Richard that he should make only one suit [of court] per year for this land.

Walter Petipas amerced 3d. for a false claim against John Packard and Alice his wife in a plea of trespass.

[79] MS: *sculpat*': Latham gives *sculpare* – to trim timber, also *stulpa – post or stake.*
[80] Margin: 'It does not lie because the essoiner did not specify a day.
[81] Margin: 'Order void because afterwards he pays a fine'.
[82] The deletion of the plaintiff's name indicates deletion of the whole entry; see the defendant's essoin above.

John of Angerhale amerced 1d. for a false claim against Adam of Angerhale in a plea of pledge, and 1d. for the same against John Goche in a like plea.

Robert Helpe amerced 2d. because he was not (?*non fuit*) the pledge of John of Angerhale; Henry Helpe 3d., John Helpe 3d., and William Isabel 2d., for the same.

William Wodebite amerced 3d. because he withheld 9d. from Agnes of Angerhale, as she complains; ordered to raise.

Agnes Wodebite amerced 3d. for a false claim against William Wodebite in a plea of debt.

John of Angerhale amerced 3d. because he disposed of villein land without leave.

William Cook caused damage in the lord's oats at Allwood with his cows; ordered; \order waived/. Hubert the lord's shepherd amerced 1d. for the same with sheep; Simon the lord's swineherd, 1d. for damage in the lord's peas with pigs, and 1d. for the same in the lord's wheat above the wood; Bartholomew Goche the keeper of the cows and Richard Banlone, 1d. each for the same. Bartholomew Goche, 2d. for damage in the lord's barley with cows. Simon the lord's swineherd, 1d. for damage in the lord's wheat with pigs, and 1d. for damage in the lord's barley. William Cook did damage in the lord's barley and peas; ordered; \order waived/. +Ordered [to attach] William Hawys and William Kembald for damage in the lord's barley; and Simon Peyntour for damage in the lord's meadow with horses and cows. Hubert the lord's shepherd amerced 3d. for damage in the lord's meadow with sheep; John Packard 1d. for damage in the lord's meadow with his cows. +Ordered [to attach] William Payn for damage in the lord's wood with sheep, and William Rampolye and John the son of Simon Rampolye for damage in the lord's wood. Robert Banlone amerced 3d. for damage in the lord's wood with horses.

The same Robert, the driver, amerced 6d. because he did not keep the oxen and stots for the plough, as he should.

John Packard amerced 1d. because he rode the lord's horse without permission.

Bartholomew Goche and Clara Heyward amerced 6d. for trespass, fornicating in the lord's manor. Clara Heyward amerced 12d. because she did not close the oast, and as a result, the malt was stolen.

Simon the lord's swineherd amerced 3d. for damage in the lord's pasture and ditches.

Surrender: John of Angerhale to John Packard and his heirs, a quarter part of a close, containing wood and pasture, called Angerhaleyard, with the reversion of a third part, which Agnes of Angerhale holds in dower, granted to him to hold by services and works, fine waived.

William Isabel amerced 6d. because he demised villein land without leave, and because he [unlawfully] detained the goods of Olivia, his mother.

Robert Helpe and the whole homage amerced 11d. because they did not reap the lord's corn in autumn, as they should do. Henry Helpe amerced 3d. because he did not reap with the lord in autumn as he should do.

John Helpe was elected to the office of reeve, fine 2s.. Henry Helpe was elected to the office of collector, fine 2s.

William Elys and Henry Littlehawe each amerced 1d. for default.

SUM 13s. 6d.

Affeerers: John of Angerhale and Robert of Angerhale

## 119.   WALSHAM Court, 3 February 1344 [HA504/1/4.32.i]

Ordered to attach William Leche to reply to Bartholomew Jerico in a plea of debt, and Ralph of Rudham chaplain, to Bartholomew in a plea of trespass.

William Rampolye amerced 2d. for unlawful detention of 3s.2d. from John of Gousle of Thetford, to his loss of 3d.; ordered to raise.

William Typetot amerced 3d. for leave to agree with Robert Typetot in a plea of trespass, pledge the hayward.

General Enquiry by John Syre, Walter Payn, William Rampolye, William Wither, Simon Peyntour, John Man, Robert Tailor, John Terwald, Stephen Cooper, Nicholas Goche, Richard Kebbil and Robert Lene.

Stephen Cooper pays 10s. fine for the office of hayward.

Surrenders: Richard Qualm to John Bolle and his heirs, a third part of ½a. of meadow in the Micklemeadow, granted to him to hold in villeinage, by services and works, fine 8d., pledge the hayward.

William Hawys to John Deeth and his heirs, a cotland in Bornscroft, containing 10p. of land, granted to him in the same form, fine 3d., pledge William Hawys.

It was ordered elsewhere to retain in the lord's hands a pightle, containing 1a. of uncultivated land, 4a. of land and ½r. of meadow, [taken] after the death of Ralph Neve, because Robert, Richard and William Warde, his kinsmen and heirs, did not come. Now Richard and William come and ask for admittance to their shares, and because Robert does not come, the whole tenement is granted to Richard and William to hold by the rod, fine 3s.4d.,[83] pledges Walter Payn and Robert Tailor.

They present that Robert Lene, when he died, held from the lord, by the rod, 2½a. of land and half a messuage, and that the lord had no heriot. Edmund Lene, Robert's brother and nearest heir, comes and pays 8s. fine for entry, pledge Stephen Cooper.

Peter Tailor amerced 3d. because his servant broke and took away the lord's hedges, pledge the hayward; Agnes Fuller 2d. for the same, pledge John Tailor because in [his] house; Amice Hereward 2d. for the same, pledge the hayward; Robert Man 3d. for the same by his wife, pledge the bailiff.

Richard Spileman amerced 1d. for damage in the lord's wood by his servant, pledge the hayward.

The servant of Thomas of Badwell took away branches from Ladyswood; ordered.

Thomas Fuller amerced 3d. for an encroachment at Staple way, digging on the common there, 4p. long and 4ft. wide; ordered etc., pledge the hayward; and 3d. for making a pit on the common, digging clay at Robhodway; ordered. Walter Fuller amerced 3d. for the same. Roger the Prior of Ixworth did the same, ordered etc.

William Gudgeon caused damage in the lord's wheat at the Nineacres with his horse; ordered etc. The farmer of the cows amerced 6d. for damage in the lord's wheat and rye in the Oldtoft and the Millwong, with cows, pledge the bailiff.

Thomas Payn of Ixworth amerced 2d. for making an unlawful way in the Oldtoft, pledge William Payn.

+Walter Rampolye amerced 1d. because he sold to John Barleyhand the reversion of a parcel of a pightle, called Sawyer's pightle, containing ½r.; ordered to take into the lord's hands, and to report the profits.

+John of Stonham amerced 1d. for waste in the lord's bondage, on the tenement

---

[83] Margin: 'and no more because heriot in last court, a cow worth 8s.'.

Goselynges, 4ft. long and 4ft. wide; ordered to take into the lord's hands, and to report the profits.

Richard Spileman, the counter-tallier and thresher, amerced 6s.8d. because he delivered to John the dairyman, out of the lord's barn, peas in the sheaf, fodder, wheat not well threshed, and chaff of barley, to the value of 3d., so they say, to the benefit of the same John, without the permission of the granger. The same John amerced 6s.8d. for receiving the said fodder and corn, pledge the bailiff.

William Pach freeman who lives on a free tenement, is a tenant of the lord in bondage, and has a daughter called Amice, who is free and holds nothing from the lord; she gave birth out of wedlock, and it is not known whether she should pay childwite,[84] or not. The jurors have a day until the next.

+It was ordered elsewhere to retain in the lord's hands a messuage ½a. of land, [taken] after the death of Ralph Neve, because William the smith and Peter Neve his kinsmen and heirs did not come to pay a fine. Now William the smith comes and asks for admittance to half of the said tenement, and he is admitted, fine 18d., pledges John Terwald and the hayward. Because Peter did not come to pay a fine, the other half shall remain in the lord's hands. It is valued at 4d. per year, in addition to services and works; and is demised to Alice Neve for her lifetime, for 6d. per year [rent], pledge Walter Payn.

Surrenders: John Man to William Patel the younger and his heirs, 4p. of uncultivated land at the Oldtoft, granted to him to hold in villeinage, by services and works, fine 2d., pledge the hayward.

John Man to Robert Lene and his heirs, ½r. of meadow in the Micklemeadow, granted to him to hold in villeinage, fine 6d., pledge the hayward.

Ordered to execute the orders of the last court, marked with a cross, and not acted upon.

SUM 40s. 8d., except 6d. annual rent

### 120. HIGH HALL Court of Nicholas de Walsham, 24 February 1344 [HA504/1/4.33.i]

William of Cranmer essoins of common suit, by William Deneys; he pledges faith.

Ralph Wybert amerced 3d. for leave to agree with Walter Petipas in a plea of debt, pledge the hayward.

John Ostreld and his pledges amerced 3d. because he did not proceed against Simon Peyntour in a plea of trespass.

Richard Banlone amerced 3d. for leave to agree with Adam of Angerhale in a plea of trespass.

Walter Petipas and his pledges amerced 3d. because he did not proceed against Ralph Wybert in a plea of debt.

John Pynfoul and William Manser each amerced 3d. for default.

Robert of Angerhale the hayward amerced 6d. because he did not execute an order of the court; ordered as elsewhere to attach William Kembald for damage in the lord's peas at Hamstale, and in his barley at Southbrook.

Henry Helpe amerced 3d. for unlawful detention of 12d. from Henry the shepherd, as he admitted in open court, the loss remitted, pledges Robert Helpe and John

---

84 MS: *heriettare*, 'to pay a heriot', inappropriate for an illegitimate birth.

Helpe; ordered to raise. Henry the shepherd in mercy for a false claim against John and Robert Helpe in a plea of debt, condoned.

The whole homage amerced 3s.4d. because they concealed the fact that Robert Banlone and Bartholomew Goche took away apples, pears and other fruits from the lord's orchard; ordered to attach Robert and Bartholomew for this trespass.

John Packard the plough-holder amerced 3d. for trespass against the lord, because by night he went out of the manor house to his own house, pledge the hayward.

William Isabel, by leave of the court, demised to William Manser 3a. of customary land, from Michaelmas next for the following five years full and complete. William Manser pays 12d. fine for having his term, pledge the hayward.

SUM 6s. 10d.

## 121. WALSHAM Court General, 12 April 1344 [HA504/1/4.32.ii]

John Deeth, defendant v Warin Bret in a plea of trespass, essoins by Robert Boton(?); he pledges faith; Warin is present.

Roger the Prior of Ixworth amerced 3d. for making an encroachment at Robhodway, digging a claypit on the common.[85]

Edmund Lene in mercy for default. Afterwards he came.

Surrenders: Richard Warde and William Warde to Matthew Gilbert and his heirs, 1½r. of land in two pieces, granted to him to hold in villeinage, by services and works, fine 12d.; and to Robert Tailor and his heirs, 1½r. of land, granted to him in the same form, fine 16d., pledge for both the hayward.

Walter Hawys to John the son of William Hawys and his heirs, a plot within a messuage, with a bakehouse built on it, 2½p. long and 1½p. wide, with ingress to and egress from the same, granted to him in the same form, fine 3d., pledge as before.

John Terwald to John the son of Edmund Patel and his heirs, ½a. of land, granted to him in the same form, fine 2s., pledge as before.

Edmund Lene and Stephen Cooper amerced 3d. for unlawful detention of 24s.4¾d. from Robert of Coney Weston ['Coneweston'] chaplain, as they acknowledged in open court, to his loss of 2s.; ordered to raise.

Surrender: Simon Peyntour to Matthew Hereward and his heirs, 1½r. of meadow in the Micklemeadow, granted to him in the same form as above, fine 12d., pledge the hayward.

Beatrice Patel gave birth out of wedlock; childwite 2s.8d. A day is given to the jurors to enquire by the next whether Amice Patel gave birth out of wedlock, or not.

Eleanor, the servant of Peter Tailor, and Matilda Herning each amerced 2d. for unlawfully gathering and taking away firewood.

John Baxter amerced 6d., Walter Rampolye 3d. and John of Foxley 3d. for brewing and selling ale in breach of the assize. Robert Lenne and George of Brockley each amerced 2d. for regrating bread. William Syre and Robert Hereward the ale-tasters each amerced 2d. because they did not perform their duties.

Robert Osbern amerced 3d. for default.

William and Robert Cook amerced 2d. because they sold to Thomas Fuller, without leave, 2r.10p. of land at the Machons; and ordered to take into the lord's hands.

---

[85] Margin: 'and no more, because afterwards it was attested that on his own soil'.

Afterwards William and Robert surrendered the tenement, to the use of Thomas Fuller; granted to him and his heirs to hold in villeinage, by services and works, fine 2s., pledge the hayward.

William Pach amerced 3d. for default.

Memorandum that Walter Rampolye acknowledges that he owes 31s. to Robert the son of William Hawys and Olivia, Robert's wife, for 8 quarters of malt bought from him, to be paid to Robert at these terms, *viz.* at Michaelmas next 15s., and at the following Michaelmas 16s., and to pay faithfully, for which he finds mainpernors, *viz.* William Rampolye, Robert Rampolye and Simon Rampolye, who commit themselves, jointly and severally, if Walter does not pay.

Olivia Patel pays 3s.4d. fine for leave to marry Robert Page of Sapiston, pledges William of Cranmer, John Man and the hayward.

Ordered to execute the orders of the last court, marked with a cross, and not acted upon.

SUM 16s. 9d.

### 122.   WALSHAM Court, 26 July 1344 [HA504/1/4.34]

Richard Kebbil, defendant v John Swete in a plea of debt, essoins by Robert Sare; he pledges faith; John is present. <Alice Kembald, defendant v Olivia Rampolye in a plea of trespass, essoins by William Kembald>.[86] Robert Crane essoins of common suit, by Robert Kembald. John Cumpyn, plaintiff v Thomas Patel in a plea of covenant, essoins by William Gobald. Richard Patel, claimant v Thomas Patel chaplain, Richard Patel the younger, William Godhous and Gundreda his wife, in a plea of land, essoins by Robert Pye.[87]

John Deeth amerced 3d. for leave to agree with Warin Bret in a plea of trespass, pledge the hayward.

The first pledges of Alice Kembald amerced 6d. because they did not have her reply to Olivia Rampolye in a plea of trespass; ordered to appoint better pledges.

Surrenders: William Hawys and Massilia his wife, she being examined in court, to John Noble and his heirs, 1a.1r. of land at Agneshedge, granted to him to hold in villeinage, by services and works, fine 4s., pledge the hayward.

William Warde the younger of Palmer street to Richard Warde his brother and his heirs, a cotland, 27ft. long and 26ft. wide, with ingress to and egress from it, granted to him in the same form, fine 6d., pledge as before.

Nicholas Goche and William of Cranmer the elder amerced 3d. for unlawful detention of 16d. from Walter the smith, to his loss of 3d.; ordered to raise.

Richard Kebbil and Peter Margery amerced 6d. for unlawful detention of 8s. from William of Cranmer the elder and Nicholas Goche, who are responsible for [the upkeep of] the church fabric (?*collectoribus op' ecclesie*), to the use of the church of Walsham, the loss is 6d.; ordered to raise. The sum of 8s. is part of a debt of 15s.; [the residue of] 7s. remains under the consideration and judgment of the lord and the townspeople, because Richard and Peter claim a share of it, having paid their fines before Sir Thomas de Wake in his sessions at [Bury] St Edmunds.

Surrenders: William Clevehog to John of Stonham and his heirs, 1½r. of land,

---

86  Margin: 'It does not lie because the essoiner does not specify a day'.
87  References to this plea recur at every court until 23 Feb. 1347.

granted to him to hold in villeinage, by services and works, fine 12d., pledge the hayward.

William Warde the younger of Palmer street to John the son of Peter Tailor, and his heirs, 1r.3p. of meadow in the Micklemeadow, granted to him in the same form, fine 12d., pledge as before.

Matthew Gilbert in mercy because he refused to take the oath as ordered, condoned.

Agnes the wife of William Cook amerced 6d. for damage in the lord's corn gathering herbage, pledge the hayward. The Prior of Ixworth in mercy for damage in the lord's rye with his geese, condoned. Hilary the servant of Robert Tailor amerced 2d. for damage in the lord's corn gathering herbage; William Wauncy 1d. for the same, pledge for both the hayward; Alice Helewys 3d. for the same, pledge the bailiff; Matthew Hereward 3d., Richard Spileman 2d., Alice Neve 1d., Nicholas Goche, John Craske, Peter Tailor, Robert Man and John Margery each amerced 3d. for the same, pledge for all the hayward.

Thomas Fuller amerced 6d. because he ploughed over the common way at Staple way, 4p. long and 7ft. wide, and 6d. for the same over the common there, 20p. long and 1½ft. wide; Robert Lene 1d. for the same, 4p. long and 1ft. wide, pledge for both the hayward.

John and Robert the sons[88] of Robert the farmer caused damage in the lord's wood, cutting down ash-trees and branches; ordered.

Robert Lene amerced 2s. for raising a fold of 4 score sheep, without leave, pledge the hayward.

William Kembald ploughed over a division between himself and Robert Hereward, 40p. long and 1ft. wide; ordered.

Robert Hereward amerced 1d. for damage in the lord's corn, gathering herbage; William Tallemache 1d. for damage in the lord's wheat in Strondescroft, pledge for both the hayward.

A day is given to William of Cranmer, William Hawys and all the others to make good pits dug on the lord's common, before the next court.

Margaret the servant of Walter Osbern amerced 6d. for damage in the lord's corn gathering herbage, pledge the bailiff; Bartholomew Jerico 6d. for the same, pledge the hayward.

Surrender: Robert Warde to William of Cranmer the elder and his heirs, 1r. of meadow in the Micklemeadow, granted to him to hold in villeinage, by services and works, fine 9d., pledge the hayward.

General Enquiry by William of Cranmer, Walter Payn, John Syre, William Rampolye, Richard Kebbil, John Terwald, Simon Peyntour, Robert Tailor, John Tailor, Matthew Hereward, Robert Lene, Nicholas Goche, William Wither and John Man.

William Hawys amerced 1d. for having 5 sheep in his fold above the fixed number.

Ralph Echeman and John Syre are elected to the office of reeve; William Cook and Thomas Dormour to the office of hayward; John Spileman and Robert Cook to the office of woodward.

Walter Osbern surrendered to the lord a piece of meadow in the Micklemeadow, 34ft. wide and [*blank*] long, and the lord granted it to him to hold for his lifetime,

---

[88] MS: 'servants', but all earlier references to John and Robert and this offence give 'sons'.

and after his death, it shall revert to Robert Lene to hold in villeinage, by services and works, fine 18d., pledge the hayward.

[SUM 17s. 4d., not stated]

### 123. HIGH HALL Court of Nicholas de Walsham, 18 October 1344 [HA504/1/4.33.ii]

[Membrane 33 is torn, and the text faded and damaged by staining: some parts of this roll, and Nos.126 and 128, are illegible. Roll no.129 is also affected.]

Henry of Hattele essoins of common suit, by William Manser; Richard Banlone of the same, by Giles Banlone.

The first pledges of Robert Banlone in mercy because they did not have him make amends to the lord for trespass, taking away apples and pears etc., condoned; ordered to appoint better pledges. The first pledges of Bartholomew Goche in mercy for the same, condoned.

Ordered as elsewhere to attach Nicholas the shepherd of Robert of Walpole for damage in the lord's oats with his sheep.

Robert of Angerhale the hayward, amerced 6d. because he did not execute the orders of the court. Ordered as elsewhere to attach William Hawys for damage in the lord's barley, and Simon Peyntour for the same in his meadows, with their horses and cows; and William Payn, William Rampolye and John the son of Simon Rampolye, for damage in the lord's woods cutting and taking away branches.

Henry Dances the rector of Westhorpe, when he died, held from the lord a messuage, by homage and fealty and services, 1½d. per year to the ward of Eye castle. Bartholomew Henry's brother and nearest heir does not come; ordered to distrain him for homage, fealty, etc.

Robert Banlone the driver of the plough amerced 18d. for defective custody of an ox, as a result of which it lost a horn; and 18d. for defective custody of the plough-oxen by night, to the lord's loss.

John Packard the plough-holder amerced 6d. because he ill-treated the plough-oxen after the time of winter work, to the lord's loss.

Margery Broun a maidservant of the manor amerced 12d. because she unlawfully took away apples and other things, contrary to the lord's orders; and 3d. because she knocked over a vat containing 3 gallons of ale, to the lord's loss; and 12d. because she took away flour from the bakehouse, to the lord's loss.

Simon Peyntour the swineherd of the manor took away fresh fish, viz. roach, [damaged], and white bread from the bakehouse, to the lord's loss.

Robert Banlone the plough-driver amerced 12d. for giving the wrong orders to Nicholas the plough-holder, as a result of which the lord lost a day.

William Wodebite amerced 3d. because he was summoned for winter work for one day, and did not come, pledge [damaged].

William Elys amerced 6d. for damage in the lord's corn, harvesting his oats badly, during two autumn reaping works, pledge the hayward; John Packard 1d. for the same.

Simon Peyntour the swineherd of the manor amerced 3d. for damage in the lord's meadow in Smallbrook with pigs; William Wodebite 2d. and John Packard 1d. for the same. The same Simon 1d. for the same in Hordeshawe with pigs. Walter Noreys the swineherd of William of Cranmer and William Hawys did the same; ordered. Walter Payn did damage in the lord's corn, in the bullimong

['bolemong'], with horses and cows, to the value of 2 sheaves, ordered. Hubert
the shepherd amerced 12d. for damage in the lord's meadow, driving a cart
loaded with various [*illeg.*], pledge Peter Goche.

William Wodebite and all his family (*familia*) amerced 1d. for making an unlawful
way outside Angerhalefield, pledge the hayward.

Robert of Angerhale amerced 3d. for trespass against the lord, breaking a (*illeg.*) in
the lord's garden.

Walter Payn caused damage in the lord's wheat in the Hamstale, to the value of
3 sheaves, and in the lord's peas at Doucedeux, 2 sheaves, ordered. John formerly
the shepherd of Robert of Walpole, did the same at Shortlond, 2 sheaves; Simon
Peyntour and others in Upstreet did the same in the same place, 1 sheaf, ordered.
The shepherds of this manor, of William Tallemache and of the Prior did the
same there, 1 sheaf, ordered. William Payn did damage in the lord's wheat at the
Sheepcote, 1 sheaf, ordered. Nicholas Deneys did the same there, 1 sheaf,
ordered. The shepherds of this manor, of the Prior and of William Hawys did the
same near Allwoodgreen, 4 sheaves, ordered. The shepherd of this manor did
damage in the lord's oats on the Thirtyacres, 2 sheaves, ordered. Thomas
Wauncy, the keeper of the oxen, amerced 6d. for damage in the lord's wheat at
Netherhawe, 6 sheaves; and 1d. for the same in the lord's barley above the wood,
1 sheaf; Robert Banlone 1d. for the same, 1 sheaf, pledge for both the hayward.

William Wodebite amerced 3d. because he was summoned for autumn work, and
did not come.

Adam of Angerhale was elected reeve, and afterwards paid 2s.6d. fine, pledge William [*sic*]. William Wodebite was elected collector, for the tenement of John
Wodebite, and took the oath.

William Wodebite amerced 6s.8d. for contempt to the lord, refusing to provide corn
for the lord's use, on the orders of [*damaged*] and John Helpe.

Simon Peyntour amerced 1d. for damage in Hordeshawe, to the value of 1d.; William Payn did the same in the lord's wheat at Trendelwood with his beasts,
ordered.

[SUM 20s. 11d.]
Affeerers: John Angerhale and Robert Angerhale

## 124.   WALSHAM Court General, 11 December 1344 [HA504/1/4.35]

William Hawys, defendant v Thomas William in a plea of debt, essoins by Robert
Kembald; he pledges faith; Thomas is present.[89]

John Swete and his pledges amerced 3d. because he did not proceed against Richard
Kebbil in a plea of debt. John Cumpyn and his pledges in mercy because he did
not proceed against Thomas Patel, in a plea of covenant, condoned. The second
pledges of Alice Kembald amerced 12d. because they did not have her reply to
Olivia Rampolye, in a plea of trespass; ordered to appoint better pledges.

+William Kembald amerced 3d. for ploughing over a division between himself and
Robert Hereward, 40p. long and 1ft. wide, pledge the hayward; ordered to make
good.

+The profits from ½a. of land of the tenement Goselynges, remaining in the lord's

---

[89]   MS: 'William'.

hands for waste in the same tenement by John of Stonham, [amount to] 15d.; ordered to retain, and to report the profits.

+The profits from 2½a. of land, taken into the lord's hands after the death of Bartholomew Patel, because Richard of Caldewell, Bartholomew's bastard son, purchased this land jointly with him, from a certain Richard Patel villein, [amount to] 6d.; ordered as above.

+The profits from 3r. of land, remaining in the lord's hands after the death of John Godhous, because John purchased this land from William Patel, Robert Totay and Richard Heryrof villeins, [amount to] 6d.; ordered as above.

+Ordered as elsewhere to attach John Withon \dead/, to reply to the lord for the illegal recovery from Richard Patel, the lord's bailiff, of 50 sheep, taken on him for services and works withheld.

+The profits from 2a. of customary land, remaining in the lord's hands because Thomas Patel sold this land to John Cumpyn by charter, without leave, [amount to] 18d.; ordered as above.

+The profits from 1a.3r. of customary land, remaining in the lord's hands because William Gobald freeman sold this land by charter to John Gobald his son, without leave [amount to] 3d.; ordered as above.

+The profits from 1½a. of customary land, remaining in the lord's hands because John Longe freeman sold this land by charter to Walter Pykhorn without leave, [amount to] 5d.; ordered as above. Upon this the jurors have a day, until the next court, to present whether the land is free or customary.

A day is given, at the request of the parties, between Richard Patel the elder, claimant, and Thomas Patel chaplain, Richard Patel the younger, William Godhous <and Gundreda, William's wife>, tenants, concerning a plea of land, until the next court, to come without essoin.

+The first pledges of John Mayheu amerced 3d. because they did not have him reply to John Spileman in a plea of trespass; ordered to appoint better pledges.

+The first pledges of John Lester amerced 3d. because they did not have him reply to Robert of Coney Weston chaplain in a plea of debt; ordered as above. Afterwards John came and placed himself etc., pledge the hayward.

+Ordered as elsewhere to attach Roger, the Prior of Ixworth, because he cultivated 1a. of customary land, of the tenement Springold, lying in the Stubbing, next to Pedderspath, and because he took away crops from this land.

+Ordered as elsewhere to attach John Nugg for trespass in the lord's warren by his servant, Richard Alot, placing snares in Ladyswood.

John Lester amerced 3d. for unlawful detention of 6s.10½d. from Ralph Spicer of [Bury] St Edmunds, as he acknowledged in open court, to the loss of 12d.; ordered to raise.

+Ordered as elsewhere to retain in the lord's hands part of a messuage and 8a. of land, which William the bastard son of Letitia Stronde purchased from Letitia with William of Cranmer the younger, as is shown in the court of 1 December 1340 [no.107], and to report the profits.

John Pynfoul amerced 1d. for trespass against John the bailiff of Sir William Tallemache, to his loss of ½d., as found by the enquiry; ordered to raise.

A day is given, at the request of the parties, between Walter the smith, plaintiff, and William Kembald, defendant, in a plea of trespass, until the next court, to come without essoin.

Alice Kembald amerced 1d. for trespass against William Wither, to his loss of 1d.; ordered to raise.

Surrender: John the son of William Hawys, to John Noble and his heirs, 1a.½r.13½p. of land and pasture at the Stonylond, granted to him to hold in villeinage, by services and works, fine 4s., pledge the hayward.

+Ordered as elsewhere to attach William Wyswyf, John Rede and Walter Doo, villeins, because they absent themselves from the lord.

Surrender: Richard Qualm to John Bolle and his heirs, 30p. of meadow, granted to him in the same form as above, fine 10d., pledge the hayward.

+Ordered as elsewhere to attach Ralph of Rudham chaplain to reply to William Hawys in a plea of trespass, and to Bartholomew Jerico in a like plea.

+Ordered as elsewhere to retain in the lord's hands 1a.3r. of customary land, which William Noreys sold by charter to John of Foxley without leave, and to report the profits.

Ordered as elsewhere to attach Olivia the daughter of Gilbert Priour, villein, because she married without leave.

+Ordered as elsewhere to attach Reginald Pynfoul for damage in Ladyswood, by his servant Hilary Typetot taking away firewood.

+Ordered as elsewhere to attach Sir William Tallemache for four autumn works, two ploughings and suit of court, for the tenement Outlawe and other tenements, [and] because he has 6 score sheep in the fold formerly of Adam Richard, in which only 60 are allowed.

Surrender: Richard Warde to John Tailor and William John's son and their heirs, 1r.3p. of meadow in the Micklemeadow, granted to him to hold in villeinage, by services and works, fine 12d., pledge the hayward.

+Ordered as elsewhere to retain in the lord's hands a piece of free land, 8p.2ft. long and 8ft. wide, which Walter the smith villein purchased from Olivia Rampolye by charter, and to report the profits.

+Ordered as elsewhere to retain in the lord's hands all the tenement which William Kembald holds, because he refused to perform the office of reeve, and to report the profits. Afterwards the tenement was released to William, at the lord's order.

Surrender: Simon Peyntour to John of Stonham and his heirs, 1r. of land, granted to him in the same form as above, fine 9d., pledge the hayward.

+Ordered as elsewhere to attach Robert the farmer of Ashfield for trespass in the lord's warren by Robert and John his sons, setting nets and other traps, and also with their dogs; and for trespass in the lord's wood by Richard and John, cutting and taking away wood. +Ordered to attach John the parson of Langham for the same, by his servants.

+Ordered as elsewhere to attach Thomas Locksmith for trespass by his servants, taking away stakes out of Ladyswood; and John of Boynhawe for the same by his wife.

+Ordered as elsewhere to retain in the lord's hands 2a. of customary land, which Agnes the widow of Adam Sket held, because she married without leave.

General Enquiry by William of Cranmer, Walter Payn, John Syre, William Rampolye, Richard Kebbil, John Terwald, Simon Peyntour, Robert Tailor, John Tailor, Robert Lene, Nicholas Goche, William Wither and John Man.

Simon Rampolye, when he died, held from the lord, 5a. of customary land and half a messuage; the lord had a calf, worth 4s., as a heriot. John, William and Roger Simon's sons are his nearest heirs, and they come and have entry by the heriot.

277

Agnes the daughter of Peter Peyntour gave birth out of wedlock; childwite 2s.8d.

John the son of Robert Warde, villein, purchased by charter a messuage 30a. of free land, in Ditton Camoys, in the fee of Sir John de Pounteneys; ordered to seize.

William the bailiff amerced 4d. for damage in the lord's barley at the Mickle-meadow; John Herning 6d., and William Pach 4d., for the same; Walter Fuller 2d. and Sir William Tallemache 3d., for the same in the tenement Strondes, pledge for all the hayward. William the swineherd of the manor amerced 1d. for damage in the lord's rye with pigs, and 1d. for damage in his barley at Strondes, pledge the bailiff.

John Hereward took away timber from the lord's bakehouse at Strondes, and Agnes the servant of Walter Goos did the same; ordered.

The goatherd amerced 2d. for damage in the lord's rye, pledge the bailiff.

Adam the rector of Westhorpe grazed his sheep where he had no right; ordered.

Thomas of the Beck amerced 2d., John Typetot 1d. and William Elys 1d., because they stored, in free tenements, corn grown on the bondage.

Robert Lene amerced 3d. because he had 12 sheep in his fold over the fixed number; William of Cranmer 3d. for the same, 10 sheep; John Herning 2d. for the same, 6 sheep, pledge for all the hayward.

John Baxter and Walter Rampolye each amerced 6d. because they brewed and sold ale in breach of the assize. Robert Lenne and George of Brockley each amerced 1d. for regrating bread. William Syre and Robert Hereward the ale-tasters each amerced 1d. because they did not perform their duties.

John Syre pays 26s.8d. fine for the office of reeve, pledge the hayward. William Cook pays 13s.4d. fine for the office of hayward.

William Hawys pays 3s.6d. fine for having a fold of 8 score sheep, 20 without fine; John Terwald 3s. for a fold of 6 score sheep; Robert Rampolye 18d. for a fold of 60 sheep; William of Cranmer 2s.6d. for a fold of 7 score sheep, 40 without fine; John Herning 18d. for a fold of 60 sheep; Robert Lene 2s. for a fold of 4 score sheep, pledge for all the hayward.

Ralph Echeman pays 26s.8d. fine for the office of reeve for the preceding year, pledges John Tailor and John Terwald.

+Ordered as elsewhere to attach John and Robert the sons of Robert the farmer for damage in the lord's wood, cutting and taking away ash trees and branches; and William Leche to reply to Bartholomew Jerico in a plea of debt, and Ralph of Rudham chaplain to the same Bartholomew in a plea of trespass.

+Ordered as elsewhere to retain in the lord's hands ½r. of land, parcel of a pightle called Sawyerspightle, because Walter Rampolye sold it to John Barleyhand without leave, and to report the profits.

+Ordered as elsewhere to retain in the lord's hands half a messuage and 1r. of land, [taken] after the death of Ralph Neve, because Peter Neve his heir and kinsman does not come to pay a fine. Afterwards it was demised to Alice Neve, to hold for her lifetime, for 6d. per year, pledge Walter Payn.

Surrenders: Matthew Hereward to Robert Hereward his son, chaplain, and his heirs, 2a. of land, 1½a. of meadow and ½a. of pasture, of which, ½a. of land lies in the croft of Walter Hereward, ½a. lies at Longelond, abutting on the messuage of John the son of Robert Tailor, ½a. lies on Brightwaldistoft, between Matthew's land and that of William Cook, and ½a. lies below Ladyswood, between the land of John Digge and Newecroftmere, the 1½a. of meadow lie in the Mickle-meadow, between the meadow of Robert Warde and that of Thomas Fuller, and

278

the ½a. of pasture lies between the messuage of the Prior of Ixworth and that of John Wauncy, abutting at one head on the king's highway called Palmer street; granted to him to hold in villeinage, by services and works, fine waived.

Walter Fuller to Robert Hereward chaplain and his heirs, 2a.3r. of land, in one piece, called the Bergh, lying between the land of Thomas Hereward and that of Alice the daughter of Robert the cooper, granted to him to hold in the same form, fine waived.

A day is given, at the request of the parties, between John Cumpyn, plaintiff, and Thomas Patel chaplain, defendant, in a plea of covenant, until the next court, to come without essoin.

+Memorandum that the lord is to be consulted concerning the fact that William Kembald holds, within his messuage, ½a. of customary land, where his barn is situated, which Simon Kembald his father exchanged with William the smith for ½a. of free land, which Walter the son of William the smith now holds, the said exchanges being made in the time of Lady Eve de Valence.

SUM 100s. 6d., except a calf, worth 4s., as a heriot

Affeerers: John Tailor and Robert Lene

## 125. WALSHAM Court General, 13 April 1345 [HA504/1/4.36]

Alice Kembald amerced 3d. for leave to agree with Olivia Rampolye in a plea of trespass, pledge the hayward.

John Hereward amerced 6d. for trespass against the lord, taking away old timber from the bakehouse Strondes, pledge as above.

John of Stonham pays 6d. fine for repossessing ½a. of land at the tenement Goselyng, remaining in the lord's hands for waste made in this tenement, pledge as above.

Nicholas Smith amerced 3d. for his false claim against Richard Spileman in a plea of debt, pledge the bailiff.

William Kembald was attached to reply to Walter the smith in a plea of trespass, concerning which Walter says that William unlawfully ploughed on his land, and reaped and took away the crop from it, to his loss of 12d.; and he produces suit. William comes and defends, saying that he has made no trespass, as he is accused, and he asks for an enquiry; the other party likewise; ordered.

Thomas William and his pledges amerced 3d. because he did not proceed against William Hawys, in a plea of debt.

Richard Patel the elder claims against Richard Patel the younger, Thomas Patel parson of the church of Thornham Parva, and William Godhous, a toft, 15a. of land, 2r. of meadow, a part of a messuage, and two parcels of two tofts, with appurtenances, in Finningham and Westhorpe. Richard, Thomas and William ask to have sight (*visum*),[90] and they have etc.; ordered.

Richard of Caldewell pays 10s. fine for having 2½a. of land out of the lord's hands, taken because this land came, by virtue of a purchase, into the hands of Richard, who is a bastard, after the death of Bartholomew Patel. Seisin is delivered to him etc., pledges Thomas Patel, Richard Patel the elder, Richard Patel the younger and John Cumpyn.

---

[90] This is assumed to be a request for sight of the rolls, which is usually expressed as 'to have the rolls scrutinised'.

Thomas Patel in mercy for leave to agree with John Cumpyn in a plea of covenant, condoned, pledge Richard Patel the elder.

Richard Warde amerced 2d. for damage in Ladyswood by his servants, taking away firewood; William Warde and Richard Spileman 2d. each for the same; John Tailor 1d. for the same by his servant; Alice Helewys 2d. for the same; pledge for all the hayward.

Thomas of Badwell overstocked the common with his sheep, and grazed where he had no right; also he caused damage with his sheep in the lord's several pasture in Cannonesbrook; ordered. Robert Lene and John Baxter each amerced 3d. for damage there with their sheep, pledge for both the hayward.

John Baxter in mercy for default. Afterwards he came.

John Tailor amerced 1d. for damage in the lord's pasture in the Smithsway with his sheep; John Terwald 3d., Thomas Fuller 2d., Alice Helewys and Ralph Echeman 1d. each, for the same, pledge for all as above.

Agnes Fuller amerced 2d. for breaking down, and taking away the lord's hedges at the Littlemeadow, and around the manor; the servant of Peter Tailor, Matilda Herning and Alice Whiteman 2d. each, for the same, pledge for all as above.

Robert Swyft amerced 1d. because his wife took away firewood at Strondes, pledge as above.

John Baxter, Walter Rampolye and John Pynfoul each amerced 6d. for brewing and selling ale in breach of the assize; Robert Lenne 3d. and George of Brockley 1d. for regrating bread in breach of the assize; Walter Risby 1d. for the same, pledge Walter Osbern, because in [his] house. William Syre and Robert Hereward the ale-tasters each amerced 2d. because they did not perform their duties.

Surrenders: William of Cranmer the elder to Thomas Fuller and Alice his wife and their heirs, 2a. of land at Neatstoft, in exchange for three pieces of land lying above Hulkeswood and at Gothelond, which Thomas and Alice Fuller and John Bonde and Avice his wife, Alice and Avice being examined in court, had surrendered to William of Cranmer. Seisin is delivered to them to hold at the lord's will, by services and works, fine 8s.[91] Thomas and Alice, she being examined in court, to John and Avice and their heirs, 1a. of land in three pieces, lying in Hulkescroft and Wyswyfcroft; seisin delivered to them in the same form, fine 2s., pledge for both parties the hayward.

Alice the daughter of Robert Warde the elder pays 13s.4d. fine for leave to marry John Aylnoth.

+William Kembald pays 3d. fine for setting a boundary between himself and Walter the smith, <and between himself and Robert Hereward at the Tounesende>, pledge the hayward. Ordered to the General Enquiry to set the boundary before the next court.

+A day was given to the General Enquiry, until the next court, to enquire concerning 3r. of land, in the lord's hands after the death of John Godhous, which John purchased from William Patel, Robert Totay and Richard Heryrof villeins, [and to certify] whether there are 3r. or 1r.; also concerning 2a. of customary land, in the lord's hands because Thomas Patel sold it to John Cumpyn by charter, without leave, whether it is all customary land or not; also concerning 1½a. of land, remaining in the lord's hands, which Walter Pykhorn purchased from John Long

---

91 Margin: 'and no more because exchange'.

by charter, whether the land is free or customary; also to apportion the tenement formerly of Agnes at the Green, [and report] how much the tenement contains, who holds it, and by what services; under penalty of 20s. \Afterwards they say concerning the 3r. of land, formerly of John Godhous, that only 1r. is held free from the lord, for services 1d., and the remainder is of the fee of other lords; concerning the 2a., formerly of Thomas Patel, that only 1r. was held from the lord by the rod. Concerning the 1½a., formerly of John Long, and the apportioning of the tenement of Agnes at the Green, they have a day until the next court, under penalty of 20s./

Cristiana the daughter of Edmund Patel pays 3s.4d. fine for leave to marry Andrew Goos, pledges Edmund Lene and William Rampolye.

Margery the daughter of William Rampolye pays 6s.8d. for leave to marry Thomas the son of William of Bacton, pledge William Rampolye.

Ordered to execute the orders of the last court, marked with a cross, and not acted upon.

[SUM 50s. 3d., not stated.]

## 126. HIGH HALL Court, 16 April 1345 [HA504/1/4.33.iii]

Walter Osbern essoins of common suit, by William of Cranmer; William Manser of the same, by Ralph Wybert; and William Elys of the same, by Robert Kembald; they all pledge faith.

Henry of Hattele in mercy because he did not warrant his essoin, condoned. Richard Banlone amerced 3d. for the same.

Nicholas Deneys amerced 1d. for damage in the lord's wheat at Sheepcote, to the value of 1 sheaf, pledge the hayward.

William Rampolye the younger and his pledges amerced 3d. because he did not proceed against Ralph Wybert in a plea of debt.

Robert Helpe, John Helpe and Henry Helpe each amerced 3d. for trespass against John of Angerhale and Adam his brother, in [illeg.] the drove-way (?chaceam) to their lands with ploughs, at the time of sowing wheat, rye, peas, oats and barley, and with carts [illeg.] spreading dung at the appropriate time, called Straytime, to their loss; ordered to raise.

Robert Hovel purchased from Adam Shepherd 1r. of land of the lord's fee; ordered.

Agnes Helpe pays a fine for leave to marry John Chapman; likewise [illeg.] for leave to marry [illeg.], pledge for both the hayward.[92]

Henry Broun, the driver of the plough, amerced 12d. because he drove an ox in the lord's plough badly (?male), to the lord's loss, pledges John Goche and Peter Goche.

Walter of Allwood amerced 3d. because he cut and took away branches of trees, for making hedges outside the manor.

Damage was caused in the lord's wood at Lenerithsdel,[93] to the value of 2d., pledge the collector.[94]

The servants of John Syre and William Cook caused damage in the lord's peas at

---

[92] Margin: amounts of both fines illegible.

[93] Margin: 'mercy 2d.', but no culprit is named. Similar wording is used in two later entries.

[94] Earlier references in this roll to this official of High Hall manor give him the title messor, translated as 'hayward'. In this, and in later references, he is given the title collector.

Kembaldslond, to the value of 1d., ordered; the servant of John Syre did damage in the lord's oats at Regway gathering herbage, ordered.

Agnes of Angerhale amerced 6d. because, two years ago, she demised to Adam Dolhale 1a. of customary land for a term of years, without leave, pledges John of Angerhale and Adam of Angerhale; ordered to take into the lord's hands, and to report the profits. The whole homage amerced 6d. for concealing this demise.

Damage was caused in the lord's several pasture by 'outside' sheep, to the value of 3d.; and to the lord's lands by unlawful roads, made by outsiders, to the lord's loss of 3d., pledge the collector.[95]

William Wodebite amerced 12d. for contempt, in that he failed to appoint a ploughholder, as ordered by the lord, pledge John Packard; John Packard 12d. for the same, pledge William Wodebite.

Ordered to execute the orders of the last court, marked with a cross, and not acted upon.

SUM 10s. 1d.

Affeerers: John Packard and John of Angerhale

### 127.   WALSHAM Court, 25 July 1345 [HA504/1/4.37]

Robert Crane essoins of common suit, by Robert Kembald; he pledged faith. Manser of Shucford, defendant v William Kembald in a plea of debt, essoins by John Pach; he pledges faith; William is present. Richard Patel the elder, claimant v Richard Patel the younger, Thomas Patel the parson of Thornham Parva, and William Godhous in a plea of land, essoins by Thomas Pye; he pledges faith.

Thomas of Badwell amerced 3d. for trespass on the lord's common with his sheep, where he had no right of common, and in the lord's several pasture in Cannonesbrook, pledge the hayward.

Walter Goos amerced 1d. for trespass, taking away wood from the bakehouse Strondes by Agnes his servant, pledge as above.

Thomas of the Beck amerced 3d. for default. Ordered to attach him to reply to Walter Cooper in pleas of debt and trespass.

William Kembald amerced 1d. for trespass against Walter the smith, to his loss of ¼d., as found by the enquiry; ordered to raise.

William Cook amerced 3d. for trespass against Robert Hereward, to his loss of 6d., as found by the enquiry; ordered to raise.

Surrender: William Rampolye to Walter the smith and his heirs, 2½r. of land within Walter's croft, in exchange for 2½r. lying within William's croft, which Walter surrenders to the use of William and his heirs; granted to each of them to hold in villeinage, by services and works, fine 2s., pledge the hayward.

Ralph Echeman amerced 2d. for damage in the lord's herbage in the Launde with his sheep; Robert Lene 6d. for the same, and 3d. for the same at the Woodway; Walter the miller and Robert Swift each amerced 1d. for the same with cows; Robert Sare and William Syre each amerced 1d. for the same at Hatchmere; Roger the Prior of Ixworth in mercy for the same in Cannonesbrook with geese, condoned; Robert Lene amerced 1d. for the same with sheep, and 3d. for the same in Westmillfield with sheep; pledge for all the hayward.

John Man amerced 12d. because he sold 1a. of land to William Rampolye, without

---

[95]  As above, amercements are shown in the margin, but the amounts are illegible.

282

leave; ordered to take into the lord's hands, and to report the profits. Memorandum that this land is sown with wheat.

Alice Helewys, who lives on the lord's bondage, gave Agnes her daughter, freewoman, in marriage to Nicholas Goche, with goods and chattels coming from the bondage, without leave. The homage say that they [*sic*] should not be amerced; the lord to be consulted. Robert Tailor gave Hilary his daughter in marriage likewise.[96]

John Terwald amerced 3d. because he had in his fold 9 sheep over the fixed number; Robert Rampolye 9d. had 31 sheep, William Hawys 18d. had 60 sheep, Robert Lene 2s. had 80 sheep, and John Herning 2d. had 7 sheep, pledge for all the hayward.

John the son of William the bailiff amerced 6d because he overstocked the lord's common with his sheep, grazing where he had no right of common, pledge the hayward.

Ralph Echeman amerced 3d. for withholding one hoeing service for 1½r. of land in Netherstreet, formerly of Robert Spileman; the same Ralph and Matthew Hereward 3d., for the same for 3r. of land formerly of the same Robert, pledge for both the hayward.

William Hawys and Richard Patel the younger were elected to the office of reeve; <Thomas Dormour>, John Spileman and Geoffrey Rath to the office of hayward; Edmund Lene and Robert Warde to the office of woodward.

Ordered to execute the orders of the last court, marked with a cross, and not acted upon.

SUM 11s. 2d.


### 128.  HIGH HALL Court, 24 September 1345 [HA504/1/4.33.iv]

Adam of Angerhale pays 6d. fine for repossessing from the lord 1a. of customary land, which was taken because Agnes his mother, two years ago, demised it to Adam Dolhale for a term of years, without leave, pledge John Helpe.

William Wodebite villein, when he died, held from the lord by services and works, a messuage 9a. of land called Aprilles, half a messuage 4½a., formerly Alwynes, and half a messuage 2½a., formerly of Walter, his father. The lord had as a heriot a stot, worth 6s.. John, Walter and John his sons are his heirs, and John and John come and have entry by the heriot, following the custom of the manor, and they swear servile fealty. Walter does not come; ordered to take his share into the lord's hands, and to report the profits. William also held for his lifetime a messuage 5a. of the tenement Grennard, by the demise of Richard Gothelarde. Richard does not come to receive the tenement; ordered to take into the lord's hands, and to report the profits. Afterwards, this tenement was granted to John Wodebite and Walter Wodebite, to hold for their lifetime by services and works, fine 2s., pledges John Packard and John Helpe.

Ordered to retain in the hands of John Wodebite a cow, a mare, a female calf, 3 quarters of wheat and 3 quarters of barley, taken upon Agnes the daughter of William Wodebite, villein, and to take more, [for her] to reply to the lord because she carted and took away chattels from her father's tenement out of the lord's villeinage, against the orders of the lord and his bailiffs.

---

[96] Margin: 'reply' against both items.

Robert Banlone, the driver of the plough, amerced 3d. for damage in the lord's wood with the stots of the manor in his custody, to the lord's loss; and 6d. for badly tending the plough-oxen in his custody. Robert amerced 3d. because he took away apples, pears and other fruits from the lord's orchard; Walter of Allwood amerced 3d. for the same by his wife.

Idonea Isabel amerced 3d. because she was summoned to reap in the autumn for money and did not come, but, against the orders of the bailiff, she reaped for Robert Hovel for money, pledge William Isabel.

William Cook did damage in the lord's wheat at Ulvesrowe, to the value of 6 sheaves; ordered; Simon Peyntour the keeper of the cows and bullocks did damage in the lord's oats at Netherhawe, to the value of 2 sheaves; ordered; Robert Banlone amerced 3d. for damage in the corn with beasts in his custody; John Fraunceys did damage in the lord's peas at Stonylond, to the value of 1 sheaf, and John Syre and Simon Cooper did the same in the lord's barley at Abels, 1 sheaf; ordered.

Richard Banlone amerced 3d. for default.

Surrender: William Wodebite into the lord's hands, by the hands of the bailiff, to the use of Agnes and Margery the daughters of John Wodebite and their heirs, 1a.1r. of land; granted to them to hold in villeinage, by services and works, fine 12d., pledges John Wodebite and John Helpe.

John, Walter and John Wodebite, the heirs of William Wodebite were summoned to work in the winter and did not come.[97]

William Isabel was elected to the office of reeve; he comes and pays a fine, pledge John Helpe. Robert Helpe was elected to the office of collector, and he took the oath.

> SUM 9s. 10d., except a stot, worth 6s., as a heriot
> Affeerers: John Packard and John of Angerhale

### 129. WALSHAM Court General, 12 November 1345 [HA504/1/4.38]

Thomas Patel the parson of the church of Thornham Parva, tenant, v Richard Patel the elder in a plea of land, essoins by Robert Joye the younger; William Godhous, [tenant], v Richard in the same plea, essoins by William Kembald; Thomas and William pledge faith; Richard is present. A day is given to Richard Patel the younger, [tenant], in the same plea. Robert Sare essoins of common suit by Robert Page; and as defendant v John Spileman in a plea of debt, by John the clerk; Robert pledges faith; John Spileman is present. <William Cook, defendant, v Robert Hereward in a plea of trespass, essoins by Nicholas Fraunceys>.[98]

Robert Crane amerced 3d. because he did not warrant his essoin.

Manser of Shucford amerced 2d. for unlawful detention of 2d. from William Kembald, as he acknowledged in open court, to the loss of 1d.; ordered to raise. Ordered to attach William Kembald to reply to Manser of Shucford in a plea of debt.

Hilary the daughter of Robert Tailor amerced 6s.8d. because she married John Patel, without leave, pledges Robert Tailor and the hayward.

---

[97] The margin is torn, and the amounts of the amercement here, and of the fine in the next item, are obliterated. It is probable that they were 12d. and 3s.4d., respectively.

[98] Margin: 'because he holds customary land'.

The second pledges of John Mayheu amerced 6d. because they did not have him reply to John Spileman, in a plea of trespass; ordered to appoint better pledges.

The first pledges of Thomas Locksmith amerced 3d. because they did not have him make amends to the lord for trespass by his servant, taking away stakes out of Ladyswood; ordered as above. Afterwards Thomas came and put himself in mercy for this trespass, pledge the hayward.

Thomas of the Beck amerced 3d. for trespass against Walter Cooper, as was found by the enquiry, depasturing Walter's herbage with his sheep, to the loss of 7d.; ordered to raise.

Agnes the daughter of Alice Helewys amerced 6s.8d. because she married Nicholas Goche, without leave, pledges Agnes' mother and the hayward.

+The profits from 1a.3r. of land, retained in the lord's hands because William Gobald freeman sold it by charter to John Gobald his son, without leave, [amount to] 12d.; ordered to retain and report the profits. +The profits from 1½a. of land, retained in the lord's hands because John Long freeman sold it by charter to Walter Pykhorn without leave, [amount to] 6d., ordered as above.

+Ordered as elsewhere to attach Roger, the Prior of Ixworth, because he cultivated 1a. of customary land of the tenement Springold, lying in the Stubbing next to the Pedderspath, and took away the crop from this land; and to attach John Nugge for trespass in the lord's warren by Richard Alot his servant setting snares in Ladyswood.

+Ordered as elsewhere to retain in the lord's hands a part of a messuage 8a. of land, which William the bastard son of Letitia Stronde purchased from Letitia, with William the son of William of Cranmer, as shown in the court of 1 December 1340 [no.107], and to report the profits.

Thomas of the Beck amerced 4d. for trespass against Walter Cooper, depasturing Walter's herbage with his sheep, as was found by the enquiry, to the loss of 9d.; ordered to raise. Walter Cooper amerced 4d. for trespass against Thomas of the Beck, depasturing Thomas' corn with his beasts, as was found by the enquiry, to the loss of 15d.; ordered to raise. Walter amerced 2d. for unlawful detention of 2 barrels from Thomas, as was found by the enquiry, to the loss of 3d.; ordered to raise.

+Ordered as elsewhere to attach William Wyswyf, John Rede and Walter Doo, villeins, because they absent themselves from the lord; and to attach Ralph of Rudham chaplain to reply to William Hawys, and Bartholomew Jerico, in pleas of trespass.

+Ordered as elsewhere to retain in the lord's hands 1a.3r. of customary land, which William Noreys sold by charter to John of Foxley without leave, and to report the profits.

+Ordered as elsewhere to attach Olivia the daughter of Gilbert Priour villein, because she married without leave; and to attach Reginald Pynfoul for damage in Ladyswood by Hilary Typetot his servant taking away firewood; and to attach Sir William Tallemache for four autumn works, two ploughings and suit of court, for the tenement Outlawe, and other [services] withheld; and because he has 6 score sheep in the fold, formerly of Adam Richard, to which only 60 sheep belong.

Adam Noble, when he died, held from the lord by services and works a messuage 3a.3½r. of land, and part of a pightle, containing 10p. of pasture; the lord had as a heriot a cow in calf, worth 8s. Thomas his son is heir to ½a. and ⅓a. of this land;

and Thomas and John, Adam's other son, are heirs to the residue of Adam's tenement. They have entry by the heriot, and they swore fealty.

Catherine Cook villein paid 2s.8d. childwite, because she gave birth outside wedlock.

The same Catherine, when she died, held from the lord, by services and works, 1a.3r. of customary land; the lord had as a heriot a cow, worth 10s. \included in the account for last year, because it came before Michaelmas/. William and Robert Cook Catherine's brothers are her heirs, and they have entry by the heriot.

Alice Helewys amerced 3d. for damage in Ladyswood with her bullocks, pledge the hayward.

William the swineherd of the manor amerced 3d. because his servant cut and took away the lord's corn in the autumn; John the goatherd and John the gooseherd each amerced 2d. for the same, pledge for all, the hayward.

Robert of Walpole grazed with his sheep and pigs where he had no right to graze, and overstocked the common with his sheep, ordered etc.

John Typetot, William Elys each amerced 1d., and Thomas of the Beck 3d., because they stored corn grown in the lord's bondage, in free tenements, pledge the hayward.

Walter Fuller amerced 2d. for damage on the banks around the manor with a cow, pledge the hayward.

John Baxter and Walter Rampolye each amerced 6d. because they brewed and sold ale in breach of the assize; John Lester 4d. and John Pynfoul 6d. for the same. Robert Lenne regrator amerced 3d. for selling bread in breach of the assize; George of Brockley and Walter of Risby 1d. each for the same, pledge for Walter, Walter Osbern, because in [his] house. William Syre and Robert Hereward the ale-tasters each amerced 2d. because they did not perform their duties.

William Cook amerced 4d. for leave to agree with Robert Hereward in a plea of trespass, in two complaints; Robert amerced 4d. for leave to agree with William in a plea of trespass, in two complaints, pledge for both the hayward.

John Rath and his pledges amerced 2d. because he did not proceed against John Pynfoul, in a plea of trespass.

John Herning and William Pach pay 2s. fine for having a fold of 4 score sheep; Robert Rampolye 18d. for a fold of 60 sheep; John Terwald 2s.6d. for a fold of 5 score sheep, pledge for all the hayward.

Thomas of the Beck amerced 6d. for leave to agree with Walter Cooper in a plea of trespass, in two complaints, pledge the hayward.

John the son of Robert Tailor and Richard Warde amerced 4d. for leave to agree with Thomas Hereward and Manser of Shucford in a plea of debt.

Robert Crane in mercy for default;[99] Richard the son of Walter of Cranmer amerced 3d. for the same; John and Thomas, Walter's [other] sons, each amerced 1½d. for the same.

Surrender: William the son of Peter Warde, to John the son of Peter Tailor and William his son and their heirs, ½r. of meadow in Micklemeadow, granted to them to hold in villeinage, by services and works, fine 6d., pledge the hayward.

William Hawys and John Tailor each pay 6s.8d. for the office of reeve, pledge the hayward.

---

99 Amount unstated.

Ordered to raise from John Angerhale[?] 20d. to the use of Robert of Drinkstone chaplain, and 12d. to the use of Edmund the brother of John [*illeg.*].

Surrender: the Prior of Ixworth to Robert Lene and his heirs, ½a. of meadow in the Micklemeadow, granted to him to hold in villeinage, by services and works, fine 2s., pledge the hayward.

William Hawys pays 2s.6d. fine for a fold of 6 score sheep, 20 without fine; William of Cranmer 2s.6d. for a fold of 7 score sheep, 40 without fine; Robert Lene pays 2s. fine for a fold of 4 score sheep; pledge for all the hayward.

+Ordered as elsewhere to retain in the lord's hands a piece of free land, 8p.2ft. long and 8¼ft. wide, which Walter the smith villein purchased from Olivia Rampolye by charter, and to report the profits.

+Ordered as elsewhere to attach Robert the farmer of Ashfield for trespass in the lord's warren by his sons Robert and John, setting nets and other traps, and also with their dogs; and for trespass in the lord's wood, cutting and taking away by Robert and John; +and to attach John the parson of Langham church for the same by his servants; and to attach John of Boynhawe for trespass against the lord by his wife taking away stakes from Ladyswood.

+Ordered as elsewhere to retain in the lord's hands 2a. of customary land which Agnes the widow of Adam Sket holds, [taken] because she married without leave, and to report the profits; +and to retain a messuage 30a. of free land in Ditton Camoys, of the fee of Sir John de Pounteneys, which John the son of Robert Warde villein purchased, and to report the profits.

+Ordered as elsewhere to attach Adam the rector of Westhorpe because he grazed with his sheep where he had no right to graze; +and to attach John and Robert the sons of Robert the farmer of Ashfield for damage in the lord's wood, cutting down and taking away an ash-tree and sticks; and to attach William Leche to reply to Bartholomew Jerico in a plea of debt; and to attach Ralph of Rudham chaplain to reply to Bartholomew in a plea of trespass.

+Ordered as elsewhere to retain in the lord's hands a parcel of a pightle, containing ½r., called Sawyer's pightle, [taken] because Walter Rampolye sold it to John Barleyhand without leave, and to report the profits; +and to retain half a messuage 1r. of land, [taken] after the death of Ralph Neve, because Peter Neve his kinsman and heir did not come to pay a fine. Afterwards, [the tenement] was demised to Alice Neve for her lifetime, for 6d. per year rent, pledge Walter Payn.

Memorandum that the lord is to be consulted concerning ½a. of customary land, which William Kembald holds within the messuage on which his barn is situated, which Simon Kembald, William's father, received from William the smith in exchange for ½a. of free land, which Walter the son of William the smith now holds; the exchange being made in the time of Lady Eve de Valence.

+A day is given to the enquiry until the next court, to enquire whether 1½a. of land, remaining in the lord's hands, which Walter Pykhorn purchased by charter from John Long, is free land or customary; and to apportion the tenement of Agnes at the Green, [and to report] how much this tenement contains, who holds it, and by what services, under penalty of 20s..

Adam Trounce, who holds customary land from the lord, amerced 12d. because he unlawfully distrained [upon] Walter the smith, Walter Rampolye and Alice wife of Simon Rampolye, and other villeins, *viz.* [taking] bullocks and cows; and he took and drove away the distraints to the messuage of Alexander de Walsham, and he kept them there, pledges William Warde and the hayward.

287

+The profits from 1a. of land, remaining in the lord's hands because John Man sold it to William Rampolye without leave, [amount to] 2s.; ordered to retain in the lord's hands, and to report the profits. Memorandum that this land was sown with wheat in the preceding year, as shown in the court roll of that year.

Ordered to attach Robert of Walpole for one ploughing service called Ploughale withheld, and for other services withheld.

SUM £4 18s., except two cows as heriots, worth 18s.,

one charged in last year's account

Affeerers: William Patel and John Spileman

# Section 5

## March 1346 – November 1350

**130.  WALSHAM Court, 24 March 1346 [HA504/1/5.1.i]**
John Margery essoins of common suit, by Peter Margery; Thomas Beck of the same,
by Thomas Swan; and Robert Crane of the same, by Robert Kembald; they
pledge faith. Manser of Shucford, plaintiff v William Kembald in a plea of debt,
essoins by Robert Hereward; he pledges faith; William is present.

Again ordered the bailiff to allow Richard Patel the younger to have sight[1] of a toft,
15a. of land, 2r. of meadow, a portion of a messuage, and two parcels of two
tofts, with appurtenances, in Finningham and Westhorpe, which Richard Patel
the elder claims against the said Richard, Thomas Patel the parson of Thornham
Parva, and William Godhous. A day is given etc.

John Spileman and his pledges amerced 2d. because he did not proceed against Robert Sare in a plea of debt; and 2d. because he did not proceed against John Mayheu in a plea of trespass, pledge the hayward.

John Noble and his pledges amerced 3d. because he did not proced against Thomas
Noble in a plea of trespass; and John amerced 3d. for leave to agree with Thomas
in this plea, pledge the hayward.

Surrenders: John the son of Robert Rampolye to John Bolle and his heirs, ½r. and
¹/₃r. of meadow, granted to him to hold in villeinage, by services and works,
fine 10d., pledge the hayward.

William the son of Peter Warde of West street to Matthew Gilbert and his heirs,
1r. of meadow, granted to him in the same form, fine 9d., pledge as before.[2]

Robert Rampolye and Agnes his wife, she being examined, to John Tailor and
William his son and their heirs, ½r. of meadow in the Micklemeadow next to
Turfpitrode ['Turpetrode'], granted to them in the same form, fine 6d., pledge as
above.

+Ordered [to attach] Mabel the daughter of Peter Springold, villein, because she
married without leave.

Agnes Crane gave birth outside wedlock; therefore childwite 2s.8d.

Alice Whiteman amerced 2d. for breaking hedges around the manor, and taking
away firewood, pledge the hayward; Catherine Brid 1d. for the same, pledge
Edmund Lene; Thomas the miller 1d. for the same, pledge Walter [Craske] the
miller; John Wauncy 1d. for the same by his servant, pledge the hayward; Sybil
Labbe 2d. for the same, pledge Simon Peyntour.

The servant of John Tailor amerced 1d. for taking away firewood out of Ladyswood,
pledge John Tailor; the servant of Alice Helewys 1d., for the same, pledge the
hayward.

---

[1]  In roll no.125 this request was assumed to refer to the rolls, but the wording here suggests that it
refers to the land. It was probably intended to refer to the claimant's evidence of title.
[2]  Tab: 'William Warde' (?15th century hand).

The first pledges of Robert of Walpole amerced 2s. because they did not have him make amends to the lord for grazing on the common of Walsham with his sheep, which lie in Westhorpe, for overstocking the common with his sheep and for grazing on the common with his pigs; also for unlawfully withholding one ploughing service at the Ploughale. Ordered to appoint better pledges. A day is given to enquire whether Robert dug and blocked a ditch at the Overway, or not.

Surrenders: Gilbert Priour and Avice his wife, she being examined in court, to John Tailor and William his son and their heirs, a cotland, 35ft. long and 28½ft. wide; granted to them to hold in villeinage, by services and customs, fine 3d., pledge the hayward. And they surrendered to the lord a cotland, 8p.4ft. long on one side, and 5p.8ft. long on the other, and 4p.5ft. wide at one head, and 14ft. wide at the other; granted to them for their lifetime. After the deaths of Gilbert and Avice the cotland shall revert to Richard, their son, and his heirs, to hold in villeinage by services and customs, fine 6d., pledges Stephen Cooper and the hayward.

A day is given, at the request of the parties, to Thomas Fuller and Alice his wife and John Bonde and Avice his wife, claimants, and Thomas Noble, tenant, in a plea of land, to come to the next court without essoin.

Surrenders: John Terwald to Robert the son of Clarice Man and his heirs, ½r. of land, below the garden of John Typetot, granted to him to hold in villeinage by services and works, fine 4d., pledge John Terwald.

William the smith to Peter Neve and his heirs, 1½r. of land and half a cotland, formerly of Ralph Neve; granted to him in the same form, fine 3s. It was ordered elsewhere to retain in the lord's hands 1½r. of land and half a messuage, taken after the death of Ralph Neve, because Peter Neve his heir did not come; Peter now comes and pays 3s. fine for entry; granted to him and his heirs to hold in the same form, pledge for both fines John Syre.

John Man pays 12d. fine to repossess, out of the lord's hands, 1a. of land, which he sold to William Rampolye without leave, pledge the hayward.

Adam Hardonn amerced 3d. for default.

Ordered to execute the orders of the last court, marked with a cross, and not acted upon.

SUM 15s. 8d.

### 131. HIGH HALL Court General of Nicholas de Walsham, 1 April 1346 [HA504/1/5.2]

Robert Sare essoins of common suit, by Richard Kebbil; Walter Osbern of the same, by William Cranmer.

It was ordered to take into the lord's hands 4a.1r. of land, with a third part of two messuages, by estimation, which William Wodebite held on the day he died, because Walter his son, one of his heirs, did not come to the last court to receive his inheritance; and to report the profits. Afterwards Walter came and paid 12d. entry fine, and the tenement was granted to him to hold in villeinage by services and works, pledges John Wodebite, John Packard and John Helpe.

Ordered as elsewhere to attach William Cook for damage in the lord's wheat at Ulvesrowe, to the value of 6 sheaves; and Simon Peyntour, keeper of the bullocks and cows, for damage in the lord's oats at Netherhawe, 3 sheaves, \condoned by the lord/; and John Frounceys for damage in the lord's peas at Stonylond, 1 sheaf; and John Syre and Simon Cooper for damage in the lord's barley at Abels,

290

2 sheaves, \condoned/. Simon Peyntour in mercy for damage in the lord's meadows in Hordeshawe with his horses and cows, pledge the hayward \condoned/.

Ordered as elsewhere to distrain Bartholomew the brother and heir of Henry
Dances, formerly the rector of Westhorpe, for homage and fealty, as shown in the
court of 18 October 1344 [no.123].

+Ordered as elsewhere to distrain Robert Hovel to show [his title to] entry into 1r. of
land of the lord's fee, which he purchased from Adam Shepherd, and for fealty.

Agnes the daughter of John Wodebite pays 10s. fine for leave to marry John the son
of Robert Rampolye; and upon this John pays a fine for entry to Agnes' tenement,[3] pledge for both the hayward; John swore fealty. The lord granted to John
the son of Robert Rampolye all the tenement, which Matilda, who was the wife
of John Wodebite, held in name of dower from the endowment of her husband, to
hold from last Michaelmas until next Michaelmas, paying 3s. per year rent,
pledge as before.

John Wodebite the younger, the son of William Wodebite, by leave of the court,
demised to Walter Wodebite his brother, all the tenement which he holds from
the lord, to hold from last Michaelmas until Michaelmas seven years hence, paying to John at Michaelmas 5s. per year. Walter shall strew the tenement with the
dung found thereon, and shall maintain it in as good a condition as he received it;
and he shall perform the services and works. He pays 3s.4d. fine for having his
term, pledges Robert Helpe and Robert of Angerhale.

Henry Trusse and Henry of Hattele each amerced 3d. for default.

Ordered [to attach] William Payn for damage in the lord's herbage at Sheepcotes
with his sheep; and John Syre and Walter Payn for the same in the lord's wheat
and herbage at Doucedeux, \condoned/; and Robert Hereward for damage with a
sow in the lord's pightle and at Gothelardsyard.

Ordered [to attach] Walter Osbern, Walter Payn, John Syre and William Payn for
making an unlawful road beyond Angerhalebrook; and William Deneys for the
same \all condoned/.

It was presented by the whole homage that three years ago waste was made in the
lord's bondage, in the tenement formerly of John Wodebite, recently held at
farm, by leave of the court, by William Wodebite, who has died since the feast of
St Peter's Chains [1 August]; [and that] the loss to the lord is 3d. The homage is
amerced 9d. because for three years they concealed, and did not present, the
waste made in this tenement.

Walter Wodebite villein amerced 18d. for contempt of the lord and his bailiffs, in
that he broke the lord's seal from his door, sealed on the lord's bondage, pledge
John Wodebite the elder.

SUM 17s. 2d., except the rent as above

Affeerers: John Packard and Robert Helpe

## 132.  WALSHAM Court General, 28 July 1346 [HA504/1/5.1.ii].

Richard Patel the younger, [co]tenant v Richard Patel the elder, claimant in a plea of
land,[4] essoins by Roger Castre; Richard Patel the elder, claimant v Thomas Patel

---

[3]  Only the one fine of 10s. is shown against this entry: it must have been intended to cover both marriage and entry fines.

[4]  MS: *unde visum* was written here, and deleted. The same words were written after a bracket linking
all these essoins. Footnote 1 to roll no.130 is relevant.

the parson of Thornham Parva, and v William Godhous, in the same plea, by Robert Sare and William Kembald [respectively]; he pledges faith.

Manser of Shucford and his pledges amerced 3d. because he did not proceed against William Kembald in a plea of debt, pledge the hayward.

Thomas Noble amerced 3d. because he unlawfully withheld ½a. of land from Thomas Fuller and Alice his wife, and John Bonde and Avice his wife; adjudged that they shall recover this land and damages from Thomas Noble; ordered to raise.

William Cook amerced 3d. for leave to agree with Robert Hereward in a plea of trespass, pledge the hayward.

Surrenders: Thomas Beck to Peter Jay and his heirs, ½a. of land at Cocksbusk, granted to him to hold in villeinage, by services and works, fine 20d., pledge the hayward.

William the son of Peter Warde to Richard Warde and his heirs, a cotland containing 4p. and three quarters of ½p. of land, granted to him in the same form, fine 4d., pledge the hayward.

Robert Warde, when he died, held from the lord, by services and works, half a messuage 13a. of land, 2a. of pasture and 1a. of wood; the lord had no heriot because Robert's best beast was seized to the use of Sir John Pountney, as a heriot for the tenement which he held in Ditton [Camoys]. John and John the sons of Richard are his heirs, and they came and refused to pay an entry fine. Ordered to take the tenement into the lord's hands, and to report the profits. Afterwards, John and John come and pay 20s. entry fine, pledge the hayward.

Agatha Long, when she died, held from the lord 1r. of land by the rod, and a part of a cottage by services and works; the lord had as a heriot a wether, before shearing, worth 18d.. Agnes [Long] her kinswoman is her nearest heir, and she has entry by the heriot.

Alice the daughter of Robert the cooper [*alias* Hereward] pays 6s.8d. for leave to marry Matthew Gilbert, pledge the hayward.

Robert Lene amerced 4d. for damage in the lord's rye at the Micklemeadow, and John Hernyng 3d. for the same, pledge for both the hayward.

John Hernyng in mercy for default; afterwards he came.

John Baxter amerced 3d. for damage in the lord's rye at the Micklemeadow, pledge the hayward. Ordered [to attach] Roger the Prior of Ixworth for the same with his pigs, and in Cannonesbrook with geese. Robert Lene amerced 6d. for damage in the lord's rye with the sheep of the manor; and the farmer of the cows of the manor 6d. for the same with geese; and William Swan 4d. for the same with pigs, pledge for all the hayward.

Robert Sare amerced 3d. for damage in Hatchmereway with a horse, and William Hawes and Robert Lene 3d. each for the same with sheep, pledge for all the hayward.

William Warde the son of Alice Warde amerced 2d., Emma Shepherd in mercy \condoned/ and Agnes Smith amerced 1d. for damage in the lord's corn gathering herbage, pledge for both the hayward.

+Ordered [to attach] Robert of Walpole because he has a ditch at the Overway, which is not cleaned out, to the common nuisance; and Adam Dolhale and John Helpe because they grazed on the common, where they had no right of common.

Robert Hereward and William Cook each amerced 3d. because they dug on the lord's common at Allwoodgreen, to the common nuisance.

+Ordered [to attach] Richard of Tendring for damage in the lord's warren taking hares.

+Ordered [to attach] Matilda the daughter of Bartholomew Patel, because she married Richard Beele of Hopton without leave.

John and Thomas the sons of Richard, the son of Letitia, amerced 4d. for default.

Thomas Julle purchased from Adam the son of Richard Shepherd a messuage ½a. of land of the lord's fee. He comes and shows the charter in due form, and swears fealty.

John Hernyng amerced 3d. for having 8 sheep in his fold over the fixed number; John Terwald 3d. for having 10 sheep, William Hawys 6d. for having 20 sheep; and William Cranmer 3d. for having 10 sheep; pledge for all the hayward.

John Baxter and Walter Rampolye each amerced 6d. because they brewed and sold ale in breach of the assize; John Syre 3d. for the same; Robert Cook in mercy for the same \condoned/. Robert Lenne amerced 2d. for regrating bread, and George Brockley 1d. for the same. William Syre and Robert Hereward the ale-tasters each amerced 2d., because they did not perform their duties.

William Syre amerced 2d. for trespass against Amice Patel, to the loss of 3d. as found by the enquiry; ordered to raise.

Ordered to summon Walter Springold, Robert Springold and John Tailor to reply to Robert Springold in a plea of land.

A day is given, at the request of the parties, to Walter Hawys, plaintiff, and Robert Sare, defendant, in a plea of trespass, to come to the next court without essoin.

Surrender: Beatrice the daughter of John Patel to John the son of John Patel and his heirs, a cottage and 1½r. of land in Upstreet, granted to him to hold in villeinage by services and works, fine 18d., pledge the hayward.

John Noble amerced 3d. for his false claim against Thomas Noble, in a plea of trespass.

Surrenders: Simon Peyntour to Robert Typetot and his heirs, 1½r. of land in the Wellfield, granted to him in the same form as above, fine 12d., pledge the hayward.

John Spileman to Robert Cook and his heirs, a piece of land 30p. long and 1½ft. wide, in exchange for a piece 30p. long and 2ft. wide, which Robert surrendered to John and his heirs; granted to them to hold in the same form as above, fine 6d., pledge the hayward.

William Deneys amerced 3d. for his false claim against John Noble in a plea of dower.

Surrender: Walter Rampolye to Robert Lene and his heirs, 1a.1½r. of land in the Millfield, granted to him in the same form as above, fine 5s., pledge the hayward.

Walter Osbern and William Payn were elected to the office of reeve. Robert Cook and Geoffrey Rath were elected to the office of hayward. Edmund Lene and Walter the smith of Upstreet were elected to the office of woodward.

Ordered to attach John Noble to reply to William Deneys in a plea of trespass.

Robert Crane amerced 3d. because he did not warrant his essoin.

Robert Lene the shepherd amerced 6s.8d. because he did not salve the sheep, as he should have done.

John the dairyman amerced 4s.6d. because he wasted the firewood in the dairy beyond measure (?*ultra modo*). Matthew Tailor custodian of the firewood, amerced 6s.8d. because he permitted the waste to be made, contrary to the lord's orders.

John Spileman, the hayward, amerced 3s.4d. because he did not lie in the lord's domain,[5] as he was ordered.

William Kembald amerced 12d. for damage in [*illeg.*]; John Tailor 3d. for the same.

Ordered to forewarn the brewers that they should sell a gallon of ale [*illeg.*] ¼d., and no more, under penalty of [*illeg.*].

John Terwald and his fellow jurors amerced 10s. because [*line illeg.*] on the tenement of Richard Patel the younger, cutting down trees, and on the tenement of Robert Shepherd chaplain, [held] at farm, for waste therein, and on the tenement of Stephen Cooper for waste made therein, cutting down the trees of Richard, Edmund and Stephen, for the said waste, etc.[6]

SUM £3 [17s.10d.], except a wether, worth 18d., as a heriot

### 133. HIGH HALL Court General of Nicholas de Walsham, 18 October 1346 [HA504/1/5.3.i]

+Robert Helpe the collector amerced 3d. because he did not execute the court's order to attach William Cook for damage in the lord's wheat; and 3d. because he did not execute the court's order to attach John Fraunceys for damage in the lord's peas. Again +ordered to attach William for damage in the lord's wheat at Ulvesrowe, 6 sheaves, and John Fraunceys for damage in the lord's peas at Stonylond, 1 sheaf, and Simon Cooper for damage in the lord's barley at Abels.

+Ordered as elsewhere to distrain Robert Hovel to show [his title for] entry into 1r. of land of the lord's fee, which he bought from Adam Shepherd, and for fealty.

+Ordered as elsewhere to attach William Payn for damage in the lord's herbage at Sheepcotes with his sheep; and Walter Payn for the same in the lord's wheat and herbage; and Robert Hereward for damage with a sow in the lord's pightle, and at Gothelardsyard.

+Ordered as elsewhere to attach Walter Payn and William Payn for making an unlawful road beyond Angerhalebrook.

The lord granted to John Man and Matilda his wife all the tenement which the said Matilda, the widow of John Wodebite, holds in dower, to hold and to keep the same, without extending the term pertaining to it, *viz.* from this day to the term of Matilda's life, and without any waste, rendering to the lord [such] services as the tenement bears, fine 3s.4d., pledges William of Cranmer and John Rampolye.

Henry Helpe and William Manser each amerced 3d. for default.

Richard Baronn and Adam, the lord's swineherds, each amerced 1d. for damage with pigs in the lord's meadow at Hordeshawe; John Packard amerced 1d. for damage in the lord's meadow at Smallbrook with his beasts.

+Ordered to attach Simon Peyntour and Richard Qualm for damage in the lord's pasture at Hordeshawe with their beasts, and +Robert Hereward for damage in the lord's wheat at Doucedeux, 4 sheaves, and +Hubert the shepherd for damage in the lord's wheat with his sheep, 1 sheaf, and +the dairymaid of the Prior of Ixworth for damage in the lord's barley, 2 sheaves.

---

5   In 1350 (roll no.155), John was heavily fined for dereliction of duty, while reeve, and again in 1351, for various offences of which one was 'that he did not lie in the manor by night, but left without leave'. This is probably a similar offence.

6   The illegible line probably refers to concealment of the waste by the jurors, but the meaning of the remainder is far from clear. This section of the membrane is badly stained and faded.

Bartholomew Goche amerced 1d. for damage in the lord's wheat at the Thirtyacres, ½ sheaf; and 1d. for damage in the lord's peas above the wood.

+Ordered to attach William Cook for damage in the lord's oats at Ulvesrowe, 1½ bushels and 1 peck, and +the servant of Robert Lene for damage in the lord's peas at Abels ['Ebeles'], 1 bushel, and +William Grocer for damage in the lord's herbage at Stonylond with his beasts, and +Robert Hereward for damage in the lord's garden, with his sow and pigs, and +John Syre for the same with his pigs.

Adam the lord's swineherd amerced 3d. for damage in the manor with the lord's pigs.

Bartholomew Goche the driver [of the plough] amerced 6d. for damage in the lord's wood with stots; and 6d. because he guarded the stots badly, and as a result one stot died, by his negligence.

Idonea Isabel pays 2s.8d. childwite, because she gave birth outside wedlock; and is amerced 6d. because she did not come to perform autumn work at the time at which she was summoned, and 6d. because she did not obey the lady's order to weave a cloth.

John Wodebite [the elder] amerced 3d. because he did not act in a proper manner (*?utiliter*), and did not perform the winter work to which he had been summoned; John Packard, Walter Wodebite, John Wodebite [the younger], Adam of Angerhale and John Rampolye each amerced 3d. for the same.

Robert of Angerhale amerced 3s.4d. because he lied and spoke maliciously about his lord.

Robert Helpe the hayward[7] amerced 6d because he did not summon workers in autumn and winter, as ordered by the lord, and 6d. because he did not order the workers to mow and stack the hay.

John Helpe amerced 3s.4d. because he advised as to what should be presented (*?ostend'*) in court, and spoke maliciously about the lord; and 12d. because he raised his fold without the lord's leave.

John Wodebite the younger amerced 3d. for his false complaint against his brothers, Walter and John.

The lord granted a day to John Rampolye to repair buildings and to make fences by the next court, under penalty of ½ mark.

John Chapman is elected to the office of reeve for his own tenement, fine 2s., pledge the hayward.

John Wodebite the elder is elected to the office of collector for the tenement formerly of Walter Wodebite [his grandfather].

SUM 22s.

Affeerers: John Packard and John of Angerhale

### 134.   WALSHAM Court General, 20 October 1346 [HA504/1/5.4]

Richard Patel the elder, claimant v Richard Patel the younger, Thomas Patel the parson of Thornham Parva, and William Godhous in a plea of land, essoins by John Cumpyn; he pledges faith; Richard, Thomas and William are present.

Walter Hawys and his pledges amerced 3d. because he did not proceed against Robert Sare in a plea of trespass, pledge the hayward.

---

7   MS: *messor*; in earlier references to him in this court, the word used is *collector*.

John Noble amerced 3d. for trespass against William Deneys, to the loss of 14d.; ordered to raise.

Robert Springold and his pledges amerced 3d. because he did not proceed against Walter Springold, Robert Springold and John Tailor in a plea of land.

Robert Lenne amerced 3d. for leave to agree with John Hawys in a plea of debt, pledge the hayward.

John Noble amerced 3d. for unlawful detention of a saddle with a girth from Thomas Noble, as found by the enquiry, to the loss of 4d.; ordered to raise.

General Enquiry by John Syre, Walter Payn, William Payn, William Wither, William Rampolye, John Pynfoul, Simon Peyntour, Robert Rampolye, Thomas Fuller, John Tailor, Richard Kebbil, Richard Patel the elder, William Cranmer the elder and Bartholomew Jerico.

Surrender: Edmund Lene to Robert Lene and his heirs, 5½p. of land within Robert's croft, in exchange for 8¾p. of land at Ayleldestoftsend, which Robert surrendered to Edmund and his heirs, granted to them to hold in villeinage by services and works, fine 8d., pledge the hayward.

William Hawys pays 2s.6d. fine for having a fold of 6 score sheep, 20 without fine.

Walter the smith amerced 3d. for trespass against John Pynfoul, to the loss of 4d.; ordered to raise. John Pynfoul amerced 3d. for trespass against Walter the smith, to the loss of 1d; ordered to raise.

Surrenders: Robert the son of William Cook to John the son of William Wauncy and his heirs, 1r. of land in the Launde, granted to him to hold in villeinage by services and works, fine 12d., pledge the hayward.

William Cook to Thomas Fuller and his heirs, 2½r. of land at the Millway, granted to him in the same form, fine 2s.6d., pledge as above.

Amice the daughter of Walter Pye pays 13s.4d. fine for leave to marry Robert Totele, pledge as above.

Robert Crane, who died since the last court, held from the lord 2½a. of land and half a messuage; the lord had no heriot because Robert had no beast. His heirs are Robert, the son of Peter Crane, and Agnes, Joan, Catherine and Cristina, the daughters of Henry Crane, and kin of Robert. Joan, Catherine and Cristina come and seek admittance to their inheritance, and entry is granted to them, fine 3s.4d. +As to the share of Agnes, she claims nothing as heir to this tenement; and as to that of Robert, the son of Peter Crane, he does not come to have entry. Ordered [to retain] in the lord's hands. \Profits 14d./

Geoffrey[8] Rath, who married Matilda Coppelowe, amerced 12d. for waste on the lord's bondage in the tenement which he holds from Matilda's dower, allowing the house to fall into ruin; ordered etc. Stephen Cooper amerced 12d. for the same in the tenement formerly of William the miller, pledge the hayward; ordered etc.

Thomas Beck, John Typetot and William Elys in mercy because they stored corn grown on the lord's bondage, in free tenements, \condoned by the lord/.

Ordered to attach Nicholas de Walsham and Thomas of Badwell because they grazed their sheep where they had no right of common.

---

[8]  MS: 'John', in error: the marriage of Geoffrey and Matilda is recorded in the court of 24 September 1331 (no.56).

Agnes Fuller amerced 3d. for damage in the lord's corn gathering corn and herbage, pledge John Tailor.

Robert Lene the shepherd amerced 6s.8d. because he milked the ewes, against the orders of the lord and his bailiffs.

William the son of Robert Lene amerced 4d., because he cut and took away the lord's barley, to the value of ½ bushel, pledge Robert Lene; John Cooper kitchen servant amerced 2s. because he cut and took away the lord's oats in the autumn, to the value of 1 peck.

Robert Shepherd chaplain sold to William the son of Robert Lene a messuage and 16a. of land, meadow and wood, without leave; ordered to take into the lord's hands, and to report the profits.[9]

John Baxter pays 9d. fine for having a fold of 30 sheep, pledge the hayward.

John Baxter, Walter Rampolye and John Syre each amerced 6d. because they brewed and sold ale in breach of the assize. Robert Lenne amerced 3d., and George of Brockley 1d., for regrating bread. William Syre and Robert Hereward the ale-tasters each amerced 2d. because they did not perform their duties.

William the servant of John Tailor amerced 2d. for damage in the lord's wood, taking away firewood; Alice the servant of Alice Helewys 1d. for the same; John Rolfes 2d., for damage in the lord's oats with foals, pledge William Wither; William Fuller 2d. for the same, pledge William Syre.

John Hernyng and William Pach pay 2s. fine for having a fold of 4 score sheep; Robert Rampolye 18d. for a fold of 60 sheep; John Terwald 12d. for a fold of 40 sheep; William Cranmer 2s. for a fold of 6 score sheep, 40 without fine; pledge for all the hayward.

Walter Osbern demised to William Rampolye half a pightle, containing ½r. of land, called Sawyerspightle; and on this, William comes and pays 6d. fine, so that the demise shall take effect, pledge the hayward.

Richard the son of Walter Cranmer, and Richard the son of Walter Qualm each amerced 3d. for default.

Surrender: Olivia the daughter of William Cook to William Cook, her brother, and his heirs, 1a.1r. of land, lying in two pieces, *viz.* at the Longelond and at Goresgate, granted to him to hold in villeinage by services and works, fine 3s.4d., pledge the hayward.

Richard Priour amerced 3d. for damage in the lord's corn by his servant [while] gathering the crop; Gilbert Priour 2d. for the same by his servant, pledge for both the hayward.

Robert Lene amerced 3s.4d. for depasturing the lord's herbage at Strondes with his sheep, pledge the hayward.

William Payn pays 26s.8d. fine for the office of reeve. Robert Cook amerced 13s.4d. for the office of hayward,[10] pledge the hayward.

Walter Rampolye surrendered to the lord a messuage in Clay street, containing 1½r.4p. of land; granted to Walter for his lifetime, and after his death, the messuage shall revert to William the son of Peter Tailor and his heirs, to hold in villeinage by services and works, fine 20s., pledges John Tailor and the hayward.

SUM 102s.

---

9 Margin: 'Void because the sale was not completed'.

10 10 Margin: 'Void because he will perform the office'.

### 135.  WALSHAM Court, 27 February 1347 [HA504/1/5.5.i]

Richard Patel the elder amerced 12d. because he did not proceed against Richard
Patel the younger, Thomas Patel the parson of Thornham Parva and William
Godhous, in a plea of land.[11]

Ordered to attach William Kembald to reply to Robert Hereward in a plea of trespass, and to William Cook in a like plea.

William Kembald was attached to reply to Robert Hereward in a plea of trespass,
concerning which Robert complains that William unlawfully ploughed land,
appropriated to himself from Robert's land at Longcroft, to his loss of 2s., and he
produces suit. William comes and defends, saying that he is not guilty; and he
asks for an enquiry, and the other party likewise; ordered etc. William was
attached to reply to William Cook in a like plea, his complaint being similar in
every respect to Robert's, and he produces suit. William Kembald defends, and
asks for an enquiry, and the other party likewise; ordered etc.

Surrenders: Thomas Beck to John Wauncy and his heirs, ½a. of land in Gorescroft,
granted to him to hold in villeinage by services and works, fine 2s., pledge the
hayward.

Peter Tailor surrendered to the lord ½a.18p. of land next to the Churchway, and
the lord granted the land to Peter, for his lifetime; after his death, it shall revert to
Isabella, Alice and Hilary, Peter's daughters, to hold in villeinage by services and
works, fine 2s., pledge as above.

Walter Osbern amerced 3d. for his false claim against John Spileman in a plea of
trespass, pledge the hayward.

John Noble amerced 2d. for leave to agree with Thomas Noble in a plea of trespass.

Surrenders: Richard Patel the elder to Ralph the son of Bartholomew Patel, and his
heirs, two tofts next to the messuage called Totayestead, containing 3r., granted
to him in the same form as above, fine 3s., pledge the hayward. And upon this,
Ralph grants that Richard shall have the benefit of the hedge of the 3r. for his
lifetime, provided that no waste is made.

Edmund Lene to John Wauncy and his heirs, 3r. of land at Thieveshedge, granted
to him in the same form, fine 2s., pledge as above.

Robert Shepherd chaplain to Emma Shepherd and her heirs, a piece of land next
to Rafelestoft, 8p. long and 10ft. wide, granted to her in the same form, fine 3d.,
pledge as above.

Simon Suter, when he died, held from the lord a third part of 2½a. of land; the lord
had no heriot, because Simon had no beast, and because he was not living on this
tenement. Robert and William, Simon's brothers, are his nearest heirs, and they
pay 18d. fine for entry, pledges Walter Payn and John Syre. Simon also held a
third part of ½a. of free land, rendering for fealty and services a third part of 2d.
per year; Robert and William are his heirs and they pay ¾d. as relief, pledges as
before.

Alice Helewys, John Spileman, Thomas Fuller and Robert Tailor each amerced 2d.
for damage in the lord's wood at Ladyswood with their cows, pledge for all the
hayward.

Ordered to attach Michael Kykeston for damage in the same place cutting down an
oak-tree and branches; John the dairyman amerced 2d. for the same taking away

---

[11] A heavy fine, but probably justified by the amount of the court's time wasted on these pleas.

firewood, pledge the bailiff; William the smith 2d. for the same by his servant, pledge the hayward; Thomas Trounce 2d. for the same, pledge Peter Neve; John Tailor 1d., and Ralph Echeman and Alice Helewys 2d. each, for the same by their servants, pledge for all the hayward.

Margaret the daughter of John Syre gave birth outside wedlock; childwite 2s.8d.

Catherine the daughter of William Rampolye pays 3s.4d. fine for leave to marry Adam Syre, pledge William Rampolye.

<Thomas Beck in mercy for withholding from the lord one ploughale>. The tenement Gores was accustomed to perform a ploughing service, called ploughale; and now Thomas Beck holds the tenement and does not perform it; ordered.

Richard the son of Walter Qualm, villein, who holds 3a. of customary land, amerced 3d. for default.

+Thomas and John the sons of Richard the son of Letitia, villeins, who hold 2a. of customary land, absent themselves from the lord, and are in default; ordered to take this land into the lord's hands, and to report the profits. \No profits except services./

+Ordered to raise from John Bonde 1 quarter of wheat, to the use of Olivia the daughter of William Cranmer, as John acknowledged in open court. On this he finds pledges to deliver the said wheat to Olivia at Easter and Whitsun next, in equal portions, *viz.* William the son of Elias Typetot and William Deneys.

John Lester in mercy for default, condoned.

+It was ordered elsewhere to retain in the lord's hands 1½a. of land, which John Long sold by charter to Walter Pykhorn without leave. Afterwards it was found that 3r. of this land are free, and therefore they are released by the lord's order. The other 3r., lying in the Millfield between the land of the rector of Gislingham and that of Walter Pykhorn, is customary land, parcel of the tenement Offenhagh; ordered to retain [the latter] 3r., and to report the profits. \Profits 6d./

Robert Lenne amerced 3d. for his false claim against William Typetot in a plea of detention of a sack.

Robert the son of Thomas Suter sold by charter to William Kembald ½a. of land below Lenerithsdel, without leave. This land is held from Nicholas de Walsham, but at some time Peter Pynfoul, villein of the lord, held the land. Ordered etc.

SUM 20s. 3¾d.

### 136. HIGH HALL Court General of Nicholas de Walsham, 21 April 1347 [HA504/1/5.3.ii]

Henry Trusse essoins of common suit, by Richard Trusse; he pledges faith.

John of Angerhale villein, who holds from the lord 2½a. of land and a quarter of a messuage of the lord's bondage, absents himself from the lord; ordered to take his tenement into the lord's hands, and to report the profits. Upon this the lord granted the tenement to Adam of Angerhale, John's brother, fine waived by the lord.

Margery Wodebite in mercy for default, condoned; Walter Wodebite amerced 3d. for the same.

John Wodebite the elder and John his brother amerced 6d. because they made waste in the lord's bondage, allowing a building on the tenement Alwynes to fall into ruin, to the value of 3d.

+Ordered to attach Robert of Walpole because his ploughman drove his plough outside the lord's wheat at Sheephouse; and +Hubert the shepherd for damage with his sheep in the same place; and +Robert Hereward and John Syre for damage with pigs in the lord's close. Richard Wynter the lord's shepherd amerced 1d. for damage in the lord's peas droving sheep, pledge the hayward.

+Ordered to attach John Machon and Nicholas Fraunceys for breaking hedges at Catherinescroft ['Catelynescroft'].

Robert Helpe in mercy because he was summoned to work and did not come, condoned.

John Wodebite the hayward amerced 6d. because he did not execute the lord's orders to collect rents and services, pledge the hayward.

Henry Helpe pays 18d. fine for having respite of suit of court from last Michaelmas to the end of the following six years, pledges John Packard and John Helpe. The same Henry, by leave of the court, demised to John Helpe 4a. of land and a quarter of a messuage, to hold from next Michaelmas to the end of the following five years; and John shall keep and maintain this tenement in the same condition as he received it, and he pays 2s. fine for having his term, pledges as above.

John Wodebite the elder, Walter Wodebite and John Wodebite the younger come into open court, and are agreed that John the elder shall have as his portion of the messuages which fell to them after the death of William, their father, the tenement called the Chesinees; Walter shall have the messuage called Aprilles; and John the younger shall have the messuage called Alwynes. John the elder shall rebuild the tenement Alwynes which his brother holds, as well as his own tenement was rebuilt, under inspection (?*per visum*) by the lord and his villeins. John, Walter and John pay 18d. fine for engrossing this apportionment, pledges John Packard and the hayward.

Ordered to attach Robert Hereward because he broke the lord's hedges making an unlawful road behind the barn; and Robert of the Peartree, to reply to Alan of Shelley in a plea of debt.

SUM 6s. 4d.

### 137.   WALSHAM Court General, 27 April 1347 [HA504/1/5.5.ii]

William Suter essoins of common suit, by William Cook; Robert Suter of the same, by Robert Hereward. William Kembald, defendant v Robert Hereward in a plea of trespass, essoins by John Bret; and v William Cook in a like plea, by Thomas Wither. He pledges faith; William Cook is present.

Thomas Fuller amerced 3d. for unlawful detention of 40s. from Robert Cook, as was found by 12 jurors in open court, to the loss of 3s.4d.; ordered to raise.

Surrenders: Simon Peyntour to the lord, ½a. of land below the garden of William Clevehog; and the lord granted this land to Simon, to hold for his lifetime by services and works. After his death, it shall revert to Richard, Simon's son, and his heirs, to hold in villeinage in the same form, fine 20d., pledge the hayward.

The same Simon to Robert the son of Elias Typetot and his heirs, ½a. of land at the Syke, granted to him to hold in the same form, fine 20d., pledge as above.

Richard Qualm to the same Robert and his heirs, ½a. of land at the Heveds, granted to him in the same form, fine 20d., pledge as above.

+Thomas Fuller amerced 2d. for unlawful detention of 4 bushels of wheat from Robert Cook, as was found by 12 jurors in open court, to the loss of 4d.; ordered to raise.

Peter Jay amerced 1d. for his false claim against William the smith in a plea of land.

Surrender: Stephen Cooper to John Tailor and William his son and their heirs, 1a. of land below the garden of John Terwald and abutting on the Churchway, granted to them in the same form as above, fine 3s., pledge the hayward.

John Baxter amerced 6d., Walter Rampolye 3d., and John Syre 6d., because they brewed and sold ale in breach of the assize. Robert Lenne, regrator, amerced 3d., and George of Brockley 1d., for selling bread in breach of the assize. William Syre and Robert Hereward the ale-tasters each amerced 2d. because they did not perform their duties.

SUM 10s. 5d.

### 138.   WALSHAM Court, 3 August 1347 [HA504/1/5.6]

John Margery essoins of common suit, by Peter Margery; he pledges faith.

William Suter and Robert Suter each amerced 3d. because they did not warrant their essoins.

Robert Hereward and his pledges amerced 1d. because he did not proceed against William Kembald in a plea of trespass; William Cook in mercy for the same in a like plea, condoned.

+Walter Hawys amerced 2d. for trespass against William Hawys in his corn and herbage, to the loss of 4d.; ordered to raise.

John Pynfoul claims against William Cranmer the younger that 3a. of land with appurtenances in Walsham are his by right, saying that Peter Pynfoul his father held the tenement as of fee and of right, and that he died seised thereof; and that after his death the tenement descends, and should descend to him as of right, as Peter's son and heir. He produces suit. William comes and asks to have sight; ordered.

Ordered to summon John Tailor and Walter and Robert, the sons of William Springold, to reply to William Cook and Robert, his brother, in a plea of land.

Surrender: Thomas Noble to John Noble and his heirs, a plot of land, 5p.35ft. long and 1p.7ft. wide at one end, and 1p.6ft. at the other, granted to him to hold in villeinage by services and works, fine 6d., pledge the hayward.

Peter Tailor amerced 2d. for damage in the lord's corn with his beasts, while gathering herbage; Emma Shepherd 2d., Agnes Smith 1d., Henry Albry, Walter Payn the younger, Robert Hereward, William Cook, Peter Neve, John Fraunceys and Nicholas Fraunceys 2d. each for the same, pledge for all the hayward.

John Robhood and Walter Fuller each amerced 3d. for digging on the lord's common, pledge for both the hayward.

Joan Crane pays 3s.4d. fine for leave to marry Thomas Gyles, pledges Manser of Shucford and Thomas Noble.

Ralph Patel villein, who died since the last court, held from the lord by the rod two portions of two tofts, containing 3r. of land; his heirs are Richard and William his brothers, who pay 2s. entry fine. He also held by the rod a third part of a messuage, a toft, and a third part of 8a. of land; Richard and William pay 3s. fine for entry, pledge for both fines Richard Patel the elder. Memorandum that he also held, with Richard and William, 4a. of free land of Scuttisfee, rendering for fealty and services 2d. per year. Richard and William are his heirs and they come.

Helewys Hereward, who died since the last court, held from the lord 1a. of land, by services and works; the lord had, as a heriot, half of a cow in calf, worth 3s.6d. Walter Hereward, husband of Helewys, will hold the tenement for his lifetime, in accordance with custom. Thereupon Walter surrendered this tenement to Thomas Hereward his brother and his heirs, to hold in villeinage by services and works,

301

and Thomas pays entry fine[12]; and Robert Hereward, the brother of Walter and Thomas, remitted and quitclaimed to Thomas all his right in this land.

Presented that Adam Conyers, who held from the lord 9a. of land of Scuttisfee, died six years and more ago. Nicholas his son and heir, aged 13 at that time, enfeoffed Robert of Walpole, William of the Chamber [*'de Camera'*] chaplain, John Gobald and Nicholas Conyers the elder of this land, for the time when he was under age. He is still under age.[13]

+Again ordered to retain in the lord's hands 1r. of customary land, which Thomas Patel sold by charter to John Cumpyn without leave, as shown in the court of 13 April 1345 [no.125], and to report the profits.[14]

+William Kembald amerced 2d. for trespass against Robert Hereward, and 2d. for the same against William Cook, ploughing over their land, the loss to each being ½d., as found by the enquiry; ordered to raise.

Surrenders: Simon Peyntour to Robert Typetot and his heirs, ½a. of land in the Syke, granted to him to hold in villeinage by services and works, fine 2s., pledge the hayward.

William Warde of West Street to Robert Lene and his heirs, 2½r. of land at Bolescote, granted to him in the same form, fine 2s.6d., pledge as above.

Presented that Robert of Walpole purchased by charter from Thomas Patel chaplain, villein, a messuage 4a. of land, 1a. of meadow and pasture in Westhorpe, Wyverstone and Bacton, and 1a. of land with a parcel of pasture adjoining in Westhorpe, called Stonylond, which were in the lord's seisin while these lands were in the hands of Thomas. Also that Thomas Patel chaplain, John Gobald and Constance Priour purchased by charter from Nicholas Conyers the elder a messuage 10a. of land and ½a. of pasture in Finningham, of which 4a. of land and pasture were formerly in the hands of William Patel and other villeins of the lord.

Walter Osbern and Robert Lene were elected to the office of reeve; Geoffrey Rath and William Smith to the office of hayward; and Manser of Shucford and Robert Rampolye to the office of woodward.

+John Man amerced 1d. for trespass against William Typetot, and William 1d. for the same against John, to the loss of 1½d. to each of them, as found by the enquiry; ordered to raise.

+Ordered as elsewhere to attach Mabel the daughter of Peter Springold, villein, because she married without leave; and to attach Adam Dolhale and John Helpe because they grazed on the common of Walsham where they had no right of common; and to attach Richard of Tendring for trespass in the lord's warren taking hares; and to attach Matilda the daughter of Bartholomew Patel because she married Richard Beele of Hopton without leave.

+The profits from 1a.3r. of land, remaining in the lord's hands because William Gobald freeman sold it by charter to John Gobald his son, without leave, [amount to] 12d. Ordered to retain in the lord's hands, and to report the profits.

+Ordered as elsewhere to attach Roger the Prior of Ixworth because he cultivated 1a. of customary land of the tenement Springolds, lying in the Stubbing next to the Pedderspath, and because he took away the crop from this land; and to attach

---

12 Margin is torn, and the amount of the fine is obliterated.

13 It is surprising that at 19 he was regarded as under age; 16 was the usual age for an heir to be admitted to his inheritance.

14 Margin: 'no profits except services'.

John Nugge for trespass by Richard Alot his servant in the lord's warren, setting snares in Ladyswood.

+Ordered as elsewhere to retain in the lord's hands part of a messuage 8a. of customary land, which William the bastard son of Letitia Stronde purchased from Letitia, with William the son of William of Cranmer, as shown in the court of 1 December 1340 [no.107]; and to report the profits.

+Ordered as elsewhere to attach William Wyswyf, <John Rede and Walter Doo>, villeins, because they absent themselves from the lord; and to attach Ralph of Rudham chaplain to reply to William Hawys in a plea of trespass, and to Bartholomew Jerico in a like plea.

+Ordered as elsewhere to retain in the lord's hands 1a.3r. of customary land, which William Noreys sold by charter to John of Foxley, without leave; and to report the profits.

+Ordered as elsewhere to attach Olivia the daughter of Gilbert Priour, villein, because she married without leave; and to attach Reginald Pynfoul for damage in Ladyswood by Hilary Typetot his servant, taking away firewood; and to attach Sir William Talemache for withholding four autumn works, two ploughings, and suit of court, for the tenement Outlagh and other tenements; and because he had 6 score sheep in the fold formerly of Adam Richard, to which only 60 belong.

+Ordered as elsewhere to retain in the lord's hands a piece of free land, 8p.2ft. long and 8ft. wide, which William the smith villein purchased by charter from Olivia Rampolye, and to report the profits.

+Ordered as elsewhere to attach Robert the farmer of Ashfield, for trespass by his sons, Robert and John, in the lord's warren setting snares and other traps, and also in the lord's wood cutting and taking away [sic];[15] also to attach John the parson of Langham for the same by his servant; and +to attach John of Boynhawe for trespass against the lord by his wife, taking away stakes out of Ladyswood.

Ordered as elsewhere to retain in the lord's hands 2a. of customary land, which Agnes the widow of Adam Sket holds, because she married without leave, and to report the profits.

+Ordered as elsewhere to retain a messuage 30a. of free land, of the fee of Sir John Pountney in Ditton Camoys, which John the son of Robert Warde purchased, and to report the profits.

+Ordered as elsewhere to attach Adam the rector of Westhorpe, because he grazed on the common of Walsham where he had no right of common; and +to attach John and Robert the servants[16] of Robert the farmer for damage in the lord's wood cutting and taking away an ash tree and sticks; and +to attach William Leche to reply to Bartholomew Jerico in a plea of trespass.

+Ordered as elsewhere to retain in the lord's hands a parcel of a pightle, containing ½r. of land, called Sawyerspightle, [taken] because Walter Rampolye sold it to John Barleyhand without leave, and to report the profits.

+Memorandum that the lord is to be consulted concerning the fact that William Kembald holds within his messuage ½a. of customary land, where his barn is

---

15 See below.

16 It would be a remarkable coincidence if the servants had the same Christian names as Robert's sons, and were guilty of the same offence as that recorded incompletely above. They were probably described as servants in error, and the last five words of this entry should have been applied to the earlier one.

situated, which Simon Kembald his father exchanged with William the smith for ½a. of free land, which Walter the son of William now holds. This exchange was made in the time of the lady Eve de Valence.

SUM 21s.

### 139.   WALSHAM Court General, 13 November 1347 [HA504/1/5.7]

William Cranmer the younger, tenant, v John Pynfoul in a plea of land, essoins by Nicholas Fraunceys, \sight/;[17] he pledges faith. John Tailor, tenant v William and Robert Cook in a plea of land, essoins by Robert Fraunceys; Walter the son of William Springold, tenant, v the same William and Robert in a like plea, essoins by John Craske, and Robert the son of William Springold, tenant, v the same William and Robert in a like plea, essoins by John Pye; they pledge faith; William and Robert Cook are present. Walter Goos, defendant, v Hugh Barker in a plea of debt, essoins by Manser of Shucford; he pledges faith; Hugh is present. John Wodebite, defendant v William Grocer in a plea of debt, essoins by John Elyot.

John Margery amerced 3d. because he did not warrant his essoin.

John Man amerced 3d. for unlawful detention of 6s.9d. from Nicholas Fraunceys, for the mainprise of Matilda Patel, to the loss of 3d.; ordered to raise.

John Spileman, the hayward, in mercy because he did not execute an order of the court, condoned.

Ordered as elsewhere to raise from William the son of Elias Typetot and William Deneys, the mainpernors of John Bonde, 1 quarter of wheat, to the use of Olivia the daughter of William Cranmer, as shown in the court of 23 February 1347 [no.135].

John Man amerced 1d. for unlawful detention of 11d. from Alice Smith, as found by the enquiry, to the loss of 1d., ordered to raise.

John Bonde amerced 3d. for unlawful detention of 3s.10d. from Adam of Shyrbourne, as he acknowledged in open court, the loss remitted, ordered to raise.

William the smith and John the son of John Patel, amerced 4d. for unlawful detention of 6s.8d. from Robert Fraunceys for the mainprise of Matilda Patel, as they acknowledged in court, loss 9d.; ordered to raise.

Thomas Fuller and his pledges in mercy because he did not proceed against Robert Cook in a plea of taking beasts, condoned.

Ordered as elsewhere to raise from Walter Hawys 4d., to the use of William Hawys, as shown in the last court.

Richard the son of Walter Qualm pays 6d. fine for respite of suit of court until Michaelmas, pledge Richard Qualm.

Surrenders: John Man to Robert the son of Elias Typetot and his heirs, 1a. of land in the Millfield, granted to him to hold in villeinage by services and works, fine 3s., pledge the hayward.

   Walter Osbern to William Syre and his heirs, 1a. of land, abutting on Trendelmerewong, granted to him to hold in the same form, fine 3s.4d., pledge the hayward.

   Nicholas Goche to Robert Lene and his heirs, 1a. of land at Stonylond, granted to him to hold in the same form, fine 3s., pledge the hayward.

---

17   This refers to William's request for sight in roll no.138.

William Rampolye to Walter the smith and his heirs, 1a. of land called Hevedacre, granted to him to hold in the same form, fine 3s., pledge the hayward.

General Enquiry by John Terwald, Richard Patel the elder, Walter Payn, William Rampolye, John Tailor, Bartholomew Jerico, Robert Lene, Robert Rampolye, Thomas Fuller, Simon Peyntour, Stephen Cooper and John Pynfoul.

The farmer of the cows amerced 12d. for damage in the lord's rye and barley with geese; William Swan 12d. for damage in the lord's peas with pigs; the farmer of the cows 5d. for the same, with cows; pledge for both the bailiff. Robert Lene 6d. for the same with lambs, and 3d. for the same in the lord's oats, at Brouneswong with sheep, pledge the hayward. Roger the Prior of Ixworth amerced 12d. for damage in the lord's several pasture with geese, and damage in breaching the lord's ditches at Churchgate, and damage in the lord's corn with pigs, pledge the hayward.

John the cowherd amerced 4d. for taking away the lord's corn in the autumn, pledge John Pach; Robert of Martlesham the woolman 3d. for receiving the stolen corn, pledge Edmund Lene.

John the goatherd amerced 3d. for taking away the lord's corn in the autumn, pledge Thomas Fuller; Thomas Fuller 3d. for receiving the stolen corn, pledge the hayward.

John the servant of the swineherd amerced 1d. for taking away the lord's corn in the autumn, pledge William Warde. Amice Hereward 2d. for the same, pledge John Terwald; John Terwald 1d. for receiving the stolen corn, pledge the hayward.

The servant of Robert Hereward amerced 3d. for taking away the lord's straw, pledge Robert Hereward; the servant of William Cook 2d. for the same, pledge the hayward. The servant of William Kembald did the same; ordered.

Joan Crane and Catherine and Cristiana, her sisters, amerced 3d. for selling to Manser of Shucford, without leave, 1a.½r. of land and a quarter part of a messuage; ordered to take into the lord's hands, and to report the profits.

Surrender: Walter Hereward to Thomas Hereward and his heirs, 1r. of land in the Bottomfield, granted to him to hold in villeinage by services and works, fine 9d., pledge the hayward.

John Typetot amerced 3d. for storing corn grown on the bondage, in a free tenement, William Elys and Peter Neve 3d. each for the same.

John Lester amerced 2d. for baking and selling bread in breach of the assize.

John Lester amerced 3d. for brewing and selling ale in breach of the assize; John Baxter 6d., Walter Rampolye 3d., John Syre 3d. and Alexander Smith 2d. for the same.

Robert Lenne and George of Brockley regrators amerced 3d. for selling bread in breach of the assize.

William Syre and Robert Hereward the ale-tasters each amerced 2d. because they did not perform their duties.

John Beck chaplain amerced 6d. for default.

Walter Osbern surrendered into the lord's hands a garden, called Godefreyespightle, containing 1½a., and the lord granted it to Walter to hold for his lifetime by services and works. After his death, the garden shall revert to Bartholomew Jerico and Alice his wife and their heirs, to hold in the same form, fine 6s., pledge the hayward. Bartholomew and Alice will and grant that Walter may cut and trim the hedges of the garden for his lifetime, without causing waste or damage.

William Hawys pays 3s. fine for a fold of 7 score sheep, of which 20 are allowed;

William Cranmer 2s.6d. for a fold of 7 score, 40 allowed; John Hernyng 18d. for a fold of 60; John Terwald 2s.6d. for a fold of 5 score; Robert Rampolye 12d. for a fold of 40; and John Baxter 6d. for a fold of 20; pledge for all the hayward.

The profits from ½a. of land below Lenerithsdel, now in the lord's hands because Robert the son of Thomas Suter sold it by charter to William Kembald, without leave, as shown in the court of 23 February 1347 [no.135], [amount to] 1d. Ordered to retain, and to report the profits.

The profits from 3r. of land, lying in the Millfield between the lands of the Rector of Gislingham and [that of] Walter Pykhorn, parcel of the tenement Offenhagh, now in the lord's hands because John Long sold it by charter to Walter Pykhorn, without leave, [amount to] 6d. Ordered as above.

The profits from 1a.3r. of land, now in the lord's hands because William Gobald freeman sold it by charter to John Gobald his son without leave, [amount to] 6d. Ordered as above.

The lord granted to John Bonecold a plot of land above the Tailorswong next to the messuage of Geoffrey Whitemor, containing 1r., to hold by the rod, rendering for services 12d. per year at the usual terms, and a hen at Christmas, and one autumn work with the lord's food.

+Ordered as elsewhere to attach Michael Kykeston for damage in the lord's wood cutting down an oak tree, and taking away its branches.

+Ordered as elsewhere to retain in the lord's hands 2a. of customary land, which Thomas and John the sons of Richard, the son of Letitia, held from the lord, because they absent themselves, and to report the profits. \No profits except services./

+Ordered as elsewhere to retain in the lord's hands 1r. of customary land, which Thomas Patel sold by charter to John Cumpyn, without leave, as shown in the court of 13 April 1345 [no.125], and to report the profits. \No profits as above./

Ordered as elsewhere to raise from William Kembald 1d. to the use of Robert Hereward and William Cook; and from John Man 1½d. to the use of William the son of Elias Typetot; and from the same William 1½d. to the use of the same John.

+Ordered as elsewhere to attach Mabel, the daughter of Peter Springold, villein, because she married without leave; and +to attach Adam Dolhale and John Helpe because they grazed on the common of Walsham, where they had no right of common; and +to attach Richard of Tendring for trespass in the lord's warren taking hares; and +to attach Matilda the daughter of Bartholomew Patel because she married Nicholas Beele of Hopton without leave; and +to attach Roger, the Prior of Ixworth, because he cultivated 1a. of customary land of the tenement Springolds, lying in the Stubbing next to the Pedderspath, and took away the crop; and +to attach John Nugg for trespass in the lord's warren by his servant Richard Alot, setting snares in Ladyswood.

+Ordered as elsewhere to retain in the lord's hands part of a messuage 8a. of land, which William the bastard son of Letitia Stronde purchased from Letitia, with William the son of William Cranmer, as shown in the court of 1 December 1340 [no.107], and to report the profits \Profits in the lord's granary/.

+Ordered as elsewhere to attach William Wyswyf because he absents himself from the lord; and to attach Ralph of Rudham chaplain to reply to William Hawys in a plea of trespass, and to Bartholomew Jerico in a like plea.

+Ordered as elsewhere to retain in the lord's hands 1a.3r. of customary land, which

William Noreys sold by charter to John of Foxley, and to report the profits. \No profits because grazed by the lord's sheep./

+Ordered as elsewhere to attach Olivia, the daughter of Gilbert Priour, villein, because she married without leave; and +to attach Reginald Pynfoul for damage in Ladyswood by his servant Hilary Typetot, taking away firewood; and +to attach Alexander de Walsham[18] for witholding four autumn works, two ploughings and suit of court for the tenement Outlawe ['Outlagh'] and other tenements; and because he has 6 score sheep in the fold, formerly of Adam Richard, to which only 60 sheep belong.

+Ordered as elsewhere to retain in the lord's hands a piece of free land, 8p.2ft. long and 8ft. wide, which Walter the smith villein purchased from Olivia Rampolye by charter, and to report the profits. \No profits except services/

Ordered as elsewhere to attach Robert the farmer of Ashfield for trespass in the lord's warren by his sons Robert and John, setting snares and other traps, and also with their dogs; and for their trespass in the lord's wood cutting and taking away.[19]

+Ordered as elsewhere to retain in the lord's hands 2a. of customary land, which Agnes the widow of Adam Sket holds, because she married without leave. \Profits in the lord's granary./

Ordered as elsewhere to attach John of Boynhawe for trespass by his wife, taking away stakes from Ladyswood.

Ordered as elsewhere to retain in the lord's hands a messuage 30a. of free land in Ditton Camoys, which John the son of Robert Warde villein purchased of the fee of Sir John de Pountney, and to report the profits.[20]

Ordered as elsewhere to attach Adam the rector of Westhorpe because he grazed his sheep on the common of Walsham, where he had no right to graze; and to attach William Leche to reply to Bartholomew Jerico in a plea of trespass.

Ordered as elsewhere to retain in the lord's hands a parcel of a pightle, containing ½r., called Sawyerspightle, because Walter Rampolye sold it to John Barleyhand without leave, and to report the profits.

Memorandum that the lord is to be consulted concerning [the fact that] William Kembald holds within his messuage ½a. of customary land, where his barn is situated, which his father Simon Kembald exchanged with William the smith villein for ½a. of free land, which Walter the son of William now holds; the exchange having been made in the time of the lady Eve de Valence.

Ordered as elsewhere to retain in the lord's hands a messuage and 16a. of land, meadow and wood, which Robert Shepherd chaplain sold without leave, and to report the profits.

Robert Lene pays 26s.8d. for the office of reeve; William the smith pays 13s.4d. for the office of hayward, pledge for both the hayward.

SUM £4 1s. 5d.

---

18 This appears to be an error; the earlier courts attribute these offences to Sir William Talemache.

19 This incomplete sentence, identical to that in a similar series of orders in roll no.138, is an illustration of the method used by the clerk; he copied the details verbatim from the earlier roll.

20 Margin: 'note (?nota)', later hand.

### 140. HIGH HALL Court of Edmund de Wells, 29 January 1348 [HA504/1/2.7.i]

William Cranmer essoins of common suit, by John Tailor; Walter Osbern of the same, by William Kembald; and William Elys of the same, by Adam Syre; they pledge faith.

Surrenders: Walter Wodebite to John Packard and his heirs, 1a. of land in West-woodfield, granted to him to hold in villeinage by services and works, fine 12d., pledge John Wodebite.[21] The same Walter to John Wodebite the elder and Letitia his wife and their heirs, 1½a. of land and pasture, of which 3r. of land and pasture lie in Alwynescroft, 1r. of land lies in two pieces at Packardsgate, and ½a. of land and pasture lies in Smallbrook opposite Alwynescroft, granted to them in the same form, fine 2s.6d., pledge John Packard. The same Walter to John Helpe and his heirs, 1r. of land abutting on Angerhaleway, granted to him in the same form, fine 6d., pledge John Packard.

Henry Trusse, who died since the last court, held from the lord 1r. of land with a cottage, rendering for fealty and services ½d. per year and suit of court. Robert Trusse chaplain his son, who is his nearest heir, does not come etc. Therefore ordered to distrain him for relief and fealty.

A day is given to John Wodebite the elder to repair a certain house on the tenement Alwynes by 1 August, pledge John Rampolye. A day is given to Walter Wodebite to repair a certain house on the tenement Aprilles by Easter, one year hence, pledge John Wodebite the elder.

William Deneys and William Payn amerced 1½d. for damage in the lord's corn, with sheep, pledge the hayward.

Presented that John Avemer the lord's bailiff sold 1 quarter of barley from the lord's corn, in breach of the lord's orders, and carried it to Whicham on the lord's horses, for his own use; and that the same John sold three heifers with calves, in breach of the lord's orders; and that in the autumn he wrongly (?*male*) harvested 7a. of peas at Doucedeux.

Robert of Angerhale pays 3d. fine for respite of suit of court until Michaelmas, pledge John Packard.

[SUM 4s. 4½d., not stated]

### 141. WALSHAM Court, 13 February 1348 [HA504/1/5.8]

Thomas Noble essoins of common suit, by Thomas Fuller; John Beck chaplain of the same, by Thomas Beck; they pledge faith.

Surrender: Walter Osbern to John Osbern and his heirs, a portion of a cotland, 21ft. long and 7ft. wide, granted to him to hold in villeinage by services and works, fine 6d., pledge the hayward.

William Cook and Robert his brother claim against John Tailor and Walter and Robert, the sons of William Springold, ½r. of land with appurtenances, as their right; John Walter and Robert ask for sight. Ordered.

Walter Goos amerced 3d. for leave to agree with Hugh Barker in a plea of debt, pledge the hayward.

The first pledges of John Wodebite amerced 6d. because they did not have him reply to William Grocer in a plea of debt. Ordered to appoint better pledges.

21 Tab: 'Walter Wodebite'.

William Kembald amerced 3d. for damage by his servant taking away the lord's straw, pledge the hayward.

+John Bonde amerced 2d. for unlawful detention from Robert [of Canteley],[22] the vicar of Pakenham, of 4s.6¾d., as he admitted in open court, damages remitted, pledges Robert Fraunceys and Thomas Fuller. Ordered to raise.

Robert Lene and his pledges amerced 2d. because he did not proceed against John Pynfoul in a plea of trespass.

John Pynfoul amerced 3d. for leave to agree with William Cranmer the younger in a plea of land, pledge the hayward. The agreement is such that John surrenders into the lord's hands all his right in the lands and tenements which William holds, of the tenement which Robert of the Peartree formerly held, as of the right of his wife Alice. And in return for this surrender, William surrenders into the lord's hands 1a. of land in the Millfield and ½r. of meadow in the Micklemeadow, to the use of John, to hold in villeinage by services and works, fine 3s.4d., pledge William Cranmer [the elder].

A day was given, at the request of the parties, between Richard the son of Andrew Patel, plaintiff, and Richard and William the sons of Bartholomew Patel, heirs of Ralph Patel, defendants, in a plea of debt, until the next court, to come without essoin.

Surrender: Walter the son of John Patel to Robert Typetot and his heirs, 1a. of land at the Holmere, granted to him to hold in villeinage by services and works, fine 3s., pledge the hayward.

Catherine Clevehog, who died since the last court, held from the lord 7a.2½r. of land; the lord had a steer, worth 4s., as a heriot. Her heirs are Agnes her daughter, married to William Clevehog the younger, freewoman, and Richard, Peter, Walter and John, the sons of Alice Clevehog, freemen and kin of Catherine, who seek admittance to the tenement. Because William Clevehog the younger and the coheirs are free, the tenement remains in the lord's hands. Afterwards, the lord granted the tenement to Agnes, Richard, Peter, Walter and John, to hold to themselves and their heirs by services and works, fine 3s.4d., pledge the hayward.

Alice Clevehog, \who was married to William Clevehog/ freewoman, died since the last court, and held from the lord half of two messuages and half of 24a. of land, by services and works; the lord had a mare, worth 4s., as a heriot. Her heirs are Richard, Peter, Walter and John, her sons, who seek admittance. William, Alice's husband, freeman seeks to hold the tenement for his lifetime, in accordance with custom and English law. The tenement remains in the lord's hands until etc. Afterwards, the lord granted it to William to hold until the full age of the heirs, fine waived by the lord.

Thomas Beck amerced 12d. because he was summoned for work at the ploughhale, and did not come, pledges the hayward and John Terwald. Ordered [to attach] Robert of Walpole for the same.

John Tailor amerced 3d. because his servant took away firewood from Ladyswood; Alice Helewys 3d. for the same, pledge for both the hayward. Richard Spileman and Ralph Echeman each amerced 1d. because they took away firewood from Ladyswood.

+Robert and William the sons of Thomas Suter, who hold 3a. of land, did not

---

[22] C. Morley, 'Catalogue of the Beneficed Clergy of Suffolk, 1086–1550', *PSIA*, vol.XXII (1936), p.42: 'Cantelee'.

perform the customs and works [due] therefrom. Ordered to take it into the lord's hands, except ½a. in the lord's hands, elsewhere.[23]

John Man amerced 3d. for default.

John Noble in mercy for unlawful detention of 5d. from Nicholas Deneys, to the loss of 1d., condoned; ordered to raise.

Robert Lenne amerced 1d. for unlawful detention of 4d. from Robert Cook, as found by the enquiry, to the loss of ½d.; ordered to raise.

Surrender: Walter Hawys to John Hawys and his heirs, 3½r. of land at the Row-esend, on condition that if Walter pays John 6s. at Michaelmas next, then Walter shall repossess the land; and if he does not, the land shall remain to John and his descendants in perpetuity. John pays 3d. fine for the engrossing of this agreement, pledge the hayward.

SUM 14s.

### 142. WALSHAM Court General, 4 June 1348 [HA504/1/5.9]

<John Man, defendant v Thomas Julle in pleas of debt and agreement, essoins by Richard Patel the younger>.[24]

John Tailor, tenant v William Cook and Robert his brother, in a plea of land, essoins by Robert Fraunceys \sight/;[25] Walter the son of William Springold, tenant v the same William and Robert in a like plea, essoins by John Spileman; Robert the son of William Springold, tenant v the same William and Robert in a like plea, by John Tolat; the tenants pledge faith; John, Walter and Robert are present.[26]

Oliver King, defendant v Robert of Herst in a plea of trespass, essoins by John Bonde; he pledges faith; Robert is present.

Richard the son of Andrew Patel and his pledges amerced 3d. because he did not proceed against Richard and William, the sons of Bartholomew Patel, in a plea of debt.

Thomas Julle and his pledges amerced 6d. because he did not proceed against John Man in pleas of debt and agreement.

John Wodebite amerced 3d. for leave to agree with William Grocer in a plea of debt, pledge the hayward.

William Cook amerced 2d. for trespass against John Maunser, to the loss of 2d.; ordered to raise. John Maunser amerced 6d. for damage against William Cook, to the loss of 1d., pledge the hayward and Manser of Shucford; ordered as above.

It was ordered elsewhere to retain in the lord's hands 3r. of land, lying in the Mill-field between the land of the Rector of Gislingham and that of Walter Pykhorn, parcel of the tenement Offenhagh, because John Long sold it by charter to Walter Pykhorn without leave. Now Walter comes into open court, and surrenders to the lord all his claim in the tenement; and the lord grants it to Walter and Richard the son of Bartholomew Patel, to hold to themselves and to Walter's heirs by the rod, fine 18d., pledge the hayward. Because the land was sold by charter, it was ordered to attach Walter to surrender the charter; he did so, and because other

---

[23] See roll no.135.

[24] Margin: 'It does not lie because the plaintiff does not proceed'.

[25] The tenants asked for sight (?of evidence of title) in the last court.

[26] John, Walter and Robert were those essoined: William and Robert Cook would have been those present.

free land was named therein, it was returned to him, to be surrendered at the lord's will, pledge Richard the son of Bartholomew Patel.

Simon Peyntour the younger amerced 2d. for trespass against Nicholas Smith, to the loss of 1d.; Waryn Bret 2d. for the same against William Smith, loss 1d., and William Smith 1d. for the same against Waryn Bret, loss ½d.; ordered to raise.

Surrenders: Avice the widow of Hugh Deneys to William Cranmer the elder and his heirs, 1½r. of land in the field called Langethweyt, granted to him to hold in villeinage by services and works, fine 12d., pledge the hayward.[27]

Robert the son of Peter Warde, to John Tailor and William his son and their heirs, 1a. of land in the field called Westcroft, next to the land of Nicholas Goche, and abutting at the south head on the land of the Prior of Ixworth, granted to them in the same form, fine 3s., pledge the hayward.

+Alice Man, when she died, held from the lord 1a.1r. of land by services and works; there was no heriot because she had no beast. Her heir is Richard her brother, who does not come; ordered.

+Hilary Coppelowe, when she died, held from the lord 1½r. of land by services and works; there was no heriot because she had no beast. Her heir is William Coppelowe her brother, who does not come; ordered.

Margaret the daughter of John Syre gave birth outside wedlock; childwite 2s.8d.

Geoffrey Stephen grazed his sheep where he had no right to do so; ordered.

Stephen Bacon, who holds the tenement formerly of Thomas of Badwell, unlawfully grazed his sheep, lying in Badwell, on the common of Walsham; ordered.

John Lester amerced 3d. because he baked and sold bread, and 3d. because he brewed and sold ale in breach of the assizes; John Baxter 6d., William Tailor 2d., Alice Smith 3d. and John Syre 3d., for brewing and selling in breach of the assize of ale; Robert Lenne regrator 3d. and George of Brockley 1d., for selling in breach of the assize of bread. William Syre and Robert Hereward the ale-tasters each amerced 3d. because they did not perform their duties.

Walter Springold the elder, who holds 2a. of land and part of a messuage, amerced 3d. for default.

William Wither in mercy because he sold to William Cranmer the elder 2½r. of land, to Walter the smith ½r., and to William Rampolye 10p. by estimation, without leave, condoned. Ordered to take into the lord's hands, and to report the profits.

Surrenders: John Bonde and Avice his wife, she being examined in court, to Thomas Fuller and his heirs, 1r. of land and wood at Wyswyfs; granted to him to hold in villeinage by services and works, fine 12d., pledge the hayward.

Agnes the widow of Henry Albry to Robert Lene and his heirs, ½a. of land in the Loundfield, granted to him in the same form, fine 20d., pledge the hayward.

William Warde the elder to Richard Warde his brother and his heirs, a piece of pasture, 4p. long and 3p. wide; granted to him in the same form, fine 3d., pledge the hayward.

Richard Kebbil amerced 2d. for his false claim against Robert Cook in a plea of trespass.

Surrenders: Agnes the widow of Henry Albry to John Tailor and William his son and their heirs, a piece of meadow, 5ft. wide, in the Micklemeadow, granted to

---

27 Tab: 'Avis le Deneys', later hand (?16th century).

them in the same form as above, fine 3d.. John Man to the same John and William and their heirs, a piece of meadow in the Micklemeadow, containing 5p., granted to them in the same form, fine 2d., pledge for both fines the hayward.

John the son of Robert Rampolye to John Bolle and his heirs, 1½r. of land, granted to him in the same form, fine 12d.. Simon Peyntour to John Bolle and his heirs, ½a. of land, granted to him in the same form, fine 18d., pledge for both fines the hayward.

Edmund Lene and Amice his wife hold a messuage 16a. of land, meadow and wood, by the demise of Robert Shepherd chaplain, for Robert's lifetime, which after Robert's death will revert to his rightful heirs. Robert came into open court and surrendered all his right and claim in the tenement; and afterwards the lord granted all the tenement, except 3r. of land in Fishpondfield, which remain in the lord's hands, to Edmund and Amice and their heirs, to hold in villeinage by the services and works which pertain to all the said tenement, on condition that the said 3r. are henceforth relieved of the services. And Edmund and Amice, who was publicly examined in court, bind themselves to give to Robert for his lifetime 18s. annually, to be paid at Michaelmas. And to this they bind all the said tenement and messuage to whomsoever to whom they shall belong. Seisin is delivered, fine £12 13s.4d.,[28] pledges Stephen Cooper and John Spileman the hayward.

It was ordered elsewhere to take into the lord's hands half of 2½a. and a quarter part of a messuage, after the death of Robert Crane, because Robert the son of Peter Crane did not come to receive the tenement, as is shown in the court of 20 October 1346 [no.134]. Now the lord grants it to Joan, Catherine and Cristiana, the daughters of Henry Crane, together with the portion of Agnes their sister, who refused to accept her share, as is shown in the same court, to hold in villeinage, fine 2s., pledge the hayward.

SUM £13 14s. 4d.

### 143.  WALSHAM Court General, 24 October 1348 [HA504/1/5.10]

The first pledges of Oliver King amerced 4d. because they did not have him reply to Robert of Herst in a plea of trespass; ordered to appoint better pledges.

The first pledges of Geoffrey Stephen amerced 3d. because they did not have him make amends to the lord for grazing his sheep where he had no right of common; ordered as above. The first pledges of Stephen Bacon in mercy for the same, grazing his sheep which lie in Badwell on the common of Walsham, condoned; ordered as above.

Adam Dolhale amerced 3d. because he grazed his beasts on the common of Walsham, where he had no right of common, pledge John Syre.

Surrenders: +William Wither to Robert and William the sons of William Cranmer the younger and their heirs, 2½r. of land in the Brookfield, granted to them to hold in villeinage by services and works, fine 2s., pledge the said William Cranmer; also to Walter the smith and his heirs, ½r. of land in the Priestscroft, granted to him in the same form, fine 5d.; also to William Rampolye and his heirs, 15p.

---

[28]  Margin: 'and no more, because 13s.4d. for the 3r., and for villein services to the lord and cutting wood for the lord in the tenement; paying 40s. annually, on All Saints Day and at the Purification'.

of land in the Millfield, granted to him in the same form, fine 4d., pledge for both the hayward.

Robert Cook and his pledges amerced 3d. because he did not proceed against John Tailor and Walter and Robert, the sons of William Springold, in a plea of land.

Surrenders: Edmund Lene to Walter the son of William Springold the younger and his heirs, 1r.12p. of land abutting on Thieveshedge, granted to him in the same form as above, fine 12d.; and to Robert, the son of the same William, and his heirs 1r.12p. in the same place, granted to him in the same form, fine 12d., pledge for both John Tailor.

General Enquiry by John Terwald, Walter Payn, William Rampolye, Simon Peyntour, John Spileman, John Tailor, Robert Rampolye, John Syre, Nicholas Goche, William Wither, Richard Kebbil and Ralph Echeman.

Surrenders: Richard Qualm to the lord, a messuage with a croft adjoining containing 1½a. called Souterscroft; granted to Richard for his lifetime, and after his death it is to revert to Walter the son of Peter Qualm and his heirs, to hold in villeinage by services and works, fine 6s., pledges Richard Qualm and the hayward.

Richard Qualm to William Patel the younger and his heirs, 32p. of land, granted to him to hold in the same form, fine 6d., pledge the hayward.

Walter Osbern, through the hands of the bailiff, to William Deneys and his heirs, 2a. of land in Eastfield, granted to him in the same form, fine 6s., pledge William Cranmer.

William Cranmer \the elder/ to Robert and William the sons of William Cranmer the younger and their heirs, a messuage 3a. of land in the croft formerly of Peter Hulke, granted to them in the same form. William Cranmer the younger to Robert and William his sons and their heirs, 1a. of land in Hulkescroft, granted to them in the same form, fine [for both transactions] 13s.4d., pledge William the elder.

John Man amerced 3d. for default. Ordered to attach him to reply to Thomas Julle in a plea of debt.

Profits: +from ½a. of land below Lenerithsdel, in the lord's hands because Robert the son of Thomas Suter sold it by charter to William Kembald without leave, as shown in the court of 23 February 1347 [no.135], [amount to] 1d. Ordered to retain and report the profits.

+from 1a.3r. of land, in the lord's hands because William Gobald freeman sold it by charter to John his son without leave, [amount to] 3d.

+from 1r. of land, in the lord's hands because Thomas Patel sold it by charter to John Cumpyn without leave, [amount to] 2d., except services.

+from 2a. of customary land held by Thomas and John the sons of Richard, son of Letitia, in the lord's hands because they absent themselves from the lord, and for services and customs withheld, nil, except services.

+from 3a. of land, [formerly] held by Robert and William, the sons of Thomas Suter, in the lord's hands because they absent themselves from the lord, and for services and customs withheld, [amount to] 12d., except services.

from 1a.1r. of land, held by Alice Man when she died, in the lord's hands because Richard, her brother and heir, does not come, nil, except services.

+from 1½r. of land, held by Hilary Coppelowe, when she died, in the lord's hands because William Coppelowe, her brother and heir, does not come, [amount to] 1d.

+from a messuage 8a. of land, in the lord's hands because William the bastard son of Letitia Stronde purchased it with William Cranmer from Letitia, as shown in the court of 1 December 1340 [no.107], in the lord's granary.

+from 1a.3r. of land, in the lord's hands because William Noreys sold it by charter by charter to John of Foxley without leave, nil, because grazed by the lord's sheep.

+from a piece of free land, 8p.2ft. long and 8ft. wide, which Walter the smith villein purchased from Olivia Rampolye, nil, except services.

+from 2a. of customary land, [formerly] held by Agnes the widow of Adam Sket, in the lord's hands because she married without leave, nil, because grazed by the lord's sheep. ['Ordered to retain and to report the profits' in all the foregoing]

Ordered as elsewhere to retain in the lord's hands a messuage 30a. of free land in Ditton Camoys, which John the son of Robert Warde villein purchased of the fee of Sir John Pountney, and to report the profits.[29]

Surrender: Simon Peyntour to Richard and John his sons and their heirs, ½a. of land in the Wellfield, granted to them to hold in villeinage by services and works, fine 20d., pledge Simon Peyntour.

John Robhood pays 3d. fine for setting a boundary between himself and Thomas Fuller, opposite the garden of Walter Hereward; ordered that it be set by the General Enquiry.

Manser of Shucford, who died since the last court, held from the lord half a cottage and 6a. of land; the lord had a cow in calf, worth 8s., as a heriot, John, Manser's son, is his nearest heir, and he has entry by the heriot.

Ordered [to attach] Roger the Prior of Ixworth because he grazed his sheep where he had no right to graze.

Alice Helewys amerced 1d. for damage with cows in Ladyswood, pledge William Cook.

Richard the goatherd amerced 12d. for unlawfully cutting and taking away the lord's corn in the autumn; John Warde 6d. for the same, pledge William Warde; Thomas Swan 6d. for the same, pledge Robert the woolman; John the dairyman, Catherine the servant of John Lester, and Henry the servant of John the dairyman, 6d. each for the same.

Catherine the servant of John Lester amerced 2d. for taking away the lord's straw; the servant of Walter Goos 3d. and the servant of Robert Sare 2d. for the same. The servants of Robert Lenne, John Spileman, Robert Man, Richard Spileman and Peter Tailor in mercy for the same,[30] pledge [for the last four] the hayward.

+The servant of Roger the Prior of Ixworth trespassed with the Prior's cart on the Oldtoftrow carting dung; ordered. The Prior did damage in Cannonesbrook with geese, and on the bank opposite the Rectory gate with oxen and bullocks, ordered.

Also he stored in a free tenement corn grown on the bondage, ordered; John Typetot and William Elys each amerced 3d. for the same.

+William the rector of Wattisfield caused damage in the lord's oats at Thwerslond with his foals; ordered.

John the dairyman amerced 4d. for damage in the lord's rye with the cows of the manor, and 2d. for the same with geese, pledge the hayward. +Roger the Prior of Ixworth did likewise with geese; ordered.

---

[29] Margin: 'Warde villein (*nativus*)', later hand (?17th century).
[30] The amount of the amercement is unknown, because the margin is torn.

Robert Lene amerced 3d. for damage in the lord's peas with the sheep of the manor, pledge the hayward.

Alice the daughter of William Hawys gave birth outside wedlock, childwite 32d.

Peter Gilbert amerced 6s.8d. for taking away from the lord's barn wheat in the chaff, estimated at ½ bushel, pledge Matthew Gilbert.

John Brook pays 6s.8d. for entry to half a messuage 7a. of land and ½a. of pasture, after the death of Roger at the Brook his father; granted to him to hold in villeinage by services and works, pledges John Terwald and William Patel the younger.

John Hawys amerced 1d. for damage in Strondescroft with a cow, pledge the hayward.

Richard Qualm amerced 3d. for obstructing the watercourse at Soutersgate, pledge the hayward; ordered to make good.

John the dairyman amerced 1d. for damage in the lord's oats on the tenement Strondes with geese; Robert Lene 2d. for the same with lambs, and 2d. for the same in the lord's woods with lambs, pledge for both the hayward.

John Lester and John Baxter each amerced 6d., William Tailor 3d. and John Syre 6d. for brewing and selling ale in breach of the assize. Robert Lenne regrator amerced 3d. and George of Brockley 2d., for selling bread in breach of the assize, pledge the hayward.

William Syre and Robert Hereward the ale-tasters amerced 2d. and 3d. respectively, because they did not perform their duties.

Alice the daughter of John Terwald pays 20s. fine for leave to marry Robert the son of William Cranmer [the younger], pledge John Terwald.

Walter Osbern amerced 3d. because he was summoned to work in the autumn and did not come; John Rath 3d. for the same, Robert Lene and Robert Springold 3d. for the same, Peter Jay, William Cranmer, William Hawys, Thomas Fuller, Thomas Dormour, Stephen Cooper and William Warde of West street each amerced 3d. for the same, pledge for all the hayward.

William Hawys pays 3s. fine for having a fold of 7 score sheep, 20 allowed; William Cranmer 2s.6d. for a fold of 7 score sheep, 40 allowed; John Hernyng 18d. for a fold of 60 sheep; John Terwald 2s.6d. for a fold of 5 score sheep; John Baxter 9d. for a fold of 30 sheep; pledge for all the hayward.

John at the Brook and Alice the widow of Roger at the Brook, by leave of the court, demised to William Patel the younger ½a. of pasture, to hold from last Michaelmas to the end of the following eight years, fine 8d.

It was ordered elsewhere to take into the lord's hands 1a.1r. of land, which Alice Man held, when she died, because Richard [Man] her brother and heir did not come. Now Richard comes and is granted entry, to hold in villeinage by services and works, fine 3s.4d., pledge Richard Qualm.

Surrender: John the son of Robert Warde the younger of West street to John Tailor and William his son, and their heirs, a piece of meadow in the Micklemeadow, 10ft. wide at one head and 11ft. wide at the other, granted to them in the same form as above, fine 6d., pledge the hayward.

Walter Osbern and John Pynfoul were elected to the office of reeve; Geoffrey Rath and William Syre to the office of hayward; Matthew Gilbert was elected woodward, and he took the oath; Walter [Craske] the miller and Thomas Noble were elected ale-tasters, and they took the oath.

William Cook amerced 3d. because he intervened against John Tailor and Walter and Robert, the sons of William Springold, in a plea of land.

Ordered to retain a mare, taken upon Walter Osbern, and to take more etc., for him to reply to John Pynfoul in a plea of trespass.

SUM £4 [12s. 3d.][31]

### 144. WALSHAM Court, 17 December 1348 [HA504/1/5.11.i]

John Beck chaplain essoins of common suit, by Thomas Beck; he pledges faith. Thomas Noble of the same, by Thomas Fuller; he pledges faith. Walter Osbern, defendant v John Pynfoul in a plea of trespass, essoins by William Kembald; he pledges faith; John is present. Robert Kembald essoins of common suit, by John Pynfoul; John Manser of the same, by John Noble; John Margery of the same, by William of Bardwell; they pledge faith.

Ordered to attach William Coppelowe to reply to Richard Peyntour in a plea of trespass. \Afterwards they agreed./

Robert Lenne amerced 3d. for default. Ordered to attach him to reply to Robert Cook in a plea of debt.

Surrenders: Alice Helewys surrenders to the lord 1½a. of land with a toft adjoining, of which the toft with a pightle, containing in all 1a., lies next to the messuage of William Wauncy, and ½a. is called Longhalfacre. The lord granted the tenement to Alice to hold for her lifetime; after her death it shall revert to William her son and his heirs, to hold in villeinage by services and works, fine 5s., pledge the hayward.

   Richard the son of Peter Warde to John Spileman and his heirs, ½r. of pasture, granted to him to hold in villeinage by services and works, fine 6d., pledge the hayward.

   Agnes Goche to John Lester and Rose, his wife, and their heirs, 3r. of land at Cocksdrit, granted to them in the same form, fine 2s.6d., pledge the hayward.

William Coppelowe amerced 2d. for leave to agree with Richard Peyntour in a plea of trespass, pledge the hayward.

Surrender: Edmund Lene to Emma Shepherd and her heirs, ½a. of land at Marlerscroft, granted to her in the same form as above, fine 18d., pledge the hayward.

John Wauncy, who died since the last court, held from the lord a cottage and 1½a. of land; the lord had a cow in calf, worth 5s., as a heriot. John and John his sons are his nearest heirs, and they have entry by the heriot.

John Hereward and Walter Marler each amerced 3d. because they uprooted the trunk of a tree on the tenement Strondes, and sold it, pledge for both the hayward.

Presented that Simon Smith villein, 20 years and more ago, held by purchase a messuage of the fee of the free tenure of Sir Alexander de Walsham; and Simon sold the messuage by charter to Agnes Stronde. Whether the sale was by the lord's leave, or not, is not known. Afterwards Agnes sold it to Sir Alexander de Walsham, who died seised thereof. Alexander, the son and heir of Sir Alexander, sold it to Henry of Saxmundham by charter; and afterwards Henry sold it by charter to Peter Neve, who now holds it. A day is given to the General Enquiry to enquire by the next court whether Simon Smith sold the tenement by the court's leave, or not.[32]

Surrender: Robert Lene surrendered to the lord 1½a. of land with a cottage and 1r. of

---

[31] A gap of 11in. follows the end of the text of this roll, and the sum is entered in the extreme corner, part of which is missing.

[32] Margin: 'Smyth villein' (*nativus*), later hand (?17th century).

meadow, of which 1r. of land, with the cottage, lies in Marlerscroft, 1r. lies in Sywardscroft, 1a. lies in the Bergh, and the meadow lies at Hevedacre. The lord granted the tenement to Robert for his lifetime; and after his death, it shall revert to Alice and Isabella, Robert's daughters, to hold for the lifetime of both of them. After the deaths of Alice and Isabella, the tenement shall revert to Robert's rightful heirs, to hold in villeinage by services and works, fine 6s., pledge the hayward.

John Man, Robert Typetot and William Typetot, tenants of the tenement formerly of John Clevehog, amerced 6d. because they withheld from the lord 1d. rent and 2 winter works.

Surrenders: William Rampolye to Walter the smith and his heirs, a third part of 2a. of land in the Millfield at Stonylond, granted to him to hold in villeinage by services and works, fine 2s., pledge the hayward.

Catherine Crane and Cristiana her sister, to Thomas the son of Giles Fuller and his heirs, a plot in a garden, 9½p.1ft. long and 2p.9ft. wide, granted to him in the same form, fine 6d., pledge the hayward.

Ordered to execute the orders of the last court, marked with a cross, and not acted upon.

SUM 19s. 5d., except the price of a cow, as a heriot

### 145. WALSHAM Court, 6 March 1349 [HA504/1/5.11.ii]

Walter Osbern amerced 2d. for leave to agree with John Pynfoul in a plea of trespass, pledge the hayward.

Surrenders: Walter Qualm and Catherine his wife, William Patel the elder and Agnes his wife, Alice the daughter of William Typetot, Robert Typetot and William his brother, they[33] being examined in court, to John Tailor and William his son and their heirs, an 8th part of 1r. of meadow in the Micklemeadow, granted to them to hold in villeinage by services and works, fine 3d. The same Walter and Catherine, William Patel and Agnes, they being examined in court, and Alice the daughter of William Typetot, to Robert the son of Elias Typetot and his heirs, 5p. of meadow in the same place, granted to him in the same form, fine 3d., pledge for both fines the hayward.

Robert the son of Clarice Man, through the hands of the bailiff, to John Terwald and his heirs, ½r. of land at Puddingsgate, granted to him in the same form, fine 3d., pledge the hayward.

Nicholas Goche to John Lester and Rose his wife and their heirs, a piece of land at Cocksdrit, 11p. long and 18ft. wide, granted to them in the same form, fine 3d., pledge the hayward.

Walter Qualm and Catherine his wife, William Patel the elder and Agnes his wife, they being examined in court, and Alice the daughter of William Typetot, to John the son of William Hawys and his heirs, 10p. of meadow in the Micklemeadow, granted to him in the same form, fine 3d., pledge the hayward.

Richard the son of Peter Warde to Walter Springold the younger and his heirs, ½r. of land at Thieveshedge, granted to him in the same form, fine 4d.; and to Robert

---

[33] 'They' probably refers only to Catherine and Agnes; the examination was to ensure that the wives were not acting under coercion from their husbands. In the next item the words occur immediately after Agnes' name.

the son of William Springold and his heirs, ½r. of land at the same place, fine 4d., pledge for both the hayward.

Geoffrey Whitemor to Robert of Martlesham the woolman and his heirs, a cottage and a garden, containing 1r. of land, at the Tailorswong, granted to him in the same form, fine 6d., pledge the hayward.

Walter Osbern to John Osbern and his heirs, a cottage, with part of a garden, containing in all 14¾p., granted to him in the same form, fine 6d., pledge the hayward.

John Tailor to Walter Springold the younger and his heirs, ½r. of meadow in the Micklemeadow, lying in two pieces in the Hevedacre and in the Upstreet half-acre, granted to him in the same form, fine 6d.; and to Robert the son of William Springold and his heirs, ½r. of meadow lying in two pieces in the same places, fine 6d., pledge for both the hayward.

John Warde the younger villein in mercy because he sold 6½a. of free land to Geoffrey Stephen without leave; ordered to take into the lord's hands, and to report the profits.

The first pledges of John Man amerced 3d. because they did not have him reply to Thomas Julle in a plea of debt; ordered to appoint better pledges. The same John amerced 12d. for default, and because he is absent from the court, in contempt thereof.

The first pledges of Robert Lenne amerced 3d. because they did not have him reply to Nicholas Wauncy in a plea of debt; and 2d. for the same to Robert Cook in a like plea; ordered to appoint better pledges.

Surrenders: Robert the son of Elias Typetot, and William his brother to John the son of William Hawys, 10p. of meadow in the Micklemeadow, in the Hevedacre; granted to him to hold in villeinage, by services and works, fine 3d., pledge the hayward.

John Tailor to the lord, a cotland, 3p. long and 3p. wide, lying between the messuage of Peter Tailor and the smithy; and also ½r. of meadow in the Micklemeadow in the Turfpitrode; the lord granted both tenements to John Tailor and William his son and their heirs, in the same form as above, fine 12d., pledge the hayward.

John Beck amerced 3d. because he did not warrant his essoin.

Ordered to raise 2s. from John Man, to the use of John Terwald, for the repair of the church.

A day was given to the General Enquiry until the next court to enquire concerning land which William Springold exchanged with Peter Springold, whether the exchange was by the court's leave or not.

SUM 7s. 7d.

## 146. HIGH HALL Court of John Talbot, parson of Rickinghall, 25 May 1349 [HA504/1/2.7.ii]

+Ordered to take into the lord's hands a cottage and 1r. of free land, which Henry Trusse freeman held from the lord, until the heir comes to do that which he should do for the same.

+Again a day was given to John Wodebite to repair a house on the tenement Alwynes until as above, pledge as above [sic]; and to Walter Wodebite to repair a house on the tenement Aprilles until as above, pledge as above [sic].

+Robert Sare freeman came into court and swore fealty to the lord for certain tenements which he holds free of the lord, and which are parcel of the tenement of John Stronde, for which services are owed, as shown in the rental. Ordered to enquire who are the tenants of these tenements.

John Goche and Peter Goche villeins, who held certain tenements from the lord in villeinage, recently died; ordered to seize until the heirs come.

William Isabel villein, who held from the lord certain tenements in villeinage, recently died; ordered to seize and to report the fruits (*de fructis*). Because William had no beast when he died, the heir will enter by a fine, following the custom of the manor.

John Chapman villein, who held from the lord in villeinage a messuage with 2a. of land, recently died; the heriot is an ewe. Agnes, John's daughter, aged three years, is his nearest heir; custody of the heir and of the land is granted to Amice John's wife,[34] until the heir's full age, to hold by customs and services. Amice swore fealty, and paid 6d. fine for having custody, pledge John Wodebite.

+William of Cranmer the elder, who held 2a. of free land of this manor, recently died; ordered to seize until etc.

Walter Osbern, who held from the lord certain tenements, recently died; ordered as above.

John Pynfoul, who held from the lord certain tenements, recently died; ordered as above.

William Deneys, who held from the lord 1a. of land, recently died. Nicholas Deneys his brother and nearest heir came and was admitted; he gives as relief 4d., a hen, 20 eggs, and one day in autumn,[35] pledge William Elys. He swore fealty.

Robert of the Peartree, who held from the lord 1a. of land \for services 1½d./, recently died; 1½d. is there as relief; ordered to seize until etc.

Robert Helpe villein, who held from the lord in villeinage a messuage 2a. of land, recently died; the heriot is a mare, worth 16d.. Robert's brothers, John, Henry and Gilbert, are his nearest heirs, and John asks to be admitted to his share of the tenement. He is admitted by the heriot, and swore fealty. Custody of the remainder of the tenement is given to him until Henry and Gilbert come etc.

William Elys came into court and swore fealty to the lord.

Margery Wodebite villein, who held from the lord in villeinage half a messuage 4a. of land, recently died. She had no beast, and Agnes Wodebite her nearest heir has entry on payment of 12d. fine, pledges John Helpe and John Packard. She swore fealty.

Adam of Angerhale is elected to the office of collector by the whole homage, and he took the oath.

SUM 22d.

## 147. WALSHAM Court General, 15 June 1349 [HA504/1/5.14]

[This roll records 103 deaths, each entry following closely the pattern of the first, which is transcribed verbatim. The transcript of the remainder is limited to the essential details.][36]

---

34  MS: 'Agnes', in error.
35  The relief is shown in the margin as '4d.'; in the text, the clerk appears to have quoted the annual rent, customs and works due from the tenement.
36  There is a space of 3½in. between the heading and the first item, presumably left by the clerk for essoins, of which there were none.

The jurors present that John Syre held from the lord on the day he died a messuage 12a. of land by services and works; and after his death the lord had a cow in calf, worth [*blank*], as a heriot. And that Adam his son is his nearest heir, and he has entry by the heriot, following the custom of the manor; and he swore fealty.

Adam Hardonn held a cottage with a garden; heriot a mare; heir is William, Adam's brother, who does not come; ordered.

Nicholas Fraunceys held a messuage 3a.1½r. of land; heriot a cow after calving; heir is Alice the daughter of Margaret Fraunceys, the wife of John Hamund, freeman, of St Edmunds, and she has entry.

Emma Fraunceys held a cottage with a garden and 1r. of land; no heriot because she had no beast; heir is John Fraunceys her brother, who declines to hold the tenement; ordered.

+Matilda Robbes held the plot of a bakehouse and ½a. of land; no heriot because she had no beast; heir is John her brother, who does not come; ordered.

John Deeth held a cotland; no heriot because he had no beast; heir is Catherine his daughter, who pays 3d. fine for entry, pledge John Fraunceys.

Walter Deneys held a messuage 5a.½r. of land; heriot a cow after calving; heir was Robert his son, who died; heriot an ewe after lambing and before shearing; Robert's heir is John his son, who has entry to the messuage 5a.½r., and a cottage and garden, formerly Robetels.

William Deneys held a messuage 8½a. of land; heriot a stot; heir is Nicholas his brother; who has entry.

Avice Deneys held 5a. of land; heriot a cow after calving; heir is Nicholas her son, who has entry.

+Juliana Deneys held 1a.1r. of land with a cottage; no heriot because she had no beast; heir is Nicholas Deneys her kinsman, who declines to have the tenement; ordered.

General Enquiry by Adam Syre, John Fraunceys, Nicholas Deneys, Robert Payn, John Noble, Walter the smith, William Typetot, Robert Typetot, Robert Rampolye, Geoffrey Rath, Thomas Hereward, Matthew Gilbert, Robert Lene, Robert Warde, William Jay and Edmund Lene.

+Walter Noreys held a messuage 3a.2½r. of land; heriot a cow; heir was Walter his son, who died before the court was held; none came to receive the tenement; ordered.

Walter Payn held three messuages and 30a. of land; heriot a mare; heir is Robert his son, who has entry.

William Payn held a messuage and 24a. of land; heriot a mare; heirs are William and John the sons of Robert Lene, his kinsmen, who have entry.

Walter the son of Geoffrey Payn held a messuage 5a. of land; no heriot; heirs are William and John his sons, who pay 2s. fine for entry, pledge Robert Lene.

William Hawys held a messuage and 40a. of land; heriot a stot; heirs are Robert and John his sons, who have entry.

John Hawys held a certain tenement, the size of which is unknown; heriot a cow; heirs are William and Robert his sons, who have entry.

Thomas Dormour held 1a.1r. of land; heriot a cow after calving; heir is unknown; ordered.

Edith the wife of Thomas Dormour held a messuage 12a. of land by estimation; heriot a cow; heir is William Swift her kinsman, who has entry.

Walter Osbern held a certain tenement, \of his own tenement as well as that of the tenement Robbes/, how much is not known; heriot a stot; none came to receive the tenement; ordered.

Bartholomew Jerico held a messuage 6a. of land; heriot a stot; heir is John his kinsman, who does not come; ordered.

John Osbern held a cottage 2½a. of land; no heriot; heir is Eleanor his kinswoman, who does not come, ordered.

+William Cranmer [the elder] held a messuage and a certain tenement by the rod; heriot a stot; heir was William his son, who afterwards died before the court was held, holding the said tenement by the rod; heriot a stot; heirs are Robert and William his sons, who had entry by the heriot. Afterwards Robert died; heriot a cow.

William Rampolye held a messuage and a certain tenement by the rod; heriot a cow; heirs are William, Robert, Walter and John, his sons, who have entry.

John, William and Roger, the sons of Simon Rampolye, held a messuage and a certain tenement; heriot an ewe, after lambing and before shearing; heir is Alice their sister, who has entry.

Surrender: William Taylor to Walter Rampolye and his heirs, through the hands of the bailiff, a messuage, granted to him to hold in villeinage by services and works, fine 2s., pledge the hayward.

Afterwards Walter Rampolye died, seised of that tenement and 4a. of land; heriot a mare; heirs are Robert Rampolye Walter's brother, Alice the daughter of Simon Rampolye, and William, Robert, Walter and John, the sons of William Rampolye, of whom Robert [Walter's] brother, Alice, Walter and John come and have entry; William and Robert the sons of William Rampolye, declined to hold the tenement, and surrendered etc.; ordered. Afterwards the tenement was granted to Robert [Walter's brother], Alice, Walter and John; fine waived.

William Wither held a messuage 5½a. of land, heriot a mare; no heir comes, ordered.

John Pynfoul held a messuage 13a. of land; heriot a stot; heir is Hilary his daughter, who has entry.

Memorandum that Agnes Longe \the wife of William Swan/ held part of a messuage 1½r. of land by the rod; the lord had no heriot; heir is John her son, but they say that William will hold the tenement for his lifetime, in accordance with the law of England.

William Elys in mercy because he was forewarned to serve the lady and refused to do so, condoned.

+John Taylor held, by the law of England, a tenement called Chequers ['Checers']; no heriot. They say that the tenement is escheat to the lord because Catherine, who was John's wife and formerly held the tenement, was a bastard; ordered.[37]

Joan, Catherine and Cristiana, the daughters of Henry Crane, held 1a.1r. of land and a quarter part of a messuage; no heriot; heirs are Eleanor Wyndilgard and Nicholas the son of Thomas Fuller. Nicholas comes and surrenders all his right to Eleanor, to hold by services and works, fine 6d. Before she died, Joan surrendered, through the hands of the bailiff, 3r. of land to John the son of Manser of Shucford, to hold in the same form, fine 9d., pledge for both the hayward.

William the smith held a messuage and a certain tenement, heriot a mare; heir is William his son, who has entry by the heriot.

---

[37] Margin: 'Excheat by bastardy', later hand (?17th century).

+Ordered to take into the lord's hands 1a. of land, which John the son of William Clevehog held, because etc., and for many defaults.

+Richard Man held 1a.1r. of land; no heriot; heir is Thomas his son, who does not come; ordered.

Alice, Agnes and Catherine, the daughters of William Typetot, held certain tenements; heriots 2 cows and a filly; heirs are Robert and William the sons of Elias Typetot, who come and have entry.

John Man held certain tenements; heriot a mare; heir is Robert his son, who has entry.

Richard Qualm held certain tenements; heriot a cow after calving; heir is Richard the son of Walter Qualm, who has entry.

Simon Peyntour held a certain tenement; heriot a cow after calving; heirs are Richard and John his sons, who have entry.

+Simon and Simon the sons of Peter Peyntour held 12a. of land by the rod; no heriot; heir is Alice their sister, who does not come; ordered.

Walter Qualm held two messuages 4a. of land; no heriot; heir is Richard the son of Walter Qualm, his nephew, who pays 20d. fine for entry, pledges Robert Rampolye and Robert Typetot.

+John at the Brook held half a messuage 7a. of land by the rod; no heriot; heir is John his kinsman, who does not come; ordered.

Agnes the wife of John Stonham held 2a. of land by the rod; heriot a cow after calving; heirs are Hilary and Isabella her daughters, but John will hold the tenement for his lifetime, following the law of England.

John Rampolye held a certain tenement by the rod; heriot a cow after calving; heir is Simon his brother, who has entry.

Agnes the wife of Robert Rampolye held a messuage 14a. of land; heriot a colt; heir is Simon her son, but Robert will hold the tenement for his lifetime.

Richard the son of Edmund Patel held half a messuage 1a. of land; no heriot; heir is John his brother, who pays 6d. fine for entry, pledge Robert Rampolye.

John Patel held a messuage and a certain tenement; heriot a cow after calving; heir is Alice his daughter, who has entry.

Edmund the son of John Patel held half a messuage 1a.1r. of land by the rod; no heriot; heirs are Walter his brother and Alice the daughter of John Patel, who pay 8d. fine for entry, pledge Robert Rampolye.

William Patel held a messuage 1a. of land by the rod; heriot a cow after calving; heir is Nicholas his son, who has entry.

+William the son of Walter Patel held a messuage 2a.1½r.10p. of land; heriot a cow after calving; heir is Cristiana his sister, who does not have entry, because William was in debt to the lord, concerning the office of hayward at Pakenham. Also he held [land] of the fee of divers lords, [whose names] are unknown. Ordered to seize.

+John Typetot held 3a. of land; heriot a cow after calving; heir is Robert his son, who has entry. Also a messuage and 2a. of free land, rendering for fealty and services 5½d. per year. Robert is nine years old; ordered etc.

Cecilia Pudding held 3a. of land by the rod; heriot a cow after calving; heir is Robert the son of John Typetot,[38] who has entry.

---

[38] Cecilia was married to John, and was Robert's mother.

Walter Hereward held a messuage 2a.1½r. of land by the rod; no heriot; heirs are Thomas his son, and John the son of Robert Hereward, who pay 12d. fine for entry, pledge the hayward.

Robert Tailor held a certain tenement by the rod; heriot a cow after calving; heirs are Peter his son, Sarah the daughter of John Tailor, and John the son of William Tailor, who have entry.

Catherine, Robert's wife, held a certain tenement; heriot a cow after calving; heirs as for Robert,[39] who have entry.

Isabella the daughter of William the miller held a messuage 2½a. of land by the rod; no heriot; heir is Robert Hereward chaplain, the son of Matthew, who pays 16d. fine for entry. Afterwards he surrendered the tenement to Matilda Robhood and her heirs; if she should die without an heir, the tenement shall revert to Robert's rightful heirs, pledge the hayward.

William Wauncy held 1a.1½r. of land with a messuage; no heriot; heirs are Walter, Robert, William, Thomas and John, the sons of John Wauncy, who do not come; ordered.

Alice the widow of Nicholas Kembald held a certain tenement; heriot a cow in calf; heirs are Robert and Thomas her sons, who have entry.

William the son of Alice Helewys held 1½a. of land by the rod; heriot a stot; heirs are Robert and Thomas his brothers, who have entry.

Robert Cook held half a messuage 17a. of land by the rod; heriot a cow in calf; heir is Olivia his daughter, who has entry.

Matthew Hereward held a certain tenement; heriot a cow; heir is Robert his son, who has entry.

Ralph Echeman held a certain tenement by the rod; heriot a cow; heir is Adam his son, who has entry.

Walter Springold held part of a messuage 2½a. of land; heriot a wether before shearing; heir is Robert his brother, who has entry.

Robert Springold held a messuage 2½a. of land by the rod; no heriot; heirs are Isabella and Hilary the daughters of John Stonham, \and Agnes the daughter of Mabel Springold, aged three years/, who pay 18d. fine for entry, pledge the hayward.

Richard Spileman held a messuage with 5a. of land; heriot a cow after calving; heir is Amice his daughter, who has entry.

Peter Gilbert held half a messuage with 2a. of land by the rod; heriot a filly; heir is Matthew his brother, who has entry.

Peter Neve held a messuage 2½r. of land by the rod; no heriot; heir is William the son of William the smith, who surrendered the tenement to the lady, who afterwards granted it to John Spileman to hold by the rod, entry fine 6d., pledge the hayward.

+Richard Patel villein held 3a. of land of the Scuttisfee, rendering for fealty and services 4d. per year; heriot a stot. Matthew his bastard son purchased the tenement jointly with Richard; and he is outlawed for felony. After Matthew's death the tenement should descend to Richard the son of Richard Patel the younger. Because Matthew is outlawed, the tenement remains in the lady's hands for his lifetime.

---

[39] Sarah and John were their grandchildren.

Richard Patel the younger and William his brother, held 3½a. of land with a messuage by the rod; heriots a stot and a wether before shearing; heir is Richard Richard's son, who has entry.[40]

Walter Syre held a certain tenement by the rod; heriot a cow after calving; heir is Adam Syre his kinsman, who has entry.

William Syre held a certain tenement by the rod; heriot a cow after calving; heir is Adam Syre his kinsman, who has entry.

Avice who was the wife of John Bonde[41] held a messuage 5a. of land; heriot a filly; heirs are Thomas, Matthew and John her sons, who have entry.

Richard Kebbil held a messuage and a certain tenement by the rod; heriot a colt; heir is John his son chaplain, who has entry.

Idonea Sare held 2½a. of land by the rod; no heriot; heir is Robert her son, who has entry, fine waived.

Rose Stronde held 5a. of land and a quarter part of a messuage; no heriot; heir is Robert the son of Robert Sare, who has entry, fine waived.

Robert Man held a messuage 1a. of land by the rod; heriot a cow after calving; heir is Robert his son, who has entry.

Walter [Craske] the miller held 1a.3r. of land with a messuage; heriot a cow after calving; heir is John his son, who has entry.

Robert Lenne held 4p. of land; no heriot; no heir comes; ordered.

Alice Lenne held 1r. of land; no heriot; no heir comes: ordered.

Stephen Cooper held a certain tenement; heriot a cow after calving; heir is Robert the son of Edmund Lene, who has entry.

Peter Tailor held a certain tenement by the rod; heriot a cow after calving; heirs are Alice his daughter \and Alexander the son of Isabella Tailor/, who have entry.

Alice the wife of Matthew Gilbert held a cottage and 5a. of land by the rod; heriot a cow after calving; heir is Robert Hereward chaplain, but Matthew will hold the tenement for his lifetime.

Thomas Fuller held a messuage and a certain tenement; heriot a cow in calf; heir is Nicholas his son, who has entry.

Surrender: Alice the wife of Thomas Fuller, through the hands of the bailiff, to Agnes her daughter and her heirs, 3r. of land and 1r. of wood in Hulkeswood with a cottage, granted to her to hold in villeinage by services and works, fine 12d., pledge the hayward.

The same Alice held [when she died] a certain tenement; heriot a cow after calving; heir is Nicholas her son, who has entry.

Walter Fuller held a messuage and a certain tenement; heriot a stot; heir is Alice the daughter of John Elys, his kinswoman, who has entry.

Agnes [née Goche] the widow of Henry Albry held a messuage 12a. of land; no heriot; heir is William Alwyne her kinsman, who pays 3s. fine for entry, pledge the hayward.

Nicholas Goche held a messuage 14a. of land; heriot a filly; heir is William Alwyne his kinsman, who has entry.

Peter Margery held a certain tenement, rendering for fealty and services 16½d. [annually]; heirs are John and Robert his sons, who come and swear fealty.

John Warde and John his brother held a messuage 16a. of land; no heriot; heirs are

---

[40] Between this entry and the next there is a blank space of 7in.

[41] As there is no mention of John holding the tenement for his lifetime, it may be that he was dead.

Robert and William the sons of Peter Warde, who pay 3s.4d. fine for entry, pledge the hayward.

Peter Jay held a messuage 16a. of land \and 3a. of land called Nunnescroft/; heriot a cow after calving; heirs are William and Robert his sons, who declined to hold the tenement; ordered.

John Tailor and William his son, held two cottages, 2a. of land, 3¾r.6p. of meadow, and one piece of meadow 5ft. wide, another 5p. (?long *damaged*), and another 10ft.wide at one head and 11ft. at the other ; heriot a cow after calving; because John and William were bastards the tenement is escheat to the lord.[42] Ordered.

Robert Hereward held ½r. of land within a messuage by the rod; heriot a cow after calving; heir is John his son, who has entry.

Olivia Cook gave birth outside wedlock, childwite 2s.8d.; Alice Patel did likewise twice, childwite 5s.4d.

John Lester amerced 2d. because he baked and sold bread in breach of the assize. Also amerced 3d. because he brewed and sold ale in breach of the assize; Alice Pye 6d. for the same.

[SUM £1 10s. 3½d., not stated]

### 148. HIGH HALL Court of Edmund de Wells and Margery de Walsham, 23 July 1349 [HA504/1/5.12.i]

William Elys essoins of common suit, by Robert Sare; he pledges faith.

Richard Banlone, when he died, held 1½r. of land by the rod; heir is Robert his son, who refuses to pay entry fine; ordered to seize, and to report the profits. Afterwards Robert pays a fine, pledges John Packard and Henry of Littlehawe.[43] He swore fealty.

Relief of 19d. [is due] following the death of Robert Sare, pledge the hayward.

John Goche, when he died, held half a messuage 6a. of land by the rod; heriot a calf; heirs are his sons, Walter aged ten years, and John two years; they have entry.

Peter Goche, when he died, held half a messuage 6a. of land by the rod; heriot a gimmer before shearing, worth 2d.; heir is John his son, aged four years, who has entry. The tenement is granted to Robert Man and Catherine his wife to hold by the rod until John's full age, fine 10d.

William Isabel, when he died, held a messuage 10a. of land by the rod; no heriot; heir is Sarah Flintard his kinswoman, \of full age/, who does not come; ordered to retain, and to report the profits.

Richard the son and heir of Robert of the Peartree, of full age, comes into court and gives 1½d. relief for 1a. of land, which he holds from the lord after his father's death, pledge John Packard.

John Pynfoul, when he died, held 2a. of land, rendering for fealty and services ½lb. of pepper per year; heir is Hilary his daughter, aged five years; ordered to take into the lord's hands, and to report the profits.

Walter Osbern, when he died, held a pightle, with 1a. of land, rendering for fealty and services 2d., one hen, 20 eggs, one ploughing and one autumn work per year; no heir comes; ordered to take into the lord's hands, and to report the profits.

+William Cranmer [the elder], when he died, held 1a. of land, rendering for fealty and services 2d., one hen, 20 eggs, one ploughing and one autumn work per year;

---

42  John's former wife Catherine was also described as a bastard in 1337 (no.86).

43  Margin: 'fine waived'.

heirs are Olivia and Hilary his kinswomen,[44] who pay 2d. relief, pledge John Packard; they swore fealty.

Adam of Angerhale, when he died, held a messuage 10a. of land by the rod; heriot a cow after calving; heir is William his kinsman, aged four years, who has entry, but does not come; ordered to take into the lord's hands, and to report the profits.

John Helpe, when he died, held a portion of a messuage 3a. of land by the rod; heriot a cow in calf; no heir comes; ordered to take into the lord's hands, and to report the profits. Alice John's widow comes and pays 6d. fine to have the tenement until the heir comes, pledge Walter Christmesse.

William Manser amerced 3d. for default.

John Wodebite pays 18d. fine for leave to marry, pledge the hayward.

\Memorandum that all the old orders which are not contained in this court are executed as above, as appears in the penultimate court./[45]

SUM 4s. 11½d.


### 149. WALSHAM Court, 1 August 1349 [HA504/1/5.13]

John Beck chaplain essoins, by John Margery; Thomas Noble of the same, by John Manser; they pledge faith.

John Fraunceys pays 6d. fine for entry to a cottage with a garden and 1r. of land, after the death of Emma Fraunceys, pledge the hayward.

It was ordered elsewhere to take into the lady's hands 4p. of land, after the death of Robert Lenne, and 1r. of land, after the death of Alice Lenne, because the heirs did not come. The lady granted all the tenement to John Terwald, fine 6d., pledge the hayward.

+William the son of William Cranmer the younger, who died since the last court, held certain tenements by the rod; heriot is a cow after calving; heirs are Olivia and Hilary his sisters, who have entry.

Walter Hawys, who died since the last court, held certain tenements by the rod; heriot is a cow after calving; heir is John his son, who has entry.

William Rampolye [the son of Simon], who died since the last court, held a quarter part of a messuage 3a. of land by the rod; no heriot, because he had no beast; heir is John his son, who pays 6d. fine for entry and custody of the heir[sic], pledge the hayward.

William Clevehog, who died since the last court, held 1½r. of land by the rod; heriot is a cow after calving; heir is Peter his son, who has entry.

Walter Patel, who died since the last court, held certain tenements by the rod; heriot is an ewe after lambing; heir is Alice the daughter of John Patel, who has entry.

Catherine at the Brook pays 4s. fine for leave to marry John Patel, pledge the hayward.

Presented that damage was done in the lady's rye at Dovehousewong, 2 bushels, and in her barley, ½ bushel.

Robert Lene amerced 6d. for damage in the lady's pasture in the Sheepsleswe, pledge the hayward.

Robert Sare, by the court's leave, demised to John Lester 7½a. of land, to hold from

---

[44] Granddaughters.

[45] This entry and the two insertions 'of full age' are in the hand of the clerk of the next court (no.151), dated 30 November 1349.

next Michaelmas to the term of four years following, full and complete, fine 12d., pledge the reeve.

Thomas Hereward and William Jay in mercy because they withdrew from the lady's service without leave, condoned.

It was ordered elsewhere to retain in the lady's hands a messuage 6a. of land after the death of Bartholomew Jerico, because the heir did not come. Adam Pidelak the son of Margery Jerico, and Thomas the son of John Pidelak came as Bartholomew's nearest heirs, and asked to be admitted to the tenement; granted to them to hold in villeinage by services and works, fine 6s.8d., pledge the hayward.

It was ordered elsewhere to retain in the lady's hands 1a.1r. of land with a cottage, after the death of Juliana Deneys, because no heir came. The lady granted the tenement to Roger Hamund of Langele, to hold to him and his successors by services and works, fine 6d., pledge the hayward. Roger finds mainpernors, *viz.* John Spileman, John Noble and William Grocer, to maintain the tenement in as good a condition as he received it, without waste or destruction.

Ordered to take into the lady's hands all the tenements which John Bolle holds, because he refused to serve her, and to report the profits.

Geoffrey Rath and John Noble are elected to the office of reeve; John Patel and William Typetot to the office of hayward; and Peter Tailor to the office of woodward.

It was ordered elsewhere to take into the lady's hands a cottage with a garden, after the death of Adam Hardonn, because William his brother and heir did not come. The lady granted the tenement to William the son of John the smith of Ixworth, to hold in villeinage by services and works, fine 2s., pledge the hayward.

It was ordered elsewhere to take into the lady's hands the tenement called Chequers, escheat to her after the death of John Tailor, which he had held for his lifetime, after the death of his wife Catherine, a bastard, as shown in the last court [no. 147]. The lady granted the tenement to Alexander the baker of Thurston, to hold in villeinage by services and works, fine waived.[46]

SUM 16s. 2d.

### 150. WALSHAM Court General, 18 November 1349, [HA504/1/5.15.i]

Nicholas Fuller, defendant v Stephen the goatherd ['le Gotherde'] in a plea of covenant, essoins by John Patel. He pledges faith; Stephen is present.

It was ordered elsewhere to take into the lady's hands a messuage 12a. of land, after the death of Simon and Simon, the sons of Peter Peyntour, because Alice their sister and heir did not come. Afterwards the lady granted the whole tenement to Alice, to hold in villeinage by services and works, fine 3s.4d., pledge John Terwald.

Adam Syre amerced 2d. for leave to agree with William Cook in a plea of trespass, pledge the hayward.

Surrender: John Pach and Eleanor his wife, she being examined in court, to John Terwald and his heirs, ½r. of land, granted to him to hold in villeinage by services and works, fine 3d., pledge the hayward.

The first pledges of Matilda Man amerced 3d. because they did not have her reply to

---

[46] Margin: 'Excheat of a tenement by bastardy', later hand (?17th century).

John Patel in a plea of covenant, pledge the hayward. Ordered to attach Matilda Man to reply to Thomas Julle in a plea of debt.

It was ordered elsewhere to take into the lady's hands a cottage and 2½a. of land, after the death of John Osbern, because Eleanor his kinswoman and heir did not come. Afterwards, the lady granted the tenement to Eleanor in the same form as above, fine 2s., pledge the hayward. Eleanor surrendered the same tenement to Nicholas Godefrey and his heirs, to hold in the same form, fine 2s., pledges the reeve and the hayward.

Surrender: Robert Rampolye [the brother of William the elder], and John and Walter, the sons of [the same] William Rampolye, to William the son of Robert Lene and his heirs, 2 parts of a messuage, formerly of Walter Rampolye; granted to him in the same form as above, fine 2s., pledge the hayward. And thereupon Robert the son of [the same] William Rampolye, surrenders all his right and claim in the said messuage.

Robert Kembald amerced 3d., Agnes Cook 2d., and William Cook 3d., for damage in Ladyswood with cows, pledge for all the hayward.

William Elys amerced 1d., Roger the Prior of Ixworth, 3d., and William Grocer 3d., because they stored corn grown on the bondage, in free tenements.

Alice the daughter of Olivia Rampolye amerced 3d. for taking away corn in the autumn.

Roger the Prior of Ixworth grazed his sheep where he had no right of common; ordered.

Margaret the widow of Richard Patel amerced 3s.4d. because she married Adam Fitzpiers without leave, pledges Richard Caldewell, John Cumpyn and John Spileman; Alice Fraunceys [Deeth] 2s. because she married Walter of Allwood without leave; Agnes Fraunceys 4s. because she married Nicholas Deneys without leave; Alice Rampolye 4s. because she married William Lene without leave, pledge for Agnes and Alice the hayward; Agnes Fuller 5s. because she married Richard Qualm without leave, pledge John Patel; Agnes Rampolye 4s. because she married Edmund Lene without leave, pledge the hayward; Catherine Gilbert 3s. because she married John Michel without leave, pledge Matthew Gilbert.

John Ryvel amerced 6d. for taking away the lady's wheat, pledge Alice Deneys, because in [her] house. Alice Deneys amerced 2d. for receiving the [same] wheat, knowing that it was stolen, pledge the hayward.

The cows of the manor damaged the lady's corn, loss 6 bushels of barley, amercement 3s.; the oxen of the manor likewise, 6d.; the pigs of the manor likewise, 4d.; the goats of the manor likewise, 3d.[47]

Walter the smith amerced 3d. for waste on the tenement Godefreys demolishing a cottage; a day was given to him to rebuild it by Michaelmas, pledge John Terwald.

Robert Hereward the rector of Heringswell and Robert Hawys purchased from John Beck chaplain a certain tenement in Walsham, formerly of John Noreys and Agnes at the Green; and they came and swore fealty, and showed the charter in due form.

John the dairyman amerced 6d. for taking away the lady's corn in the autumn.

Alice Pye paid 9d. fine for having a fold of 30 sheep.

---

[47] MS does not say who was amerced; it may have been the individual custodians or the reeve, who was responsible for all of them.

Alice Pye and John Lester each amerced 6d. for breaking the assize of ale; John Manser 4d. for the same. George of Brockley amerced 1d. for regrating bread. Thomas Noble the ale-taster amerced 2d. because he did not perform his duties; John the miller was elected to the office.

William Grocer amerced 2s. because he took away a quernstone and a brass pot, pledge the hayward. A day is given to enquire concerning more.

It was ordered elsewhere to take into the lord's hands 1½a. of land, which John the son of William Clevehog held, because he absented himself and for many defaults. John comes and pays 6d. fine to repossess the land; granted to him to hold in villeinage by services and works, pledge William Typetot.

Surrender: John the son of William Clevehog to William Typetot and his heirs, 1r. of land, granted to him in the same form, fine 6d., pledge the hayward.

It was ordered elsewhere to take into the lady's hands half a messuage 1a.1r. of land, after the death of Robert Springold, because his nearest heir, Agnes the daughter of Mabel Springold, was aged three years. The lady granted the tenement to Walter Petyt, Agnes' father, to hold until her full age, pledges John Spileman and Robert Springold. \Walter came and refused to hold the tenement; ordered to retain, and to report the profits./

At the court of 15 June [no.147] it was presented that Alice the wife of Matthew Gilbert held a cottage 5a. of land, that the lady had a heriot, that Robert Hereward chaplain was her heir, and that Matthew will hold the tenement for life. Thereupon Robert comes and surrenders all his right and claim therein, and remits and quitclaims to Matthew and his heirs, to hold in the same form as above, fine 12d., pledge the hayward.

It was ordered elsewhere to take into the lady's hands a messuage with a garden, after the death of Alice Lenne, because no heir came. The lady granted the tenement to John Terwald and his heirs, in the same form as above, fine 12d., pledge the hayward .

Eleanor the widow of William Wither surrendered to the lady a messuage with a garden, and 10a. of land and 1r. of meadow. The lady granted the whole tenement to John at the Meadow, of Little Ashfield, and Eleanor, to hold to them and the heirs lawfully procreated of their bodies; and if they die without such heirs, the tenement shall revert to John's rightful heirs, to hold in villeinage by services and works; they pay a fine for entry. Eleanor pays a fine for leave to marry John,[48] pledge John Spileman.

Thomas Kembald amerced 3d. for default.

Peter the son of Robert Tailor amerced 3d. for trespass against William Alwyne, to the loss of 8d., as found by the enquiry; ordered to raise.

General Enquiry by John Terwald, Adam Syre, Robert Payn, Nicholas Deneys, William Typetot, Robert Typetot, Robert Rampolye, Richard Peyntour, Walter the smith, John Noble, Robert Lene and Edmund Lene.

Richard Priour amerced 3d. because he sold to Alexander the baker a cottage with a garden of the lady's bondage, without leave; ordered to seize, and to report the profits.

Richard Priour amerced 3d. for default.

+A day is given, at the request of the parties, between Adam Pidelak, plaintiff and

---

[48] Margin: 'fine 26s.8d.'; this covered the entry fine and that for leave to marry.

John Noble, defendant, in a plea of trespass until the next court, to come without essoin.

+Ordered as elsewhere to retain in the lady's hands the plot of a bakehouse and ½a. of land, [taken] after the death of Matilda Robbes, because John her brother and heir did not come, and to report the profits. \Profits in the account./

+The profits from a messuage 3a.2½r. of land, in the lady's hands after the death of Walter Noreys, [amount to] 6d.; ordered to retain and report the profits.

+The profits from a messuage 5½a. of land, in the lady's hands after the death of William Wyther, [amount to] 5d.; ordered as above.

+The profits from 1a. 1r. of land, in the lady's hands after the death of Richard Man, [amount] to 1d.; ordered as above.

+The profits from a messuage 2a. of free land, in the lady's hands after the death of John Typetot, because Robert his son is under age, [amount to] 12d.; ordered as above.

SUM 79s. 4d.

### 151.   HIGH HALL Court of Edmund de Wells and Margery de Walsham, 30 November 1349 [HA504/1/5.12.ii]

Olivia Cranmer essoins of common suit, by William Elys; Henry Hattele, of the same, by William Manser; they pledge faith.

+Ordered to retain in the lords' hands a messuage 10a. of \ware/ land, which William Isabel held, until etc.

Ordered to retain in the lords' hands 2a. of land, which John Pynfoul held by knight's service, until etc. Afterwards the lords granted the tenement to Adam Syre, to hold until the full age of the heir, rendering services and customs therefrom, as shown in the last court.

Ordered to retain in the lords' hands a pightle 1a. of land, which Walter Osbern held, until etc.

+Ordered to retain in the lords' hands a messuage 10a. of villein land, which Adam of Angerhale held, until etc.

+Again a day was given to John Wodebite the elder to repair a house on the tenement Alwynes by 1 August, pledge John Packard; and to +Walter Wodebite to repair a house on the tenement Aprilles by 1 August, pledge John Wodebite the elder.

Robert Barker amerced 3d. for default, and 11d. because he was summoned for ploughing work at the time of sowing wheat, and did not come.

Robert Angerhale amerced 3d. for default.

The whole homage present that Olivia Cranmer and Hilary her sister damaged the lords' barley \in the field called Abovethewood/ with 16 cows and bullocks, to the value of 7 bushels; ordered to raise, pledges Nicholas Deneys and Edmund Lene; that John Noble did the same there with two cows, 1 bushel, ordered to raise.

The Prior of Ixworth damaged the lords' wheat at the Hulver \with his cows/, 2 sheaves; and in the Thirtyacres with his sheep, 3 sheaves; ordered to raise.

<Edmund Lene damaged the lords' oats at Angerhalefield with his horses, 1 bushel; John Packard and John Wodebite did the same with their beasts, ½ bushel each; ordered>.[49]

---

[49]  Deleted because in the next court.

+Adam Sire and Alice Hereward damaged the lord's barley at Stonylond with their beasts, ½ bushel each; ordered to raise. Adam Sire amerced 3d. for damage in the ox pasture with sheep and pigs.

Agnes Wodebite \the daughter of William Wodebite/, villein, married without leave. Agnes the daughter of John Wodebite did the same; ordered to seize all the tenements which they hold in villeinage, until etc.[50]

[SUM 1s. 8d., not stated]


### 152. WALSHAM Court, 3 February 1350, [HA504/1/5.15.ii]

Stephen the goatherd and his pledges amerced 3d. because he did not proceed against Nicholas Fuller in a plea of covenant.

Matilda Man amerced 1d. for leave to agree with John Patel in a plea of covenant, pledge the hayward.

Thomas Julle amerced 1d. for his false claim against Matilda Man in a plea of debt, pledge the hayward.

The first pledges of Roger the Prior of Ixworth amerced 3d. because he grazes his sheep where he has no right; ordered to appoint better pledges.

John Hardheved the miller amerced 2d. for leave to agree with Nicholas Patel in a plea of trespass, pledge John Spileman.

Peter Tailor amerced 2d. for leave to agree with Richard Qualm in a plea of trespass, pledge John Terwald.

Richard Priour amerced 3d. because he abused Edmund Lene villein, outside the court, in contempt of the lady, pledge John Terwald.

Alice at the Brook amerced 3s.4d. because she married William Warde without leave, pledge John Spileman; likewise, Agnes Goche to Peter Warde, 3s.4d.; Amice, the daughter of Richard Spileman, to Stephen Swilepot, 3s.; Alice, the widow of Simon Rampolye, to Robert Payn, 5s.; pledge for all the hayward.

Matilda Robhood gave birth outside wedlock, childwite 2s.8d.

Edmund de Wells the rector of Beccles damaged the lady's wheat at Currescroft with his pigs, cows and sheep; ordered.

Richard Qualm amerced 1d. for damage in the lady's wheat on the Oldtoft with cows; ordered. Olivia Cranmer in mercy for the same, condoned.

Robert the farmer amerced 1d. for damage in Ladyswood with a colt; William Piers 1d. for the same, pledge for both the hayward.

Edmund Lene amerced 1d. for damage in the lady's wheat on Ayleldestoft with sheep; Agnes Cook 1d. for the same, pledge for both the hayward; Nicholas Fuller 1d. for the same, pledge Richard Qualm; Cristiana Lene and Agnes Goche 1d. each for the same, pledge the hayward.

John the lady's shepherd amerced 3d. for damage in her wheat at Northawegate, pledge John Spileman.

Ordered [to attach] John Robetel villein, who absents himself from the lady and is living in Bacton ['Baketon'].

Surrenders: John Kebbil chaplain to John Terwald and his heirs, 1r. of meadow in the Micklemeadow, granted to him to hold in villeinage by services and works, fine 6d.; and to John the son of Manser of Shucford and his heirs, 1r. and a third

---

[50] Margin: 'enrolled in the next court'.

part of 2r. of land, granted to him in the same form, fine 10d., pledge for both the hayward.

Richard the son of Gilbert Priour to John Hardheved the miller and his heirs, a cottage with a garden, 8p.4ft. long on one side and 5p.8ft. on the other, and 4p.5ft. wide at one head and 14ft. at the other, granted to him in the same form, fine 12d., pledge the hayward.

SUM 21s. 10d.

### 153.   HIGH HALL Court of Edmund de Wells, 1 June 1350 [HA504/1/5.16.i]

William Manser essoins of common suit, by Henry of Hattele; Adam Sire of the same, by William Elys; they pledge faith.

John Trusse, who purchased from Robert his brother 1r. of land of the lord's fee, in a messuage in Westhorpe, next to the messuage of William Payn chaplain, swore fealty, and found a pledge to show the charter at the next court, *viz.* John Packard.

+The profits from a pightle and 1a. of land, in the lord's hands after the death of Walter Osbern, because no heir came;[51] ordered to retain, and report the profits.

Agnes the daughter of John Wodebite pays 2s. fine for leave to marry Edmund Lene, pledges John Wodebite and John Packard.

Amice Helpe to pay a fine for leave to marry Adam Dolet, condoned; ordered to distrain Adam for fealty and for entry to the tenement which he holds by the right of his wife.

Agnes Chapman freewoman, who holds 1a. of customary land, gave birth outside wedlock, childwite,[52] pledge Edmund Lene.

Ordered [to attach] Adam Sire for trespass against the lord by his sow killing 10 unshorn sheep, and for damage by the same sow in a stack of peas.

John Packard freeman, who holds customary land, married without leave; Alice Helpe freewoman, who holds customary land, married John Packard without leave, both in mercy.

Agnes Chapman surrendered all her right in the tenement which she holds in dower after the death of her husband Gilbert Helpe the younger, to Gilbert the son of Gilbert Helpe the elder, and John the son of John Helpe; granted to them to hold in villeinage, fine 6d., pledge John Packard.

[SUM 2s. 6d., not stated]

### 154.   HIGH HALL Court of Edmund de Wells, 29 September 1350, [HA504/1/5.16.ii]

Henry of Hattele essoins of common suit, by Henry of Littlehawe, he pledges faith.

William Manser amerced 3d. because he did not warrant his essoin. Adam Syre in mercy for the same. \Afterwards he came/.

The first pledges of John Trusse amerced 3d. because they did not have him show the charter by which he purchased 1r. of land from Robert Trusse; ordered to appoint better pledges.

Ordered to take into the lord's hands 1a. of land, which Adam Dolet holds by the right of his wife Amice, because he refuses to pay entry fine. Afterwards he came and paid 3d. fine for entry, pledge John Packard.

---

[51] Margin: 'services and works'.
[52] No amount is given for this fine, or for the amercements of John Packard and Alice Helpe. This is probably because the tenants were free, and the lord's right to levy these fines was in doubt.

+John Wodebite amerced 3d. because he did not repair a house on the tenement Alwynes as he undertook, pledge John Packard; ordered to repair.

+Walter Wodebite amerced 3d. because he did not repair a house on the tenement Aprilles as he undertook, pledge John Wodebite; ordered to repair.

Edmund Lene caused damage in the lord's oats at Angerhalefield with his horses, to the loss of 1 bushel, pledge John Wodebite; John Packard and John Wodebite did the same, to the loss of ½ bushel each; ordered to raise, pledge each for the other.

Ordered to attach Agnes the daughter of William Wodebite villein because she married without leave, and lives in Hinderclay ['Hildercle'].

John Trusse amerced 1d. for default. <William Manser in mercy for the same.> [see above]

Edmund Lene amerced 6d. because he was summoned to work in autumn and did not come, pledge John Wodebite; John Packard 3d. for the same, pledge the hayward.

The cowherd of the manor caused damage in the lord's barley above the wood, 4 sheaves; and in the lord's wheat at Netherhawe, 2 bushels; ordered.

The cowherd of the Prior of Ixworth caused damage in the lord's barley at the Hulver, 2 bushels; ordered.

+The cowherd of the Prior, Adam Sire, Walter of Allwood and the swineherd of the manor caused damage in the peas at the Henbels [?Abels], with their beasts, ordered.

Walter Wodebite amerced 3d. because he was summoned to work in autumn, and did not come, pledge the hayward.

Nicholas Deneys and William Clevehog caused damage in the oats on Kembaldslond, 4 sheaves; ordered. John Packard caused damage in the lord's oats at Helpeswood with cows, 2 bushels, pledge the hayward.

The keeper of the oxen and cows caused damage in the lord's peas at Helpeswood, ½ bushel.

Robert Banlone caused damage in the lord's oats at Newhawe, 1 sheaf; and in his peas at Westhorpe, 1 bushel.

+John Wodebite amerced 3d. for waste made on his tenement demolishing a certain house, pledge the hayward; ordered to rebuild. Edmund Lene 3d. for the same, pledge John Wodebite; ordered as above.

John Packard was elected to the office of reeve, but declined to perform that office; Ordered to seize all the tenements which he holds from the lord, and to report the profits.

John Wodebite was elected to the office of hayward for the tenement Aprilles, and took the oath.

[SUM 2s. 10d., not stated]

## 155.   WALSHAM Court General, 11 November 1350 [HA504/1/5.17.i]

John Patel in mercy for default. Afterwards he came.

William Jay and his pledges amerced 2d. because he did not proceed against William Godyene ['Guggeon'] in a plea of trespass.

The first pledges of Roger the Prior of Ixworth amerced 12d. because they did not have him make amends for damage in the lady's rye with his pigs; ordered to appoint better pledges.

+The profit from ½a. of land, now in the lady's hands because Edmund Lene sold it to William Lene without leave, is nothing, except the services. Ordered to retain, and report the profits.

+Ordered to attach John Robetel villein because he absents himself from the lady, and lives in Bacton.

+Ordered to attach Edmund de Wells, the rector of Beccles, for trespass in the lady's warren taking a hare.

+Ordered to attach Henry Breton and William and Walter his brothers, villeins, because they absent themselves from the lady.

+Ordered to attach Adam Fitzpiers to make good waste in the bondage on the tenement formerly of Richard Patel the younger.

+Walter the smith amerced 6d. because he did not make good waste in the tenement Godefreys as he undertook; ordered to make good.

+Ordered to attach Robert of Walpole for withholding a boonwork in the autumn, called Reapale, with one man going; and +to attach William Larke for the same.

A day is given, at the request of the parties, between John Robhood, plaintiff and Peter Tailor, defendant, in a plea of trespass, until the next court, to come without essoin.

+Ordered as elsewhere to retain in the lady's hands the plot of a bakehouse and ½a. of land, [taken] after the death of Matilda Robbes, because John her brother and heir did not come, and to report the profits.[53]

+Ordered to retain in the lady's hands a messuage 3a.2½r. of land, [taken] after the death of Walter Noreys, because no heir came, and to report the profits.

+The profit from a messuage 5½a. of land, in the lady's hands after the death of William Wither, because no heir came; ordered.

+The profit from 1a.1r. of land, in the lady's hands after the death of Richard Man, because Thomas his son and heir did not came; ordered.

+The profit from a messuage 2a. of free land, in the lady's hands after the death of John Typetot, because Robert his son and heir is under age; ordered.

Thomas Hereward and Alice his wife amerced 3d. for their false claim against Nicholas Fuller in a plea of land.

William Godyene amerced 3d. for breaking an agreement with William Jay, as found by the enquiry, to the loss of 3s.5d.; ordered to raise.

Hilary the daughter of William Cranmer [the younger] pays 13s.4d. fine for leave to marry John the son of Peter Margery, pledge the hayward.

Matilda Robhood pays 5s. fine for leave to marry William Cook, pledge the hayward.

John Noble amerced 1d. for his false claim against John Rampolye in a plea of trespass.

Cristiana Springold and Joan the daughter of Bartholomew Patel gave birth outside wedlock; childwyt 2s.8d. each.

Thomas Lorence amerced 2d. for damage in Ladyswood with his beasts, pledge John Lene; John Lester 4d. for the same, pledge John Terwald; John of Banham 12d. for the same, pledge Robert Springold; the dairymaid of the manor 3d. for the same, pledge the reeve; the keeper of the cows of the manor 3d. for the same, pledge the reeve \waived because no keeper/.

Massilia Hawys amerced 1d. for damage with beasts in the close called Master

---

[53] Margin: against this and the next four items: 'profits nil except services'.

John's, pledge John Terwald; Richard Priour, Robert Sare and Alice Pye, 2d. each for the same, pledge the hayward; John Hardheved 1d. for the same, pledges the hayward and William Typetot; Cristiana Lene 1d. for the same, pledge the reeve.

William Lene in mercy because he was summoned to work in autumn and did not come \condoned because in the lady's service/; John Rampolye amerced 2d., Nicholas Fuller 2d., Thomas Hereward 1d. and Robert Hernyng 1d. for the same, pledge for all the hayward.

Thomas Hereward the thresher in mercy because he withdrew from the lady's service \condoned because he did what he should have done/.

Roger the Prior of Ixworth grazed his sheep where he has no right of common; ordered.

Massilia Hawys in mercy because she raised a fold without leave. \Afterwards she paid 3s.6d. fine, for a fold of 80 sheep, of which 20 are without fine, as in past years./ Robert Hereward chaplain amerced 2s. because he raised a fold without leave, pledge for both the hayward; ordered.

John Lester and Alice Pye each amerced 3d. because they brewed and sold ale in breach of the assize; Robert Rampolye 1d. for the same, pledge for Alice and Robert the hayward. Thomas Noble and John Craske the ale-tasters each amerced 1d. because they did not perform their duties; John at the Meadow elected in place of Thomas Noble.

+Adam Fitzpiers and Margaret his wife amerced 6d. because they demised the tenement of Richard Patel the younger to Robert Tanne for a term of years, without leave; ordered to take into the lady's hands, and to report the profits.

Surrender: John Noble to John the son of John Pach and his heirs, 1r. of land in the Millfield, granted to him to hold in villeinage by services and works, fine 3d., pledge the hayward.

John Spileman the reeve amerced 40s. because he did not perform his duties in a proper manner, and as a result a great part of the lady's corn died in the autumn, to her loss, pledges John Terwald and Adam Syre.

Damage was done in Ladyswood by oxen, cows and other animals; amercement waived.

Nicholas Godefrey villein in mercy because he absents himself, and refuses to serve the lady as a thresher, condoned.

It was ordered elsewhere to take into the lady's hands 3½r.16p. of meadow, and a piece of meadow 5ft. wide, another piece containing 5p., and another 10ft. wide at one head and 11ft. wide at the other, escheat to the lady after the deaths of John Tailor and William his son, because they were bastards. Now the lady grants all this tenement to John Bolle, to hold to him and his heirs in villeinage by services and works, fine 36s., pledge the hayward.[54]

Ordered as elsewhere to retain in the lady's hands two cottages, [taken] after the deaths of John Tailor and William his son, escheat because they were bastards; and a certain tenement after the death of Walter Osbern, as much of his own tenement as of the tenement Robbes, how much is not yet known, because no heir comes; and half a messuage 7a. of land, after the death of John at the Brook, because no heir comes; and a messuage 2a.1½r.10p. of land, and other tenements

---

54 Margin: 'Excheat', later hand (?17th century).

of the fee of various lords, how many is not known, after the death of William, the son of Walter Patel, because Walter was in debt to the lady from the time when he was the hayward at Pakenham; and 6½a. of free land which John Warde the younger sold to Geoffrey Stephen without leave; and ½a. of land below Lenerithsdel which Robert the son of Thomas Suter sold by charter to William Kembald without leave; and 1a.3r. of land, which William Gobald freeman sold by charter to John his son, without leave; and 1r. of land which Thomas Patel sold by charter to John Cumpyn without leave; and 2a. of customary land which Thomas and John the sons of Richard, the son of Letitia, held from the lady, because they absent themselves; and 3a. of land which Robert and William the sons of Thomas Suter held, because they absent themselves, and for services and works withheld; and 1r. of land, after the death of Hilary Coppelowe, because William her brother and heir does not come; and a messuage 8a. of land which William the bastard son of Letitia Stronde purchased from Letitia, as shown in the court of 1 December 1340 [no.107]; and 1a.3r. of land which William Noreys sold by charter to John of Foxley without leave; and a piece of free land, 7p.2ft. long and 8ft. wide, which Walter the smith villein purchased from Olivia Rampolye; and 2a. of land, which Agnes Sket held, because she married without leave; and a messuage and [blank] of land, meadow and wood, after the death of Agnes Sket, because John her son is under age, viz. [blank] years; and to report the profits.[55]

SUM 111s. 11d.

---

[55] Margin: 'Profits in the account of last year, and in the lady's granary, except services'.

# GLOSSARY

Abbreviations:

*MED*   *Middle English Dictionary*
*OED*   *Oxford English Dictionary*
*Latham*  R.E. Latham, *Revised Medieval Latin Word List* (London 1965)

Where the subject of a definition occurs very rarely, the numbers of the courts where it appears are shown in or at the end of the definition, e.g. '(nos. 42 and 43)' under 'Aid'.

**Account** (*compotus*): annual statement prepared by the reeve of all moneys received and expended on the lord's behalf, and of his crops and livestock

**Affeerer**: one of two tenants appointed by each manorial court to advise the steward on the level of amercements (q.v.)

**Aid**: payment demanded from a feudal vassal by his lord, limited by Magna Carta to three uses, namely to make the lord's eldest son a knight (nos.42 and 43), to marry his eldest daughter and to help him pay a relief (q.v.) to his superior lord (*OED*). Also payment due from a certain tenement for a specific use e.g. 'to the light of the Blessed Virgin Mary' (no.6); see also **Sheriff's Aid**

**Ale, Assize of**, see **Bread and Ale, Assizes of**

**Ale-taster**, one of two officials appointed to regulate the quality and price of ale brewed and sold in the vill

**Amercement**: penalty in money or in kind for an offence against the lord or the court, as advised by the affeerers; see Introduction, under 'The Courts, Procedures' p.9

**Assizes of Bread and Ale**: see **Bread and Ale, Assizes of**

**Attachment**: seizure of a person or his possessions to ensure his compliance with the court's orders

**Bailiff**: agent or official of the lord of the manor; see Editorial Methods p.22

**Bondage**, see **Villeinage**

**Boonwork**: labour service on the lord's land and crops owed to the lord of the manor at peak periods, and always at the time of harvest and ploughing. These works, sometimes called 'love-works', were additional to all other services pertaining to the tenants' holdings; see **Ploughale** and **Reapale**

**Bounds**, see **Metes and bounds**

**Bread and Ale, Assizes of**: regulation by statute of the baking of bread, the brewing of ale, and the sale of each

**Bullimong** ('Bolemong'): mixture of crops grown together for cattle-feed, e.g. oats, beans and peas

**Capital lord(s) of the fee**: lord or lords superior to the lord of a fee which has been subdivided among yet other lords: the process known as subinfeudation. This phrase is used as a proviso in contemporary charters transferring free or customary land, for example, thus: 'rendering annually to the capital lords of the fee the lawful, due and accustomed services therefrom, for all services, aids, customs, suits of court and secular demands'. Later the words after 'therefrom' are replaced with 'etc.', and it is in this form that the phrase is used in the Walsham rolls, probably copied from charters which had been temporarily surrendered to the lord. In later centuries, the clause appears to have been no more than an all-embracing form of words to cover all payments and duties due to any lord, comparable with the more modern phrase 'without prejudice'; see **Fee, Knight's**.

**Capital messuage**: messuage in which the the owner or tenant of more than one messuage had his own dwelling, his chief messuage; see **Messuage**

**Carucate**: notional area of land taken for fiscal purposes to be that which could be worked by one plough team in a season; the fiscal value of 1 carucate was taken as 120 fiscal acres; see also **Old acre** and **Ware land**.

**Castle ward** or **guard**: tax paid in commutation of the service whereby a tenant was required to assist in the defence of the lord's castle, owed in Walsham manor to Norwich castle, in High Hall to Eye castle (no.123); sometimes called 'wardpenny'

**Chaplain** (*capellanus*): ordained priest without a parochial benefice

**Chapman**: small trader, usually selling his wares at markets or fairs, a pedlar. William the chapman appears in several High Hall courts in Section 2 as 'William the son of Reginald the chapman', whose surname is given in court no.1 as *mercator*, for which the only meaning in Latham is 'merchant'.

**Charter**: deed of covenant between parties to a land transaction, used as proof of title

**Chevage**: annual payment by villeins permitted to live outside the manor, to acknowledge their subservience to the lord

**Childwite**: fine paid to the lord when an unmarried villein gave birth to a child: in Walsham the fine was levied on the woman or her father; *OED* suggests that the putative father paid.

**Collector**: official responsible for collecting fines, rents and other monies for the lord, and for keeping the tallies of expenditure, also known as the 'hayward' (*messor*); see Introduction under 'Court Officials' p.7.

**Cosp**: hasp, cross-piece of the handle of a garden fork, or the head of a plough

**Cotland** (*cotagium*): smallholding, usually including a cottage

**Countertallier** (*contratalliator*): holder of a counter-tally used to confirm the other half of a tally retained by the tallier, or his employer

**Croft**: enclosed plot of land, often adjacent to a house; see also **Toft**

**Cullet**, see **Sheep**

**Customary tenure**: tenure of land for which suit of court at specified courts, annual rent and services are owed to the lord

**Customs and works**: the dues to the lord by which customary tenements were held

**Customs of the manor**: customs of land tenure, inheritance, dower, etc., of land measurement, and of tithe payment, 'from time immemorial'. The Walsham customs were set down in the 1577 Survey, and are recorded by Dodd.[1]

**Day, given by the court**: the time limit specified for the settlement of a claim or dispute, usually by the next court, sometimes called 'love day'

---

[1]   Dodd, *Field Book of Walsham le Willows*, pp.49–51.

**Default**: failure to perform an obligatory duty, usually to attend court

**Deforcement**: taking and keeping land from the lawful owner or tenant

**Delivery of prisoners**, see **Gaol delivery**

**Demesne**: land held for the lord's own use, sometimes attached to the manor house

**Demise**: to grant, convey or transfer land other than villein land

**Distrain**: to confiscate a person's land or goods to force him to meet an obligation, e.g. to appear in court to answer a complaint

**Dower**: right of a widow to hold for her lifetime part of her late husband's land; by the law of England one third, by the custom of Walsham a half

**Dredge**: mixture of grains sown together, especially oats and barley

**Easement**: right or privilege of access across the land of another person

**Enfeoffment**: action by which the ownership of land held in fee is transferred to another's 'use', that is 'benefit'

**Engross**: to record in a formal document, e.g. a court roll

**Escheat**: land that falls to the lord by forfeiture

**Essoin**: excuse for absence from court; to offer such an excuse on behalf of the absentee

**Farm**: rent paid annually in money or in kind, without any other services

**Farmer of the cows of the manor**: one who pays a fine to lease the lord's herd

**Fealty**: oath of fidelity to his lord sworn by a tenant in court

**Fee, Capital lords of**, see **Capital lords of the fee**

**Fee of the lord**: all the land which the lord held from his superior lord, either a vassal holding the land of the tenant in chief (q.v.) or the tenant in chief himself

**Fee, Knight's**: land with which a newly-dubbed knight was enfeoffed to provide him with the income to equip himself for military service owed by his lord. These estates tended to become fragmented, as can be seen in court no.63 where Sir Hugh Hovel is to be distrained to swear fealty for half of a quarter of a knight's fee in Wyverstone, which he holds from the lord of Walsham manor.[2]

**Fine**: payment made to the lord in return for a specific concession e.g. entry to a tenement, leave to marry, etc.

**Fold, The lord's**: moveable enclosure of land, made of hurdles, in which tenants had to keep their animals by night

**Fold, Liberty of**: right to graze a fixed number of sheep in a specified area, the rent for which was 6d. per score

**Foddercorn**: corn grown for cattle-feed (no.9)

**Frank-marriage**: tenure by which a man and his wife held land granted to them by the father or other near relative of the wife, the estate being heritable to the 4th generation of their heirs, without service other than fealty (*OED*) (no.41)

**Fugitive**: villein who absents himself from the manor without leave

**Full age**: age at which heirs were able to enter their inheritance; in Walsham, usually 16 years

**Furlong**: division of an unenclosed field, not of standard dimensions

**Gannocker**: keeper of an ale-house, retailer of ale

**Gavelkind**, see **Partible inheritance**

**Gimmer**, see **Sheep**

---

2  For a detailed study of this topic, see the essay entitled 'The Knight and the Knight's Fee in England' by Sally Harvey, in *Peasants, Knights and Heretics*, ed. R.H. Hilton (Cambridge 1976).

**Hayward** (*messor*): annually elected manorial official; for duties see Introduction under 'Court Officials' p.7

**Herbage**: growth of grass or green vegetables

**Heriot**: customary payment to the lord of the best beast of a deceased tenant of villein land

**Hogget**, see **Sheep**

**Homage**, also **The whole homage**: body of persons owing allegiance in the manor court; all who owed homage, fealty and suit of court (*OED*)

**Illegal Recovery**, see **Recovery**

**Inheritance, Partible**, see **Partible inheritance**

**Knighting of lord's eldest son**, see **Aid**

**Knight's fee**, see **Fee, Knight's**

**Lanksetel**: long bench, or settle, usually with arms and high back (*OED*)

**Law Merchant**: law based on the customs of merchants, usually administered in special courts such as those of markets and fairs

**Law, Wager of**: procedure for settlement of dispute; see Introduction under 'The Courts, Procedures' pp.10–11

**Love-day**, see **Day**

**Mainpernor**: a surety; one who accepts responsibility for the fulfilment of a covenant by another person; **Mainprise**: action of a mainpernor

**Mark**: unit of monetary value, originally equal to that of 8 ounces of gold at 20 pence per ounce = 13s.4d.; not a coin, though later coins of the value of ½ mark were minted

**Marry, Fine for leave to**: customary payment due to the lord from the daughter of a villein, sometimes called 'merchet'

**Maslin**: mixed grains sown together, especially rye with wheat

**Messuage**: tenement on which a dwelling is built

**Metes and bounds**: designation of boundaries by measurement and markers

**Mollond**: land on which rent was paid in commutation of services and customs ('molland' *OED*)

**Mortuary**: customary gift to the parish priest of a beast from the effects of a deceased parishioner

**Multure**: proportion of a tenant's grain, taken by the miller in return for milling it

**Old acre**: fiscal acre, 120th part of a carucate (q.v.); see also **Ware land**

**Pannage**: feeding of pigs in woodland, the right or privilege to do so; acorns or beechmast on which the pigs fed

**Parker**: in Walsham, the official responsible for the control of stray animals within the manor, and custody of them and others taken into the lord's hands, in the pound (q.v.). In manors where the lord's land included a park, its maintenance was the parker's function; the duties he performed in Walsham were those of a pindar.

**Partible inheritance**: described in the custumary thus: 'that if any tenant dies seised of his copy lands and tenements, the same to be equally divided and parted amongst all his sons, according to the law of gavelkind'[3]

**Pightle**: enclosed plot of land, usually small

---

[3]  Dodd, *Field Book of Walsham le Willows*, p.50.

**Ploughhale** ('plowale'): boonwork at ploughtime when ale and food were provided by the lord

**Posnet**: cooking pot with handle and three legs

**Pound:** enclosure in which stray animals and those taken in distraint were penned

**Quitclaim**: formal renunciation of title to land

**Reapale** ('repale'): boonwork at harvest when ale and food were provided by the lord

**Recognition**: grace payment made jointly by all the tenants to a new lord of the manor at his first court, but often remitted

**Recovery** (*rescussio*): taking of impounded animals or goods, attached or distrained, from the lord's possession without leave

**Reeve** (*prepositus*): annually elected manorial official; for duties, see Introduction under 'Court Officials' p.7

**Regrating**: the offence of buying-up market commodities, especially victuals, in order to sell again at a profit at the same or a neighbouring market (*OED*). A similar offence, called 'forestalling', concerned the sale, before the market opened, of commodities bought outside. By action against offenders, the courts exercised effective control over the price of food. All the references to regrating in the rolls relate to sales of bread or ale, the prices of which were regulated by statute. **Regrater** or **Regrator**: one who regrates

**Relief**: payment made to the lord by the heir of a free tenant on entry to his inheritance

**Remit**, see **Quitclaim**

**Rental**: document listing all the customary tenements, with the name of each tenant; sometimes dimensions, rents, customs and services due were also listed

**Resetting** (*receptamentum*): unlawful receiving or harbouring of goods or animals (no.6)

**Respite**: postponement, adjournment

**Rod**: symbol of the lord's authority used to ratify transfers of land, except that held at the lord's will; also as a badge of office for those holding temporary authority, e.g. supervision of labourers (no.46)

**Sacrist**: official charged with the custody of sacred vessels, relics, vestments, books, etc. of a church or religious house (*OED*)

**Salving of sheep**: smearing with mixture of grease, or butter, and turpentine, or tar, to control infestation with ticks, etc.

**Seisin, Delivery of**: symbolic transfer of possession of land in the court, e.g. by the rod (q.v.)

**Serjeant** (*serviens*): manorial official whose duties were similar to those of an under-bailiff

**Services**, see **Customs and works**

**Severalty**: land exclusively held by an individual, not held jointly with others

**Sheep**

> **Sheep of the cullet**: best sheep chosen from the flock; 'cull' meant to select the fattest sheep
>
> **Gimmer**: ewe between its first and second shearing
>
> **Hogget**: sheep before its first shearing, a yearling
>
> **Sheep, Salving of**; see **Salving**
>
> **Wether**: castrated male sheep

**Sheriff's aid**; annual payment due from a manor to the sheriff of the shire. In the Liberty of St Edmund it was paid to the abbot; Walsham owed 4s. per year (no.62).[4]

**Shytenesyeld**: no definition of this word has been traced, but the context suggests that it was a payment, the 'y' possibly being intended as 'g'. *MED* gives 'shitten' meaning shut-in, as in 'Shitten Saturday', when Christ was shut in the sepulchre: 'shytenesyeld' may relate to this meaning (no.102).

**Stot**: draught horse

**Straytime**: time for rounding up stray animals

**Suit of court**: customary obligation of a tenant to attend the court of his lord

**Templars**: members of religious and military order founded in 1118 and suppressed in 1312

**Tenement**: land which is held of another by any form of tenure, a holding

**Term, To have a**: to have the lease of a tenement for an agreed period

**Tester**: canopy over a bed, of wood or fabric

**Toft**: enclosure on which a house and its outbuildings stand, or formerly stood; as in 'toft and croft'

**Vill** (*villa*): territorial unit for taxation under the feudal system, consisting of a village and its subsidiary hamlets, roughly equating to a modern parish (*OED*). For the asssessment of Danegeld, Blackbourne Hundred was divided into 14 'letes', one of which comprised the vills of Walsham, Ashfield Magna and Ashfield Parva; Walsham owed half of the sum due from the lete.[5]

**Villein**: person of unfree status; see Introduction under 'The Tenants' pp.14–17

**Villeinage**: status of a villein, or of land tenure at the lord's will, by services and works on the lord's land at his summons

**Ward service**: see **Castle ward**

**Ware land**: the word 'ware' appears only once, in describing a ten-acre holding of the late William Isabel (no.151). This tenement was probably part of 40 acres belonging to the Abbey, shown in Abbot Samson's Kalendar as 'ware acres'. The word has a fiscal meaning, similar to 'old acre' (q.v.).[6]

**Warren, Liberty of**: privilege granted by the sovereign to keep and hunt small game e.g. hares, partridges and rabbits

**Wether**, see **Sheep**

**Woodward**: manorial official responsible for maintenance of the lord's woodland and hedges, and for the prevention of poaching

**Works**, see **Customs and works**

---

[4] R.H.C. Davis, ed., *The Kalendar of Abbot Samson of Bury St Edmunds* (London 1954), p.50.
[5] Davis, *The Kalendar*, p.xix.
[6] Davis, *The Kalendar*, p.xxxviii.

# Index of Persons

Please note that more than one reference may be found on the page cited.

Abbreviations used: br. brother, d. daughter, hus. husband, kin. kinsman, m. married, n. nephew, sis. sister, s. son, w. wife, wid. widow

# Index of Places

This index does not include references to places outside Walsham which form part of names cited in the Index of Persons, such as Richard of Wortham; where place names follow a surname, as in Gilbert Helpe of Westhorpe, they are included.

# Index of Subjects

As is customary, this index is arranged in alphabetical order, but five categories of reference, covering the main business of the court, are segregated. They are Crops, Land and Tenements, Livestock, Services and Works (Customs), and Stockmen, and appropriate references are listed under these headings. Cross references are included. *Passim* is used as sparingly as was deemed reasonable.

Absence from the manor: 31, 44, 50, 60, 112, 114, 118, 120, 126, 129, 130, 136, 179, 199, 208, 218, 229, 230, 234, 239, 248, 254, 256, 260, 262, 263, 266, 277, 285, 299, 303, 306, 313, 329, 331, 334, 336
   chevage, 31, 44, 56, 58, 70, 84, 110, 112, 114, 118, 120, 127, 130, 166, 172, 184, 189, 262
Account (*compotus*): 116n, 118, 129, 130, 149, 183, 199, 267, 286, 288, 330, 336n, parchment for, not brought to court, 99, 267
Acquittals: *sine die*, 48, 60, 105, 112, 114, 117n, 127, 143, 145, 147, 150, 153, 167, 177, 200, other, 94, 110, 112, 122, 164
Affeerers, 7, 9, 49, 78, 88, 89, 90, 91, 93, 108, 109, 111, 114, 125, 180, 183, 188, 191, 195, 199, 209, 211, 213, 214, 217, 221, 222, 223, 226, 228, 232, 237, 241, 244, 256, 259, 263, 264, 268, 275, 279, 282, 284, 288, 291, 295
Aids: to knight lord's eldest son, 109, 110, 112, 114, 118, 121,130, to Virgin Mary's light in church, 51, sheriff's aid, 155, 157
Ale: Assize of, breach by brewers, 37, 52, 61, 79, 82, 104, 116, 124, 144, 148, 154, 160, 163, 174, 179, 187, 190, 198, 206, 213, 220, 225, 230, 236, 240, 243, 247, 255, 258, 265, 271, 278, 280, 286, 293, 297, 301, 305, 311, 315, 325, 329, 335
   by gannockers (vendors), 37, 79, 82, 104, 116, 125, 144, 148, 154, 160, 163, 174, 179, 187, 190, 198, 206, 225, 230, 236, 240, 243, 255, 258, 265, 271, 278, 280, 286, 293, 297, 301, 305, 311, 315, 325, 335
   measures not marked by seal, 125, disputes concerning, 131, 254, bought for Wm.Lene's funeral, 135
Ale-tasters: election of, 104, 225, 240, 262, 315, 329, 335, deprived of office, 104, 225, 240, 335, neglect of duties, 104, 116, 124, 148, 154, 160, 163, 174, 179, 187, 190. 198, 213, 220, 230, 236, 240, 243, 247, 255, 258, 265, 271, 278, 280, 286, 293, 297, 301, 305, 311, 315, 329, 335, not sent for, 113, 116, 125, 155, 187, 266

Amercement: *passim*, condoned/waived, because poor, 37, 86, 102, 115, 190, 194, 206, 208, 220, 251, 242, 243, 247, 249, 258, because infirm, 117, 124, no reason given, 80, 101, 104, 108, 113, 115, 116, 119, 122, 124, 125, 127, 129, 131n, 133, 138, 139, 140, 144, 147, 149, 154, 155, 163, 166, 167, 169, 172, 175, 179, 181, 182, 183, 192, 198, 200, 201, 202, 205, 206, 209, 217, 218, 219, 222, 226, 227, 229, 233, 234, 235, 237, 241, 244, 246, 250, 251, 259, 263, 264, 265, 271, 273, 274, 275, 280, 281, 282, 290, 291, 292, 293, 296, 299, 300, 301, 304, 310, 311, 312, 321, 327, 331, 332, 335
Apples, *see* Fruit
Apple trees, *see* Trees
Appropriation, *see* Encroachment
Ash trees, *see* Trees
Assault: beating, 153, 226, and drawing blood, 245
Attachment: *passim*, by the body, 45, 50, 52, 58, 166, 172, 179, 182, 197, by chattels, *see* Chattels
Attorney, 155, 159, 214
Autumn work, *see* **Services**, Reaping
Bailiff/serjeant, 45, 51, 54, 59, 63, 65, 66, 68, 71, 74, 83n, 87, 92, 93, 94, 103, 107, 109, 110, 112, 114, 116, 119, 121, 130, 136, 145, 161, 170, 183, 187, 190, 197, 203, 208, 209, 214, 221, 226, 229, 231, 232, 241, 242, 245, 247, 255, 257, 260, 261, 263, 269, 270, 273, 276, 278, 279, 283, 308
Bakehouse, 229, 230, 271, 274, 278, 279, 282, 320
Banks (*fossata*), 158, 160, 181, 184, 200, 286, 314
Barley, *see* **Crops**
Barrels, *see* Household goods
Bastards, 135, 236, 239, 246, 248, 253, 254, 264, 266, 276, 279, 285, 303, 306, 313, 321, 323, 325, 327, 335
Beans, *see* **Crops**
Bequests, 125, 128, 135
Births out of wedlock: childwite paid, 70, 89, 90, 111, 119, 122, 163, 178, 181, 190, 197, 216,